The Writings of Tertullian
Volume I
By Tertullian
This Edition Edited by Anthony Uyl

Woodstock, Ontario, Canada 2017

The Writings of Tertullian - Volume I

The Writings of Tertullian - Volume I
By Tertullian (c. 160-c. 230)
This Edition Edited by Anthony Uyl

Originally Edited By Philip Schaff (1819-1893) (Editor)
And Allan Menzies (1845-1916) (Editor)

Originally Published As:
The Writings of the Fathers Down to A.D. 325
Ante-Nicene Fathers Volume 3
Latin Christianity: Its Founder, Tertullian
I. Apologetic; II. Anti-Marcion; III. Ethical

Originally Published By:
T&T Clark, Edinburgh
And WM. B. Eerdmans Publishing Company, Grand Rapids, Michigan

The text of The Writings of Tertullian - Volume I is all in the Public Domain. The covers, background, layout and Devoted Publishing logo are Copyright ©2017 Devoted Publishing. This edition is published by Devoted Publishing a division of 2165467 Ontario Inc.

**What kind of philosophies do you have?
Let us know!**

Visit our online store: www.devotedpublishing.com
Contact us at: devotedpub@hotmail.com
Visit us on Facebook: @DevotedPublishing

Published in Woodstock, Ontario, Canada 2017

For bulk educational rates, please contact us at the above email address.

ISBN: 978-1-77356-156-1

Table of Contents

Preface 11
Part First 12
   Introductory Note 12
      Footnotes: 20
I - Apology 23
   The Apology [77] 23
   Chapter I 23
   Chapter II 24
   Chapter III 25
   Chapter IV 26
   Chapter V 27
   Chapter VI 27
   Chapter VII 28
   Chapter VIII 29
   Chapter IX 30
   Chapter X 31
   Chapter XI 32
   Chapter XII 33
   Chapter XIII 33
   Chapter XIV 34
   Chapter XV 34
   Chapter XVI 35
   Chapter XVII 36
   Chapter XVIII 36
   Chapter XIX 37
   Chapter XX 37
   Chapter XXI 38
   Chapter XXII 40
   Chapter XXIII 41
   Chapter XXIV 42
   Chapter XXV 43
   Chapter XXVI 44
   Chapter XXVII 44
   Chapter XXVIII 44
   Chapter XXIX 45
   Chapter XXX 45
   Chapter XXXI 46
   Chapter XXXII 46
   Chapter XXXIII 46

Chapter XXXIV 46
Chapter XXXV 47
Chapter XXXVI 48
Chapter XXXVII 48
Chapter XXXVIII 49
Chapter XXXIX 49
Chapter XL 50
Chapter XLI 51
Chapter XLII 51
Chapter XLIII 52
Chapter XLIV 52
Chapter XLV 52
Chapter XLVI 53
Chapter XLVII 54
Chapter XLVIII 55
Chapter XLIX 56
Chapter L 57
Elucidations 58
   Footnotes: 61
II - On Idolatry 63
Chapter I - Wide Scope of the Word Idolatry 63
Chapter II - Idolatry in Its More Limited Sense. Its Copiousness 63
Chapter III - Idolatry: Origin and Meaning of the Name 64
Chapter IV - Idols Not to Be Made, Much Less Worshipped. Idols and Idol-Makers in the Same Category 64
Chapter V [185] - Sundry Objections or Excuses Dealt with 65
Chapter VI - Idolatry Condemned by Baptism. To Make an Idol Is, in Fact, to Worship It 65
Chapter VII - Grief of the Faithful at the Admission of Idol-Makers into the Church; Nay, Even into the Ministry 66
Chapter VIII - Other Arts Made Subservient to Idolatry. Lawful Means of Gaining a Livelihood Abundant 66
Chapter IX - Professions of Some Kinds Allied to Idolatry. Of Astrology in Particular 66
Chapter X - Of Schoolmasters and Their Difficulties 67
Chapter XI - Connection Between Covetousness and Idolatry. Certain Trades, However Gainful, to Be Avoided 68
Chapter XII - Further Answers to the Plea, How Am I to Live? 69
Chapter XIII - Of the Observance of Days Connected with Idolatry 69
Chapter XIV - Of Blasphemy. One of St. Paul's Sayings 70
Chapter XV - Concerning Festivals in Honour of Emperors, Victories, and the Like 70
Chapter XVI - Concerning Private Festivals 71
Chapter XVII - The Cases of Servants and Other Officials. What Offices a Christian Man May Hold 72

Chapter XVIII - Dress as Connected with Idolatry...72

Chapter XIX - Concerning Military Service...73

Chapter XX - Concerning Idolatry in Words..73

Chapter XXI - Of Silent Acquiescence in Heathen Formularies..74

Chapter XXII - Of Accepting Blessing in the Name of Idols..74

Chapter XXIII - Written Contracts in the Name of Idols. Tacit Consent..................................74

Chapter XXIV - General Conclusion..75

Elucidations..75

   Footnotes:..76

III - The Shows, or De Spectaculis [347] 81

  Chapter I..81

  Chapter II...81

  Chapter III..82

  Chapter IV...83

  Chapter V..83

  Chapter VI...83

  Chapter VII..84

  Chapter VIII..84

  Chapter IX...85

  Chapter X..85

  Chapter XI...86

  Chapter XII..86

  Chapter XIII..86

  Chapter XIV..87

  Chapter XV...87

  Chapter XVI..87

  Chapter XVII...88

  Chapter XVIII...88

  Chapter XIX..88

  Chapter XX...89

  Chapter XXI..89

  Chapter XXII..89

  Chapter XXIII...90

  Chapter XXIV..90

  Chapter XXV..90

  Chapter XXVI..91

  Chapter XXVII...91

  Chapter XXVIII..91

  Chapter XXIX..92

  Chapter XXX...92

   Footnotes:...92

IV - The Chaplet, or De Corona [380] 94

- Chapter I 94
- Chapter II 94
- Chapter III 95
- Chapter IV 95
- Chapter V 96
- Chapter VI 96
- Chapter VII 97
- Chapter VIII 98
- Chapter IX 98
- Chapter X 98
- Chapter XI 99
- Chapter XII 100
- Chapter XIII 101
- Chapter XIV 102
- Chapter XV 102
- Elucidations 102
  - Footnotes: 103

V - To Scapula [446] 105

- Chapter I 105
- Chapter II 105
- Chapter III 106
- Chapter IV 106
- Chapter V 107
- Elucidations 107
  - Footnotes: 108

VI - Ad Nationes [458] 109

- Book I 109
- Chapter I [459] - The Hatred Felt by the Heathen Against the Christians is Unjust, Because Based on Culpable Ignorance 109
- Chapter II [475] - The Heathen Perverted Judgment in the Trial of Christians. They Would Be More Consistent If They Dispensed with All Form of Trial. Tertullian Urges This with Much Indignation 110
- Chapter III [487] -- The Great Offence in the Christians Lies in Their Very Name. The Name Vindicated 110
- Chapter IV [502] - The Truth Hated in the Christians; So in Measure Was It, of Old, in Socrates. The Virtues of the Christians 111
- Chapter V [522] - The Inconsistent Life of Any False Christian No More Condemns True Disciples of Christ, Than a Passing Cloud Obscures a Summer Sky 112
- Chapter VI [531] - The Innocence of the Christians Not Compromised by the Iniquitous Laws Which Were Made Against Them 113
- Chapter VII [545] - The Christians Defamed. A Sarcastic Description of Fame; Its Deception and Atrocious Slanders of the Christians Lengthily Described 113

Chapter VIII [585] - The Calumny Against the Christians Illustrated in the Discovery of Psammetichus. Refutation of the Story 115

Chapter IX [595] - The Christians are Not the Cause of Public Calamities: There Were Such Troubles Before Christianity 116

Chapter X [604] - The Christians are Not the Only Contemners of the Gods. Contempt of Them Often Displayed by Heathen Official Persons. Homer Made the Gods Contemptible 117

Chapter XI [651] - The Absurd Cavil of the Ass's Head Disposed of 119

Chapter XII [654] - The Charge of Worshipping a Cross. The Heathens Themselves Made Much of Crosses in Sacred Things; Nay, Their Very Idols Were Formed on a Crucial Frame 120

Chapter XIII [672] - The Charge of Worshipping the Sun Met by a Retort 121

Chapter XIV [679] - The Vile Calumny About Onocoetes Retorted on the Heathen by Tertullian 121

Chapter XV [686] - The Charge of Infanticide Retorted on the Heathen 121

Chapter XVI [698] - Other Charges Repelled by the Same Method. The Story of the Noble Roman Youth and His Parents 122

Chapter XVII [715] - The Christian Refusal to Swear by the Genius of Cæsar. Flippancy and Irreverence Retorted on the Heathen 123

Chapter XVIII [732] - Christians Charged with an Obstinate Contempt of Death. Instances of the Same are Found Amongst the Heathen 123

Chapter XIX [750] - If Christians and the Heathen Thus Resemble Each Other, There is Great Difference in the Grounds and Nature of Their Apparently Similar Conduct 124

Chapter XX - Truth and Reality Pertain to Christians Alone. The Heathen Counselled to Examine and Embrace It 125

    Footnotes: 125

Book II [773] 131

Chapter I - The Heathen Gods from Heathen Authorities. Varro Has Written a Work on the Subject. His Threefold Classification. The Changeable Character of that Which Ought to Be Fixed and Certain 131

Chapter II - Philosophers Had Not Succeeded in Discovering God. The Uncertainty and Confusion of Their Speculations 132

Chapter III - The Physical Philosophers Maintained the Divinity of the Elements; The Absurdity of the Tenet Exposed 133

Chapter IV - Wrong Derivation of the Word Θεός. The Name Indicative of the True Deity. God Without Shape and Immaterial. Anecdote of Thales 134

Chapter V - The Physical Theory Continued. Further Reasons Advanced Against the Divinity of the Elements 135

Chapter VI - The Changes of the Heavenly Bodies, Proof that They are Not Divine. Transition from the Physical to the Mythic Class of Gods 136

Chapter VII - The Gods of the Mythic Class. The Poets a Very Poor Authority in Such Matters. Homer and the Mythic Poets. Why Irreligious 136

Chapter VIII - The Gods of the Different Nations. Varro's Gentile Class. Their Inferiority. A Good Deal of This Perverse Theology Taken from Scripture. Serapis a Perversion of Joseph 137

Chapter IX - The Power of Rome. Romanized Aspect of All the Heathen Mythology. Varro's Threefold Distribution Criticised. Roman Heroes (Æneas Included,) Unfavourably Reviewed 138

Chapter X - A Disgraceful Feature of the Roman Mythology. It Honours Such Infamous Characters as Larentina 139

Chapter XI - The Romans Provided Gods for Birth, Nay, Even Before Birth, to Death. Much Indelicacy in This System 140

Chapter XII [976] - The Original Deities Were Human--With Some Very Questionable Characteristics.

Saturn or Time Was Human. Inconsistencies of Opinion About Him 140

  Chapter XIII [1011] - The Gods Human at First. Who Had the Authority to Make Them Divine? Jupiter Not Only Human, But Immoral 142

  Chapter XIV - Gods, Those Which Were Confessedly Elevated to the Divine Condition, What Pre-Eminent Right Had They to Such Honour? Hercules an Inferior Character 143

  Chapter XV - The Constellations and the Genii Very Indifferent Gods. The Roman Monopoly of Gods Unsatisfactory. Other Nations Require Deities Quite as Much 144

  Chapter XVI - Inventors of Useful Arts Unworthy of Deification. They Would Be the First to Acknowledge a Creator. The Arts Changeable from Time to Time, and Some Become Obsolete ... 144

  Chapter XVII [1081] - Conclusion, the Romans Owe Not Their Imperial Power to Their Gods. The Great God Alone Dispenses Kingdoms, He is the God of the Christians 145

  Appendix - A Fragment Concerning the Execrable Gods of the Heathen 146

  Elucidation 147

    Footnotes: 147

VII - An Answer to the Jews [1126] 153

  Chapter I - Occasion of Writing. Relative Position of Jews and Gentiles Illustrated 153

  Chapter II - The Law Anterior to Moses 153

  Chapter III - Of Circumcision and the Supercession of the Old Law 155

  Chapter IV - Of the Observance of the Sabbath 156

  Chapter V - Of Sacrifices 157

  Chapter VI - Of the Abolition and the Abolisher of the Old Law 157

  Chapter VII - The Question Whether Christ Be Come Taken Up 158

  Chapter VIII - Of the Times of Christ's Birth and Passion, and of Jerusalem's Destruction 159

  Chapter IX - Of the Prophecies of the Birth and Achievements of Christ 161

  Chapter X - Concerning the Passion of Christ, and Its Old Testament Predictions and Adumbrations
  164

  Chapter XI - Further Proofs, from Ezekiel. Summary of the Prophetic Argument Thus Far 166

  Chapter XII - Further Proofs from the Calling of the Gentiles 167

  Chapter XIII - Argument from the Destruction of Jerusalem and Desolation of Judea 167

  Chapter XIV - Conclusion. Clue to the Error of the Jews 169

    Footnotes: 171

VIII - The Soul's Testimony [1477] 178

  Chapter I 178

  Chapter II 179

  Chapter III 179

  Chapter IV 180

  Chapter V 181

  Chapter VI 181

  Elucidations 182

    Footnotes: 182

IX - A Treatise on the Soul [1489] 184

  Chapter I - It is Not to the Philosophers that We Resort for Information About the Soul But to God.
  [1490]
  184

Chapter II - The Christian Has Sure and Simple Knowledge Concerning the Subject Before Us.....185

Chapter III - The Soul's Origin Defined Out of the Simple Words of Scripture 186

Chapter IV - In Opposition to Plato, the Soul Was Created and Originated at Birth. After settling the origin of the soul, its condition or state comes up next..187

Chapter V - Probable View of the Stoics, that the Soul Has a Corporeal Nature..............................187

Chapter VI - The Arguments of the Platonists for the Soul's Incorporeality, Opposed, Perhaps Frivolously 188

Chapter VII - The Soul's Corporeality Demonstrated Out of the Gospels 189

Chapter VIII - Other Platonist Arguments Considered 189

Chapter IX - Particulars of the Alleged Communication to a Montanist Sister................................190

Chapter X - The Simple Nature of the Soul is Asserted with Plato. The Identity of Spirit and Soul.191

Chapter XI - Spirit--A Term Expressive of an Operation of the Soul, Not of Its Nature 192

Chapter XII - Difference Between the Mind and the Soul, and the Relation Between Them 193

Chapter XIII - The Soul's Supremacy..194

Chapter XIV - The Soul Variously Divided by the Philosophers; This Division is Not a Material Dissection..194

Chapter XV - The Soul's Vitality and Intelligence. Its Character and Seat in Man..........................195

Chapter XVI - The Soul's Parts. Elements of the Rational Soul 196

Chapter XVII - The Fidelity of the Senses, Impugned by Plato, Vindicated by Christ Himself 197

Chapter XVIII - Plato Suggested Certain Errors to the Gnostics. Functions of the Soul..................198

Chapter XIX - The Intellect Coeval with the Soul in the Human Being. An Example from Aristotle. Converted into Evidence Favourable to These Views 200

Chapter XX - The Soul, as to Its Nature Uniform, But Its Faculties Variously Developed. Varieties Only Accidental...201

Chapter XXI - As Free-Will Actuates an Individual So May His Character Change.......................202

Chapter XXII - Recapitulation. Definition of the Soul 203

Chapter XXIII - The Opinions of Sundry Heretics Which Originate Ultimately with Plato.............203

Chapter XXIV - Plato's Inconsistency. He Supposes the Soul Self-Existent, Yet Capable of Forgetting What Passed in a Previous State..204

Chapter XXV - Tertullian Refutes, Physiologically, the Notion that the Soul is Introduced After Birth 205

Chapter XXVI - Scripture Alone Offers Clear Knowledge on the Questions We Have Been Controverting 207

Chapter XXVII - Soul and Body Conceived, Formed and Perfected in Element Simultaneously 207

Chapter XXVIII - The Pythagorean Doctrine of Transmigration Sketched and Censured...............208

Chapter XXIX - The Pythagorean Doctrine Refuted by Its Own First Principle, that Living Men are Formed from the Dead..209

Chapter XXX - Further Refutation of the Pythagorean Theory 210

Chapter XXXI - Further Exposure of Transmigration, Its Inextricable Embarrassment 210

Chapter XXXII - Empedocles Increased the Absurdity of Pythagoras by Developing the Posthumous Change of Men into Various Animals 211

Chapter XXXIII - The Judicial Retribution of These Migrations Refuted with Raillery 213

Chapter XXXIV - These Vagaries Stimulated Some Profane Corruptions of Christianity. The Profanity of Simon Magus Condemned..214

Chapter XXXV - The Opinions of Carpocrates, Another Offset from the Pythagorean Dogmas, Stated and Confuted 215

Chapter XXXVI - The Main Points of Our Author's Subject. On the Sexes of the Human Race 216

Chapter XXXVII - On the Formation and State of the Embryo. Its Relation with the Subject of This Treatise..................216

Chapter XXXVIII - On the Growth of the Soul. Its Maturity Coincident with the Maturity of the Flesh in Man..................217

Chapter XXXIX - The Evil Spirit Has Marred the Purity of the Soul from the Very Birth 218

Chapter XL - The Body of Man Only Ancillary to the Soul in the Commission of Evil 218

Chapter XLI - Notwithstanding the Depravity of Man's Soul by Original Sin, There is Yet Left a Basis Whereon Divine Grace Can Work for Its Recovery by Spiritual Regeneration..................219

Chapter XLII - Sleep, the Mirror of Death, as Introductory to the Consideration of Death 219

Chapter XLIII - Sleep a Natural Function as Shown by Other Considerations, and by the Testimony of Scripture..................220

Chapter XLIV - The Story of Hermotimus, and the Sleeplessness of the Emperor Nero. No Separation of the Soul from the Body Until Death 221

Chapter XLV - Dreams, an Incidental Effect of the Soul's Activity. Ecstasy 222

Chapter XLVI - Diversity of Dreams and Visions. Epicurus Thought Lightly of Them, Though Generally Most Highly Valued. Instances of Dreams..................222

Chapter XLVII - Dreams Variously Classified. Some are God-Sent, as the Dreams of Nebuchadnezzar; Others Simply Products of Nature..................224

Chapter XLVIII - Causes and Circumstances of Dreams. What Best Contributes to Efficient Dreaming..................224

Chapter XLIX - No Soul Naturally Exempt from Dreams..................225

Chapter L - The Absurd Opinion of Epicurus and the Profane Conceits of the Heretic Menander on Death, Even Enoch and Elijah Reserved for Death..................225

Chapter LI - Death Entirely Separates the Soul from the Body 226

Chapter LII - All Kinds of Death a Violence to Nature, Arising from Sin.--Sin an Intrusion Upon Nature as God Created It 227

Chapter LIII - The Entire Soul Being Indivisible Remains to the Last Act of Vitality; Never Partially or Fractionally Withdrawn from the Body..................227

Chapter LIV - Whither Does the Soul Retire When It Quits the Body? Opinions of Philosophers All More or Less Absurd. The Hades of Plato..................228

Chapter LV - The Christian Idea of the Position of Hades; The Blessedness of Paradise Immediately After Death. The Privilege of the Martyrs 229

Chapter LVI - Refutation of the Homeric View of the Soul's Detention from Hades Owing to the Body's Being Unburied. That Souls Prematurely Separated from the Body Had to Wait for Admission into Hades Also Refuted..................230

Chapter LVII - Magic and Sorcery Only Apparent in Their Effects. God Alone Can Raise the Dead 231

Chapter LVIII - Conclusion. Points Postponed. All Souls are Kept in Hades Until the Resurrection, Anticipating Their Ultimate Misery or Bliss 232

   Footnotes:..................233

Preface

We present a volume widely differing, in its contents, from those which have gone before; it contains the works of the great founder of Latin Christianity, the versatile and brilliant Tertullian. Not all his works, indeed, for they could not be contained in one of our books. This book, however, considerably overruns the promised number of pages, and gives three complete parts of Tertullian's writings, according to the classification of our Editor-in-chief. The Fourth volume will begin with the fourth class of his works, those which exhibit our author's ascetic ideas and the minor morals of the Primitive Christians, that collection being closed by the four treatises which were written in support of a defined and schismatical Montanism.

The Editor-in-chief has been in active correspondence with representative men of divers theological schools, hoping to secure their co-operation in editorial work.

As yet, however, the result has not enabled us to announce more than one additional collaborator: the rapidity with which the successive volumes must be furnished proving an almost insurmountable obstacle in the way of securing as co-workers, divines actively engaged in professional duties and literary tasks. The sympathy and encouragement which have been expressed by all with whom a correspondence has been opened, have been most cheering. To the Rev. Dr. Riddle, of Hartford, well known as one of the most learned of the AmericaHærn Revisers of the New Testament, we are indebted for his consent to edit one of the concluding volumes of the Series, accompanying it with a Bibliographical Review of the entire Literature of the Patrologia of the Ante-Nicene period: supplying therein a compendious view of all the writers upon this period and of the latest critical editions of the Ante-Nicene authors themselves. The editor-in-chief will continue his annotations and the usual prefaces, in Professor Riddle's volume, but will be relieved, in some degree, of the laborious and minute attention to details which earlier volumes have necessarily exacted.

It is needful to remind the reader that he possesses in this volume what has long been a desideratum among divines. The crabbed Latin of the great Tertullian has been thought to defy translation: and the variety and uncertain dates of his works have rendered classification and arrangement almost an equal difficulty. But here is the work achieved by competent hands, and now, for the first time, reduced to orderly and methodical plan. We have little doubt that the student on comparing our edition with that of the Edinburgh Series, will congratulate himself on the great gain of the arrangement; and we trust the original matter with which it is illustrated may be found not less acceptable.

Part First

Introductory Note

[a.d. 145-220.] When our Lord repulsed the woman of Canaan (Matt. xv. 22) with apparent harshness, he applied to her people the epithet dogs, with which the children of Israel had thought it piety to reproach them. When He accepted her faith and caused it to be recorded for our learning, He did something more: He reversed the curse of the Canaanite and showed that the Church was designed "for all people;" Catholic alike for all time and for all sorts and conditions of men.

Thus the North-African Church was loved before it was born: the Good Shepherd was gently leading those "that were with young."

Here was the charter of those Christians to be a Church, who then were Canaanites in the land of their father Ham.

It is remarkable indeed that among these pilgrims and strangers to the West the first elements of Latin Christianity come into view. Even at the close of the Second Century the Church in Rome is an inconsiderable, though prominent, member of the great confederation of Christian Churches which has its chief seats in Alexandria and Antioch, and of which the entire Literature is Greek. It is an African presbyter who takes from Latin Christendom the reproach of theological and literary barrenness and begins the great work in which, upon his foundations, Cyprian and Augustine built up, with incomparable genius, that Carthaginian School of Christian thought by which Latin Theology was dominated for centuries. It is important to note (1.) that providentially not one of these illustrious doctors died in Communion with the Roman See, pure though it was and venerable at that time; and (2.) that to the works of Augustine the Reformation in Germany and Continental Europe was largely due; while (3.) the specialties of the Anglican Reformation were, in like proportion, due to the writings of Tertullian and Cyprian. The hinges of great and controlling destinies for Western Europe and our own America are to be found in the period we are now approaching.

The merest school-boy knows much of the history of Carthage, and how the North Africans became Roman citizens. How they became Christians is not so clear. A melancholy destiny has enveloped Carthage from the outset, and its glory and greatness as a Christian See were transient indeed. It blazed out all at once in Tertullian, after about a century of missionary labours had been exerted upon its creation: and having given a Minucius Felix, an Arnobius and a Lactantius to adorn the earliest period of Western Ecclesiastical learning, in addition to its nobler luminaries, it rapidly declined. At the beginning of the Third Century, at a council presided over by Agrippinus, Bishop of Carthage, there were present not less than seventy bishops of the Province. A period of cruel persecutions followed, and the African Church received a baptism of blood.

Tertullian was born a heathen, and seems to have been educated at Rome, where he probably practiced as a jurisconsult. We may, perhaps, adopt most of the ideas of Allix, as conjecturally probable, and assign his birth to a.d. 145. He became a Christian about 185, and a presbyter about 190. The period of his strict orthodoxy very nearly expires with the century. He lived to an extreme old age, and some suppose even till a.d. 240. More probably we must adopt the date preferred by recent writers, a.d. 220.

It seems to be the fashion to treat of Tertullian as a Montanist, and only incidentally to celebrate his services to the Catholic Orthodoxy of Western Christendom. Were I his biographer I should reverse this course, as a mere act of justice, to say nothing of gratitude to a man of splendid intellect, to whom the filial spirit of Cyprian accorded the loving tribute of a disciple, and whose genius stamped itself upon the very words of Latin theology, and prepared the language for the labours of a Jerome. In creating the Vulgate, and so lifting the Western Churches into a position of intellectual equality with the East, the latter as well as St. Augustine himself were debtors to Tertullian in a degree not to be estimated by any other than the Providential Mind that inspired his brilliant career as a Christian.

In speaking of Tatian I laid the base for what I wished to say of Tertullian. Let God only be their judge; let us gratefully recognize the debt we owe to them. Let us read them, as we read the works of King Solomon. We must, indeed, approve of the discipline of the Primitive Age, which allowed of no compromises. The Church was struggling for existence, and could not permit any man to become her master.

The more brilliant the intellect, the more dangerous to the poor Church were its perversions of her Testimony.

Before the heathen tribunals, and in the market-places, it would not answer to let Christianity appear double-tongued. The orthodoxy of the Church, not less than her children, was undergoing an ordeal of fire.

It seems a miracle that her Testimony preserved its unity, and that heresy was branded as such by the instinct of the Faithful. Poor Tertullian was cut off by his own act. The weeping Church might bewail him as David mourned for Absalom, but like David, she could not give the Ark of God into other hands than those of the loyal and the true. I have set the writings of Tertullian in a natural and logical order [1], so as to aid the student, and to relieve him from the distractions of such an arrangement as one finds in Oehler's edition.

Valuable as it is, the practical use of it is irritating and confusing. The reader of that edition may turn to the slightly differing schemes of Neander and Kaye, for a theoretical order of the works; but here he will find a classification which will aid his inquiries. He will find, first, those works which connect with the Apologists of the former volumes of this series: which illustrate the Church's position toward the outside world, the Jews as well as the Gentiles. Next come those works which contend with internal differences and heresies. And then, those which reflect the morals and manners of Christians. These are classed with some reference to their degrees of freedom from the Montanistic taint, and are followed, last of all, by the few tracts which belong to the melancholy period of his lapse, and are directed against the Church's orthodoxy.

Let it be borne in mind, that if this sad close of Tertullian's career cannot be extenuated, the later history of Latin Christianity forbids us to condemn him, in the tones which proceeded from the Virgin Church with authority, and which the law of her testimony and the instinct of self-preservation forced her to utter. Let us reflect that St. Bernard and after him the Schoolmen, whom we so deservedly honour, separated themselves far more absolutely than ever Tertullian did from the orthodoxy of Primitive Christendom. The schism which withdrew the West from Communion with the original seats of Christendom, and from Nicene Catholicity, was formidable beyond all expression, in comparison with Tertullian's entanglements with a delusion which the See of Rome itself had momentarily patronized. Since the Council of Trent, not a theologian of the Latins has been free from organic heresies, compared with which the fanaticism of our author was a trifling aberration. Since the late Council of the Vatican, essential Montanism has become organized in the Latin Churches: for what are the new revelations and oracles of the pontiff but the deliria of another claimant to the voice and inspiration of the Paraclete? Poor Tertullian! The sad influences of his decline and folly have been fatally felt in all the subsequent history of the West, but, surely subscribers to the Modern Creed of the Vatican have reason to "speak gently of their father's fall." To Döllinger, with the "Old Catholic" remnant only, is left the right to name the Montanists heretics, or to upbraid Tertullian as a lapser from Catholicity. [2]

From Dr. Holmes, I append the following Introductory Notice: [3]

(I.) Quintus Septimius Florens Tertullianus, as our author is called in the mss. of his works, is thus noticed by Jerome in his Catalogus Scriptorum Ecclesiasticorum: [4] "Tertullian, a presbyter, the first Latin writer after Victor and Apollonius, was a native of the province of Africa and city of Carthage, the son of a proconsular centurion:

he was a man of a sharp and vehement temper, flourished under Severus and Antoninus Caracalla, and wrote numerous works, which (as they are generally known) I think it unnecessary to particularize.

I saw at Concordia, in Italy, an old man named Paulus. He said that when young he had met at Rome with an aged amanuensis of the blessed Cyprian, who told him that Cyprian never passed a day without reading some portion of Tertullian's works, and used frequently to say, Give me my master, meaning Tertullian. After remaining a presbyter of the church until he had attained the middle age of life, Tertullian was, by the envy and contumelious treatment of the Roman clergy, driven to embrace the opinions of Montanus, which he has mentioned in several of his works under the title of the New Prophecy....He is reported to have lived to a very advanced age, and to have composed many other works which are not extant." We add Bishop Kaye's notes on this extract, in an abridged shape: "The correctness of some parts of this account has been questioned. Doubts have been entertained whether Tertullian was a presbyter, although these have solely arisen from Roman Catholic objections to a married priesthood; for it is certain that he was married, there being among his works two treatises addressed to his wife....Another question has been raised respecting the place where Tertullian officiated as a presbyter--whether at Carthage or at Rome. That he at one time resided at Carthage may be inferred from Jerome's statement, and is rendered certain by several passages of his own writings. Allix supposes that the notion of his having been a presbyter of the Roman Church owed its rise to what Jerome said of the envy and abuse of the Roman clergy impelling him to espouse the party of Montanus.

Optatus, [5] and the author of the work de Hæresibus, which Sirmond edited under the title of Prædestinatus, expressly call him a Carthaginian presbyter. Semler, however, in a dissertation inserted in his edition of Tertullian's works,[6] contends that he was a presbyter of the Roman Church. Eusebius[7] tells us that he was accurately acquainted with the Roman laws, and on other accounts a distinguished person at Rome.[8] Tertullian displays, moreover, a knowledge of the proceedings of the Roman Church with respect to Marcion and Valentinus, who were once members of it, which could scarcely have been obtained by one who had not himself been numbered amongst its presbyters.[9] Semler admits that, after Tertullian seceded from the church, he left and returned to Carthage. Jerome does not inform us whether Tertullian was born of Christian parents, or was converted to Christianity. There are passages in his writings[10] which seem to imply that he had been a Gentile; yet he may perhaps mean to describe, not his own condition, but that of Gentiles in general, before their conversion. Allix and the majority of commentators understand them literally, as well as some other passages in which he speaks of his own infirmities and sinfulness. His writings show that he flourished at the period specified by Jerome--that is, during the reigns of Severus and Antoninus Caracalla, or between the years a.d. 193 and 216; but they supply no precise information respecting the date of his birth, or any of the principal occurrences of his life. Allix places his birth about 145 or 150; his conversion to Christianity about a.d. 185; his marriage about 186; his admission to the priesthood[11] about 192; his adoption of the opinions of Montanus about 199; and his death about a.d. 220. But these dates, it must be understood, rest entirely on conjecture."[12]

(II.) Tertullian's work against Marcion, as it happens, is, as to its date, the best authenticated--perhaps the only well authenticated--particular connected with the author's life. He himself[13] mentions the fifteenth year of the reign of Severus as the time when he was writing the work: "Ad xv. jam Severi imperatoris." This agrees with Jerome's Chronicle, where occurs this note: "Anno 2223 Severi xv° Tertullianus...celebratur."[14] This year is assigned to the year of our Lord 207;[15] but notwithstanding the certainty of this date, it is far from clear that it describes more than the time of the publication of the first book. On the contrary, it is nearly certain that the other books, although connected manifestly enough in the author's argument and purpose (compare the initial and the final chapters of the several books), were yet issued at separate times. Noesselt[16] shows that between the Book i. and Books ii.-iv. Tertullian issued his De Præscript. Hæret., and previous to Book v. he published his tracts, De Carne Christi and De Resurrectione Carnis. After giving the incontestable date of the xv. of Severus for the first book, he says it is a mistake to suppose that the other books were published with it. He adds: "Although we cannot undertake to determine whether Tertullian issued his Books ii., iii., iv., against Marcion, together or separately, or in what year, we yet venture to affirm that Book v. appeared apart from the rest. For the tract De Resurr. Carnis appears from its second chapter to have been published after the tract De Carne Christi, in which latter work (chap. vii.) he quotes a passage from the fourth book against Marcion.

But in his Book v. against Marcion (chap. x.), he refers to his work De Resurr. Carnis; which circumstance makes it evident that Tertullian published his Book v. at a different time from his Book iv. In his Book i. he announces his intention (chap. i.) of some time or other completing his tract De Præscript. Hæret., but in his book De Carne Christi (chap. ii.), he mentions how he had completed it,--a conclusive proof that his Book i. against Marcion preceded the other books."

(III.) Respecting Marcion himself, the most formidable heretic who had as yet opposed revealed truth, enough will turn up in this treatise, with the notes which we have added in explanation, to satisfy the reader. It will, however, be convenient to give here a few introductory particulars of him. Tertullian[17] mentions Marcion as being, with Valentinus, in communion with the Church at Rome, "under the episcopate of the blessed Eleutherus." He goes on to charge them with "ever-restless curiosity, with which they infected even the brethren;" and informs us that they were more than once put out of communion--"Marcion, indeed, with the 200 sesterces which he brought into the church."[18] He goes on to say, that "being at last condemned to the banishment of a perpetual separation, they sowed abroad the poisons of their doctrines. Afterwards, when Marcion, having professed penitence, agreed to the terms offered to him, that he should receive reconciliation on condition that he brought back to the church the rest also, whom he had trained up for perdition, he was prevented by death." He was a native of Sinope in Pontus, of which city, according to an account preserved by Epiphanius,[19] which, however, is somewhat doubtful, his father was bishop, and of high character both for his orthodoxy and exemplary practice. He came to Rome soon after the death of Hyginus, probably about a.d. 141 or 142; and soon after his arrival he adopted the heresy of Cerdon.[20]

(IV.) It is an interesting question as to what edition of the Holy Scriptures Tertullian used in his very copious quotations. It may at once be asserted that he did not cite from the Hebrew, although some writers have claimed for him, among his varied learning, a knowledge of the sacred language. Bp. Kaye observes, page 61, n. 1, that "he sometimes speaks as if he was acquainted with Hebrew," and refers to the Anti-Marcion iv. 39, the Adv. Praxeam v., and the Adv. Judæos ix. Be this as it may, it is manifest that Tertullian's Scripture passages never resemble the Hebrew, but in nearly every instance the Septuagint, whenever, as is most frequently the case, that version differs from the original. In the New Testament there is, as might be expected, a tolerably close conformity to the Greek. There is, however, it must be allowed, a sufficiently frequent variation from the letter of both the Greek Testaments to justify Semler's suspicion that Tertullian always quoted from the old Latin version, [21] whatever that might have been, which was current in the African church in the second and third centuries. The most valuable part of Semler's Dissertatio de varia et incerta indole Librorum Q. S. F. Tertulliani is his investigation of this very point. In section iv. he endeavours to prove this proposition: "Hic scriptor [22] non in manibus habuit Græcos libros sacros;" and he states his conclusion thus: "Certissimum est nec Tertullianum nec Cyprianum nec ullum scriptorem e Latinis illis ecclesiasticis provocare unquam ad Græcorum librorum auctoritatem si vel maxime obscura aut contraria lectio occurreret;" and again: "Ex his satis certum est, Latinos satis diu secutos fuisse auctoritatem suorum librorum adversus Græcos, nec concessisse nisi serius, cum Augustini et Hieronymi nova auctoritas juvare videretur." It is not ignorance of Greek which is imputed to Tertullian, for he is said to have well understood that language, and even to have composed in it. He probably followed the Latin, as writers now usually quote the authorized English, as being current and best known among their readers. Independent feeling, also, would have weight with such a temper as Tertullian's, to say nothing of the suspicion which largely prevailed in the African branch of the Latin church, that the Greek copies of the Scriptures were much corrupted by the heretics, who were chiefly, if not wholly, Greeks or Greek-speaking persons.

(V.) Whatever perverting effect Tertullian's secession to the sect of Montanus [23] may have had on his judgment in his latest writings, it did not vitiate the work against Marcion. With a few trivial exceptions, this treatise may be read by the strictest Catholic without any feeling of annoyance. His lapse to Montanism is set down conjecturally as having taken place a.d. 199. Jerome, we have seen, attributed the event to his quarrel with the Roman clergy, but this is at least doubtful; nor must it be forgotten that Tertullian's mind seems to have been peculiarly suited by nature [24] to adopt the mystical notions and ascetic principles of Montanus. It is satisfactory to find that, on the whole, "the authority of Tertullian," as the learned Dr. Burton says, "upon great points of doctrine is considered to be little, if at all, affected by his becoming a Montanist." (Lectures on Eccl. Hist. vol. ii. p. 234.) Besides the different works which are expressly mentioned in the notes of this volume, recourse has been had by the translator to Dupin's Hist. Eccl. Writers (trans.), vol. i. pp. 69-86; Tillemont's Mèmoires Hist. Eccl. iii. 85-103; Dr. Smith's Greek and Roman Biography, articles "Marcion" and "Tertullian;" Schaff's article, in Herzog's Cyclopædia, on "Tertullian;" Munter's Primordia Eccl. Africanæ, pp. 118-150; Robertson's Church Hist. vol. i. pp. 70-77; Dr. P. Schaff's Hist. of Christian Church (New York, 1859, pp. 511-519), and Archdeacon Evans' Biography of the Early Church, vol. i. (Lives of "Marcion," pp. 93-122, and "Tertullian," pp. 325-363). This last work, though of a popular cast, shows a good deal of research and learning, expressed in the pleasant style of the once popular author of The Rectory of Vale Head. The translator has mentioned these works, because they are all quite accessible to the general reader, and will give him adequate information concerning the subject treated in the present volume.

To this introduction of Dr. Holmes must be added that of Mr. Thelwall, the translator of the Third volume in the Edinburgh Series, as follows:

To arrange chronologically the works (especially if numerous) of an author whose own date is known with tolerable precision, is not always or necessarily easy: witness the controversies as to the succession of St. Paul's epistles. To do this in the case of an author whose own date is itself a matter of controversy may therefore be reasonably expected to be still less so; and such is the predicament of him who attempts to perform this task for Tertullian. I propose to give a specimen or two of the difficulties with which the task is beset; and then to lay before the reader briefly a summary of the results at which eminent scholars, who have devoted much time and thought to the subject, have arrived. Such a course, I think, will at once afford him means of judging of the absolute impossibility of arriving at definite certainty in the matter; and induce him to excuse me if I prefer furnishing him with materials from which to deduce his own conclusions, rather than venturing on an ex cathedra decision on so doubtful a subject.

I. The book, as Dr. Holmes has reminded us, [25] of the date of which we seem to have the surest evidence, is Adv. Marc. i. This book was in course of writing, as its author himself (c. 15) tells us, "in the fifteenth year of the empire of Severus." Now this date would be clear if there were no doubt as to which year of our Ἥρα corresponds to Tertullian's fifteenth of Severus. Pamelius, however, says Dr. Holmes, makes it a.d. 208; Clinton, (whose authority is more recent and better,) 207.

2. Another book which promises to give some clue to its date is the de Pallio. [26] The writer uses these phrases: "præsentis imperii triplex virtus;" "Deo tot Augustis in unum favente;" which show that there were at the time three persons unitedly bearing the title Augusti--not Cæsares only, but the still higher Augusti;--while the remainder of that context, as well as the opening of c. 1, indicates a time of peace of some considerable duration; a time of plenty; and a time during and previous to which great changes had taken place in the general aspect of the Roman Empire, and some particular traitor had been discovered and frustrated. Such a combination of circumstances might seem to fix the date with some degree of assurance. But unhappily, as Kaye reminds us, [27] commentators cannot agree as to who the three Augusti are. Some say Severus, Caracalla, and Albinus; some say Severus, Caracalla, and

Geta.

Hence we have a difference of some twelve years or thereabouts in the computations. For Albinus was defeated by Severus in person, and fell by his own hand, in a.d. 197; and Geta, Severus' second son, brother of Caracalla, was not associated by his father with himself and his other son as Augustus until a.d. 208, though he had received the title of Cæsar ten years before, in the same year in which Caracalla had received that of Augustus. [28] For my own part, I may perhaps be allowed to say that I should incline to agree, like Salmasius, with those who assign the later date. The limits of the present Introduction forbid my entering at large into my reasons for so doing. I am, however, supported in it by the authority of Neander. [29] In one point, though, I should hesitate to agree with Oehler, who appears to follow Salmasius and others herein,--namely, in understanding the expression "et cacto et rubo subdolæ familiaritatis convulso" of Albinus. It seems to me the words might with more propriety be applied to Plautianus; and that in the word "familiaritatis" we may see (after Tertullian's fashion) a play upon the meaning, with a reference not only to the long-standing but mischievous intimacy which existed between Severus and his countryman (perhaps fellow-townsman) Plautianus, who for his harshness and cruelty is fitly compared to the prickly cactus.

He alludes likewise to the alliance which this ambitious prætorian præfect had contrived to contract with the family of the emperor, by the marriage of his daughter Plautilla to Caracalla,--an event which, as it turned out, led to his own death. Thus in the "rubo" there may be a reference to the ambitious and conceited "bramble" of Jotham's parable, [30] and perhaps, too, to the "thistle" of Jehoash's.[31] If this be so, the date would be at least approximately fixed, as Plautianus did not marry his daughter to Caracalla till a.d. 203, and was himself put to death in the following year, 204, while Geta, as we have seen, was made Augustus in 208.

3. The date of the Apology, however, is perhaps at once the most contested, and the most strikingly illustrative of the difficulties to which allusion has been made.

It is not surprising that its date should have been more disputed than that of other pieces, inasmuch as it is the best known, and (for some reasons) the most interesting and famous, of all our author's productions. In fact, the dates assigned to it by different authorities vary from Mosheim's 198 to that suggested by the very learned Allix, who assigns it to 217. [32]

4. Once more.

In the tract de Monogamia (c. 3) the author says that since the date of St. Paul's first Epistle to the Corinthians "about 160 years had elapsed."

Here, again, did we only know with certainty the precise date of that epistle, we could ascertain "about" the date of the tract. But (a) the date of the epistle is itself variously given, Burton giving it as early as a.d. 52, Michaelis and Mill as late as 57; and (b) Tertullian only says, "Armis circiter clx. exinde productis;" while the way in which, in the ad Natt., within the short space of three chapters, he states first [33] that 250, and then (in c. 9) that 300, years had not elapsed since the rise of the Christian name, leads us to think that here again [34] he only desires to speak in round numbers, meaning perhaps more than 150, but less than 170.

These specimens must suffice, though it might be easy to add to them. There is, however, another classification of our author's writings which has been attempted. Finding the haplessness of strict chronological accuracy, commentators have seized on the idea that peradventure there might be found at all events some internal marks by which to determine which of them were written before, which after, the writer's secession to Montanism. It may be confessed that this attempt has been somewhat more successful than the other. Yet even here there are two formidable obstacles standing in our way. The first and greatest is, that the natural temper of Tertullian was from the first so akin to the spirit of Montanism, that, unless there occur distinct allusions to the "New Prophecy," or expressions specially connected with Montanistic phraseology, the general tone of any treatise is not a very safe guide. The second is, that the subject-matter of some of the treatises is not such as to afford much scope for the introduction of the peculiarities of a sect which professed to differ in discipline only, not doctrine, from the church at large.

Still the result of this classification seems to show one important feature of agreement between commentators, however they may differ upon details; and that is, that considerably the larger part of our author's rather voluminous productions [35] must have been subsequent to his lamented secession. I think the best way to give the reader means for forming his own judgment will be, as I have said, to lay before him in parallel columns a tabular view of the disposition of the books by Dr. Neander and Bishop Kaye. These two modern writers, having given particular care to the subject, bringing to bear upon it all the advantages derived from wide reading, eminent abilities, and a diligent study of the works of preceding writers on the same questions, [36] have a special right to be heard upon the matter in hand; and I think, if I may be allowed to say so, that, for calm judgment, and minute acquaintance with his author, I shall not be accused of undue partiality if I express my opinion that, as far as my own observation goes, the palm must be awarded to the Bishop. In this view I am supported by the fact that the accomplished Professor Ramsay, [37] follows Dr. Kaye's arrangement. I premise that Dr. Neander adopts a threefold division, into:

1. Writings which were occasioned by the relation of the Christians to the heathen, and refer to their vindication of Christianity against the heathen; attacks on heathenism; the sufferings and conduct of Christians under persecution; and the intercourse of Christians with heathens:
2. Writings which relate to Christian and church life, and to ecclesiastical discipline:
3. The dogmatic and dogmatico-controversial treatises.
And under each head he subdivides into:
a. Pre-Montanist writings; b. Post-Montanist writings:

thus leaving no room for what Kaye calls "works respecting which nothing certain can be pronounced." For the sake of clearness, this order has not been followed in the table. On the other side, it will be seen that Dr. Kaye, while not assuming to speak with more than a reasonable probability, is careful so to arrange the treatises under each head as to show the order, so far as it is discoverable, in which the books under that head were published; i.e., if one book is quoted in another book, the book so quoted, if distinctly referred to as already before the world, is plainly anterior to that in which it is quoted. Thus, then, have:

Neander.
I. Pre-Montanist.
1. De Poenitentia.
2. De Oratione.
3. De Baptismo.
4. Ad Uxorem i.
5. Ad Uxorem ii.
6. Ad Martyres.
7. De Patientia.
8. De Spectaculis.
9. De Idololatria.
10. 11. Ad Nationes i. ii.
12. Apologeticus.
13. De Testimonio Animæ.
14. De Præscr. Hæreticorum.
15. De Cult. Fem. i.
16. De Cult. Fem. ii.
II. Montanist.
17-21. Adv. Marc. i. ii. iii. iv. v.
22. De Anima.
23. De Carne Christi.
24. De Res. Carn.
25. De Cor. Mil.
26. De Virg. Vel.
27. De Ex. Cast.
28. De Monog.
29. De Jejuniis.
30. De Pudicitia.
31. De Pallio.
32. Scorpiace.
33. Ad Scapulam.
34. Adv. Valentinianos.
35. Adv. Hermogenem.
36. Adv. Praxeam.
37. Adv. Judæos.
38. De Fuga in Persecutione.

Kaye.
I. Pre-Montanist (probably).
1. De Poenitentia.[38]
2. De Oratione.
3. De Baptismo.
4. Ad Uxorem i.
5. Ad Uxorem ii.
6. Ad Martyres.
7. De Patientia.
8. Adv. Judæos.

9. De Præscr. Hæreticorum. [39]

II. Montanist (certainly).

10. Adv. Marc. i.
11. Adv. Marc. ii. [40]
12. De Anima. [41]
13. Adv. Marc. iii.
14. Adv. Marc. iv. [42]
15. De Carne Christi. [43]
16. De Resurrectione Carnis. [44]
17. Adv. Marc. v.
18. Adv. Praxeam.
19. Scorpiace. [45]
20. De Corona Militis.
21. De Virginibus Velandis.
22. De Exhortatione Castitatis.
23. De Fuga in Persecutione.
24. De Monogamia. [46]
25. De Jejuniis.
26. De Pudicitia.

III. Montanist (probably).

27. Adv. Valentinianos.
28. Ad Scapulam.
29. De Spectaculis. [47]
30. De Idololatria.
31. De Cultu Feminarum i.
32. De Cultu Feminarum ii.

IV. Works respecting which nothing certain can be pronounced.

33. The Apology. [48]
34. Ad Nationes i.
35. Ad Nationes ii.
36. De Testimonio Animæ.
37. De Pallio.
38. Adv. Hermogenem.

A comparison of these two lists will show that the difference between the two great authorities is, as Kaye remarks, "not great; and with respect to some of the tracts on which we differ, the learned author expresses himself with great diffidence." [49] The main difference, in fact, is that which affects two tracts upon kindred subjects, the de Spectaculis, and Idololatria, the de Cultu Feminarum (a subject akin to the other two), and the adv. Judæos. With reference to all these, except the last, to which I believe the Archdeacon does not once refer, the Bishop's opinion appears to have the support of Archdeacon Evans, whose learned and interesting essay, referred to in the note, appears in a volume published in 1837. Dr. Kaye's Lectures, on which his book is founded, were delivered in 1825.

Of the date of his first edition I am not aware. Dr. Neander's Antignostikus also first appeared in 1825. The preface to his second edition bears date July 1, 1849 [50]. As to the adv. Judæos, I confess I agree with Neander in thinking that, at all events from the beginning of c. 9, it is spurious.

If it be urged that Jerome expressly quotes it as Tertullian's, I reply, Jerome so quotes it, I believe, when he is expounding Daniel. Now all that the adv. Jud. has to say about Daniel ends with the end of c. 8. It is therefore quite compatible with the fact thus stated to recognize the earlier half of the book as genuine, and to reject the rest, beginning, as it happens, just after the eighth chapter, as spurious. Perhaps Dr. Neander's Jewish birth and training peculiarly fit him to be heard on this question. Nor do I think Professor Ramsay (in the article above alluded to) has quite seen the force of Kaye's own remarks on Neander. [51] What he does say is equally creditable to his candour and his accuracy; namely: "The instances alleged by Dr. Neander, in proof of this position, are undoubtedly very remarkable; but if the concluding chapters of the tract are spurious, no ground seems to be left for asserting that the genuine portion was posterior to the third Book against Marcion, [52] --and none, consequently, for asserting that it was written by a Montanist." With which remark I must draw these observations on the genuine extant works of Tertullian to a close.

The next point to which a brief reference must be made is the lost works of Tertullian, lists of these are given both by Oehler and by Kaye, viz.:

1. A Book on Aaron's Robes: mentioned by Jerome, Epist. 128, ad Fabiolam de Veste Sacerdotali (tom. ii. p. 586, Opp. ed. Bened.).
2. A Book on the Superstition of the Age. [53]

3. A Book on the Submission of the Soul.

4. A Book on the Flesh and the Soul.

Nos. 2, 3, and 4 are known only by their titles, which are found in the Index to Tertullian's works given in the Codex Agobardi; but the tracts themselves are not extant in the ms., which appears to have once contained--

5. A Book on Paradise, named in the Index, and referred to in de Anima 55, adv. Marc. iii. 12; and

6. A Book on the Hope of the Faithful: also named in the Index, and referred to adv. Marc. iii. 24; and by Jerome in his account of Papias, [54] and on Ezek. xxxvi.; [55] and by Gennadius of Marseilles. [56]

7. Six Books on Ecstasy, with a seventh in reply to Apollonius: [57] see Jerome. [58] See, too, J. A. Fabricius on the words of the unknown author whom the Jesuit Sirmond edited under the name Prædestinatus; who gathers thence that "Soter, pope of the City, [59] and Apollonius, bishop [60] of the Ephesians, wrote a book against the Montanists; in reply to whom Tertullian, a Carthaginian presbyter, wrote." J. Pamelius thinks these seven books were originally published in Greek.

8. A Book in reply to the Apellesites (i.e. the followers of Apelles [61]): referred to in de Carne Christi, c. 8.

9. A Book on the Origin [62] of the Soul, in reply to Hermogenes: referred to in de Anima, cc. 1, 3, 22, 24.

10. A Book on Fate: referred to by Fulgentius Planciades, p. 562, Merc.; also referred to as either written, or intended to be written, by Tertullian himself, de Anima, c. 20. Jerome [63] states that there was extant, or had been extant, a book on Fate under the name of Minucius Felix, written indeed by a perspicuous author, but not in the style of Minucius Felix. This, Pamelius judged, should perhaps be rather ascribed to Tertullian.

11. A Book on the Trinity. Jerome [64] says: "Novatian wrote....a large volume on the Trinity, as if making an epitome of a work of Tertullian's, which most men not knowing regard it as Cyprian's." Novatian's book stood in Tertullian's name in the mss. of J. Gangneius, who was the first to edit it; in a Malmesbury ms. which Sig. Gelenius used; and in others.

12. A Book addressed to a Philosophic Friend on the Straits of Matrimony. Both Kaye and Oehler [65] are in doubt whether Jerome's words, [66] by which some have been led to conclude that Tertullian wrote some book or books on this and kindred subjects, really imply as much, or whether they may not refer merely to those tracts and passages in his extant writings which touch upon such matters. Kaye hesitates to think that the "Book to a Philosophic Friend" is the same as the de Exhortatione Castitatis, because Jerome says Tertullian wrote on the subject of celibacy "in his youth;" but as Cave takes what Jerome elsewhere says of Tertullian's leaving the Church "about the middle of his age" to mean his spiritual age, the same sense might attach to his words here too, and thus obviate the Bishop's difficulty.

There are some other works which have been attributed to Tertullian--on Circumcision; on Animals Clean and Unclean; on the truth that God is a Judge--which Oehler likewise rejects, believing that the expressions of Jerome refer only to passages in the Anti-Marcion and other extant works. To Novatian Jerome does ascribe a distinct work on Circumcision, [67] and this may (comp. 11, just above) have given rise to the view that Tertullian had written one also.

There were, moreover, three treatises at least written by Tertullian in Greek. They are:

1. A Book on Public Shows. See de Cor. c. 6.

2. A Book on Baptism. See de Bapt. c. 15.

3. A Book on the Veiling of Virgins. See de V. V. c. 1.

Oehler adds that J. Pamelius, in his epistle dedicatory to Philip II. of Spain, makes mention of a Greek copy of Tertullian in the library of that king. This report, however, since nothing has ever been seen or heard of the said copy from that time, Oehler judges to be erroneous. [68]

It remains briefly to notice the confessedly spurious works which the editions of Tertullian generally have appended to them. With these Kaye does not deal. The fragment, adv. omnes Hæreses, Oehler attributes to Victorinus Petavionensis, i.e., Victorinus bishop of Pettaw, on the Drave, in Austrian Styria. It was once thought he ought to be called Pictaviensis, i.e. of Poictiers; but John Launoy [69] has shown this to be an error.

Victorinus is said by Jerome to have "understood Greek better than Latin; hence his works are excellent for the sense, but mean as to the style." [70] Cave believes him to have been a Greek by birth. Cassiodorus [71] states him to have been once a professor of rhetoric. Jerome's statement agrees with the style of the tract in question; and Jerome distinctly says Victorinus did write adversus omnes Hæreses. Allix leaves the question of its authorship quite uncertain. If Victorinus be the author, the book falls clearly within the Ante-Nicene period; for Victorinus fell a martyr in the Diocletian persecution, probably about a.d. 303.

The next fragment--"Of the Execrable Gods of the Heathens"--is of quite uncertain authorship.

Oehler would attribute it "to some declaimer not quite ignorant of Tertullian's writings," but certainly not to Tertullian himself.

Lastly we come to the metrical fragments. Concerning these, it is perhaps impossible to assign them to their rightful owners.

Oehler has not troubled himself much about them; but he seems to regard the Jonah as worthy of more regard than the rest, for he seems to have intended giving more labour to its editing at some future time. Whether he has ever done so, or given us his German version of Tertullian's own works, which, "si Deus adjuverit," he distinctly promises in his preface, I do not know. Perhaps the best thing to be done under the circumstances is to give the judgment of the learned Peter Allix. It may be premised that by the celebrated George Fabricius [72] --who published his great work, Poetarum Veterum Ecclesiasticorum Opera Christiana, etc., in 1564--the Five Books in Reply to Marcion, and the Judgment of the Lord, are ascribed to Tertullian, the Genesis and Sodom to Cyprian. Pamelius likewise seems to have ascribed the Five Books, the Jonah, and the Sodom [73] to Tertullian; and according to Lardner, Bishop Bull likewise attributed the Five Books to him. [74] They have been generally ascribed to the Victorinus above mentioned. Tillemont, among others, thinks they may well enough be his. [75] Rigaltius is content to demonstrate that they are not Tertullian's, but leaves the real authorship without attempting to decide it. Of the others the same eminent critic says, "They seem to have been written at Carthage, at an age not far removed from Tertullian's." [76] Allix, after observing that Pamelius is inconsistent with himself in attributing the Genesis and Sodom at one time to Tertullian, at another to Cyprian, rejects both views equally, and assigns the Genesis with some confidence to Salvian, a presbyter of Marseilles, whose "floruit" Cave gives cir. 440, a contemporary of Gennadius, and a copious author. To this it is, Allix thinks, that Gennadius alludes in his Catalogue of Illustrious Men, c. 77.

The Judgment of the Lord Allix ascribes to one Verecundus, an African bishop, whose date he finds it difficult to decide exactly. He refers to two of the name: one Bishop of Tunis, whom Victor of Tunis in his chronicle mentions as having died in exile at Chalcedon a.d. 552; the other Bishop of Noba, who visited Carthage with many others a.d. 482, at the summons of King Huneric, to answer there for their faith;--and would ascribe the poem to the former, thinking that he finds an allusion to it in the article upon that Verecundus in the de Viris Illustribus of Isidore of Seville.

Oehler agrees with him. The Five Books Allix seems to hint may be attributed to some imitator of the Victorinus of Pettaw named above. Oehler attributes them rather to one Victorinus, or Victor, of Marseilles, a rhetorician, who died a.d. 450. He appears in G. Fabricius as Claudius Marius Victorinus, writer of a Commentary on Genesis, and an epistle ad Salomonem Abbata, both in verse, and of some considerable length.

Footnotes:

1. Elucidation I.
2. The notes of Dr. Holmes were bracketted, and I have been forced to remove this feature, as brackets are tokens in this edition of the contributions of American editors. The perpetual recurrence of brackets in his translations has led me to improve the page by parenthetical marks instead, which answer as well and rarely can be mistaken for the author's parentheses, while these disfigure the printer's work much less. I have sometimes substituted italics for brackets, where an inconsiderable word, like and or for, was bracketted by the translator. In every case that I have noted, an intelligent reader will readily perceive such instances; but a critic who may wish to praise, or condemn, should carefully compare the Edinburgh pages with our own. I found them so painful to the eye and so needlessly annoying to the reader, that I have taken the responsibility of making what seems to me a very great typographical improvement.
3. (I.) Concerning Tertullian; (II.) Concerning his Work against Marcion, its date, etc.; (III.) Concerning Marcion; (IV.) Concerning Tertullian's Bible; (V.) Influence of his Montanism on his writings.
4. We quote Bishop Kaye's translation of Jerome's article; see his Account of the Writings of Tertullian, pp. 5-8.
5. Adv. Parmenianum, i.
6. Chap. ii.
7. Eccl. Hist., ii. 2.
8. Valesius, however, supposes the historian's words τῶν μάλιστα ἐπὶ 'Ρώμης λαμπρῶν to mean, that Tertullian had obtained distinction among Latin writers.
9. See De Præscript. Hæretic. xxx.
10. De Poenitentia, i. Hoc genus hominum, quod et ipsi retro fuimus, cæci, sine Domini lumine, naturâ tenus norunt; De Fuga in Persecutione, vi. Nobis autem et via nationum patet, in quâ et inventi sumus; Adv. Marcionem, iii. 21. Et nationes, quod sumus nos; Apolog. xviii. Hæc et nos risimus aliquando; de vestris fuimus; also De Spectac. xix.
11. [Kaye, p. 9. A fair view of this point.]
12. These notes of Bishop Kaye may be found, in their fuller form, in his work on Tertullian, pp. 8-12.
13. Book i., chap. xv.
14. Jerome probably took this date as the central period, when Tertullian "flourished," because of its being the only clearly authenticated one, and because also (it may

be) of the importance and fame of the Treatise against Marcion.

15. So Clinton, Fasti Romani, i. 204; or 208, Pamelius, Vita Tertull.

16. In his treatise, De vera ætate ac doctrina script. Tertulliani, sections 28, 45.

17. De Præscript. Hæret. xxx.

18. Comp. Adv. Marcionem, iv. 4.

19. I., Adv. Hæret. xlii. 1.

20. Dr. Burton's Lectures on Eccl. Hist. of First Three Centuries, ii. 105-109.

21. Or versions.

22. Tertullianus.

23. Vincentius Lirinensis, in his celebrated Commonitorium, expresses the opinion of Catholic churchmen concerning Tertullian thus: "Tertullian, among the Latins, without controversy, is the chief of all our writers. For who was more learned than he? Who in divinity or humanity more practised? For, by a certain wonderful capacity of mind, he attained to and understood all philosophy, all the sects of philosophers, all their founders and supporters, all their systems, all sorts of histories and studies.

And for his wit, was he not so excellent, so grave, so forcible, that he scarce ever undertook the overthrow of any position, but either by quickness of wit he undermined, or by weight of reason he crushed it? Further, who is able to express the praises which his style of speech deserves, which is fraught (I know none like it) with that cogency of reason, that such as it cannot persuade, it compels to assent; whose so many words almost are so many sentences; whose so many senses, so many victories? This know Marcion and Apelles, Praxeas and Hermogenes, Jews, Gentiles, Gnostics, and divers others, whose blasphemous opinions he hath overthrown with his many and great volumes, as it had been thunderbolts. And yet this man after all, this Tertullian, not retaining the Catholic doctrine--that is, the old faith--hath discredited with his later error his worthy writings," etc.--Chap. xxiv. (Oxford trans. chap. xviii.)

24. Neander's introduction to his Antignostikus should be read in connection with this topic. He powerfully delineates the disposition of Tertullian and the character of Montanism, and attributes his secession to that sect not to outward causes, but to "his internal congeniality of mind."

But, inasmuch as a man's subjective development is very much guided by circumstances, it is not necessary, in agreeing with Neander, to disbelieve some such account as Jerome has given us of Tertullian (Neander's Antignostikus, etc. Bohn's trans., vol. ii. pp. 200-207).

25. Introductory Notice to the Anti-Marcion, pp. xiii., xiv.

26. In the end of Chapter Second.

27. Eccl. Hist. illust. from Tertullian's Writings, p. 36 sqq. (ed. 3, Lond. 1845).

28. See Kaye, as above.

29. Antignostikus, p. 424 (Bohn's tr., ed. 1851).

30. See Judg. ix. 2 sqq.

31. See 2 Kings (4 Kings in LXX. and Vulg.) xiv. 9.

32. Here, again, our limits forbid a discussion; but the allusion to the Rhone having "scarcely yet lost the stain of blood" which we find in the ad. Natt. i. 17, compared with Apol. 35, seems to favour the idea of those who date the ad. Natt. earlier than the Apology, and consider the latter as a kind of new edition of the former: while it would fix the date of the ad. Natt. as not certainly earlier than 197, in which year (as we have seen) Albinus died. The fatal battle took place on the banks of the Rhone.

33. In c. 7.

34. Viz. in the de Monog.

35. It looks strange to see Tertullian's works referred to as consisting of "about thirty short treatises" in Murdock's note on Moshiem. See the ed. of the Eccl. Hist. by Dr. J. Seaton Reid, p. 65, n. 2, Lond. and Bel. 1852.

36. This last qualification is very specially observable in Dr. Kaye.

37. In his article on Tertullian in Smith's Dict. of Biog. and Myth.

38. Referred to apparently in de Pudic. ad init.-Tr.

39. The de Præscr. is ref. to in adv. Marc. i.; adv Prax. 2; de Carne Christi, 2; adv. Hermog. 1.

40. Ref. to in de Res. Carn. 2, 14; Scorp. 5; de Anima, 21. The only mark, as the learned Bishop's remarks imply, for fixing the date of publication as Montanistic, is the fact that Tertullian alludes, in the opening sentences, to B. i. Hence B. ii. could not, in its present form, have appeared till after B. i.

Now B. i. contains evident marks of Montanism: see the last chapter, for instance. But the writer speaks (in the same passage) of B. ii. as being the treatise, the ill fate of which in its unfinished condition he there relates--at least such seems the legitimate sense of his words--now remodelled. Hence, when originally written, it may not have been Montanistic.--Tr.

41. Ref. to in de Res. Carn. 2, 17, 45; comp. cc. 18, 21.

42. Ref. to in de Carn. Chr. 7.

43. Ref. to in de Res. Carn. 2.

44. See the beginning and end of the de Carne Christi.--Tr.

Ref. to in adv. Marc. v. 10.

45. In c. 4 Tertullian speaks as if he had already refuted all the heretics.

46. Ref. to in de Jej. c. 1.

47. Ref. to in de Idolol. 13; in de Cult. Fem. i. 8. In the de Cor. 6 is a reference to the Greek tract de Spectaculis by our author.

48. Archdeacon Evans, in his Biography of the Early Church (in the Theological Library), suggests that the success which the Apology met with, or at least the fame it brought its author, may have been the occasion of Tertullian's visit to Rome. He rejects entirely the supposition that Tertullian was a presbyter of the Roman church; nor does he think Eusebius' words, καὶ τῶν μάλιστα ἐπὶ Ῥώμης λαμπρῶν (Eccl. Hist. ii. 2. 47 ad fin., 48 ad init.), sufficiently plain to be relied on. One thing does seem pretty plain, that the rendering of them which Rufinus gives, and Valesius follows, "inter nostros" (sc. Latinos) "Scriptores admodum clarus," cannot be correct.

That we find a famous Roman lawyer Tertullianus, or Tertyllianus, among the writers fragments of whom are preserved in the Pandects, Neander reminds us; but (as he says) it by no means follows, even if it could be proved that the date of the said lawyer corresponded with the supposed date of our Tertullian, that they were identical.

Still it is worth bearing in mind, especially as a similarity of language exists, or has been thought to exist, between the jurist and the Christian author. And the juridical language and tone of our author do seem to point to his having--though Mr. Evans regards that as doubtful--been a trained lawyer.--Tr.

49. Kaye, as above. Pref. to 2d ed. pp. xxi. xxii. incorporated in the 3d ed., which I always quote.

50. i.e., four years after Kaye's third.

51. See Pref. 2d ed. p. xix. n. 9.

52. It being from that book that the quotations are taken which make up the remainder of the tract, as Semler, worthless as his theories are, has well shown.

53. "Sæculi" or "of the world," or perhaps "of heathenism."

54. Catal. Scrippt. Eccles. c. 18.

55. P. 952, tom. iii. Opp. ed. Bened.

56. De Ecclesiæ dogmatibus, c. 55.

57. Referred to in Adv. Marc. iv. 22.

So Kaye thinks; but perhaps the reference is doubtful. See, however, the passage in Dr. Holmes' translation in the present series, with his note thereon.

58. De Scriptt. Eccles. 53, 24, 40.

59. i.e., Rome.

60. Antistes.

61. A Marcionite at one time: he subsequently set up a sect of his own. He is mentioned in the adv. omn. Hær. c. 6.

62. Censu.

63. Catal. Scrippt. Eccles. c. 58.

64. Catal. Scrippt. Eccles. c. 70.

65. Oehler speaks more decidedly than Kaye.

66. Epist. ad Eustochium de Custodia Virginitatis, p. 37, tom. iv. Opp. ed. Bened.; adv. Jovin. i. p. 157, tom. iv. Opp. ed. Bened.

67. In the Catal. Scrippt. Eccles.

68. "Mendacem" is his word. I know not whether he intends to charge Pamelius with wilful fraud.

69. Doctor of the Sorbonne, said by Bossuet to have proved himself "a semi-Pelagian and Jansenist!" born in 1603, in Normandy, died in 1678.

70. Jer. de Vir. Illust. c. 74.

71. B. 470, d. 560.

72. He must not be confounded with the still more famous John Albert Fabricius of the next century, referred to in p. xv. above.

73. Whole of these metrical fragments.

74. Lardner, Credibility, vol. iii. p. 169, under "Victorinus of Pettaw," ed. Kippis, Lond. 1838.

75. See Lardner, as above.

76. See Migne, who prefixes this judgment of Rig. to the de Judicio Domini.

I - Apology

[Translated by the Rev. S. Thelwall, Late Scholar of Christ's College, Cantab.]

The Apology [77]

Chapter I

Rulers of the Roman Empire, if, seated for the administration of justice on your lofty tribunal, under the gaze of every eye, and occupying there all but the highest position in the state, you may not openly inquire into and sift before the world the real truth in regard to the charges made against the Christians; if in this case alone you are afraid or ashamed to exercise your authority in making public inquiry with the carefulness which becomes justice; if, finally, the extreme severities inflicted on our people in recently private judgments, stand in the way of our being permitted to defend ourselves before you, you cannot surely forbid the Truth to reach your ears by the secret pathway of a noiseless book. [78] She has no appeals to make to you in regard of her condition, for that does not excite her wonder. She knows that she is but a sojourner on the earth, and that among strangers she naturally finds foes; and more than this, that her origin, her dwelling-place, her hope, her recompense, her honours, are above. One thing, meanwhile, she anxiously desires of earthly rulers--not to be condemned unknown. What harm can it do to the laws, supreme in their domain, to give her a hearing?

Nay, for that part of it, will not their absolute supremacy be more conspicuous in their condemning her, even after she has made her plea? But if, unheard, sentence is pronounced against her, besides the odium of an unjust deed, you will incur the merited suspicion of doing it with some idea that it is unjust, as not wishing to hear what you may not be able to hear and condemn.

We lay this before you as the first ground on which we urge that your hatred to the name of Christian is unjust.

And the very reason which seems to excuse this injustice (I mean ignorance) at once aggravates and convicts it.

For what is there more unfair than to hate a thing of which you know nothing, even though it deserve to be hated?

Hatred is only merited when it is known to be merited. But without that knowledge, whence is its justice to be vindicated? for that is to be proved, not from the mere fact that an aversion exists, but from acquaintance with the subject. When men, then, give way to a dislike simply because they are entirely ignorant of the nature of the thing disliked, why may it not be precisely the very sort of thing they should not dislike? So we maintain that they are both ignorant while they hate us, and hate us unrighteously while they continue in ignorance, the one thing being the result of the other either way of it. The proof of their ignorance, at once condemning and excusing their injustice, is this, that those who once hated Christianity because they knew nothing about it, no sooner come to know it than they all lay down at once their enmity.

From being its haters they become its disciples. By simply getting acquainted with it, they begin now to hate what they had formerly been, and to profess what they had formerly hated; and their numbers are as great as are laid to our charge. The outcry is that the State is filled with Christians--that they are in the fields, in the citadels, in the islands: they make lamentation, as for some calamity, that both sexes, every age and condition, even high rank, are passing over to the profession of the Christian faith; and yet for all, their minds are not awakened to the thought of some good they have failed to notice in it. They must not allow any truer suspicions to cross their minds; they have no desire to make closer trial. Here alone the curiosity of human nature slumbers. They like to be ignorant, though to others the knowledge has been bliss.

Anacharsis reproved the rude venturing to criticise the cultured; how much more this judging of those who know, by men who are entirely ignorant, might he have denounced! Because they already dislike, they want to know no more. Thus they prejudge that of which they are ignorant to be such, that, if they came to know it, it could no longer be the object of their aversion; since, if inquiry finds nothing worthy of dislike, it is certainly proper to cease from an unjust dislike, while if its bad character comes plainly out, instead of the detestation entertained for it being thus diminished, a stronger reason for perseverance in that detestation is obtained, even under the authority of justice itself. But, says one, a thing is not good merely because multitudes go over to it; for how many have the bent of their nature towards whatever is bad! how many go astray into ways of error! It is undoubted. Yet a thing that is thoroughly evil, not even those whom it carries away venture to defend as good. Nature throws a veil either of fear or shame over all evil. For instance, you find that criminals are eager to conceal themselves, avoid appearing in public, are in trepidation when they are caught, deny their guilt, when they are accused; even when they are put to the rack, they do not easily or always confess; when there is no doubt about their condemnation, they grieve for what they have done. In their self-communings they admit their being impelled by sinful dispositions, but they lay the blame either on fate or on the stars. They are unwilling to acknowledge that the thing is theirs, because they own that it is wicked. But what is there like this in the Christian's case? The only shame or regret he feels, is at not having been a Christian earlier. If he is pointed out, he glories in it; if he is accused, he offers no defence; interrogated, he makes voluntary confession; condemned he renders thanks. What sort of evil thing is this, which wants all the ordinary peculiarities of evil--fear, shame, subterfuge, penitence, lamenting?

What! is that a crime in which the criminal rejoices? to be accused of which is his ardent wish, to be punished for which is his felicity? You cannot call it madness, you who stand convicted of knowing nothing of the matter.

Chapter II

If, again, it is certain that we are the most wicked of men, why do you treat us so differently from our fellows, that is, from other criminals, it being only fair that the same crime should get the same treatment? When the charges made against us are made against others, they are permitted to make use both of their own lips and of hired pleaders to show their innocence. They have full opportunity of answer and debate; in fact, it is against the law to condemn anybody undefended and unheard. Christians alone are forbidden to say anything in exculpation of themselves, in defence of the truth, to help the judge to a righteous decision; all that is cared about is having what the public hatred demands-- the confession of the name, not examination of the charge: while in your ordinary judicial investigations, on a man's confession of the crime of murder, or sacrilege, or incest, or treason, to take the points of which we are accused, you are not content to proceed at once to sentence,--you do not take that step till you thoroughly examine the circumstances of the confession--what is the real character of the deed, how often, where, in what way, when he has done it, who were privy to it, and who actually took part with him in it. Nothing like this is done in our case, though the falsehoods disseminated about us ought to have the same sifting, that it might be found how many murdered children each of us had tasted; how many incests each of us had shrouded in darkness; what cooks, what dogs had been witness of our deeds. Oh, how great the glory of the ruler who should bring to light some Christian who had devoured a hundred infants! But, instead of that, we find that even inquiry in regard to our case is forbidden. For the younger Pliny, when he was ruler of a province, having condemned some Christians to death, and driven some from their stedfastness, being still annoyed by their great numbers, at last sought the advice of Trajan, [79] the reigning emperor, as to what he was to do with the rest, explaining to his master that, except an obstinate disinclination to offer sacrifices, he found in the religious services nothing but meetings at early morning for singing hymns to Christ and [80] God, and sealing home their way of life by a united pledge to be faithful to their religion, forbidding murder, adultery, dishonesty, and other crimes. Upon this Trajan wrote back that Christians were by no means to be sought after; but if they were brought before him, they should be punished. O miserable deliverance,--under the necessities of the case, a self-contradiction! It forbids them to be sought after as innocent, and it commands them to be punished as guilty. It is at once merciful and cruel; it passes by, and it punishes. Why dost thou play a game of evasion upon thyself, O Judgment?

If thou condemnest, why dost thou not also inquire. If thou does not inquire, why dost thou not also absolve? Military stations are distributed through all the provinces for tracking robbers. Against traitors and public foes every man is a soldier; search is made even for their confederates and accessories. The Christian alone must not be sought, though he may be brought and accused before the judge; as if a search had any other end than that in view! And so you condemn the man for whom nobody wished a search to be made when he is presented to you, and who even now does not deserve punishment, I suppose, because of his guilt, but because, though forbidden to be sought, he was found. And then, too, you do not in that case deal with us in the ordinary way of judicial proceedings against offenders; for, in the case of others denying, you apply the torture to make them confess--Christians alone you torture, to make them deny; whereas, if we were guilty of any crime, we should be sure to deny it, and you with your tortures would force us to confession. Nor indeed should you hold that our crimes require no such investigation merely on the ground that you are convinced by our confession of the name that the deeds were done,--you who are daily wont, though you know well enough what murder is, none the less to extract from the confessed murderer a full account of how the crime was perpetrated. So that with all the greater perversity you act, when, holding our crimes proved by our confession of the name of Christ, you drive us by torture to fall from our confession, that, repudiating the name, we may in like manner repudiate also the crimes with which, from that same confession, you had assumed that we were chargeable. I suppose, though you believe us to be the worst of mankind, you do not wish us to perish.

For thus, no doubt, you are in the habit of bidding the murderer deny, and of ordering the man guilty of sacrilege to the rack if he persevere in his acknowledgment! Is that the way of it? But if thus you do not deal with us as criminals, you declare us thereby innocent, when as innocent you are anxious that we do not persevere in a confession which you know will bring on us a condemnation of necessity, not of justice, at your hands. "I am a Christian," the man cries out. He tells you what he is; you wish to hear from him what he is not. Occupying your place of authority to extort the truth, you do your utmost to get lies from us. "I am," he says, "that which you ask me if I am. Why do you torture me to sin? I confess, and you put me to the rack. What would you do if I denied? Certainly you give no ready credence to others when they deny. When we deny, you believe at once. Let this perversity of yours lead you to suspect that there is some hidden power in the case under whose influence you act against the forms, against the nature of public justice, even against the very laws themselves. For, unless I am greatly mistaken, the laws enjoin offenders to be searched out, and not to be hidden away. They lay it down that persons who own a crime are to be condemned, not acquitted. The decrees of the senate, the commands of your chiefs, lay this clearly down. The power of which you are servants is a civil, not a tyrannical domination.

Among tyrants, indeed, torments used to be inflicted even as punishments: with you they are mitigated to a means of questioning alone. Keep to your law in these as necessary till confession is obtained; and if the torture is anticipated by confession, there will be no occasion for it: sentence should be passed; the criminal should be given over to the penalty which is his due, not released. Accordingly, no one is eager for the acquittal of the guilty; it is not right to desire that, and so no one is ever compelled to deny. Well, you think the Christian a man of every crime, an enemy of the gods, of the emperor, of the laws, of good morals, of all nature; yet you compel him to deny, that you may acquit him, which without him denial you could not do. You play fast and loose with the laws. You wish him to deny his guilt, that you may, even against his will, bring him out blameless and free from all guilt in reference to the past! Whence is this strange perversity on your part? How is it you do not reflect that a spontaneous confession is greatly more worthy of credit than a compelled denial; or consider whether, when compelled to deny, a man's denial may not be in good faith, and whether acquitted, he may not, then and there, as soon as the trial is over, laugh at your hostility, a Christian as much as ever? Seeing, then, that in everything you deal differently with us than with other criminals, bent upon the one object of taking from us our name (indeed, it is ours no more if we do what Christians never do), it is made perfectly clear that there is no crime of any kind in the case, but merely a name which a certain system, ever working against the truth, pursues with its enmity, doing this chiefly with the object of securing that men may have no desire to know for certain what they know for certain they are entirely ignorant of. Hence, too, it is that they believe about us things of which they have no proof, and they are disinclined to have them looked into, lest the charges, they would rather take on trust, are all proved to have no foundation, that the name so hostile to that rival power--its crimes presumed, not proved--may be condemned simply on its own confession. So we are put to the torture if we confess, and we are punished if we persevere, and if we deny we are acquitted, because all the contention is about a name. Finally, why do you read out of your tablet-lists that such a man is a Christian?

Why not also that he is a murderer?

And if a Christian is a murderer, why not guilty, too, of incest, or any other vile thing you believe of us? In our case alone you are either ashamed or unwilling to mention the very names of our crimes-- If to be called a "Christian" does not imply any crime, the name is surely very hateful, when that of itself is made a crime.

Chapter III

What are we to think of it, that most people so blindly knock their heads against the hatred of the Christian name; that when they bear favourable testimony to any one, they mingle with it abuse of the name he bears?

"A good man," says one, "is Gaius Seius, only that he is a Christian." So another, "I am astonished that a wise man like Lucius should have suddenly become a Christian." Nobody thinks it needful to consider whether Gaius is not good and Lucius wise, on this very account that he is a Christian; or a Christian, for the reason that he is wise and good. They praise what they know, they abuse what they are ignorant of, and they inspire their knowledge with their ignorance; though in fairness you should rather judge of what is unknown from what is known, than what is known from what is unknown.

Others, in the case of persons whom, before they took the name of Christian, they had known as loose, and vile, and wicked, put on them a brand from the very thing which they praise.

In the blindness of their hatred, they fall foul of their own approving judgment! "What a woman she was! how wanton! how gay! What a youth he was! how profligate! how libidinous!--they have become Christians!" So the hated name is given to a reformation of character. Some even barter away their comforts for that hatred, content to bear injury, if they are kept free at home from the object of their bitter enmity.

The wife, now chaste, the husband, now no longer jealous, casts out of his house; the son, now obedient, the father, who used to be so patient, disinherits; the servant, now faithful, the master, once so mild, commands away from his presence; it is a high offence for any one to be reformed by the detested name. Goodness is of less value than hatred of Christians. Well now, if there is this dislike of the name, what blame can you attach to names? What accusation can you bring against mere designations, save that something in the word sounds either barbarous, or unlucky, or scurrilous, or unchaste? But Christian, so far as the meaning of the word is concerned, is derived from anointing. Yes, and even when it is wrongly pronounced by you "Chrestianus" (for you do not even know accurately the name you hate), it comes from sweetness and benignity. You hate, therefore, in the guiltless, even a guiltless name. But the special ground of dislike to the sect is, that it bears the name of its Founder. Is there anything new in a religious sect getting for its followers a designation from its master? Are not the philosophers called from the founders of their systems--Platonists, Epicureans, Pythagoreans? Are not the Stoics and Academics so called also from the places in which they assembled and stationed themselves? and are not physicians named from Erasistratus, grammarians from Aristarchus, cooks even from Apicius? And yet the bearing of the name, transmitted from the original institutor with whatever he has instituted, offends no one. No doubt, if it is proved that the sect is a bad one, and so its founder bad as well, that will prove that the name is bad and deserves our aversion, in respect of the character both of the sect and its author. Before, therefore, taking up a dislike to the name, it behoved you to consider the sect in the author, or the author in the sect. But now, without any sifting and knowledge of either, the mere name is made matter of accusation, the mere name is assailed, and a sound alone brings condemnation on a sect and its author both, while of both you are ignorant, because they have such and such a designation, not because they are convicted of anything wrong.

Chapter IV

And so, having made these remarks as it were by way of preface, that I might show in its true colours the injustice of the public hatred against us, I shall now take my stand on the plea of our blamelessness; and I shall not only refute the things which are objected to us, but I shall also retort them on the objectors, that in this way all may know that Christians are free from the very crimes they are so well aware prevail among themselves, that they may at the same time be put to the blush for their accusations against us,--accusations I shall not say of the worst of men against the best, but now, as they will have it, against those who are only their fellows in sin. We shall reply to the accusation of all the various crimes we are said to be guilty of in secret, such as we find them committing in the light of day, and as being guilty of which we are held to be wicked, senseless, worthy of punishment, deserving of ridicule. But since, when our truth meets you successfully at all points, the authority of the laws as a last resort is set up against it, so that it is either said that their determinations are absolutely conclusive, or the necessity of obedience is, however unwillingly, preferred to the truth, I shall first, in this matter of the laws grapple with you as with their chosen protectors. Now first, when you sternly lay it down in your sentences, "It is not lawful for you to exist," and with unhesitating rigour you enjoin this to be carried out, you exhibit the violence and unjust domination of mere tyranny, if you deny the thing to be lawful, simply on the ground that you wish it to be unlawful, not because it ought to be. But if you would have it unlawful because it ought not to be lawful, without doubt that should have no permission of law which does harm; and on this ground, in fact, it is already determined that whatever is beneficial is legitimate. Well, if I have found what your law prohibits to be good, as one who has arrived at such a previous opinion, has it not lost its power to debar me from it, though that very thing, if it were evil, it would justly forbid to me? If your law has gone wrong, it is of human origin, I think; it has not fallen from heaven. Is it wonderful that man should err in making a law, or come to his senses in rejecting it? Did not the Lacedæmonians amend the laws of Lycurgus himself, thereby inflicting such pain on their author that he shut himself up, and doomed himself to death by starvation? Are you not yourselves every day, in your efforts to illumine the darkness of antiquity, cutting and hewing with the new axes of imperial rescripts and edicts, that whole ancient and rugged forest of your laws? Has not Severus, that most resolute of rulers, but yesterday repealed the ridiculous Papian laws [81] which compelled people to have children before the Julian laws allow matrimony to be contracted, and that though they have the authority of age upon their side? There were laws, too, in old times, that parties against whom a decision had been given might be cut in pieces by their creditors; however, by common consent that cruelty was afterwards erased from the statutes, and the capital penalty turned into a brand of shame. By adopting the plan of confiscating a debtor's goods, it was sought rather to pour the blood in blushes over his face than to pour it out.

How many laws lie hidden out of sight which still require to be reformed! For it is neither the number of their years nor the dignity of their maker that commends them, but simply that they are just; and therefore, when their injustice is recognized, they are deservedly condemned, even though they condemn.

Why speak we of them as unjust? nay, if they punish mere names, we may well call them irrational. But if they punish acts, why in our case do they punish acts solely on the ground of a name, while in others they must have them proved not from the name, but from the wrong done? I am a practiser of incest (so they say); why do they not inquire into it? I am an infant-killer; why do they not apply the torture to get from me the truth? I am guilty of crimes against the gods, against the Cæsars; why am I, who am able to clear myself, not allowed to be heard on my own behalf? No law forbids the sifting of the crimes which it prohibits, for a judge never inflicts a righteous vengeance if he is not well assured that a crime has been committed; nor does a citizen render a true subjection to the law, if he does not know the nature of the thing on which the punishment is inflicted. It is not enough that a law is just, nor that the judge should be convinced of its justice; those from whom obedience is expected should have that conviction too. Nay, a law lies under strong suspicions which does not care to have itself tried and approved: it is a positively wicked law, if, unproved, it tyrannizes over men.

Chapter V

To say a word about the origin of laws of the kind to which we now refer, there was an old decree that no god should be consecrated by the emperor till first approved by the senate. Marcus Æmilius had experience of this in reference to his god Alburnus.

And this, too, makes for our case, that among you divinity is allotted at the judgment of human beings. Unless gods give satisfaction to men, there will be no deification for them: the god will have to propitiate the man. Tiberius [82] accordingly, in whose days the Christian name made its entry into the world, having himself received intelligence from Palestine of events which had clearly shown the truth of Christ's divinity, brought the matter before the senate, with his own decision in favour of Christ.

The senate, because it had not given the approval itself, rejected his proposal. Cæsar held to his opinion, threatening wrath against all accusers of the Christians. Consult your histories; you will there find that Nero was the first who assailed with the imperial sword the Christian sect, making progress then especially at Rome.

But we glory in having our condemnation hallowed by the hostility of such a wretch. For any one who knows him, can understand that not except as being of singular excellence did anything bring on it Nero's condemnation.

Domitian, too, a man of Nero's type in cruelty, tried his hand at persecution; but as he had something of the human in him, he soon put an end to what he had begun, even restoring again those whom he had banished. Such as these have always been our persecutors,--men unjust, impious, base, of whom even you yourselves have no good to say, the sufferers under whose sentences you have been wont to restore. But among so many princes from that time to the present day, with anything of divine and human wisdom in them, point out a single persecutor of the Christian name.

So far from that, we, on the contrary, bring before you one who was their protector, as you will see by examining the letters of Marcus Aurelius, that most grave of emperors, in which he bears his testimony that that Germanic drought was removed by the rains obtained through the prayers of the Christians who chanced to be fighting under him.

And as he did not by public law remove from Christians their legal disabilities, yet in another way he put them openly aside, even adding a sentence of condemnation, and that of greater severity, against their accusers. What sort of laws are these which the impious alone execute against us--and the unjust, the vile, the bloody, the senseless, the insane? which Trajan to some extent made naught by forbidding Christians to be sought after; which neither a Hadrian, though fond of searching into all things strange and new, nor a Vespasian, though the subjugator of the Jews, nor a Pius, nor a Verus, ever enforced? It should surely be judged more natural for bad men to be eradicated by good princes as being their natural enemies, than by those of a spirit kindred with their own.

Chapter VI

I would now have these most religious protectors and vindicators of the laws and institutions of their fathers, tell me, in regard to their own fidelity and the honour, and submission they themselves show to ancestral institutions, if they have departed from nothing--if they have in nothing gone out of the old paths--if they have not put aside whatsoever is most useful and necessary as rules of a virtuous life. What has become of the laws repressing expensive and ostentatious ways of living? which forbade more than a hundred asses to be expended on a supper, and more than one fowl to be set on the table at a time, and that not a fatted one; which expelled a patrician from the senate on the serious ground, as it was counted, of aspiring to be too great, because he had acquired ten pounds of silver; which put down the theatres as quickly as they arose to debauch the manners of the people; which did not permit the insignia of official dignities or of noble birth to be rashly or with impunity usurped? For I see the Centenarian suppers must now bear the name, not from the hundred asses, but from the hundred sestertia [83] expended on them; and that mines of silver are made into dishes (it were little if this applied only to senators, and not to freedmen or even mere whip-spoilers [84]). I see, too, that neither is a single theatre enough, nor are theatres unsheltered: no doubt it was that immodest pleasure might not be torpid in the wintertime, the Lacedæmonians invented their woollen cloaks for the plays. I see now no difference between the dress of matrons and prostitutes. In regard to women, indeed, those laws of your fathers, which used to be such an encouragement to modesty and sobriety, have also fallen into desuetude, when a woman had yet known no gold upon her save on the finger, which, with the bridal ring, her husband had sacredly pledged to himself; when the abstinence of women from wine was carried so far, that a matron, for opening the compartments of a wine cellar, was starved to death by her friends,--while in the times of Romulus, for merely tasting wine, Mecenius killed his wife, and suffered nothing for the deed. With reference to this also, it was the custom of women to kiss their relatives, that they might be detected by their breath. Where is that happiness of married life, ever so desirable, which distinguished our earlier manners, and as the result of which for about 600 years there was not among us a single divorce? Now, women have every member of the body heavy laden with gold; wine-bibbing is so common among them, that the kiss is never offered with their will; and as for divorce, they long for it as though it were the natural consequence of marriage. The laws, too, your fathers in their wisdom had enacted concerning the very gods themselves, you their most loyal children have rescinded.

The consuls, by the authority of the senate, banished Father Bacchus and his mysteries not merely from the city, but from the whole of Italy. The consuls Piso and Gabinius, no Christians surely, forbade Serapis, and Isis, and Arpocrates, with their dogheaded friend, [85] admission into the Capitol--in the act casting them out from the assembly of the gods--overthrow their altars, and expelled them from the country, being anxious to prevent the vices of their base and lascivious religion from spreading. These, you have restored, and conferred highest honours on them. What has come to your religion--of the veneration due by you to your ancestors? In your dress, in your food, in your style of life, in your opinions, and last of all in your very speech, you have renounced your progenitors. You are always praising antiquity, and yet every day you have novelties in your way of living. From your having failed to maintain what you should, you make it clear, that, while you abandon the good ways of your fathers, you retain and guard the things you ought not. Yet the very tradition of your fathers, which you still seem so faithfully to defend, and in which you find your principal matter of accusation against the Christians--I mean zeal in the worship of the gods, the point in which antiquity has mainly erred--although you have rebuilt the altars of Serapis, now a Roman deity, and to Bacchus, now become a god of Italy, you offer up your orgies,--I shall in its proper place show that you despise, neglect, and overthrow, casting entirely aside the authority of the men of old. I go on meantime to reply to that infamous charge of secret crimes, clearing my way to things of open day.

Chapter VII

Monsters of wickedness, we are accused of observing a holy rite in which we kill a little child and then eat it; in which, after the feast, we practise incest, the dogs--our pimps, forsooth, overturning the lights and getting us the shamelessness of darkness for our impious lusts. This is what is constantly laid to our charge, and yet you take no pains to elicit the truth of what we have been so long accused. Either bring, then, the matter to the light of day if you believe it, or give it no credit as having never inquired into it. On the ground of your double dealing, we are entitled to lay it down to you that there is no reality in the thing which you dare not expiscate. You impose on the executioner, in the case of Christians, a duty the very opposite of expiscation: he is not to make them confess what they do, but to make them deny what they are. We date the origin of our religion, as we have mentioned before, from the reign of Tiberius. Truth and the hatred of truth come into our world together. As soon as truth appears, it is regarded as an enemy. It has as many foes as there are strangers to it:

the Jews, as was to be looked for, from a spirit of rivalry; the soldiers, out of a desire to extort money; our very domestics, by their nature. We are daily beset by foes, we are daily betrayed; we are oftentimes surprised in our meetings and congregations. Whoever happened withal upon an infant wailing, according to the common story? Whoever kept for the judge, just as he had found them, the gory mouths of Cyclops and Sirens? Whoever found any traces of uncleanness in their wives? Where is the man who, when he had discovered such atrocities, concealed them; or, in the act of dragging the culprits before the judge, was bribed into silence? If we always keep our secrets, when were our proceedings made known to the world?

Nay, by whom could they be made known?

Not, surely, by the guilty parties themselves; even from the very idea of the thing, the fealty of silence being ever due to mysteries. The Samothracian and Eleusinian make no disclosures--how much more will silence be kept in regard to such as are sure, in their unveiling, to call forth punishment from man at once, while wrath divine is kept in store for the future?

If, then, Christians are not themselves the publishers of their crime, it follows of course it must be strangers.

And whence have they their knowledge, when it is also a universal custom in religious initiations to keep the profane aloof, and to beware of witnesses, unless it be that those who are so wicked have less fear than their neighbors? Every one knows what sort of thing rumour is. It is one of your own sayings, that "among all evils, none flies so fast as rumour." Why is rumour such an evil thing? Is it because it is fleet? Is it because it carries information? Or is it because it is in the highest degree mendacious?--a thing, not even when it brings some truth to us, without a taint of falsehood, either detracting, or adding, or changing from the simple fact? Nay more, it is the very law of its being to continue only while it lies, and to live but so long as there is no proof; for when the proof is given, it ceases to exist; and, as having done its work of merely spreading a report, it delivers up a fact, and is henceforth held to be a fact, and called a fact.

And then no one says, for instance, "They say that it took place at Rome," or, "There is a rumour that he has obtained a province," but, "He has got a province," and, "It took place at Rome." Rumour, the very designation of uncertainty, has no place when a thing is certain. Does any but a fool put his trust in it? For a wise man never believes the dubious. Everybody knows, however zealously it is spread abroad, on whatever strength of asseveration it rests, that some time or other from some one fountain it has its origin. Thence it must creep into propagating tongues and ears; and a small seminal blemish so darkens all the rest of the story, that no one can determine whether the lips, from which it first came forth, planted the seed of falsehood, as often happens, from a spirit of opposition, or from a suspicious judgment, or from a confirmed, nay, in the case of some, an inborn, delight in lying. It is well that time brings all to light, as your proverbs and sayings testify, by a provision of Nature, which has so appointed things that nothing long is hidden, even though rumour has not disseminated it.

It is just then as it should be, that fame for so long a period has been alone aware of the crimes of Christians.

This is the witness you bring against us--one that has never been able to prove the accusation it some time or other sent abroad, and at last by mere continuance made into a settled opinion in the world; so that I confidently appeal to Nature herself, ever true, against those who groundlessly hold that such things are to be credited.

Chapter VIII

See now, we set before you the reward of these enormities. They give promise of eternal life. Hold it meanwhile as your own belief. I ask you, then, whether, so believing, you think it worth attaining with a conscience such as you will have. Come, plunge your knife into the babe, enemy of none, accused of none, child of all; or if that is another's work, simply take your place beside a human being dying before he has really lived, await the departure of the lately given soul, receive the fresh young blood, saturate your bread with it, freely partake. The while as you recline at table, take note of the places which your mother and your sister occupy; mark them well, so that when the dog-made darkness has fallen on you, you may make no mistake, for you will be guilty of a crime--unless you perpetrate a deed of incest. Initiated and sealed into things like these, you have life everlasting. Tell me, I pray you, is eternity worth it? If it is not, then these things are not to be credited.

Even although you had the belief, I deny the will; and even if you had the will, I deny the possibility. Why then can others do it, if you cannot? why cannot you, if others can? I suppose we are of a different nature--are we Cynopæ or Sciapodes? [86] You are a man yourself as well as the Christian: if you cannot do it, you ought not to believe it of others, for a Christian is a man as well as you. But the ignorant, forsooth, are deceived and imposed on. They were quite unaware of anything of the kind being imputed to Christians, or they would certainly have looked into it for themselves, and searched the matter out. Instead of that, it is the custom for persons wishing initiation into sacred rites, I think, to go first of all to the master of them, that he may explain what preparations are to be made. Then, in this case, no doubt he would say, "You must have a child still of tender age, that knows not what it is to die, and can smile under thy knife; bread, too, to collect the gushing blood; in addition to these, candlesticks, and lamps, and dogs--with tid-bits to draw them on to the extinguishing of the lights:

above all things, you will require to bring your mother and your sister with you." But what if mother and sister are unwilling? or if there be neither the one nor the other? What if there are Christians with no Christian relatives? He will not be counted, I suppose, a true follower of Christ, who has not a brother or a son. And what now, if these things are all in store for them without their knowledge?

At least afterwards they come to know them; and they bear with them, and pardon them. They fear, it may be said, lest they have to pay for it if they let the secret out: nay, but they will rather in that case have every claim to protection; they will even prefer, one might think, dying by their own hand, to living under the burden of such a dreadful knowledge. Admit that they have this fear; yet why do they still persevere? For it is plain enough that you will have no desire to continue what you would never have been, if you had had previous knowledge of it.

Chapter IX

That I may refute more thoroughly these charges, I will show that in part openly, in part secretly, practices prevail among you which have led you perhaps to credit similar things about us. Children were openly sacrificed in Africa to Saturn as lately as the proconsulship of Tiberius, who exposed to public gaze the priests suspended on the sacred trees overshadowing their temple--so many crosses on which the punishment which justice craved overtook their crimes, as the soldiers of our country still can testify who did that very work for that proconsul. And even now that sacred crime still continues to be done in secret. It is not only Christians, you see, who despise you; for all that you do there is neither any crime thoroughly and abidingly eradicated, nor does any of your gods reform his ways. When Saturn did not spare his own children, he was not likely to spare the children of others; whom indeed the very parents themselves were in the habit of offering, gladly responding to the call which was made on them, and keeping the little ones pleased on the occasion, that they might not die in tears. At the same time, there is a vast difference between homicide and parricide. A more advanced age was sacrificed to Mercury in Gaul. I hand over the Tauric fables to their own theatres. Why, even in that most religious city of the pious descendants of Æneas, there is a certain Jupiter whom in their games they lave with human blood. It is the blood of a beast-fighter, you say. Is it less, because of that, the blood of a man?[87] Or is it viler blood because it is from the veins of a wicked man? At any rate it is shed in murder. O Jove, thyself a Christian, and in truth only son of thy father in his cruelty! But in regard to child murder, as it does not matter whether it is committed for a sacred object, or merely at one's own self-impulse--although there is a great difference, as we have said, between parricide and homicide--I shall turn to the people generally. How many, think you, of those crowding around and gaping for Christian blood,--how many even of your rulers, notable for their justice to you and for their severe measures against us, may I charge in their own consciences with the sin of putting their offspring to death? As to any difference in the kind of murder, it is certainly the more cruel way to kill by drowning, or by exposure to cold and hunger and dogs. A maturer age has always preferred death by the sword. In our case, murder being once for all forbidden, we may not destroy even the foetus in the womb, while as yet the human being derives blood from other parts of the body for its sustenance. To hinder a birth is merely a speedier man-killing; nor does it matter whether you take away a life that is born, or destroy one that is coming to the birth. That is a man which is going to be one; you have the fruit already in its seed. As to meals of blood and such tragic dishes, read--I am not sure where it is told (it is in Herodotus, I think)--how blood taken from the arms, and tasted by both parties, has been the treaty bond among some nations. I am not sure what it was that was tasted in the time of Catiline. They say, too, that among some Scythian tribes the dead are eaten by their friends. But I am going far from home. At this day, among ourselves, blood consecrated to Bellona, blood drawn from a punctured thigh and then partaken of, seals initiation into the rites of that goddess. Those, too, who at the gladiator shows, for the cure of epilepsy, quaff with greedy thirst the blood of criminals slain in the arena, as it flows fresh from the wound, and then rush off--to whom do they belong? those, also, who make meals on the flesh of wild beasts at the place of combat--who have keen appetites for bear and stag? That bear in the struggle was bedewed with the blood of the man whom it lacerated:

that stag rolled itself in the gladiator's gore. The entrails of the very bears, loaded with as yet undigested human viscera, are in great request. And you have men rifting up man-fed flesh? If you partake of food like this, how do your repasts differ from those you accuse us Christians of? And do those, who, with savage lust, seize on human bodies, do less because they devour the living? Have they less the pollution of human blood on them because they only lick up what is to turn into blood? They make meals, it is plain, not so much of infants, as of grown-up men. Blush for your vile ways before the Christians, who have not even the blood of animals at their meals of simple and natural food; who abstain from things strangled and that die a natural death, for no other reason than that they may not contract pollution, so much as from blood secreted in the viscera. To clench the matter with a single example, you tempt Christians with sausages of blood, just because you are perfectly aware that the thing by which you thus try to get them to transgress they hold unlawful.[88] And how unreasonable it is to believe that those, of whom you are convinced that they regard with horror the idea of tasting the blood of oxen, are eager after blood of men; unless, mayhap, you have tried it, and found it sweeter to the taste! Nay, in fact, there is here a test you should apply to discover Christians, as well as the fire-pan and the censer. They should be proved by their appetite for human blood, as well as by their refusal to offer sacrifice; just as otherwise they should be affirmed to be free of Christianity by their refusal to taste of blood, as by their sacrificing; and there would be no want of blood of men, amply supplied as that would be in the trial and condemnation of prisoners. Then who are more given to the crime of incest than those who have enjoyed the instruction of Jupiter himself? Ctesias tells us that the Persians have illicit intercourse with their mothers.

The Macedonians, too, are suspected on this point; for on first hearing the tragedy of OEdipus they made mirth of the incest-doer's grief, exclaiming, ἤλαυνε εἰς τὴν μητέρα. Even now reflect what opportunity there is for mistakes leading to incestuous comminglings--your promiscuous looseness supplying the materials. You first of all expose your children, that they may be taken up by any compassionate passer-by, to whom they are quite unknown; or you give them away, to be adopted by those who will do better to them the part of parents. Well, some time or other, all memory of the alienated progeny must be lost; and when once a mistake has been made, the transmission of incest thence will still go on--the race and the crime creeping on together. Then, further, wherever you are--at home, abroad, over the seas--your lust is an attendant, whose general indulgence, or even its indulgence in the most limited scale, may easily and unwittingly anywhere beget children, so that in this way a progeny scattered about in the commerce of life may have intercourse with those who are their own kin, and have no notion that there is any incest in the case. A persevering and stedfast chastity has protected us from anything like this:

keeping as we do from adulteries and all post-matrimonial unfaithfulness, we are not exposed to incestuous mishaps. Some of us, making matters still more secure, beat away from them entirely the power of sensual sin, by a virgin continence, still boys in this respect when they are old.

If you would but take notice that such sins as I have mentioned prevail among you, that would lead you to see that they have no existence among Christians. The same eyes would tell you of both facts. But the two blindnesses are apt to go together; so that those who do not see what is, think they see what is not. I shall show it to be so in everything. But now let me speak of matters which are more clear.

Chapter X

"You do not worship the gods," you say; "and you do not offer sacrifices for the emperors." Well, we do not offer sacrifice for others, for the same reason that we do not for ourselves,--namely, that your gods are not at all the objects of our worship.

So we are accused of sacrilege and treason. This is the chief ground of charge against us--nay, it is the sum-total of our offending; and it is worthy then of being inquired into, if neither prejudice nor injustice be the judge, the one of which has no idea of discovering the truth, and the other simply and at once rejects it. We do not worship your gods, because we know that there are no such beings.

This, therefore, is what you should do:

you should call on us to demonstrate their non-existence, and thereby prove that they have no claim to adoration; for only if your gods were truly so, would there be any obligation to render divine homage to them. And punishment even were due to Christians, if it were made plain that those to whom they refused all worship were indeed divine. But you say, They are gods. We protest and appeal from yourselves to your knowledge; let that judge us; let that condemn us, if it can deny that all these gods of yours were but men. If even it venture to deny that, it will be confuted by its own books of antiquities, from which it has got its information about them, bearing witness to this day, as they plainly do, both of the cities in which they were born, and the countries in which they have left traces of their exploits, as well as where also they are proved to have been buried.

Shall I now, therefore, go over them one by one, so numerous and so various, new and old, barbarian, Grecian, Roman, foreign, captive and adopted, private and common, male and female, rural and urban, naval and military? It were useless even to hunt out all their names: so I may content myself with a compend; and this not for your information, but that you may have what you know brought to your recollection, for undoubtedly you act as if you had forgotten all about them. No one of your gods is earlier than Saturn: from him you trace all your deities, even those of higher rank and better known. What, then, can be proved of the first, will apply to those that follow. So far, then, as books give us information, neither the Greek Diodorus or Thallus, neither Cassius Severus or Cornelius Nepos, nor any writer upon sacred antiquities, have ventured to say that Saturn was any but a man: so far as the question depends on facts, I find none more trustworthy than those--that in Italy itself we have the country in which, after many expeditions, and after having partaken of Attic hospitalities, Saturn settled, obtaining cordial welcome from Janus, or, as the Salii will have it, Janis. The mountain on which he dwelt was called Saturnius; the city he founded is called Saturnia to this day; last of all, the whole of Italy, after having borne the name of Oenotria, was called Saturnia from him.

He first gave you the art of writing, and a stamped coinage, and thence it is he presides over the public treasury.

But if Saturn were a man, he had undoubtedly a human origin; and having a human origin, he was not the offspring of heaven and earth. As his parents were unknown, it was not unnatural that he should be spoken of as the son of those elements from which we might all seem to spring. For who does not speak of heaven and earth as father and mother, in a sort of way of veneration and honour? or from the custom which prevails among us of saying that persons of whom we have no knowledge, or who make a sudden appearance, have fallen from the skies? In this way it came about that Saturn, everywhere a sudden and unlooked-for guest, got everywhere the name of the Heaven-born. For even the common folk call persons whose stock is unknown, sons of earth. I say nothing of how men in these rude times were wont to act, when they were impressed by the look of any stranger happening to appear among them, as though it were divine, since even at this day men of culture make gods of those whom, a day or two before, they acknowledged to be dead men by their public mourning for them. Let these notices of Saturn, brief as they are, suffice. It will thus also be proved that Jupiter is as certainly a man, as from a man he sprung; and that one after another the whole swarm is mortal like the primal stock.

Chapter XI

And since, as you dare not deny that these deities of yours once were men, you have taken it on you to assert that they were made gods after their decease, let us consider what necessity there was for this. In the first place, you must concede the existence of one higher God--a certain wholesale dealer in divinity, who has made gods of men.

For they could neither have assumed a divinity which was not theirs, nor could any but one himself possessing it have conferred it on them. If there was no one to make gods, it is vain to dream of gods being made when thus you have no god-maker. Most certainly, if they could have deified themselves, with a higher state at their command, they never would have been men. If, then, there be one who is able to make gods, I turn back to an examination of any reason there may be for making gods at all; and I find no other reason than this, that the great God has need of their ministrations and aids in performing the offices of Deity. But first it is an unworthy idea that He should need the help of a man, and in fact a dead man, when, if He was to be in want of this assistance from the dead, He might more fittingly have created some one a god at the beginning.

Nor do I see any place for his action.

For this entire world-mass--whether self-existent and uncreated, as Pythagoras maintains, or brought into being by a creator's hands, as Plato holds--was manifestly, once for all in its original construction, disposed, and furnished, and ordered, and supplied with a government of perfect wisdom. That cannot be imperfect which has made all perfect. There was nothing waiting on for Saturn and his race to do. Men will make fools of themselves if they refuse to believe that from the very first rain poured down from the sky, and stars gleamed, and light shone, and thunders roared, and Jove himself dreaded the lightnings you put in his hands; that in like manner before Bacchus, and Ceres, and Minerva, nay before the first man, whoever that was, every kind of fruit burst forth plentifully from the bosom of the earth, for nothing provided for the support and sustenance of man could be introduced after his entrance on the stage of being. Accordingly, these necessaries of life are said to have been discovered, not created.

But the thing you discover existed before; and that which had a pre-existence must be regarded as belonging not to him who discovered it, but to him who made it, for of course it had a being before it could be found. But if, on account of his being the discoverer of the vine, Bacchus is raised to godship, Lucullus, who first introduced the cherry from Pontus into Italy, has not been fairly dealt with; for as the discoverer of a new fruit, he has not, as though he were its creator, been awarded divine honours.

Wherefore, if the universe existed from the beginning, thoroughly furnished with its system working under certain laws for the performance of its functions, there is, in this respect, an entire absence of all reason for electing humanity to divinity; for the positions and powers which you have assigned to your deities have been from the beginning precisely what they would have been, although you had never deified them.

But you turn to another reason, telling us that the conferring of deity was a way of rewarding worth. And hence you grant, I conclude, that the god-making God is of transcendent righteousness,--one who will neither rashly, improperly, nor needlessly bestow a reward so great. I would have you then consider whether the merits of your deities are of a kind to have raised them to the heavens, and not rather to have sunk them down into lowest depths of Tartarus,--the place which you regard, with many, as the prison-house of infernal punishments. For into this dread place are wont to be cast all who offend against filial piety, and such as are guilty of incest with sisters, and seducers of wives, and ravishers of virgins, and boy-polluters, and men of furious tempers, and murderers, and thieves, and deceivers; all, in short, who tread in the footsteps of your gods, not one of whom you can prove free from crime or vice, save by denying that they had ever a human existence. But as you cannot deny that, you have those foul blots also as an added reason for not believing that they were made gods afterwards. For if you rule for the very purpose of punishing such deeds; if every virtuous man among you rejects all correspondence, converse, and intimacy with the wicked and base, while, on the other hand, the high God has taken up their mates to a share of His majesty, on what ground is it that you thus condemn those whose fellow-actors you adore? Your goodness is an affront in the heavens. Deify your vilest criminals, if you would please your gods. You honour them by giving divine honours to their fellows. But to say no more about a way of acting so unworthy, there have been men virtuous, and pure, and good. Yet how many of these nobler men you have left in the regions of doom! as Socrates, so renowned for his wisdom, Aristides for his justice, Themistocles for his warlike genius, Alexander for his sublimity of soul, Polycrates for his good fortune, Croesus for his wealth, Demosthenes for his eloquence. Which of these gods of yours is more remarkable for gravity and wisdom than Cato, more just and warlike than Scipio? which of them more magnanimous than Pompey, more prosperous than Sylla, of greater wealth than Crassus, more eloquent than Tullius? How much better it would have been for the God Supreme to have waited that He might have taken such men as these to be His heavenly associates, prescient as He must have surely been of their worthier character! He was in a hurry, I suppose, and straightway shut heaven's gates; and now He must surely feel ashamed at these worthies murmuring over their lot in the regions below.

Chapter XII

But I pass from these remarks, for I know and I am going to show what your gods are not, by showing what they are. In reference, then, to these, I see only names of dead men of ancient times; I hear fabulous stories; I recognize sacred rites founded on mere myths.

As to the actual images, I regard them as simply pieces of matter akin to the vessels and utensils in common use among us, or even undergoing in their consecration a hapless change from these useful articles at the hands of reckless art, which in the transforming process treats them with utter contempt, nay, in the very act commits sacrilege; so that it might be no slight solace to us in all our punishments, suffering as we do because of these same gods, that in their making they suffer as we do themselves. You put Christians on crosses and stakes: [89] what image is not formed from the clay in the first instance, set on cross and stake?

The body of your god is first consecrated on the gibbet. You tear the sides of Christians with your claws; but in the case of your own gods, axes, and planes, and rasps are put to work more vigorously on every member of the body. We lay our heads upon the block; before the lead, and the glue, and the nails are put in requisition, your deities are headless. We are cast to the wild beasts, while you attach them to Bacchus, and Cybele, and Cælestis. We are burned in the flames; so, too, are they in their original lump. We are condemned to the mines; from these your gods originate. We are banished to islands; in islands it is a common thing for your gods to have their birth or die. If it is in this way a deity is made, it will follow that as many as are punished are deified, and tortures will have to be declared divinities. But plain it is these objects of your worship have no sense of the injuries and disgraces of their consecrating, as they are equally unconscious of the honours paid to them. O impious words! O blasphemous reproaches! Gnash your teeth upon us--foam with maddened rage against us--ye are the persons, no doubt, who censured a certain Seneca speaking of your superstition at much greater length and far more sharply! In a word, if we refuse our homage to statues and frigid images, the very counterpart of their dead originals, with which hawks, and mice, and spiders are so well acquainted, does it not merit praise instead of penalty, that we have rejected what we have come to see is error? We cannot surely be made out to injure those who we are certain are nonentities. What does not exist, is in its nonexistence secure from suffering.

Chapter XIII

"But they are gods to us," you say. And how is it, then, that in utter inconsistency with this, you are convicted of impious, sacrilegious, and irreligious conduct to them, neglecting those you imagine to exist, destroying those who are the objects of your fear, making mock of those whose honour you avenge? See now if I go beyond the truth. First, indeed, seeing you worship, some one god, and some another, of course you give offence to those you do not worship. You cannot continue to give preference to one without slighting another, for selection implies rejection. You despise, therefore, those whom you thus reject; for in your rejection of them, it is plain you have no dread of giving them offence. For, as we have already shown, every god depended on the decision of the senate for his godhead. No god was he whom man in his own counsels did not wish to be so, and thereby condemned. The family deities you call Lares, you exercise a domestic authority over, pledging them, selling them, changing them--making sometimes a cooking-pot of a Saturn, a firepan of a Minerva, as one or other happens to be worn down, or broken in its long sacred use, or as the family head feels the pressure of some more sacred home necessity. In like manner, by public law you disgrace your state gods, putting them in the auction-catalogue, and making them a source of revenue. Men seek to get the Capitol, as they seek to get the herb market, under the voice of the crier, under the auction spear, under the registration of the quæstor.

Deity is struck off and farmed out to the highest bidder. But indeed lands burdened with tribute are of less value; men under the assessment of a poll-tax are less noble; for these things are the marks of servitude. In the case of the gods, on the other hand, the sacredness is great in proportion to the tribute which they yield; nay, the more sacred is a god, the larger is the tax he pays. Majesty is made a source of gain. Religion goes about the taverns begging. You demand a price for the privilege of standing on temple ground, for access to the sacred services; there is no gratuitous knowledge of your divinities permitted--you must buy their favours with a price. What honours in any way do you render to them that you do not render to the dead? You have temples in the one case just as in the other; you have altars in the one case as in the other. Their statues have the same dress, the same insignia. As the dead man had his age, his art, his occupation, so it is with the deity. In what respect does the funeral feast differ from the feast of Jupiter? or the bowl of the gods from the ladle of the manes? or the undertaker from the soothsayer, as in fact this latter personage also attends upon the dead? With perfect propriety you give divine honours to your departed emperors, as you worship them in life. The gods will count themselves indebted to you; nay, it will be matter of high rejoicing among them that their masters are made their equals.

But when you adore Larentina, a public prostitute--I could have wished that it might at least have been Lais or Phryne--among your Junos, and Cereses, and Dianas; when you instal in your Pantheon Simon Magus, [90] giving him a statue and the title of Holy God; when you make an infamous court page a god of the sacred synod, although your ancient deities are in reality no better, they will still think themselves affronted by you, that the privilege antiquity conferred on them alone, has been allowed to others.

Chapter XIV

I wish now to review your sacred rites; and I pass no censure on your sacrificing, when you offer the worn-out, the scabbed, the corrupting; when you cut off from the fat and the sound the useless parts, such as the head and the hoofs, which in your house you would have assigned to the slaves or the dogs; when of the tithe of Hercules you do not lay a third upon his altar (I am disposed rather to praise your wisdom in rescuing something from being lost); but turning to your books, from which you get your training in wisdom and the nobler duties of life, what utterly ridiculous things I find!--that for Trojans and Greeks the gods fought among themselves like pairs of gladiators; that Venus was wounded by a man, because she would rescue her son Æneas when he was in peril of his life from the same Diomede; that Mars was almost wasted away by a thirteen months' imprisonment; that Jupiter was saved by a monster's aid from suffering the same violence at the hands of the other gods; that he now laments the fate of Sarpedon, now foully makes love to his own sister, recounting (to her) former mistresses, now for a long time past not so dear as she. After this, what poet is not found copying the example of his chief, to be a disgracer of the gods? One gives Apollo to king Admetus to tend his sheep; another hires out the building labours of Neptune to Laomedon. A well-known lyric poet, too--Pindar, I mean--sings of Æsculapius deservedly stricken with lightning for his greed in practising wrongfully his art.

A wicked deed it was of Jupiter--if he hurled the bolt--unnatural to his grandson, and exhibiting envious feeling to the Physician. Things like these should not be made public if they are true; and if false, they should not be fabricated among people professing a great respect for religion.

Nor indeed do either tragic or comic writers shrink from setting forth the gods as the origin of all family calamities and sins. I do not dwell on the philosophers, contenting myself with a reference to Socrates, who, in contempt of the gods, was in the habit of swearing by an oak, and a goat, and a dog. In fact, for this very thing Socrates was condemned to death, that he overthrew the worship of the gods. Plainly, at one time as well as another, that is, always truth is disliked. However, when rueing their judgment, the Athenians inflicted punishment on his accusers, and set up a golden image of him in a temple, the condemnation was in the very act rescinded, and his witness was restored to its former value. Diogenes, too, makes utter mock of Hercules and the Roman cynic Varro brings forward three hundred Joves, or Jupiters they should be called, all headless.

Chapter XV

Others of your writers, in their wantonness, even minister to your pleasures by vilifying the gods. Examine those charming farces of your Lentuli and Hostilii, whether in the jokes and tricks it is the buffoons or the deities which afford you merriment; such farces I mean as Anubis the Adulterer, and Luna of the masculine gender, and Diana under the lash, and the reading the will of Jupiter deceased, and the three famishing Herculeses held up to ridicule. Your dramatic literature, too, depicts all the vileness of your gods.

The Sun mourns his offspring [91] cast down from heaven, and you are full of glee; Cybele sighs after the scornful swain, [92] and you do not blush; you brook the stage recital of Jupiter's misdeeds, and the shepherd [93] judging Juno, Venus, and Minerva. Then, again, when the likeness of a god is put on the head of an ignominious and infamous wretch, when one impure and trained up for the art in all effeminacy, represents a Minerva or a Hercules, is not the majesty of your gods insulted, and their deity dishonored? Yet you not merely look on, but applaud. You are, I suppose, more devout in the arena, where after the same fashion your deities dance on human blood, on the pollutions caused by inflicted punishments, as they act their themes and stories, doing their turn for the wretched criminals, except that these, too, often put on divinity and actually play the very gods. We have seen in our day a representation of the mutilation of Attis, that famous god of Pessinus, and a man burnt alive as Hercules. We have made merry amid the ludicrous cruelties of the noonday exhibition, at Mercury examining the bodies of the dead with his hot iron; we have witnessed Jove's brother, [94] mallet in hand, dragging out the corpses of the gladiators. But who can go into everything of this sort? If by such things as these the honour of deity is assailed, if they go to blot out every trace of its majesty, we must explain them by the contempt in which the gods are held, alike by those who actually do them, and by those for whose enjoyment they are done. This it will be said, however, is all in sport. But if I add--it is what all know and will admit as readily to be the fact--that in the temples adulteries are arranged, that at the altars pimping is practised, that often in the houses of the temple-keepers and priests, under the sacrificial fillets, and the sacred hats, [95] and the purple robes, amid the fumes of incense, deeds of licentiousness are done, I am not sure but your gods have more reason to complain of you than of Christians. It is certainly among the votaries of your religion that the perpetrators of sacrilege are always found, for Christians do not enter your temples even in the day-time. Perhaps they too would be spoilers of them, if they worshipped in them. What then do they worship, since their objects of worship are different from yours? Already indeed it is implied, as the corollary from their rejection of the lie, that they render homage to the truth; nor continue longer in an error which they have given up in the very fact of recognizing it to be an error.

Take this in first of all, and when we have offered a preliminary refutation of some false opinions, go on to derive from it our entire religious system.

Chapter XVI

For, like some others, you are under the delusion that our god is an ass's head. [96] Cornelius Tacitus first put this notion into people's minds. In the fifth book of his histories, beginning the (narrative of the) Jewish war with an account of the origin of the nation; and theorizing at his pleasure about the origin, as well as the name and the religion of the Jews, he states that having been delivered, or rather, in his opinion, expelled from Egypt, in crossing the vast plains of Arabia, where water is so scanty, they were in extremity from thirst; but taking the guidance of the wild asses, which it was thought might be seeking water after feeding, they discovered a fountain, and thereupon in their gratitude they consecrated a head of this species of animal. And as Christianity is nearly allied to Judaism, from this, I suppose, it was taken for granted that we too are devoted to the worship of the same image.

But the said Cornelius Tacitus (the very opposite of tacit in telling lies) informs us in the work already mentioned, that when Cneius Pompeius captured Jerusalem, he entered the temple to see the arcana of the Jewish religion, but found no image there. Yet surely if worship was rendered to any visible object, the very place for its exhibition would be the shrine; and that all the more that the worship, however unreasonable, had no need there to fear outside beholders.

For entrance to the holy place was permitted to the priests alone, while all vision was forbidden to others by an outspread curtain. You will not, however, deny that all beasts of burden, and not parts of them, but the animals entire, are with their goddess Epona objects of worship with you.

It is this, perhaps, which displeases you in us, that while your worship here is universal, we do homage only to the ass. Then, if any of you think we render superstitious adoration to the cross, in that adoration he is sharer with us. If you offer homage to a piece of wood at all, it matters little what it is like when the substance is the same: it is of no consequence the form, if you have the very body of the god.

And yet how far does the Athenian Pallas differ from the stock of the cross, or the Pharian Ceres as she is put up uncarved to sale, a mere rough stake and piece of shapeless wood? Every stake fixed in an upright position is a portion of the cross; we render our adoration, if you will have it so, to a god entire and complete. We have shown before that your deities are derived from shapes modelled from the cross.

But you also worship victories, for in your trophies the cross is the heart of the trophy. [97] The camp religion of the Romans is all through a worship of the standards, a setting the standards above all gods. Well, as those images decking out the standards are ornaments of crosses.

All those hangings of your standards and banners are robes of crosses. I praise your zeal: you would not consecrate crosses unclothed and unadorned. Others, again, certainly with more information and greater verisimilitude, believe that the sun is our god. We shall be counted Persians perhaps, though we do not worship the orb of day painted on a piece of linen cloth, having himself everywhere in his own disk. The idea no doubt has originated from our being known to turn to the east in prayer. [98] But you, many of you, also under pretence sometimes of worshipping the heavenly bodies, move your lips in the direction of the sunrise. In the same way, if we devote Sun-day to rejoicing, from a far different reason than Sun-worship, we have some resemblance to those of you who devote the day of Saturn to ease and luxury, though they too go far away from Jewish ways, of which indeed they are ignorant. But lately a new edition of our god has been given to the world in that great city: it originated with a certain vile man who was wont to hire himself out to cheat the wild beasts, and who exhibited a picture with this inscription: The God of the Christians, born of an ass. [99] He had the ears of an ass, was hoofed in one foot, carried a book, [100] and wore a toga. Both the name and the figure gave us amusement. But our opponents ought straightway to have done homage to this biformed divinity, for they have acknowledged gods dog-headed and lion-headed, with horn of buck and ram, with goat-like loins, with serpent legs, with wings sprouting from back or foot. These things we have discussed ex abundanti, that we might not seem willingly to pass by any rumor against us unrefuted. Having thoroughly cleared ourselves, we turn now to an exhibition of what our religion really is.

Chapter XVII

The object of our worship is the One God, [101] He who by His commanding word, His arranging wisdom, His mighty power, brought forth from nothing this entire mass of our world, with all its array of elements, bodies, spirits, for the glory of His majesty; whence also the Greeks have bestowed on it the name of Κόσμος. The eye cannot see Him, though He is (spiritually) visible. He is incomprehensible, though in grace He is manifested. He is beyond our utmost thought, though our human faculties conceive of Him. He is therefore equally real and great. But that which, in the ordinary sense, can be seen and handled and conceived, is inferior to the eyes by which it is taken in, and the hands by which it is tainted, and the faculties by which it is discovered; but that which is infinite is known only to itself. This it is which gives some notion of God, while yet beyond all our conceptions-- our very incapacity of fully grasping Him affords us the idea of what He really is.

He is presented to our minds in His transcendent greatness, as at once known and unknown. And this is the crowning guilt of men, that they will not recognize One, of whom they cannot possibly be ignorant. Would you have the proof from the works of His hands, so numerous and so great, which both contain you and sustain you, which minister at once to your enjoyment, and strike you with awe; or would you rather have it from the testimony of the soul itself? Though under the oppressive bondage of the body, though led astray by depraving customs, though enervated by lusts and passions, though in slavery to false gods; yet, whenever the soul comes to itself, as out of a surfeit, or a sleep, or a sickness, and attains something of its natural soundness, it speaks of God; using no other word, because this is the peculiar name of the true God.

"God is great and good"--"Which may God give," are the words on every lip. It bears witness, too, that God is judge, exclaiming, "God sees," and, "I commend myself to God," and, "God will repay me." O noble testimony of the soul by nature [102] Christian! Then, too, in using such words as these, it looks not to the Capitol, but to the heavens. It knows that there is the throne of the living God, as from Him and from thence itself came down.

Chapter XVIII

But, that we might attain an ampler and more authoritative knowledge at once of Himself, and of His counsels and will, God has added a written revelation for the behoof of every one whose heart is set on seeking Him, that seeking he may find, and finding believe, and believing obey. For from the first He sent messengers into the world,--men whose stainless righteousness made them worthy to know the Most High, and to reveal Him,--men abundantly endowed with the Holy Spirit, that they might proclaim that there is one God only who made all things, who formed man from the dust of the ground (for He is the true Prometheus who gave order to the world by arranging the seasons and their course),--these have further set before us the proofs He has given of His majesty in His judgments by floods and fires, the rules appointed by Him for securing His favour, as well as the retribution in store for the ignoring, forsaking and keeping them, as being about at the end of all to adjudge His worshippers to everlasting life, and the wicked to the doom of fire at once without ending and without break, raising up again all the dead from the beginning, reforming and renewing them with the object of awarding either recompense. Once these things were with us, too, the theme of ridicule. We are of your stock and nature: men are made, not born, Christians. The preachers of whom we have spoken are called prophets, from the office which belongs to them of predicting the future. Their words, as well as the miracles which they performed, that men might have faith in their divine authority, we have still in the literary treasures they have left, and which are open to all. Ptolemy, surnamed Philadelphus, the most learned of his race, a man of vast acquaintance with all literature, emulating, I imagine, the book enthusiasm of Pisistratus, among other remains of the past which either their antiquity or something of peculiar interest made famous, at the suggestion of Demetrius Phalereus, who was renowned above all grammarians of his time, and to whom he had committed the management of these things, applied to the Jews for their writings--I mean the writings peculiar to them and in their tongue, which they alone possessed, for from themselves, as a people dear to God for their fathers' sake, their prophets had ever sprung, and to them they had ever spoken. Now in ancient times the people we call Jews bare the name of Hebrews, and so both their writings and their speech were Hebrew. But that the understanding of their books might not be wanting, this also the Jews supplied to Ptolemy; for they gave him seventy-two interpreters--men whom the philosopher Menedemus, the well-known asserter of a Providence, regarded with respect as sharing in his views. The same account is given by Aristæus. So the king left these works unlocked to all, in the Greek language. [103] To this day, at the temple of Serapis, the libraries of Ptolemy are to be seen, with the identical Hebrew originals in them. The Jews, too, read them publicly. Under a tribute-liberty, they are in the habit of going to hear them every Sabbath. Whoever gives ear will find God in them; whoever takes pains to understand, will be compelled to believe.

Chapter XIX

Their high antiquity, first of all, claims authority for these writings.

With you, too, it is a kind of religion to demand belief on this very ground. Well, all the substances, all the materials, the origins, classes, contents of your most ancient writings, even most nations and cities illustrious in the records of the past and noted for their antiquity in books of annals,--the very forms of your letters, those revealers and custodiers of events, nay (I think I speak still within the mark), your very gods themselves, your very temples and oracles, and sacred rites, are less ancient than the work of a single prophet, in whom you have the thesaurus of the entire Jewish religion, and therefore too of ours. If you happen to have heard of a certain Moses, I speak first of him: he is as far back as the Argive Inachus; by nearly four hundred years--only seven less--he precedes Danaus, your most ancient name; while he antedates by a millennium the death of Priam. I might affirm, too, that he is five hundred years earlier than Homer, and have supporters of that view. The other prophets also, though of later date, are, even the most recent of them, as far back as the first of your philosophers, and legislators, and historians.

It is not so much the difficulty of the subject, as its vastness, that stands in the way of a statement of the grounds on which these statements rest; the matter is not so arduous as it would be tedious. It would require the anxious study of many books, and the fingers busy reckoning.

The histories of the most ancient nations, such as the Egyptians, the Chaldeans, the Phoenicians, would need to be ransacked; the men of these various nations who have information to give, would have to be called in as witnesses. Manetho the Egyptian, and Berosus the Chaldean, and Hieromus the Phoenician king of Tyre; their successors too, Ptolemy the Mendesian, and Demetrius Phalereus, and King Juba, and Apion, and Thallus, and their critic the Jew Josephus, the native vindicator of the ancient history of his people, who either authenticates or refutes the others. Also the Greek censors' lists must be compared, and the dates of events ascertained, that the chronological connections may be opened up, and thus the reckonings of the various annals be made to give forth light. We must go abroad into the histories and literature of all nations. And, in fact, we have already brought the proof in part before you, in giving those hints as to how it is to be effected. But it seems better to delay the full discussion of this, lest in our haste we do not sufficiently carry it out, or lest in its thorough handling we make too lengthened a digression.

Chapter XX

To make up for our delay in this, we bring under your notice something of even greater importance; we point to the majesty of our Scriptures, if not to their antiquity. If you doubt that they are as ancient as we say, we offer proof that they are divine.

And you may convince yourselves of this at once, and without going very far. Your instructors, the world, and the age, and the event, are all before you.

All that is taking place around you was fore-announced; all that you now see with your eye was previously heard by the ear. The swallowing up of cities by the earth; the theft of islands by the sea; wars, bringing external and internal convulsions; the collision of kingdoms with kingdoms; famines and pestilences, and local massacres, and widespread desolating mortalities; the exaltation of the lowly, and the humbling of the proud; the decay of righteousness, the growth of sin, the slackening interest in all good ways; the very seasons and elements going out of their ordinary course, monsters and portents taking the place of nature's forms--it was all foreseen and predicted before it came to pass. While we suffer the calamities, we read of them in the Scriptures; as we examine, they are proved. Well, the truth of a prophecy, I think, is the demonstration of its being from above.

Hence there is among us an assured faith in regard to coming events as things already proved to us, for they were predicted along with what we have day by day fulfilled. They are uttered by the same voices, they are written in the same books--the same Spirit inspires them. All time is one to prophecy foretelling the future. Among men, it may be, a distinction of times is made while the fulfilment is going on: from being future we think of it as present, and then from being present we count it as belonging to the past. How are we to blame, I pray you, that we believe in things to come as though they already were, with the grounds we have for our faith in these two steps?

Chapter XXI

But having asserted that our religion is supported by the writings of the Jews, the oldest which exist, though it is generally known, and we fully admit that it dates from a comparatively recent period-- no further back indeed than the reign of Tiberius--a question may perhaps be raised on this ground about its standing, as if it were hiding something of its presumption under shadow of an illustrious religion, one which has at any rate undoubted allowance of the law, or because, apart from the question of age, we neither accord with the Jews in their peculiarities in regard to food, nor in their sacred days, nor even in their well-known bodily sign, nor in the possession of a common name, which surely behoved to be the case if we did homage to the same God as they. Then, too, the common people have now some knowledge of Christ, and think of Him as but a man, one indeed such as the Jews condemned, so that some may naturally enough have taken up the idea that we are worshippers of a mere human being. But we are neither ashamed of Christ--for we rejoice to be counted His disciples, and in His name to suffer-- nor do we differ from the Jews concerning God. We must make, therefore, a remark or two as to Christ's divinity. In former times the Jews enjoyed much of God's favour, when the fathers of their race were noted for their righteousness and faith. So it was that as a people they flourished greatly, and their kingdom attained to a lofty eminence; and so highly blessed were they, that for their instruction God spake to them in special revelations, pointing out to them beforehand how they should merit His favor and avoid His displeasure. But how deeply they have sinned, puffed up to their fall with a false trust in their noble ancestors, turning from God's way into a way of sheer impiety, though they themselves should refuse to admit it, their present national ruin would afford sufficient proof. Scattered abroad, a race of wanderers, exiles from their own land and clime, they roam over the whole world without either a human or a heavenly king, not possessing even the stranger's right to set so much as a simple footstep in their native country. The sacred writers withal, in giving previous warning of these things, all with equal clearness ever declared that, in the last days of the world, God would, out of every nation, and people, and country, choose for Himself more faithful worshippers, upon whom He would bestow His grace, and that indeed in ampler measure, in keeping with the enlarged capacities of a nobler dispensation.

Accordingly, He appeared among us, whose coming to renovate and illuminate man's nature was pre-announced by God--I mean Christ, that Son of God. And so the supreme Head and Master of this grace and discipline, the Enlightener and Trainer of the human race, God's own Son, was announced among us, born--but not so born as to make Him ashamed of the name of Son or of His paternal origin. It was not His lot to have as His father, by incest with a sister, or by violation of a daughter or another's wife, a god in the shape of serpent, or ox, or bird, or lover, for his vile ends transmuting himself into the gold of Danaus. They are your divinities upon whom these base deeds of Jupiter were done. But the Son of God has no mother in any sense which involves impurity; she, whom men suppose to be His mother in the ordinary way, had never entered into the marriage bond. [104] But, first, I shall discuss His essential nature, and so the nature of His birth will be understood. We have already asserted that God made the world, and all which it contains, by His Word, and Reason, and Power. It is abundantly plain that your philosophers, too, regard the Λόγος--that is, the Word and Reason--as the Creator of the universe. For Zeno lays it down that he is the creator, having made all things according to a determinate plan; that his name is Fate, and God, and the soul of Jupiter, and the necessity of all things. Cleanthes ascribes all this to spirit, which he maintains pervades the universe. And we, in like manner, hold that the Word, and Reason, and Power, by which we have said God made all, have spirit as their proper and essential substratum, in which the Word has in being to give forth utterances, and reason abides to dispose and arrange, and power is over all to execute. We have been taught that He proceeds forth from God, and in that procession He is generated; so that He is the Son of God, and is called God from unity of substance with God.

For God, too, is a Spirit. Even when the ray is shot from the sun, it is still part of the parent mass; the sun will still be in the ray, because it is a ray of the sun--there is no division of substance, but merely an extension. Thus Christ is Spirit of Spirit, and God of God, as light of light is kindled.[105] The material matrix remains entire and unimpaired, though you derive from it any number of shoots possessed of its qualities; so, too, that which has come forth out of God is at once God and the Son of God, and the two are one. In this way also, as He is Spirit of Spirit and God of God, He is made a second in manner of existence--in position, not in nature; and He did not withdraw from the original source, but went forth.

This ray of God, then, as it was always foretold in ancient times, descending into a certain virgin, and made flesh in her womb, is in His birth God and man united. The flesh formed by the Spirit is nourished, grows up to manhood, speaks, teaches, works, and is the Christ. Receive meanwhile this fable, if you choose to call it so--it is like some of your own--while we go on to show how Christ's claims are proved, and who the parties are with you by whom such fables have been set a going to overthrow the truth, which they resemble. The Jews, too, were well aware that Christ was coming, as those to whom the prophets spake. Nay, even now His advent is expected by them; nor is there any other contention between them and us, than that they believe the advent has not yet occurred. For two comings of Christ having been revealed to us:

a first, which has been fulfilled in the lowliness of a human lot; a second, which impends over the world, now near its close, in all the majesty of Deity unveiled; and, by misunderstanding the first, they have concluded that the second--which, as matter of more manifest prediction, they set their hopes on-- is the only one. It was the merited punishment of their sin not to understand the Lord's first advent: for if they had, they would have believed; and if they had believed, they would have obtained salvation. They themselves read how it is written of them that they are deprived of wisdom and understanding--of the use of eyes and ears. [106] As, then, under the force of their pre-judgment, they had convinced themselves from His lowly guise that Christ was no more than man, it followed from that, as a necessary consequence, that they should hold Him a magician from the powers which He displayed,--expelling devils from men by a word, restoring vision to the blind, cleansing the leprous, reinvigorating the paralytic, summoning the dead to life again, making the very elements of nature obey Him, stilling the storms and walking on the sea; proving that He was the Λόγος of God, that primordial first-begotten Word, accompanied by power and reason, and based on Spirit,--that He who was now doing all things by His word, and He who had done that of old, were one and the same. But the Jews were so exasperated by His teaching, by which their rulers and chiefs were convicted of the truth, chiefly because so many turned aside to Him, that at last they brought Him before Pontius Pilate, at that time Roman governor of Syria; and, by the violence of their outcries against Him, extorted a sentence giving Him up to them to be crucified. He Himself had predicted this; which, however, would have signified little had not the prophets of old done it as well. And yet, nailed upon the cross, He exhibited many notable signs, by which His death was distinguished from all others. At His own free-will, He with a word dismissed from Him His spirit, anticipating the executioner's work. In the same hour, too, the light of day was withdrawn, when the sun at the very time was in his meridian blaze. Those who were not aware that this had been predicted about Christ, no doubt thought it an eclipse. You yourselves have the account of the world-portent still in your archives. [107] Then, when His body was taken down from the cross and placed in a sepulchre, the Jews in their eager watchfulness surrounded it with a large military guard, lest, as He had predicted His resurrection from the dead on the third day, His disciples might remove by stealth His body, and deceive even the incredulous. But, lo, on the third day there a was a sudden shock of earthquake, and the stone which sealed the sepulchre was rolled away, and the guard fled off in terror:

Without a single disciple near, the grave was found empty of all but the clothes of the buried One. But nevertheless, the leaders of the Jews, whom it nearly concerned both to spread abroad a lie, and keep back a people tributary and submissive to them from the faith, gave it out that the body of Christ had been stolen by His followers. For the Lord, you see, did not go forth into the public gaze, lest the wicked should be delivered from their error; that faith also, destined to a great reward, might hold its ground in difficulty. But He spent forty days with some of His disciples down in Galilee, a region of Judea, instructing them in the doctrines they were to teach to others.

Thereafter, having given them commission to preach the gospel through the world, He was encompassed with a cloud and taken up to heaven,--a fact more certain far than the assertions of your Proculi concerning Romulus. [108] All these things Pilate did to Christ; and now in fact a Christian in his own convictions, he sent word of Him to the reigning Cæsar, who was at the time Tiberius.

Yes, and the Cæsars too would have believed on Christ, if either the Cæsars had not been necessary for the world, or if Christians could have been Cæsars. His disciples also, spreading over the world, did as their Divine Master bade them; and after suffering greatly themselves from the persecutions of the Jews, and with no unwilling heart, as having faith undoubting in the truth, at last by Nero's cruel sword sowed the seed of Christian blood at Rome. [109] Yes, and we shall prove that even your own gods are effective witnesses for Christ.

It is a great matter if, to give you faith in Christians, I can bring forward the authority of the very beings on account of whom you refuse them credit. Thus far we have carried out the plan we laid down. We have set forth this origin of our sect and name, with this account of the Founder of Christianity. Let no one henceforth charge us with infamous wickedness; let no one think that it is otherwise than we have represented, for none may give a false account of his religion. For in the very fact that he says he worships another god than he really does, he is guilty of denying the object of his worship, and transferring his worship and homage to another; and, in the transference, he ceases to worship the god he has repudiated. We say, and before all men we say, and torn and bleeding under your tortures, we cry out, "We worship God through Christ." Count Christ a man, if you please; by Him and in Him God would be known and be adored.

If the Jews object, we answer that Moses, who was but a man, taught them their religion; against the Greeks we urge that Orpheus at Pieria, Musæus at Athens, Melampus at Argos, Trophonius in Boeotia, imposed religious rites; turning to yourselves, who exercise sway over the nations, it was the man Numa Pompilius who laid on the Romans a heavy load of costly superstitions. Surely Christ, then, had a right to reveal Deity, which was in fact His own essential possession, not with the object of bringing boors and savages by the dread of multitudinous gods, whose favour must be won into some civilization, as was the case with Numa; but as one who aimed to enlighten men already civilized, and under illusions from their very culture, that they might come to the knowledge of the truth. Search, then, and see if that divinity of Christ be true. If it be of such a nature that the acceptance of it transforms a man, and makes him truly good, there is implied in that the duty of renouncing what is opposed to it as false; especially and on every ground that which, hiding itself under the names and images of dead, the labours to convince men of its divinity by certain signs, and miracles, and oracles.

Chapter XXII

And we affirm indeed the existence of certain spiritual essences; nor is their name unfamiliar. The philosophers acknowledge there are demons; Socrates himself waiting on a demon's will. Why not? since it is said an evil spirit attached itself specially to him even from his childhood--turning his mind no doubt from what was good. The poets are all acquainted with demons too; even the ignorant common people make frequent use of them in cursing. In fact, they call upon Satan, the demon-chief, in their execrations, as though from some instinctive soul-knowledge of him. Plato also admits the existence of angels. The dealers in magic, no less, come forward as witnesses to the existence of both kinds of spirits. We are instructed, moreover, by our sacred books how from certain angels, who fell of their own free-will, there sprang a more wicked demon-brood, condemned of God along with the authors of their race, and that chief we have referred to. It will for the present be enough, however, that some account is given of their work.

Their great business is the ruin of mankind. So, from the very first, spiritual wickedness sought our destruction. They inflict, accordingly, upon our bodies diseases and other grievous calamities, while by violent assaults they hurry the soul into sudden and extraordinary excesses. Their marvellous subtleness and tenuity give them access to both parts of our nature. As spiritual, they can do no harm; for, invisible and intangible, we are not cognizant of their action save by its effects, as when some inexplicable, unseen poison in the breeze blights the apples and the grain while in the flower, or kills them in the bud, or destroys them when they have reached maturity; as though by the tainted atmosphere in some unknown way spreading abroad its pestilential exhalations. So, too, by an influence equally obscure, demons and angels breathe into the soul, and rouse up its corruptions with furious passions and vile excesses; or with cruel lusts accompanied by various errors, of which the worst is that by which these deities are commended to the favour of deceived and deluded human beings, that they may get their proper food of flesh-fumes and blood when that is offered up to idol-images. What is daintier food to the spirit of evil, than turning men's minds away from the true God by the illusions of a false divination? And here I explain how these illusions are managed. Every spirit is possessed of wings. This is a common property of both angels and demons. So they are everywhere in a single moment; the whole world is as one place to them; all that is done over the whole extent of it, it is as easy for them to know as to report. Their swiftness of motion is taken for divinity, because their nature is unknown. Thus they would have themselves thought sometimes the authors of the things which they announce; and sometimes, no doubt, the bad things are their doing, never the good. The purposes of God, too, they took up of old from the lips of the prophets, even as they spoke them; and they gather them still from their works, when they hear them read aloud. Thus getting, too, from this source some intimations of the future, they set themselves up as rivals of the true God, while they steal His divinations.

But the skill with which their responses are shaped to meet events, your Croesi and Pyrrhi know too well. On the other hand, it was in that way we have explained, the Pythian was able to declare that they were cooking a tortoise [110] with the flesh of a lamb; in a moment he had been to Lydia. From dwelling in the air, and their nearness to the stars, and their commerce with the clouds, they have means of knowing the preparatory processes going on in these upper regions, and thus can give promise of the rains which they already feel.

Very kind too, no doubt, they are in regard to the healing of diseases. For, first of all, they make you ill; then, to get a miracle out of it, they command the application of remedies either altogether new, or contrary to those in use, and straightway withdrawing hurtful influence, they are supposed to have wrought a cure. What need, then, to speak of their other artifices, or yet further of the deceptive power which they have as spirits: of these Castor apparitions, [111] of water carried by a sieve, and a ship drawn along by a girdle, and a beard reddened by a touch, all done with the one object of showing that men should believe in the deity of stones, and not seek after the only true God?

Chapter XXIII

Moreover, if sorcerers call forth ghosts, and even make what seem the souls of the dead to appear; if they put boys to death, in order to get a response from the oracle; if, with their juggling illusions, they make a pretence of doing various miracles; if they put dreams into people's minds by the power of the angels and demons whose aid they have invited, by whose influence, too, goats and tables are made to divine,--how much more likely is this power of evil to be zealous in doing with all its might, of its own inclination, and for its own objects, what it does to serve the ends of others! Or if both angels and demons do just what your gods do, where in that case is the pre-eminence of deity, which we must surely think to be above all in might? Will it not then be more reasonable to hold that these spirits make themselves gods, giving as they do the very proofs which raise your gods to godhead, than that the gods are the equals of angels and demons? You make a distinction of places, I suppose, regarding as gods in their temple those whose divinity you do not recognize elsewhere; counting the madness which leads one man to leap from the sacred houses, to be something different from that which leads another to leap from an adjoining house; looking on one who cuts his arms and secret parts as under a different furor from another who cuts his throat. The result of the frenzy is the same, and the manner of instigation is one. But thus far we have been dealing only in words:

We now proceed to a proof of facts, in which we shall show that under different names you have real identity.

Let a person be brought before your tribunals, who is plainly under demoniacal possession. The wicked spirit, bidden to speak by a follower of Christ, [112] will as readily make the truthful confession that he is a demon, as elsewhere he has falsely asserted that he is a god.

Or, if you will, let there be produced one of the god-possessed, as they are supposed, who, inhaling at the altar, conceive divinity from the fumes, who are delivered of it by retching, who vent it forth in agonies of gasping. Let that same Virgin Cælestis herself the rain-promiser, let Æsculapius discoverer of medicines, ready to prolong the life of Socordius, and Tenatius, and Asclepiodotus, now in the last extremity, if they would not confess, in their fear of lying to a Christian, that they were demons, then and there shed the blood of that most impudent follower of Christ. What clearer than a work like that? what more trustworthy than such a proof?

The simplicity of truth is thus set forth; its own worth sustains it; no ground remains for the least suspicion.

Do you say that it is done by magic, or some trick of that sort? You will not say anything of the sort, if you have been allowed the use of your ears and eyes. For what argument can you bring against a thing that is exhibited to the eye in its naked reality? If, on the one hand, they are really gods, why do they pretend to be demons? Is it from fear of us? In that case your divinity is put in subjection to Christians; and you surely can never ascribe deity to that which is under authority of man, nay (if it adds aught to the disgrace) of its very enemies. If, on the other hand, they are demons or angels, why, inconsistently with this, do they presume to set themselves forth as acting the part of gods? For as beings who put themselves out as gods would never willingly call themselves demons, if they were gods indeed, that they might not thereby in fact abdicate their dignity; so those whom you know to be no more than demons, would not dare to act as gods, if those whose names they take and use were really divine. For they would not dare to treat with disrespect the higher majesty of beings, whose displeasure they would feel was to be dreaded. So this divinity of yours is no divinity; for if it were, it would not be pretended to by demons, and it would not be denied by gods.

But since on both sides there is a concurrent acknowledgment that they are not gods, gather from this that there is but a single race--I mean the race of demons, the real race in both cases.

Let your search, then, now be after gods; for those whom you had imagined to be so you find to be spirits of evil. The truth is, as we have thus not only shown from our own gods that neither themselves nor any others have claims to deity, you may see at once who is really God, and whether that is He and He alone whom we Christians own; as also whether you are to believe in Him, and worship Him, after the manner of our Christian faith and discipline. But at once they will say, Who is this Christ with his fables? is he an ordinary man? is he a sorcerer? was his body stolen by his disciples from its tomb? is he now in the realms below? or is he not rather up in the heavens, thence about to come again, making the whole world shake, filling the earth with dread alarms, making all but Christians wail--as the Power of God, and the Spirit of God, as the Word, the Reason, the Wisdom, and the Son of God? Mock as you like, but get the demons if you can to join you in your mocking; let them deny that Christ is coming to judge every human soul which has existed from the world's beginning, clothing it again with the body it laid aside at death; let them declare it, say, before your tribunal, that this work has been allotted to Minos and Rhadamanthus, as Plato and the poets agree; let them put away from them at least the mark of ignominy and condemnation. They disclaim being unclean spirits, which yet we must hold as indubitably proved by their relish for the blood and fumes and foetid carcasses of sacrificial animals, and even by the vile language of their ministers. Let them deny that, for their wickedness condemned already, they are kept for that very judgment-day, with all their worshippers and their works. Why, all the authority and power we have over them is from our naming the name of Christ, and recalling to their memory the woes with which God threatens them at the hands of Christ as Judge, and which they expect one day to overtake them. Fearing Christ in God, and God in Christ, they become subject to the servants of God and Christ. So at our touch and breathing, overwhelmed by the thought and realization of those judgment fires, they leave at our command the bodies they have entered, unwilling, and distressed, and before your very eyes put to an open shame. You believe them when they lie; give credit to them, then, when they speak the truth about themselves. No one plays the liar to bring disgrace upon his own head, but for the sake of honour rather. You give a readier confidence to people making confessions against themselves, than denials in their own behalf. It has not been an unusual thing, accordingly, for those testimonies of your deities to convert men to Christianity; for in giving full belief to them, we are led to believe in Christ. Yes, your very gods kindle up faith in our Scriptures, they build up the confidence of our hope. You do homage, as I know, to them also with the blood of Christians. On no account, then, would they lose those who are so useful and dutiful to them, anxious even to hold you fast, lest some day or other as Christians you might put them to the rout,--if under the power of a follower of Christ, who desires to prove to you the Truth, it were at all possible for them to lie.

Chapter XXIV

This whole confession of these beings, in which they declare that they are not gods, and in which they tell you that there is no God but one, the God whom we adore, is quite sufficient to clear us from the crime of treason, chiefly against the Roman religion. For if it is certain the gods have no existence, there is no religion in the case. If there is no religion, because there are no gods, we are assuredly not guilty of any offence against religion. Instead of that, the charge recoils on your own head: worshipping a lie, you are really guilty of the crime you charge on us, not merely by refusing the true religion of the true God, but by going the further length of persecuting it. But now, granting that these objects of your worship are really gods, is it not generally held that there is one higher and more potent, as it were the world's chief ruler, endowed with absolute power and majesty? For the common way is to apportion deity, giving an imperial and supreme domination to one, while its offices are put into the hands of many, as Plato describes great Jupiter in the heavens, surrounded by an array at once of deities and demons. It behooves us, therefore, to show equal respect to the procurators, prefects, and governors of the divine empire. And yet how great a crime does he commit, who, with the object of gaining higher favour with the Cæsar, transfers his endeavours and his hopes to another, and does not confess that the appellation of God as of Emperor belongs only to the Supreme Head, when it is held a capital offence among us to call, or hear called, by the highest title any other than Cæsar himself! Let one man worship God, another Jupiter; let one lift suppliant hands to the heavens, another to the altar of Fides; let one--if you choose to take this view of it--count in prayer the clouds, and another the ceiling panels; let one consecrate his own life to his God, and another that of a goat. For see that you do not give a further ground for the charge of irreligion, by taking away religious liberty, [113] and forbidding free choice of deity, so that I may no longer worship according to my inclination, but am compelled to worship against it. Not even a human being would care to have unwilling homage rendered him; and so the very Egyptians have been permitted the legal use of their ridiculous superstition, liberty to make gods of birds and beasts, nay, to condemn to death any one who kills a god of their sort. Every province even, and every city, has its god. Syria has Astarte, Arabia has Dusares, the Norici have Belenus, Africa has its Cælestis, Mauritania has its own princes. I have spoken, I think, of Roman provinces, and yet I have not said their gods are Roman; for they are not worshipped at Rome any more than others who are ranked as deities over Italy itself by municipal consecration, such as Delventinus of Casinum, Visidianus of Narnia, Ancharia of Asculum, Nortia of Volsinii, Valentia of Ocriculum, Hostia of Satrium, Father Curis of Falisci, in honour of whom, too, Juno got her surname. In, fact, we alone are prevented having a religion of our own. We give offence to the Romans, we are excluded from the rights and privileges of Romans, because we do not worship the gods of Rome. It is well that there is a God of all, whose we all are, whether we will or no. But with you liberty is given to worship any god but the true God, as though He were not rather the God all should worship, to whom all belong.

Chapter XXV

I think I have offered sufficient proof upon the question of false and true divinity, having shown that the proof rests not merely on debate and argument, but on the witness of the very beings whom you believe are gods, so that the point needs no further handling. However, having been led thus naturally to speak of the Romans, I shall not avoid the controversy which is invited by the groundless assertion of those who maintain that, as a reward of their singular homage to religion, the Romans have been raised to such heights of power as to have become masters of the world; and that so certainly divine are the beings they worship, that those prosper beyond all others, who beyond all others honour them. [114] This, forsooth, is the wages the gods have paid the Romans for their devotion. The progress of the empire is to be ascribed to Sterculus, the Mutunus, and Larentina! For I can hardly think that foreign gods would have been disposed to show more favour to an alien race than to their own, and given their own fatherland, in which they had their birth, grew up to manhood, became illustrious, and at last were buried, over to invaders from another shore! As for Cybele, if she set her affections on the city of Rome as sprung of the Trojan stock saved from the arms of Greece, she herself forsooth being of the same race,--if she foresaw her transference [115] to the avenging people by whom Greece the conqueror of Phrygia was to be subdued, let her look to it (in regard of her native country's conquest by Greece). Why, too, even in these days the Mater Magna has given a notable proof of her greatness which she has conferred as a boon upon the city; when, after the loss to the State of Marcus Aurelius at Sirmium, on the sixteenth before the Kalends of April, that most sacred high priest of hers was offering, a week after, impure libations of blood drawn from his own arms, and issuing his commands that the ordinary prayers should be made for the safety of the emperor already dead. O tardy messengers! O sleepy despatches! through whose fault Cybele had not an earlier knowledge of the imperial decease, that the Christians might have no occasion to ridicule a goddess so unworthy. Jupiter, again, would surely never have permitted his own Crete to fall at once before the Roman Fasces, forgetful of that Idean cave and the Corybantian cymbals, and the sweet odour of her who nursed him there. Would he not have exalted his own tomb above the entire Capitol, that the land which covered the ashes of Jove might rather be the mistress of the world? Would Juno have desired the destruction of the Punic city, beloved even to the neglect of Samos, and that by a nation of Æneadæ? As to that I know, "Here were her arms, here was her chariot, this kingdom, if the Fates permit, the goddess tends and cherishes to be mistress of the nations." [116] Jove's hapless wife and sister had no power to prevail against the Fates! "Jupiter himself is sustained by fate." And yet the Romans have never done such homage to the Fates, which gave them Carthage against the purpose and the will of Juno, as to the abandoned harlot Larentina. It is undoubted that not a few of your gods have reigned on earth as kings. If, then, they now possess the power of bestowing empire, when they were kings themselves, from whence had they received their kingly honours? Whom did Jupiter and Saturn worship? A Sterculus, I suppose. But did the Romans, along with the native-born inhabitants, afterwards adore also some who were never kings? In that case, however, they were under the reign of others, who did not yet bow down to them, as not yet raised to godhead. It belongs to others, then, to make gift of kingdoms, since there were kings before these gods had their names on the roll of divinities. But how utterly foolish it is to attribute the greatness of the Roman name to religious merits, since it was after Rome became an empire, or call it still a kingdom, that the religion she professes made its chief progress! Is it the case now? Has its religion been the source of the prosperity of Rome? Though Numa set agoing an eagerness after superstitious observances, yet religion among the Romans was not yet a matter of images or temples. It was frugal in its ways, its rites were simple, and there were no capitols struggling to the heavens; but the altars were offhand ones of turf, and the sacred vessels were yet of Samian earthen-ware, and from these the odours rose, and no likeness of God was to be seen. For at that time the skill of the Greeks and Tuscans in image-making had not yet overrun the city with the products of their art. The Romans, therefore, were not distinguished for their devotion to the gods before they attained to greatness; and so their greatness was not the result of their religion. Indeed, how could religion make a people great who have owed their greatness to their irreligion? For, if I am not mistaken, kingdoms and empires are acquired by wars, and are extended by victories. More than that, you cannot have wars and victories without the taking, and often the destruction, of cities. That is a thing in which the gods have their share of calamity. Houses and temples suffer alike; there is indiscriminate slaughter of priests and citizens; the hand of rapine is laid equally upon sacred and on common treasure. Thus the sacrileges of the Romans are as numerous as their trophies. They boast as many triumphs over the gods as over the nations; as many spoils of battle they have still, as there remain images of captive deities. And the poor gods submit to be adored by their enemies, and they ordain illimitable empire to those whose injuries rather than their simulated homage should have had retribution at their hands. But divinities unconscious are with impunity dishonoured, just as in vain they are adored. You certainly never can believe that devotion to religion has evidently advanced to greatness a people who, as we have put it, have either grown by injuring religion, or have injured religion by their growth. Those, too, whose kingdoms have become part of the one great whole of the Roman empire, were not without religion when their kingdoms were taken from them.

Chapter XXVI

Examine then, and see if He be not the dispenser of kingdoms, who is Lord at once of the world which is ruled, and of man himself who rules; if He have not ordained the changes of dynasties, with their appointed seasons, who was before all time, and made the world a body of times; if the rise and the fall of states are not the work of Him, under whose sovereignty the human race once existed without states at all.

How do you allow yourselves to fall into such error? Why, the Rome of rural simplicity is older than some of her gods; she reigned before her proud, vast Capitol was built. The Babylonians exercised dominion, too, before the days of the Pontiffs; and the Medes before the Quindecemvirs; and the Egyptians before the Salii; and the Assyrians before the Luperci; and the Amazons before the Vestal Virgins. And to add another point: if the religions of Rome give empire, ancient Judea would never have been a kingdom, despising as it did one and all these idol deities; Judea, whose God you Romans once honoured with victims, and its temple with gifts, and its people with treaties; and which would never have been beneath your sceptre but for that last and crowning offence against God, in rejecting and crucifying Christ.

Chapter XXVII

Enough has been said in these remarks to confute the charge of treason against your religion: for we cannot be held to do harm to that which has no existence. When we are called therefore to sacrifice, we resolutely refuse, relying on the knowledge we possess, by which we are well assured of the real objects to whom these services are offered, under profaning of images and the deification of human names. Some, indeed, think it a piece of insanity that, when it is in our power to offer sacrifice at once, and go away unharmed, holding as ever our convictions, we prefer an obstinate persistence in our confession to our safety. You advise us, forsooth, to take unjust advantage of you; but we know whence such suggestions come, who is at the bottom of it all, and how every effort is made, now by cunning suasion, and now by merciless persecution, to overthrow our constancy. No other than that spirit, half devil and half angel, who, hating us because of his own separation from God, and stirred with envy for the favour God has shown us, turns your minds against us by an occult influence, moulding and instigating them to all that perversity in judgment, and that unrighteous cruelty, which we have mentioned at the beginning of our work, when entering on this discussion. For, though the whole power of demons and kindred spirits is subject to us, yet still, as ill-disposed slaves sometimes conjoin contumacy with fear, and delight to injure those of whom they at the same time stand in awe, so is it here.

For fear also inspires hatred.

Besides, in their desperate condition, as already under condemnation, it gives them some comfort, while punishment delays, to have the usufruct of their malignant dispositions. And yet, when hands are laid on them, they are subdued at once, and submit to their lot; and those whom at a distance they oppose, in close quarters they supplicate for mercy. So when, like insurrectionary workhouses, or prisons, or mines, or any such penal slaveries, they break forth against us their masters, they know all the while that they are not a match for us, and just on that account, indeed, rush the more recklessly to destruction. We resist them, unwillingly, as though they were equals, and contend against them by persevering in that which they assail; and our triumph over them is never more complete than when we are condemned for resolute adherence to our faith.

Chapter XXVIII

But as it was easily seen to be unjust to compel freemen against their will to offer sacrifice (for even in other acts of religious service a willing mind is required), it should be counted quite absurd for one man to compel another to do honour to the gods, when he ought ever voluntarily, and in the sense of his own need, to seek their favour, lest in the liberty which is his right he should be ready to say, "I want none of Jupiter's favours; pray who art thou? Let Janus meet me with angry looks, with whichever of his faces he likes; what have you to do with me?" You have been led, no doubt, by these same evil spirits to compel us to offer sacrifice for the well-being of the emperor; and you are under a necessity of using force, just as we are under an obligation to face the dangers of it.

This brings us, then, to the second ground of accusation, that we are guilty of treason against a majesty more august; for you do homage with a greater dread and an intenser reverence to Cæsar, than Olympian Jove himself. And if you knew it, upon sufficient grounds. For is not any living man better than a dead one, whoever he be? But this is not done by you on any other ground than regard to a power whose presence you vividly realize; so that also in this you are convicted of impiety to your gods, inasmuch as you show a greater reverence to a human sovereignty than you do to them. Then, too, among you, people far more readily swear a false oath in the name of all the gods, than in the name of the single genius of Cæsar.

Chapter XXIX

Let it be made clear, then, first of all, if those to whom sacrifice is offered are really able to protect either emperor or anybody else, and so adjudge us guilty of treason, if angels and demons, spirits of most wicked nature, do any good, if the lost save, if the condemned give liberty, if the dead (I refer to what you know well enough) defend the living. For surely the first thing they would look to would be the protection of their statues, and images, and temples, which rather owe their safety, I think, to the watch kept by Cæsar's guards. Nay, I think the very materials of which these are made come from Cæsar's mines, and there is not a temple but depends on Cæsar's will. Yes, and many gods have felt the displeasure of the Cæsar. It makes for my argument if they are also partakers of his favour, when he bestows on them some gift or privilege. How shall they who are thus in Cæsar's power, who belong entirely to him, have Cæsar's protection in their hands, so that you can imagine them able to give to Cæsar what they more readily get from him? This, then, is the ground on which we are charged with treason against the imperial majesty, to wit, that we do not put the emperors under their own possessions; that we do not offer a mere mock service on their behalf, as not believing their safety rests in leaden hands. But you are impious in a high degree who look for it where it is not, who seek it from those who have it not to give, passing by Him who has it entirely in His power. Besides this, you persecute those who know where to seek for it, and who, knowing where to seek for it, are able as well to secure it.

Chapter XXX

For we offer prayer for the safety of our princes to the eternal, the true, the living God, whose favour, beyond all others, they must themselves desire.

They know from whom they have obtained their power; they know, as they are men, from whom they have received life itself; they are convinced that He is God alone, on whose power alone they are entirely dependent, to whom they are second, after whom they occupy the highest places, before and above all the gods. Why not, since they are above all living men, and the living, as living, are superior to the dead? They reflect upon the extent of their power, and so they come to understand the highest; they acknowledge that they have all their might from Him against whom their might is nought. Let the emperor make war on heaven; let him lead heaven captive in his triumph; let him put guards on heaven; let him impose taxes on heaven! He cannot. Just because he is less than heaven, he is great. For he himself is His to whom heaven and every creature appertains. He gets his sceptre where he first got his humanity; his power where he got the breath of life. Thither we lift our eyes, with hands outstretched, because free from sin; with head uncovered, for we have nothing whereof to be ashamed; finally, without a monitor, because it is from the heart we supplicate. Without ceasing, for all our emperors we offer prayer.

We pray for life prolonged; for security to the empire; for protection to the imperial house; for brave armies, a faithful senate, a virtuous people, the world at rest, whatever, as man or Cæsar, an emperor would wish. These things I cannot ask from any but the God from whom I know I shall obtain them, both because He alone bestows them and because I have claims upon Him for their gift, as being a servant of His, rendering homage to Him alone, persecuted for His doctrine, offering to Him, at His own requirement, that costly and noble sacrifice of prayer [117] despatched from the chaste body, an unstained soul, a sanctified spirit, not the few grains of incense a farthing buys[118] --tears of an Arabian tree,--not a few drops of wine,--not the blood of some worthless ox to which death is a relief, and, in addition to other offensive things, a polluted conscience, so that one wonders, when your victims are examined by these vile priests, why the examination is not rather of the sacrificers than the sacrifices. With our hands thus stretched out and up to God, rend us with your iron claws, hang us up on crosses, wrap us in flames, take our heads from us with the sword, let loose the wild beasts on us,--the very attitude of a Christian praying is one of preparation for all punishment. [119] Let this, good rulers, be your work: wring from us the soul, beseeching God on the emperor's behalf. Upon the truth of God, and devotion to His name, put the brand of crime.

Chapter XXXI

But we merely, you say, flatter the emperor, and feign these prayers of ours to escape persecution. Thank you for your mistake, for you give us the opportunity of proving our allegations. Do you, then, who think that we care nothing for the welfare of Cæsar, look into God's revelations, examine our sacred books, which we do not keep in hiding, and which many accidents put into the hands of those who are not of us. Learn from them that a large benevolence is enjoined upon us, even so far as to supplicate God for our enemies, and to beseech blessings on our persecutors. [120] Who, then, are greater enemies and persecutors of Christians, than the very parties with treason against whom we are charged? Nay, even in terms, and most clearly, the Scripture says, "Pray for kings, and rulers, and powers, that all may be peace with you." [121] For when there is disturbance in the empire, if the commotion is felt by its other members, surely we too, though we are not thought to be given to disorder, are to be found in some place or other which the calamity affects.

Chapter XXXII

There is also another and a greater necessity for our offering prayer in behalf of the emperors, nay, for the complete stability of the empire, and for Roman interests in general. For we know that a mighty shock impending over the whole earth--in fact, the very end of all things threatening dreadful woes--is only retarded by the continued existence of the Roman empire. [122] We have no desire, then, to be overtaken by these dire events; and in praying that their coming may be delayed, we are lending our aid to Rome's duration. More than this, though we decline to swear by the genii of the Cæsars, we swear by their safety, which is worth far more than all your genii. Are you ignorant that these genii are called "Dæmones," and thence the diminutive name "Dæmonia" is applied to them? We respect in the emperors the ordinance of God, who has set them over the nations.

We know that there is that in them which God has willed; and to what God has willed we desire all safety, and we count an oath by it a great oath. But as for demons, that is, your genii, we have been in the habit of exorcising them, not of swearing by them, and thereby conferring on them divine honour.

Chapter XXXIII

But why dwell longer on the reverence and sacred respect of Christians to the emperor, whom we cannot but look up to as called by our Lord to his office?

So that on valid grounds I might say Cæsar is more ours than yours, for our God has appointed him. Therefore, as having this propriety in him, I do more than you for his welfare, not merely because I ask it of Him who can give it, or because I ask it as one who deserves to get it, but also because, in keeping the majesty of Cæsar within due limits, and putting it under the Most High, and making it less than divine, I commend him the more to the favour of Deity, to whom I make him alone inferior. But I place him in subjection to one I regard as more glorious than himself.

Never will I call the emperor God, and that either because it is not in me to be guilty of falsehood; or that I dare not turn him into ridicule; or that not even himself will desire to have that high name applied to him. If he is but a man, it is his interest as man to give God His higher place. Let him think it enough to bear the name of emperor.

That, too, is a great name of God's giving. To call him God, is to rob him of his title. If he is not a man, emperor he cannot be. Even when, amid the honours of a triumph, he sits on that lofty chariot, he is reminded that he is only human. A voice at his back keeps whispering in his ear, "Look behind thee; remember thou art but a man." And it only adds to his exultation, that he shines with a glory so surpassing as to require an admonitory reference to his condition. [123] It adds to his greatness that he needs such a reminiscence, lest he should think himself divine.

Chapter XXXIV

Augustus, the founder of the empire, would not even have the title Lord; for that, too, is a name of Deity. For my part, I am willing to give the emperor this designation, but in the common acceptation of the word, and when I am not forced to call him Lord as in God's place. But my relation to him is one of freedom; for I have but one true Lord, the God omnipotent and eternal, who is Lord of the emperor as well. How can he, who is truly father of his country, be its lord?

The name of piety is more grateful than the name of power; so the heads of families are called fathers rather than lords. Far less should the emperor have the name of God. We can only profess our belief that he is that by the most unworthy, nay, a fatal flattery; it is just as if, having an emperor, you call another by the name, in which case will you not give great and unappeasable offence to him who actually reigns?--an offence he, too, needs to fear on whom you have bestowed the title. Give all reverence to God, if you wish Him to be propitious to the emperor. Give up all worship of, and belief in, any other being as divine. Cease also to give the sacred name to him who has need of God himself. If such adulation is not ashamed of its lie, in addressing a man as divine, let it have some dread at least of the evil omen which it bears. It is the invocation of a curse, to give Cæsar the name of god before his apotheosis.

Chapter XXXV

This is the reason, then, why Christians are counted public enemies: that they pay no vain, nor false, nor foolish honours to the emperor; that, as men believing in the true religion, they prefer to celebrate their festal days with a good conscience, instead of with the common wantonness. It is, forsooth, a notable homage to bring fires and couches out before the public, to have feasting from street to street, to turn the city into one great tavern, to make mud with wine, to run in troops to acts of violence, to deeds of shamelessness to lust allurements! What! is public joy manifested by public disgrace? Do things unseemly at other times beseem the festal days of princes? Do they who observe the rules of virtue out of reverence for Cæsar, for his sake turn aside from them? Shall piety be a license to immoral deeds, and shall religion be regarded as affording the occasion for all riotous extravagance? Poor we, worthy of all condemnation! For why do we keep the votive days and high rejoicings in honour of the Cæsars with chastity, sobriety, and virtue? Why, on the day of gladness, do we neither cover our door-posts with laurels, nor intrude upon the day with lamps? It is a proper thing, at the call of a public festivity, to dress your house up like some new brothel. [124] However, in the matter of this homage to a lesser majesty, in reference to which we are accused of a lower sacrilege, because we do not celebrate along with you the holidays of the Cæsars in a manner forbidden alike by modesty, decency, and purity,--in truth they have been established rather as affording opportunities for licentiousness than from any worthy motive;--in this matter I am anxious to point out how faithful and true you are, lest perchance here also those who will not have us counted Romans, but enemies of Rome's chief rulers, be found themselves worse than we wicked Christians! I appeal to the inhabitants of Rome themselves, to the native population of the seven hills: does that Roman vernacular of theirs ever spare a Cæsar? The Tiber and the wild beasts' schools bear witness. Say now if nature had covered our hearts with a transparent substance through which the light could pass, whose hearts, all graven over, would not betray the scene of another and another Cæsar presiding at the distribution of a largess? And this at the very time they are shouting, "May Jupiter take years from us, and with them lengthen like to you,"--words as foreign to the lips of a Christian as it is out of keeping with his character to desire a change of emperor. But this is the rabble, you say; yet, as the rabble, they still are Romans, and none more frequently than they demand the death of Christians. [125] Of course, then, the other classes, as befits their higher rank, are religiously faithful.

No breath of treason is there ever in the senate, in the equestrian order, in the camp, in the palace.

Whence, then, came a Cassius, a Niger, an Albinus? Whence they who beset the Cæsar [126] between the two laurel groves? Whence they who practised wrestling, that they might acquire skill to strangle him? Whence they who in full armour broke into the palace, [127] more audacious than all your Tigerii and Parthenii. [128] If I mistake not, they were Romans; that is, they were not Christians. Yet all of them, on the very eve of their traitorous outbreak, offered sacrifices for the safety of the emperor, and swore by his genius, one thing in profession, and another in the heart; and no doubt they were in the habit of calling Christians enemies of the state. Yes, and persons who are now daily brought to light as confederates or approvers of these crimes and treasons, the still remnant gleanings after a vintage of traitors, with what verdant and branching laurels they clad their door-posts, with what lofty and brilliant lamps they smoked their porches, with what most exquisite and gaudy couches they divided the Forum among themselves; not that they might celebrate public rejoicings, but that they might get a foretaste of their own votive seasons in partaking of the festivities of another, and inaugurate the model and image of their hope, changing in their minds the emperor's name. The same homage is paid, dutifully too, by those who consult astrologers, and soothsayers, and augurs, and magicians, about the life of the Cæsars,--arts which, as made known by the angels who sinned, and forbidden by God, Christians do not even make use of in their own affairs. But who has any occasion to inquire about the life of the emperor, if he have not some wish or thought against it, or some hopes and expectations after it? For consultations of this sort have not the same motive in the case of friends as in the case of sovereigns. The anxiety of a kinsman is something very different from that of a subject.

Chapter XXXVI

If it is the fact that men bearing the name of Romans are found to be enemies of Rome, why are we, on the ground that we are regarded as enemies, denied the name of Romans? We may be at once Romans and foes of Rome, when men passing for Romans are discovered to be enemies of their country.

So the affection, and fealty, and reverence, due to the emperors do not consist in such tokens of homage as these, which even hostility may be zealous in performing, chiefly as a cloak to its purposes; but in those ways which Deity as certainly enjoins on us, as they are held to be necessary in the case of all men as well as emperors. Deeds of true heart-goodness are not due by us to emperors alone. We never do good with respect of persons; for in our own interest we conduct ourselves as those who take no payment either of praise or premium from man, but from God, who both requires and remunerates an impartial benevolence. [129] We are the same to emperors as to our ordinary neighbors. For we are equally forbidden to wish ill, to do ill, to speak ill, to think ill of all men. The thing we must not do to an emperor, we must not do to any one else: what we would not do to anybody, a fortiori, perhaps we should not do to him whom God has been pleased so highly to exalt.

Chapter XXXVII

If we are enjoined, then, to love our enemies, as I have remarked above, whom have we to hate? If injured, we are forbidden to retaliate, lest we become as bad ourselves: who can suffer injury at our hands? In regard to this, recall your own experiences. How often you inflict gross cruelties on Christians, partly because it is your own inclination, and partly in obedience to the laws! How often, too, the hostile mob, paying no regard to you, takes the law into its own hand, and assails us with stones and flames! With the very frenzy of the Bacchanals, they do not even spare the Christian dead, but tear them, now sadly changed, no longer entire, from the rest of the tomb, from the asylum we might say of death, cutting them in pieces, rending them asunder. Yet, banded together as we are, ever so ready to sacrifice our lives, what single case of revenge for injury are you able to point to, though, if it were held right among us to repay evil by evil, a single night with a torch or two could achieve an ample vengeance? But away with the idea of a sect divine avenging itself by human fires, or shrinking from the sufferings in which it is tried. If we desired, indeed, to act the part of open enemies, not merely of secret avengers, would there be any lacking in strength, whether of numbers or resources?

The Moors, the Marcomanni, the Parthians themselves, or any single people, however great, inhabiting a distinct territory, and confined within its own boundaries, surpasses, forsooth, in numbers, one spread over all the world! We are but of yesterday, and we have filled every place among you--cities, islands, fortresses, towns, market-places, the very camp, tribes, companies, palace, senate, forum,--we have left nothing to you but the temples of your gods. For what wars should we not be fit, not eager, even with unequal forces, we who so willingly yield ourselves to the sword, if in our religion it were not counted better to be slain than to slay? Without arms even, and raising no insurrectionary banner, but simply in enmity to you, we could carry on the contest with you by an ill-willed severance alone. For if such multitudes of men were to break away from you, and betake themselves to some remote corner of the world, why, the very loss of so many citizens, whatever sort they were, would cover the empire with shame; nay, in the very forsaking, vengeance would be inflicted. Why, you would be horror-struck at the solitude in which you would find yourselves, at such an all-prevailing silence, and that stupor as of a dead world. You would have to seek subjects to govern. You would have more enemies than citizens remaining. For now it is the immense number of Christians which makes your enemies so few,--almost all the inhabitants of your various cities being followers of Christ. [130] Yet you choose to call us enemies of the human race, rather than of human error.

Nay, who would deliver you from those secret foes, ever busy both destroying your souls and ruining your health?

Who would save you, I mean, from the attacks of those spirits of evil, which without reward or hire we exorcise?

This alone would be revenge enough for us, that you were henceforth left free to the possession of unclean spirits.

But instead of taking into account what is due to us for the important protection we afford you, and though we are not merely no trouble to you, but in fact necessary to your well-being, you prefer to hold us enemies, as indeed we are, yet not of man, but rather of his error.

Chapter XXXVIII

Ought not Christians, therefore, to receive not merely a somewhat milder treatment, but to have a place among the law-tolerated societies, seeing they are not chargeable with any such crimes as are commonly dreaded from societies of the illicit class? For, unless I mistake the matter, the prevention of such associations is based on a prudential regard to public order, that the state may not be divided into parties, which would naturally lead to disturbance in the electoral assemblies, the councils, the curiæ, the special conventions, even in the public shows by the hostile collisions of rival parties; especially when now, in pursuit of gain, men have begun to consider their violence an article to be bought and sold. But as those in whom all ardour in the pursuit of glory and honour is dead, we have no pressing inducement to take part in your public meetings; nor is there aught more entirely foreign to us than affairs of state. We acknowledge one all-embracing commonwealth--the world. We renounce all your spectacles, as strongly as we renounce the matters originating them, which we know were conceived of superstition, when we give up the very things which are the basis of their representations.

Among us nothing is ever said, or seen, or heard, which has anything in common with the madness of the circus, the immodesty of the theatre, the atrocities of the arena, the useless exercises of the wrestling-ground. Why do you take offence at us because we differ from you in regard to your pleasures?

If we will not partake of your enjoyments, the loss is ours, if there be loss in the case, not yours. We reject what pleases you. You, on the other hand, have no taste for what is our delight. The Epicureans were allowed by you to decide for themselves one true source of pleasure--I mean equanimity; the Christian, on his part, has many such enjoyments--what harm in that?

Chapter XXXIX

I shall at once go on, then, to exhibit the peculiarities of the Christian society, that, as I have refuted the evil charged against it, I may point out its positive good. [131] We are a body knit together as such by a common religious profession, by unity of discipline, and by the bond of a common hope. We meet together as an assembly and congregation, that, offering up prayer to God as with united force, we may wrestle with Him in our supplications. This violence God delights in. We pray, too, for the emperors, for their ministers and for all in authority, for the welfare of the world, for the prevalence of peace, for the delay of the final consummation. [132] We assemble to read our sacred writings, if any peculiarity of the times makes either forewarning or reminiscence needful. [133] However it be in that respect, with the sacred words we nourish our faith, we animate our hope, we make our confidence more stedfast; and no less by inculcations of God's precepts we confirm good habits. In the same place also exhortations are made, rebukes and sacred censures are administered. For with a great gravity is the work of judging carried on among us, as befits those who feel assured that they are in the sight of God; and you have the most notable example of judgment to come when any one has sinned so grievously as to require his severance from us in prayer, in the congregation and in all sacred intercourse. The tried men of our elders preside over us, obtaining that honour not by purchase, but by established character. There is no buying and selling of any sort in the things of God. Though we have our treasure-chest, it is not made up of purchase-money, as of a religion that has its price. On the monthly day, [134] if he likes, each puts in a small donation; but only if it be his pleasure, and only if he be able: for there is no compulsion; all is voluntary. These gifts are, as it were, piety's deposit fund. For they are not taken thence and spent on feasts, and drinking-bouts, and eating-houses, but to support and bury poor people, to supply the wants of boys and girls destitute of means and parents, and of old persons confined now to the house; such, too, as have suffered shipwreck; and if there happen to be any in the mines, or banished to the islands, or shut up in the prisons, for nothing but their fidelity to the cause of God's Church, they become the nurslings of their confession. But it is mainly the deeds of a love so noble that lead many to put a brand upon us. See, they say, how they love one [135] another, for themselves are animated by mutual hatred; how they are ready even to die for one another, for they themselves will sooner put to death. And they are wroth with us, too, because we call each other brethren; for no other reason, as I think, than because among themselves names of consanguinity are assumed in mere pretence of affection.

But we are your brethren as well, by the law of our common mother nature, though you are hardly men, because brothers so unkind. At the same time, how much more fittingly they are called and counted brothers who have been led to the knowledge of God as their common Father, who have drunk in one spirit of holiness, who from the same womb of a common ignorance have agonized into the same light of truth! But on this very account, perhaps, we are regarded as having less claim to be held true brothers, that no tragedy makes a noise about our brotherhood, or that the family possessions, which generally destroy brotherhood among you, create fraternal bonds among us. One in mind and soul, we do not hesitate to share our earthly goods with one another. All things are common among us but our wives. We give up our community where it is practised alone by others, who not only take possession of the wives of their friends, but most tolerantly also accommodate their friends with theirs, following the example, I believe, of those wise men of ancient times, the Greek Socrates and the Roman Cato, who shared with their friends the wives whom they had married, it seems for the sake of progeny both to themselves and to others; whether in this acting against their partners' wishes, I am not able to say. Why should they have any care over their chastity, when their husbands so readily bestowed it away? O noble example of Attic wisdom, of Roman gravity--the philosopher and the censor playing pimps! What wonder if that great love of Christians towards one another is desecrated by you!

For you abuse also our humble feasts, on the ground that they are extravagant as well as infamously wicked.

To us, it seems, applies the saying of Diogenes: "The people of Megara feast as though they were going to die on the morrow; they build as though they were never to die!" But one sees more readily the mote in another's eye than the beam in his own.

Why, the very air is soured with the eructations of so many tribes, and curiæ, and decuriæ. The Salii cannot have their feast without going into debt; you must get the accountants to tell you what the tenths of Hercules and the sacrificial banquets cost; the choicest cook is appointed for the Apaturia, the Dionysia, the Attic mysteries; the smoke from the banquet of Serapis will call out the firemen. Yet about the modest supper-room of the Christians alone a great ado is made.

Our feast explains itself by its name.

The Greeks call it agapè, i.e., affection. Whatever it costs, our outlay in the name of piety is gain, since with the good things of the feast we benefit the needy; not as it is with you, do parasites aspire to the glory of satisfying their licentious propensities, selling themselves for a belly-feast to all disgraceful treatment,--but as it is with God himself, a peculiar respect is shown to the lowly. If the object of our feast be good, in the light of that consider its further regulations. As it is an act of religious service, it permits no vileness or immodesty. The participants, before reclining, taste first of prayer to God. As much is eaten as satisfies the cravings of hunger; as much is drunk as befits the chaste.

They say it is enough, as those who remember that even during the night they have to worship God; they talk as those who know that the Lord is one of their auditors. After manual ablution, and the bringing in of lights, each [136] is asked to stand forth and sing, as he can, a hymn to God, either one from the holy Scriptures or one of his own composing,--a proof of the measure of our drinking. As the feast commenced with prayer, so with prayer it is closed. We go from it, not like troops of mischief-doers, nor bands of vagabonds, nor to break out into licentious acts, but to have as much care of our modesty and chastity as if we had been at a school of virtue rather than a banquet. Give the congregation of the Christians its due, and hold it unlawful, if it is like assemblies of the illicit sort: by all means let it be condemned, if any complaint can be validly laid against it, such as lies against secret factions. But who has ever suffered harm from our assemblies? We are in our congregations just what we are when separated from each other; we are as a community what we are individuals; we injure nobody, we trouble nobody. When the upright, when the virtuous meet together, when the pious, when the pure assemble in congregation, you ought not to call that a faction, but a curia--[i.e., the court of God.]

Chapter XL

On the contrary, they deserve the name of faction who conspire to bring odium on good men and virtuous, who cry out against innocent blood, offering as the justification of their enmity the baseless plea, that they think the Christians the cause of every public disaster, of every affliction with which the people are visited.

If the Tiber rises as high as the city walls, if the Nile does not send its waters up over the fields, if the heavens give no rain, if there is an earthquake, if there is famine or pestilence, straightway the cry [137] is, "Away with the Christians to the lion!"

What! shall you give such multitudes to a single beast? Pray, tell me how many calamities befell the world and particular cities before Tiberius reigned--before the coming, that is, of Christ? We read of the islands of Hiera, and Anaphe, and Delos, and Rhodes, and Cos, with many thousands of human beings, having been swallowed up. Plato informs us that a region larger than Asia or Africa was seized by the Atlantic Ocean. An earthquake, too, drank up the Corinthian sea; and the force of the waves cut off a part of Lucania, whence it obtained the name of Sicily. These things surely could not have taken place without the inhabitants suffering by them. But where--I do not say were Christians, those despisers of your gods--but where were your gods themselves in those days, when the flood poured its destroying waters over all the world, or, as Plato thought, merely the level portion of it?

For that they are of later date than that calamity, the very cities in which they were born and died, nay, which they founded, bear ample testimony; for the cities could have no existence at this day unless as belonging to postdiluvian times. Palestine had not yet received from Egypt its Jewish swarm (of emigrants), nor had the race from which Christians sprung yet settled down there, when its neighbors

Sodom and Gomorrah were consumed by fire from heaven. The country yet smells of that conflagration; and if there are apples there upon the trees, it is only a promise to the eye they give--you but touch them, and they turn to ashes. Nor had Tuscia and Campania to complain of Christians in the days when fire from heaven overwhelmed Vulsinii, and Pompeii was destroyed by fire from its own mountain.

No one yet worshipped the true God at Rome, when Hannibal at Cannæ counted the Roman slain by the pecks of Roman rings. Your gods were all objects of adoration, universally acknowledged, when the Senones closely besieged the very Capitol. And it is in keeping with all this, that if adversity has at any time befallen cities, the temples and the walls have equally shared in the disaster, so that it is clear to demonstration the thing was not the doing of the gods, seeing it also overtook themselves. The truth is, the human race has always deserved ill at God's hand.

First of all, as undutiful to Him, because when it knew Him in part, it not only did not seek after Him, but even invented other gods of its own to worship; and further, because, as the result of their willing ignorance of the Teacher of righteousness, the Judge and Avenger of sin, all vices and crimes grew and flourished. But had men sought, they would have come to know the glorious object of their seeking; and knowledge would have produced obedience, and obedience would have found a gracious instead of an angry God. They ought then to see that the very same God is angry with them now as in ancient times, before Christians were so much as spoken of. It was His blessings they enjoyed--created before they made any of their deities: and why can they not take it in, that their evils come from the Being whose goodness they have failed to recognize? They suffer at the hands of Him to whom they have been ungrateful. And, for all that is said, if we compare the calamities of former times, they fall on us more lightly now, since God gave Christians to the world; for from that time virtue put some restraint on the world's wickedness, and men began to pray for the averting of God's wrath. In a word, when the summer clouds give no rain, and the season is matter of anxiety, you indeed--full of feasting day by day, and ever eager for the banquet, baths and taverns and brothels always busy--offer up to Jupiter your rain-sacrifices; you enjoin on the people barefoot processions; you seek heaven at the Capitol; you look up to the temple-ceilings for the longed-for clouds--God and heaven not in all your thoughts. We, dried up with fastings, and our passions bound tightly up, holding back as long as possible from all the ordinary enjoyments of life, rolling in sackcloth and ashes, assail heaven with our importunities--touch God's heart--and when we have extorted divine compassion, why, Jupiter gets all the honour!

Chapter XLI

You, therefore, are the sources of trouble in human affairs; on you lies the blame of public adversities, since you are ever attracting them--you by whom God is despised and images are worshipped. It should surely seem the more natural thing to believe that it is the neglected One who is angry, and not they to whom all homage is paid; or most unjustly they act, if, on account of the Christians, they send trouble on their own devotees, whom they are bound to keep clear of the punishments of Christians. But this, you say, hits your God as well, since He permits His worshippers to suffer on account of those who dishonour Him. But admit first of all His providential arrangings, and you will not make this retort. For He who once for all appointed an eternal judgment at the world's close, does not precipitate the separation, which is essential to judgment, before the end.

Meanwhile He deals with all sorts of men alike, so that all together share His favours and reproofs. His will is, that outcasts and elect should have adversities and prosperities in common, that we should have all the same experience of His goodness and severity. Having learned these things from His own lips, we love His goodness, we fear His wrath, while both by you are treated with contempt; and hence the sufferings of life, so far as it is our lot to be overtaken by them, are in our case gracious admonitions, while in yours they are divine punishments. We indeed are not the least put about: for, first, only one thing in this life greatly concerns us, and that is, to get quickly out of it; and next, if any adversity befalls us, it is laid to the door of your transgressions. Nay, though we are likewise involved in troubles because of our close connection with you, we are rather glad of it, because we recognize in it divine foretellings, which, in fact, go to confirm the confidence and faith of our hope. But if all the evils you endure are inflicted on you by the gods you worship out of spite to us, why do you continue to pay homage to beings so ungrateful, and unjust; who, instead of being angry with you, should rather have been aiding and abetting you by persecuting Christians--keeping you clear of their sufferings?

Chapter XLII

But we are called to account as harm-doers on another [138] ground, and are accused of being useless in the affairs of life. How in all the world can that be the case with people who are living among you, eating the same food, wearing the same attire, having the same habits, under the same necessities of existence? We are not Indian Brahmins or Gymnosophists, who dwell in woods and exile themselves from ordinary human life. We do not forget the debt of gratitude we owe to God, our Lord and Creator; we reject no creature of His hands, though certainly we exercise restraint upon ourselves, lest of any gift of His we make an immoderate or sinful use. So we sojourn with you in the world, abjuring neither forum, nor shambles, nor bath, nor booth, nor workshop, nor inn, nor weekly market, nor any other places of commerce. We sail with you, and fight with you, [139] and till the ground with you; and in like manner we unite with you in your traffickings--even in the various arts we make public property of our works for your benefit. How it is we seem useless in your ordinary business, living with you and by you as we do, I am not able to understand. But if I do not frequent your religious ceremonies, I am still on the sacred day a man. I do not at the Saturnalia bathe myself at dawn, that I may not lose both day and night; yet I bathe at a decent and healthful hour, which preserves me both in heat and blood. I can be rigid and pallid like you after ablution when I am dead. I do not recline in public at the feast of Bacchus, after the manner of the beast-fighters at their final banquet.

Yet of your resources I partake, wherever I may chance to eat. I do not buy a crown for my head. What matters it to you how I use them, if nevertheless the flowers are purchased? I think it more agreeable to have them free and loose, waving all about. Even if they are woven into a crown, we smell the crown with our nostrils: let those look to it who scent the perfume with their hair. We do not go to your spectacles; yet the articles that are sold there, if I need them, I will obtain more readily at their proper places. We certainly buy no frankincense. If the Arabias complain of this, let the Sabæans be well assured that their more precious and costly merchandise is expended as largely in the burying of Christians [140] as in the fumigating of the gods. At any rate, you say, the temple revenues are every day falling off. [141] how few now throw in a contribution! In truth, we are not able to give alms both to your human and your heavenly mendicants; nor do we think that we are required to give any but to those who ask for it. Let Jupiter then hold out his hand and get, for our compassion spends more in the streets than yours does in the temples. But your other taxes will acknowledge a debt of gratitude to Christians; for in the faithfulness which keeps us from fraud upon a brother, we make conscience of paying all their dues: so that, by ascertaining how much is lost by fraud and falsehood in the census declarations--the calculation may easily be made--it would be seen that the ground of complaint in one department of revenue is compensated by the advantage which others derive.

Chapter XLIII

I will confess, however, without hesitation, that there are some who in a sense may complain of Christians that they are a sterile race:

as, for instance, pimps, and panders, and bath-suppliers; assassins, and poisoners, and sorcerers; soothsayers, too, diviners, and astrologers. But it is a noble fruit of Christians, that they have no fruits for such as these.

And yet, whatever loss your interests suffer from the religion we profess, the protection you have from us makes amply up for it. What value do you set on persons, I do not here urge who deliver you from demons, I do not urge who for your sakes present prayers before the throne of the true God, for perhaps you have no belief in that--but from whom you can have nothing to fear?

Chapter XLIV

Yes, and no one considers what the loss is to the common weal,--a loss as great as it is real, no one estimates the injury entailed upon the state, when, men of virtue as we are, we are put to death in such numbers; when so many of the truly good suffer the last penalty. And here we call your own acts to witness, you who are daily presiding at the trials of prisoners, and passing sentence upon crimes. Well, in your long lists of those accused of many and various atrocities, has any assassin, any cutpurse, any man guilty of sacrilege, or seduction, or stealing bathers' clothes, his name entered as being a Christian too? Or when Christians are brought before you on the mere ground of their name, is there ever found among them an ill-doer of the sort? It is always with your folk the prison is steaming, the mines are sighing, the wild beasts are fed: it is from you the exhibitors of gladiatorial shows always get their herds of criminals to feed up for the occasion. You find no Christian there, except simply as being such; or if one is there as something else, a Christian he is no longer. [142]

Chapter XLV

We, then, alone are without crime. Is there ought wonderful in that, if it be a very necessity with us? For a necessity indeed it is. Taught of God himself what goodness is, we have both a perfect knowledge of it as revealed to us by a perfect Master; and faithfully we do His will, as enjoined on us by a Judge we dare not despise. But your ideas of virtue you have got from mere human opinion; on human authority, too, its obligation rests: hence your system of practical morality is deficient, both in the fulness and authority requisite to produce a life of real virtue. Man's wisdom to point out what is good, is no greater than his authority to exact the keeping of it; the one is as easily deceived as the other is despised. And so, which is the ampler rule, to say, "Thou shalt not kill," or to teach, "Be not even angry?" Which is more perfect, to forbid adultery, or to restrain from even a single lustful look?

Which indicates the higher intelligence, interdicting evil-doing, or evil-speaking? Which is more thorough, not allowing an injury, or not even suffering an injury done to you to be repaid? Though withal you know that these very laws also of yours, which seem to lead to virtue, have been borrowed from the law of God as the ancient model.

Of the age of Moses we have already spoken. But what is the real authority of human laws, when it is in man's power both to evade them, by generally managing to hide himself out of sight in his crimes, and to despise them sometimes, if inclination or necessity leads him to offend?

Think of these things, too, in the light of the brevity of any punishment you can inflict--never to last longer than till death. On this ground Epicurus makes light of all suffering and pain, maintaining that if it is small, it is contemptible; and if it is great, it is not long-continued.

No doubt about it, we, who receive our awards under the judgment of an all-seeing God, and who look forward to eternal punishment from Him for sin,--we alone make real effort to attain a blameless life, under the influence of our ampler knowledge, the impossibility of concealment, and the greatness of the threatened torment, not merely long-enduring but everlasting, fearing Him, whom he too should fear who the fearing judges,--even God, I mean, and not the proconsul.

Chapter XLVI

We have sufficiently met, as I think, the accusation of the various crimes on the ground of which these fierce demands are made for Christian blood.

We have made a full exhibition of our case; and we have shown you how we are able to prove that our statement is correct, from the trustworthiness, I mean, and antiquity of our sacred writings, and from the confession likewise of the powers of spiritual wickedness themselves.

Who will venture to undertake our refutation; not with skill of words, but, as we have managed our demonstration, on the basis of reality? But while the truth we hold is made clear to all, unbelief meanwhile, at the very time it is convinced of the worth of Christianity, which has now become well known for its benefits as well as from the intercourse of life, takes up the notion that it is not really a thing divine, but rather a kind of philosophy.

These are the very things, it says, the philosophers counsel and profess--innocence, justice, patience, sobriety, chastity. Why, then, are we not permitted an equal liberty and impunity for our doctrines as they have, with whom, in respect of what we teach, we are compared? or why are not they, as so like us, not pressed to the same offices, for declining which our lives are imperilled? For who compels a philosopher to sacrifice or take an oath, or put out useless lamps at midday? Nay, they openly overthrow your gods, and in their writings they attack your superstitions; and you applaud them for it. Many of them even, with your countenance, bark out against your rulers, and are rewarded with statues and salaries, instead of being given to the wild beasts. And very right it should be so. For they are called philosophers, not Christians. This name of philosopher has no power to put demons to the rout. Why are they not able to do that too? since philosophers count demons inferior to gods. Socrates used to say, "If the demon grant permission." Yet he, too, though in denying the existence of your divinities he had a glimpse of the truth, at his dying ordered a cock to be sacrificed to Æsculapius, I believe in honour of his father, [143] for Apollo pronounced Socrates the wisest of men. Thoughtless Apollo! testifying to the wisdom of the man who denied the existence of his race. In proportion to the enmity the truth awakens, you give offence by faithfully standing by it; but the man who corrupts and makes a mere pretence of it precisely on this ground gains favour with its persecutors. The truth which philosophers, these mockers and corrupters of it, with hostile ends merely affect to hold, and in doing so deprave, caring for nought but glory, Christians both intensely and intimately long for and maintain in its integrity, as those who have a real concern about their salvation. So that we are like each other neither in our knowledge nor our ways, as you imagine.

For what certain information did Thales, the first of natural philosophers, give in reply to the inquiry of Croesus regarding Deity, the delay for further thought so often proving in vain?

There is not a Christian workman but finds out God, and manifests Him, and hence assigns to Him all those attributes which go to constitute a divine being, though Plato affirms that it is far from easy to discover the Maker of the universe; and when He is found, it is difficult to make Him known to all. But if we challenge you to comparison in the virtue of chastity, I turn to a part of the sentence passed by the Athenians against Socrates, who was pronounced a corrupter of youth. The Christian confines himself to the female sex. I have read also how the harlot Phryne kindled in Diogenes the fires of lust, and how a certain Speusippus, of Plato's school, perished in the adulterous act. The Christian husband has nothing to do with any but his own wife. Democritus, in putting out his eyes, because he could not look on women without lusting after them, and was pained if his passion was not satisfied, owns plainly, by the punishment he inflicts, his incontinence.

But a Christian with grace-healed eyes is sightless in this matter; he is mentally blind against the assaults of passion. If I maintain our superior modesty of behaviour, there at once occurs to me Diogenes with filth-covered feet trampling on the proud couches of Plato, under the influence of another pride: the Christian does not even play the proud man to the pauper. If sobriety of spirit be the virtue in debate, why, there are Pythagoras at Thurii, and Zeno at Priene, ambitious of the supreme power:

the Christian does not aspire to the ædileship. If equanimity be the contention, you have Lycurgus choosing death by self-starvation, because the Lacons had made some emendation of his laws: the Christian, even when he is condemned, gives thanks. [144] If the comparison be made in regard to trustworthiness, Anaxagoras denied the deposit of his enemies: the Christian is noted for his fidelity even among those who are not of his religion.

If the matter of sincerity is to be brought to trial, Aristotle basely thrust his friend Hermias from his place:

the Christian does no harm even to his foe. With equal baseness does Aristotle play the sycophant to Alexander, instead of exercising to keep him in the right way, and Plato allows himself to be bought by Dionysius for his belly's sake. Aristippus in the purple, with all his great show of gravity, gives way to extravagance; and Hippias is put to death laying plots against the state: no Christian ever attempted such a thing in behalf of his brethren, even when persecution was scattering them abroad with every atrocity.

But it will be said that some of us, too, depart from the rules of our discipline. In that case, however, we count them no longer Christians; but the philosophers who do such things retain still the name and the honour of wisdom.

So, then, where is there any likeness between the Christian and the philosopher? between the disciple of Greece and of heaven? between the man whose object is fame, and whose object is life? between the talker and the doer? between the man who builds up and the man who pulls down? between the friend and the foe of error? between one who corrupts the truth, and one who restores and teaches it? between its chief and its custodier?

Chapter XLVII

Unless I am utterly mistaken, there is nothing so old as the truth; and the already proved antiquity of the divine writings is so far of use to me, that it leads men more easily to take it in that they are the treasure-source whence all later wisdom has been taken. And were it not necessary to keep my work to a moderate size, I might launch forth also into the proof of this. What poet or sophist has not drunk at the fountain of the prophets? Thence, accordingly, the philosophers watered their arid minds, so that it is the things they have from us which bring us into comparison with them. For this reason, I imagine, philosophy was banished by certain states--I mean by the Thebans, by the Spartans also, and the Argives--its disciples sought to imitate our doctrines; and ambitious, as I have said, of glory and eloquence alone, if they fell upon anything in the collection of sacred Scriptures which displeased them, in their own peculiar style of research, they perverted it to serve their purpose: for they had no adequate faith in their divinity to keep them from changing them, nor had they any sufficient understanding of them, either, as being still at the time under veil--even obscure to the Jews themselves, whose peculiar possession they seemed to be. For so, too, if the truth was distinguished by its simplicity, the more on that account the fastidiousness of man, too proud to believe, set to altering it; so that even what they found certain they made uncertain by their admixtures.

Finding a simple revelation of God, they proceeded to dispute about Him, not as He had revealed to them, but turned aside to debate about His properties, His nature, His abode. Some assert Him to be incorporeal; others maintain He has a body,--the Platonists teaching the one doctrine, and the Stoics the other.

Some think that He is composed of atoms, others of numbers: such are the different views of Epicurus and Pythagoras. One thinks He is made of fire; so it appeared to Heraclitus. The Platonists, again, hold that He administers the affairs of the world; the Epicureans, on the contrary, that He is idle and inactive, and, so to speak, a nobody in human things. Then the Stoics represent Him as placed outside the world, and whirling round this huge mass from without like a potter; while the Platonists place Him within the world, as a pilot is in the ship he steers. So, in like manner, they differ in their views about the world itself, whether it is created or uncreated, whether it is destined to pass away or to remain for ever. So again it is debated concerning the nature of the soul, which some contend is divine and eternal, while others hold that it is dissoluble. According to each one's fancy, He has introduced either something new, or refashioned the old. Nor need we wonder if the speculations of philosophers have perverted the older Scriptures. Some of their brood, with their opinions, have even adulterated our new-given Christian revelation, and corrupted it into a system of philosophic doctrines, and from the one path have struck off many and inexplicable by-roads. [145] And I have alluded to this, lest any one becoming acquainted with the variety of parties among us, this might seem to him to put us on a level with the philosophers, and he might condemn the truth from the different ways in which it is defended. But we at once put in a plea in bar against these tainters of our purity, asserting that this is the rule of truth which comes down from Christ by transmission through His companions, to whom we shall prove that those devisers of different doctrines are all posterior. Everything opposed to the truth has been got up from the truth itself, the spirits of error carrying on this system of opposition. By them all corruptions of wholesome discipline have been secretly instigated; by them, too, certain fables have been introduced, that, by their resemblance to the truth, they might impair its credibility, or vindicate their own higher claims to faith; so that people might think Christians unworthy of credit because the poets or philosophers are so, or might regard the poets and philosophers as worthier of confidence from their not being followers of Christ. Accordingly, we get ourselves laughed at for proclaiming that God will one day judge the world. For, like us, the poets and philosophers set up a judgment-seat in the realms below.

And if we threaten Gehenna, which is a reservoir of secret fire under the earth for purposes of punishment, we have in the same way derision heaped on us. For so, too, they have their Pyriphlegethon, a river of flame in the regions of the dead. And if we speak of Paradise, [146] the place of heavenly bliss appointed to receive the spirits of the saints, severed from the knowledge of this world by that fiery zone as by a sort of enclosure, the Elysian plains have taken possession of their faith. Whence is it, I pray you have all this, so like us, in the poets and philosophers?

The reason simply is, that they have been taken from our religion. But if they are taken from our sacred things, as being of earlier date, then ours are the truer, and have higher claims upon belief, since even their imitations find faith among you. If they maintain their sacred mysteries to have sprung from their own minds, in that case ours will be reflections of what are later than themselves, which by the nature of things is impossible, for never does the shadow precede the body which casts it, or the image the reality. [147]

Chapter XLVIII

Come now, if some philosopher affirms, as Laberius holds, following an opinion of Pythagoras, that a man may have his origin from a mule, a serpent from a woman, and with skill of speech twists every argument to prove his view, will he not gain acceptance for and work in some the conviction that, on account of this, they should even abstain from eating animal food? May any one have the persuasion that he should so abstain, lest by chance in his beef he eats of some ancestor of his? But if a Christian promises the return of a man from a man, and the very actual Gaius from Gaius, [148] the cry of the people will be to have him stoned; they will not even so much as grant him a hearing. If there is any ground for the moving to and fro of human souls into different bodies, why may they not return into the very substance they have left, seeing this is to be restored, to be that which had been? They are no longer the very things they had been; for they could not be what they were not, without first ceasing to be what they had been. If we were inclined to give all rein upon this point, discussing into what various beasts one and another might probably be changed, we would need at our leisure to take up many points. But this we would do chiefly in our own defence, as setting forth what is greatly worthier of belief, that a man will come back from a man--any given person from any given person, still retaining his humanity; so that the soul, with its qualities unchanged, may be restored to the same condition, thought not to the same outward framework. Assuredly, as the reason why restoration takes place at all is the appointed judgment, every man must needs come forth the very same who had once existed, that he may receive at God's hands a judgment, whether of good desert or the opposite. And therefore the body too will appear; for the soul is not capable of suffering without the solid substance (that is, the flesh; and for this reason, also) that it is not right that souls should have all the wrath of God to bear: they did not sin without the body, within which all was done by them. But how, you say, can a substance which has been dissolved be made to reappear again?

Consider thyself, O man, and thou wilt believe in it! Reflect on what you were before you came into existence. Nothing. For if you had been anything, you would have remembered it. You, then, who were nothing before you existed, reduced to nothing also when you cease to be, why may you not come into being again out of nothing, at the will of the same Creator whose will created you out of nothing at the first? Will it be anything new in your case? You who were not, were made; when you cease to be again, you shall be made. Explain, if you can, your original creation, and then demand to know how you shall be re-created. Indeed, it will be still easier surely to make you what you were once, when the very same creative power made you without difficulty what you never were before. There will be doubts, perhaps, as to the power of God, of Him who hung in its place this huge body of our world, made out of what had never existed, as from a death of emptiness and inanity, animated by the Spirit who quickens all living things, its very self the unmistakable type of the resurrection, that it might be to you a witness--nay, the exact image of the resurrection.

Light, every day extinguished, shines out again; and, with like alternation, darkness succeeds light's outgoing. The defunct stars re-live; the seasons, as soon as they are finished, renew their course; the fruits are brought to maturity, and then are reproduced. The seeds do not spring up with abundant produce, save as they rot and dissolve away;--all things are preserved by perishing, all things are refashioned out of death. Thou, man of nature so exalted, if thou understandest thyself, taught even by the Pythian [149] words, lord of all these things that die and rise,--shalt thou die to perish evermore? Wherever your dissolution shall have taken place, whatever material agent has destroyed you, or swallowed you up, or swept you away, or reduced you to nothingness, it shall again restore you. Even nothingness is His who is Lord of all. You ask, Shall we then be always dying, and rising up from death? If so the Lord of all things had appointed, you would have to submit, though unwillingly, to the law of your creation. But, in fact, He has no other purpose than that of which He has informed us. The Reason which made the universe out of diverse elements, so that all things might be composed of opposite substances in unity--of void and solid, of animate and inanimate, of comprehensible and incomprehensible, of light and darkness, of life itself and death--has also disposed time into order, by fixing and distinguishing its mode, according to which this first portion of it, which we inhabit from the beginning of the world, flows down by a temporal course to a close; but the portion which succeeds, and to which we look forward continues forever. When, therefore, the boundary and limit, that millennial interspace, has been passed, when even the outward fashion of the world itself--which has been spread like a veil over the eternal economy, equally a thing of time--passes away, then the whole human race shall be raised again, to have its dues meted out according as it has merited in the period of good or evil, and thereafter to have these paid out through the immeasurable ages of eternity. Therefore after this there is neither death nor repeated resurrections, but we shall be the same that we are now, and still unchanged--the servants of God, ever with God, clothed upon with the proper substance of eternity; but the profane, and all who are not true worshippers of God, in like manner shall be consigned to the punishment of everlasting fire--that fire which, from its very nature indeed, directly ministers to their incorruptibility. The philosophers are familiar as well as we with the distinction between a common and a secret fire. Thus that which is in common use is far different from that which we see in divine judgments, whether striking as thunderbolts from heaven, or bursting up out of the earth through mountain-tops; for it does not consume what it scorches, but while it burns it repairs. So the mountains continue ever burning; and a person struck by lighting is even now kept safe from any destroying flame. A notable proof this of the fire eternal! a notable example of the endless judgment which still supplies punishment with fuel! The mountains burn, and last. How will it be with the wicked and the enemies of God? [150]

Chapter XLIX

These are what are called presumptuous speculations in our case alone; in the philosophers and poets they are regarded as sublime speculations and illustrious discoveries. They are men of wisdom, we are fools. They are worthy of all honour, we are folk to have the finger pointed at; nay, besides that, we are even to have punishments inflicted on us. But let things which are the defence of virtue, if you will, have no foundation, and give them duly the name of fancies, yet still they are necessary; let them be absurd if you will, yet they are of use: they make all who believe them better men and women, under the fear of never-ending punishment and the hope of never-ending bliss.

It is not, then, wise to brand as false, nor to regard as absurd, things the truth of which it is expedient to presume.

On no ground is it right positively to condemn as bad what beyond all doubt is profitable. Thus, in fact, you are guilty of the very presumption of which you accuse us, in condemning what is useful. It is equally out of the question to regard them as nonsensical; at any rate, if they are false and foolish, they hurt nobody. For they are just (in that case) like many other things on which you inflict no penalties--foolish and fabulous things, I mean, which, as quite innocuous, are never charged as crimes or punished. But in a thing of the kind, if this be so indeed, we should be adjudged to ridicule, not to swords, and flames, and crosses, and wild beasts, in which iniquitous cruelty not only the blinded populace exults and insults over us, but in which some of you too glory, not scrupling to gain the popular favour by your injustice. As though all you can do to us did not depend upon our pleasure.

It is assuredly a matter of my own inclination, being a Christian. Your condemnation, then, will only reach me in that case, if I wish to be condemned; but when all you can do to me, you can do only at my will, all you can do is dependent on my will, and is not in your power. The joy of the people in our trouble is therefore utterly reasonless.

For it is our joy they appropriate to themselves, since we would far rather be condemned than apostatize from God; on the contrary, our haters should be sorry rather than rejoice, as we have obtained the very thing of our own choice.

Tertullian

Chapter L

In that case, you say, why do you complain of our persecutions? You ought rather to be grateful to us for giving you the sufferings you want. Well, it is quite true that it is our desire to suffer, but it is in the way that the soldier longs for war. No one indeed suffers willingly, since suffering necessarily implies fear and danger.

Yet the man who objected to the conflict, both fights with all his strength, and when victorious, he rejoices in the battle, because he reaps from it glory and spoil. It is our battle to be summoned to your tribunals that there, under fear of execution, we may battle for the truth. But the day is won when the object of the struggle is gained. This victory of ours gives us the glory of pleasing God, and the spoil of life eternal. But we are overcome. Yes, when we have obtained our wishes. Therefore we conquer in dying; [151] we go forth victorious at the very time we are subdued. Call us, if you like, Sarmenticii and Semaxii, because, bound to a half-axle stake, we are burned in a circle-heap of fagots. This is the attitude in which we conquer, it is our victory-robe, it is for us a sort of triumphal car. Naturally enough, therefore, we do not please the vanquished; on account of this, indeed, we are counted a desperate, reckless race. But the very desperation and recklessness you object to in us, among yourselves lift high the standard of virtue in the cause of glory and of fame. Mucius of his own will left his right hand on the altar: what sublimity of mind! Empedocles gave his whole body at Catana to the fires of Ætna: what mental resolution! A certain foundress of Carthage gave herself away in second marriage to the funeral pile: what a noble witness of her chastity! Regulus, not wishing that his one life should count for the lives of many enemies, endured these crosses over all his frame: how brave a man--even in captivity a conqueror! Anaxarchus, when he was being beaten to death by a barley-pounder, cried out, "Beat on, beat on at the case of Anaxarchus; no stroke falls on Anaxarchus himself." O magnanimity of the philosopher, who even in such an end had jokes upon his lips! I omit all reference to those who with their own sword, or with any other milder form of death, have bargained for glory.

Nay, see how even torture contests are crowned by you. The Athenian courtezan, having wearied out the executioner, at last bit off her tongue and spat it in the face of the raging tyrant, that she might at the same time spit away her power of speech, nor be longer able to confess her fellow-conspirators, if even overcome, that might be her inclination. Zeno the Eleatic, when he was asked by Dionysius what good philosophy did, on answering that it gave contempt of death, was all unquailing, given over to the tyrant's scourge, and sealed his opinion even to the death. We all know how the Spartan lash, applied with the utmost cruelty under the very eyes of friends encouraging, confers on those who bear it honor proportionate to the blood which the young men shed. O glory legitimate, because it is human, for whose sake it is counted neither reckless foolhardiness, nor desperate obstinacy, to despise death itself and all sorts of savage treatment; for whose sake you may for your native place, for the empire, for friendship, endure all you are forbidden to do for God!

And you cast statues in honour of persons such as these, and you put inscriptions upon images, and cut out epitaphs on tombs, that their names may never perish. In so far you can by your monuments, you yourselves afford a sort of resurrection to the dead. Yet he who expects the true resurrection from God, is insane, if for God he suffers!

But go zealously on, good presidents, you will stand higher with the people if you sacrifice the Christians at their wish, kill us, torture us, condemn us, grind us to dust; your injustice is the proof that we are innocent. Therefore God suffers that we thus suffer; for but very lately, in condemning a Christian woman to the leno rather than to the leo you made confession that a taint on our purity is considered among us something more terrible than any punishment and any death. [152] Nor does your cruelty, however exquisite, avail you; it is rather a temptation to us.

The oftener we are mown down by you, the more in number we grow; the blood of Christians is seed. [153] Many of your writers exhort to the courageous bearing of pain and death, as Cicero in the Tusculans, as Seneca in his Chances, as Diogenes, Pyrrhus, Callinicus; and yet their words do not find so many disciples as Christians do, teachers not by words, but by their deeds. That very obstinacy you rail against is the preceptress. For who that contemplates it, is not excited to inquire what is at the bottom of it? who, after inquiry, does not embrace our doctrines? and when he has embraced them, desires not to suffer that he may become partaker of the fulness of God's grace, that he may obtain from God complete forgiveness, by giving in exchange his blood? For that secures the remission of all offences. On this account it is that we return thanks on the very spot for your sentences. As the divine and human are ever opposed to each other, when we are condemned by you, we are acquitted by the Highest.

Elucidations

I.

(Arrangement, supra.)

The arrangement I have adopted in editing these Edinburgh Translations of Tertullian is a practical one. It will be found logical and helpful to the student, who is referred to the Prefatory pages of this volume for an Elucidation of the difficulties, with which any arrangement of these treatises is encumbered. For, first, an attempt to place them in chronological order is out of the question; [154] and, second, all efforts to separate precisely the Orthodox from the Montanistic or Montanist works of our author have hitherto defied the acumen of critics.

It would be mere empiricism for me to attempt an original classification in the face of questions which even experts have been unable to determine.

If we bear in mind, however, a few guiding facts, we shall see that difficulties are less than might appear, assuming our object to be a practical one. (1.) Only four of these essays were written against Orthodoxy; (2.) five more are reckoned as wholly uncertain, which amounts to saying that they are not positively heretical. (3.) Again, five are colourless, as to Montanism, and hence should be reputed Orthodox.

(4.) Of others, written after the influences of Montanism had, more or less, tainted his doctrine, the whole are yet valuable and some are noble defences of the Catholic Faith. (5.) Finally eight or ten of his treatises were written while he was a Catholic, and are precious contributions to the testimony of the Primitive Church.

From these facts, we may readily conclude that the mass of Tertullian's writings is Orthodox.

Some of them are to be read with caution; others, again, must be rejected for their heresy; but yet all are most instructive historically, and as defining even by errors "the faith once delivered to the Saints." I propose to note those which require caution as we pass them in review. Those written against the Church are classed by themselves, at the end of the list, and all the rest may be read with confidence. A most interesting inquiry arises in connection with the quotations from Scripture to be found in our author. Did a Latin version exist in his day, or does he translate from the Greek of the New Testament and the LXX? A paradoxical writer (Semler) contends that Tertullian "never used a Greek ms." (see Kaye, p. 106.) But Tertullian's rugged Latin betrays everywhere his familiarity with Greek idioms and forms of thought. He wrote, also, in Greek, and there is no reason to doubt that he knew the Greek Scriptures primarily, if he knew any Greek whatever. Possibly we owe to Tertullian the primordia of the Old African Latin Versions, some of which seem to have contained the disputed text 1 John v. 7; of which more when we come to the Praxeas. For the present in the absence of definite evidence we must infer that Tertullian usually translated from the LXX, and from the originals of the New Testament. But Mosheim thinks the progress of the Gospel in the West was now facilitated by the existence of Latin Versions.

Observe, also, Kaye's important note, p. 293, and his reference to Lardner, Cred. xxvii. 19.

II.

(Address to Magistrates, cap. i)

The Apology comes first in order, on logical grounds. It is classed with our author's orthodox works by Neander, and pronounced colourless by Kaye. It is the noblest of his productions in its purpose and spirit, and it falls in with the Primitive System of Apologetics. I have placed next in order to it several treatises, mostly unblemished, which are of the same character; which defend the cause of Christians against Paganism, against Gentile Philosophy, and against Judaism; closing this portion by the two books Ad Nationes, which may be regarded as a recapitulation of the author's arguments, especially those to be found in the Apology. In these successive works, as compared with those of Justin Martyr, we obtain a fair view of the progressive relations of the Church with the Roman Empire and with divers antagonistic systems in the East and West.

III.

(History of Christians, cap. ii)

The following Chronological outline borrowed from the Benedictines and from Bishop Kaye, will prove serviceable here. [155]

Tertullian born (circa) a.d. 150.
Tertullian converted (surmise) 185.
Tertullian married (say) 186.
Tertullian ordained presbyter (circa) 192.
Tertullian lapsed (circa) 200.
Tertullian deceased (extreme surmise) 240.

The Imperial history of his period may be thus arranged:
Birth of Caracalla a.d. 188.
Birth of Geta 189.
Reign of Severus 193.
Defeat of Niger 195.
Caracalla made a Cæsar 196.
Capture of Byzantium 196.
Defeat of Albinus 197.
Geta made a Cæsar 198.
Caracalla called Augustus 198.
Caracalla associated in the Empire 198.
War against the Parthians 198.
Severus returns from the war 203.
Celebration of the Secular Games 204.
Plautianus put to death (circa) 205.
Geta called Augustus 208.
War in Britain 208.
Wall of Severus 210.
Death of Severus 211.

IV.

(Tiberius, capp. v. and xxiv)

A fair examination of what has been said on this subject, pro and con, may be found in Kaye's Tertullian, [156] pp. 102-105. In his abundant candour this author leans to the doubters, but in stating the case he seems to me to fortify the position of Lardner and Mosheim.

What the brutal Tiberius may have thought or done with respect to Pilate's report concerning the holy victim of his judicial injustice is of little importance to the believer.

Nevertheless, as matter of history it deserves attention. Great stress is to be placed on the fact that Tertullian was probably a jurisconsult, familiar with the Roman archives, and influenced by them in his own acceptance of Divine Truth. It is not supposable that such a man would have hazarded his bold appeal to the records, in remonstrating with the Senate and in the very faces of the Emperor and his colleagues, had he not known that the evidence was irrefragable.

V.

(The darkness at the Crucifixion, cap. xxi)

Kaye disappoints us (p. 150) in his slight notice of this most interesting subject. Without attempting to discuss the story of Phlegon and other points which afford Gibbon an opportunity for misplaced sneering, such as even a Pilate would have rebuked, while it may be well to recall the exposition of Milman, [157] at the close of Gibbon's fifteenth chapter, I must express my own preference for another view. This will be found candidly summed up and stated, in the Speaker's Commentary, in the concise note on St. Matt. xxvii. 45.

VI.

(Numbers of the Faithful, cap. xxxvii)

Kaye, as usual, gives this vexed question a candid survey. [158] Making all allowances, however, I accept the conjecture of some reputable authorities, that there were 2,000,000 of Christians, in the bounds of the Roman Empire at the close of the Second Century. So mightily grew the testimony of Jesus and prevailed. When we reflect that only a century intervened between the times of Tertullian and the conversion of the Roman Emperor, it is not easy to regard our author's language as merely that of fervid genius and of rhetorical hyperbole. He could not have ventured upon exaggeration without courting scorn as well as defeat.

What he affirms is probable in the nature of the case. Were it otherwise, then the conditions, which, in a single century rendered it possible for Constantine to effect the greatest revolution in mind and manners that has ever been known among men, would be a miracle compared with which that of his alleged Vision of the Cross sinks into insignificance. To this subject it will be necessary to recur hereafter.

VII.

(Christian usages, cap. xxxix)

A candid review of the matters discussed in this chapter will be found in Kaye (pp. 146, 209.) The important fact is there clearly stated that "the primitive Christians scrupulously complied with the decree pronounced by the Apostles at Jerusalem in abstaining from things strangled and from blood"

(Acts xv. 20). On this subject consult the references given in the Speaker's Commentary, ad locum. The Greeks, to their honour, still maintain this prohibition, but St. Augustine's great authority relaxed the Western scruples on this matter, for he regarded it as a decree of temporary obligation, while the Hebrew and Gentile Christians were in peril of misunderstanding and estrangement. [159]

On the important question as to the cessation of miracles Kaye takes a somewhat original position. But see his interesting discussion and that of the late Professor Hey, in Kaye's Tertullian, pp. 80-102, 151-161. I do not think writers on these subjects have sufficiently distinguished between miracles properly so called, and providences vouchsafed in answer to prayer. There was no miracle in the case of the Thundering Legion, assuming the story to be true; and I dare to affirm that marked answers to prayer, by providential interpositions, but wholly distinct from miraculous agencies, have never ceased among those who "ask in the Son's Name." Such interpositions are often preternatural only; that is, they economize certain powers which, though natural in themselves, lie outside of the System of Nature with which we happen to be familiar. This distinction has been overlooked.

VIII.

(Multitudes, cap. xl)

Note the words--"multitudes to a single beast." Can it be possible that Tertullian would use such language to the magistrates, if he knew that such sentences were of rare occurrence? The disposition of our times to minimize the persecutions of our Christian forefathers calls upon us to note such references, all the more important because occurring obiter and mentioned as notorious. Note also, the closing chapter of this Apology, and reference to the outcries of the populace, in Cap. xxxv. [160] See admirable remarks on the benefits derived by the Church from the sufferings of Christian martyrs, with direct reference to Tertullian, Wordsworth, Church Hist. to Council of Nicæa, cap. xxiv., p. 374.

IX.

(Christian manners, cap. xlii)

A study of the manners of Christians, in the Ante-Nicene Age, as sketched by the unsparing hand of Tertullian, will convince any unprejudiced mind of the mighty power of the Holy Ghost, in framing such characters out of heathen originals. When, under Montanistic influences our severely ascetic author complains of the Church's corruptions, and turns inside-out the whole estate of the faithful, we see all that can be pressed on the other side; but, this very important chapter must be borne in mind, together with the closing sentence of chap. xliv., as evidence that whatever might be said by a rigid disciplinarian, the Church, as compared with our day, was still a living embodiment of Philippians iv. 8.

X.

(Paradise, cap. xlvii)

See Kaye, p. 248. Our author seems not always consistent with himself in his references to the Places of departed spirits. Kaye thinks he identifies Paradise with the Heaven of the Most High, in one place (the De Exhort. Cast., xiii.) where he probably confuses the Apostle's ideas, in Galatians v. 12, and Ephesians v. 5. Commonly, however, though he is not consistent with himself, this would be his scheme:--

1. The Inferi, or Hades, where the soul of Dives was in one continent and that of Lazarus in another, with a gulf between. Our author places "Abraham's bosom" in Hades.

2. Paradise. In Hades, but in a superior and more glorious region. This more blessed abode was opened to the souls of the martyrs and other greater saints, at our Lord's descent into the place of the dead. After the General Resurrection and Judgment, there remain:

1. Gehenna, for the lost, prepared for the devil and his angels.

2. The Heaven of Heavens, the eternal abode of the righteous, in the vision of the Lord and His Eternal Joy.

Tertullian's variations on this subject will force us to recur to it hereafter; but, here it may be noted that the confusions of Latin Christianity received their character in this particular, from the genius of our author. Augustine caught from him a certain indecision about the terms and places connected with the state of the departed which has continued, to this day, to perplex theologians in the West. Taking advantage of such confusions, the stupendous Roman system of "Purgatory" was fabricated in the middle ages; but the Greeks never accepted it, and it differs fundamentally from what the earlier Latin Fathers, including Tertullian, have given us as speculations.

XI.

(The Leo and the Leno, cap. l)

Here we find the alliterative and epigrammatic genius of Tertullian anticipating a similar poetic charm in Augustine. The Christian maid or matron preferred the Leo to the leno; to be devoured rather than to be debauched. Our author wrests a tribute to the chastity of Christian women from the cruelty of their judges, who recognizing this fact, were accustomed as a refinement of their injustice to give sentence against them, refusing the mercy of a horrible death, by committing them to the ravisher: "damnando Christianam ad lenonem potius quam ad leonem."

XII.

(The Seed of the Church, cap. I)

Kaye has devoted a number of his pages [161] to the elucidation of this subject, not only showing the constancy of the martyrs, but illustrating the fact that Christians, like St. Paul, were forced to "die daily," even when they were not subjected to the fiery trial. He who confessed himself a Christian made himself a social outcast. All manner of outrages and wrongs could be committed against him with impunity. Rich men, who had joined themselves to Christ, [162] were forced to accept "the spoiling of their goods." Brothers denounced brothers, and husbands their wives; "a man's foes were they of his own household." But the Church triumphed through suffering, and "out of weakness was made strong."

Footnotes:

77. [Great diversity exists among the critics as to the date of this Apology; see Kaye, pp. xvi. 48, 65. Mosheim says, a.d. 198, Kaye a.d. 204.]

78. Elucidation II.

79. [For chronological dates in our author's age, see Elucidation III. Tertullian places an interval of 115 years, 6 months, and 15 days between Tiberius and Antoninus Pius. See Answer to the Jews, cap. vii. infra.]

80. Another reading is "ut Deo," as God.

81. [A reference in which Kaye sees no reason to doubt that the Apology was written during the reign under the emperor. See Kaye's Tertullian, p. 49.]

82. [Elucidation IV.]

83. As = 2-1/8 farthings. Sestertium = £7, 16s. 3d.

84. Slaves still bearing the marks of the scourge.

85. Anubis.

86. Fabulous monsters.

87. [Another example of what Christianity was doing for man as man.]

88. [See Elucidation VII., p. 58, infra in connection with usages in cap. xxxix.]

89. [Inconsistent this with Gibbon's minimizing theory of the number of the Christian martyrs.]

Elucidation VIII.

90. [Confirming the statement of Justin Martyr. See Vol. I., p. 187, note 1, and p. 193, this Series.]

91. Phaethon.

92. Atys or Attis.

93. Paris.

94. Pluto.

95. ["Sacred hats and purple robes and incense fumes" have been associated with the same crimes, alas! in widely different relations.]

96. [Caricatures of the Crucifixion are extant which show how greedily the heathen had accepted this profane idea.]

97. [A premonition of the Labarum.]

98. [As noted by Clement of Alexandria. See p. 535, Vol. II., and note.]

99. Onocoites. If with Oehler, Onochoietes, the meaning is "asinarius sacerdos" (Oehler).

100. Referring evidently to the Scriptures; and showing what the Bible was to the early Christians.

101. [Kaye, p. 168. Remarks on natural religion.]

102. [Though we are not by nature good, in our present estate; this is elsewhere demonstrated by Tertullian, as see cap. xviii.]

103. [Kaye, p. 291. See Elucidation I. Also Vol. II., p. 334.]

104. [That is, by the consummation of her marriage with Joseph.]

105. [Language common among Christians, and adopted afterwards into the Creed.]

106. Isa. vi. 10.

107. Elucidation V.

108. Proculus was a Roman senator who affirmed that Romulus had appeared to him after his death.

109. [Chapter l. at close. "The blood of Christians is the seed of the Church."]

110. Herodotus, I. 47. [See Wilberforce's Five Empires, p. 67.]

111. [Castor and Pollux. Imitated in saint worship.]

112. [This testimony must be noted as something of which Tertullian confidently challenges denial.]

113. [Observe our author's assertion that in its own nature, worship must be a voluntary act, and note this expression libertatem religionis.]

114. [See Augustine's City of God, III. xvii. p. 95, Ed. Migne.]

115. Her image was taken from Pessinus to Rome.

116. [Familiar reference to Virgil, Æneid, I. 15.]

117. Heb. x. 22. [See cap. xlii. infra. p. 49.]

118. [Once more this reflection on the use of material incense, which is common to

The Writings of Tertullian - Volume I

119. [A reference to kneeling, which see the de Corona cap. 3, infra. Christians are represented as standing at prayer, in the delineations of the Catacombs.

But, see Nicene Canon, xx.]
120. Matt. v. 44.
121. 1 Tim. ii. 2.
122. [Cap. xxxix. infra. And see Kaye, pp. 20, 348. A subject of which more hereafter.]
123. [A familiar story of Alexander is alluded to.]
124. [Note this reference to a shameless custom of the heathen in Rome and elsewhere.]
125. [See cap. l. and Note on cap. xl. infra.]
126. Commodus.
127. To murder Pertinax.
128. Tigerius and Parthenius were among the murderers of Commodus.
129. [Cap. ix. p. 25, note 1 supra. Again, Christian democracy, "honouring all men."]
130. [Elucidation VI.]
131. [Elucidation VII.]
132. [Chap. xxxii. supra p. 43.]
133. [An argument for Days of Public Thanksgiving, Fasting and the like.]
134. [On ordinary Sundays, "they laid by in store," apparently: once a month they offered.]
135. [A precious testimony, though the caviller asserts that afterwards the heathen used this expression derisively.]
136. [Or, perhaps--"One is prompted to stand forth and bring to God, as every one can, whether from the Holy Scriptures, or of his own mind"--i.e. according to his taste.]
137. [Christianos ad leonem. From what class, chiefly, see cap. xxxv. supra. Elucidation VIII.]
138. [Elucidation IX. See Kaye, p. 361.]
139. [The occupation of a soldier was regarded as lawful therefore. But see, afterwards, the De Corona cap. xi.]
140. [An interesting fact as to the burial-rites of Early Christians. As to incense, see cap. xxx. supra. p. 42.]
141. An index of the growth of Christianity.
142. [An appeal so defiant that its very boldness confirms this tribute to the character of our Christian fathers, p. 42.]
143. [Tertullian's exposition of this enigmatical fact (see the Phædo) is better than divers other ingenious theories.]
144. [John xxi. 19. A pious habit which long survived among Christians, when learning that death was at hand: as in Shakespeare's Henry IV., "Laud be to God, ev'n there my life must end." See 1 Thess. v. 18.]
145. [See Irenæus, vol. i. p. 377 this Series.]
146. [Elucidation X.]
147. True, in the sense that a shadow cannot be projected by a body not yet existent.
148. [i.e., Caius, used (like John Doe with us) in Roman Law.]
149. Know thyself. [Juvenal, xi. 27, on which see great wealth of reference in J.E.B. Mayor's Juvenal (xiii. Satires), and note especially, Bernard, Serm. De Divers xl. 3. In Cant. Cantic. xxxvi. 5-7.]
150. [Our author's philosophy may be at fault, but his testimony is not to be mistaken.]
151. [Vicimus cum occidimur.]
152. [Elucidation XI.]
153. [Elucidation XII.]
154. Kaye, p. 36. Also, p. 8, supra.
155. Kaye (following L'Art de verifier les Dates) pp. 11 and 456.
156. My references are to the Third Edition, London, Rivingtons, 1845.
157. In his edition of The Decline and Fall, Vol. I., p. 589, American reprint.
158. pp. 85-88.
159. Ep. ad Faust. xxxii. 13. and see Conybeare and Howson.
160. Compare Kaye on Mosheim, p. 107.
161. pp. 129-140.
162. Even under Commodus, vol. ii. p. 598, this series.

II - On Idolatry

[Translated by the Rev. S. Thelwall.]

Chapter I - Wide Scope of the Word Idolatry

The principal crime of the human race, the highest guilt charged upon the world, the whole procuring cause of judgment, is idolatry. [163] For, although each single fault retains its own proper feature, although it is destined to judgment under its own proper name also, yet it is marked off under the general account of idolatry. Set aside names, examine works, the idolater is likewise a murderer. Do you inquire whom he has slain? If it contributes ought to the aggravation of the indictment, no stranger nor personal enemy, but his own self. By what snares? Those of his error. By what weapon? The offence done to God. By how many blows? As many as are his idolatries. He who affirms that the idolater perishes not, [164] will affirm that the idolater has not committed murder. Further, you may recognize in the same crime [165] adultery and fornication; for he who serves false gods is doubtless an adulterer [166] of truth, because all falsehood is adultery.

So, too, he is sunk in fornication.

For who that is a fellow-worker with unclean spirits, does not stalk in general pollution and fornication? And thus it is that the Holy Scriptures [167] use the designation of fornication in their upbraiding of idolatry. The essence of fraud, I take it, is, that any should seize what is another's, or refuse to another his due; and, of course, fraud done toward man is a name of greatest crime. Well, but idolatry does fraud to God, by refusing to Him, and conferring on others, His honours; so that to fraud it also conjoins contumely. But if fraud, just as much as fornication and adultery, entails death, then, in these cases, equally with the former, idolatry stands unacquitted of the impeachment of murder. After such crimes, so pernicious, so devouring of salvation, all other crimes also, after some manner, and separately disposed in order, find their own essence represented in idolatry. In it also are the concupiscences of the world. For what solemnity of idolatry is without the circumstance of dress and ornament? In it are lasciviousnesses and drunkennesses; since it is, for the most part, for the sake of food, and stomach, and appetite, that these solemnities are frequented. In it is unrighteousness. For what more unrighteous than it, which knows not the Father of righteousness?

In it also is vanity, since its whole system is vain. In it is mendacity, for its whole substance is false. Thus it comes to pass, that in idolatry all crimes are detected, and in all crimes idolatry. Even otherwise, since all faults savour of opposition to God, and there is nothing which savours of opposition to God which is not assigned to demons and unclean spirits, whose property idols are; doubtless, whoever commits a fault is chargeable with idolatry, for he does that which pertains to the proprietors of idols.

Chapter II - Idolatry in Its More Limited Sense. Its Copiousness

But let the universal names of crimes withdraw to the specialities of their own works; let idolatry remain in that which it is itself. Sufficient to itself is a name so inimical to God, a substance of crime so copious, which reaches forth so many branches, diffuses so many veins, that from this name, for the greatest part, is drawn the material of all the modes in which the expansiveness of idolatry has to be foreguarded against by us, since in manifold wise it subverts the servants of God; and this not only when unperceived, but also when cloaked over.

Most men simply regard idolatry as to be interpreted in these senses alone, viz.: if one burn incense, or immolate a victim, or give a sacrificial banquet, or be bound to some sacred functions or priesthoods; just as if one were to regard adultery as to be accounted in kisses, and in embraces, and in actual fleshly contact; or murder as to be reckoned only in the shedding forth of blood, and in the actual taking away of life. But how far wider an extent the Lord assigns to those crimes we are sure: when He defines adultery to consist even in concupiscence, [168] "if one shall have cast an eye lustfully on," and stirred his soul with immodest commotion; when He judges murder [169] to consist even in a word of curse or of reproach, and in every impulse of anger, and in the neglect of charity toward a brother just as

John teaches, [170] that he who hates his brother is a murderer.

Else, both the devil's ingenuity in malice, and God the Lord's in the Discipline by which He fortifies us against the devil's depths, [171] would have but limited scope, if we were judged only in such faults as even the heathen nations have decreed punishable.

How will our "righteousness abound above that of the Scribes and Pharisees," as the Lord has prescribed, [172] unless we shall have seen through the abundance of that adversary quality, that is, of unrighteousness? But if the head of unrighteousness is idolatry, the first point is, that we be fore-fortified against the abundance of idolatry, while we recognise it not only in its palpable manifestations.

Chapter III - Idolatry: Origin and Meaning of the Name

Idol in ancient times there was none. Before the artificers of this monstrosity had bubbled into being, [173] temples stood solitary and shrines empty, just as to the present day in some places traces of the ancient practice remain permanently. Yet idolatry used to be practised, not under that name, but in that function; for even at this day it can be practised outside a temple, and without an idol.

But when the devil introduced into the world artificers of statues and of images, and of every kind of likenesses, that former rude business of human disaster attained from idols both a name and a development. Thenceforward every art which in any way produces an idol instantly became a fount of idolatry. For it makes no difference whether a moulder cast, or a carver grave, or an embroiderer weave the idol; because neither is it a question of material, whether an idol be formed of gypsum, or of colors, or of stone, or of bronze, [174] or of silver, or of thread. For since even without an idol idolatry is committed, when the idol is there it makes no difference of what kind it be, of what material, or what shape; lest any should think that only to be held an idol which is consecrated in human shape. To establish this point, the interpretation of the word is requisite. Eidos, in Greek, signifies form; eidolon, derived diminutively from that, by an equivalent process in our language, makes formling. [175] Every form or formling, therefore, claims to be called an idol. Hence idolatry is "all attendance and service about every idol." Hence also, every artificer of an idol is guilty of one and the same crime, [176] unless, the People [177] which consecrated for itself the likeness of a calf, and not of a man, fell short of incurring the guilt of idolatry. [178]

Chapter IV - Idols Not to Be Made, Much Less Worshipped. Idols and Idol-Makers in the Same Category

God prohibits an idol as much to be made as to be worshipped. In so far as the making what may be worshipped is the prior act, so far is the prohibition to make (if the worship is unlawful) the prior prohibition. For this cause--the eradicating, namely, of the material of idolatry--the divine law proclaims, "Thou shalt make no idol;" [179] and by conjoining, "Nor a similitude of the things which are in the heaven, and which are in the earth, and which are in the sea," has interdicted the servants of God from acts of that kind all the universe over. Enoch had preceded, predicting that "the demons, and the spirits of the angelic apostates, [180] would turn into idolatry all the elements, all the garniture of the universe, all things contained in the heaven, in the sea, in the earth, that they might be consecrated as God, in opposition to God." All things, therefore, does human error worship, except the Founder of all Himself.

The images of those things are idols; the consecration of the images is idolatry. Whatever guilt idolatry incurs, must necessarily be imputed to every artificer of every idol. In short, the same Enoch fore-condemns in general menace both idol-worshippers and idol-makers together. And again:

"I swear to you, sinners, that against the day of perdition of blood [181] repentance is being prepared. Ye who serve stones, and ye who make images of gold, and silver, and wood, and stones and clay, and serve phantoms, and demons, and spirits in fanes, [182] and all errors not according to knowledge, shall find no help from them." But Isaiah [183] says, "Ye are witnesses whether there is a God except Me." "And they who mould and carve out at that time were not: all vain! who do that which liketh them, which shall not profit them!" And that whole ensuing discourse sets a ban as well on the artificers as the worshippers:

the close of which is, "Learn that their heart is ashes and earth, and that none can free his own soul." In which sentence David equally includes the makers too. "Such," says he, "let them become who make them." [184] And why should I, a man of limited memory, suggest anything further? Why recall anything more from the Scriptures? As if either the voice of the Holy Spirit were not sufficient; or else any further deliberation were needful, whether the Lord cursed and condemned by priority the artificers of those things, of which He curses and condemns the worshippers!

Chapter V [185] - Sundry Objections or Excuses Dealt with

We will certainly take more pains in answering the excuses of artificers of this kind, who ought never to be admitted into the house of God, if any have a knowledge of that Discipline. [186] To begin with, that speech, wont to be cast in our teeth, "I have nothing else whereby to live," may be more severely retorted, "You have, then, whereby to live?"

If by your own laws, what have you to do with God?" [187] Then, as to the argument they have the hardihood to bring even from the Scriptures, "that the apostle has said, As each has been found, so let him persevere.'" [188] We may all, therefore, persevere in sins, as the result of that interpretation! for there is not any one of us who has not been found as a sinner, since no other cause was the source of Christ's descent than that of setting sinners free. Again, they say the same apostle has left a precept, according to his own example, "That each one work with his own hands for a living." [189] If this precept is maintained in respect to all hands, I believe even the bath-thieves [190] live by their hands, and robbers themselves gain the means to live by their hands; forgers, again, execute their evil handwritings, not of course with their feet, but hands; actors, however, achieve a livelihood not with hands alone, but with their entire limbs. Let the Church, therefore, stand open to all who are supported by their hands and by their own work; if there is no exception of arts which the Discipline of God receives not. But some one says, in opposition to our proposition of "similitude being interdicted," "Why, then, did Moses in the desert make a likeness of a serpent out of bronze?" The figures, which used to be laid as a groundwork for some secret future dispensation, not with a view to the repeal of the law, but as a type of their own final cause, stand in a class by themselves. Otherwise, if we should interpret these things as the adversaries of the law do, do we, too, as the Marcionites do, ascribe inconsistency to the Almighty, whom they[191] in this manner destroy as being mutable, while in one place He forbids, in another commands? But if any feigns ignorance of the fact that that effigy of the serpent of bronze, after the manner of one uphung, denoted the shape of the Lord's cross, [192] which was to free us from serpents--that is, from the devil's angels--while, through itself, it hanged up the devil slain; or whatever other exposition of that figure has been revealed to worthier men [193] no matter, provided we remember the apostle affirms that all things happened at that time to the People [194] figuratively. [195] It is enough that the same God, as by law He forbade the making of similitude, did, by the extraordinary precept in the case of the serpent, interdict similitude. [196] If you reverence the same God, you have His law, "Thou shalt make no similitude." [197] If you look back, too, to the precept enjoining the subsequently made similitude, do you, too, imitate Moses: make not any likeness in opposition to the law, unless to you, too, God have bidden it. [198]

Chapter VI - Idolatry Condemned by Baptism. To Make an Idol Is, in Fact, to Worship It

If no law of God had prohibited idols to be made by us; if no voice of the Holy Spirit uttered general menace no less against the makers than the worshippers of idols; from our sacrament itself we would draw our interpretation that arts of that kind are opposed to the faith. For how have we renounced the devil and his angels, if we make them? What divorce have we declared from them, I say not with whom, but dependent on whom, we live? What discord have we entered into with those to whom we are under obligation for the sake of our maintenance? Can you have denied with the tongue what with the hand you confess? unmake by word what by deed you make? preach one God, you who make so many? preach the true God, you who make false ones? "I make," says one, "but I worship not;" as if there were some cause for which he dare not worship, besides that for which he ought not also to make,--the offence done to God, namely, in either case.

Nay, you who make, that they may be able to be worshipped, do worship; and you worship, not with the spirit of some worthless perfume, but with your own; nor at the expense of a beast's soul, but of your own. To them you immolate your ingenuity; to them you make your sweat a libation; to them you kindle the torch of your forethought. More are you to them than a priest, since it is by your means they have a priest; your diligence is their divinity. [199] Do you affirm that you worship not what you make? Ah! but they affirm not so, to whom you slay this fatter, more precious and greater victim, your salvation.

Chapter VII - Grief of the Faithful at the Admission of Idol-Makers into the Church; Nay, Even into the Ministry

A whole day the zeal of faith will direct its pleadings to this quarter: bewailing that a Christian should come from idols into the Church; should come from an adversary workshop into the house of God; should raise to God the Father hands which are the mothers of idols; should pray to God with the hands which, out of doors, are prayed to in opposition to God; should apply to the Lord's body those hands which confer bodies on demons. Nor is this sufficient. Grant that it be a small matter, if from other hands they receive what they contaminate; but even those very hands deliver to others what they have contaminated. Idol-artificers are chosen even into the ecclesiastical order. Oh wickedness! Once did the Jews lay brands on Christ; these mangle His body daily.

Oh hands to be cut off! Now let the saying, "If thy hand make thee do evil, amputate it," [200] see to it whether it were uttered by way of similitude merely. What hands more to be amputated than those in which scandal is done to the Lord's body?

Chapter VIII - Other Arts Made Subservient to Idolatry. Lawful Means of Gaining a Livelihood Abundant

There are also other species of very many arts which, although they extend not to the making of idols, yet, with the same criminality, furnish the adjuncts without which idols have no power. For it matters not whether you erect or equip: if you have embellished his temple, altar, or niche; if you have pressed out gold-leaf, or have wrought his insignia, or even his house:

work of that kind, which confers not shape, but authority, is more important. If the necessity of maintenance [201] is urged so much, the arts have other species withal to afford means of livelihood, without outstepping the path of discipline, that is, without the confiction of an idol. The plasterer knows both how to mend roofs, and lay on stuccoes, and polish a cistern, and trace ogives, and draw in relief on party-walls many other ornaments beside likenesses. The painter, too, the marble mason, the bronze-worker, and every graver whatever, knows expansions [202] of his own art, of course much easier of execution. For how much more easily does he who delineates a statue overlay a sideboard! [203] How much sooner does he who carves a Mars out of a lime-tree, fasten together a chest!

No art but is either mother or kinswoman of some neighbour [204] art: nothing is independent of its neighbour. The veins of the arts are many as are the concupiscences of men.

"But there is difference in wages and the rewards of handicraft;" therefore there is difference, too, in the labour required. Smaller wages are compensated by more frequent earning. How many are the party-walls which require statues? How many the temples and shrines which are built for idols? But houses, and official residences, and baths, and tenements, how many are they?

Shoe- and slipper-gilding is daily work; not so the gilding of Mercury and Serapis. Let that suffice for the gain [205] of handicrafts. Luxury and ostentation have more votaries than all superstition.

Ostentation will require dishes and cups more easily than superstition. Luxury deals in wreaths, also, more than ceremony. When, therefore, we urge men generally to such kinds of handicrafts as do not come in contact with an idol indeed and with the things which are appropriate to an idol; since, moreover, the things which are common to idols are often common to men too; of this also we ought to beware that nothing be, with our knowledge, demanded by any person from our idols' service.

For if we shall have made that concession, and shall not have had recourse to the remedies so often used, I think we are not free of the contagion of idolatry, we whose (not unwitting) hands [206] are found busied in the tendence, or in the honour and service, of demons.

Chapter IX - Professions of Some Kinds Allied to Idolatry. Of Astrology in Particular

We observe among the arts [207] also some professions liable to the charge of idolatry. Of astrologers there should be no speaking even; [208] but since one in these days has challenged us, defending on his own behalf perseverance in that profession, I will use a few words. I allege not that he honours idols, whose names he has inscribed on the heaven, [209] to whom he has attributed all God's power; because men, presuming that we are disposed of by the immutable arbitrament of the stars, think on that account that God is not to be sought after. One proposition I lay down: that those angels, the deserters from God, the lovers of women, [210] were likewise the discoverers of this curious art, on that account also condemned by God. Oh divine sentence, reaching even unto the earth in its vigour, whereto the unwitting render testimony! The astrologers are expelled just like their angels. The city and Italy are interdicted to the astrologers, just as heaven to their angels.[211] There is the same penalty of exclusion for disciples and masters. "But Magi and astrologers came from the east." [212] We know the mutual alliance of magic and astrology. The interpreters of the stars, then, were the first to announce Christ's birth the first to present Him "gifts." By this bond, [must] I imagine, they put Christ under obligation to themselves?

What then? Shall therefore the religion of those Magi act as patron now also to astrologers? Astrology now-a-days, forsooth, treats of Christ--is the science of the stars of Christ; not of Saturn, or Mars, and whomsoever else out of the same class of the dead [213] it pays observance to and preaches? But, however, that science has been allowed until the Gospel, in order that after Christ's birth no one should thence forward interpret any one's nativity by the heaven. For they therefore offered to the then infant Lord that frankincense and myrrh and gold, to be, as it were, the close of worldly [214] sacrifice and glory, which Christ was about to do away. What, then?

The dream--sent, doubtless, of the will of God--suggested to the same Magi, namely, that they should go home, but by another way, not that by which they came. It means this: that they should not walk in their ancient path. [215] Not that Herod should not pursue them, who in fact did not pursue them; unwitting even that they had departed by another way, since he was withal unwitting by what way they came. Just so we ought to understand by it the right Way and Discipline. And so the precept was rather, that thence forward they should walk otherwise. So, too, that other species of magic which operates by miracles, emulous even in opposition to Moses, [216] tried God's patience until the Gospel.

For thenceforward Simon Magus, just turned believer, (since he was still thinking somewhat of his juggling sect; to wit, that among the miracles of his profession he might buy even the gift of the Holy Spirit through imposition of hands) was cursed by the apostles, and ejected from the faith.[217] Both he and that other magician, who was with Sergius Paulus, (since he began opposing himself to the same apostles) was mulcted with loss of eyes. [218] The same fate, I believe, would astrologers, too, have met, if any had fallen in the way of the apostles. But yet, when magic is punished, of which astrology is a species, of course the species is condemned in the genus. After the Gospel, you will nowhere find either sophists, Chaldeans, enchanters, diviners, or magicians, except as clearly punished. "Where is the wise, where the grammarian, where the disputer of this age? Hath not God made foolish the wisdom of this age?" [219] You know nothing, astrologer, if you know not that you should be a Christian. If you did know it, you ought to have known this also, that you should have nothing more to do with that profession of yours which, of itself, fore-chants the climacterics of others, and might instruct you of its own danger. There is no part nor lot for you in that system of yours. [220] He cannot hope for the kingdom of the heavens, whose finger or wand abuses [221] the heaven.

Chapter X - Of Schoolmasters and Their Difficulties

Moreover, we must inquire likewise touching schoolmasters; nor only of them, but also all other professors of literature. Nay, on the contrary, we must not doubt that they are in affinity with manifold idolatry: first, in that it is necessary for them to preach the gods of the nations, to express their names, genealogies, honourable distinctions, all and singular; and further, to observe the solemnities and festivals of the same, as of them by whose means they compute their revenues. What schoolmaster, without a table of the seven idols, [222] will yet frequent the Quinquatria? The very first payment of every pupil he consecrates both to the honour and to the name of Minerva; so that, even though he be not said "to eat of that which is sacrificed to idols" [223] nominally (not being dedicated to any particular idol), he is shunned as an idolater.

What less of defilement does he recur on that ground, [224] than a business brings which, both nominally and virtually, is consecrated publicly to an idol? The Minervalia are as much Minerva's, as the Saturnalia Saturn's; Saturn's, which must necessarily be celebrated even by little slaves at the time of the Saturnalia. New-year's gifts likewise must be caught at, and the Septimontium kept; and all the presents of Midwinter and the feast of Dear Kinsmanship must be exacted; the schools must be wreathed with flowers; the flamens' wives and the ædiles sacrifice; the school is honoured on the appointed holy-days. The same thing takes place on an idol's birthday; every pomp of the devil is frequented. Who will think that these things are befitting to a Christian master, [225] unless it be he who shall think them suitable likewise to one who is not a master?

We know it may be said, "If teaching literature is not lawful to God's servants, neither will learning be likewise;" and, "How could one be trained unto ordinary human intelligence, or unto any sense or action whatever, since literature is the means of training for all life? How do we repudiate secular studies, without which divine studies cannot be pursued?"

Let us see, then, the necessity of literary erudition; let us reflect that partly it cannot be admitted, partly cannot be avoided. Learning literature is allowable for believers, rather than teaching; for the principle of learning and of teaching is different. If a believer teach literature, while he is teaching doubtless he commends, while he delivers he affirms, while he recalls he bears testimony to, the praises of idols interspersed therein. He seals the gods themselves with this name;[226] whereas the Law, as we have said, prohibits "the names of gods to be pronounced,"[227] and this name [228] to be conferred on vanity. [229] Hence the devil gets men's early faith built up from the beginnings of their erudition. Inquire whether he who catechizes about idols commit idolatry. But when a believer learns these things, if he is already capable of understanding what idolatry is, he neither receives nor allows them; much more if he is not yet capable. Or, when he begins to understand, it behoves him first to understand what he has previously learned, that is, touching God and the faith. Therefore he will reject those things, and will not receive them; and will be as safe as one who from one who knows it not, knowingly accepts poison, but does not drink it. To him necessity is attributed as an excuse, because he has no other way to learn. Moreover, the not teaching literature is as much easier than the not learning, as it is easier, too, for the pupil not to attend, than for the master not to frequent, the rest of the defilements incident to the schools from public and scholastic solemnities.

Chapter XI - Connection Between Covetousness and Idolatry. Certain Trades, However Gainful, to Be Avoided

If we think over the rest of faults, tracing them from their generations, let us begin with covetousness, "a root of all evils," [230] wherewith, indeed, some having been ensnared, "have suffered shipwreck about faith." [231] Albeit covetousness is by the same apostle called idolatry.[232] In the next place proceeding to mendacity, the minister of covetousness (of false swearing I am silent, since even swearing is not lawful [233])--is trade adapted for a servant of God? But, covetousness apart, what is the motive for acquiring? When the motive for acquiring ceases, there will be no necessity for trading. Grant now that there be some righteousness in business, secure from the duty of watchfulness against covetousness and mendacity; I take it that that trade which pertains to the very soul and spirit of idols, which pampers every demon, falls under the charge of idolatry. Rather, is not that the principal idolatry? If the selfsame merchandises--frankincense, I mean, and all other foreign productions--used as sacrifice to idols, are of use likewise to men for medicinal ointments, to us Christians also, over and above, for solaces of sepulture, let them see to it. At all events, while the pomps, while the priesthoods, while the sacrifices of idols, are furnished by dangers, by losses, by inconveniences, by cogitations, by runnings to and fro, or trades, what else are you demonstrated to be but an idols' agent? Let none contend that, in this way, exception may be taken to all trades. All graver faults extend the sphere for diligence in watchfulness proportionably to the magnitude of the danger; in order that we may withdraw not only from the faults, but from the means through which they have being. For although the fault be done by others, it makes no difference if it be by my means. In no case ought I to be necessary to another, while he is doing what to me is unlawful. Hence I ought to understand that care must be taken by me, lest what I am forbidden to do be done by my means. In short, in another cause of no lighter guilt I observe that fore-judgment. In that I am interdicted from fornication, I furnish nothing of help or connivance to others for that purpose; in that I have separated my own flesh itself from stews, I acknowledge that I cannot exercise the trade of pandering, or keep that kind of places for my neighbour's behoof.

So, too, the interdiction of murder shows me that a trainer of gladiators also is excluded from the Church; nor will any one fail to be the means of doing what he subministers to another to do. Behold, here is a more kindred fore-judgment: if a purveyor of the public victims come over to the faith, will you permit him to remain permanently in that trade? or if one who is already a believer shall have undertaken that business, will you think that he is to be retained in the Church?

No, I take it; unless any one will dissemble in the case of a frankincense-seller too. In sooth, the agency of blood pertains to some, that of odours to others. If, before idols were in the world, idolatry, hitherto shapeless, used to be transacted by these wares; if, even now, the work of idolatry is perpetrated, for the most part, without the idol, by burnings of odours; the frankincense-seller is a something even more serviceable even toward demons, for idolatry is more easily carried on without the idol, than without the ware of the frankincense-seller. [234] Let us interrogate thoroughly the conscience of the faith itself. With what mouth will a Christian frankincense-seller, if he shall pass through temples, with what mouth will he spit down upon and blow out the smoking altars, for which himself has made provision? With what consistency will he exorcise his own foster-children, [235] to whom he affords his own house as store-room?

Indeed, if he shall have ejected a demon, [236] let him not congratulate himself on his faith, for he has not ejected an enemy; he ought to have had his prayer easily granted by one whom he is daily feeding. [237] No art, then, no profession, no trade, which administers either to equipping or forming idols, can be free from the title of idolatry; unless we interpret idolatry to be altogether something else than the service of idol-tendence.

Chapter XII - Further Answers to the Plea, How Am I to Live?

In vain do we flatter ourselves as to the necessities of human maintenance, if--after faith sealed [238] --we say, "I have no means to live?" [239] For here I will now answer more fully that abrupt proposition. It is advanced too late. For after the similitude of that most prudent builder,[240] who first computes the costs of the work, together with his own means, lest, when he has begun, he afterwards blush to find himself spent, deliberation should have been made before. But even now you have the Lord's sayings, as examples taking away from you all excuse.

For what is it you say? "I shall be in need." But the Lord calls the needy "happy." [241] "I shall have no food." But "think not," says He, "about food;" [242] and as an example of clothing we have the lilies. [243] "My work was my subsistence." Nay, but "all things are to be sold, and divided to the needy." [244] "But provision must be made for children and posterity." "None, putting his hand on the plough, and looking back, is fit" for work. [245] "But I was under contract." "None can serve two lords." [246] If you wish to be the Lord's disciple, it is necessary you "take your cross, and follow the Lord:" [247] your cross; that is, your own straits and tortures, or your body only, which is after the manner of a cross. Parents, wives, children, will have to be left behind, for God's sake. [248] Do you hesitate about arts, and trades, and about professions likewise, for the sake of children and parents? Even there was it demonstrated to us, that both "dear pledges," [249] and handicrafts, and trades, are to be quite left behind for the Lord's sake; while James and John, called by the Lord, do leave quite behind both father and ship; [250] while Matthew is roused up from the toll-booth; [251] while even burying a father was too tardy a business for faith. [252] None of them whom the Lord chose to Him said, "I have no means to live." Faith fears not famine. It knows, likewise, that hunger is no less to be contemned by it for God's sake, than every kind of death. It has learnt not to respect life; how much more food? [You ask] "How many have fulfilled these conditions?" But what with men is difficult, with God is easy. [253] Let us, however, comfort ourselves about the gentleness and clemency of God in such wise, as not to indulge our "necessities" up to the point of affinities with idolatry, but to avoid even from afar every breath of it, as of a pestilence. [And this] not merely in the cases forementioned, but in the universal series of human superstition; whether appropriated to its gods, or to the defunct, or to kings, as pertaining to the selfsame unclean spirits, sometimes through sacrifices and priesthoods, sometimes through spectacles and the like, sometimes through holy-days.

Chapter XIII - Of the Observance of Days Connected with Idolatry

But why speak of sacrifices and priesthoods? Of spectacles, moreover, and pleasures of that kind, we have already filled a volume of their own. [254] In this place must be handled the subject of holidays and other extraordinary solemnities, which we accord sometimes to our wantonness, sometimes to our timidity, in opposition to the common faith and Discipline. The first point, indeed, on which I shall join issue is this:

whether a servant of God ought to share with the very nations themselves in matters of his kind either in dress, or in food, or in any other kind of their gladness. "To rejoice with the rejoicing, and grieve with the grieving," [255] is said about brethren by the apostle when exhorting to unanimity. But, for these purposes, "There is nought of communion between light and darkness,"[256] between life and death or else we rescind what is written, "The world shall rejoice, but ye shall grieve." [257] If we rejoice with the world, there is reason to fear that with the world we shall grieve too. But when the world rejoices, let us grieve; and when the world afterward grieves, we shall rejoice. Thus, too, Eleazar [258] in Hades, [259] (attaining refreshment in Abraham's bosom) and the rich man, (on the other hand, set in the torment of fire) compensate, by an answerable retribution, their alternate vicissitudes of evil and good.

There are certain gift-days, which with some adjust the claim of honour, with others the debt of wages. "Now, then," you say, "I shall receive back what is mine, or pay back what is another's." If men have consecrated for themselves this custom from superstition, why do you, estranged as you are from all their vanity, participate in solemnities consecrated to idols; as if for you also there were some prescript about a day, short of the observance of a particular day, to prevent your paying or receiving what you owe a man, or what is owed you by a man? Give me the form after which you wish to be dealt with.

For why should you skulk withal, when you contaminate your own conscience by your neighbour's ignorance?

If you are not unknown to be a Christian, you are tempted, and you act as if you were not a Christian against your neighbour's conscience; if, however, you shall be disguised withal, [260] you are the slave of the temptation. At all events, whether in the latter or the former way, you are guilty of being "ashamed of God." [261] But "whosoever shall be ashamed of Me in the presence of men, of him will I too be ashamed," says He, "in the presence of my Father who is in the heavens." [262]

Chapter XIV - Of Blasphemy. One of St. Paul's Sayings

But, however, the majority (of Christians) have by this time induced the belief in their mind that it is pardonable if at any time they do what the heathen do, for fear "the Name be blasphemed." Now the blasphemy which must quite be shunned by us in every way is, I take it, this: If any of us lead a heathen into blasphemy with good cause, either by fraud, or by injury, or by contumely, or any other matter of worthy complaint, in which "the Name" is deservedly impugned, so that the Lord, too, be deservedly angry.

Else, if of all blasphemy it has been said, "By your means My Name is blasphemed," [263] we all perish at once; since the whole circus, with no desert of ours, assails "the Name" with wicked suffrages. Let us cease (to be Christians) and it will not be blasphemed! On the contrary, while we are, let it be blasphemed: in the observance, not the overstepping, of discipline; while we are being approved, not while we are being reprobated. Oh blasphemy, bordering on martyrdom, which now attests me to be a Christian, [264] while for that very account it detests me! The cursing of well-maintained Discipline is a blessing of the Name.

"If," says he, "I wished to please men, I should not be Christ's servant." [265] But the same apostle elsewhere bids us take care to please all: "As I," he says, "please all by all means." [266] No doubt he used to please them by celebrating the Saturnalia and New-year's day!

[Was it so] or was it by moderation and patience? by gravity, by kindness, by integrity? In like manner, when he is saying, "I have become all things to all, that I may gain all," [267] does he mean "to idolaters an idolater?" "to heathens a heathen?" "to the worldly worldly?" But albeit he does not prohibit us from having our conversation with idolaters and adulterers, and the other criminals, saying, "Otherwise ye would go out from the world," [268] of course he does not so slacken those reins of conversation that, since it is necessary for us both to live and to mingle with sinners, we may be able to sin with them too. Where there is the intercourse of life, which the apostle concedes, there is sinning, which no one permits. To live with heathens is lawful, to die with them [269] is not. Let us live with all; [270] let us be glad with them, out of community of nature, not of superstition. We are peers in soul, not in discipline; fellow-possessors of the world, not of error.

But if we have no right of communion in matters of this kind with strangers, how far more wicked to celebrate them among brethren! Who can maintain or defend this? The Holy Spirit upbraids the Jews with their holy-days. "Your Sabbaths, and new moons, and ceremonies," says He, "My soul hateth." [271] By us, to whom Sabbaths are strange, [272] and the new moons and festivals formerly beloved by God, the Saturnalia and New-year's and Midwinter's festivals and Matronalia are frequented--presents come and go--New-year's gifts--games join their noise--banquets join their din! Oh better fidelity of the nations to their own sect, which claims no solemnity of the Christians for itself! Not the Lord's day, not Pentecost, even if they had known them, would they have shared with us; for they would fear lest they should seem to be Christians. We are not apprehensive lest we seem to be heathens! If any indulgence is to be granted to the flesh, you have it. I will not say your own days, [273] but more too; for to the heathens each festive day occurs but once annually:

you have a festive day every eighth day. [274] Call out the individual solemnities of the nations, and set them out into a row, they will not be able to make up a Pentecost. [275]

Chapter XV - Concerning Festivals in Honour of Emperors, Victories, and the Like

Examples of the Three Children and Daniel.

But "let your works shine," saith He; [276] but now all our shops and gates shine!

You will now-a-days find more doors of heathens without lamps and laurel-wreaths than of Christians. What does the case seem to be with regard to that species (of ceremony) also? If it is an idol's honour, without doubt an idol's honour is idolatry. If it is for a man's sake, let us again consider that all idolatry is for man's sake; [277] let us again consider that all idolatry is a worship done to men, since it is generally agreed even among their worshippers that aforetime the gods themselves of the nations were men; and so it makes no difference whether that superstitious homage be rendered to men of a former age or of this. Idolatry is condemned, not on account of the persons which are set up for worship, but on account of those its observances, which pertain to demons. "The things which are Cæsar's are to be rendered to Cæsar." [278] It is enough that He set in apposition thereto, "and to God the things which are God's." What things, then, are Cæsar's? Those, to wit, about which the consultation was then held, whether the poll-tax should be furnished to Cæsar or no. Therefore, too, the Lord demanded that the money should be shown Him, and inquired about the image, whose it was; and when He had heard it was Cæsar's, said, "Render to Cæsar what are Cæsar's, and what are God's to God;" that is, the image of Cæsar, which is on the coin, to Cæsar, and the image of God, which is on man, [279] to God; so as to render to Cæsar indeed money, to God yourself. Otherwise, what will be God's, if all things are Cæsar's? "Then," do you say, "the lamps before my doors, and the laurels on my posts are an honour to God?" They are there of course, not because they are an honour to God, but to him who is honour in God's stead by ceremonial observances of that kind, so far as is manifest, saving the religious performance, which is in secret appertaining to demons. For we ought to be sure if there are any whose notice it escapes through ignorance of this world's literature, that there are among the Romans even gods of entrances; Cardea (Hinge-goddess), called after hinges, and Forculus (Door-god) after doors, and Limentinus (Threshold-god) after the threshold, and Janus himself (Gate-god) after the gate: and of course we know that, though names be empty and feigned, yet, when they are drawn down into superstition, demons and every unclean spirit seize them for themselves, through the bond of consecration. Otherwise demons have no name individually, but they there find a name where they find also a token. Among the Greeks likewise we read of Apollo Thyræus, i.e. of the door, and the Antelii, or Anthelii, demons, as presiders over entrances. These things, therefore, the Holy Spirit foreseeing from the beginning, fore-chanted, through the most ancient prophet Enoch, that even entrances would come into superstitious use. For we see too that other entrances [280] are adored in the baths. But if there are beings which are adored in entrances, it is to them that both the lamps and the laurels will pertain. To an idol you will have done whatever you shall have done to an entrance. In this place I call a witness on the authority also of God; because it is not safe to suppress whatever may have been shown to one, of course for the sake of all. I know that a brother was severely chastised, the same night, through a vision, because on the sudden announcement of public rejoicings his servants had wreathed his gates.

And yet himself had not wreathed, or commanded them to be wreathed; for he had gone forth from home before, and on his return had reprehended the deed.

So strictly are we appraised with God in matters of this kind, even with regard to the discipline of our family. [281] Therefore, as to what relates to the honours due to kings or emperors, we have a prescript sufficient, that it behoves us to be in all obedience, according to the apostle's precept, [282] "subject to magistrates, and princes, and powers;" [283] but within the limits of discipline, so long as we keep ourselves separate from idolatry. For it is for this reason, too, that that example of the three brethren has forerun us, who, in other respects obedient toward king Nebuchodonosor rejected with all constancy the honour to his image, [284] proving that whatever is extolled beyond the measure of human honour, unto the resemblance of divine sublimity, is idolatry.

So too, Daniel, in all other points submissive to Darius, remained in his duty so long as it was free from danger to his religion; [285] for, to avoid undergoing that danger, he feared the royal lions no more than they the royal fires. Let, therefore, them who have no light, light their lamps daily; let them over whom the fires of hell are imminent, affix to their posts, laurels doomed presently to burn:

to them the testimonies of darkness and the omens of their penalties are suitable. You are a light of the world, [286] and a tree ever green. [287] If you have renounced temples, make not your own gate a temple. I have said too little. If you have renounced stews, clothe not your own house with the appearance of a new brothel.

Chapter XVI - Concerning Private Festivals

Touching the ceremonies, however, of private and social solemnities--as those of the white toga, of espousals, of nuptials, of name-givings--I should think no danger need be guarded against from the breath of the idolatry which is mixed up with them. For the causes are to be considered to which the ceremony is due. Those above-named I take to be clean in themselves, because neither manly garb, nor the marital ring or union, descends from honours done to any idol. In short, I find no dress cursed by God, except a woman's dress on a man: [288] for "cursed," saith He, "is every man who clothes himself in woman's attire." The toga, however, is a dress of manly name as well as of manly use. [289] God no more prohibits nuptials to be celebrated than a name to be given. "But there are sacrifices appropriated to these occasions." Let me be invited, and let not the title of the ceremony be "assistance at a sacrifice," and the discharge of my good offices is at the service of my friends. Would that it were "at their service" indeed, and that we could escape seeing what is unlawful for us to do. But since the evil one has so surrounded the world with idolatry, it will be lawful for us to be present at some ceremonies which see us doing service to a man, not to an idol.

Clearly, if invited unto priestly function and sacrifice, I will not go, for that is service peculiar to an idol; but neither will I furnish advice, or expense, or any other good office in a matter of that kind. If it is on account of the sacrifice that I be invited, and stand by, I shall be partaker of idolatry; if any other cause conjoins me to the sacrificer, I shall be merely a spectator of the sacrifice. [290]

Chapter XVII - The Cases of Servants and Other Officials. What Offices a Christian Man May Hold

But what shall believing servants or children [291] do? officials likewise, when attending on their lords, or patrons, or superiors, when sacrificing? Well, if any one shall have handed the wine to a sacrificer, nay, if by any single word necessary or belonging to a sacrifice he shall have aided him, he will be held to be a minister of idolatry. Mindful of this rule, we can render service even "to magistrates and powers," after the example of the patriarchs and the other forefathers, [292] who obeyed idolatrous kings up to the confine of idolatry. Hence arose, very lately, a dispute whether a servant of God should take the administration of any dignity or power, if he be able, whether by some special grace, or by adroitness, to keep himself intact from every species of idolatry; after the example that both Joseph and Daniel, clean from idolatry, administered both dignity and power in the livery and purple of the prefecture of entire Egypt or Babylonia. And so let us grant that it is possible for any one to succeed in moving, in whatsoever office, under the mere name of the office, neither sacrificing nor lending his authority to sacrifices; not farming out victims; not assigning to others the care of temples; not looking after their tributes; not giving spectacles at his own or the public charge, or presiding over the giving them; making proclamation or edict for no solemnity; not even taking oaths: moreover (what comes under the head of power), neither sitting in judgment on any one's life or character, for you might bear with his judging about money; neither condemning nor fore-condemning; [293] binding no one, imprisoning or torturing no one--if it is credible that all this is possible.

Chapter XVIII - Dress as Connected with Idolatry

But we must now treat of the garb only and apparatus of office. There is a dress proper to every one, as well for daily use as for office and dignity. That famous purple, therefore, and the gold as an ornament of the neck, were, among the Egyptians and Babylonians, ensigns of dignity, in the same way as bordered, or striped, or palm-embroidered togas, and the golden wreaths of provincial priests, are now; but not on the same terms. For they used only to be conferred, under the name of honour, on such as deserved the familiar friendship of kings (whence, too, such used to be styled the "purpled-men" [294] of kings, just as among us, [295] some, from their white toga, are called "candidates" [296]); but not on the understanding that that garb should be tied to priesthoods also, or to any idol-ceremonies. For if that were the case, of course men of such holiness and constancy [297] would instantly have refused the defiled dresses; and it would instantly have appeared that Daniel had been no zealous slave to idols, nor worshipped Bel, nor the dragon, which long after did appear. That purple, therefore, was simple, and used not at that time to be a mark of dignity [298] among the barbarians, but of nobility. [299] For as both Joseph, who had been a slave, and Daniel, who through [300] captivity had changed his state, attained the freedom of the states of Babylon and Egypt through the dress of barbaric nobility; [301] so among us believers also, if need so be, the bordered toga will be proper to be conceded to boys, and the stole to girls, [302] as ensigns of birth, not of power; of race, not of office; of rank, not of superstition. But the purple, or the other ensigns of dignities and powers, dedicated from the beginning to idolatry engrafted on the dignity and the powers, carry the spot of their own profanation; since, moreover, bordered and striped togas, and broad-barred ones, are put even on idols themselves; and fasces also, and rods, are borne before them; and deservedly, for demons are the magistrates of this world: they bear the fasces and the purples, the ensigns of one college. What end, then, will you advance if you use the garb indeed, but administer not the functions of it? In things unclean, none can appear clean. If you put on a tunic defiled in itself, it perhaps may not be defiled through you; but you, through it, will be unable to be clean. Now by this time, you who argue about "Joseph" and "Daniel," know that things old and new, rude and polished, begun and developed, slavish and free, are not always comparable. For they, even by their circumstances, were slaves; but you, the slave of none, [303] in so far as you are the slave of Christ alone, [304] who has freed you likewise from the captivity of the world, will incur the duty of acting after your Lord's pattern.

That Lord walked in humility and obscurity, with no definite home: for "the Son of man," said He, "hath not where to lay His head;" [305] unadorned in dress, for else He had not said, "Behold, they who are clad in soft raiment are in kings' houses;" [306] in short, inglorious in countenance and aspect, just as Isaiah withal had fore-announced. [307] If, also, He exercised no right of power even over His own followers, to whom He discharged menial ministry; [308] if, in short, though conscious of His own kingdom, [309] He shrank back from being made a king, [310] He in the fullest manner gave His own an example for turning coldly from all the pride and garb, as well of dignity as of power. For if they were to be used, who would rather have used them than the Son of God? What kind and what number of fasces would escort Him? what kind of purple would bloom from His shoulders? what kind of gold would beam from His head, had He not judged the glory of the world to be alien both to Himself and to His? Therefore what He was unwilling to accept, He has rejected; what He rejected, He has condemned; what He condemned, He has counted as part of the devil's pomp.

For He would not have condemned things, except such as were not His; but things which are not God's, can be no other's but the devil's. If you have forsworn "the devil's pomp," [311] know that whatever there you touch is idolatry.

Let even this fact help to remind you that all the powers and dignities of this world are not only alien to, but enemies of, God; that through them punishments have been determined against God's servants; through them, too, penalties prepared for the impious are ignored.

But "both your birth and your substance are troublesome to you in resisting idolatry." [312] For avoiding it, remedies cannot be lacking; since, even if they be lacking, there remains that one by which you will be made a happier magistrate, not in the earth, but in the heavens. [313]

Chapter XIX - Concerning Military Service

In that last section, decision may seem to have been given likewise concerning military service, which is between dignity and power. [314] But now inquiry is made about this point, whether a believer may turn himself unto military service, and whether the military may be admitted unto the faith, even the rank and file, or each inferior grade, to whom there is no necessity for taking part in sacrifices or capital punishments. There is no agreement between the divine and the human sacrament, [315] the standard of Christ and the standard of the devil, the camp of light and the camp of darkness. One soul cannot be due to two masters--God and Cæsar. And yet Moses carried a rod, [316] and Aaron wore a buckle, [317] and John (Baptist) is girt with leather [318] and Joshua the son of Nun leads a line of march; and the People warred: if it pleases you to sport with the subject. But how will a Christian man war, nay, how will he serve even in peace, without a sword, which the Lord has taken away? [319] For albeit soldiers had come unto John, and had received the formula of their rule; [320] albeit, likewise, a centurion had believed; [321] still the Lord afterward, in disarming Peter, unbe**d every soldier.

No dress is lawful among us, if assigned to any unlawful action.

Chapter XX - Concerning Idolatry in Words

But, however, since the conduct according to the divine rule is imperilled, not merely by deeds, but likewise by words, (for, just as it is written, "Behold the man and his deeds;" [322] so, "Out of thy own mouth shalt thou be justified" [323]), we ought to remember that, even in words, also the inroad of idolatry must be foreguarded against, either from the defect of custom or of timidity. The law prohibits the gods of the nations from being named, [324] not of course that we are not to pronounce their names, the speaking of which common intercourse extorts from us: for this must very frequently be said, "You find him in the temple of Æsculapius;" and, "I live in Isis Street;" and, "He has been made priest of Jupiter;" and much else after this manner, since even on men names of this kind are bestowed. I do not honour Saturnus if I call a man so, by his own name. I honour him no more than I do Marcus, if I call a man Marcus. But it says, "Make not mention of the name of other gods, neither be it heard from thy mouth."[325] The precept it gives is this, that we do not call them gods. For in the first part of the law, too, "Thou shalt not," saith He, "use the name of the Lord thy God in a vain thing," [326] that is, in an idol. [327] Whoever, therefore, honours an idol with the name of God, has fallen into idolatry.

But if I speak of them as gods, something must be added to make it appear that I do not call them gods. For even the Scripture names "gods," but adds "their," viz. "of the nations:" just as David does when he had named "gods," where he says, "But the gods of the nations are demons." [328] But this has been laid by me rather as a foundation for ensuing observations.

However, it is a defect of custom to say, "By Hercules, So help me the god of faith;" [329] while to the custom is added the ignorance of some, who are ignorant that it is an oath by Hercules. Further, what will an oath be, in the name of gods whom you have forsworn, but a collusion of faith with idolatry? For who does not honour them in whose name he swears?

Chapter XXI - Of Silent Acquiescence in Heathen Formularies

But it is a mark of timidity, when some other man binds you in the name of his gods, by the making of an oath, or by some other form of attestation, and you, for fear of discovery, [330] remain quiet. For you equally, by remaining quiet, affirm their majesty, by reason of which majesty you will seem to be bound.

What matters it, whether you affirm the gods of the nations by calling them gods, or by hearing them so called?

Whether you swear by idols, or, when adjured by another, acquiesce? Why should we not recognize the subtleties of Satan, who makes it his aim that, what he cannot effect by our mouth, he may effect by the mouth of his servants, introducing idolatry into us through our ears? At all events, whoever the adjurer is, he binds you to himself either in friendly or unfriendly conjunction. If in unfriendly, you are now challenged unto battle, and know that you must fight. If in friendly, with how far greater security will you transfer your engagement unto the Lord, that you may dissolve the obligation of him through whose means the Evil One was seeking to annex you to the honour of idols, that is, to idolatry!

All sufferance of that kind is idolatry.

You honour those to whom, when imposed as authorities, you have rendered respect. I know that one (whom the Lord pardon!), when it had been said to him in public during a law-suit, "Jupiter be wroth with you," answered, "On the contrary, with you." What else would a heathen have done who believed Jupiter to be a god? For even had he not retorted the malediction by Jupiter (or other such like), yet, by merely returning a curse, he would have confirmed the divinity of Jove, showing himself irritated by a malediction in Jove's name. For what is there to be indignant at, (if cursed) in the name of one whom you know to be nothing? For if you rave, you immediately affirm his existence, and the profession of your fear will be an act of idolatry. How much more, while you are returning the malediction in the name of Jupiter himself, are you doing honour to Jupiter in the same way as he who provoked you! But a believer ought to laugh in such cases, not to rave; nay, according to the precept, [331] not to return a curse in the name of God even, but dearly to bless in the name of God, that you may both demolish idols and preach God, and fulfil discipline.

Chapter XXII - Of Accepting Blessing in the Name of Idols

Equally, one who has been initiated into Christ will not endure to be blessed in the name of the gods of the nations, so as not always to reject the unclean benediction, and to cleanse it out for himself by converting it Godward.

To be blessed in the name of the gods of the nations is to be cursed in the name of God. If I have given an alms, or shown any other kindness, and the recipient pray that his gods, or the Genius of the colony, may be propitious to me, my oblation or act will immediately be an honour to idols, in whose name he returns me the favour of blessing. But why should he not know that I have done it for God's sake; that God may rather be glorified, and demons may not be honoured in that which I have done for the sake of God? If God sees that I have done it for His sake, He equally sees that I have been unwilling to show that I did it for His sake, and have in a manner made His precept [332] a sacrifice to idols. Many say, "No one ought to divulge himself;" but I think neither ought he to deny himself. For whoever dissembles in any cause whatever, by being held as a heathen, does deny; and, of course, all denial is idolatry, just as all idolatry is denial, whether in deeds or in words. [333]

Chapter XXIII - Written Contracts in the Name of Idols. Tacit Consent

But there is a certain species of that class, doubly sharpened in deed and word, and mischievous on either side, although it flatter you, as if it were free of danger in each; while it does not seem to be a deed, because it is not laid hold of as a word. In borrowing money from heathens under pledged [334] securities, Christians give a guarantee under oath, and deny themselves to have done so. Of course, the time of the prosecution, and the place of the judgment seat, and the person of the presiding judge, decide that they knew themselves to have so done. [335] Christ prescribes that there is to be no swearing. "I wrote," says the debtor, "but I said nothing. It is the tongue, not the written letter, which kills."

Here I call Nature and Conscience as my witnesses: Nature, because even if the tongue in dictating remains motionless and quiet, the hand can write nothing which the soul has not dictated; albeit even to the tongue itself the soul may have dictated either something conceived by itself, or else something delivered by another. Now, lest it be said, "Another dictated," I here appeal to Conscience whether, what another dictated, the soul entertains, [336] and transmits unto the hand, whether with the concomitance or the inaction of the tongue. Enough, that the Lord has said faults are committed in the mind and the conscience. If concupiscence or malice have ascended into a man's heart, He saith it is held as a deed. [337] You therefore have given a guarantee; which clearly has "ascended into your heart," which you can neither contend you were ignorant of nor unwilling; for when you gave the guarantee, you knew that you did it; when you knew, of course you were willing: you did it as well in act as in thought; nor can you by the lighter charge exclude the heavier, [338] so as to say that it is clearly rendered false, by giving a guarantee for what you do not actually perform. "Yet I have not denied, because I have not sworn." But you have sworn, since, even if you had done no such thing, you would still be said to swear, if you have even consented to so doing. Silence of voice is an unavailing plea in a case of writing; and muteness of sound in a case of letters. For Zacharias, when punished with a temporary privation of voice, holds colloquy with his mind, and, passing by his bootless tongue, with the help of his hands dictates from his heart, and without his mouth pronounces the name of his son. [339] Thus, in his pen there speaks a hand clearer than every sound, in his waxen tablet there is heard a letter more vocal that every mouth. [340] Inquire whether a man have spoken who is understood to have spoken. [341] Pray we the Lord that no necessity for that kind of contract may ever encompass us; and if it should so fall out, may He give our brethren the means of helping us, or give us constancy to break off all such necessity, lest those denying letters, the substitutes for our mouth, be brought forward against us in the day of judgment, sealed with the seals, not now of witnesses, but of angels!

Chapter XXIV - General Conclusion

Amid these reefs and inlets, amid these shallows and straits of idolatry, Faith, her sails filled by the Spirit of God, navigates; safe if cautious, secure if intently watchful. But to such as are washed overboard is a deep whence is no out-swimming; to such as are run aground is inextricable shipwreck; to such as are engulphed is a whirlpool, where there is no breathing--even in idolatry. All waves thereof whatsoever suffocate; every eddy thereof sucks down unto Hades. Let no one say, "Who will so safely foreguard himself? We shall have to go out of the world!" [342] As if it were not as well worth while to go out, as to stand in the world as an idolater!

Nothing can be easier than caution against idolatry, if the fear of it be our leading fear; any "necessity" whatever is too trifling compared to such a peril. The reason why the Holy Spirit did, when the apostles at that time were consulting, relax the bond and yoke for us, [343] was that we might be free to devote ourselves to the shunning of idolatry. This shall be our Law, the more fully to be administered the more ready it is to hand; (a Law) peculiar to Christians, by means whereof we are recognised and examined by heathens. This Law must be set before such as approach unto the Faith, and inculcated on such as are entering it; that, in approaching, they may deliberate; observing it, may persevere; not observing it, may renounce their name. [344] We will see to it, if, after the type of the Ark, there shall be in the Church raven, kite, dog, and serpent. At all events, an idolater is not found in the type of the Ark: no animal has been fashioned to represent an idolater. Let not that be in the Church which was not in the Ark. [345]

Elucidations

I.
(The Second Commandment)

Tertullian's teaching agrees with that of Clement of Alexandria [346] and with all the Primitive Fathers. But compare the Trent Catechism, (chapter ii., quest. 17.)--"Nor let any one suppose that this commandment prohibits the arts of painting, modelling or sculpture, for, in the Scriptures we are informed that God himself commanded images of cherubim, and also of the brazen serpent, to be made, etc." So far, the comparison is important, because while our author limits any inference from this instance as an exception, this Catechism turns it into a rule: and so far, we are only looking at the matter with reference to Art. But, the Catechism, (quest. xxiii. xxiv.), goes on to teach that images of the Saints, etc. ought to be made and honoured "as a holy practice." It affirms, also, that it is a practice which has been attended with the greatest advantage to the faithful: which admits of a doubt, especially when the honour thus mentioned is everywhere turned into worship, precisely like that offered to the Brazen Serpent, when the People "burned incense to it," and often much more. But even this is not my point; for that Catechism, with what verity need not be argued, affirms, also, that this doctrine "derives confirmation from the monuments of the Apostolic age, the general Councils of the Church, and the writings of so many most holy and learned Fathers, who are of one accord upon the subject." Doubtless they are "of one accord," but all the other way.

II.
(Military service, cap. xix)
This chapter must prepare us for a much more sweeping condemnation of the military profession in the De Spectaculis and the De Corona; but Neander's judgment seems to me very just. The Corona, itself, is rather Montanistic than Montanist, in the opinion of some critics, among whom Gibbon is not to count for much, for the reasons given by Kaye (p. 52), and others hardly less obvious. Surely, if this ascetic opinion and some similar instances were enough to mark a man as a heretic, what are we to say of the thousand crotchets maintained by good Christians, in our day?

III.
(Passive idolatry, cap. xxii)
Neander's opinion as to the freedom of De Idololatria from Montanistic taint, is mildly questioned by Bp. Kaye, chiefly on the ground of the agreement of this chapter with the extravagances of the Scorpiace. He thinks "the utmost pitch" of such extravagance is reached in the positions here taken. But Neander's judgment seems to me preferable. Lapsers usually give tokens of the bent of their minds, and unconsciously betray their inclinations before they themselves see whither they are tending.

Thus they become victims of their own plausible self-deceptions.

IV.
(Tacit consents and reservations, cap. xxiii)
It cannot be doubted that apart from the specific case which Tertullian is here maintaining, his appeal to conscience is maintained by reason, by the Morals of the Fathers and by Holy Scripture. Now compare with this the Morality which has been made dogmatic, among Latins, by the elevation of Liguori to the dignities of a "Saint" and a "Doctor of the Church." Even Cardinal Newman cannot accept it without reservations, so thoroughly does it commit the soul to fraud and hypocrisy.

See Liguori, Opp. Tom. II., pp. 34-44, and Meyrick, Moral Theology of the Church of Rome, London, 1855.

Republished, with an Introduction, by the Editor of this Series, Baltimore, 1857. Also Newman, Apologia, p. 295 et seqq.

Footnotes:

163. [This solemn sentence vindicates the place I have given to the De Idololatria in the order adopted for this volume.

After this and the Apology come three treatises confirming its positions, and vindicating the principles of Christians in conflict with Idolatry, the great generic crime of a world lying in wickedness. These three are the De Spectaculis, the De Corona and the Ad Scapulam. The De Spectaculis was written after this treatise, in which indeed it is mentioned (Cap. xiii.), but logically it follows, illustrates and enforces it.

Hence my practical plan: which will be concluded by a scheme (conjectural in part) of chronological order in which precision is affirmed by all critics to be impossible, but, by which we may reach approximate accuracy, with great advantage. The De Idololatria is free from Montanism. But see Kaye, p. xvi.]

164. Lit., "has not perished," as if the perishing were already complete; as, of course, it is judicially as soon as the guilt is incurred, though not actually.

165. i.e., in idolatry.

166. A play on the word: we should say, "an adulterator."

167. Oehler refers to Ezek. xxiii.; but many other references might be given--in the Pentateuch and Psalms, for instance.

168. Matt. v. 28.

169. Matt. v. 22.

170. 1 John. iii. 15.

171. Rev. ii. 24.

172. Matt. v. 20.

173. "Boiled out," "bubbled out."

174. Or, brass.

175. i.e., a little form.

176. Idolatry, namely.

177. [Capitalized to mark its emphatic sense, i.e., the People of God = the Jews.]

178. See Ex. xxxii.; and compare 1 Cor. x. 7, where the latter part of Ex. xxxii. 6 is quoted.

179. Lev. xxvi. 1; Ex. xx. 4; Deut. v. 8. It must of course be borne in mind that Tertullian has defined the meaning of the word idol in the former chapter, and speaks with reference to that definition.

180. Compare de Oratione, c. 23, and de Virg. Vel. c. 7.

181. "Sanguinis perditionis:" such is the reading of Oehler and others. If it be correct, probably the phrase "perdition of blood" must be taken as equivalent to "bloody perdition," after the Hebrew fashion. Compare, for similar instances, 2 Sam. xvi. 7; Ps. v. 6; xxvi.

9; lv. 23; Ezek. xxii. 2, with the marginal readings. But Fr. Junius would read, "Of blood and of perdition"--sanguinis et perditionis. Oehler's own interpretation of the reading he gives--"blood-shedding"--appears unsatisfactory.

182. "In fanis." This is Oehler's reading on conjecture. Other readings are--infamis, infamibus, insanis, infernis.

183. Isa. xliv. 8 et seqq.

184. Ps. cxv. 8. In our version, "They that make them are like unto them." Tertullian again agrees with the LXX.

185. Cf. chaps. viii. and xii.

186. i.e., the Discipline of the house of God, the Church. Oehler reads, "eam disciplinam," and takes the meaning to be that no artificer of this class should be admitted into the Church, if he applies for admittance, with a knowledge of the law of God referred to in the former chapters, yet persisting in his unlawful craft. Fr. Junius would read, "ejus disciplinam."

187. i.e., If laws of your own, and not the will and law of God, are the source and means of your life, you owe no thanks and no obedience to God, and therefore need not seek admittance into His house (Oehler).

188. 1 Cor. vii. 20. In Eng. ver., "Let every man abide in the same calling wherein he was called."

189. 1 Thess. iv. 11; 2 Thess. iii. 6-12.

190. i.e., thieves who frequented the public baths, which were a favorite resort at Rome.

191. The Marcionites.

192. [The argument amounts to this, that symbols were not idols:

yet even so, God only could ordain symbols that were innocent. The Nehushtan of King Hezekiah teaches us the "peril of Idolatry" (2 Kings xviii. 4) and that even a divine symbol may be destroyed justly if it be turned to a violation of the Second Commandment.]

193. [On which see Dr. Smith, Dict. of the Bible, ad vocem "Serpent."]

194. i.e., the Jewish people, who are generally meant by the expression "the People" in the singular number in Scripture. We shall endeavour to mark that distinction by writing the word, as here, with a capital.

195. See 1 Cor. x. 6, 11.

196. On the principle that the exception proves the rule. As Oehler explains it: "By the fact of the extraordinary precept in that particular case, God gave an indication that likeness-making had before been forbidden and interdicted by Him."

197. Ex. xx. 4, etc. [The absurd "brazen serpent" which I have seen in the Church of St. Ambrose, in Milan, is with brazen hardihood affirmed to be the identical serpent which Moses lifted up in the wilderness. But it lacks all symbolic character, as it is not set upon a pole nor in any way fitted to a cross. It greatly resembles a vane set upon a pivot.]

198. [Elucidation I.]

199. i.e., Unless you made them, they would not exist, and therefore [would not be regarded as divinities; therefore] your diligence gives them their divinity.

200. Matt. xviii. 8.

201. See chaps. v. and xii.

202. See chap. ii., "The expansiveness of idolatry."

203. Abacum. The word has various meanings; but this, perhaps, is its most general use: as, for instance, in Horace and Juvenal.

204. Alterius = ἕτερον which in the New Testament is = to "neighbour" in Rom. xiii. 8, etc. [Our author must have borne in mind Cicero's beautiful words--"Etenim omnes artes quæ ad humanitatem pertinent habent quoddam commune vinculum," etc. Pro Archia, i. tom. x. p. 10. Ed. Paris, 1817.]

205. Quæstum. Another reading is "questum," which would require us to translate "plaint."

206. "Quorum manus non ignorantium," i.e., "the hands of whom not unwitting;" which may be rendered as above, because in English, as in the Latin, in adjective "unwitting" belongs to the "whose," not to the "hands."

207. "Ars" in Latin is very generally used to mean "a scientific art." [See Titus iii. 14. English margin.]

208. See Eph. v. 11, 12, and similar passages.

209. i.e., by naming the stars after them.

210. Comp. chap. iv., and the references there given. The idea seems founded on an ancient reading found in the Codex Alexandrinus of the LXX. in Gen. vi. 2, "angels of God," for "sons of God."

211. See Tac. Ann. ii. 31, etc. (Oehler.)

212. See Matt. ii.

213. Because the names of the heathen divinities, which used to be given to the stars, were in many cases only names of dead men deified.

214. Or, heathenish.

215. Or, sect.

216. See Ex. vii., viii., and comp. 2 Tim. iii. 8.

217. See Acts viii. 9-24.

218. See Acts xiii. 6-11.

219. 1 Cor. i. 20.

220. See Acts viii. 21.

221. See 1 Cor. vii. 31, "They that use this world as not abusing it." The astrologer abuses the heavens by putting the heavenly bodies to a sinful use.

222. i.e., the seven planets.
223. See 1 Cor. viii. 10.
224. i.e., because "he does not nominally eat," etc.
225. [Note the Christian Schoolmaster, already distinguished as such, implying the existence and the character of Christian schools. Of which, learn more from the Emperor Julian, afterwards.]
226. i.e., the name of gods.
227. Ex. xxiii. 13; Josh. xxiii. 7; Ps. xvi. 4; Hos. ii. 17; Zech. xiii. 2.
228. i.e., the name of God.
229. i.e., on an idol, which, as Isaiah says, is "vanity."
230. 1 Tim. vi. 10.
231. 1 Tim. i. 19.
232. Col. iii. 5. It has been suggested that for "quamvis" we should read "quum bis;" i.e., "seeing covetousness is twice called," etc. The two places are Col. iii. 5, and Eph. v. 5.
233. Matt. v. 34-37; Jas. v. 12.
234. [The aversion of the early Christian Fathers passim to the ceremonial use of incense finds one explanation here.]
235. i.e., the demons, or idols, to whom incense is burned.
236. i.e., from one possessed.
237. i.e., The demon, in gratitude for the incense which the man daily feeds him with, ought to depart out of the possessed at his request.
238. i.e., in baptism.
239. See above, chaps. v. and viii. [One is reminded here of the famous pleasantry of Dr. Johnson; see Boswell.]
240. See Luke xiv. 28-30.
241. Luke vi. 20.
242. Matt. vi. 25, 31, etc.; Luke xii. 22-24.
243. Matt. vi. 28; Luke xii. 28.
244. Matt. xix. 21; Luke xviii. 22.
245. Luke ix. 62, where the words are, "is fit for the kingdom of God."
246. Matt. vi. 24; Luke xvi. 13.
247. Matt. xvi. 24; Mark viii. 34; Luke ix. 23; xiv. 27.
248. Luke xiv. 26; Mark x. 29, 30; Matt. xix. 27-30. Compare these texts with Tertullian's words, and see the testimony he thus gives to the deity of Christ.
249. i.e., any dear relations.
250. Matt. iv. 21, 22; Mark i. 19, 20; Luke v. 10, 11.
251. Matt. ix. 9; Mark ii. 14; Luke v. 29.
252. Luke ix. 59, 60.
253. Matt. xix. 26; Luke i. 37; xviii. 27.
254. The treatise De Spectaculis [soon to follow, in this volume.]
255. Rom. xii. 15.
256. See 2 Cor. vi. 14. In the De Spect.

xxvi. Tertullian has the same quotation (Oehler). And there, too, he adds, as here, "between life and death."
257. John xvi. 20. It is observable that Tertullian here translates κόσμον by "seculum."
258. i.e., Lazarus, Luke xvi. 19-31.
259. "Apud inferos," used clearly here by Tertullian of a place of happiness. Augustine says he never finds it so used in Scripture. See Ussher's "Answer to a Jesuit" on the Article, "He descended into hell." [See Elucid. X. p. 59, supra.]
260. i.e., if you are unknown to be a Christian: "dissimulaberis." This is Oehler's reading; but Latinius and Fr. Junis would read "Dissimulaveris," ="if you dissemble the fact" of being a Christian, which perhaps is better.
261. So Mr. Dodgson renders very well.
262. Matt. x. 33; Mark viii. 38; Luke ix. 26; 2 Tim. ii. 12.
263. Isa. lii. 5; Ezek. xxxvi. 20, 23. Cf. 2 Sam. xii. 14; Rom. ii. 24.
264. [This play on the words is literally copied from the original--"quæ tunc me testatur Christianum, cum propter ea me detestatur."]
265. St. Paul. Gal. i. 10.
266. 1 Cor. x. 32, 33.
267. 1 Cor. ix. 22.
268. 1 Cor. v. 10.
269. i.e., by sinning (Oehler), for "the wages of sin is death."
270. There seems to be a play on the word "convivere" (whence "convivium," etc.), as in Cic. de Sen. xiii.
271. Isa. i. 14, etc.
272. [This is noteworthy. In the earlier days sabbaths (Saturdays) were not unobserved, but, it was a concession pro tempore, to Hebrew Christians.]
273. i.e., perhaps your own birthdays. [See cap. xvi. infra.]
Oehler seems to think it means, "all other Christian festivals beside Sunday."
274. ["An Easter Day in every week."--Keble.]
275. i.e., a space of fifty days, see Deut. xvi. 10; and comp. Hooker, Ecc. Pol. iv. 13, 7, ed. Keble.
276. Matt. v. 16.
277. See chap. ix. p. 152, note 4.
278. Matt. xxii. 21; Mark xii. 17; Luke xx. 25.
279. See Gen. i. 26, 27; ix. 6; and comp. 1 Cor. xi. 7.
280. The word is the same as that for "the mouth" of a river, etc. Hence Oehler supposes the "entrances" or "mouths" here referred to to be the mouths of fountains, where nymphs were supposed to dwell. Nympha is supposed to be the same word as

Lympha. See Hor. Sat. i. 5, 97; and Macleane's note.

281. [He seems to refer to some Providential event, perhaps announced in a dream, not necessarily out of the course of common occurrences.]

282. Rom. xiii. 1, etc.; 1 Pet. ii, 13, 14.

283. Tit. iii. 1.

284. Dan. iii.

285. Dan. vi.

286. Matt. v. 14; Phil. ii. 15.

287. Ps. i. 1-3; xcii. 12-15.

288. Tertullian should have added, "and a man's on a woman." See Deut. xxii. 5. Moreover, the word "cursed" is not used there, but "abomination" is.

289. Because it was called toga virilis-- "the manly toga."

290. [1 Cor. viii. The law of the inspired apostle seems as rigorous here and in 1 Cor. x. 27-29.]

291. This is Oehler's reading; Regaltius and Fr. Junius would read "liberti" = freedmen. I admit that in this instance I prefer their reading; among other reasons it answers better to "patronis" ="patrons."

292. Majores. Of course the word may be rendered simply "ancients;" but I have kept the common meaning "forefathers."

293. "The judge condemns, the legislator fore-condemns."--Rigaltius (Oehler.)

294. Or, "purpurates."

295. [Not us Christians, but us Roman citizens.]

296. Or, "white-men."

297. Or, "consistency."

298. i.e., Official character.

299. Or, "free" or "good" "birth."

300. Or, "during."

301. i.e., the dress was the sign that they had obtained it.

302. I have departed from Oehler's reading here, as I have not succeeded in finding that the "stola" was a boy's garment; and, for grammatical reasons, the reading of Gelenius and Pamelius (which I have taken) seems best.

303. See 1 Cor. ix. 19.

304. St. Paul in his epistle glories in the title, "Paul, a slave," or "bondman," "of Christ Jesus."

305. Luke ix. 58; Matt. viii. 20.

306. Matt. xi. 8; Luke vii. 25.

307. Isa. liii. 2.

308. See John xiii. 1-17.

309. See John xviii. 36.

310. John vi. 15.

311. In baptism.

312. i.e., From your birth and means, you will be expected to fill offices which are in some way connected with idolatry.

313. i.e., Martyrdom (La Cerda, quoted by Oehler).

For the idea of being "a magistrate in the heavens," [sitting on a throne] compare such passages as Matt. xix. 28; Luke xxii. 28, 30; 1 Cor. vi. 2, 3; Rev. ii. 26, 27; iii. 21.

314. Elucidation II.

315. "Sacramentum" in Latin is, among other meanings, "a military oath."

316. "Virgam." The vine switch, or rod, in the Roman army was a mark of the centurion's (i.e., captain's) rank.

317. To fasten the ephod; hence the buckle worn by soldiers here referred to would probably be the belt buckle. Buckles were sometimes given as military rewards (White and Riddle).

318. As soldiers with belts.

319. Matt. xxvi. 52; 2 Cor. x. 4; John xviii. 36.

320. See Luke iii. 12, 13.

321. Matt. viii. 5, etc.; Luke vii. 1, etc.

322. Neither Oehler nor any editor seems to have discovered the passage here referred to.

323. Matt. xii. 37.

324. Ex. xxiii. 13. [St. Luke, nevertheless, names Castor and Pollux, Acts xxviii. 2., on our author's principle.]

325. Ex. xxiii. 13.

326. Ex. xx. 7.

327. Because Scripture calls idols "vanities" and "vain things." See 2 Kings xvii. 15, Ps. xxiv. 4, Isa. lix. 4, Deut. xxxii. 21, etc.

328. Ps. xcvi. 5. The LXX. in whose version ed. Tisch. it is Ps. xcv. read δαιμόνια, like Tertullian. Our version has "idols."

329. Mehercule. Medius Fidius. I have given the rendering of the latter, which seems preferred by Paley (Ov. Fast. vi. 213, note), who considers it = me dius (i.e., Deus) fidius juvet.

Smith (Lat. Dict. s.v.) agrees with him, and explains it, me deus fidius servet. White and Riddle (s.v.) take the me (which appears to be short) as a "demonstrative" particle or prefix, and explain, "By the God of truth!" "As true as heaven," "Most certainly."

330. i.e., for fear of being discovered to be a Christian (Oehler).

331. See Matt. v. 44, 1 Pet. iii. 9, etc.

332. i.e., the precept which enjoins me to "do good and lend."

333. Elucidation III.

334. Or, "mortgaged."

335. This is, perhaps, the most obscure and difficult passage in the entire treatise. I have followed Oehler's reading, and given what appears to be his sense; but the readings are widely different, and it is doubtful whether any is correct. I can scarcely, however, help thinking that the "se negant" here, and the "tamen non negavi" below, are to be

connected with the "puto autem nec negare" at the end of the former chapter; and that the true rendering is rather: "And [by so doing] deny themselves," i.e., deny their Christian name and faith. "Doubtless a time of persecution," such as the present time is--or "of prosecution," which would make very good sense--"and the place of the tribunal, and the person of the presiding judge, require them to know themselves," i.e., to have no shuffling or disguise. I submit this rendering with diffidence; but it does seem to me to suit the context better, and to harmonize better with the "Yet I have not denied," i.e., my name and faith, which follows, and with the "denying letters" which are mentioned at the end of the chapter.--Tr.

336. Mr. Dodgson renders "conceiveth;" and the word is certainly capable of that meaning.

337. See Matt. v. 28.

338. Oehler understands "the lighter crime" or "charge" to be "swearing;" the "heavier," to be "denying the Lord Christ."

339. See Luke i. 20, 22, 62, 63.

340. This is how Mr. Dodgson renders, and the rendering agrees with Oehler's punctuation. [So obscure however, is Dodgson's rendering that I have slightly changed the punctuation, to clarify it, and subjoin Oehler's text.] But perhaps we may read thus: "He speaks in his pen; he is heard in his waxen tablet: the hand is clearer than every sound; the letter is more vocal than every mouth." [Oehler reads thus: "Cum manibus suis a corde dictat et nomen filii sine ore pronuntiat: loquitur in stilo, auditur in cera manus omni sono clarior, littera omni ore vocalior." I see no difficulty here.]

341. Elucidation IV.

342. 1 Cor. v. 10.

343. Acts xv. 1-31.

344. i.e., cease to be Christians (Rigalt., referred to by Oehler).

345. [General references to Kaye (3d edition), which will be useful to those consulting that author's Tertullian, for Elucidations of the De Idololatria, are as follows: Preface, p. xxiii. Then, pp. 56, 141, 206, 231, 300, 360, 343, 360 and 362.]

346. See vol. II., p. 186, this series.

III - The Shows, or De Spectaculis [347]
[Translated by the Rev. S. Thelwall.]

Chapter I

Ye Servants of God, about to draw near to God, that you may make solemn consecration of yourselves to Him, [348] seek well to understand the condition of faith, the reasons of the Truth, the laws of Christian Discipline, which forbid among other sins of the world, the pleasures of the public shows. Ye who have testified and confessed [349] that you have done so already, review the subject, that there may be no sinning whether through real or wilful ignorance.

For such is the power of earthly pleasures, that, to retain the opportunity of still partaking of them, it contrives to prolong a willing ignorance, and bribes knowledge into playing a dishonest part. To both things, perhaps, some among you are allured by the views of the heathens who in this matter are wont to press us with arguments, such as these: (1) That the exquisite enjoyments of ear and eye we have in things external are not in the least opposed to religion in the mind and conscience; and (2) That surely no offence is offered to God, in any human enjoyment, by any of our pleasures, which it is not sinful to partake of in its own time and place, with all due honour and reverence secured to Him. But this is precisely what we are ready to prove:

That these things are not consistent with true religion and true obedience to the true God. There are some who imagine that Christians, a sort of people ever ready to die, are trained into the abstinence they practise, with no other object than that of making it less difficult to despise life, the fastenings to it being severed as it were. They regard it as an art of quenching all desire for that which, so far as they are concerned, they have emptied of all that is desirable; and so it is thought to be rather a thing of human planning and foresight, than clearly laid down by divine command. It were a grievous thing, forsooth, for Christians, while continuing in the enjoyment of pleasures so great, to die for God! It is not as they say; though, if it were, even Christian obstinacy might well give all submission to a plan so suitable, to a rule so excellent.

Chapter II

Then, again, every one is ready with the argument [350] that all things, as we teach, were created by God, and given to man for his use, and that they must be good, as coming all from so good a source; but that among them are found the various constituent elements of the public shows, such as the horse, the lion, bodily strength, and musical voice. It cannot, then, be thought that what exists by God's own creative will is either foreign or hostile to Him; and if it is not opposed to Him, it cannot be regarded as injurious to His worshippers, as certainly it is not foreign to them.

Beyond all doubt, too, the very buildings connected with the places of public amusement, composed as they are of rocks, stones, marbles, pillars, are things of God, who has given these various things for the earth's embellishment; nay, the very scenes are enacted under God's own heaven. How skilful a pleader seems human wisdom to herself, especially if she has the fear of losing any of her delights--any of the sweet enjoyments of worldly existence! In fact, you will find not a few whom the imperilling of their pleasures rather than their life holds back from us.

For even the weakling has no strong dread of death as a debt he knows is due by him; while the wise man does not look with contempt on pleasure, regarding it as a precious gift--in fact, the one blessedness of life, whether to philosopher or fool. Now nobody denies what nobody is ignorant of--for Nature herself is teacher of it--that God is the Maker of the universe, and that it is good, and that it is man's by free gift of its Maker. But having no intimate acquaintance with the Highest, knowing Him only by natural revelation, and not as His "friends"--afar off, and not as those who have been brought nigh to Him--men cannot but be in ignorance alike of what He enjoins and what He forbids in regard to the administration of His world. They must be ignorant, too, of the hostile power which works against Him, and perverts to wrong uses the things His hand has formed; for you cannot know either the will or the adversary of a God you do not know. We must not, then, consider merely by whom all things were made, but by whom they have been perverted. We shall find out for what use they were made at first, when we find for what they were not. There is a vast difference between the corrupted state and that of primal purity, just because there is a vast difference between the Creator and the corrupter. Why, all sorts of evils, which as indubitably evils even the heathens prohibit, and against which they guard themselves, come from the works of God. Take, for instance, murder, whether committed by iron, by poison, or by magical enchantments. Iron and herbs and demons are all equally creatures of God. Has the Creator, withal, provided these things for man's destruction? Nay, He puts His interdict on every sort of man-killing by that one summary precept, "Thou shalt not kill." Moreover, who but God, the Maker of the world, put in its gold, brass, silver, ivory, wood, and all the other materials used in the manufacture of idols? Yet has He done this that men may set up a worship in opposition to Himself? On the contrary idolatry in His eyes is the crowning sin. What is there offensive to God which is not God's? But in offending Him, it ceases to be His; and in ceasing to be His, it is in His eyes an offending thing. Man himself, guilty as he is of every iniquity, is not only a work of God--he is His image, and yet both in soul and body he has severed himself from his Maker. For we did not get eyes to minister to lust, and the tongue for speaking evil with, and ears to be the receptacle of evil speech, and the throat to serve the vice of gluttony, and the belly to be gluttony's ally, and the genitals for unchaste excesses, and hands for deeds of violence, and the feet for an erring life; or was the soul placed in the body that it might become a thought-manufactory of snares, and fraud, and injustice? I think not; for if God, as the righteous exactor of innocence, hates everything like malignity--if He hates utterly such plotting of evil, it is clear beyond a doubt, that, of all things that have come from His hand, He has made none to lead to works which He condemns, even though these same works may be carried on by things of His making; for, in fact, it is the one ground of condemnation, that the creature misuses the creation. We, therefore, who in our knowledge of the Lord have obtained some knowledge also of His foe--who, in our discovery of the Creator, have at the same time laid hands upon the great corrupter, ought neither to wonder nor to doubt that, as the prowess of the corrupting and God-opposing angel overthrew in the beginning the virtue of man, the work and image of God, the possessor of the world, so he has entirely changed man's nature--created, like his own, for perfect sinlessness--into his own state of wicked enmity against his Maker, that in the very thing whose gift to man, but not to him, had grieved him, he might make man guilty in God's eyes, and set up his own supremacy. [351]

Chapter III

Fortified by this knowledge against heathen views, let us rather turn to the unworthy reasonings of our own people; for the faith of some, either too simple or too scrupulous, demands direct authority from Scripture for giving up the shows, and holds out that the matter is a doubtful one, because such abstinence is not clearly and in words imposed upon God's servants. Well, we never find it expressed with the same precision, "Thou shalt not enter circus or theatre, thou shalt not look on combat or show;" as it is plainly laid down, "Thou shalt not kill; thou shalt not worship an idol; thou shalt not commit adultery or fraud." [352] But we find that that first word of David bears on this very sort of thing:

"Blessed," he says, "is the man who has not gone into the assembly of the impious, nor stood in the way of sinners, nor sat in the seat of scorners." [353] Though he seems to have predicted beforehand of that just man, that he took no part in the meetings and deliberations of the Jews, taking counsel about the slaying of our Lord, yet divine Scripture has ever far-reaching applications: after the immediate sense has been exhausted, in all directions it fortifies the practice of the religious life, so that here also you have an utterance which is not far from a plain interdicting of the shows. If he called those few Jews an assembly of the wicked, how much more will he so designate so vast a gathering of heathens! Are the heathens less impious, less sinners, less enemies of Christ, than the Jews were then? And see, too, how other things agree. For at the shows they also stand in the way. For they call the spaces between the seats going round the amphitheatre, and the passages which separate the people running down, ways. The place in the curve where the matrons sit is called a chair. Therefore, on the contrary, it holds, unblessed is he who has entered any council of wicked men, and has stood in any way of sinners, and has sat in any chair of scorners. We may understand a thing as spoken generally, even when it requires a certain special interpretation to be given to it. For some things spoken with a special reference contain in them general truth. When God admonishes the Israelites of their duty, or sharply reproves them, He has surely a reference to all men; when He threatens destruction to Egypt and Ethiopia, He surely precondemns every sinning nation, whatever. If, reasoning from species to genus, every nation that sins against them is an Egypt and Ethiopia; so also, reasoning from genus to species, with reference to the origin of shows, every show is an assembly of the wicked.

Chapter IV

Lest any one think that we are dealing in mere argumentative subtleties, I shall turn to that highest authority of our "seal" itself. When entering the water, we make profession of the Christian faith in the words of its rule; we bear public testimony that we have renounced the devil, his pomp, and his angels. Well, is it not in connection with idolatry, above all, that you have the devil with his pomp and his angels? from which, to speak briefly--for I do not wish to dilate--you have every unclean and wicked spirit. If, therefore, it shall be made plain that the entire apparatus of the shows is based upon idolatry, beyond all doubt that will carry with it the conclusion that our renunciatory testimony in the laver of baptism has reference to the shows, which, through their idolatry, have been given over to the devil, and his pomp, and his angels. We shall set forth, then, their several origins, in what nursing-places they have grown to manhood; next the titles of some of them, by what names they are called; then their apparatus, with what superstitions they are observed; (then their places, to what patrons they are dedicated;) then the arts which minister to them, to what authors they are traced. If any of these shall be found to have had no connection with an idol-god, it will be held as free at once from the taint of idolatry, and as not coming within the range of our baptismal abjuration. [354]

Chapter V

In the matter of their origins, as these are somewhat obscure and but little known to many among us, our investigations must go back to a remote antiquity, and our authorities be none other than books of heathen literature.

Various authors are extant who have published works on the subject. The origin of the games as given by them is this. Timæus tells us that immigrants from Asia, under the leadership of Tyrrhenus, who, in a contest about his native kingdom, had succumbed to his brother, settled down in Etruria. Well, among other superstitious observances under the name of religion, they set up in their new home public shows. The Romans, at their own request, obtain from them skilled performers--the proper seasons--the name too, for it is said they are called Ludi, from Lydi. And though Varro derives the name of Ludi from Ludus, that is, from play, as they called the Luperci also Ludii, because they ran about making sport; still that sporting of young men belongs, in his view, to festal days and temples, and objects of religious veneration. However, it is of little consequence the origin of the name, when it is certain that the thing springs from idolatry. The Liberalia, under the general designation of Ludi, clearly declared the glory of Father Bacchus; for to Bacchus these festivities were first consecrated by grateful peasants, in return for the boon he conferred on them, as they say, making known the pleasures of wine. Then the Consualia were called Ludi, and at first were in honour of Neptune, for Neptune has the name of Consus also. Thereafter Romulus dedicated the Equiria to Mars, though they claim the Consualia too for Romulus, on the ground that he consecrated them to Consus, the god, as they will have it, of counsel; of the counsel, forsooth, in which he planned the rape of the Sabine virgins for wives to his soldiers. An excellent counsel truly; and still I suppose reckoned just and righteous by the Romans themselves, I may not say by God. This goes also to taint the origin: you cannot surely hold that to be good which has sprung from sin, from shamelessness, from violence, from hatred, from a fratricidal founder, from a son of Mars. Even now, at the first turning-post in the circus, there is a subterranean altar to this same Consus, with an inscription to this effect:

"Consus, great in counsel, Mars, in battle mighty tutelar deities." The priests of the state sacrifice at it on the nones of July; the priest of Romulus and the Vestals on the twelfth before the Kalends of September. In addition to this, Romulus instituted games in honor of Jupiter Feretrius on the Tarpeian Hill, according to the statement Piso has handed down to us, called both Tarpeian and Capitoline. After him Numa Pompilius instituted games to Mars and Robigo (for they have also invented a goddess of rust); then Tullus Hostilius; then Ancus Martius; and various others in succession did the like. As to the idols in whose honour these games were established, ample information is to be found in the pages of Suetonius Tranquillus.

But we need say no more to prove the accusation of idolatrous origin.

Chapter VI

To the testimony of antiquity is added that of later games instituted in their turn, and betraying their origin from the titles which they bear even at the present day, in which it is imprinted as on their very face, for what idol and for what religious object games, whether of the one kind or the other, were designed. You have festivals bearing the name of the great Mother [355] and Apollo of Ceres too, and Neptune, and Jupiter Latiaris, and Flora, all celebrated for a common end; the others have their religious origin in the birthdays and solemnities of kings, in public successes in municipal holidays.

There are also testamentary exhibitions, in which funeral honours are rendered to the memories of private persons; and this according to an institution of ancient times. For from the first the "Ludi" were regarded as of two sons, sacred and funereal, that is in honour of the heathen deities and of the dead. But in the matter of idolatry, it makes no difference with us under what name or title it is practised, while it has to do with the wicked spirits whom we abjure.

If it is lawful to offer homage to the dead, it will be just as lawful to offer it to their gods: you have the same origin in both cases; there is the same idolatry; there is on our part the same solemn renunciation of all idolatry.

Chapter VII

The two kinds of public games, then, have one origin; and they have common names, as owning the same parentage. So, too, as they are equally tainted with the sin of idolatry, their foundress, they must needs be like each other in their pomp. But the more ambitious preliminary display of the circus games to which the name procession specially belongs, is in itself the proof to whom the whole thing appertains, in the many images the long line of statues, the chariots of all sorts, the thrones, the crowns, the dresses. What high religious rites besides, what sacrifices precede, come between, and follow. How many guilds, how many priesthoods, how many offices are set astir, is known to the inhabitants of the great city in which the demon convention has its headquarters. If these things are done in humbler style in the provinces, in accordance with their inferior means, still all circus games must be counted as belonging to that from which they are derived; the fountain from which they spring defiles them. The tiny streamlet from its very spring-head, the little twig from its very budding, contains in it the essential nature of its origin. It may be grand or mean, no matter, any circus procession whatever is offensive to God.

Though there be few images to grace it, there is idolatry in one; though there be no more than a single sacred car, it is a chariot of Jupiter: anything of idolatry whatever, whether meanly arrayed or modestly rich and gorgeous, taints it in its origin.

Chapter VIII

To follow out my plan in regard to places: the circus is chiefly consecrated to the Sun, whose temple stands in the middle of it, and whose image shines forth from its temple summit; for they have not thought it proper to pay sacred honours underneath a roof to an object they have itself in open space. Those who assert that the first spectacle was exhibited by Circe, and in honour of the Sun her father, as they will have it, maintain also the name of circus was derived from her. Plainly, then, the enchantress did this in the name of the parties whose priestess she was--I mean the demons and spirits of evil. What an aggregation of idolatries you see, accordingly, in the decoration of the place! Every ornament of the circus is a temple by itself. The eggs are regarded as sacred to the Castors, by men who are not ashamed to profess faith in their production from the egg of a swan, which was no other than Jupiter himself. The Dolphins vomit forth in honour of Neptune. Images of Sessia, so called as the goddess of sowing; of Messia, so called as the goddess of reaping; of Tutulina, so called as the fruit-protecting deity--load the pillars. In front of these you have three altars to these three gods--Great, Mighty, Victorious.

They reckon these of Samo-Thrace.

The huge Obelisk, as Hermeteles affirms, is set up in public to the Sun; its inscription, like its origin, belongs to Egyptian superstition. Cheerless were the demon-gathering without their Mater Magna; and so she presides there over the Euripus. Consus, as we have mentioned, lies hidden under ground at the Murcian Goals. These two sprang from an idol. For they will have it that Murcia is the goddess of love; and to her, at that spot, they have consecrated a temple. See, Christian, how many impure names have taken possession of the circus! You have nothing to do with a sacred place which is tenanted by such multitudes of diabolic spirits. And speaking of places, this is the suitable occasion for some remarks in anticipation of a point that some will raise. What, then, you say; shall I be in danger of pollution if I go to the circus when the games are not being celebrated? There is no law forbidding the mere places to us.

For not only the places for show-gatherings, but even the temples, may be entered without any peril of his religion by the servant of God, if he has only some honest reason for it, unconnected with their proper business and official duties. Why, even the streets and the market-place, and the baths, and the taverns, and our very dwelling-places, are not altogether free from idols. Satan and his angels have filled the whole world. It is not by merely being in the world, however, that we lapse from God, but by touching and tainting ourselves with the world's sins. I shall break with my Maker, that is, by going to the Capitol or the temple of Serapis to sacrifice or adore, as I shall also do by going as a spectator to the circus and the theatre. The places in themselves do not contaminate, but what is done in them; from this even the places themselves, we maintain, become defiled.

The polluted things pollute us.

It is on this account that we set before you to whom places of the kind are dedicated, that we may prove the things which are done in them to belong to the idol-patrons to whom the very places are sacred. [356]

Chapter IX

Now as to the kind of performances peculiar to the circus exhibitions. In former days equestrianism was practised in a simple way on horseback, and certainly its ordinary use had nothing sinful in it; but when it was dragged into the games, it passed from the service of God into the employment of demons.

Accordingly this kind of circus performances is regarded as sacred to Castor and Pollux, to whom, Stesichorus tells us, horses were given by Mercury. And Neptune, too, is an equestrian deity, by the Greeks called Hippius.

In regard to the team, they have consecrated the chariot and four to the sun; the chariot and pair to the moon.

But, as the poet has it, "Erichthonius first dared to yoke four horses to the chariot, and to ride upon its wheels with victorious swiftness." Erichthonius, the son of Vulcan and Minerva, fruit of unworthy passion upon earth, is a demon-monster, nay, the devil himself, and no mere snake. But if Trochilus the Argive is maker of the first chariot, he dedicated that work of his to Juno. If Romulus first exhibited the four-horse chariot at Rome, he too, I think, has a place given him among idols, at least if he and Quirinus are the same. But as chariots had such inventors, the charioteers were naturally dressed, too, in the colours of idolatry; for at first these were only two, namely white and red,--the former sacred to the winter with its glistening snows, the latter sacred to the summer with its ruddy sun: but afterwards, in the progress of luxury as well as of superstition, red was dedicated by some to Mars, and white by others to the Zephyrs, while green was given to Mother Earth, or spring, and azure to the sky and sea, or autumn. But as idolatry of every kind is condemned by God, that form of it surely shares the condemnation which is offered to the elements of nature.

Chapter X

Let us pass on now to theatrical exhibitions, which we have already shown have a common origin with the circus, and bear like idolatrous designations--even as from the first they have borne the name of "Ludi," and equally minister to idols.

They resemble each other also in their pomp, having the same procession to the scene of their display from temples and altars, and that mournful profusion of incense and blood, with music of pipes and trumpets, all under the direction of the soothsayer and the undertaker, those two foul masters of funeral rites and sacrifices. So as we went on from the origin of the "Ludi" to the circus games, we shall now direct our course thence to those of the theatre, beginning with the place of exhibition. At first the theatre was properly a temple of Venus; and, to speak briefly, it was owing to this that stage performances were allowed to escape censure, and got a footing in the world. For ofttimes the censors, in the interests of morality, put down above all the rising theatres, foreseeing, as they did, that there was great danger of their leading to a general profligacy; so that already, from this accordance of their own people with us, there is a witness to the heathen, and in the anticipatory judgment of human knowledge even a confirmation of our views. Accordingly Pompey the Great, less only than his theatre, when he had erected that citadel of all impurities, fearing some time or other censorial condemnation of his memory, superposed on it a temple of Venus; and summoning by public proclamation the people to its consecration, he called it not a theatre, but a temple, "under which," said he, "we have placed tiers of seats for viewing the shows." So he threw a veil over a structure on which condemnation had been often passed, and which is ever to be held in reprobation, by pretending that it was a sacred place; and by means of superstition he blinded the eyes of a virtuous discipline. But Venus and Bacchus are close allies. These two evil spirits are in sworn confederacy with each other, as the patrons of drunkenness and lust. So the theatre of Venus is as well the house of Bacchus: for they properly gave the name of Liberalia also to other theatrical amusements--which besides being consecrated to Bacchus (as were the Dionysia of the Greeks), were instituted by him; and, without doubt, the performances of the theatre have the common patronage of these two deities. That immodesty of gesture and attire which so specially and peculiarly characterizes the stage are consecrated to them--the one deity wanton by her sex, the other by his drapery; while its services of voice, and song, and lute, and pipe, belong to Apollos, and Muses, and Minervas, and Mercuries. You will hate, O Christian, the things whose authors must be the objects of your utter detestation. So we would now make a remark about the arts of the theatre, about the things also whose authors in the names we execrate. We know that the names of the dead are nothing, as are their images; but we know well enough, too, who, when images are set up, under these names carry on their wicked work, and exult in the homage rendered to them, and pretend to be divine--none other than spirits accursed, than devils. We see, therefore, that the arts also are consecrated to the service of the beings who dwell in the names of their founders; and that things cannot be held free from the taint of idolatry whose inventors have got a place among the gods for their discoveries. Nay, as regards the arts, we ought to have gone further back, and barred all further argument by the position that the demons, predetermining in their own interests from the first, among other evils of idolatry, the pollutions of the public shows, with the object of drawing man away from his Lord and binding him to their own service, carried out their purpose by bestowing on him the artistic gifts which the shows require. For none but themselves would have made provision and preparation for the objects they had in view; nor would they have given the arts to the world by any but those in whose names, and images, and histories they set up for their own ends the artifice of consecration.

Chapter XI

In fulfilment of our plan, let us now go on to consider the combats. Their origin is akin to that of the games (ludi). Hence they are kept as either sacred or funereal, as they have been instituted in honour of the idol-gods of the nations or of the dead.

Thus, too, they are called Olympian in honour of Jupiter, known at Rome as the Capitoline; Nemean, in honour of Hercules; Isthmian, in honour of Neptune; the rest mortuarii, as belonging to the dead. What wonder, then, if idolatry pollutes the combat-parade with profane crowns, with sacerdotal chiefs, with attendants belonging to the various colleges, last of all with the blood of its sacrifices? To add a completing word about the "place"--in the common place for the college of the arts sacred to the Muses, and Apollo, and Minerva, and also for that of the arts dedicated to Mars, they with contest and sound of trumpet emulate the circus in the arena, which is a real temple--I mean of the god whose festivals it celebrates. The gymnastic arts also originated with their Castors, and Herculeses, and Mercuries.

Chapter XII

It remains for us to examine the "spectacle" most noted of all, and in highest favour. It is called a dutiful service (munus), from its being an office, for it bears the name of "officium" as well as "munus." The ancients thought that in this solemnity they rendered offices to the dead; at a later period, with a cruelty more refined, they somewhat modified its character.

For formerly, in the belief that the souls of the departed were appeased by human blood, they were in the habit of buying captives or slaves of wicked disposition, and immolating them in their funeral obsequies. Afterwards they thought good to throw the veil of pleasure over their iniquity.[357] Those, therefore, whom they had provided for the combat, and then trained in arms as best they could, only that they might learn to die, they, on the funeral day, killed at the places of sepulture. They alleviated death by murders. Such is the origin of the "Munus." But by degrees their refinement came up to their cruelty; for these human wild beasts could not find pleasure exquisite enough, save in the spectacle of men torn to pieces by wild beasts. Offerings to propitiate the dead then were regarded as belonging to the class of funeral sacrifices; and these are idolatry: for idolatry, in fact, is a sort of homage to the departed; the one as well as the other is a service to dead men. Moreover, demons have abode in the images of the dead. To refer also to the matter of names, though this sort of exhibition has passed from honours of the dead to honours of the living, I mean, to quæstorships and magistracies--to priestly offices of different kinds; yet, since idolatry still cleaves to the dignity's name, whatever is done in its name partakes of its impurity. The same remark will apply to the procession of the "Munus," as we look at that in the pomp which is connected with these honours themselves; for the purple robes, the fasces, the fillets, the crowns, the proclamations too, and edicts, the sacred feasts of the day before, are not without the pomp of the devil, without invitation of demons. What need, then, of dwelling on the place of horrors, which is too much even for the tongue of the perjurer? For the amphitheatre [358] is consecrated to names more numerous and more dire [359] than is the Capitol itself, temple of all demons as it is. There are as many unclean spirits there as it holds men. To conclude with a single remark about the arts which have a place in it, we know that its two sorts of amusement have for their patrons Mars and Diana.

Chapter XIII

We have, I think, faithfully carried out our plan of showing in how many different ways the sin of idolatry clings to the shows, in respect of their origins, their titles, their equipments, their places of celebration, their arts; and we may hold it as a thing beyond all doubt, that for us who have twice [360] renounced all idols, they are utterly unsuitable. "Not that an idol is anything," [361] as the apostle says, but that the homage they render is to demons, who are the real occupants of these consecrated images, whether of dead men or (as they think) of gods. On this account, therefore, because they have a common source--for their dead and their deities are one--we abstain from both idolatries.

Nor do we dislike the temples less than the monuments: we have nothing to do with either altar, we adore neither image; we do not offer sacrifices to the gods, and we make no funeral oblations to the departed; nay, we do not partake of what is offered either in the one case or the other, for we cannot partake of God's feast and the feast of devils. [362] If, then, we keep throat and belly free from such defilements, how much more do we withhold our nobler parts, our ears and eyes, from the idolatrous and funereal enjoyments, which are not passed through the body, but are digested in the very spirit and soul, whose purity, much more than that of our bodily organs, God has a right to claim from us.

Chapter XIV

Having sufficiently established the charge of idolatry, which alone ought to be reason enough for our giving up the shows, let us now ex abundanti look at the subject in another way, for the sake of those especially who keep themselves comfortable in the thought that the abstinence we urge is not in so many words enjoined, as if in the condemnation of the lusts of the world there was not involved a sufficient declaration against all these amusements. For as there is a lust of money, or rank, or eating, or impure enjoyment, or glory, so there is also a lust of pleasure. But the show is just a sort of pleasure. I think, then, that under the general designation of lusts, pleasures are included; in like manner, under the general idea of pleasures, you have as a specific class the "shows." But we have spoken already of how it is with the places of exhibition, that they are not polluting in themselves, but owing to the things that are done in them from which they imbibe impurity, and then spirt it again on others.

Chapter XV

Having done enough, then, as we have said, in regard to that principal argument, that there is in them all the taint of idolatry--having sufficiently dealt with that, let us now contrast the other characteristics of the show with the things of God. God has enjoined us to deal calmly, gently, quietly, and peacefully with the Holy Spirit, because these things are alone in keeping with the goodness of His nature, with His tenderness and sensitiveness, and not to vex Him with rage, ill-nature, anger, or grief. Well, how shall this be made to accord with the shows? For the show always leads to spiritual agitation, since where there is pleasure, there is keenness of feeling giving pleasure its zest; and where there is keenness of feeling, there is rivalry giving in turn its zest to that.

Then, too, where you have rivalry, you have rage, bitterness, wrath and grief, with all bad things which flow from them--the whole entirely out of keeping with the religion of Christ. For even suppose one should enjoy the shows in a moderate way, as befits his rank, age or nature, still he is not undisturbed in mind, without some unuttered movings of the inner man. No one partakes of pleasures such as these without their strong excitements; no one comes under their excitements without their natural lapses. These lapses, again, create passionate desire. If there is no desire, there is no pleasure, and he is chargeable with trifling who goes where nothing is gotten; in my view, even that is foreign to us. Moreover, a man pronounces his own condemnation in the very act of taking his place among those with whom, by his disinclination to be like them, he confesses he has no sympathy. It is not enough that we do no such things ourselves, unless we break all connection also with those who do. "If thou sawest a thief," says the Scripture, "thou consentedst with him."[363] Would that we did not even inhabit the same world with these wicked men! But though that wish cannot be realized, yet even now we are separate from them in what is of the world; for the world is God's, but the worldly is the devil's.

Chapter XVI

Since, then, all passionate excitement is forbidden us, we are debarred from every kind of spectacle, and especially from the circus, where such excitement presides as in its proper element. See the people coming to it already under strong emotion, already tumultuous, already passion-blind, already agitated about their bets. The prætor is too slow for them: their eyes are ever rolling as though along with the lots in his urn; then they hang all eager on the signal; there is the united shout of a common madness. Observe how "out of themselves" they are by their foolish speeches. "He has thrown it!" they exclaim; and they announce each one to his neighbour what all have seen. I have clearest evidence of their blindness; they do not see what is really thrown. They think it a "signal cloth," but it is the likeness of the devil cast headlong from on high. And the result accordingly is, that they fly into rages, and passions, and discords, and all that they who are consecrated to peace ought never to indulge in. Then there are curses and reproaches, with no cause of hatred; there are cries of applause, with nothing to merit them.

What are the partakers in all this--not their own masters--to obtain of it for themselves? unless, it may be, that which makes them not their own: they are saddened by another's sorrow, they are gladdened by another's joy. Whatever they desire on the one hand, or detest on the other, is entirely foreign to themselves. So love with them is a useless thing, and hatred is unjust. Or is a causeless love perhaps more legitimate than a causeless hatred? God certainly forbids us to hate even with a reason for our hating; for He commands us to love our enemies. God forbids us to curse, though there be some ground for doing so, in commanding that those who curse us we are to bless. But what is more merciless than the circus, where people do not spare even their rulers and fellow-citizens? If any of its madnesses are becoming elsewhere in the saints of God, they will be seemly in the circus too; but if they are nowhere right, so neither are they there.

Chapter XVII

Are we not, in like manner, enjoined to put away from us all immodesty?

On this ground, again, we are excluded from the theatre, which is immodesty's own peculiar abode, where nothing is in repute but what elsewhere is disreputable. So the best path to the highest favour of its god is the vileness which the Atellan [364] gesticulates, which the buffoon in woman's clothes exhibits, destroying all natural modesty, so that they blush more readily at home than at the play, which finally is done from his childhood on the person of the pantomime, that he may become an actor. The very harlots, too, victims of the public lust, are brought upon the stage, their misery increased as being there in the presence of their own sex, from whom alone they are wont to hide themselves:

they are paraded publicly before every age and every rank--their abode, their gains, their praises, are set forth, and that even in the hearing of those who should not hear such things. I say nothing about other matters, which it were good to hide away in their own darkness and their own gloomy caves, lest they should stain the light of day. Let the Senate, let all ranks, blush for very shame! Why, even these miserable women, who by their own gestures destroy their modesty, dreading the light of day, and the people's gaze, know something of shame at least once a year. But if we ought to abominate all that is immodest, on what ground is it right to hear what we must not speak? For all licentiousness of speech, nay, every idle word, is condemned by God.

Why, in the same way, is it right to look on what it is disgraceful to do? How is it that the things which defile a man in going out of his mouth, are not regarded as doing so when they go in at his eyes and ears--when eyes and ears are the immediate attendants on the spirit--and that can never be pure whose servants-in-waiting are impure? You have the theatre forbidden, then, in the forbidding of immodesty.

If, again, we despise the teaching of secular literature as being foolishness in God's eyes, our duty is plain enough in regard to those spectacles, which from this source derive the tragic or comic play. If tragedies and comedies are the bloody and wanton, the impious and licentious inventors of crimes and lusts, it is not good even that there should be any calling to remembrance the atrocious or the vile. What you reject in deed, you are not to bid welcome to in word.

Chapter XVIII

But if you argue that the racecourse is mentioned in Scripture, I grant it at once. But you will not refuse to admit that the things which are done there are not for you to look upon: the blows, and kicks, and cuffs, and all the recklessness of hand, and everything like that disfiguration of the human countenance, which is nothing less than the disfiguration of God's own image. You will never give your approval to those foolish racing and throwing feats, and yet more foolish leapings; you will never find pleasure in injurious or useless exhibitions of strength; certainly you will not regard with approval those efforts after an artificial body which aim at surpassing the Creator's work; and you will have the very opposite of complacency in the athletes Greece, in the inactivity of peace, feeds up. And the wrestler's art is a devil's thing. The devil wrestled with, and crushed to death, the first human beings.

Its very attitude has power in it of the serpent kind, firm to hold--tortures to clasp--slippery to glide away.

You have no need of crowns; why do you strive to get pleasures from crowns?

Chapter XIX

We shall now see how the Scriptures condemn the amphitheatre. If we can maintain that it is right to indulge in the cruel, and the impious, and the fierce, let us go there. If we are what we are said to be, let us regale ourselves there with human blood. It is good, no doubt, to have the guilty punished. Who but the criminal himself will deny that? And yet the innocent can find no pleasure in another's sufferings:

he rather mourns that a brother has sinned so heinously as to need a punishment so dreadful. But who is my guarantee that it is always the guilty who are adjudged to the wild beasts, or to some other doom, and that the guiltless never suffer from the revenge of the judge, or the weakness of the defence, or the pressure of the rack? How much better, then, is it for me to remain ignorant of the punishment inflicted on the wicked, lest I am obliged to know also of the good coming to untimely ends--if I may speak of goodness in the case at all! At any rate, gladiators not chargeable with crime are offered in sale for the games, that they may become the victims of the public pleasure. Even in the case of those who are judicially condemned to the amphitheatre, what a monstrous thing it is, that, in undergoing their punishment, they, from some less serious delinquency, advance to the criminality of manslayers! But I mean these remarks for heathen. As to Christians, I shall not insult them by adding another word as to the aversion with which they should regard this sort of exhibition; though no one is more able than myself to set forth fully the whole subject, unless it be one who is still in the habit of going to the shows. I would rather withal be incomplete than set memory a-working. [365]

Chapter XX

How vain, then--nay, how desperate--is the reasoning of persons, who, just because they decline to lose a pleasure, hold out that we cannot point to the specific words or the very place where this abstinence is mentioned, and where the servants of God are directly forbidden to have anything to do with such assemblies! I heard lately a novel defence of himself by a certain play-lover. "The sun," said he, "nay, God Himself, looks down from heaven on the show, and no pollution is contracted." Yes, and the sun, too, pours down his rays into the common sewer without being defiled. As for God, would that all crimes were hid from His eye, that we might all escape judgment! But He looks on robberies too; He looks on falsehoods, adulteries, frauds, idolatries, and these same shows; and precisely on that account we will not look on them, lest the All-seeing see us. You are putting on the same level, O man, the criminal and the judge; the criminal who is a criminal because he is seen, and the Judge who is a Judge because He sees.

Are we set, then, on playing the madman outside the circus boundaries? Outside the gates of the theatre are we bent on lewdness, outside the course on arrogance, and outside the amphitheatre on cruelty, because outside the porticoes, the tiers and the curtains, too, God has eyes? Never and nowhere is that free from blame which God ever condemns; never and nowhere is it right to do what you may not do at all times and in all places.

It is the freedom of the truth from change of opinion and varying judgments which constitutes its perfection, and gives it its claims to full mastery, unchanging reverence, and faithful obedience. That which is really good or really evil cannot be ought else. But in all things the truth of God is immutable.

Chapter XXI

The heathen, who have not a full revelation of the truth, for they are not taught of God, hold a thing evil and good as it suits self-will and passion, making that which is good in one place evil in another, and that which is evil in one place in another good. So it strangely happens, that the same man who can scarcely in public lift up his tunic, even when necessity of nature presses him, takes it off in the circus, as if bent on exposing himself before everybody; the father who carefully protects and guards his virgin daughter's ears from every polluting word, takes her to the theatre himself, exposing her to all its vile words and attitudes; he, again, who in the streets lays hands on or covers with reproaches the brawling pugilist, in the arena gives all encouragement to combats of a much more serious kind; and he who looks with horror on the corpse of one who has died under the common law of nature, in the amphitheatre gazes down with most patient eyes on bodies all mangled and torn and smeared with their own blood; nay, the very man who comes to the show, because he thinks murderers ought to suffer for their crime, drives the unwilling gladiator to the murderous deed with rods and scourges; and one who demands the lion for every manslayer of deeper dye, will have the staff for the savage swordsman, and rewards him with the cap of liberty. Yes and he must have the poor victim back again, that he may get a sight of his face--with zest inspecting near at hand the man whom he wished torn in pieces at safe distance from him: so much the more cruel he if that was not his wish.

Chapter XXII

What wonder is there in it? Such inconsistencies as these are just such as we might expect from men, who confuse and change the nature of good and evil in their inconstancy of feeling and fickleness in judgment. Why, the authors and managers of the spectacles, in that very respect with reference to which they highly laud the charioteers, and actors, and wrestlers, and those most loving gladiators, to whom men prostitute their souls, women too their bodies, slight and trample on them, though for their sakes they are guilty of the deeds they reprobate; nay, they doom them to ignominy and the loss of their rights as citizens, excluding them from the Curia, and the rostra, from senatorial and equestrian rank, and from all other honours as well as certain distinctions. What perversity! They have pleasure in those whom yet they punish; they put all slights on those to whom, at the same time, they award their approbation; they magnify the art and brand the artist. What an outrageous thing it is, to blacken a man on account of the very things which make him meritorious in their eyes! Nay, what a confession that the things are evil, when their authors, even in highest favour, are not without a mark of disgrace upon them!

Chapter XXIII

Seeing, then, man's own reflections, even in spite of the sweetness of pleasure, lead him to think that people such as these should be condemned to a hapless lot of infamy, losing all the advantages connected with the possession of the dignities of life, how much more does the divine righteousness inflict punishment on those who give themselves to these arts! Will God have any pleasure in the charioteer who disquiets so many souls, rouses up so many furious passions, and creates so many various moods, either crowned like a priest or wearing the colours of a pimp, decked out by the devil that he may be whirled away in his chariot, as though with the object of taking off Elijah? Will He be pleased with him who applies the razor to himself, and completely changes his features; who, with no respect for his face, is not content with making it as like as possible to Saturn and Isis and Bacchus, but gives it quietly over to contumelious blows, as if in mockery of our Lord? The devil, forsooth, makes it part, too, of his teaching, that the cheek is to be meekly offered to the smiter. In the same way, with their high shoes, he has made the tragic actors taller, because "none can add a cubit to his stature." [366] His desire is to make Christ a liar. And in regard to the wearing of masks, I ask is that according to the mind of God, who forbids the making of every likeness, and especially then the likeness of man who is His own image? The Author of truth hates all the false; He regards as adultery all that is unreal.

Condemning, therefore, as He does hypocrisy in every form, He never will approve any putting on of voice, or sex, or age; He never will approve pretended loves, and wraths, and groans, and tears. Then, too, as in His law it is declared that the man is cursed who attires himself in female garments,[367] what must be His judgment of the pantomime, who is even brought up to play the woman! And will the boxer go unpunished? I suppose he received these cæstus-scars, and the thick skin of his fists, and these growths upon his ears, at his creation! God, too, gave him eyes for no other end than that they might be knocked out in fighting! I say nothing of him who, to save himself, thrusts another in the lion's way, that he may not be too little of a murderer when he puts to death that very same man on the arena.

Chapter XXIV

In how many other ways shall we yet further show that nothing which is peculiar to the shows has God's approval, or without that approval is becoming in God's servants? If we have succeeded in making it plain that they were instituted entirely for the devil's sake, and have been got up entirely with the devil's things (for all that is not God's, or is not pleasing in His eyes, belongs to His wicked rival), this simply means that in them you have that pomp of the devil which in the "seal" of our faith we abjure. We should have no connection with the things which we abjure, whether in deed or word, whether by looking on them or looking forward to them; but do we not abjure and rescind that baptismal pledge, when we cease to bear its testimony? Does it then remain for us to apply to the heathen themselves. Let them tell us, then, whether it is right in Christians to frequent the show. Why, the rejection of these amusements is the chief sign to them that a man has adopted the Christian faith. If any one, then, puts away the faith's distinctive badge, he is plainly guilty of denying it. What hope can you possibly retain in regard to a man who does that? When you go over to the enemy's camp, you throw down your arms, desert the standards and the oath of allegiance to your chief:

you cast in your lot for life or death with your new friends.

Chapter XXV

Seated where there is nothing of God, will one be thinking of his Maker? Will there be peace in his soul when there is eager strife there for a charioteer?

Wrought up into a frenzied excitement, will he learn to be modest? Nay, in the whole thing he will meet with no greater temptation than that gay attiring of the men and women. The very intermingling of emotions, the very agreements and disagreements with each other in the bestowment of their favours, where you have such close communion, blow up the sparks of passion. And then there is scarce any other object in going to the show, but to see and to be seen.

When a tragic actor is declaiming, will one be giving thought to prophetic appeals? Amid the measures of the effeminate player, will he call up to himself a psalm? And when the athletes are hard at struggle, will he be ready to proclaim that there must be no striking again? And with his eye fixed on the bites of bears, and the sponge-nets of the net-fighters, can he be moved by compassion? May God avert from His people any such passionate eagerness after a cruel enjoyment!

For how monstrous it is to go from God's church to the devil's--from the sky to the stye, [368] as they say; to raise your hands to God, and then to weary them in the applause of an actor; out of the mouth, from which you uttered Amen over the Holy Thing, to give witness in a gladiator's favour; to cry "forever" to any one else but God and Christ!

Chapter XXVI

Why may not those who go into the temptations of the show become accessible also to evil spirits? We have the case of the woman--the Lord Himself is witness--who went to the theatre, and came back possessed. In the outcasting, [369] accordingly, when the unclean creature was upbraided with having dared to attack a believer, he firmly replied, [370] "And in truth I did it most righteously, for I found her in my domain." Another case, too, is well known, in which a woman had been hearing a tragedian, and on the very night she saw in her sleep a linen cloth--the actor's name being mentioned at the same time with strong disapproval--and five days after that woman was no more. How many other undoubted proofs we have had in the case of persons who, by keeping company with the devil in the shows, have fallen from the Lord! For no one can serve two masters. [371] What fellowship has light with darkness, life with death? [372]

Chapter XXVII

We ought to detest these heathen meetings and assemblies, if on no other account than that there God's name is blasphemed--that the cry "To the lions!" is daily raised against us [373] --that from thence persecuting decrees are wont to emanate, and temptations are sent forth. What will you do if you are caught in that heaving tide of impious judgments? Not that there any harm is likely to come to you from men: nobody knows that you are a Christian; but think how it fares with you in heaven. For at the very time the devil is working havoc in the church, do you doubt that the angels are looking down from above, and marking every man, who speaks and who listens to the blaspheming word, who lends his tongue and who lends his ears to the service of Satan against God? Shall you not then shun those tiers where the enemies of Christ assemble, that seat of all that is pestilential, and the very super incumbent atmosphere all impure with wicked cries? Grant that you have there things that are pleasant, things both agreeable and innocent in themselves; even some things that are excellent. Nobody dilutes poison with gall and hellebore: the accursed thing is put into condiments well seasoned and of sweetest taste. So, too, the devil puts into the deadly draught which he prepares, things of God most pleasant and most acceptable. Everything there, then, that is either brave, noble, loud-sounding, melodious, or exquisite in taste, hold it but as the honey drop of a poisoned cake; nor make so much of your taste for its pleasures, as of the danger you run from its attractions.

Chapter XXVIII

With such dainties as these let the devil's guests be feasted. The places and the times, the inviter too, are theirs. Our banquets, our nuptial joys, are yet to come. We cannot sit down in fellowship with them, as neither can they with us.

Things in this matter go by their turns.

Now they have gladness and we are troubled. "The world," says Jesus, "shall rejoice; ye shall be sorrowful." [374] Let us mourn, then, while the heathen are merry, that in the day of their sorrow we may rejoice; lest, sharing now in their gladness, we share then also in their grief. Thou art too dainty, Christian, if thou wouldst have pleasure in this life as well as in the next; nay, a fool thou art, if thou thinkest this life's pleasures to be really pleasures. The philosophers, for instance, give the name of pleasure to quietness and repose; in that they have their bliss; in that they find entertainment: they even glory in it. You long for the goal, and the stage, and the dust, and the place of combat!

I would have you answer me this question: Can we not live without pleasure, who cannot but with pleasure die? For what is our wish but the apostle's, to leave the world, and be taken up into the fellowship of our Lord? [375] You have your joys where you have your longings.

Chapter XXIX

Even as things are, if your thought is to spend this period of existence in enjoyments, how are you so ungrateful as to reckon insufficient, as not thankfully to recognize the many and exquisite pleasures God has bestowed upon you? For what more delightful than to have God the Father and our Lord at peace with us, than revelation of the truth than confession of our errors, than pardon of the innumerable sins of our past life? What greater pleasure than distaste of pleasure itself, contempt of all that the world can give, true liberty, a pure conscience, a contented life, and freedom from all fear of death? What nobler than to tread under foot the gods of the nations--to exorcise evil spirits [376] --to perform cures--to seek divine revealings--to live to God? These are the pleasures, these the spectacles that befit Christian men--holy, everlasting, free. Count of these as your circus games, fix your eyes on the courses of the world, the gliding seasons, reckon up the periods of time, long for the goal of the final consummation, defend the societies of the churches, be startled at God's signal, be roused up at the angel's trump, glory in the palms of martyrdom. If the literature of the stage delight you, we have literature in abundance of our own--plenty of verses, sentences, songs, proverbs; and these not fabulous, but true; not tricks of art, but plain realities.

Would you have also fightings and wrestlings? Well, of these there is no lacking, and they are not of slight account. Behold unchastity overcome by chastity, perfidy slain by faithfulness, cruelty stricken by compassion, impudence thrown into the shade by modesty: these are the contests we have among us, and in these we win our crowns. Would you have something of blood too? You have Christ's.

Chapter XXX

But what a spectacle is that fast-approaching advent [377] of our Lord, now owned by all, now highly exalted, now a triumphant One! What that exultation of the angelic hosts! What the glory of the rising saints! What the kingdom of the just thereafter! What the city New Jerusalem![378] Yes, and there are other sights: that last day of judgment, with its everlasting issues; that day unlooked for by the nations, the theme of their derision, when the world hoary with age, and all its many products, shall be consumed in one great flame! How vast a spectacle then bursts upon the eye! What there excites my admiration? what my derision?

Which sight gives me joy? which rouses me to exultation?--as I see so many illustrious monarchs, whose reception into the heavens was publicly announced, groaning now in the lowest darkness with great Jove himself, and those, too, who bore witness of their exultation; governors of provinces, too, who persecuted the Christian name, in fires more fierce than those with which in the days of their pride they raged against the followers of Christ. What world's wise men besides, the very philosophers, in fact, who taught their followers that God had no concern in ought that is sublunary, and were wont to assure them that either they had no souls, or that they would never return to the bodies which at death they had left, now covered with shame before the poor deluded ones, as one fire consumes them! Poets also, trembling not before the judgment-seat of Rhadamanthus or Minos, but of the unexpected Christ! I shall have a better opportunity then of hearing the tragedians, louder-voiced in their own calamity; of viewing the play-actors, much more "dissolute" in the dissolving flame; of looking upon the charioteer, all glowing in his chariot of fire; of beholding the wrestlers, not in their gymnasia, but tossing in the fiery billows; unless even then I shall not care to attend to such ministers of sin, in my eager wish rather to fix a gaze insatiable on those whose fury vented itself against the Lord. "This," I shall say, "this is that carpenter's or hireling's son, that Sabbath-breaker, that Samaritan and devil-possessed! This is He whom you purchased from Judas! This is He whom you struck with reed and fist, whom you contemptuously spat upon, to whom you gave gall and vinegar to drink! This is He whom His disciples secretly stole away, that it might be said He had risen again, or the gardener abstracted, that his lettuces might come to no harm from the crowds of visitants!" What quæstor or priest in his munificence will bestow on you the favour of seeing and exulting in such things as these? And yet even now we in a measure have them by faith in the picturings of imagination. But what are the things which eye has not seen, ear has not heard, and which have not so much as dimly dawned upon the human heart? Whatever they are, they are nobler, I believe, than circus, and both theatres, [379] and every race-course.

Footnotes:

347. [It is the opinion of Dr. Neander that this treatise proceeded from our author before his lapse: but Bp. Kaye (p. xvi.) finds some exaggerated expressions in it, concerning the military life, which savour of Montanism. Probably they do, but had he written the tract as a professed Montanist, they would have been much less ambiguous, in all probability. At all events, a work so colourless that doctors can disagree about even its shading, must be regarded as practically orthodox.

Exaggerated expressions are but the characteristics of the author's genius. We find the like in all writers of strongly marked individuality.

Neander dates this treatise circa a.d. 197. That it was written at Carthage is the conviction of Kaye and Dr. Allix; see Kaye, p. 55.]

348. [He speaks of Catechumens, called elsewhere Novitioli. See Bunsen, Hippol. III. Church and House-book, p. 5.]

349. [Here he addresses the Fideles or Communicants, as we call them.]

350. [Kaye (p. 366), declares that all the arguments urged in this tract are comprised in two sentences of the Apology, cap. 38.]

351. [For the demonology of this treatise, compare capp. 10, 12, 13, 23, and see Kaye's full but condensed statement (pp. 201-204), in his account of the writings, etc.]

352. Ex. xx. 14.

353. Ps. i. 1. [Kaye's censure of this use of the text, (p. 366) seems to me gratuitous.]

354. [Neander argues with great force that in referring to Scripture and not at all to the "new Prophecy," our author shows his orthodoxy. We may add " that highest authority" to which he appeals in this chapter.]

355. [Cybele.]

356. [Very admirable reflections on this chapter may be found in Kaye, pp. 362-3.]

357. [The authority of Tertullian, in this matter, is accepted by the critics, as of historic importance.]

358. [Though this was probably written at Carthage, his reference to the Flavian theatre in this place is plain from the immediate comparison with the Capitol.]

359. [To the infernal deities and first of all to Pluto. See vol. I. note 6, p. 131, this Series.]

360. [Bunsen, Hippol. Vol. III. pp. 20-22.]

361. 1 Cor. viii. 4.

362. 1 Cor. x. 21.

363. Ps. xlix. 18. [This chapter bears on modern theatres.]

364. [The ludi Atellani were so called from Atella, in Campania, where a vast amphitheatre delighted the inhabitants. Juvenal, Sat. vi. 71. The like disgrace our times.]

365. [See Kaye, p. 11. This expression is thought to confirm the probability of Tertullian's original Gentilism.]

366. Matt. vi. 27.

367. Deut. xxii.

368. [De Cælo in Cænum: (sic) Oehler.]

369. [The exorcism. For the exorcism in Baptism, see Bunsen, Hippol. iii. 19.]

370. See Neander's explanation in Kaye, p. xxiii. But, let us observe the entire simplicity with which our author narrates a sort of incident known to the apostles. Acts xvi. 16.]

371. Matt. vi. 24.

372. 2 Cor. iv. 14.

373. [Observe--"daily raised." On this precarious condition of the Christians, in their daily life, see the calm statement of Kaye, pp. 110, 111.

374. John xvi. 20.

375. Phil. i. 23.

376. [See cap. 26, supra.
On this claim to such powers still remaining in the church. See Kaye, p. 89.]

377. [Kaye, p. 20. He doubtless looked for a speedy appearance of the Lord: and note the apparent expectation of a New Jerusalem, on earth, before the Consummation and Judgment.]

378. [This New Jerusalem gives Bp. Kaye (p. 55) "decisive proof" of Montanism, especially as compared with the Third Book against Marcion. I cannot see it, here.]

379. Viz., the theatre and amphitheatre. [This concluding chapter, which Gibbon delights to censure, because its fervid rhetoric so fearfully depicts the punishments of Christ's enemies, "appears to Dr. Neander to contain a beautiful specimen of lively faith and Christian confidence." See Kaye, p. xxix.]

IV - The Chaplet, or De Corona [380]

Chapter I

Very lately it happened thus: while the bounty of our most excellent emperors [381] was dispensed in the camp, the soldiers, laurel-crowned, were approaching. One of them, more a soldier of God, more stedfast than the rest of his brethren, who had imagined that they could serve two masters, his head alone uncovered, the useless crown in his hand--already even by that peculiarity known to every one as a Christian--was nobly conspicuous. Accordingly, all began to mark him out, jeering him at a distance, gnashing on him near at hand. The murmur is wafted to the tribune, when the person had just left the ranks. The tribune at once puts the question to him, Why are you so different in your attire? He declared that he had no liberty to wear the crown with the rest.

Being urgently asked for his reasons, he answered, I am a Christian. O soldier! boasting thyself in God. Then the case was considered and voted on; the matter was remitted to a higher tribunal; the offender was conducted to the prefects. At once he put away the heavy cloak, his disburdening commenced; he loosed from his foot the military shoe, beginning to stand upon holy ground; [382] he gave up the sword, which was not necessary either for the protection of our Lord; from his hand likewise dropped the laurel crown; and now, purple-clad with the hope of his own blood, shod with the preparation of the gospel, girt with the sharper word of God, completely equipped in the apostles' armour, and crowned more worthily with the white crown of martyrdom, he awaits in prison the largess of Christ. Thereafter adverse judgments began to be passed upon his conduct--whether on the part of Christians I do not know, for those of the heathen are not different--as if he were headstrong and rash, and too eager to die, because, in being taken to task about a mere matter of dress, he brought trouble on the bearers of the Name, [383] --he, forsooth, alone brave among so many soldier-brethren, he alone a Christian. It is plain that as they have rejected the prophecies of the Holy Spirit, [384] they are also purposing the refusal of martyrdom. So they murmur that a peace so good and long is endangered for them. Nor do I doubt that some are already turning their back on the Scriptures, are making ready their luggage, are equipped for flight from city to city; for that is all of the gospel they care to remember. I know, too, their pastors are lions in peace, deer in the fight. As to the questions asked for extorting confessions from us, we shall teach elsewhere.

Now, as they put forth also the objection--But where are we forbidden to be crowned?--I shall take this point up, as more suitable to be treated of here, being the essence, in fact, of the present contention. So that, on the one hand, the inquirers who are ignorant, but anxious, may be instructed; and on the other, those may be refuted who try to vindicate the sin, especially the laurel-crowned Christians themselves, to whom it is merely a question of debate, as if it might be regarded as either no trespass at all, or at least a doubtful one, because it may be made the subject of investigation.

That it is neither sinless nor doubtful, I shall now, however, show.

Chapter II

I affirm that not one of the Faithful has ever a crown upon his head, except at a time of trial. That is the case with all, from catechumens to confessors and martyrs, [385] or (as the case may be) deniers. Consider, then, whence the custom about which we are now chiefly inquiring got its authority. But when the question is raised why it is observed, it is meanwhile evident that it is observed. Therefore that can neither be regarded as no offence, or an uncertain one, which is perpetrated against a practice which is capable of defence, on the ground even of its repute, and is sufficiently ratified by the support of general acceptance. It is undoubted, so that we ought to inquire into the reason of the thing; but without prejudice to the practice, not for the purpose of overthrowing it, but rather of building it up, that you may all the more carefully observe it, when you are also satisfied as to its reason. But what sort of procedure is it, for one to be bringing into debate a practice, when he has fallen from it, and to be seeking the explanation of his having ever had it, when he has left it off? Since, although he may wish to seem on this account desirous to investigate it, that he may show that he has not done wrong in giving it up, it is evident that he nevertheless transgressed previously in its presumptuous observance.

If he has done no wrong to-day in accepting the crown he offended before in refusing it. This treatise, therefore, will not be for those who not in a proper condition for inquiry, but for those who, with the real desire of getting instruction, bring forward, not a question for debate, but a request for advice. For it is from this desire that a true inquiry always proceeds; and I praise the faith which has believed in the duty of complying with the rule, before it has learned the reason of it. An easy thing it is at once to demand where it is written that we should not be crowned.

But is it written that we should be crowned? Indeed, in urgently demanding the warrant of Scripture in a different side from their own, men prejudge that the support of Scripture ought no less to appear on their part. For if it shall be said that it is lawful to be crowned on this ground, that Scripture does not forbid it, it will as validly be retorted that just on this ground is the crown unlawful, because the Scripture does not enjoin it. What shall discipline do? Shall it accept both things, as if neither were forbidden? Or shall it refuse both, as if neither were enjoined? But "the thing which is not forbidden is freely permitted." I should rather say [386] that what has not been freely allowed is forbidden.

Chapter III

And how long shall we draw the saw to and fro through this line, when we have an ancient practice, which by anticipation has made for us the state, i.e., of the question? If no passage of Scripture has prescribed it, assuredly custom, which without doubt flowed from tradition, has confirmed it. For how can anything come into use, if it has not first been handed down?

Even in pleading tradition, written authority, you say, must be demanded. Let us inquire, therefore, whether tradition, unless it be written, should not be admitted. Certainly we shall say that it ought not to be admitted, if no cases of other practices which, without any written instrument, we maintain on the ground of tradition alone, and the countenance thereafter of custom, affords us any precedent.

To deal with this matter briefly, I shall begin with baptism. [387] When we are going to enter the water, but a little before, in the presence of the congregation and under the hand of the president, we solemnly profess that we disown the devil, and his pomp, and his angels. Hereupon we are thrice immersed, making a somewhat ampler pledge than the Lord has appointed in the Gospel. Then when we are taken up (as new-born children), [388] we taste first of all a mixture of milk and honey, and from that day we refrain from the daily bath for a whole week. We take also, in congregations before daybreak, and from the hand of none but the presidents, the sacrament of the Eucharist, which the Lord both commanded to be eaten at meal-times, and enjoined to be taken by all alike. [389] As often as the anniversary comes round, we make offerings for the dead as birthday honours. We count fasting or kneeling in worship on the Lord's day to be unlawful. We rejoice in the same privilege also from Easter to Whitsunday. We feel pained should any wine or bread, even though our own, be cast upon the ground.

At every forward step and movement, at every going in and out, when we put on our clothes and shoes, when we bathe, when we sit at table, when we light the lamps, on couch, on seat, in all the ordinary actions of daily life, we trace upon the forehead the sign. [390]

Chapter IV

If, for these and other such rules, you insist upon having positive Scripture injunction, you will find none. Tradition will be held forth to you as the originator of them, custom as their strengthener, and faith as their observer. That reason will support tradition, and custom, and faith, you will either yourself perceive, or learn from some one who has. Meanwhile you will believe that there is some reason to which submission is due. I add still one case more, as it will be proper to show you how it was among the ancients also. Among the Jews, so usual is it for their women to have the head veiled, that they may thereby be recognised. I ask in this instance for the law. I put the apostle aside. If Rebecca at once drew down her veil, when in the distance she saw her betrothed, this modesty of a mere private individual could not have made a law, or it will have made it only for those who have the reason which she had. Let virgins alone be veiled, and this when they are coming to be married, and not till they have recognised their destined husband. If Susanna also, who was subjected to unveiling on her trial, [391] furnishes an argument for the veiling of women, I can say here also, the veil was a voluntary thing. She had come accused, ashamed of the disgrace she had brought on herself, properly concealing her beauty, even because now she feared to please. But I should not suppose that, when it was her aim to please, she took walks with a veil on in her husband's avenue. Grant, now, that she was always veiled. In this particular case, too, or, in fact, in that of any other, I demand the dress-law.

If I nowhere find a law, it follows that tradition has given the fashion in question to custom, to find subsequently (its authorization in) the apostle's sanction, from the true interpretation of reason. This instances, therefore, will make it sufficiently plain that you can vindicate the keeping of even unwritten tradition established by custom; the proper witness for tradition when demonstrated by long-continued observance. [392] But even in civil matters custom is accepted as law, when positive legal enactment is wanting; and it is the same thing whether it depends on writing or on reason, since reason is, in fact, the basis of law. But, (you say), if reason is the ground of law, all will now henceforth have to be counted law, whoever brings it forward, which shall have reason as its ground. [393] Or do you think that every believer is entitled to originate and establish a law, if only it be such as is agreeable to God, as is helpful to discipline, as promotes salvation, when the Lord says, "But why do you not even of your own selves judge what is right?" [394] And not merely in regard to a judicial sentence, but in regard to every decision in matters we are called on to consider, the apostle also says, "If of anything you are ignorant, God shall reveal it unto you;" [395] he himself, too, being accustomed to afford counsel though he had not the command of the Lord, and to dictate of himself [396] as possessing the Spirit of God who guides into all truth. Therefore his advice has, by the warrant of divine reason, become equivalent to nothing less than a divine command. Earnestly now inquire of this teacher, [397] keeping intact your regard for tradition, from whomsoever it originally sprang; nor have regard to the author, but to the authority, and especially that of custom itself, which on this very account we should revere, that we may not want an interpreter; so that if reason too is God's gift, you may then learn, not whether custom has to be followed by you, but why.

Chapter V

The argument for Christian practices becomes all the stronger, when also nature, which is the first rule of all, supports them. Well, she is the first who lays it down that a crown does not become the head. But I think ours is the God of nature, who fashioned man; and, that he might desire, (appreciate, become partaker of) the pleasures afforded by His creatures, endowed him with certain senses, (acting) through members, which, so to speak, are their peculiar instruments. The sense of hearing he has planted in the ears; that of sight, lighted up in the eyes; that of taste, shut up in the mouth; that of smell, wafted into the nose; that of touch, fixed in the tips of the fingers. By means of these organs of the outer man doing duty to the inner man, the enjoyments of the divine gifts are conveyed by the senses to the soul. [398] What, then, in flowers affords you enjoyment? For it is the flowers of the field which are the peculiar, at least the chief, material of crowns. Either smell, you say, or colour, or both together. What will be the senses of colour and smell? Those of seeing and smelling, I suppose. What members have had these senses allotted to them? The eyes and the nose, if I am not mistaken.

With sight and smell, then, make use of flowers, for these are the senses by which they are meant to be enjoyed; use them by means of the eyes and nose, which are the members to which these senses belong. You have got the thing from God, the mode of it from the world; but an extraordinary mode does not prevent the use of the thing in the common way. Let flowers, then, both when fastened into each other and tied together in thread and rush, be what they are when free, when loose--things to be looked at and smelt. You count it a crown, let us say, when you have a bunch of them bound together in a series, that you may carry many at one time that you may enjoy them all at once.

Well, lay them in your bosom if they are so singularly pure, and strew them on your couch if they are so exquisitely soft, and consign them to your cup if they are so perfectly harmless.

Have the pleasure of them in as many ways as they appeal to your senses. But what taste for a flower, what sense for anything belonging to a crown but its band, have you in the head, which is able neither to distinguish colour, nor to inhale sweet perfumes, nor to appreciate softness? It is as much against nature to long after a flower with the head, as it is to crave food with the ear, or sound with the nostril. But everything which is against nature deserves to be branded as monstrous among all men; but with us it is to be condemned also as sacrilege against God, the Lord and Creator of nature.

Chapter VI

Demanding then a law of God, you have that common one prevailing all over the world, engraven on the natural tables to which the apostle too is wont to appeal, as when in respect of the woman's veil he says, "Does not even Nature teach you?" [399] --as when to the Romans, affirming that the heathen do by nature those things which the law requires, [400] he suggests both natural law and a law-revealing nature. Yes, and also in the first chapter of the epistle he authenticates nature, when he asserts that males and females changed among themselves the natural use of the creature into that which is unnatural, [401] by way of penal retribution for their error.

We first of all indeed know God Himself by the teaching of Nature, calling Him God of gods, taking for granted that He is good, and invoking Him as Judge. Is it a question with you whether for the enjoyment of His creatures, Nature should be our guide, that we may not be carried away in the direction in which the rival of God has corrupted, along with man himself, the entire creation which had been made over to our race for certain uses, whence the apostle says that it too unwillingly became subject to vanity, completely bereft of its original character, first by vain, then by base, unrighteous, and ungodly uses? It is thus, accordingly, in the pleasures of the shows, that the creature is dishonoured by those who by nature indeed perceive that all the materials of which shows are got up belong to God, but lack the knowledge to perceive as well that they have all been changed by the devil. But with this topic we have, for the sake of our own play-lovers, sufficiently dealt, and that, too, in a work in Greek. [402]

Chapter VII

Let these dealers in crowns then recognize in the meantime the authority of Nature, on the ground of a common sense as human beings, and the certifications of their peculiar religion, as, according to the last chapter, worshippers of the God of nature; and, as it were, thus over and above what is required, let them consider those other reasons to which forbid us wearing crowns, especially on the head, and indeed crowns of every sort. For we are obliged to turn from the rule of Nature, which we share with mankind in general, that we may maintain the whole peculiarity of our Christian discipline, in relation also to other kinds of crowns which seem to have been provided for different uses, as being composed of different substances, lest, because they do not consist of flowers, the use of which nature has indicated (as it does in the case of this military laurel one itself), they may be thought not to come under the prohibition of our sect, since they have escaped any objections of nature. I see, then, that we must go into the matter both with more research, and more fully, from its beginnings on through its successive stages of growth to its more erratic developments. For this we need to turn to heathen literature, for things belonging to the heathen must be proved from their own documents. The little of this I have acquired, will, I believe, be enough.

If there really was a Pandora, whom Hesiod mentions as the first of women, hers was the first head the graces crowned, for she received gifts from all the gods whence she got her name Pandora. But Moses, a prophet, not a poet-shepherd, shows us the first woman Eve having her loins more naturally girt about with leaves than her temples with flowers.

Pandora, then, is a myth. And so we have to blush for the origin of the crown, even on the ground of the falsehood connected with it; and, as will soon appear, on the ground no less of its realities. For it is an undoubted fact that certain persons either originated the thing, or shed lustre on it. Pherecydes relates that Saturn was the first who wore a crown; Diodorus, that Jupiter, after conquering the Titans, was honoured with this gift by the rest of the gods. To Priapus also the same author assigns fillets; and to Ariadne a garland of gold and of Indian gems, the gift of Vulcan, afterwards of Bacchus, and subsequently turned into a constellation. Callimachus has put a vine crown upon Juno. So too at Argos, her statue, vine-wreathed, with a lion's skin placed beneath her feet, exhibits the stepmother exulting over the spoils of her two step-sons. Hercules displays upon his head sometimes poplar, sometimes wild-olive, sometimes parsley. You have the tragedy of Cerberus; you have Pindar; and besides Callimachus, who mentions that Apollo, too when he had killed the Delphic serpent, as a suppliant, put on a laurel garland; for among the ancients suppliants were wont to be crowned. Harpocration argues that Bacchus the same as Osiris among the Egyptians, was designedly crowned with ivy, because it is the nature of ivy to protect the brain against drowsiness. But that in another way also Bacchus was the originator of the laurel crown (the crown) in which he celebrated his triumph over the Indians, even the rabble acknowledge, when they call the days dedicated to him the "great crown." If you open, again, the writings of the Egyptian Leo, you learn that Isis was the first who discovered and wore ears of corn upon her head--a thing more suited to the belly. Those who want additional information will find an ample exposition of the subject in Claudius Saturninus, a writer of distinguished talent who treats this question also, for he has a book on crowns, so explaining their beginnings as well as causes, and kinds, and rites, that you find all that is charming in the flower, all that is beautiful in the leafy branch, and every sod or vine-shoot has been dedicated to some head or other; making it abundantly clear how foreign to us we should judge the custom of the crowned head, introduced as it was by, and thereafter constantly managed for the honour of, those whom the world has believed to be gods. If the devil, a liar from the beginning, is even in this matter working for his false system of godhead (idolatry), he had himself also without doubt provided for his god-lie being carried out. What sort of thing, then, must that be counted among the people of the true God, which was brought in by the nations in honour of the devil's candidates, and was set apart from the beginning to no other than these; and which even then received its consecration to idolatry by idols and in idols yet alive?

Not as if an idol were anything, but since the things which others offer up to idols belong to demons. But if the things which others offer to them belong to demons how much more what idols offered to themselves, when they were in life! The demons themselves, doubtless, had made provision for themselves by means of those whom they had possessed, while in a state of desire and craving, before provision had been actually made.

Chapter VIII

Hold fast in the meantime this persuasion, while I examine a question which comes in our way. For I already hear it is said, that many other things as well as crowns have been invented by those whom the world believes to be gods, and that they are notwithstanding to be met with both in our present usages and in those of early saints, and in the service of God, and in Christ Himself, who did His work as man by no other than these ordinary instrumentalities of human life. Well, let it be so; nor shall I inquire any further back into the origin of this things. Let Mercury have been the first who taught the knowledge of letters; I will own that they are requisite both for the business and commerce of life, and for performing our devotion to God. Nay, if he also first strung the chord to give forth melody, I will not deny, when listening to David, that this invention has been in use with the saints, and has ministered to God. Let Æsculapius have been the first who sought and discovered cures: Esaias [403] mentions that he ordered Hezekiah medicine when he was sick. Paul, too, knows that a little wine does the stomach good.[404] Let Minerva have been the first who built a ship: I shall see Jonah and the apostles sailing. Nay, there is more than this: for even Christ, we shall find, has ordinary raiment; Paul, too, has his cloak. [405] If at once, of every article of furniture and each household vessel, you name some god of the world as the originator, well, I must recognise Christ, both as He reclines on a couch, and when He presents a basin for the feet of His disciples, and when He pours water into it from a ewer, and when He is girt about with a linen towel [406] --a garment specially sacred to Osiris. It is thus in general I reply upon the point, admitting indeed that we use along with others these articles, but challenging that this be judged in the light of the distinction between things agreeable and things opposed to reason, because the promiscuous employment of them is deceptive, concealing the corruption of the creature, by which it has been made subject to vanity. For we affirm that those things only are proper to be used, whether by ourselves or by those who lived before us, and alone befit the service of God and Christ Himself, which to meet the necessities of human life supply what is simply; useful and affords real assistance and honourable comfort, so that they may be well believed to have come from God's own inspiration, who first of all no doubt provided for and taught and ministered to the enjoyment, I should suppose, of His own man. As for the things which are out of this class, they are not fit to be used among us, especially those which on that account indeed are not to be found either with the world, or in the ways of Christ.

Chapter IX

In short, what patriarch, what prophet, what Levite, or priest, or ruler, or at a later period what apostle, or preacher of the gospel, or bishop, do you ever find the wearer of a crown? [407] I think not even the temple of God itself was crowned; as neither was the ark of the testament, nor the tabernacle of witness, nor the altar, nor the candlestick crowned though certainly, both on that first solemnity of the dedication, and in that second rejoicing for the restoration, crowning would have been most suitable if it were worthy of God. But if these things were figures of us (for we are temples of God, and altars, and lights, and sacred vessels), this too they in figure set forth, that the people of God ought not to be crowned. The reality must always correspond with the image. If, perhaps, you object that Christ Himself was crowned, to that you will get the brief reply: Be you too crowned, as He was; you have full permission. Yet even that crown of insolent ungodliness was not of any decree of the Jewish people. It was a device of the Roman soldiers, taken from the practice of the world,--a practice which the people of God never allowed either on the occasion of public rejoicing or to gratify innate luxury: so they returned from the Babylonish captivity with timbrels, and flutes, and psalteries, more suitably than with crowns; and after eating and drinking, uncrowned, they rose up to play. Neither would the account of the rejoicing nor the exposure of the luxury have been silent touching the honour or dishonour of the crown. Thus too Isaiah, as he says, "With timbrels, and psalteries, and flutes they drink wine," [408] would have added "with crowns," if this practice had ever had place in the things of God.

Chapter X

So, when you allege that the ornaments of the heathen deities are found no less with God, with the object of claiming among these for general use the head-crown, you already lay it down for yourself, that we must not have among us, as a thing whose use we are to share with others, what is not to be found in the service of God. Well, what is so unworthy of God indeed as that which is worthy of an idol? But what is so worthy of an idol as that which is also worthy of a dead man? For it is the privilege of the dead also to be thus crowned, as they too straightway become idols, both by their dress and the service of deification, which (deification) is with us a second idolatry. Wanting, then, the sense, it will be theirs to use the thing for which the sense is wanting, just as if in full possession of the sense they wished to abuse it.

When there ceases to be any reality in the use, there is no distinction between using and abusing.

Who can abuse a thing, when the precipient nature with which he wishes to carry out his purpose is not his to use it? The apostle, moreover, forbids us to abuse, while he would more naturally have taught us not to use, unless on the ground that, where there is no sense for things, there is no wrong use of them.

But the whole affair is meaningless, and is, in fact, a dead work so far as concerns the idols; though, without doubt, a living one as respects the demons [409] to whom the religious rite belongs. "The idols of the heathen," says David, "are silver and gold." "They have eyes, and see not; a nose, and smell not; hands, and they will not handle." [410] By means of these organs, indeed, we are to enjoy flowers; but if he declares that those who make idols will be like them, they already are so who use anything after the style of idol adornings. "To the pure all things are pure: so, likewise, all things to the impure are impure;" [411] but nothing is more impure than idols.

The substances are themselves as creatures of God without impurity, and in this their native state are free to the use of all; but the ministries to which in their use they are devoted, makes all the difference; for I, too, kill a cock for myself, just as Socrates did for Æsculapius; and if the smell of some place or other offends me, I burn the Arabian product myself, but not with the same ceremony, nor in the same dress, nor with the same pomp, with which it is done to idols. [412] If the creature is defiled by a mere word, as the apostle teaches, "But if any one say, This is offered in sacrifice to idols, you must not touch it," [413] much more when it is polluted by the dress, and rites, and pomp of what is offered to the gods. Thus the crown also is made out to be an offering to idols; [414] for with this ceremony, and dress, and pomp, it is presented in sacrifice to idols, its originators, to whom its use is specially given over, and chiefly on this account, that what has no place among the things of God may not be admitted into use with us as with others.

Wherefore the apostle exclaims, "Flee idolatry:" [415] certainly idolatry whole and entire he means. Reflect on what a thicket it is, and how many thorns lie hid in it.

Nothing must be given to an idol, and so nothing must be taken from one. If it is inconsistent with faith to recline in an idol temple, what is it to appear in an idol dress? What communion have Christ and Belial? Therefore flee from it; for he enjoins us to keep at a distance from idolatry--to have no close dealings with it of any kind. Even an earthly serpent sucks in men at some distance with its breath.

Going still further, John says, "My little children, keep yourselves from idols," [416] --not now from idolatry, as if from the service of it, but from idols--that is, from any resemblance to them: for it is an unworthy thing that you, the image of the living God, should become the likeness of an idol and a dead man. Thus far we assert, that this attire belongs to idols, both from the history of its origin, and from its use by false religion; on this ground, besides, that while it is not mentioned as connected with the worship of God, it is more and more given over to those in whose antiquities, as well as festivals and services, it is found. In a word, the very doors, the very victims and altars, the very servants and priests, are crowned. You have, in Claudius, the crowns of all the various colleges of priests. We have added also that distinction between things altogether different from each other--things, namely, agreeable, and things contrary to reason--in answer to those who, because there happens to be the use of some things in common, maintain the right of participation in all things. With reference to this part of the subject, therefore, it now remains that the special grounds for wearing crowns should be examined, that while we show these to be foreign, nay, even opposed to our Christian discipline, we may demonstrate that none of them have any plea of reason to support it, on the basis of which this article of dress might be vindicated as one in whose use we can participate, as even some others may whose instances are cast up to us.

Chapter XI

To begin with the real ground of the military crown, I think we must first inquire whether warfare is proper at all for Christians. What sense is there in discussing the merely accidental, when that on which it rests is to be condemned? Do we believe it lawful for a human oath [417] to be superadded to one divine, for a man to come under promise to another master after Christ, and to abjure father, mother, and all nearest kinsfolk, whom even the law has commanded us to honour and love next to God Himself, to whom the gospel, too, holding them only of less account than Christ, has in like manner rendered honour? Shall it be held lawful to make an occupation of the sword, when the Lord proclaims that he who uses the sword shall perish by the sword?

And shall the son of peace take part in the battle when it does not become him even to sue at law? And shall he apply the chain, and the prison, and the torture, and the punishment, who is not the avenger even of his own wrongs?

Shall he, forsooth, either keep watch-service for others more than for Christ, or shall he do it on the Lord's day, when he does not even do it for Christ Himself? And shall he keep guard before the temples which he has renounced? And shall he take a meal where the apostle has forbidden him? [418] And shall he diligently protect by night those whom in the day-time he has put to flight by his exorcisms, leaning and resting on the spear the while with which Christ's side was pierced? Shall he carry a flag, [419] too, hostile to Christ? And shall he ask a watchword from the emperor who has already received one from God? Shall he be disturbed in death by the trumpet of the trumpeter, who expects to be aroused by the angel's trump? And shall the Christian be burned according to camp rule, when he was not permitted to burn incense to an idol, when to him Christ remitted the punishment of fire?

Then how many other offences there are involved in the performances of camp offices, which we must hold to involve a transgression of God's law, you may see by a slight survey. The very carrying of the name over from the camp of light to the camp of darkness is a violation of it. Of course, if faith comes later, and finds any preoccupied with military service, their case is different, as in the instance of those whom John used to receive for baptism, and of those most faithful centurions, I mean the centurion whom Christ approves, and the centurion whom Peter instructs; yet, at the same time, when a man has become a believer, and faith has been sealed, there must be either an immediate abandonment of it, which has been the course with many; or all sorts of quibbling will have to be resorted to in order to avoid offending God, and that is not allowed even outside of military service; [420] or, last of all, for God the fate must be endured which a citizen-faith has been no less ready to accept. Neither does military service hold out escape from punishment of sins, or exemption from martyrdom. Nowhere does the Christian change his character. There is one gospel, and the same Jesus, who will one day deny every one who denies, and acknowledge every one who acknowledges God,--who will save, too, the life which has been lost for His sake; but, on the other hand, destroy that which for gain has been saved to His dishonour. With Him the faithful citizen is a soldier, just as the faithful soldier is a citizen. [421] A state of faith admits no plea of necessity; they are under no necessity to sin, whose one necessity is, that they do not sin. For if one is pressed to the offering of sacrifice and the sheer denial of Christ by the necessity of torture or of punishment, yet discipline does not connive even at that necessity; because there is a higher necessity to dread denying and to undergo martyrdom, than to escape from suffering, and to render the homage required. In fact, an excuse of this sort overturns the entire essence of our sacrament, removing even the obstacle to voluntary sins; for it will be possible also to maintain that inclination is a necessity, as involving in it, forsooth, a sort of compulsion. I have, in fact, disposed of this very allegation of necessity with reference to the pleas by which crowns connected with official position are vindicated, in support of which it is in common use, since for this very reason offices must be either refused, that we may not fall into acts of sin, or martyrdoms endured that we may get quit of offices. Touching this primary aspect of the question, as to the unlawfulness even of a military life itself, I shall not add more, that the secondary question may be restored to its place. Indeed, if, putting my strength to the question, I banish from us the military life, I should now to no purpose issue a challenge on the matter of the military crown. Suppose, then, that the military service is lawful, as far as the plea for the crown is concerned. [422]

Chapter XII

But I first say a word also about the crown itself. This laurel one is sacred to Apollo or Bacchus--to the former as the god of archery, to the latter as the god of triumphs. In like manner Claudius teaches; when he tells us that soldiers are wont too to be wreathed in myrtle. For the myrtle belongs to Venus, the mother of the Æneadæ, the mistress also of the god of war, who, through Ilia and the Romuli is Roman.

But I do not believe that Venus is Roman as well as Mars, because of the vexation the concubine gave her. [423] When military service again is crowned with olive, the idolatry has respect to Minerva, who is equally the goddess of arms--but got a crown of the tree referred to, because of the peace she made with Neptune. In these respects, the superstition of the military garland will be everywhere defiled and all-defiling. And it is further defiled, I should think, also in the grounds of it. Lo the yearly public pronouncing of vows, what does that bear on its face to be?

It takes place first in the part of the camp where the general's tent is, and then in the temples. In addition to the places, observe the words also:

"We vow that you, O Jupiter, will then have an ox with gold-decorated horns." What does the utterance mean? Without a doubt the denial (of Christ). Albeit the Christian says nothing in these places with the mouth, he makes his response by having the crown on his head. The laurel is likewise commanded (to be used) at the distribution of the largess. So you see idolatry is not without its gain, selling, as it does, Christ for pieces of gold, as Judas did for pieces of silver. Will it be "Ye cannot serve God and mammon" [424] to devote your energies to mammon, and to depart from God? Will it be "Render unto Cæsar the things which are Cæsar's, and unto God the things which are God's," [425] not only not to render the human being to God, but even to take the denarius from Cæsar? Is the laurel of the triumph made of leaves, or of corpses? Is it adorned with ribbons, or with tombs? Is it bedewed with ointments, or with the tears of wives and mothers? It may be of some Christians too; [426] for Christ is also among the barbarians. [427] Has not he who has carried (a crown for) this cause on his head, fought even against himself?

Another son of service belongs to the royal guards. And indeed crowns are called (Castrenses), as belonging to the camp; Munificæ likewise, from the Cæsarean functions they perform. But even then you are still the soldier and the servant of another; and if of two masters, of God and Cæsar: but assuredly then not of Cæsar, when you owe yourself to God, as having higher claims, I should think, even in matters in which both have an interest.

Chapter XIII

For state reasons, the various orders of the citizens also are crowned with laurel crowns; but the magistrates besides with golden ones, as at Athens, and at Rome. Even to those are preferred the Etruscan. This appellation is given to the crowns which, distinguished by their gems and oak leaves of gold, they put on, with mantles having an embroidery of palm branches, to conduct the chariots containing the images of the gods to the circus. There are also provincial crowns of gold, needing now the larger heads of images instead of those of men. But your orders, and your magistracies, and your very place of meeting, the church, are Christ's. You belong to Him, for you have been enrolled in the books of life. [428] There the blood of the Lord serves for your purple robe, and your broad stripe is His own cross; there the axe is already laid to the trunk of the tree; [429] there is the branch out of the root of Jesse. [430] Never mind the state horses with their crown. Your Lord, when, according to the Scripture, He would enter Jerusalem in triumph, had not even an ass of His own. These (put their trust) in chariots, and these in horses; but we will seek our help in the name of the Lord our God. [431] From so much as a dwelling in that Babylon of John's Revelation [432] we are called away; much more then from its pomp. The rabble, too, are crowned, at one time because of some great rejoicing for the success of the emperors; at another, on account of some custom belonging to municipal festivals. For luxury strives to make her own every occasion of public gladness. But as for you, you are a foreigner in this world, a citizen of Jerusalem, the city above. Our citizenship, the apostle says, is in heaven. [433] You have your own registers, your own calendar; you have nothing to do with the joys of the world; nay, you are called to the very opposite, for "the world shall rejoice, but ye shall mourn." [434] And I think the Lord affirms, that those who mourn are happy, not those who are crowned.

Marriage, too, decks the bridegroom with its crown; and therefore we will not have heathen brides, lest they seduce us even to the idolatry with which among them marriage is initiated.

You have the law from the patriarchs indeed; you have the apostle enjoining people to marry in the Lord. [435] You have a crowning also on the making of a freeman; but you have been already ransomed by Christ, and that at a great price.

How shall the world manumit the servant of another? Though it seems to be liberty, yet it will come to be found bondage. In the world everything is nominal, and nothing real.

For even then, as ransomed by Christ, you were under no bondage to man; and now, though man has given you liberty, you are the servant of Christ. If you think freedom of the world to be real, so that you even seal it with a crown, you have returned to the slavery of man, imagining it to be freedom; you have lost the freedom of Christ, fancying it is slavery. Will there be any dispute as to the cause of crown-wearing, which contests in the games in their turn supply, and which, both as sacred to the gods and in honour of the dead, their own reason at once condemns? It only remains, that the Olympian Jupiter, and the Nemean Hercules, and the wretched little Archemorus, and the hapless Antinous, should be crowned in a Christian, that he himself may become a spectacle disgusting to behold. We have recounted, as I think, all the various causes of the wearing of the crown, and there is not one which has any place with us: all are foreign to us, unholy, unlawful, having been abjured already once for all in the solemn declaration of the sacrament. For they were of the pomp of the devil and his angels, offices of the world, [436] honours, festivals, popularity huntings, false vows, exhibitions of human servility, empty praises, base glories, and in them all idolatry, even in respect of the origin of the crowns alone, with which they are all wreathed. Claudius will tell us in his preface, indeed, that in the poems of Homer the heaven also is crowned with constellations, and that no doubt by God, no doubt for man; therefore man himself, too, should be crowned by God.

But the world crowns brothels, and baths, and bakehouses, and prisons, and schools, and the very amphitheatres, and the chambers where the clothes are stripped from dead gladiators, and the very biers of the dead. How sacred and holy, how venerable and pure is this article of dress, determine not from the heaven of poetry alone, but from the traffickings of the whole world.

But indeed a Christian will not even dishonour his own gate with laurel crowns, if so be he knows how many gods the devil has attached to doors; Janus so-called from gate, Limentinus from threshold, Forcus and Carna from leaves and hinges; among the Greeks, too, the Thyræan Apollo, and the evil spirits, the Antelii.

Chapter XIV

Much less may the Christian put the service of idolatry on his own head--nay, I might have said, upon Christ, since Christ is the Head of the Christian man--(for his head) is as free as even Christ is, under no obligation to wear a covering, not to say a band. But even the head which is bound to have the veil, I mean woman's, as already taken possession of by this very thing, is not open also to a band. She has the burden of her own humility to bear. If she ought not to appear with her head uncovered on account of the angels, [437] much more with a crown on it will she offend those (elders) who perhaps are then wearing crowns above. [438] For what is a crown on the head of a woman, but beauty made seductive, but mark of utter wantonness,--a notable casting away of modesty, a setting temptation on fire?

Therefore a woman, taking counsel from the apostles' foresight, [439] will not too elaborately adorn herself, that she may not either be crowned with any exquisite arrangement of her hair.

What sort of garland, however, I pray you, did He who is the Head of the man and the glory of the woman, Christ Jesus, the Husband of the church, submit to in behalf of both sexes? Of thorns, I think, and thistles,--a figure of the sins which the soil of the flesh brought forth for us, but which the power of the cross removed, blunting, in its endurance by the head of our Lord, death's every sting. Yes, and besides the figure, there is contumely with ready lip, and dishonour, and infamy, and the ferocity involved in the cruel things which then disfigured and lacerated the temples of the Lord, that you may now be crowned with laurel, and myrtle, and olive, and any famous branch, and which is of more use, with hundred-leaved roses too, culled from the garden of Midas, and with both kinds of lily, and with violets of all sorts, perhaps also with gems and gold, so as even to rival that crown of Christ which He afterwards obtained. For it was after the gall He tasted the honeycomb [440] and He was not greeted as King of Glory in heavenly places till He had been condemned to the cross as King of the Jews, having first been made by the Father for a time a little less than the angels, and so crowned with glory and honour. If for these things, you owe your own head to Him, repay it if you can, such as He presented His for yours; or be not crowned with flowers at all, if you cannot be with thorns, because you may not be with flowers.

Chapter XV

Keep for God His own property untainted; He will crown it if He choose. Nay, then, He does even choose. He calls us to it. To him who conquers He says, "I will give a crown of life." [441] Be you, too, faithful unto death, and fight you, too, the good fight, whose crown the apostle [442] feels so justly confident has been laid up for him. The angel [443] also, as he goes forth on a white horse, conquering and to conquer, receives a crown of victory; and another [444] is adorned with an encircling rainbow (as it were in its fair colours)--a celestial meadow. In like manner, the elders sit crowned around, crowned too with a crown of gold, and the Son of Man Himself flashes out above the clouds. If such are the appearances in the vision of the seer, of what sort will be the realities in the actual manifestation?

Look at those crowns. Inhale those odours. Why condemn you to a little chaplet, or a twisted headband, the brow which has been destined for a diadem? For Christ Jesus has made us even kings to God and His Father. What have you in common with the flower which is to die? You have a flower in the Branch of Jesse, upon which the grace of the Divine Spirit in all its fulness rested--a flower undefiled, unfading, everlasting, by choosing which the good soldier, too, has got promotion in the heavenly ranks. Blush, ye fellow-soldiers of his, henceforth not to be condemned even by him, but by some soldier of Mithras, who, at his initiation in the gloomy cavern, in the camp, it may well be said, of darkness, when at the sword's point a crown is presented to him, as though in mimicry of martyrdom, and thereupon put upon his head, is admonished to resist and cast it off, and, if you like, transfer it to his shoulder, saying that Mithras is his crown. And thenceforth he is never crowned; and he has that for a mark to show who he is, if anywhere he be subjected to trial in respect of his religion; and he is at once believed to be a soldier of Mithras if he throws the crown away--if he say that in his god he has his crown. Let us take note of the devices of the devil, who is wont to ape some of God's things with no other design than, by the faithfulness of his servants, to put us to shame, and to condemn us.

Elucidations

I.
(Usages)

Here a reference to Bunsen's Hippolytus, vol. III., so often referred to in the former volume, will be useful. A slight metaphrase will bring out the sense, perhaps, of this most interesting portrait of early Christian usages.

In baptism, we use trine immersion, in honour of the trinal Name, after renouncing the devil and

Tertullian

his angels and the pomps and vanities of his kingdom. [445] But this trinal rite is a ceremonial amplification of what is actually commanded.

It was heretofore tolerated in some places that communicants should take each one his portion, with his own hand, but now we suffer none to receive this sacrament except at the hand of the minister.

By our Lord's own precept and example, it may be received at the hour of ordinary meals, and alike by all the faithful whether men or women, yet we usually do this in our gatherings before daybreak. Offerings are made in honour of our departed friends, on the anniversaries of their deaths, which we esteem their true birthdays, as they are born to a better life.

We kneel at other times, but on the Lord's day, and from the Paschal Feast to Pentecost we stand in prayer, nor do we count it lawful to fast on Sundays. We are concerned if even a particle of the wine or bread, made ours, in the Lord's Supper, falls to the ground, by our carelessness. In all the ordinary occasions of life we furrow our foreheads with the sign of the Cross, in which we glory none the less because it is regarded as our shame by the heathen in presence of whom it is a profession of our faith.

He owns there is no Scripture for any of these usages, in which there was an amplifying of the precepts of Christ. Let us note there was yet no superstitious usage even of this sign of the Cross. It was an act by which, in suffering "shame for Jesus' name," they fortified themselves against betraying the Master. It took the place, be it remembered, of innumerable heathen practices, and was a protest against them.

It meant--"God forbid that I should glory, save in the Cross." I express no personal opinion as to this observance, but give the explanation which the early Christians would have given. Tertullian touched with Montanism, but not yet withdrawn from Catholic Communion, pleads the common cause of believers.

II.
(Traditions, cap. iv)

The traditions here argued for respect things in their nature indifferent.

And as our author asserts the long continuance of such usages to be their chief justification, it is evident that he supposed them common from the Sub-apostolic age. There is nothing here to justify amplifications and traditions which, subsequently, came in like a flood to change principles of the Faith once delivered to the Saints.

Even in his little plea for Montanistic revelations of some possible novelties, he pre-supposes that reason must be subject to Scripture and Apostolic Law.

In a word, his own principle of "Prescription" must be honoured even in things indifferent; if novel they are not Catholic.

Footnotes:

380. [Kaye, apparently accepting the judgment of Dr. Neander, assigns this treatise to a.d. 204. The bounty here spoken of, then, must be that dispensed in honour of the victories over the Parthians, under Severus.]

381. "Emperors." The Emperor Severus associated his two sons with him in the possession of the imperial power; Caracalla in the year 198, Geta in 208.--Tr.

382. [A touch of our author's genius, inspired by the Phrygian enthusiasm for martyrdom. The ground on which a martyr treads begins to be holy, even before the sacrifice, and in loosing his shoe the victim consecrates the spot and at the same time pays it homage.]

383. [The name of Christ: and the Antiochian name of Christians.]

384. [Gibbon will have it that the De Corona was written while Tertullian was orthodox, but this reference to the Montanist notion of "New Prophecy" seems to justify the decision of critics against Gibbon, who, as Kaye suggests (p. 53) was anxious to make Christianity itself responsible for military insubordination and for offences against Imperial Law.]

385. [Kaye (p. 231) notes this as a rare instance of classing Catechumens among "the Faithful."]

386. [This is said not absolutely but in contrast with extreme license; but it shows the Supremacy of Scripture. Compare De Monogam, cap. 4.]

387. [Elucidation I., and see Bunsen's Church and House Book, pp. 19-24.]

388. [There is here an allusion to the Roman form of recognizing a lawful child. The father, taking up the new-born infant, gave him adoption into the family, and recognised him as a legitimate son and heir.]

389. [Men and women, rich and poor.]

390. i.e., of the Cross.

391. Vulgate, Dan. xiii. 32. [See Apocrypha, Hist. of Susanna, v. 32.]

392. [Observe it must (1.) be based on Apostolic grounds; (2.) must not be a novelty, but derived from a time "to which the memory of men runneth not contrary."]

393. [I slightly amend the translation to bring out the force of an objection to which our author gives a Montanistic reply.]

394. Luke xii. 27.
395. Phil. iii. 15.
396. [See luminous remarks in Kaye, pp. 371-373.]
397. [This teacher, i.e., right reason, under the guidance of the Holy Ghost.

He is here foisting in a plea for the "New Prophecy," apparently, and this is one of the most decided instances in the treatise.]
398. Kaye [p. 187,] has some valuable remarks on this testimony to the senses in Christian Philosophy, and compares Cicero, I. Tusc. cap. xx. or xlvi.]
399. 1 Cor. xi. 14.
400. Rom. ii. 14.
401. Rom. i. 26.
402. [Plays were regarded as pomps renounced in Baptism.]
403. Isa. xxxviii. 21.
404. 1 Tim. v. 23.
405. 2 Tim. iv. 13. [This is a useful comment as showing what this φαιλόνη was. Our author translates it by pænula. Of which more when we reach the De Pallio.]
406. John xiii. 1-5.
407. [But see Eusebius, Hist. B. v., cap. 24, whose story is examined by Lardner, Cred., vol. iv., p. 448.]
408. Isa. v. 12.
409. [Compare De Idololatria, cap. xv., p. 70, supra.]
410. Ps. cxv. 4-8.
411. Tit. i. 15.
412. [He seems to know no use for incense except for burials and for fumigation.]
413. 1 Cor. x. 28.
414. [Kaye (p. 362) defends our author against Barbeyrac's animadversions, by the maxim, "put yourself in his place" i.e. among the abominations of Paganism.]
415. 1 Cor. x. 14.
416. 1 John v. 21.
417. [He plays on this word Sacramentum. Is the military sacrament to be added to the Lord's?]
418. 1 Cor. viii. 10.
419. [Vexillum. Such words as these prepared for the Labarum.]
420. "Outside of the military service." By substituting ex militia for the corresponding words extra militiam, as has been proposed by Rigaltius, the sentence acquires a meaning such that desertion from the army is suggested as one of the methods by which a soldier who has become a Christian may continue faithful to Jesus. But the words extra militiam are a genuine part of the text. There is no good ground, therefore, for the statement of Gibbon:

"Tertullian (de Corona Militis, c. xi.) suggests to them the expedient of deserting; a counsel which, if it had been generally known, was not very proper to conciliate the favour of the emperors toward the Christian sect."--Tr.
421. "The faithful," etc.; i.e., the kind of occupation which any one has cannot be pleaded by him as a reason for not doing all that Christ has enjoined upon His people.--Tr.
422. [He was not yet quite a Montanist.]
423. i.e., Ilia.
424. Matt. vi. 24.
425. Matt. xxii. 21.
426. [Such considerations may account for our author's abandonment of what he says in the Apology; which compare in capp. xlii. and xxxix.]
427. [Et apud barbaros enim Christus. See Kaye's argument, p. 87.]
428. Phil. iv. 3.
429. Matt. iii. 10.
430. Isa. xi. 1.
431. Ps. xx. 7.
432. Rev. xviii. 4. [He understands this of Rome.]
433. Phil. iii. 20.
434. John xvi. 20.
435. 1 Cor. vii. 39.
436. [A suggestive interpretation of the baptismal vow, of which see Bunsen, Hippol., Vol. III., p. 20.]
437. 1 Cor. xi. 10. [Does he here play on the use of the word angels in the Revelation? He seems to make it = elders.]
438. Rev. iv. 4.
439. 1 Tim. ii. 9; 1 Pet. iii. 3.
440. [A very striking collocation of Matt. xxvii. 34, and Luke xxiv. 42.]
441. Rev. ii. 10; Jas. i. 22.
442. 2 Tim. iv. 8.
443. Rev. vi. 2.
444. Rev. x. 1.
445. See Kaye, pp. 408-415.

V – To Scapula [446]

[Translated by the Rev. S. Thelwall.]

Chapter I

We are not in any great perturbation or alarm about the persecutions we suffer from the ignorance of men; for we have attached ourselves to this sect, fully accepting the terms of its covenant, so that, as men whose very lives are not their own, we engage in these conflicts, our desire being to obtain God's promised rewards, and our dread lest the woes with which He threatens an unchristian life should overtake us. Hence we shrink not from the grapple with your utmost rage, coming even forth of our own accord to the contest; and condemnation gives us more pleasure than acquittal. We have sent, therefore, this tract to you in no alarm about ourselves, but in much concern for you and for all our enemies, to say nothing of our friends. For our religion commands us to love even our enemies, and to pray for those who persecute us, aiming at a perfection all its own, and seeking in its disciples something of a higher type than the commonplace goodness of the world. For all love those who love them; it is peculiar to Christians alone to love those that hate them. Therefore mourning over your ignorance, and compassionating human error, and looking on to that future of which every day shows threatening signs, necessity is laid on us to come forth in this way also, that we may set before you the truths you will not listen to openly.

Chapter II

We are worshippers of one God, of whose existence and character Nature teaches all men; at whose lightnings and thunders you tremble, whose benefits minister to your happiness. You think that others, too, are gods, whom we know to be devils.

However, it is a fundamental human right, a privilege of nature, that every man should worship according to his own convictions: one man's religion neither harms nor helps another man. It is assuredly no part of religion to compel religion--to which free-will and not force should lead us--the sacrificial victims even being required of a willing mind. You will render no real service to your gods by compelling us to sacrifice. For they can have no desire of offerings from the unwilling, unless they are animated by a spirit of contention, which is a thing altogether undivine. Accordingly the true God bestows His blessings alike on wicked men and on His own elect; upon which account He has appointed an eternal judgment, when both thankful and unthankful will have to stand before His bar. Yet you have never detected us--sacrilegious wretches though you reckon us to be--in any theft, far less in any sacrilege. But the robbers of your temples, all of them swear by your gods, and worship them; they are not Christians, and yet it is they who are found guilty of sacrilegious deeds. We have not time to unfold in how many other ways your gods are mocked and despised by their own votaries. So, too, treason is falsely laid to our charge, though no one has ever been able to find followers of Albinus, or Niger, or Cassius, among Christians; while the very men who had sworn by the genii of the emperors, who had offered and vowed sacrifices for their safety, who had often pronounced condemnation on Christ's disciples, are till this day found traitors to the imperial throne. A Christian is enemy to none, least of all to the Emperor of Rome, whom he knows to be appointed by his God, and so cannot but love and honour; and whose well-being moreover, he must needs desire, with that of the empire over which he reigns so long as the world shall stand--for so long as that shall Rome continue. [447] To the emperor, therefore, we render such reverential homage as is lawful for us and good for him; regarding him as the human being next to God who from God has received all his power, and is less than God alone. And this will be according to his own desires. For thus--as less only than the true God--he is greater than all besides. Thus he is greater than the very gods themselves, even they, too, being subject to him. We therefore sacrifice for the emperor's safety, but to our God and his, and after the manner God has enjoined, in simple prayer. For God, Creator of the universe, has no need of odours or of blood. These things are the food of devils. [448] But we not only reject those wicked spirits: we overcome them; we daily hold them up to contempt; we exorcise them from their victims, as multitudes can testify. So all the more we pray for the imperial well-being, as those who seek it at the hands of Him who is able to bestow it. And one would think it must be abundantly clear to you that the religious system under whose rules we act is one inculcating a divine patience; since, though our numbers are so great--constituting all but the majority in every city--we conduct ourselves so quietly and modestly; I might perhaps say, known rather as individuals than as organized communities, and remarkable only for the reformation of our former vices. For far be it from us to take it ill that we have laid on us the very things we wish, or in any way plot the vengeance at our own hands, which we expect to come from God.

Chapter III

However, as we have already remarked, it cannot but distress us that no state shall bear unpunished the guilt of shedding Christian blood; as you see, indeed, in what took place during the presidency of Hilarian, for when there had been some agitation about places of sepulture for our dead, and the cry arose, "No areæ--no burial-grounds for the Christians," it came that their own areæ,[449] their threshing-floors, were a-wanting, for they gathered in no harvests. As to the rains of the bygone year, it is abundantly plain of what they were intended to remind men--of the deluge, no doubt, which in ancient times overtook human unbelief and wickedness; and as to the fires which lately hung all night over the walls of Carthage, they who saw them know what they threatened; and what the preceding thunders pealed, they who were hardened by them can tell. All these things are signs of God's impending wrath, which we must needs publish and proclaim in every possible way; and in the meanwhile we must pray it may be only local. Sure are they to experience it one day in its universal and final form, who interpret otherwise these samples of it. That sun, too, in the metropolis of Utica,[450] with light all but extinguished, was a portent which could not have occurred from an ordinary eclipse, situated as the lord of day was in his height and house. You have the astrologers, consult them about it. We can point you also to the deaths of some provincial rulers, who in their last hours had painful memories of their sin in persecuting the followers of Christ.[451] Vigellius Saturninus, who first here used the sword against us, lost his eyesight.

Claudius Lucius Herminianus in Cappadocia, enraged that his wife had become a Christian, had treated the Christians with great cruelty: well, left alone in his palace, suffering under a contagious malady, he boiled out in living worms, and was heard exclaiming, "Let nobody know of it, lest the Christians rejoice, and Christian wives take encouragement." Afterwards he came to see his error in having tempted so many from their stedfastness by the tortures he inflicted, and died almost a Christian himself. In that doom which overtook Byzantium,[452] Cæcilius Capella could not help crying out, "Christians, rejoice!" Yes, and the persecutors who seem to themselves to have acted with impunity shall not escape the day of judgment. For you we sincerely wish it may prove to have been a warning only, that, immediately after you had condemned Mavilus of Adrumetum to the wild beasts, you were overtaken by those troubles, and that even now for the same reason you are called to a blood-reckoning. But do not forget the future.

Chapter IV

We who are without fear ourselves are not seeking to frighten you, but we would save all men if possible by warning them not to fight with God.[453] You may perform the duties of your charge, and yet remember the claims of humanity; if on no other ground than that you are liable to punishment yourself, (you ought to do so). For is not your commission simply to condemn those who confess their guilt, and to give over to the torture those who deny? You see, then, how you trespass yourselves against your instructions to wring from the confessing a denial. It is, in fact, an acknowledgment of our innocence that you refuse to condemn us at once when we confess. In doing your utmost to extirpate us, if that is your object, it is innocence you assail.

But how many rulers, men more resolute and more cruel than you are, have contrived to get quit of such causes altogether,--as Cincius Severus, who himself suggested the remedy at Thysdris, pointing out how the Christians should answer that they might secure an acquittal; as Vespronius Candidus, who dismissed from his bar a Christian, on the ground that to satisfy his fellow-citizens would break the peace of the community; as Asper, who, in the case of a man who gave up his faith under slight infliction of the torture, did not compel the offering of sacrifice, having owned before, among the advocates and assessors of court, that he was annoyed at having had to meddle with such a case. Pudens, too, at once dismissed a Christian who was brought before him, perceiving from the indictment that it was a case of vexatious accusation; tearing the document in pieces, he refused so much as to hear him without the presence of his accuser, as not being consistent with the imperial commands.

All this might be officially brought under your notice, and by the very advocates, who are themselves also under obligations to us, although in court they give their voice as it suits them.

The clerk of one of them who was liable to be thrown upon the ground by an evil spirit, was set free from his affliction; as was also the relative of another, and the little boy of a third.

How many men of rank (to say nothing of common people) have been delivered from devils, and healed of diseases!

Even Severus himself, the father of Antonine, was graciously mindful of the Christians; for he sought out the Christian Proculus, surnamed Torpacion, the steward of Euhodias, and in gratitude for his having once cured him by anointing, he kept him in his palace till the day of his death. [454] Antonine, too, brought up as he was on Christian milk, was intimately acquainted with this man. Both women and men of highest rank, whom Severus knew well to be Christians, were not merely permitted by him to remain uninjured; but he even bore distinguished testimony in their favour, and gave them publicly back to us from the hands of a raging populace. Marcus Aurelius also, in his expedition to Germany, by the prayers his Christian soldiers offered to God, got rain in that well-known thirst. [455] When, indeed, have not droughts been put away by our kneelings and our fastings? At times like these, moreover, the people crying to "the God of gods, the alone Omnipotent," under the name of Jupiter, have borne witness to our God. Then we never deny the deposit placed in our hands; we never pollute the marriage bed; we deal faithfully with our wards; we give aid to the needy; we render to none evil for evil. As for those who falsely pretend to belong to us, and whom we, too, repudiate, let them answer for themselves. In a word, who has complaint to make against us on other grounds? To what else does the Christian devote himself, save the affairs of his own community, which during all the long period of its existence no one has ever proved guilty of the incest or the cruelty charged against it?

It is for freedom from crime so singular, for a probity so great, for righteousness, for purity, for faithfulness, for truth, for the living God, that we are consigned to the flames; for this is a punishment you are not wont to inflict either on the sacrilegious, or on undoubted public enemies, or on the treason-tainted, of whom you have so many.

Nay, even now our people are enduring persecution from the governors of Legio and Mauritania; but it is only with the sword, as from the first it was ordained that we should suffer. But the greater our conflicts, the greater our rewards.

Chapter V

Your cruelty is our glory. Only see you to it, that in having such things as these to endure, we do not feel ourselves constrained to rush forth to the combat, if only to prove that we have no dread of them, but on the contrary, even invite their infliction.

When Arrius Antoninus was driving things hard in Asia, the whole Christians of the province, in one united band, presented themselves before his judgment-seat; on which, ordering a few to be led forth to execution, he said to the rest, "O miserable men, if you wish to die, you have precipices or halters." If we should take it into our heads to do the same thing here, what will you make of so many thousands, of such a multitude of men and women, persons of every sex and every age and every rank, when they present themselves before you?

How many fires, how many swords will be required? What will be the anguish of Carthage itself, which you will have to decimate, [456] as each one recognises there his relatives and companions, as he sees there it may be men of your own order, and noble ladies, and all the leading persons of the city, and either kinsmen or friends of those of your own circle? Spare thyself, if not us poor Christians! Spare Carthage, if not thyself! Spare the province, which the indication of your purpose has subjected to the threats and extortions at once of the soldiers and of private enemies.

We have no master but God. He is before you, and cannot be hidden from you, but to Him you can do no injury. But those whom you regard as masters are only men, and one day they themselves must die. Yet still this community will be undying, for be assured that just in the time of its seeming overthrow it is built up into greater power. For all who witness the noble patience of its martyrs, as struck with misgivings, are inflamed with desire to examine into the matter in question;[457] and as soon as they come to know the truth, they straightway enrol themselves its disciples.

Elucidations

I.
(Scapula, cap. i)

Scapula was Proconsul of Carthage, and though its date is conjectural (a.d. 217), this work gives valuable indices of its time and circumstances. It was composed after the death of Severus, to whom there is an allusion in chapter iv., after the destruction of Byzantium (a.d. 196), to which there is a reference in chapter iii.; and Dr. Allix suggests, after the dark day of Utica (a.d. 210) which he supposes to be referred to in the same chapter. Cincius Severus, who is mentioned in chapter iv., was put to death by Severus, a.d. 198.

II.
(Caractacus, cap. ii., note 2)

Mr. Lewin (St. Paul, ii. 397), building on the fascinating theory of Archdeacon Williams, thinks St. Paul's Claudia (Qu. Gladys?) may very well have been the daughter of Caradoc, with whose noble character we are made acquainted by Tacitus. (Annals xii. 36.) And Archdeacon Williams gives us very strong reason to believe he was a Christian. He may very well have lived to behold the Coliseum completed. What more natural then, in view of the cruelty against Christians there exercised, for the expressions with which he is credited? In this case his words contain an eloquent ambiguity, which Christians would appreciate, and which may have been in our author's mind when he says--"quousque sæculum stabit." To those who looked for the Second Advent, daily, this did not mean what the heathen might suppose.

Bede's version of the speech (See Du Cange, II., 407.,) is this: "Quandiu stabit Colyseus--stabit et Roma: Quando cadet Colysevs--cadet et Roma: Quando cadet Roma--cadet et mundus."

Footnotes:

446. [See Elucidation I. Written late in our author's life, this tract contains no trace of Montanism, and shows that his heart was with the common cause of all Christians. Who can give up such an Ephraim without recalling the words of inspired love for the erring?-- Jer. xxxi. 20; Hos. xi. 8.]

447. [Kaye points out our author's inconsistencies on this matter.

If Caractacus ever made the speech ascribed to him (Bede, or Gibbon, cap. lxxi.) it would confirm the opinion of those who make him a convert to Christ: "Quando cadet Roma, cadet et mundus." Elucidation II.]

448. [On this sort of Demonology see Kaye, pp. 203-207, with his useful references. See De Spectaculis, p. 80, supra.]

449. [An obvious play on the ambiguity of this word.]

450. [Notes of the time when this was written. See Kaye, p. 57.]

451. [Christians remembered Herod (Acts xii. 23) very naturally; but we may reserve remarks on such instances till we come to Lactantius. But see Kaye (p. 102) who speaks unfavourably of them.]

452. [Notes of the time when this was written. See Kaye, p. 57.]

453. [Our author uses the Greek (μὴ θεομαχεῖν) but not textually of Acts v. 39.]

454. [Another note of time. a.d. 211. See Kaye, as before.]

455. [Compare Vol. I., p. 187, this Series.]

456. [Compare De Fuga, cap. xii.

It is incredible that our author could exaggerate in speaking to the chief magistrate of Carthage.]

457. [Mosheim's strange oversight, in neglecting to include such considerations, in accounting for the growth of the church, is justly censured by Kaye, p. 124.]

VI – Ad Nationes [458]

Book I
[Translated by Dr. Holmes.]

Chapter I [459] - The Hatred Felt by the Heathen Against the Christians is Unjust, Because Based on Culpable Ignorance

One proof of that ignorance of yours, which condemns [460] whilst it excuses [461] your injustice, is at once apparent in the fact, that all who once shared in your ignorance and hatred (of the Christian religion), as soon as they have come to know it, leave off their hatred when they cease to be ignorant; nay more, they actually themselves become what they had hated, and take to hating what they had once been. Day after day, indeed, you groan over the increasing number of the Christians. Your constant cry is, that the state is beset (by us); that Christians are in your fields, in your camps, in your islands. You grieve over it as a calamity, that each sex, every age--in short, every rank--is passing over from you to us; yet you do not even after this set your minds upon reflecting whether there be not here some latent good.

You do not allow yourselves in suspicions which may prove too true, [462] nor do you like ventures which may be too near the mark. [463] This is the only instance in which human curiosity grows torpid. You love to be ignorant of what other men rejoice to have discovered; you would rather not know it, because you now cherish your hatred as if you were aware that, (with the knowledge,) your hatred would certainly come to an end. Still, [464] if there shall be no just ground for hatred, it will surely be found to be the best course to cease from the past injustice.

Should, however, a cause have really existed there will be no diminution of the hatred, which will indeed accumulate so much the more in the consciousness of its justice; unless it be, forsooth,[465] that you are ashamed to cast off your faults, [466] or sorry to free yourselves from blame. [467] I know very well with what answer you usually meet the argument from our rapid increase. [468] That indeed must not, you say, be hastily accounted a good thing which converts a great number of persons, and gains them over to its side. I am aware how the mind is apt to take to evil courses. How many there are which forsake virtuous living!

How many seek refuge in the opposite!

Many, no doubt; [469] nay, very many, as the last days approach. [470] But such a comparison as this fails in fairness of application; for all are agreed in thinking thus of the evil-doer, so that not even the guilty themselves, who take the wrong side, and turn away from the pursuit of good to perverse ways, are bold enough to defend evil as good. [471] Base things excite their fear, impious ones their shame. In short, they are eager for concealment, they shrink from publicity, they tremble when caught; when accused, they deny; even when tortured, they do not readily or invariably confess (their crime); at all events, [472] they grieve when they are condemned.

They reproach themselves for their past life; their change from innocence to an evil disposition they even attribute to fate. They cannot say that it is not a wrong thing, therefore they will not admit it to be their own act. As for the Christians, however, in what does their case resemble this? No one is ashamed; no one is sorry, except for his former (sins). [473] If he is pointed at (for his religion), he glories in it; if dragged to trial, he does not resist; if accused, he makes no defence. When questioned, he confesses; when condemned, he rejoices. What sort of evil is this, in which the nature of evil comes to a standstill? [474]

Chapter II [475] - The Heathen Perverted Judgment in the Trial of Christians. They Would Be More Consistent If They Dispensed with All Form of Trial. Tertullian Urges This with Much Indignation

In this case you actually [476] conduct trials contrary to the usual form of judicial process against criminals; for when culprits are brought up for trial, should they deny the charge, you press them for a confession by tortures. When Christians, however, confess without compulsion, you apply the torture to induce them to deny. What great perverseness is this, when you stand out against confession, and change the use of the torture, compelling the man who frankly acknowledges the charge [477] to evade it, and him who is unwilling, to deny it? You, who preside for the purpose of extorting truth, demand falsehood from us alone that we may declare ourselves not to be what we are. I suppose you do not want us to be bad men, and therefore you earnestly wish to exclude us from that character. To be sure, [478] you put others on the rack and the gibbet, to get them to deny what they have the reputation of being. Now, when they deny (the charge against them), you do not believe them but on our denial, you instantly believe us. If you feel sure that we are the most injurious of men, why, even in processes against us, are we dealt with by you differently from other offenders? I do not mean that you make no account of [479] either an accusation or a denial (for your practice is not hastily to condemn men without an indictment and a defence); but, to take an instance in the trial of a murderer, the case is not at once ended, or the inquiry satisfied, on a man's confessing himself the murderer.

However complete his confession, [480] you do not readily believe him; but over and above this, you inquire into accessory circumstances--how often had he committed murder; with what weapons, in what place, with what plunder, accomplices, and abettors after the fact [481] (was the crime perpetrated)--to the end that nothing whatever respecting the criminal might escape detection, and that every means should be at hand for arriving at a true verdict. In our case, on the contrary, [482] whom you believe to be guilty of more atrocious and numerous crimes, you frame your indictments [483] in briefer and lighter terms. I suppose you do not care to load with accusations men whom you earnestly wish to get rid of, or else you do not think it necessary to inquire into matters which are known to you already. It is, however, all the more perverse that you compel us to deny charges about which you have the clearest evidence. But, indeed, [484] how much more consistent were it with your hatred of us to dispense with all forms of judicial process, and to strive with all your might not to urge us to say "No," and so have to acquit the objects of your hatred; but to confess all and singular the crimes laid to our charge, that your resentments might be the better glutted with an accumulation of our punishments, when it becomes known how many of those feasts each one of us may have celebrated, and how many incests we may have committed under cover of the night! What am I saying? Since your researches for rooting out our society must needs be made on a wide scale, you ought to extend your inquiry against our friends and companions. Let our infanticides and the dressers (of our horrible repasts) be brought out,--ay, and the very dogs which minister to our (incestuous) nuptials; [485] then the business (of our trial) would be without a fault. Even to the crowds which throng the spectacles a zest would be given; for with how much greater eagerness would they resort to the theatre, when one had to fight in the lists who had devoured a hundred babies! For since such horrid and monstrous crimes are reported of us, they ought, of course, to be brought to light, lest they should seem to be incredible, and the public detestation of us should begin to cool. For most persons are slow to believe such things, [486] feeling a horrible disgust at supposing that our nature could have an appetite for the food of wild beasts, when it has precluded these from all concubinage with the race of man.

Chapter III [487] -- The Great Offence in the Christians Lies in Their Very Name. The Name Vindicated

Since, therefore, you who are in other cases most scrupulous and persevering in investigating charges of far less serious import, relinquish your care in cases like ours, which are so horrible, and of such surpassing sin that impiety is too mild a word for them, by declining to hear confession, which should always be an important process for those who conduct judicial proceedings; and failing to make a full inquiry, which should be gone into by such as sue for a condemnation, it becomes evident that the crime laid to our charge consists not of any sinful conduct, but lies wholly in our name. If, indeed, [488] any real crimes were clearly adducible against us, their very names would condemn us, if found applicable, [489] so that distinct sentences would be pronounced against us in this wise: Let that murderer, or that incestuous criminal, or whatever it be that we are charged with, be led to execution, be crucified, or be thrown to the beasts.

Your sentences, however, [490] import only that one has confessed himself a Christian. No name of a crime stands against us, but only the crime of a name. Now this in very deed is neither more nor less than [491] the entire odium which is felt against us.

The name is the cause: some mysterious force intensified by your ignorance assails it, so that you do not wish to know for certain that which for certain you are sure you know nothing of; and therefore, further, you do not believe things which are not submitted to proof, and, lest they should be easily refuted, [492] you refuse to make inquiry, so that the odious name is punished under the presumption of (real) crimes. In order, therefore, that the issue may be withdrawn from the offensive name, we are compelled to deny it; then upon our denial we are acquitted, with an entire absolution [493] for the past: we are no longer murderers, no longer incestuous, because we have lost that name. [494] But since this point is dealt with in a place of its own, [495] do you tell us plainly why you are pursuing this name even to extirpation? What crime, what offence, what fault is there in a name? For you are barred by the rule [496] which puts it out of your power to allege crimes (of any man), which no legal action moots, no indictment specifies, no sentence enumerates. In any case which is submitted to the judge, [497] inquired into against the defendant, responded to by him or denied, and cited from the bench, I acknowledge a legal charge.

Concerning, then, the merit of a name, whatever offence names may be charged with, whatever impeachment words may be amenable to, I for my part [498] think, that not even a complaint is due to a word or a name, unless indeed it has a barbarous sound, or smacks of ill-luck, or is immodest, or is indecorous for the speaker, or unpleasant to the hearer.

These crimes in (mere) words and names are just like barbarous words and phrases, which have their fault, and their solecism, and their absurdity of figure. The name Christian, however, so far as its meaning goes, bears the sense of anointing. Even when by a faulty pronunciation you call us "Chrestians" (for you are not certain about even the sound of this noted name), you in fact lisp out the sense of pleasantness and goodness. [499] You are therefore vilifying [500] in harmless men even the harmless name we bear, which is not inconvenient for the tongue, nor harsh to the ear, nor injurious to a single being, nor rude for our country, being a good Greek word, as many others also are, and pleasant in sound and sense. Surely, surely, [501] names are not things which deserve punishment by the sword, or the cross, or the beasts.

Chapter IV [502] - The Truth Hated in the Christians; So in Measure Was It, of Old, in Socrates. The Virtues of the Christians

But the sect, you say, is punished in the name of its founder. Now in the first place it is, no doubt, a fair and usual custom that a sect should be marked out by the name of its founder, since philosophers are called Pythagoreans and Platonists after their masters; in the same way physicians are called after Erasistratus, and grammarians after Aristarchus. If, therefore, a sect has a bad character because its founder was bad, it is punished [503] as the traditional bearer [504] of a bad name. But this would be indulging in a rash assumption. The first step was to find out what the founder was, that his sect might be understood, instead of hindering [505] inquiry into the founder's character from the sect. But in our case, [506] by being necessarily ignorant of the sect, through your ignorance of its founder, or else by not taking a fair survey of the founder, because you make no inquiry into his sect, you fasten merely on the name, just as if you vilified in it both sect and founder, whom you know nothing of whatever. And yet you openly allow your philosophers the right of attaching themselves to any school, and bearing its founder's name as their own; and nobody stirs up any hatred against them, although both in public and in private they bark out [507] their bitterest eloquence against your customs, rites, ceremonies, and manner of life, with so much contempt for the laws, and so little respect for persons, that they even flaunt their licentious words[508] against the emperors themselves with impunity.

And yet it is the truth, which is so troublesome to the world, that these philosophers affect, but which Christians possess: they therefore who have it in possession afford the greater displeasure, because he who affects a thing plays with it; he who possesses it maintains it. For example, [509] Socrates was condemned on that side (of his wisdom) in which he came nearest in his search to the truth, by destroying your gods. Although the name of Christian was not at that time in the world, yet truth was always suffering condemnation. Now you will not deny that he was a wise man, to whom your own Pythian (god) had borne witness. Socrates, he said, was the wisest of men. Truth overbore Apollo, and made him pronounce even against himself since he acknowledged that he was no god, when he affirmed that that was the wisest man who was denying the gods. However, [510] on your principle he was the less wise because he denied the gods, although, in truth, he was all the wiser by reason of this denial. It is just in the same way that you are in the habit of saying of us: "Lucius Titius is a good man, only he is a Christian;" while another says; "I wonder that so worthy[511] a man as Caius Seius has become a Christian." [512] According to [513] the blindness of their folly men praise what they know, (and) blame what they are ignorant of; and that which they know, they vitiate by that which they do not know. It occurs to none (to consider) whether a man is not good and wise because he is a Christian, or therefore a Christian because he is wise and good, although it is more usual in human conduct to determine obscurities by what is manifest, than to prejudice what is manifest by what is obscure.

Some persons wonder that those whom they had known to be unsteady, worthless, or wicked before they bore this [514] name, have been suddenly converted to virtuous courses; and yet they better know how to wonder (at the change) than to attain to it; others are so obstinate in their strife as to do battle with their own best interests, which they have it in their power to secure by intercourse [515] with that hated name. I know more than one [516] husband, formerly anxious about their wives' conduct, and unable to bear even mice to creep into their bed-room without a groan of suspicion, who have, upon discovering the cause of their new assiduity, and their unwonted attention to the duties of home, [517] offered the entire loan of their wives to others,[518] disclaimed all jealousy, (and) preferred to be the husbands of she-wolves than of Christian women: they could commit themselves to a perverse abuse of nature, but they could not permit their wives to be reformed for the better! A father disinherited his son, with whom he had ceased to find fault. A master sent his slave to bridewell, [519] whom he had even found to be indispensable to him. As soon as they discovered them to be Christians, they wished they were criminals again; for our discipline carries its own evidence in itself, nor are we betrayed by anything else than our own goodness, just as bad men also become conspicuous [520] by their own evil. Else how is it that we alone are, contrary to the lessons of nature, branded as very evil because of our good? For what mark do we exhibit except the prime wisdom, [521] which teaches us not to worship the frivolous works of the human hand; the temperance, by which we abstain from other men's goods; the chastity, which we pollute not even with a look; the compassion, which prompts us to help the needy; the truth itself, which makes us give offence; and liberty, for which we have even learned to die? Whoever wishes to understand who the Christians are, must needs employ these marks for their discovery.

Chapter V [522] - The Inconsistent Life of Any False Christian No More Condemns True Disciples of Christ, Than a Passing Cloud Obscures a Summer Sky

As to your saying of us that we are a most shameful set, and utterly steeped in luxury, avarice, and depravity, we will not deny that this is true of some. It is, however, a sufficient testimonial for our name, that this cannot be said of all, not even of the greater part of us. It must happen even in the healthiest and purest body, that a mole should grow, or a wart arise on it, or freckles disfigure it. Not even the sky itself is clear with so perfect [523] a serenity as not to be flecked with some filmy cloud. [524] A slight spot on the face, because it is obvious in so conspicuous a part, only serves to show purity of the entire complexion. The goodness of the larger portion is well attested by the slender flaw.

But although you prove that some of our people are evil, you do not hereby prove that they are Christians.

Search and see whether there is any sect to which (a partial shortcoming) is imputed as a general stain. [525] You are accustomed in conversation yourselves to say, in disparagement of us, "Why is so-and-so deceitful, when the Christians are so self-denying? why merciless, when they are so merciful?" You thus bear your testimony to the fact that this is not the character of Christians, when you ask, in the way of a retort, [526] how men who are reputed to be Christians can be of such and such a disposition. There is a good deal of difference between an imputation and a name,[527] between an opinion and the truth. For names were appointed for the express purpose of setting their proper limits between mere designation and actual condition. [528] How many indeed are said to be philosophers, who for all that do not fulfil the law of philosophy? All bear the name in respect of their profession; but they hold the designation without the excellence of the profession, and they disgrace the real thing under the shallow pretence of its name. Men are not straightway of such and such a character, because they are said to be so; but when they are not, it is vain to say so of them: they only deceive people who attach reality to a name, when it is its consistency with fact which decides the condition implied in the name. [529] And yet persons of this doubtful stamp do not assemble with us, neither do they belong to our communion: by their delinquency they become yours once more [530] since we should be unwilling to mix even with them whom your violence and cruelty compelled to recant. Yet we should, of course, be more ready to have included amongst us those who have unwillingly forsaken our discipline than wilful apostates. However, you have no right to call them Christians, to whom the Christians themselves deny that name, and who have not learned to deny themselves.

Chapter VI [531] - The Innocence of the Christians Not Compromised by the Iniquitous Laws Which Were Made Against Them

Whenever these statements and answers of ours, which truth suggests of its own accord, press and restrain your conscience, which is the witness of its own ignorance, you betake yourselves in hot haste to that poor altar of refuge, [532] the authority of the laws, because these, of course, would never punish the offensive [533] sect, if their deserts had not been fully considered by those who made the laws. Then what is it which has prevented a like consideration on the part of those who put the laws in force, when, in the case of all other crimes which are similarly forbidden and punished by the laws, the penalty is not inflicted [534] until it is sought by regular process? [535] Take, [536] for instance, the case of a murderer or an adulterer. An examination is ordered touching the particulars [537] of the crime, even though it is patent to all what its nature [538] is. Whatever wrong has been done by the Christian ought to be brought to light.

No law forbids inquiry to be made; on the contrary, inquiry is made in the interest of the laws.[539] For how are you to keep the law by precautions against that which the law forbids, if you neutralize the carefulness of the precaution by your failing to perceive [540] what it is you have to keep? No law must keep to itself [541] the knowledge of its own righteousness, [542] but (it owes it) to those from whom it claims obedience. The law, however, becomes an object of suspicion when it declines to approve itself.

Naturally enough, [543] then, are the laws against the Christians supposed to be just and deserving of respect and observance, just as long as men remain ignorant of their aim and purport; but when this is perceived, their extreme injustice is discovered, and they are deservedly rejected with abhorrence, [544] along with (their instruments of torture)--the swords, the crosses, and the lions. An unjust law secures no respect. In my opinion, however, there is a suspicion among you that some of these laws are unjust, since not a day passes without your modifying their severity and iniquity by fresh deliberations and decisions.

Chapter VII [545] - The Christians Defamed. A Sarcastic Description of Fame; Its Deception and Atrocious Slanders of the Christians Lengthily Described

Whence comes it to pass, you will say to us, that such a character could have been attributed to you, as to have justified the lawmakers perhaps by its imputation? Let me ask on my side, what voucher they had then, or you now, for the truth of the imputation? (You answer,) Fame. Well, now, is not this--

"Fama malum, quo non aliud velocius ullum?" [546]

Now, why a plague, [547] if it be always true? It never ceases from lying; nor even at the moment when it reports the truth is it so free from the wish to lie, as not to interweave the false with the true, by processes of addition, diminution, or confusion of various facts. Indeed, [548] such is its condition, that it can only continue to exist while it lies. For it lives only just so long as it fails to prove anything. As soon as it proves itself true, it falls; and, as if its office of reporting news were at an end, it quits its post: thenceforward the thing is held to be a fact, and it passes under that name. No one, then, says, to take an instance, "The report is that this happened at Rome," or, "The rumour goes that he has got a province;" but, "He has got a province," and, "This happened at Rome." Nobody mentions a rumour except at an uncertainty, because nobody can be sure of a rumour, but only of certain knowledge; and none but a fool believes a rumour, because no wise man puts faith in an uncertainty. In however wide a circuit [549] a report has been circulated, it must needs have originated some time or other from one mouth; afterwards it creeps on somehow to ears and tongues which pass it on [550] and so obscures the humble error in which it began, that no one considers whether the mouth which first set it a-going disseminated a falsehood,--a circumstance which often happens either from a temper of rivalry, or a suspicious turn, or even the pleasure of feigning news. It is, however, well that time reveals all things, as your own sayings and proverbs testify; yea, as nature herself attests, which has so ordered it that nothing lies hid, not even that which fame has not reported. See, now, what a witness [551] you have suborned against us: it has not been able up to this time to prove the report it set in motion, although it has had so long a time to recommend it to our acceptance. This name of ours took its rise in the reign of Augustus; under Tiberius it was taught with all clearness and publicity; [552] under Nero it was ruthlessly condemned, [553] and you may weigh its worth and character even from the person of its persecutor. If that prince was a pious man, then the Christians are impious; if he was just, if he was pure, then the Christians are unjust and impure; if he was not a public enemy, we are enemies of our country: what sort of men we are, our persecutor himself shows, since he of course punished what produced hostility to himself. [554] Now, although every other institution which existed under Nero has been destroyed, yet this of ours has firmly remained-- righteous, it would seem, as being unlike the author (of its persecution). Two hundred and fifty years, then, have not yet passed since our life began. During the interval there have been so many criminals; so many crosses have obtained immortality; [555] so many infants have been slain; so many loaves steeped in blood; so many extinctions of candles; [556] so many dissolute marriages. And up to the present time it is mere report which fights against the Christians. No doubt it has a strong support in the wickedness of the human mind, and utters its falsehoods with more success among cruel and savage men. For the more inclined you are to maliciousness, the more ready are you to believe evil; in short, men more easily believe the evil that is false, than the good which is true. Now, if injustice has left any place within you for the exercise of prudence in investigating the truth of reports, justice of course demanded that you should examine by whom the report could have been spread among the multitude, and thus circulated through the world. For it could not have been by the Christians themselves, I suppose, since by the very constitution and law of all mysteries the obligation of silence is imposed. How much more would this be the case in such (mysteries as are ascribed to us), which, if divulged, could not fail to bring down instant punishment from the prompt resentment of men! Since, therefore, the Christians are not their own betrayers, it follows that it must be strangers. Now I ask, how could strangers obtain knowledge of us, when even true and lawful mysteries exclude every stranger from witnessing them, unless illicit ones are less exclusive? Well, then, it is more in keeping with the character of strangers both to be ignorant (of the true state of a case), and to invent (a false account). Our domestic servants (perhaps) listened, and peeped through crevices and holes, and stealthily got information of our ways.

What, then, shall we say when our servants betray them to you? [557] It is better, (to be sure,) [558] for us all not to be betrayed by any; but still, if our practices be so atrocious, how much more proper is it when a righteous indignation bursts asunder even all ties of domestic fidelity?

How was it possible for it to endure what horrified the mind and affrighted the eye? This is also a wonderful thing, both that he who was so overcome with impatient excitement as to turn informer, [559] did not likewise desire to prove (what he reported), and that he who heard the informer's story did not care to see for himself, since no doubt the reward [560] is equal both for the informer who proves what he reports, and for the hearer who convinces himself of the credibility [561] of what he hears. But then you say that (this is precisely what has taken place):

first came the rumour, then the exhibition of the proof; first the hearsay, then the inspection; and after this, fame received its commission. Now this, I must say, [562] surpasses all admiration, that that was once for all detected and divulged which is being for ever repeated, unless, forsooth, we have by this time ceased from the reiteration of such things [563] (as are alleged of us). But we are called still by the same (offensive) name, and we are supposed to be still engaged in the same practices, and we multiply from day to day; the more [564] we are, the more become we objects of hatred. Hatred increases as the material for it increases. Now, seeing that the multitude of offenders is ever advancing, how is it that the crowd of informers does not keep equal pace therewith? To the best of my belief, even our manner of life [565] has become better known; you know the very days of our assemblies; therefore we are both besieged, and attacked, and kept prisoners actually in our secret congregations. Yet who ever came upon a half-consumed corpse (amongst us)? Who has detected the traces of a bite in our blood-steeped loaf? Who has discovered, by a sudden light invading our darkness, any marks of impurity, I will not say of incest, (in our feasts)? If we save ourselves by a bribe [566] from being dragged out before the public gaze with such a character, how is it that we are still oppressed? We have it indeed in our own power not to be thus apprehended at all; for who either sells or buys information about a crime, if the crime itself has no existence? But why need I disparagingly refer to [567] strange spies and informers, when you allege against us such charges as we certainly do not ourselves divulge with very much noise--either as soon as you hear of them, if we previously show them to you, or after you have yourselves discovered them, if they are for the time concealed from you? For no doubt, [568] when any desire initiation in the mysteries, their custom is first to go to the master or father of the sacred rites.

Then he will say (to the applicant), You must bring an infant, as a guarantee for our rites, to be sacrificed, as well as some bread to be broken and dipped in his blood; you also want candles, and dogs tied together to upset them, and bits of meat to rouse the dogs.

Moreover, a mother too, or a sister, is necessary for you. What, however, is to be said if you have neither? I suppose in that case you could not be a genuine Christian. Now, do let me ask you, Will such things, when reported by strangers, bear to be spread about (as charges against us)? It is impossible for such persons to understand proceedings in which they take no part. [569] The first step of the process is perpetrated with artifice; our feasts and our marriages are invented and detailed [570] by ignorant persons, who had never before heard about Christian mysteries. And though they afterwards cannot help acquiring some knowledge of them, it is even then as having to be administered by others whom they bring on the scene. [571] Besides, how absurd is it that the profane know mysteries which the priest knows not!

They keep them all to themselves, then, [572] and take them for granted; and so these tragedies, (worse than those) of Thyestes or OEdipus, do not at all come forth to light, nor find their way [573] to the public. Even more voracious bites take nothing away from the credit [574] of such as are initiated, whether servants or masters. If, however, none of these allegations can be proved to be true, how incalculable must be esteemed the grandeur (of that religion) which is manifestly not overbalanced even by the burden of these vast atrocities! O ye heathen; who have and deserve our pity, [575] behold, we set before you the promise which our sacred system offers. It guarantees eternal life to such as follow and observe it; on the other hand, it threatens with the eternal punishment of an unending fire those who are profane and hostile; while to both classes alike is preached a resurrection from the dead.

We are not now concerned [576] about the doctrine of these (verities), which are discussed in their proper place. [577] Meanwhile, however, believe them, even as we do ourselves, for I want to know whether you are ready to reach them, as we do, through such crimes. Come, whosoever you are, plunge your sword into an infant; or if that is another's office, then simply gaze at the breathing creature [578] dying before it has lived; at any rate, catch its fresh [579] blood in which to steep your bread; then feed yourself without stint; and whilst this is going on, recline.

Carefully distinguish the places where your mother or your sister may have made their bed; mark them well, in order that, when the shades of night have fallen upon them, putting of course to the test the care of every one of you, you may not make the awkward mistake of alighting on somebody else: [580] you would have to make an atonement, if you failed of the incest. When you have effected all this, eternal life will be in store for you. I want you to tell me whether you think eternal life worth such a price. No, indeed, [581] you do not believe it: even if you did believe it, I maintain that you would be unwilling to give (the fee); or if willing, would be unable. But why should others be able if you are unable? Why should you be able if others are unable?

What would you wish impunity (and) eternity to stand you in? [582] Do you suppose that these (blessings) can be bought by us at any price? Have Christians teeth of a different sort from others? Have they more ample jaws? [583] Are they of different nerve for incestuous lust? I trow not. It is enough for us to differ from you in condition [584] by truth alone.

Chapter VIII [585] - The Calumny Against the Christians Illustrated in the Discovery of Psammetichus. Refutation of the Story

We are indeed said to be the "third race" of men. What, a dog-faced race? [586] Or broadly shadow-footed? [587] Or some subterranean [588] Antipodes? If you attach any meaning to these names, pray tell us what are the first and the second race, that so we may know something of this "third."

Psammetichus thought that he had hit upon the ingenious discovery of the primeval man. He is said to have removed certain new-born infants from all human intercourse, and to have entrusted them to a nurse, whom he had previously deprived of her tongue, in order that, being completely exiled from all sound of the human voice, they might form their speech without hearing it; and thus, deriving it from themselves alone, might indicate what that first nation was whose speech was dictated by nature. Their first utterance was Bekkos, a word which means "bread" in the language of Phrygia: the Phrygians, therefore, are supposed to be the first of the human race. [589] But it will not be out of place if we make one observation, with a view to show how your faith abandons itself more to vanities than to verities. Can it be, then, at all credible that the nurse retained her life, after the loss of so important a member, the very organ of the breath of life, [590] --cut out, too, from the very root, with her throat [591] mutilated, which cannot be wounded even on the outside without danger, and the putrid gore flowing back to the chest, and deprived for so long a time of her food? Come, even suppose that by the remedies of a Philomela she retained her life, in the way supposed by wisest persons, who account for the dumbness not by cutting out the tongue, but from the blush of shame; if on such a supposition she lived, she would still be able to blurt out some dull sound. And a shrill inarticulate noise from opening the mouth only, without any modulation of the lips, might be forced from the mere throat, though there were no tongue to help. This, it is probable, the infants readily imitated, and the more so because it was the only sound; only they did it a little more neatly, as they had tongues; [592] and then they attached to it a definite signification. Granted, then, that the Phrygians were the earliest race, it does not follow that the Christians are the third. For how many other nations come regularly after the Phrygians? Take care, however, lest those whom you call the third race should obtain the first rank, since there is no nation indeed which is not Christian. Whatever nation, therefore, was the first, is nevertheless Christian now.[593] It is ridiculous folly which makes you say we are the latest race, and then specifically call us the third. But it is in respect of our religion, [594] not of our nation, that we are supposed to be the third; the series being the Romans, the Jews, and the Christians after them. Where, then, are the Greeks? or if they are reckoned amongst the Romans in regard to their superstition (since it was from Greece that Rome borrowed even her gods), where at least are the Egyptians, since these have, so far as I know, a mysterious religion peculiar to themselves? Now, if they who belong to the third race are so monstrous, what must they be supposed to be who preceded them in the first and the second place?

Chapter IX [595] - The Christians are Not the Cause of Public Calamities: There Were Such Troubles Before Christianity

But why should I be astonished at your vain imputations?

Under the same natural form, malice and folly have always been associated in one body and growth, and have ever opposed us under the one instigator of error. [596] Indeed, I feel no astonishment; and therefore, as it is necessary for my subject, I will enumerate some instances, that you may feel the astonishment by the enumeration of the folly into which you fall, when you insist on our being the causes of every public calamity or injury. If the Tiber has overflowed its banks, if the Nile has remained in its bed, if the sky has been still, or the earth been in commotion, if death[597] has made its devastations, or famine its afflictions, your cry immediately is, "This is the fault [598] of the Christians!" As if they who fear the true God could have to fear a light thing, or at least anything else (than an earthquake or famine, or such visitations). [599] I suppose it is as despisers of your gods that we call down on us these strokes of theirs. As we have remarked already, [600] three hundred years have not yet passed in our existence; but what vast scourges before that time fell on all the world, on its various cities and provinces! what terrible wars, both foreign and domestic! what pestilences, famines, conflagrations, yawnings, and quakings of the earth has history recorded! [601] Where were the Christians, then, when the Roman state furnished so many chronicles of its disasters? Where were the Christians when the islands Hiera, Anaphe, and Delos, and Rhodes, and Cea were desolated with multitudes of men? or, again, when the land mentioned by Plato as larger than Asia or Africa was sunk in the Atlantic Sea? or when fire from heaven overwhelmed Volsinii, and flames from their own mountain consumed Pompeii? when the sea of Corinth was engulphed by an earthquake? when the whole world was destroyed by the deluge? Where then were (I will not say the Christians, who despise your gods, but) your gods themselves, who are proved to be of later origin than that great ruin by the very places and cities in which they were born, sojourned, and were buried, and even those which they founded?

For else they would not have remained to the present day, unless they had been more recent than that catastrophe.

If you do not care to peruse and reflect upon these testimonies of history, the record of which affects you differently from us, [602] in order especially that you may not have to tax your gods with extreme injustice, since they injure even their worshippers on account of their despisers, do you not then prove yourselves to be also in the wrong, when you hold them to be gods, who make no distinction between the deserts of yourselves and profane persons? If, however, as it is now and then very vainly said, you incur the chastisement of your gods because you are too slack in our extirpation, you then have settled the question [603] of their weakness and insignificance; for they would not be angry with you for loitering over our punishment, if they could do anything themselves,--although you admit the same thing indeed in another way, whenever by inflicting punishment on us you seem to be avenging them. If one interest is maintained by another party, that which defends is the greater of the two. What a shame, then, must it be for gods to be defended by a human being!

Chapter X [604] - The Christians are Not the Only Contemners of the Gods. Contempt of Them Often Displayed by Heathen Official Persons. Homer Made the Gods Contemptible

Pour out now all your venom; fling against this name of ours all your shafts of calumny: I shall stay no longer to refute them; but they shall by and by be blunted, when we come to explain our entire discipline. [605] I shall content myself now indeed with plucking these shafts out of our own body, and hurling them back on yourselves. The same wounds which you have inflicted on us by your charges I shall show to be imprinted on yourselves, that you may fall by your own swords and javelins. [606] Now, first, when you direct against us the general charge of divorcing ourselves from the institutions of our forefathers, consider again and again whether you are not yourselves open to that accusation in common with us. For when I look through your life and customs, lo, what do I discover but the old order of things corrupted, nay, destroyed by you?

Of the laws I have already said, that you are daily supplanting them with novel decrees and statutes. As to everything else in your manner of life, how great are the changes you have made from your ancestors--in your style, your dress, your equipage, your very food, and even in your speech; for the old-fashioned you banish, as if it were offensive to you! Everywhere, in your public pursuits and private duties, antiquity is repealed; all the authority of your forefathers your own authority has superseded. To be sure, [607] you are for ever praising old customs; but this is only to your greater discredit, for you nevertheless persistently reject them. How great must your perverseness have been, to have bestowed approbation on your ancestors' institutions, which were too inefficient to be lasting, all the while that you were rejecting the very objects of your approbation! But even that very heir-loom [608] of your forefathers, which you seem to guard and defend with greatest fidelity, in which you actually [609] find your strongest grounds for impeaching us as violators of the law, and from which your hatred of the Christian name derives all its life--I mean the worship of the gods--I shall prove to be undergoing ruin and contempt from yourselves no less than [610] (from us),--unless it be that there is no reason for our being regarded as despisers of the gods like yourselves, on the ground that nobody despises what he knows has absolutely no existence.

What certainly exists can be despised.

That which is nothing, suffers nothing. From those, therefore, to whom it is an existing thing,[611] must necessarily proceed the suffering which affects it. All the heavier, then, is the accusation which burdens you who believe that there are gods and (at the same time) despise them, who worship and also reject them, who honour and also assail them. One may also gather the same conclusion from this consideration, above all:

since you worship various gods, some one and some another, you of course despise those which you do not worship.

A preference for the one is not possible without slighting the other, and no choice can be made without a rejection.

He who selects some one out of many, has already slighted the other which he does not select. But it is impossible that so many and so great gods can be worshipped by all.

Then you must have exercised your contempt (in this matter) even at the beginning, since indeed you were not then afraid of so ordering things, that all the gods could not become objects of worship to all. For those very wise and prudent ancestors of yours, whose institutions you know not how to repeal, especially in respect of your gods, are themselves found to have been impious. I am much mistaken, if they did not sometimes decree that no general should dedicate a temple, which he may have vowed in battle, before the senate gave its sanction; as in the case of Marcus Æmilius, who had made a vow to the god Alburnus. Now is it not confessedly the greatest impiety, nay, the greatest insult, to place the honour of the Deity at the will and pleasure of human judgment, so that there cannot be a god except the senate permit him? Many times have the censors destroyed [612] (a god) without consulting the people.

Father Bacchus, with all his ritual, was certainly by the consuls, on the senate's authority, cast not only out of the city, but out of all Italy; whilst Varro informs us that Serapis also, and Isis, and Arpocrates, and Anubis, were excluded from the Capitol, and that their altars which the senate had thrown down were only restored by the popular violence. The Consul Gabinius, however, on the first day of the ensuing January, although he gave a tardy consent to some sacrifices, in deference to the crowd which assembled, because he had failed to decide about Serapis and Isis, yet held the judgment of the senate to be more potent than the clamour of the multitude, and forbade the altars to be built. Here, then, you have amongst your own forefathers, if not the name, at all events the procedure, [613] of the Christians, which despises the gods.

If, however, you were even innocent of the charge of treason against them in the honour you pay them, I still find that you have made a consistent advance in superstition as well as impiety.

For how much more irreligious are you found to be! There are your household gods, the Lares and the Penates, which you possess [614] by a family consecration: [615] you even tread them profanely under foot, you and your domestics, by hawking and pawning them for your wants or your whims. Such insolent sacrilege might be excusable, if it were not practised against your humbler deities; as it is, the case is only the more insolent. There is, however, some consolation for your private household gods under these affronts, that you treat your public deities with still greater indignity and insolence. First of all, you advertise them for auction, submit them to public sale, knock them down to the highest bidder, when you every five years bring them to the hammer among your revenues. For this purpose you frequent the temple of Serapis or the Capitol, hold your sales there, [616] conclude your contracts, [617] as if they were markets, with the well-known [618] voice of the crier, (and) the self-same levy [619] of the quæstor. Now lands become cheaper when burdened with tribute, and men by the capitation tax diminish in value (these are the well-known marks of slavery).

But the gods, the more tribute they pay, become more holy; or rather, [620] the more holy they are, the more tribute do they pay. Their majesty is converted into an article of traffic; men drive a business with their religion; the sanctity of the gods is beggared with sales and contracts. You make merchandise of the ground of your temples, of the approach to your altars, of your offerings, [621] of your sacrifices. [622] You sell the whole divinity (of your gods). You will not permit their gratuitous worship. The auctioneers necessitate more repairs [623] than the priests.

It was not enough that you had insolently made a profit of your gods, if we would test the amount of your contempt; and you are not content to have withheld honour from them, you must also depreciate the little you do render to them by some indignity or other. What, indeed, do you do by way of honouring your gods, which you do not equally offer to your dead? You build temples for the gods, you erect temples also to the dead; you build altars for the gods, you build them also for the dead; you inscribe the same superscription over both; you sketch out the same lineaments for their statues--as best suits their genius, or profession, or age; you make an old man of Saturn, a beardless youth of Apollo; you form a virgin from Diana; in Mars you consecrate a soldier, a blacksmith in Vulcan. No wonder, therefore, if you slay the same victims and burn the same odours for your dead as you do for your gods. What excuse can be found for that insolence which classes the dead of whatever sort [624] as equal with the gods? Even to your princes there are assigned the services of priests and sacred ceremonies, and chariots, [625] and cars, and the honours of the solisternia and the lectisternia, holidays and games. Rightly enough, [626] since heaven is open to them; still it is none the less contumelious to the gods: in the first place, because it could not possibly be decent that other beings should be numbered with them, even if it has been given to them to become divine after their birth; in the second place, because the witness who beheld the man caught up into heaven [627] would not forswear himself so freely and palpably before the people, if it were not for the contempt felt about the objects sworn to both by himself and those [628] who allow the perjury. For these feel of themselves, that what is sworn to is nothing; and more than that, they go so far as to fee the witness, because he had the courage to publicly despise the avengers of perjury. Now, as to that, who among you is pure of the charge of perjury?

By this time, indeed, there is an end to all danger in swearing by the gods, since the oath by Cæsar carries with it more influential scruples, which very circumstance indeed tends to the degradation of your gods; for those who perjure themselves when swearing by Cæsar are more readily punished than those who violate an oath to a Jupiter. But, of the two kindred feelings of contempt and derision, contempt is the more honourable, having a certain glory in its arrogance; for it sometimes proceeds from confidence, or the security of consciousness, or a natural loftiness of mind. Derision, however, is a more wanton feeling, and so far it points more directly [629] to a carping insolence. Now only consider what great deriders of your gods you show yourselves to be! I say nothing of your indulgence of this feeling during your sacrificial acts, how you offer for your victims the poorest and most emaciated creatures; or else of the sound and healthy animals only the portions which are useless for food, such as the heads and hoofs, or the plucked feathers and hair, and whatever at home you would have thrown away. I pass over whatever may seem to the taste [630] of the vulgar and profane to have constituted the religion [631] of your forefathers; but then the most learned and serious classes (for seriousness and wisdom to some extent [632] profess [633] to be derived from learning) are always, in fact, the most irreverent towards your gods; and if their learning ever halts, it is only to make up for the remissness by a more shameful invention of follies and falsehoods about their gods. I will begin with that enthusiastic fondness which you show for him from whom every depraved writer gets his dreams, to whom you ascribe as much honour as you derogate from your gods, by magnifying him who has made such sport of them. I mean Homer by this description. He it is, in my opinion, who has treated the majesty of the Divine Being on the low level of human condition, imbuing the gods with the falls [634] and the passions of men; who has pitted them against each other with varying success, like pairs of gladiators: he wounds Venus with an arrow from a human hand; he keeps Mars a prisoner in chains for thirteen months, with the prospect of

Tertullian

perishing; [635] he parades [636] Jupiter as suffering a like indignity from a crowd of celestial (rebels;) or he draws from him tears for Sarpedon; or he represents him wantoning with Juno in the most disgraceful way, advocating his incestuous passion for her by a description and enumeration of his various amours. Since then, which of the poets has not, on the authority of their great prince, calumniated the gods, by either betraying truth or feigning falsehood? Have the dramatists also, whether in tragedy or comedy, refrained from making the gods the authors [637] of the calamities and retributions (of their plays)? I say nothing of your philosophers, whom a certain inspiration of truth itself elevates against the gods, and secures from all fear in their proud severity and stern discipline. Take, for example, [638] Socrates. In contempt of your gods, he swears by an oak, and a dog, and a goat.

Now, although he was condemned to die for this very reason, the Athenians afterwards repented of that condemnation, and even put to death his accusers. By this conduct of theirs the testimony of Socrates is replaced at its full value, and I am enabled to meet you with this retort, that in his case you have approbation bestowed on that which is now-a-days reprobated in us.

But besides this instance there is Diogenes, who, I know not to what extent, made sport of Hercules; whilst Varro, that Diogenes of the Roman cut, [639] introduces to our view some three hundred Joves, or, as they ought to be called, Jupiters, [640] (and all) without heads. Your other wanton wits [641] likewise minister to your pleasures by disgracing the gods. Examine carefully the sacrilegious [642] beauties of your Lentuli and Hostii; now, is it the players or your gods who become the objects of your mirth in their tricks and jokes? Then, again, with what pleasure do you take up the literature of the stage, which describes all the foul conduct of the gods! Their majesty is defiled in your presence in some unchaste body. The mask of some deity, at your will, [643] covers some infamous paltry head. The Sun mourns for the death of his son by a lightning-flash amid your rude rejoicing. Cybele sighs for a shepherd who disdains her, without raising a blush on your cheek; and you quietly endure songs which celebrate [644] the gallantries of Jove. You are, of course, possessed of a more religious spirit in the show of your gladiators, when your gods dance, with equal zest, over the spilling of human blood, (and) over those filthy penalties which are at once their proof and plot for executing your criminals, or else (when) your criminals are punished personating the gods themselves. [645] We have often witnessed in a mutilated criminal your god of Pessinum, Attis; a wretch burnt alive has personated Hercules. We have laughed at the sport of your mid-day game of the gods, when Father Pluto, Jove's own brother, drags away, hammer in hand, the remains of the gladiators; when Mercury, with his winged cap and heated wand, tests with his cautery whether the bodies were really lifeless, or only feigning death.

Who now can investigate every particular of this sort although so destructive of the honour of the Divine Being, and so humiliating to His majesty? They all, indeed, have their origin [646] in a contempt (of the gods), on the part both of those who practise [647] these personations, as well as of those [648] who are susceptible of being so represented. [649] I hardly know, therefore, whether your gods have more reason to complain of yourselves or of us. After despising them on the one hand, you flatter them on the other; if you fail in any duty towards them, you appease them with a fee; [650] in short, you allow yourselves to act towards them in any way you please. We, however, live in a consistent and entire aversion to them.

Chapter XI [651] - The Absurd Cavil of the Ass's Head Disposed of

In this matter we are (said to be) guilty not merely of forsaking the religion of the community, but of introducing a monstrous superstition; for some among you have dreamed that our god is an ass's head,--an absurdity which Cornelius Tacitus first suggested. In the fourth book of his histories,[652] where he is treating of the Jewish war, he begins his description with the origin of that nation, and gives his own views respecting both the origin and the name of their religion. He relates that the Jews, in their migration in the desert, when suffering for want of water, escaped by following for guides some wild asses, which they supposed to be going in quest of water after pasture, and that on this account the image of one of these animals was worshipped by the Jews. From this, I suppose, it was presumed that we, too, from our close connection with the Jewish religion, have ours consecrated under the same emblematic form. The same Cornelius Tacitus, however,--who, to say the truth, is most loquacious in falsehood--forgetting his later statement, relates how Pompey the Great, after conquering the Jews and capturing Jerusalem, entered the temple, but found nothing in the shape of an image, though he examined the place carefully. Where, then, should their God have been found? Nowhere else, of course, than in so memorable a temple which was carefully shut to all but the priests, and into which there could be no fear of a stranger entering. But what apology must I here offer for what I am going to say, when I have no other object at the moment than to make a passing remark or two in a general way which shall be equally applicable to yourselves? [653] Suppose that our God, then, be an asinine person, will you at all events deny that you possess the same characteristics with ourselves in that matter? (Not their heads only, but) entire asses, are, to be sure, objects of adoration to you, along with their tutelar Epona; and all herds, and cattle, and beasts you consecrate, and their stables into the bargain!

This, perhaps, is your grievance against us, that, when surrounded by cattle-worshippers of every kind we are simply devoted to asses!

Chapter XII [654] - The Charge of Worshipping a Cross. The Heathens Themselves Made Much of Crosses in Sacred Things; Nay, Their Very Idols Were Formed on a Crucial Frame

As for him who affirms that we are "the priesthood of a cross," [655] we shall claim him [656] as our co-religionist. [657] A cross is, in its material, a sign of wood; amongst yourselves also the object of worship is a wooden figure. Only, whilst with you the figure is a human one, with us the wood is its own figure.

Never mind [658] for the present what is the shape, provided the material is the same: the form, too, is of no importance, [659] if so be it be the actual body of a god.

If, however, there arises a question of difference on this point what, (let me ask,) is the difference between the Athenian Pallas, or the Pharian Ceres, and wood formed into a cross, [660] when each is represented by a rough stock, without form, and by the merest rudiment of a statue [661] of unformed wood? Every piece of timber [662] which is fixed in the ground in an erect position is a part of a cross, and indeed the greater portion of its mass.

But an entire cross is attributed to us, with its transverse beam, [663] of course, and its projecting seat. Now you have the less to excuse you, for you dedicate to religion only a mutilated imperfect piece of wood, while others consecrate to the sacred purpose a complete structure. The truth, however, after all is, that your religion is all cross, as I shall show. You are indeed unaware that your gods in their origin have proceeded from this hated cross. [664] Now, every image, whether carved out of wood or stone, or molten in metal, or produced out of any other richer material, must needs have had plastic hands engaged in its formation. Well, then, this modeller,[665] before he did anything else, [666] hit upon the form of a wooden cross, because even our own body assumes as its natural position the latent and concealed outline of a cross. Since the head rises upwards, and the back takes a straight direction, and the shoulders project laterally, if you simply place a man with his arms and hands outstretched, you will make the general outline of a cross. Starting, then, from this rudimental form and prop, [667] as it were, he applies a covering of clay, and so gradually completes the limbs, and forms the body, and covers the cross within with the shape which he meant to impress upon the clay; then from this design, with the help of compasses and leaden moulds, he has got all ready for his image which is to be brought out into marble, or clay, or whatever the material be of which he has determined to make his god. (This, then, is the process:) after the cross-shaped frame, the clay; after the clay, the god.

In a well-understood routine, the cross passes into a god through the clayey medium. The cross then you consecrate, and from it the consecrated (deity) begins to derive his origin. [668] By way of example, let us take the case of a tree which grows up into a system of branches and foliage, and is a reproduction of its own kind, whether it springs from the kernel of an olive, or the stone of a peach, or a grain of pepper which has been duly tempered under ground. Now, if you transplant it, or take a cutting off its branches for another plant, to what will you attribute what is produced by the propagation?

Will it not be to the grain, or the stone, or the kernel? Because, as the third stage is attributable to the second, and the second in like manner to the first, so the third will have to be referred to the first, through the second as the mean. We need not stay any longer in the discussion of this point, since by a natural law every kind of produce throughout nature refers back its growth to its original source; and just as the product is comprised in its primal cause, so does that cause agree in character with the thing produced. Since, then, in the production of your gods, you worship the cross which originates them, here will be the original kernel and grain, from which are propagated the wooden materials of your idolatrous images. Examples are not far to seek. Your victories you celebrate with religious ceremony[669] as deities; and they are the more august in proportion to the joy they bring you. The frames on which you hang up your trophies must be crosses: these are, as it were, the very core of your pageants. [670] Thus, in your victories, the religion of your camp makes even crosses objects of worship; your standards it adores, your standards are the sanction of its oaths; your standards it prefers before Jupiter himself. But all that parade [671] of images, and that display of pure gold, are (as so many) necklaces of the crosses. In like manner also, in the banners and ensigns, which your soldiers guard with no less sacred care, you have the streamers (and) vestments of your crosses. You are ashamed, I suppose, to worship unadorned and simple crosses.

Tertullian

Chapter XIII [672] - The Charge of Worshipping the Sun Met by a Retort

Others, with greater regard to good manners, it must be confessed, suppose that the sun is the god of the Christians, because it is a well-known fact that we pray towards the east, or because we make Sunday a day of festivity.

What then? Do you do less than this? Do not many among you, with an affectation of sometimes worshipping the heavenly bodies likewise, move your lips in the direction of the sunrise? It is you, at all events, who have even admitted the sun into the calendar of the week; and you have selected its day, [673] in preference to the preceding day [674] as the most suitable in the week [675] for either an entire abstinence from the bath, or for its postponement until the evening, or for taking rest and for banqueting. By resorting to these customs, you deliberately deviate from your own religious rites to those of strangers. For the Jewish feasts on the Sabbath and "the Purification," [676] and Jewish also are the ceremonies of the lamps, [677] and the fasts of unleavened bread, and the "littoral prayers," [678] all which institutions and practices are of course foreign from your gods. Wherefore, that I may return from this digression, you who reproach us with the sun and Sunday should consider your proximity to us. We are not far off from your Saturn and your days of rest.

Chapter XIV [679] - The Vile Calumny About Onocoetes Retorted on the Heathen by Tertullian

Report has introduced a new calumny respecting our God. Not so long ago, a most abandoned wretch in that city of yours, [680] a man who had deserted indeed his own religion--a Jew, in fact, who had only lost his skin, flayed of course by wild beasts, [681] against which he enters the lists for hire day after day with a sound body, and so in a condition to lose his skin [682] --carried about in public a caricature of us with this label: Onocoetes. [683] This (figure) had ass's ears, and was dressed in a toga with a book, having a hoof on one of his feet. And the crowd believed this infamous Jew. For what other set of men is the seed-plot [684] of all the calumny against us?

Throughout the city, therefore, Onocoetes is all the talk. As, however, it is less then "a nine days' wonder," [685] and so destitute of all authority from time, and weak enough from the character of its author, I shall gratify myself by using it simply in the way of a retort. Let us then see whether you are not here also found in our company. Now it matters not what their form may be, when our concern is about deformed images. You have amongst you gods with a dog's head, and a lion's head, with the horns of a cow, and a ram, and a goat, goat-shaped or serpent-shaped, and winged in foot, head, and back. Why therefore brand our one God so conspicuously? Many an Onocoetes is found amongst yourselves.

Chapter XV [686] - The Charge of Infanticide Retorted on the Heathen

Since we are on a par in respect of the gods, it follows that there is no difference between us on the point of sacrifice, or even of worship, [687] if I may be allowed to make good our comparison from another sort of evidence. We begin our religious service, or initiate our mysteries, with slaying an infant. As for you, since your own transactions in human blood and infanticide have faded from your memory, you shall be duly reminded of them in the proper place; we now postpone most of the instances, that we may not seem to be everywhere [688] handling the selfsame topics. Meanwhile, as I have said, the comparison between us does not fail in another point of view. For if we are infanticides in one sense, you also can hardly be deemed such in any other sense; because, although you are forbidden by the laws to slay new-born infants, it so happens that no laws are evaded with more impunity or greater safety, with the deliberate knowledge of the public, and the suffrages [689] of this entire age. [690] Yet there is no great difference between us, only you do not kill your infants in the way of a sacred rite, nor (as a service) to God. But then you make away with them in a more cruel manner, because you expose them to the cold and hunger, and to wild beasts, or else you get rid of them by the slower death of drowning. If, however, there does occur any dissimilarity between us in this matter, [691] you must not overlook the fact that it is your own dear children [692] whose life you quench; and this will supplement, nay, abundantly aggravate, on your side of the question, whatever is defective in us on other grounds. Well, but we are said to sup off our impious sacrifice! Whilst we postpone to a more suitable place [693] whatever resemblance even to this practice is discoverable amongst yourselves, we are not far removed from you in voracity.

If in the one case there is unchastity, and in ours cruelty, we are still on the same footing (if I may so far admit our guilt [694]) in nature, where cruelty is always found in concord with unchastity. But, after all, what do you less than we; or rather, what do you not do in excess of us?

I wonder whether it be a small matter to you [695] to pant for human entrails, because you devour full-grown men alive? Is it, forsooth, only a trifle to lick up human blood, when you draw out [696] the blood which was destined to live? Is it a light thing in your view to feed on an infant, when you consume one wholly before it is come to the birth? [697]

Chapter XVI [698] - Other Charges Repelled by the Same Method. The Story of the Noble Roman Youth and His Parents

I am now come to the hour for extinguishing the lamps, and for using the dogs, and practising the deeds of darkness. And on this point I am afraid I must succumb to you; for what similar accusation shall I have to bring against you? But you should at once commend the cleverness with which we make our incest look modest, in that we have devised a spurious night, [699] to avoid polluting the real light and darkness, and have even thought it right to dispense with earthly lights, and to play tricks also with our conscience. For whatever we do ourselves, we suspect in others when we choose (to be suspicious). As for your incestuous deeds, on the contrary, [700] men enjoy them at full liberty, in the face of day, or in the natural night, or before high Heaven; and in proportion to their successful issue is your own ignorance of the result, since you publicly indulge in your incestuous intercourse in the full cognizance of broad day-light. (No ignorance, however, conceals our conduct from our eyes,) for in the very darkness we are able to recognise our own misdeeds. The Persians, you know very well, [701] according to Ctesias, live quite promiscuously with their mothers, in full knowledge of the fact, and without any horror; whilst of the Macedonians it is well known that they constantly do the same thing, and with perfect approbation: for once, when the blinded [702] OEdipus came upon their stage, they greeted him with laughter and derisive cheers. The actor, taking off his mask in great alarm, said, "Gentlemen, have I displeased you?" "Certainly not," replied the Macedonians, "you have played your part well enough; but either the author was very silly, if he invented (this mutilation as an atonement for the incest), or else OEdipus was a great fool for his pains if he really so punished himself;" and then they shouted out one to the other, Ἥλσυνε εἰς τὴν μητέρα. But how insignificant, (say you,) is the stain which one or two nations can make on the whole world! As for us, we of course have infected the very sun, polluted the entire ocean! Quote, then, one nation which is free from the passions which allure the whole race of men to incest! If there is a single nation which knows nothing of concubinage through the necessity of age and sex--to say nothing of lust and licentiousness--that nation will be a stranger to incest. If any nature can be found so peculiarly removed from the human state as to be liable neither to ignorance, nor error, nor misfortune, that alone may be adduced with any consistency as an answer to the Christians. Reflect, therefore, on the licentiousness which floats about amongst men's passions [703] as if they were the winds, and consider whether there be any communities which the full and strong tides of passion fail to waft to the commission of this great sin. In the first place, when you expose your infants to the mercy of others, or leave them for adoption to better parents than yourselves, do you forget what an opportunity for incest is furnished, how wide a scope is opened for its accidental commission? Undoubtedly, such of you as are more serious from a principle of self-restraint and careful reflection, abstain from lusts which could produce results of such a kind, in whatever place you may happen to be, at home or abroad, so that no indiscriminate diffusion of seed, or licentious reception thereof, will produce children to you unawares, such as their very parents, or else other children, might encounter in inadvertent incest, for no restraint from age is regarded in (the importunities of) lust. All acts of adultery, all cases of fornication, all the licentiousness of public brothels, whether committed at home or perpetrated out of doors, [704] serve to produce confusions of blood and complications of natural relationship, [705] and thence to conduce to incest; from which consummation your players and buffoons draw the materials of their exhibitions. It was from such a source, too, that so flagrant a tragedy recently burst upon the public as that which the prefect Fuscianus had judicially to decide. A boy of noble birth, who, by the unintentional neglect of his attendants, [706] had strolled too far from home, was decoyed by some passers-by, and carried off. The paltry Greek [707] who had the care of him, or somebody else, [708] in true Greek fashion, had gone into the house and captured him. Having been taken away into Asia, he is brought, when arrived at full age, back to Rome, and exposed for sale. His own father buys him unawares, and treats him as a Greek. [709] Afterwards, as was his wont, the youth is sent by his master into the fields, chained as a slave. [710] Thither the tutor and the nurse had already been banished for punishment. The whole case is represented to them; they relate each other's misfortunes: they, on the one hand, how they had lost their ward when he was a boy; he, on the other hand, that he had been lost from his boyhood. But they agreed in the main, that he was a native of Rome of a noble family; perhaps he further gave sure proofs of his identity.

Accordingly, as God willed it for the purpose of fastening a stain upon that age, a presentiment about the time excites him, the periods exactly suit his age, even his eyes help to recall [711] his features, some peculiar marks on his body are enumerated. His master and mistress, who are now no other than his own father and mother, anxiously urge a protracted inquiry. The slave-dealer is examined, the unhappy truth is all discovered. When their wickedness becomes manifest, the parents find a remedy for their despair by hanging themselves; to their son, who survives the miserable calamity, their property is awarded by the prefect, not as an inheritance, but as the wages of infamy and incest. That one case was a sufficient example for public exposure [712] of the sins of this sort which are secretly perpetrated among you. Nothing happens among men in solitary isolation. But, as it seems to me, it is only in a solitary case that such a charge can be drawn out against us, even in the mysteries of our religion. You ply us evermore with this charge; [713] yet there are like delinquencies to be traced amongst you, even in your ordinary course of life. [714]

Chapter XVII [715] - The Christian Refusal to Swear by the Genius of Cæsar. Flippancy and Irreverence Retorted on the Heathen

As to your charges of obstinacy and presumption, whatever you allege against us, even in these respects, there are not wanting points in which you will bear a comparison with us. Our first step in this contumacious conduct concerns that which is ranked by you immediately after [716] the worship due to God, that is, the worship due to the majesty of the Cæsars, in respect of which we are charged with being irreligious towards them, since we neither propitiate their images nor swear by their genius. We are called enemies of the people. Well, be it so; yet at the same time (it must not be forgotten, that) the emperors find enemies amongst you heathen, and are constantly getting surnames to signalize their triumphs--one becoming Parthicus, [717] and another Medicus and Germanicus. [718] On this head [719] the Roman people must see to it who they are amongst whom [720] there still remain nations which are unsubdued and foreign to their rule. But, at all events, you are of us, [721] and yet you conspire against us. (In reply, we need only state) a well-known fact, [722] that we acknowledge the fealty of Romans to the emperors. No conspiracy has ever broken out from our body: no Cæsar's blood has ever fixed a stain upon us, in the senate or even in the palace; no assumption of the purple has ever in any of the provinces been affected by us. The Syrias still exhale the odours of their corpses; still do the Gauls [723] fail to wash away (their blood) in the waters of their Rhone. Your allegations of our insanity [724] I omit, because they do not compromise the Roman name. But I will grapple with [725] the charge of sacrilegious vanity, and remind you of [726] the irreverence of your own lower classes, and the scandalous lampoons [727] of which the statues are so cognizant, and the sneers which are sometimes uttered at the public games, [728] and the curses with which the circus resounds.

If not in arms, you are in tongue at all events always rebellious. But I suppose it is quite another affair to refuse to swear by the genius of Cæsar?

For it is fairly open to doubt as to who are perjurers on this point, when you do not swear honestly[729] even by your gods. Well, we do not call the emperor God; for on this point sannam facimus,[730] as the saying is. But the truth is, that you who call Cæsar God both mock him, by calling him what he is not, and curse him, because he does not want to be what you call him. For he prefers living to being made a god. [731]

Chapter XVIII [732] - Christians Charged with an Obstinate Contempt of Death. Instances of the Same are Found Amongst the Heathen

The rest of your charge of obstinacy against us you sum up in this indictment, that we boldly refuse neither your swords, nor your crosses, nor your wild beasts, nor fire, nor tortures, such is our obduracy and contempt of death. But (you are inconsistent in your charges); for in former times amongst your own ancestors all these terrors have come in men's intrepidity [733] not only to be despised, but even to be held in great praise. How many swords there were, and what brave men were willing to suffer by them, it were irksome to enumerate. [734] (If we take the torture) of the cross, of which so many instances have occurred, exquisite in cruelty, your own Regulus readily initiated the suffering which up to his day was without a precedent; [735] a queen of Egypt used wild beasts of her own (to accomplish her death); [736] the Carthaginian woman, who in the last extremity of her country was more courageous than her husband Asdrubal, [737] only followed the example, set long before by Dido herself, of going through fire to her death. Then, again, a woman of Athens defied the tyrant, exhausted his tortures, and at last, lest her person and sex might succumb through weakness, she bit off her tongue and spat out of her mouth the only possible instrument of a confession which was now out of her power. [738] But in your own instance you account such deeds glorious, in ours obstinate.

Annihilate now the glory of your ancestors, in order that you may thereby annihilate us also. Be content from henceforth to repeal the praises of your forefathers, in order that you may not have to accord commendation to us for the same (sufferings). Perhaps (you will say) the character of a more robust age may have rendered the spirits of antiquity more enduring. Now, however, (we enjoy) the blessing of quietness and peace; so that the minds and dispositions of men (should be) more tolerant even towards strangers. Well, you rejoin, be it so: you may compare yourselves with the ancients; we must needs pursue with hatred all that we find in you offensive to ourselves, because it does not obtain currency [739] among us. Answer me, then, on each particular case by itself. I am not seeking for examples on a uniform scale. [740] Since, forsooth, the sword through their contempt of death produced stories of heroism amongst your ancestors, it is not, of course,[741] from love of life that you go to the trainers sword in hand and offer yourselves as gladiators, [742] (nor) through fear of death do you enrol your names in the army. [743] Since an ordinary [744] woman makes her death famous by wild beasts, it cannot but be of your own pure accord that you encounter wild beasts day after day in the midst of peaceful times. Although no longer any Regulus among you has raised a cross as the instrument of his own crucifixion, yet a contempt of the fire has even now displayed itself, [745] since one of yourselves very lately has offered for a wager [746] to go to any place which may be fixed upon and put on the burning shirt.[747] If a woman once defiantly danced beneath the scourge, the same feat has been very recently performed again by one of your own (circus-) hunters [748] as he traversed the appointed course, not to mention the famous sufferings of the Spartans. [749]

Chapter XIX [750] - If Christians and the Heathen Thus Resemble Each Other, There is Great Difference in the Grounds and Nature of Their Apparently Similar Conduct

Here end, I suppose, your tremendous charges of obstinacy against the Christians. Now, since we are amenable to them in common with yourselves, it only remains that we compare the grounds which the respective parties have for being personally derided. All our obstinacy, however, is with you a foregone conclusion, [751] based on our strong convictions; for we take for granted [752] a resurrection of the dead. Hope in this resurrection amounts to [753] a contempt of death. Ridicule, therefore, as much as you like the excessive stupidity of such minds as die that they may live; but then, in order that you may be able to laugh more merrily, and deride us with greater boldness, you must take your sponge, or perhaps your tongue, and wipe away those records of yours every now and then cropping out, [754] which assert in not dissimilar terms that souls will return to bodies. But how much more worthy of acceptance is our belief which maintains that they will return to the same bodies! And how much more ridiculous is your inherited conceit, [755] that the human spirit is to reappear in a dog, or a mule, or a peacock! Again, we affirm that a judgment has been ordained by God according to the merits of every man. This you ascribe to Minos and Rhadamanthus, while at the same time you reject Aristides, who was a juster judge than either.

By the award of the judgment, we say that the wicked will have to spend an eternity in endless fire, the pious and innocent in a region of bliss. In your view likewise an unalterable condition is ascribed to the respective destinations of Pyriphlegethon [756] and Elysium. Now they are not merely your composers of myth and poetry who write songs of this strain; but your philosophers also speak with all confidence of the return of souls to their former state, [757] and of the twofold award [758] of a final judgment.

Chapter XX - Truth and Reality Pertain to Christians Alone. The Heathen Counselled to Examine and Embrace It

How long therefore, O most unjust heathen, will you refuse to acknowledge us, and (what is more) to execrate your own (worthies), since between us no distinction has place, because we are one and the same? Since you do not (of course) hate what you yourselves are, give us rather your right hands in fellowship, unite your salutations, [759] mingle your embraces, sanguinary with the sanguinary, incestuous with the incestuous, conspirators with conspirators, obstinate and vain with those of the selfsame qualities. In company with each other, we have been traitors to the majesty of the gods; and together do we provoke their indignation. You too have your "third race;" [760] not indeed third in the way of religious rite, [761] but a third race in sex, and, made up as it is of male and female in one, it is more fitted to men and women (for offices of lust). [762] Well, then, do we offend you by the very fact of our approximation and agreement?

Being on a par is apt to furnish unconsciously the materials for rivalry. Thus "a potter envies a potter, and a smith a smith." [763] But we must now discontinue this imaginary confession. [764] Our conscience has returned to the truth, and to the consistency of truth. For all those points which you allege [765] (against us) will be really found in ourselves alone; and we alone can rebut them, against whom they are adduced, by getting you to listen [766] to the other side of the question, whence that full knowledge is learnt which both inspires counsel and directs the judgment.

Now it is in fact your own maxim, that no one should determine a cause without hearing both sides of it; and it is only in our own case that you neglect (the equitable principle). You indulge to the full [767] that fault of human nature, that those things which you do not disallow in yourselves you condemn in others, or you boldly charge [768] against others those things the guilt of which [769] you retain a lasting consciousness of [770] in yourselves. The course of life in which you will choose to occupy yourselves is different from ours: whilst chaste in the eyes of others, you are unchaste towards your own selves; whilst vigorous against vice out of doors, you succumb to it at home. This is the injustice (which we have to suffer), that, knowing truth, we are condemned by those who know it not; free from guilt, we are judged by those who are implicated in it. Remove the mote, or rather the beam, out of your own eye, that you may be able to extract the mote from the eyes of others. Amend your own lives first, that you may be able to punish the Christians. Only so far as you shall have effected your own reformation, will you refuse to inflict punishment on them--nay, so far will you have become Christians yourselves; and as you shall have become Christians, so far will you have compassed your own amendment of life. Learn what that is which you accuse in us, and you will accuse no longer; search out what that is which you do not accuse in yourselves, and you will become self-accusers. From these very few and humble remarks, so far as we have been able to open out the subject to you, you will plainly get some insight into (your own) error, and some discovery of our truth. Condemn that truth if you have the heart, [771] but only after you have examined it; and approve the error still, if you are so minded, [772] only first explore it. But if your prescribed rule is to love error and hate truth, why, (let me ask,) do you not probe to a full discovery the objects both of your love and your hatred?

Footnotes:

458. [As a recapitulation I insert this here to close this class of argument for the reasons following.] This treatise resembles The Apology, both in its general purport as a vindication of Christianity against heathen prejudice, and in many of its expressions and statements. So great is the resemblance that this shorter work has been thought by some to have been a first draft of the longer and perfect one. Tertullian, however, here addresses his expostulations to the general public, while in The Apology it is the rulers and magistrates of the empire whom he seeks to influence. [Dr. Allix conjectures the date of this treatise to be about a.d. 217. See Kaye, p. 50.]

459. Compare The Apology, c. i.

460. Revincit. "Condemnat" is Tertullian's word in The Apology, i.

461. Defendit. "Excusat" in Apol.

462. Non licet rectius suspicari.

463. Non lubet propius experiri.

464. At quin.

465. Nisi si.

466. Emendari pudet.

467. Excusari piget.

468. Redundantiæ nostræ.

469. Bona fide.

470. Pro extremitatibus temporum.

471. Or perhaps, "to maintain evil in preference to good."

472. Certe.

473. Pristinorum. In the corresponding passage (Apol. i.) the phrase is, "nisi plane retro non fuisse," i.e., "except that he was not a Christian long ago."

474. Cessat.
475. Comp. c. ii. of The Apology.
476. Ipsi.
477. Gratis reum.
478. Sane.
479. Neque spatium commodetis.
480. Quanquam confessis.
481. Receptoribus, "concealers" of the crime.
482. Porro.
483. Elogia.
484. Immo.
485. We have for once departed from Oehler's text, and preferred Rigault's: "Perducerentur infantarii et coci, ipsi canes pronubi, emendata esset res." The sense is evident from The Apology, c. vii.: "It is said that we are guilty of most horrible crimes; that in the celebration of our sacrament we put a child to death, which we afterward devour, and at the end of our banquet revel in incest; that we employ dogs as ministers of our impure delights, to overthrow the candles, and thus to provide darkness, and remove all shame which might interfere with these impious lusts" (Chevalier's translation). These calumnies were very common, and are noticed by Justin Martyr, Minucius Felix, Eusebius, Athenagoras, and Origen, who attributes their origin to the Jews.

Oehler reads infantariæ, after the Agobardine codex and editio princeps, and quotes Martial (Epigr. iv. 88), where the word occurs in the sense of an inordinate love of children.
486. Nam et plerique fidem talium temperant.
487. Comp. The Apology, cc. i. and ii.
488. Adeo si.
489. Si accommodarent.
490. Porro.
491. Hæc ratio est.
492. Reprobentur.
493. Impunitate.
494. i.e., the name "Christians."
495. By the "suo loco," Tertullian refers to The Apology.
496. Præscribitur vobis.
497. Præsidi.
498. Ego.
499. Χρηστός means both "pleasant" and "good;" and the heathen founded this word with the sacred name Χριστός.
500. Detinetis.
501. Et utique.
502. See The Apology, c. iii.
503. Plectitur.
504. Tradux.
505. Retinere.
506. At nunc.
507. Elatrent.
508. Libertatem suam, "their liberty of speech."
509. Denique.
510. Porro.
511. Gravem, "earnest."
512. Comp. The Apology, c. iii.
513. Pro.
514. i.e., the Christian.
515. De commercio.
516. Unum atque alium. The sense being plural, we have so given it all through.
517. Captivitatis (as if theirs was a self-inflicted captivity at home).
518. Omnem uxorem patientiam obtulisse (comp. Apology, middle of c. xxxix.).
519. In ergastulum.
520. Radiant.
521. He means the religion of Christ, which he in b. ii. c. ii. contrasts with "the mere wisdom" of the philosophers.
522. Compare The Apology, cc. ii. xliv. xlvi.
523. Colata, "filtered" [or "strained"--Shaks.]
524. Ut non alicujus nubiculæ flocculo resignetur. This picturesque language defies translation.
525. Malitiæ.
526. Dum retorquetis.
527. Inter crimen et nomen.
528. Inter dici et esse.
529. Status nominis.
530. Denuo.
531. Compare The Apology, c. iv.
532. Ad arulam quandam.
533. Istam.
534. Cessat, "loiters."
535. Requiratur.
536. Lege.
537. Ordo.
538. Genus.
539. Literally, "holding the inquiry makes for the laws."
540. Per defectionem agnoscendi.
541. Sibi debet.
542. Justitiæ suæ.
543. Merito.
544. Despuuntur.
545. Comp. The Apology, cc. vii, viii.
546. Æneid. iv. 174. "Fame, than which never plague that runs Its way more swiftly wins."--Conington.
547. "A plague" = malum.
548. Quid? quod "Yea more."
549. Ambitione.
550. Traduces.
551. Prodigiam. The word is "indicem" in The Apology.
552. Disciplina ejus illuxit.
553. Damnatio invaluit.
554. Æmula sibi.
555. Divinitatem consecutæ.

556. See above, c. ii. note.
557. i.e., What is the value of such evidence?
558. We have inserted this phrase as the sentence is strongly ironical.
559. Deferre, an infinitive of purpose, of which construction of our author Oehler gives examples.
560. Fructus.
561. Si etiam sibi credat.
562. Quidem.
563. Talia factitare.
564. We read "quo," and not "quod," because.
565. Conversatio.
566. This refers to a calumny which the heathen frequently spread about the Christians.
567. Detrectem or simply "treat of," "refer to," like the simple verb "tractare."
568. The irony of all this passage is evident.
569. Diversum opus.
570. Subjiciuntur "are stealthily narrated."
571. Inducunt.
572. It is difficult to see what this "tacent igitur" means without referring to the similar passage in The Apology (end of c. viii.), which supplies a link wanted in the context.

"At all events," says he, "they know this afterward, and yet submit to it, and allow it. They fear to be punished, while, if they proclaimed the truth, they would deserve universal approbation."

Tertullian here states what the enemies of the Christians used to allege against them. After discovering the alleged atrocities of their secret assemblies, they kept their knowledge forsooth to themselves, being afraid of the consequences of a disclosure, etc.

573. We have for convenience treated "protrahunt" (q.d. "nor do they report them") as a neuter verb.
574. Even worse than Thyestean atrocities would be believed of them.
575. Miseræ atque miserandæ.
576. Viderimus.
577. See below, in c. xix.
578. Animam.
579. Rudem, "hardly formed."
580. Extraneam.
581. Immo idcirco.
582. Quanto constare.
583. "An alii ordines dentium Christianorum, et alii specus faucium?" (literally, "Have Christians other sets of teeth, and other caverns of jaws?") This seems to refer to voracious animals like the shark, whose terrible teeth, lying in several rows, and greediness to swallow anything, however incongruous, that comes in its way, are well-known facts in natural history.
584. Positione.
585. Compare The Apology, c. viii.
586. Cynopæ. This class would furnish the unnatural "teeth," and "jaws," just referred to.
587. Sciapodes with broad feet producing a large shade; suited for the "incestuous lust" above mentioned.
588. Literally, "which come up from under ground."
589. Tertullian got this story from Herodotus, ii. 2.
590. Ipsius animæ organo.
591. Faucibus.
592. Utpote linguatuli.
593. This is one of the passages which incidentally show how widely spread was Christianity.
594. De Superstitione.
595. Comp. The Apology, cc. xl. xli. [And Augustine, Civ. Dei. iii.]
596. By the "manceps erroris" he means the devil.
597. Libitina.
598. Christianorum meritum, which with "sit" may also, "Let the Christians have their due." In The Apology the cry is, "Christianos ad leonem."
599. We insert this after Oehler. Tertullian's words are, "Quasi modicum habeant aut aliud metuere qui Deum verum."
600. See above, c. vii.
601. Sæculum digessit.
602. Aliter vobis renuntiata.
603. Absolutum est.
604. Comp. The Apology, cc. xii. xiii. xiv. xv.
605. See The Apology (passim), especially cc. xvi.-xxiv., xxx.-xxxvi., and xxxix.
606. Admentationibus.
607. Plane.
608. Traditum.
609. Vel.
610. Perinde a vobis.
611. Quibus est.
612. Adsolaverunt, "thrown to the ground;" "floored."
613. Sectam. [Rather--"A Christian secession."]
614. Perhibetis.
615. Domestica consecratione, i.e., "for family worship."
616. Addicitur.
617. Conducitur.
618. Eadem.
619. Exactione, "as excise duty for the treasury."
620. Immo.
621. "In money," stipibus.

622. " Victims. "
623. Plus refigitur.
624. Utut mortuos.
625. Tensæ.
626. Plane.
627. Rigaltius has the name Proculus in his text; but Tertullian refers not merely to that case but to a usual functionary, necessary in all cases of deification.
628. Oehler reads "ei" (of course for "ii"); Rigalt. reads "ii."
629. Denotatior ad.
630. Gulæ, "Depraved taste."
631. Prope religionem convenire, "to have approximated to."
632. Quatenus.
633. Credunt, one would expect "creduntur" ("are supposed"), which is actually read by Gothofredus.
634. Or, "circumstances" (casibus).
635. Fortasse periturum.
636. Traducit, perhaps "degrades."
637. Ut dei præfarentur. Oehler explains the verb "præfari" to mean "auctorem esse et tanquam caput."
638. Denique.
639. Stili.
640. Tertullian gives the comic plural "Juppiteres."
641. Ingenia.
642. Because appropriating to themselves the admiration which was due to the gods.
643. Cujuslibet dei.
644. Sustinetis modulari.
645. It is best to add the original of this almost unintelligible passage:
"Plane religiosiores estis in gladiatorum cavea, ubi super sanguinem humanum, supra inquinamenta poenarum proinde saltant dei vestri argumenta et historias nocentibus erogandis, aut in ipsis deis nocentes puniuntur." Some little light may be derived from the parallel passage of the Apology (c. xv.), which is expressed somewhat less obscurely. Instead of the words in italics, Tertullian there substitutes these: "Argumenta et historias noxiis ministrantes, nisi quod et ipsos deos vestros sæpe noxii induunt"-- "whilst furnishing the proofs and the plots for (executing) criminals, only that the said criminals often act the part of your gods themselves."
Oehler refers, in illustration of the last clause, to the instance of the notorious robber Laureolus, who personated Prometheus; others, again, personated Laureolus himself: some criminals had to play the part of Orpheus; others of Mutius Scævola. It will be observed that these executions were with infamous perverseness set off with scenic show, wherein the criminal enacted some violent death in yielding up his own life. The indignant irony of the whole passage, led off by the "plane religiosiores estis," is evident.
646. Censentur.
647. Factitant.
648. i.e., the gods themselves.
649. Redimitis.
650. Redimitis.
651. Comp. The Apology, c. xvi.
652. In The Apology (c. xvi.) the reference is to "the fifth book." This is correct. Book v. c. 3, is meant.
653. In vobis, for "in vos" ex pari transferendorum.
654. Comp. The Apology, c. xvi.
655. Crucis antistites.
656. Erit.
657. Consacraneus.
658. Viderint.
659. Viderit.
660. Stipite crucis.
661. Solo staticulo. The use of wood in the construction of an idol is mentioned afterward.
662. Omne robur.
663. Antemna. See our Anti-Marcion, p. 156. Ed. Edinburgh.
664. De isto patibulo.
665. Plasta.
666. In primo.
667. Statumini.
668. Comp. The Apology, c. xii.: "Every image of a god has been first constructed on a cross and stake, and plastered with cement. The body of your god is first dedicated upon a gibbet."
669. Veneramini.
670. Tropæum, for "tropæorum." We have given the sense rather than the words of this awkward sentence.
671. Suggestus.
672. Comp. The Apology, c. xvi.
673. Sunday.
674. Saturday.
675. Ex diebus.
676. On the "Coena pura," see our Anti-Marcion, p. 386, note 4.
677. See Lev. xxiv. 2; also 2 Chron. xiii. 11. Witsius (Ægyptiaca, ii. 16, 17) compares the Jewish with the Egyptian "ritus lucernarum."
678. Tertullian, in his tract de Jejun. xvi., speaks of the Jews praying (after the loss of their temple, and in their dispersion) in the open air, "per omne litus."
679. Comp. The Apology, c. xvi.
680. In ista civitate, Rome.
681. This is explained in the passage of The Apology (xvi.): "He had for money exposed himself with criminals to fight with wild beasts."
682. Decutiendus, from a jocular word,

"decutire."

683. This curious word is compounded of ὄνος, an ass, and κοιᾶσθαι, which Hesychius explains by ἱερᾶσθαι, to act as a priest. The word therefore means, "asinarius sacerdos," "an ass of a priest." Calumnious enough; but suited to the vile occasion, and illustrative of the ribald opposition which Christianity had to encounter.

684. We take Rigaltius' reading, "seminarium."

685. Tanquam hesternum.

686. Comp. The Apology, c. ix.

687. Sacri.

688. He refers in this passage to his Apology, especially c. ix.

689. Tabellis.

690. Unius ætatis. This Oehler explains by "per unam jam totam hanc ætatem."

691. Genere.

692. Pignora, scil. amoris.

693. See Apology, c. ix.

694. Si forte.

695. Parum scilicet?

696. Elicitis.

697. Infantem totum præcocum.

698. Comp. The Apology, c. ix.

699. Adulteram noctem.

700. Ceterum.

701. Plane.

702. Trucidatus oculos.

703. Errores.

704. Sive stativo vel ambulatorio titulo.

705. Compagines generis.

706. Comitum.

707. Græculus.

708. "Aliquis" is here understood.

709. Utitur Græco, i.e., cinædo, "for purposes of lust."

710. Or, "is sent into the country, and put into prison."

711. Aliquid recordantur.

712. Publicæ eruptionis.

713. Intentatis.

714. Vestris non sacramentis, with a hyphen, "your non-mysteries."

715. Comp. The Apology, c. xxxv.

716. Secunda.

717. Severus, in a.d. 198.

718. These titles were borne by Caracalla.

719. Or, "topic"--hoc loco.

720. i.e., whether among the Christians or the heathen.

721. A cavil of the heathen.

722. Sane.

723. Galliæ.

724. Vesaniæ.

725. Conveniam.

726. Recognoscam.

727. Festivos libellos.

728. A concilio.

729. Ex fide.

730. Literally, "we make faces."

731. Comp. The Apology, c. xxxiii., p. 37, supra, and Minucius Felix, Octavius, c. xxiii. [Vol. IV. this Series.]

732. Comp., The Apology, c. 50 [p. 54, infra.]

733. A virtute didicerunt.

734. With the "piget prosequi" to govern the preceding oblique clause, it is unnecessary to suppose (with Oehler) the omission here of some verb like "erogavit."

735. Novitatem...dedicavit.

736. Tertullian refers to Cleopatra's death also in his tract ad Mart. c. iv. [See this Vol. infra.]

737. This case is again referred to in this treatise (p. 138), and in ad Mart c. iv. [See this Volume, infra.]

738. Eradicatæ confessionis. [See p. 55, supra.]

739. Non invenitur.

740. Eadem voce.

741. Utique. The ironical tone of Tertullian's answer is evident.

742. Gladio ad lanistas auctoratis.

743. We follow Oehler in giving the clause this negative turn; he renders it: "Tretet nicht aus Furcht vor dem Tode ins Kriegsheer ein."

744. Alicui.

745. Jam evasit.

746. Auctoravit.

747. Vestiendum incendiale tunica.

748. Inter venatorios: "venatores circi" (Oehler).

749. "Doubtless the stripes which the Spartans endured with such firmness, aggravated by the presence of their nearest relatives, who encouraged them, conferred honour upon their family."--Apology, c. 50. [See p. 55, supra.]

750. Compare The Apology, cc. xlvii. xlviii. xlix. [This Vol., supra.]

751. Præstruitur.

752. Præsumimus.

753. Est.

754. Interim.

755. Traditum.

756. The heathen hell, Tartarus or Orcus.

757. Reciprocatione.

758. Distributione.

759. Compingite oscula.

760. Eunuchs (Rigalt.).

761. As the Christians were held to be; coming after (1) the heathen, (2) the Jews. See above, c. viii., and Scorpiace, c. x.

762. Eunuchs (Rigalt.).

763. An oft-quoted proverb in ancient writers. It occurs in Hesiod (Opp. et Dies) 25.

764. Literally, "cease henceforth, O,

simulated confession."
    765. Omnia ista.
    766. This seems to be the force of the "agnitione," which Oehler renders "auditione."
    767. Satisfacitis.
    768. Jactetis.
    769. Quorum reatum.
    770. Memineritis.
    771. Si potestis.
    772. Si putatis.

Book II [773]

Chapter I - The Heathen Gods from Heathen Authorities. Varro Has Written a Work on the Subject. His Threefold Classification. The Changeable Character of that Which Ought to Be Fixed and Certain

Our defence requires that we should at this point discuss with you the character of your gods, O ye heathen, fit objects of our pity, [774] appealing even to your own conscience to determine whether they be truly gods, as you would have it supposed, or falsely, as you are unwilling to have proved. [775] Now this is the material part of human error, owing to the wiles of its author, that it is never free from the ignorance of error, [776] whence your guilt is all the greater.

Your eyes are open, yet they see not; your ears are unstopped, yet they hear not; though your heart beats, it is yet dull, nor does your mind understand [777] that of which it is cognizant. [778] If indeed the enormous perverseness (of your worship) could [779] be broken up [780] by a single demurrer, we should have our objection ready to hand in the declaration [781] that, as we know all those gods of yours to have been instituted by men, all belief in the true Deity is by this very circumstance brought to nought; [782] because, of course, nothing which some time or other had a beginning can rightly seem to be divine. But the fact is, [783] there are many things by which tenderness of conscience is hardened into the callousness of wilful error. Truth is beleaguered with the vast force (of the enemy), and yet how secure she is in her own inherent strength! And naturally enough [784] when from her very adversaries she gains to her side whomsoever she will, as her friends and protectors, and prostrates the entire host of her assailants. It is therefore against these things that our contest lies--against the institutions of our ancestors, against the authority of tradition, [785] the laws of our governors, and the reasonings of the wise; against antiquity, custom, submission; [786] against precedents, prodigies, miracles,--all which things have had their part in consolidating that spurious [787] system of your gods. Wishing, then, to follow step by step your own commentaries which you have drawn out of your theology of every sort (because the authority of learned men goes further with you in matters of this kind than the testimony of facts), I have taken and abridged the works of Varro; [788] for he in his treatise Concerning Divine Things, collected out of ancient digests, has shown himself a serviceable guide [789] for us. Now, if I inquire of him who were the subtle inventors [790] of the gods, he points to either the philosophers, the peoples, or the poets. For he has made a threefold distinction in classifying the gods: one being the physical class, of which the philosophers treat; another the mythic class, which is the constant burden of [791] the poets; the third, the gentile class, which the nations have adopted each one for itself. When, therefore, the philosophers have ingeniously composed their physical (theology) out of their own conjectures, when the poets have drawn their mythical from fables, and the (several) nations have forged their gentile (polytheism) according to their own will, where in the world must truth be placed? In the conjectures? Well, but these are only a doubtful conception. In the fables? But they are at best an absurd story. In the popular accounts? [792] This sort of opinion, [793] however, is only promiscuous [794] and municipal. Now all things with the philosophers are uncertain, because of their variation with the poets all is worthless, because immoral; with the nations all is irregular and confused, because dependent on their mere choice.

The nature of God, however, if it be the true one with which you are concerned, is of so definite a character as not to be derived from uncertain speculations, [795] nor contaminated with worthless fables, nor determined by promiscuous conceits. It ought indeed to be regarded, as it really is, as certain, entire, universal, because it is in truth the property of all. Now, what god shall I believe? One that has been gauged by vague suspicion? One that history [796] has divulged? One that a community has invented? It would be a far worthier thing if I believed no god, than one which is open to doubt, or full of shame, or the object of arbitrary selection. [797]

Chapter II - Philosophers Had Not Succeeded in Discovering God. The Uncertainty and Confusion of Their Speculations

But the authority of the physical philosophers is maintained among you [798] as the special property[799] of wisdom. You mean of course, that pure and simple wisdom of the philosophers which attests its own weakness mainly by that variety of opinion which proceeds from an ignorance of the truth. Now what wise man is so devoid of truth, as not to know that God is the Father and Lord of wisdom itself and truth? Besides, there is that divine oracle uttered by Solomon: "The fear of the Lord," says he, "is the beginning of wisdom." [800] But [801] fear has its origin in knowledge; for how will a man fear that of which he knows nothing? Therefore he who shall have the fear of God, even if he be ignorant of all things else, if he has attained to the knowledge and truth of God, [802] will possess full and perfect wisdom.

This, however, is what philosophy has not clearly realized. For although, in their inquisitive disposition to search into all kinds of learning, the philosophers may seem to have investigated the sacred Scriptures themselves for their antiquity, and to have derived thence some of their opinions; yet because they have interpolated these deductions they prove that they have either despised them wholly or have not fully believed them, for in other cases also the simplicity of truth is shaken[803] by the over-scrupulousness of an irregular belief, [804] and that they therefore changed them, as their desire of glory grew, into products of their own mind. The consequence of this is, that even that which they had discovered degenerated into uncertainty, and there arose from one or two drops of truth a perfect flood of argumentation. For after they had simply [805] found God, they did not expound Him as they found Him, but rather disputed about His quality, and His nature, and even about His abode. The Platonists, indeed, (held) Him to care about worldly things, both as the disposer and judge thereof. The Epicureans regarded Him as apathetic [806] and inert, and (so to say) a non-entity. [807] The Stoics believed Him to be outside of the world; the Platonists, within the world.

The God whom they had so imperfectly admitted, they could neither know nor fear; and therefore they could not be wise, since they wandered away indeed from the beginning of wisdom," that is, "the fear of God." Proofs are not wanting that among the philosophers there was not only an ignorance, but actual doubt, about the divinity. Diogenes, when asked what was taking place in heaven, answered by saying, "I have never been up there." Again, whether there were any gods, he replied, "I do not know; only there ought to be gods." [808] When Croesus inquired of Thales of Miletus what he thought of the gods, the latter having taken some time [809] to consider, answered by the word "Nothing."

Even Socrates denied with an air of certainty [810] those gods of yours. [811] Yet he with a like certainty requested that a cock should be sacrificed to Æsculapius. And therefore when philosophy, in its practice of defining about God, is detected in such uncertainty and inconsistency, what "fear" could it possibly have had of Him whom it was not competent [812] clearly to determine? We have been taught to believe of the world that it is god. [813] For such the physical class of theologizers conclude it to be, since they have handed down such views about the gods that Dionysius the Stoic divides them into three kinds. The first, he supposes, includes those gods which are most obvious, as the Sun, Moon, and Stars; the next, those which are not apparent, as Neptune; the remaining one, those which are said to have passed from the human state to the divine, as Hercules and Amphiaraus. In like manner, Arcesilaus makes a threefold form of the divinity--the Olympian, the Astral, the Titanian--sprung from Coelus and Terra; from which through Saturn and Ops came Neptune, Jupiter, and Orcus, and their entire progeny. Xenocrates, of the Academy, makes a twofold division--the Olympian and the Titanian, which descend from Coelus and Terra. Most of the Egyptians believe that there are four gods--the Sun and the Moon, the Heaven and the Earth. Along with all the supernal fire Democritus conjectures that the gods arose. Zeno, too, will have it that their nature resembles it. Whence Varro also makes fire to be the soul of the world, that in the world fire governs all things, just as the soul does in ourselves. But all this is most absurd. For he says, Whilst it is in us, we have existence; but as soon as it has left us, we die. Therefore, when fire quits the world in lightning, the world comes to its end.

Chapter III - The Physical Philosophers Maintained the Divinity of the Elements; The Absurdity of the Tenet Exposed

From these developments of opinion, we see that your [814] physical class of philosophers are driven to the necessity of contending that the elements are gods, since it alleges that other gods are sprung from them; for it is only from gods that gods could be born. Now, although we shall have to examine these other gods more fully in the proper place, in the mythic section of the poets, yet, inasmuch as we must meanwhile treat of them in their connection with the present class, [815] we shall probably even from their present class, [816] when once we turn to the gods themselves, succeed in showing that they can by no means appear to be gods who are said to be sprung from the elements; so that we have at once a presumption [817] that the elements are not gods, since they which are born of the elements are not gods. In like manner, whilst we show that the elements are not gods, we shall, according to the law of natural relationship, [818] get a presumptive argument that they cannot rightly be maintained to be gods whose parents (in this case the elements) are not gods. It is a settled point [819] that a god is born of a god, and that what lacks divinity [820] is born of what is not divine. Now, so far as [821] the world of which your philosophers treat [822] (for I apply this term to the universe in the most comprehensive sense [823]) contains the elements, ministering to them as its component parts (for whatever its own condition may be, the same of course will be that of its elements and constituent portions), it must needs have been formed either by some being, according to the enlightened view [824] of Plato, or else by none, according to the harsh opinion [825] of Epicurus; and since it was formed, by having a beginning, it must also have an end. That, therefore, which at one time before its beginning had no existence, and will by and by after its end cease to have an existence, cannot of course, by any possibility, seem to be a god, wanting as it does that essential character of divinity, eternity, which is reckoned to be [826] without beginning, and without end. If, however, it [827] is in no wise formed, and therefore ought to be accounted divine--since, as divine, it is subject neither to a beginning nor an end of itself--how is it that some assign generation to the elements, which they hold to be gods, when the Stoics deny that anything can be born of a god? Likewise, how is it that they wish those beings, whom they suppose to be born of the elements, to be regarded as gods, when they deny that a god can be born?

Now, what must hold good of the universe [828] will have to be predicated of the elements, I mean of heaven, and of earth, and of the stars, and of fire, which Varro has vainly proposed that you should believe [829] to be gods, and the parents of gods, contrary to that generation and nativity which he had declared to be impossible in a god. Now this same Varro had shown that the earth and the stars were animated. [830] But if this be the case, they must needs be also mortal, according to the condition [831] of animated nature; for although the soul is evidently immortal, this attribute is limited to it alone: it is not extended to that with which it is associated, that is, the body. Nobody, however, will deny that the elements have body, since we both touch them and are touched by them, and we see certain bodies fall down from them. If, therefore, they are animated, laying aside the principle [832] of a soul, as befits their condition as bodies, they are mortal--of course not immortal. And yet whence is it that the elements appear to Varro to be animated?

Because, forsooth, the elements have motion. And then, in order to anticipate what may be objected on the other side, that many things else have motion--as wheels, as carriages, as several other machines--he volunteers the statement that he believes only such things to be animated as move of themselves, without any apparent mover or impeller from without, like the apparent mover of the wheel, or propeller of the carriage, or director of the machine. If, then, they are not animated, they have no motion of themselves. Now, when he thus alleges a power which is not apparent, he points to what it was his duty to seek after, even the creator and controller of the motion; for it does not at once follow that, because we do not see a thing, we believe that it does not exist. Rather, it is necessary the more profoundly to investigate what one does not see, in order the better to understand the character of that which is apparent. Besides if (you admit) only the existence of those things which appear and are supposed to exist simply because they appear, how is it that you also admit them to be gods which do not appear? If, moreover, those things seem to have existence which have none, why may they not have existence also which do not seem to have it? Such, for instance, as the Mover [833] of the heavenly beings. Granted, then, that things are animated because they move of themselves, and that they move of themselves when they are not moved by another:

still it does not follow that they must straightway be gods, because they are animated, nor even because they move of themselves; else what is to prevent all animals whatever being accounted gods, moving as they do of themselves? This, to be sure, is allowed to the Egyptians, but their superstitious vanity has another basis. [834]

Chapter IV - Wrong Derivation of the Word Θεός. The Name Indicative of the True Deity. God Without Shape and Immaterial. Anecdote of Thales

Some affirm that the gods (i.e. θεοί) were so called because the verbs θέειν and σείσθαι signify to run and to be moved. [835] This term, then, is not indicative of any majesty, for it is derived from running and motion, not from any dominion [836] of godhead. But inasmuch as the Supreme God whom we worship is also designated Θεός, without however the appearance of any course or motion in Him, because He is not visible to any one, it is clear that that word must have had some other derivation, and that the property of divinity, innate in Himself, must have been discovered. Dismissing, then, that ingenious interpretation, it is more likely that the gods were not called θεοί from running and motion, but that the term was borrowed from the designation of the true God; so that you gave the name θεοί to the gods, whom you had in like manner forged for yourselves.

Now, that this is the case, a plain proof is afforded in the fact that you actually give the common appellation θεοί to all those gods of yours, in whom there is no attribute of course or motion indicated. When, therefore, you call them both θεοί and immoveable with equal readiness, there is a deviation as well from the meaning of the word as from the idea [837] of godhead, which is set aside [838] if measured by the notion of course and motion. But if that sacred name be peculiarly significant of deity, and be simply true and not of a forced interpretation [839] in the case of the true God, but transferred in a borrowed sense [840] to those other objects which you choose to call gods, then you ought to show to us [841] that there is also a community of character between them, so that their common designation may rightly depend on their union of essence. But the true God, on the sole ground that He is not an object of sense, is incapable of being compared with those false deities which are cognizable to sight and sense (to sense indeed is sufficient); for this amounts to a clear statement of the difference between an obscure proof and a manifest one. Now, since the elements are obvious to all, (and) since God, on the contrary, is visible to none, how will it be in your power from that part which you have not seen to pass to a decision on the objects which you see? Since, therefore, you have not to combine them in your perception or your reason, why do you combine them in name with the purpose of combining them also in power?

For see how even Zeno separates the matter of the world from God: he says that the latter has percolated through the former, like honey through the comb. God, therefore, and Matter are two words (and) two things. Proportioned to the difference of the words is the diversity of the things; the condition also of matter follows its designation. Now if matter is not God, because its very appellation teaches us so, how can those things which are inherent in matter--that is, the elements--be regarded as gods, since the component members cannot possibly be heterogeneous from the body? But what concern have I with physiological conceits? It were better for one's mind to ascend above the state of the world, not to stoop down to uncertain speculations. Plato's form for the world was round. Its square, angular shape, such as others had conceived it to be, he rounded off, I suppose, with compasses, from his labouring to have it believed to be simply without a beginning.[842] Epicurus, however, who had said, "What is above us is nothing to us," wished notwithstanding to have a peep at the sky, and found the sun to be a foot in diameter.

Thus far you must confess [843] men were niggardly in even celestial objects.

In process of time their ambitious conceptions advanced, and so the sun too enlarged its disk.[844] Accordingly, the Peripatetics marked it out as a larger world. [845] Now, pray tell me, what wisdom is there in this hankering after conjectural speculations?

What proof is afforded to us, notwithstanding the strong confidence of its assertions, by the useless affectation of a scrupulous curiosity, [846] which is tricked out with an artful show of language? It therefore served Thales of Miletus quite right, when, star-gazing as he walked with all the eyes he had, he had the mortification of falling [847] into a well, and was unmercifully twitted by an Egyptian, who said to him, "Is it because you found nothing on earth to look at, that you think you ought to confine your gaze to the sky?" His fall, therefore, is a figurative picture of the philosophers; of those, I mean, [848] who persist in applying [849] their studies to a vain purpose, since they indulge a stupid curiosity on natural objects, which they ought rather (intelligently to direct) to their Creator and Governor.

Chapter V - The Physical Theory Continued. Further Reasons Advanced Against the Divinity of the Elements

Why, then, do we not resort to that far more reasonable [850] opinion, which has clear proof of being derived from men's common sense and unsophisticated deduction? [851] Even Varro bears it in mind, when he says that the elements are supposed to be divine, because nothing whatever is capable, without their concurrence, [852] of being produced, nourished, or applied to the sustenance [853] of man's life and of the earth, since not even our bodies and souls could have sufficed in themselves without the modification [854] of the elements. By this it is that the world is made generally habitable,--a result which is harmoniously secured [855] by the distribution into zones, [856] except where human residence has been rendered impracticable by intensity of cold or heat. On this account, men have accounted as gods--the sun, because it imparts from itself the light of day, ripens the fruit with its warmth, and measures the year with its stated periods; the moon, which is at once the solace of the night and the controller of the months by its governance; the stars also, certain indications as they are of those seasons which are to be observed in the tillage of our fields; lastly, the very heaven also under which, and the earth over which, as well as the intermediate space within which, all things conspire together for the good of man. Nor is it from their beneficent influences only that a faith in their divinity has been deemed compatible with the elements, but from their opposite qualities also, such as usually happen from what one might call[857] their wrath and anger--as thunder, and hail, and drought, and pestilential winds, floods also, and openings of the ground, and earthquakes: these are all fairly enough [858] accounted gods, whether their nature becomes the object of reverence as being favourable, or of fear because terrible--the sovereign dispenser, [859] in fact, [860] both of help and of hurt. But in the practical conduct of social life, this is the way in which men act and feel: they do not show gratitude or find fault with the very things from which the succour or the injury proceeds, so much as with them by whose strength and power the operation of the things is effected. For even in your amusements you do not award the crown as a prize to the flute or the harp, but to the musician who manages the said flute or harp by the power of his delightful skill. [861] In like manner, when one is in ill-health, you do not bestow your acknowledgments on the flannel wraps, [862] or the medicines, or the poultices, but on the doctors by whose care and prudence the remedies become effectual.

So again, in untoward events, they who are wounded with the sword do not charge the injury on the sword or the spear, but on the enemy or the robber; whilst those whom a falling house covers do not blame the tiles or the stones, but the oldness of the building; as again shipwrecked sailors impute their calamity not to the rocks and waves, but to the tempest. And rightly too; for it is certain that everything which happens must be ascribed not to the instrument with which, but to the agent by whom, it takes place; inasmuch as he is the prime cause of the occurrence, [863] who appoints both the event itself and that by whose instrumentality it comes to pass (as there are in all things these three particular elements-- the fact itself, its instrument, and its cause), because he himself who wills the occurrence of a thing comes into notice [864] prior to the thing which he wills, or the instrument by which it occurs. On all other occasions therefore, your conduct is right enough, because you consider the author; but in physical phenomena your rule is opposed to that natural principle which prompts you to a wise judgment in all other cases, removing out of sight as you do the supreme position of the author, and considering rather the things that happen, than him by whom they happen. Thus it comes to pass that you suppose the power and the dominion to belong to the elements, which are but the slaves and functionaries.

Now do we not, in thus tracing out an artificer and master within, expose the artful structure of their slavery [865] out of the appointed functions of those elements to which you ascribe (the attributes) of power? [866] But gods are not slaves; therefore whatever things are servile in character are not gods. Otherwise [867] they should prove to us that, according to the ordinary course of things, liberty is promoted by irregular licence, [868] despotism by liberty, and that by despotism divine power is meant. For if all the (heavenly bodies) overhead forget not [869] to fulfil their courses in certain orbits, in regular seasons, at proper distances, and at equal intervals--appointed in the way of a law for the revolutions of time, and for directing the guidance thereof--can it fail to result [870] from the very observance of their conditions and the fidelity of their operations, that you will be convinced both by the recurrence of their orbital courses and the accuracy of their mutations, when you bear in mind how ceaseless is their recurrence, that a governing power presides over them, to which the entire management of the world [871] is obedient, reaching even to the utility and injury of the human race? For you cannot pretend that these (phenomena) act and care for themselves alone, without contributing anything to the advantage of mankind, when you maintain that the elements are divine for no other reason than that you experience from them either benefit or injury to yourself. For if they benefit themselves only, you are under no obligation to them.

Chapter VI - The Changes of the Heavenly Bodies, Proof that They are Not Divine. Transition from the Physical to the Mythic Class of Gods

Come now, do you allow that the Divine Being not only has nothing servile in His course, but exists in unimpaired integrity, and ought not to be diminished, or suspended, or destroyed? Well, then, all His blessedness [872] would disappear, if He were ever subject to change. Look, however, at the stellar bodies; they both undergo change, and give clear evidence of the fact. The moon tells us how great has been its loss, as it recovers its full form; [873] its greater losses you are already accustomed to measure in a mirror of water; [874] so that I need not any longer believe in any wise what magians have asserted. The sun, too, is frequently put to the trial of an eclipse. Explain as best you may the modes of these celestial casualties, it is impossible [875] for God either to become less or to cease to exist. Vain, therefore, are [876] those supports of human learning, which, by their artful method of weaving conjectures, belie both wisdom and truth.

Besides, [877] it so happens, indeed, according to your natural way of thinking, that he who has spoken the best is supposed to have spoken most truly, instead of him who has spoken the truth being held to have spoken the best. Now the man who shall carefully look into things, will surely allow it to be a greater probability that those [878] elements which we have been discussing are under some rule and direction, than that they have a motion of their own, and that being under government they cannot be gods. If, however, one is in error in this matter, it is better to err simply than speculatively, like your physical philosophers. But, at the same time, [879] if you consider the character of the mythic school, (and compare it with the physical,) the error which we have already seen frail men [880] making in the latter is really the more respectable one, since it ascribes a divine nature to those things which it supposes to be superhuman in their sensibility, whether in respect of their position, their power, their magnitude, or their divinity. For that which you suppose to be higher than man, you believe to be very near to God.

Chapter VII - The Gods of the Mythic Class. The Poets a Very Poor Authority in Such Matters. Homer and the Mythic Poets. Why Irreligious

But to pass to the mythic class of gods, which we attributed to the poets, [881] I hardly know whether I must only seek to put them on a par with our own human mediocrity, or whether they must be affirmed to be gods, with proofs of divinity, like the African Mopsus and the Boeotian Amphiaraus. I must now indeed but slightly touch on this class, of which a fuller view will be taken in the proper place. [882] Meanwhile, that these were only human beings, is clear from the fact that you do not consistently call them gods, but heroes. Why then discuss the point? Although divine honours had to be ascribed to dead men, it was not to them as such, of course. Look at your own practice, when with similar excess of presumption you sully heaven with the sepulchres of your kings: is it not such as are illustrious for justice, virtue, piety, and every excellence of this sort, that you honour with the blessedness of deification, contented even to incur contempt if you forswear yourselves [883] for such characters? And, on the other hand, do you not deprive the impious and disgraceful of even the old prizes of human glory, tear up [884] their decrees and titles, pull down their statues, and deface [885] their images on the current coin? Will He, however, who beholds all things, who approves, nay, rewards the good, prostitute before all men [886] the attribute of His own inexhaustible grace and mercy? And shall men be allowed an especial mount of care and righteousness, that they may be wise [887] in selecting and multiplying [888] their deities? Shall attendants on kings and princes be more pure than those who wait on the Supreme God? [889] You turn your back in horror, indeed, on outcasts and exiles, on the poor and weak, on the obscurely born and the low-lived; [890] but yet you honour, even by legal sanctions, [891] unchaste men, adulterers, robbers, and parricides. Must we regard it as a subject of ridicule or indignation, that such characters are believed to be gods who are not fit to be men? Then, again, in this mythic class of yours which the poets celebrate, how uncertain is your conduct as to purity of conscience and the maintenance thereof!

For whenever we hold up to execration the wretched, disgraceful and atrocious (examples) of your gods, you defend them as mere fables, on the pretence of poetic licence; whenever we volunteer a silent contempt [892] of this said [893] poetic licence, then you are not only troubled with no horror of it, but you go so far as [894] to show it respect, and to hold it as one of the indispensable (fine) arts; nay, [895] you carry out the studies of your higher classes [896] by its means, as the very foundation [897] of your literature. Plato was of opinion that poets ought to be banished, as calumniators of the gods; (he would even have) Homer himself expelled from his republic, although, as you are aware, [898] he was the crowned head of them all. But while you admit and retain them thus, why should you not believe them when they disclose such things respecting your gods? And if you do believe your poets, how is it that you worship such gods (as they describe)?

If you worship them simply because you do not believe the poets, why do you bestow praise on such lying authors, without any fear of giving offence to those whose calumniators you honour? A regard for truth [899] is not, of course, to be expected of poets.

But when you say that they only make men into gods after their death, do you not admit that before death the said gods were merely human? Now what is there strange in the fact, that they who were once men are subject to the dishonour [900] of human casualties, or crimes, or fables?

Do you not, in fact, put faith in your poets, when it is in accordance with their rhapsodies [901] that you have arranged in some instances your very rituals? How is it that the priestess of Ceres is ravished, if it is not because Ceres suffered a similar outrage? Why are the children of others sacrificed to Saturn, [902] if it is not because he spared not his own?

Why is a male mutilated in honour of the Idæan goddess Cybele, unless it be that the (unhappy) youth who was too disdainful of her advances was castrated, owing to her vexation at his daring to cross her love? [903] Why was not Hercules "a dainty dish" to the good ladies of Lanuvium, if it was not for the primeval offence which women gave to him? The poets, no doubt, are liars. Yet it is not because of their telling us that [904] your gods did such things when they were human beings, nor because they predicated divine scandals [905] of a divine state, since it seemed to you more credible that gods should exist, though not of such a character, than that there should be such characters, although not gods.

Chapter VIII - The Gods of the Different Nations. Varro's Gentile Class. Their Inferiority. A Good Deal of This Perverse Theology Taken from Scripture. Serapis a Perversion of Joseph

There remains the gentile class of gods amongst the several nations: [906] these were adopted out of mere caprice, not from the knowledge of the truth; and our information about them comes from the private notions of different races. God, I imagine, is everywhere known, everywhere present, powerful everywhere--an object whom all ought to worship, all ought to serve. Since, then, it happens that even they, whom all the world worships in common, fail in the evidence of their true divinity, how much more must this befall those whom their very votaries [907] have not succeeded in discovering! For what useful authority could possibly precede a theology of so defective a character as to be wholly unknown to fame?

How many have either seen or heard of the Syrian Atargatis, the African Coelestis, the Moorish Varsutina, the Arabian Obodas and Dusaris, or the Norican Belenus, or those whom Varro mentions--Deluentinus of Casinum, Visidianus of Narnia, Numiternus of Atina, or Ancharia of Asculum? And who have any clear notions [908] of Nortia of Vulsinii? [909] There is no difference in the worth of even their names, apart from the human surnames which distinguish them. I laugh often enough at the little coteries of gods [910] in each municipality, which have their honours confined within their own city walls. To what lengths this licence of adopting gods has been pushed, the superstitious practices of the Egyptians show us; for they worship even their native [911] animals, such as cats, crocodiles, and their snake. It is therefore a small matter that they have also deified a man--him, I mean, whom not Egypt only, or Greece, but the whole world worships, and the Africans swear by; about whose state also all that helps our conjectures and imparts to our knowledge the semblance of truth is stated in our own (sacred) literature. For that Serapis of yours was originally one of our own saints called Joseph. [912] The youngest of his brethren, but superior to them in intellect, he was from envy sold into Egypt, and became a slave in the family of Pharaoh king of the country. [913] Importuned by the unchaste queen, when he refused to comply with her desire, she turned upon him and reported him to the king, by whom he is put into prison.

There he displays the power of his divine inspiration, by interpreting aright the dreams of some (fellow-prisoners).

Meanwhile the king, too, has some terrible dreams. Joseph being brought before him, according to his summons, was able to expound them.

Having narrated the proofs of true interpretation which he had given in the prison, he opens out his dream to the king:

those seven fat-fleshed and well-favoured kine signified as many years of plenty; in like manner, the seven lean-fleshed animals predicted the scarcity of the seven following years.

He accordingly recommends precautions to be taken against the future famine from the previous plenty. The king believed him. The issue of all that happened showed how wise he was, how invariably holy, and now how necessary. So Pharaoh set him over all Egypt, that he might secure the provision of corn for it, and thenceforth administer its government. They called him Serapis, from the turban [914] which adorned his head. The peck-like [915] shape of this turban marks the memory of his corn-provisioning; whilst evidence is given that the care of the supplies was all on his head, [916] by the very ears of corn which embellish the border of the head-dress. For the same reason, also, they made the sacred figure of a dog, [917] which they regard (as a sentry) in Hades, and put it under his right hand, because the care of the Egyptians was concentrated [918] under his hand. And they put at his side Pharia,[919] whose name shows her to have been the king's daughter. For in addition to all the rest of his kind gifts and rewards, Pharaoh had given him his own daughter in marriage. Since, however, they had begun to worship both wild animals and human beings, they combined both figures under one form Anubis, in which there may rather be seen clear proofs of its own character and condition enshrined [920] by a nation at war with itself, refractory [921] to its kings, despised among foreigners, with even the appetite of a slave and the filthy nature of a dog.

Chapter IX - The Power of Rome. Romanized Aspect of All the Heathen Mythology. Varro's Threefold Distribution Criticised. Roman Heroes (Æneas Included,) Unfavourably Reviewed

Such are the more obvious or more remarkable points which we had to mention in connection with Varro's threefold distribution of the gods, in order that a sufficient answer might seem to be given touching the physical, the poetic, and the gentile classes. Since, however, it is no longer to the philosophers, nor the poets, nor the nations that we owe the substitution of all (heathen worship for the true religion) although they transmitted the superstition, but to the dominant Romans, who received the tradition and gave it wide authority, another phase of the widespread error of man must now be encountered by us; nay, another forest must be felled by our axe, which has obscured the childhood of the degenerate worship [922] with germs of superstitions gathered from all quarters. Well, but even the gods of the Romans have received from (the same) Varro a threefold classification into the certain, the uncertain, and the select. What absurdity! What need had they of uncertain gods, when they possessed certain ones? Unless, forsooth, they wished to commit themselves to [923] such folly as the Athenians did; for at Athens there was an altar with this inscription: "To the unknown gods." [924] Does, then, a man worship that which he knows nothing of? Then, again, as they had certain gods, they ought to have been contented with them, without requiring select ones. In this want they are even found to be irreligious! For if gods are selected as onions are, [925] then such as are not chosen are declared to be worthless. Now we on our part allow that the Romans had two sets of gods, common and proper; in other words, those which they had in common with other nations, and those which they themselves devised. And were not these called the public and the foreign [926] gods? Their altars tell us so; there is (a specimen) of the foreign gods at the fane of Carna, of the public gods in the Palatium. Now, since their common gods are comprehended in both the physical and the mythic classes, we have already said enough concerning them. I should like to speak of their particular kinds of deity. We ought then to admire the Romans for that third set of the gods of their enemies, [927] because no other nation ever discovered for itself so large a mass of superstition. Their other deities we arrange in two classes: those which have become gods from human beings, and those which have had their origin in some other way. Now, since there is advanced the same colourable pretext for the deification of the dead, that their lives were meritorious, we are compelled to urge the same reply against them, that no one of them was worth so much pains.

Their fond [928] father Æneas, in whom they believed, was never glorious, and was felled with a stone [929] --a vulgar weapon, to pelt a dog withal, inflicting a wound no less ignoble! But this Æneas turns out [930] a traitor to his country; yes, quite as much as Antenor. And if they will not believe this to be true of him, he at any rate deserted his companions when his country was in flames, and must be held inferior to that woman of Carthage, [931] who, when her husband Hasdrubal supplicated the enemy with the mild pusillanimity of our Æneas, refused to accompany him, but hurrying her children along with her, disdained to take her beautiful self and father's noble heart [932] into exile, but plunged into the flames of the burning Carthage, as if rushing into the embraces of her (dear but) ruined country. Is he "pious Æneas" for (rescuing) his young only son and decrepit old father, but deserting Priam and Astyanax? But the Romans ought rather to detest him; for in defence of their princes and their royal [933] house, they surrender [934] even children and wives, and every dearest pledge. [935] They deify the son of Venus, and this with the full knowledge and consent of her husband Vulcan, and without opposition from even

Juno. Now, if sons have seats in heaven owing to their piety to their parents, why are not those noble youths [936] of Argos rather accounted gods, because they, to save their mother from guilt in the performance of some sacred rites, with a devotion more than human, yoked themselves to her car and dragged her to the temple? Why not make a goddess, for her exceeding piety, of that daughter [937] who from her own breasts nourished her father who was famishing in prison? What other glorious achievement can be related of Æneas, but that he was nowhere seen in the fight on the field of Laurentum? Following his bent, perhaps he fled a second time as a fugitive from the battle. [938] In like manner, Romulus posthumously becomes a god. Was it because he founded the city? Then why not others also, who have built cities, counting even [939] women? To be sure, Romulus slew his brother in the bargain, and trickishly ravished some foreign virgins. Therefore of course he becomes a god, and therefore a Quirinus ("god of the spear"), because then their fathers had to use the spear [940] on his account. What did Sterculus do to merit deification? If he worked hard to enrich the fields stercoribus,[941] (with manure,) Augias had more dung than he to bestow on them. If Faunus, the son of Picus, used to do violence to law and right, because struck with madness, it was more fit that he should be doctored than deified. [942] If the daughter of Faunus so excelled in chastity, that she would hold no conversation with men, it was perhaps from rudeness, or a consciousness of deformity, or shame for her father's insanity. How much worthier of divine honour than this "good goddess" [943] was Penelope, who, although dwelling among so many suitors of the vilest character, preserved with delicate tact the purity which they assailed! There is Sanctus, too, [944] who for his hospitality had a temple consecrated to him by king Plotius; and even Ulysses had it in his power to have bestowed one more god upon you in the person of the most refined Alcinous.

Chapter X - A Disgraceful Feature of the Roman Mythology. It Honours Such Infamous Characters as Larentina

I hasten to even more abominable cases. Your writers have not been ashamed to publish that of Larentina.

She was a hired prostitute, whether as the nurse of Romulus, and therefore called Lupa, because she was a prostitute, or as the mistress of Hercules, now deceased, that is to say, now deified. They [945] relate that his temple-warder [946] happened to be playing at dice in the temple alone; and in order to represent a partner for himself in the game, in the absence of an actual one, he began to play with one hand for Hercules and the other for himself. (The condition was,) that if he won the stakes from Hercules, he should with them procure a supper and a prostitute; if Hercules, however, proved the winner, I mean his other hand, then he should provide the same for Hercules. The hand of Hercules won. That achievement might well have been added to his twelve labours!

The temple-warden buys a supper for the hero, and hires Larentina to play the whore. The fire which dissolved the body of even a Hercules [947] enjoyed the supper, and the altar consumed everything. Larentina sleeps alone in the temple; and she a woman from the brothel, boasts that in her dreams she had submitted herself to the pleasure of Hercules; [948] and she might possibly have experienced this, as it passed through her mind, in her sleep. In the morning, on going out of the temple very early, she is solicited by a young man--"a third Hercules," so to speak. [949] He invites her home. She complies, remembering that Hercules had told her that it would be for her advantage.

He then, to be sure, obtains permission that they should be united in lawful wedlock (for none was allowed to have intercourse with the concubine of a god without being punished for it); the husband makes her his heir. By and by, just before her death, she bequeathed to the Roman people the rather large estate which she had obtained through Hercules. After this she sought deification for her daughters too, whom indeed the divine Larentina ought to have appointed her heirs also. The gods of the Romans received an accession in her dignity. For she alone of all the wives of Hercules was dear to him, because she alone was rich; and she was even far more fortunate than Ceres, who contributed to the pleasure of the (king of the) dead. [950] After so many examples and eminent names among you, who might not have been declared divine? Who, in fact, ever raised a question as to his divinity against Antinous? [951] Was even Ganymede more grateful and dear than he to (the supreme god) who loved him?

According to you, heaven is open to the dead. You prepare [952] a way from Hades to the stars.

Prostitutes mount it in all directions, so that you must not suppose that you are conferring a great distinction upon your kings.

Chapter XI - The Romans Provided Gods for Birth, Nay, Even Before Birth, to Death. Much Indelicacy in This System

And you are not content to assert the divinity of such as were once known to you, whom you heard and handled, and whose portraits have been painted, and actions recounted, and memory retained amongst you; but men insist upon consecrating with a heavenly life [953] I know not what incorporeal, inanimate shadows, and the mere names of things--dividing man's entire existence amongst separate powers even from his conception in the womb: so that there is a god Consevius,[954] to preside over concubital generation; and Fluviona,[955] to preserve the (growth of the) infant in the womb; after these come Vitumnus and Sentinus,[956] through whom the babe begins to have life and its earliest sensation; then Diespiter,[957] by whose office the child accomplishes its birth. But when women begin their parturition, Candelifera also comes in aid, since childbearing requires the light of the candle; and other goddesses there are [958] who get their names from the parts they bear in the stages of travail. There were two Carmentas likewise, according to the general view: to one of them, called Postverta, belonged the function of assisting the birth of the introverted child; while the other, Prosa,[959] executed the like office for the rightly born.

The god Farinus was so called from (his inspiring) the first utterance; while others believed in Locutius from his gift of speech. Cunina [960] is present as the protector of the child's deep slumber, and supplies to it refreshing rest. To lift them (when fallen) [961] there is Levana, and along with her Rumina.[962] It is a wonderful oversight that no gods were appointed for cleaning up the filth of children. Then, to preside over their first pap and earliest drink you have Potina and Edula; [963] to teach the child to stand erect is the work of Statina, [964] whilst Adeona helps him to come to dear Mamma, and Abeona to toddle off again; then there is Domiduca, [965] (to bring home the bride;) and the goddess Mens, to influence the mind to either good or evil. [966] They have likewise Volumnus and Voleta, [967] to control the will; Paventina, (the goddess) of fear; Venilia, of hope; [968] Volupia, of pleasure; [969] Præstitia, of beauty.[970] Then, again, they give his name to Peragenor, [971] from his teaching men to go through their work; to Consus, from his suggesting to them counsel. Juventa is their guide on assuming the manly gown, and "bearded Fortune" when they come to full manhood. [972] If I must touch on their nuptial duties, there is Afferenda whose appointed function is to see to the offering of the dower; but fie on you! you have your Mutunus [973] and Tutunus and Pertunda [974] and Subigus and the goddess Prema and likewise Perfica. [975] O spare yourselves, ye impudent gods! No one is present at the secret struggles of married life. Those very few persons who have a wish that way, go away and blush for very shame in the midst of their joy.

Chapter XII [976] - The Original Deities Were Human--With Some Very Questionable Characteristics. Saturn or Time Was Human. Inconsistencies of Opinion About Him

Now, how much further need I go in recounting your gods--because I want to descant on the character of such as you have adopted? It is quite uncertain whether I shall laugh at your absurdity, or upbraid you for your blindness. For how many, and indeed what, gods shall I bring forward? Shall it be the greater ones, or the lesser? The old ones, or the novel? The male, or the female? The unmarried, or such as are joined in wedlock? The clever, or the unskilful? The rustic or the town ones? The national or the foreign? For the truth is, [977] there are so many families, so many nations, which require a catalogue[978] (of gods), that they cannot possibly be examined, or distinguished, or described. But the more diffuse the subject is, the more restriction must we impose on it. As, therefore, in this review we keep before us but one object--that of proving that all these gods were once human beings (not, indeed, to instruct you in the fact, [979] for your conduct shows that you have forgotten it)--let us adopt our compendious summary from the most natural method[980] of conducting the examination, even by considering the origin of their race. For the origin characterizes all that comes after it. Now this origin of your gods dates, [981] I suppose, from Saturn. And when Varro mentions Jupiter, Juno, and Minerva, as the most ancient of the gods, it ought not to have escaped our notice, that every father is more ancient than his sons, and that Saturn therefore must precede Jupiter, even as Coelus does Saturn, for Saturn was sprung from Coelus and Terra. I pass by, however, the origin of Coelus and Terra. They led in some unaccountable way [982] single lives, and had no children. Of course they required a long time for vigorous growth to attain to such a stature. [983] By and by, as soon as the voice of Coelus began to break,[984] and the breasts of Terra to become firm, [985] they contract marriage with one another.

I suppose either Heaven [986] came down to his spouse, or Earth went up to meet her lord. Be that as it may, Earth conceived seed of Heaven, and when her year was fulfilled brought forth Saturn in a wonderful manner. Which of his parents did he resemble? Well, then, even after parentage began, [987] it is certain [988] that they had no child previous to Saturn, and only one daughter afterwards--Ops; thenceforth they ceased to procreate. The truth is, Saturn castrated Coelus as he was sleeping. We read this name Coelus as of the masculine gender. And for the matter of that, how could he be a father unless he were a male? But with what instrument was the castration effected? He had a scythe. What, so early as that? For Vulcan was not yet an artificer in iron. The widowed Terra, however, although still quite young, was in no hurry [989] to marry another. Indeed, there was no second Coelus for her. What but Ocean offers her an embrace? But he savours of brackishness, and she has been accustomed to fresh water. [990] And so Saturn is the sole male child of Coelus and Terra. When grown to puberty, he marries his own sister. No laws as yet prohibited incest, nor punished parricide.

Then, when male children were born to him, he would devour them; better himself (should take them) than the wolves, (for to these would they become a prey) if he exposed them. He was, no doubt, afraid that one of them might learn the lesson of his father's scythe. When Jupiter was born in course of time, he was removed out of the way: [991] (the father) swallowed a stone instead of the son, as was pretended. This artifice secured his safety for a time; but at length the son, whom he had not devoured, and who had grown up in secret, fell upon him, and deprived him of his kingdom. Such, then, is the patriarch of the gods whom Heaven [992] and Earth produced for you, with the poets officiating as midwives. Now some persons with a refined [993] imagination are of opinion that, by this allegorical fable of Saturn, there is a physiological representation of Time: (they think) that it is because all things are destroyed by Time, that Coelus and Terra were themselves parents without having any of their own, and that the (fatal) scythe was used, and that (Saturn) devoured his own offspring, because he, [994] in fact, absorbs within himself all things which have issued from him. They call in also the witness of his name; for they say that he is called Κρόνος in Greek, meaning the same thing as χρόνος. [995] His Latin name also they derive from seed-sowing; [996] for they suppose him to have been the actual procreator--that the seed, in fact, was dropt down from heaven to earth by his means. They unite him with Ops, because seeds produce the affluent treasure (Opem) of actual life, and because they develope with labour (Opus). Now I wish that you would explain this metaphorical [997] statement. It was either Saturn or Time. If it was Time, how could it be Saturn? If he, how could it be Time? For you cannot possibly reckon both these corporeal subjects [998] as co-existing in one person. What, however, was there to prevent your worshipping Time under its proper quality? Why not make a human person, or even a mythic man, an object of your adoration, but each in its proper nature not in the character of Time? What is the meaning of that conceit of your mental ingenuity, if it be not to colour the foulest matters with the feigned appearance of reasonable proofs? [999] Neither, on the one hand, do you mean Saturn to be Time, because you say he is a human being; nor, on the other hand, whilst portraying him as Time, do you on that account mean that he was ever human. No doubt, in the accounts of remote antiquity your god Saturn is plainly described as living on earth in human guise. Anything whatever may obviously be pictured as incorporeal which never had an existence; there is simply no room for such fiction, where there is reality. Since, therefore, there is clear evidence that Saturn once existed, it is in vain that you change his character. He whom you will not deny to have once been man, is not at your disposal to be treated anyhow, nor can it be maintained that he is either divine or Time. In every page of your literature the origin [1000] of Saturn is conspicuous. We read of him in Cassius Severus and in the Corneliuses, Nepos and Tacitus, [1001] and, amongst the Greeks also, in Diodorus, and all other compilers of ancient annals.[1002] No more faithful records of him are to be traced than in Italy itself. For, after (traversing) many countries, and (enjoying) the hospitality of Athens, he settled in Italy, or, as it was called, OEnotria, having met with a kind welcome from Janus, or Janes, [1003] as the Salii call him. The hill on which he settled had the name Saturnius, whilst the city which he founded [1004] still bears the name Saturnia; in short, the whole of Italy once had the same designation. Such is the testimony derived from that country which is now the mistress of the world: whatever doubt prevails about the origin of Saturn, his actions tell us plainly that he was a human being. Since, therefore, Saturn was human, he came undoubtedly from a human stock; and more, because he was a man, he, of course, came not of Coelus and Terra. Some people, however, found it easy enough to call him, whose parents were unknown, the son of those gods from whom all may in a sense seem to be derived. For who is there that does not speak under a feeling of reverence of the heaven and the earth as his own father and mother? Or, in accordance with a custom amongst men, which induces them to say of any who are unknown or suddenly apparent, that "they came from the sky?"

Hence it happened that, because a stranger appeared suddenly everywhere, it became the custom to call him a heaven-born man, [1005] --just as we also commonly call earth-born all those whose descent is unknown. I say nothing of the fact that such was the state of antiquity, when men's eyes and minds were so habitually rude, that they were excited by the appearance of every newcomer as if it were that of a god: much more would this be the case with a king, and that the primeval one.

I will linger some time longer over the case of Saturn, because by fully discussing his primordial history I shall beforehand furnish a compendious answer for all other cases; and I do not wish to omit the more convincing testimony of your sacred literature, the credit of which ought to be the greater in proportion to its antiquity.

Now earlier than all literature was the Sibyl; that Sibyl, I mean, who was the true prophetess of truth, from whom you borrow their title for the priests of your demons. She in senarian verse expounds the descent of Saturn and his exploits in words to this effect: "In the tenth generation of men, after the flood had overwhelmed the former race, reigned Saturn, and Titan, and Japetus, the bravest of the sons of Terra and Coelus." Whatever credit, therefore, is attached to your older writers and literature, and much more to those who were the simplest as belonging to that age,[1006] it becomes sufficiently certain that Saturn and his family [1007] were human beings. We have in our possession, then, a brief principle which amounts to a prescriptive rule about their origin serving for all other cases, to prevent our going wrong in individual instances. The particular character [1008] of a posterity is shown by the original founders of the race--mortal beings (come) from mortals, earthly ones from earthly; step after step comes in due relation [1009] --marriage, conception, birth--country, settlements, kingdoms, all give the clearest proofs. [1010] They, therefore who cannot deny the birth of men, must also admit their death; they who allow their mortality must not suppose them to be gods.

Chapter XIII [1011] - The Gods Human at First. Who Had the Authority to Make Them Divine? Jupiter Not Only Human, But Immoral

Manifest cases, indeed, like these have a force peculiarly their own. Men like Varro and his fellow-dreamers admit into the ranks of the divinity those whom they cannot assert to have been in their primitive condition anything but men; (and this they do) by affirming that they became gods after their death. Here, then, I take my stand. If your gods were elected [1012] to this dignity and deity, [1013] just as you recruit the ranks of your senate, you cannot help conceding, in your wisdom, that there must be some one supreme sovereign who has the power of selecting, and is a kind of Cæsar; and nobody is able to confer [1014] on others a thing over which he has not absolute control. Besides, if they were able to make gods of themselves after their death, pray tell me why they chose to be in an inferior condition at first? Or, again, if there is no one who made them gods, how can they be said to have been made such, if they could only have been made by some one else? There is therefore no ground afforded you for denying that there is a certain wholesale distributor[1015] of divinity. Let us accordingly examine the reasons for despatching mortal beings to heaven. I suppose you will produce a pair of them. Whoever, then, is the awarder (of the divine honours), exercises his function, either that he may have some supports, or defences, or it may be even ornaments to his own dignity; or from the pressing claims of the meritorious, that he may reward all the deserving. No other cause is it permitted us to conjecture. Now there is no one who, when bestowing a gift on another, does not act with a view to his own interest or the other's. This conduct, however, cannot be worthy of the Divine Being, inasmuch as His power is so great that He can make gods outright; whilst His bringing man into such request, on the pretence that he requires the aid and support of certain, even dead persons, is a strange conceit, since He was able from the very first to create for Himself immortal beings. He who has compared human things with divine will require no further arguments on these points. And yet the latter opinion ought to be discussed, that God conferred divine honours in consideration of meritorious claims. Well, then, if the award was made on such grounds, if heaven was opened to men of the primitive age because of their deserts, we must reflect that after that time no one was worthy of such honour; except it be, that there is now no longer such a place for any one to attain to. Let us grant that anciently men may have deserved heaven by reason of their great merits. Then let us consider whether there really was such merit. Let the man who alleges that it did exist declare his own view of merit.

Since the actions of men done in the very infancy of time [1016] are a valid claim for their deification, you consistently admitted to the honour the brother and sister who were stained with the sin of incest--Ops and Saturn. Your Jupiter too, stolen in his infancy, was unworthy of both the home and the nutriment accorded to human beings; and, as he deserved for so bad a child, he had to live in Crete. [1017] Afterwards, when full-grown, he dethrones his own father, who, whatever his parental character may have been, was most prosperous in his reign, king as he was of the golden age. Under him, a stranger to toil and want, peace maintained its joyous and gentle sway; under him--

"Nulli subigebant arva coloni;" [1018]
"No swains would bring the fields beneath their sway;" [1019]

and without the importunity of any one the earth would bear all crops spontaneously. [1020] But he hated a father who had been guilty of incest, and had once mutilated his [1021] grandfather. And yet, behold, he himself marries his own sister; so that I should suppose the old adage was made for him: Τοῦ πατρὸς τὸ παιδίον--"Father's own child." There was "not a pin to choose" between the father's piety and the son's. If the laws had been just even at that early time, [1022] Jupiter ought to have been "sewed up in both sacks." [1023] After this corroboration of his lust with incestuous gratification, why should he hesitate to indulge himself lavishly in the lighter excesses of adultery and debauchery? Ever since [1024] poetry sported thus with his character, in some such way as is usual when a runaway slave [1025] is posted up in public, we have been in the habit of gossiping without restraint [1026] of his tricks [1027] in our chat with passers-by; [1028] sometimes sketching him out in the form of the very money which was the fee of his debauchery--as when (he personated) a bull, or rather paid the money's worth of one, [1029] and showered (gold) into the maiden's chamber, or rather forced his way in with a bribe; [1030] sometimes (figuring him) in the very likenesses of the parts which were acted [1031] --as the eagle which ravished (the beautiful youth), [1032] and the swan which sang (the enchanting song). [1033] Well now, are not such fables as these made up of the most disgusting intrigues and the worst of scandals? or would not the morals and tempers of men be likely to become wanton from such examples? In what manner demons, the offspring of evil angels who have been long engaged in their mission, have laboured to turn men [1034] aside from the faith to unbelief and to such fables, we must not in this place speak of to any extent. As indeed the general body [1035] (of your gods), which took their cue [1036] from their kings, and princes, and instructors,[1037] was not of the self-same nature, it was in some other way [1038] that similarity of character was exacted by their authority. But how much the worst of them was he who (ought to have been, but) was not, the best of them? By a title peculiar to him, you are indeed in the habit of calling Jupiter "the Best," [1039] whilst in Virgil he is "Æquus Jupiter." [1040] All therefore were like him--incestuous towards their own kith and kin, unchaste to strangers, impious, unjust! Now he whom mythic story left untainted with no conspicuous infamy, was not worthy to be made a god.

Chapter XIV - Gods, Those Which Were Confessedly Elevated to the Divine Condition, What Pre-Eminent Right Had They to Such Honour? Hercules an Inferior Character

But since they will have it that those who have been admitted from the human state to the honours of deification should be kept separate from others, and that the distinction which Dionysius the Stoic drew should be made between the native and the factitious [1041] gods, I will add a few words concerning this last class also. I will take Hercules himself for raising the gist of a reply[1042] (to the question) whether he deserved heaven and divine honours? For, as men choose to have it, these honours are awarded to him for his merits. If it was for his valour in destroying wild beasts with intrepidity, what was there in that so very memorable? Do not criminals condemned to the games, though they are even consigned to the contest of the vile arena, despatch several of these animals at one time, and that with more earnest zeal? If it was for his world-wide travels, how often has the same thing been accomplished by the rich at their pleasant leisure, or by philosophers in their slave-like poverty? [1043] Is it forgotten that the cynic Asclepiades on a single sorry cow, [1044] riding on her back, and sometimes nourished at her udder, surveyed [1045] the whole world with a personal inspection?

Even if Hercules visited the infernal regions, who does not know that the way to Hades is open to all? If you have deified him on account of his much carnage and many battles, a much greater number of victories was gained by the illustrious Pompey, the conqueror of the pirates who had not spared Ostia itself in their ravages; and (as to carnage), how many thousands, let me ask, were cooped up in one corner of the citadel [1046] of Carthage, and slain by Scipio?

Wherefore Scipio has a better claim to be considered a fit candidate for deification [1047] than Hercules. You must be still more careful to add to the claims of (our) Hercules his debaucheries with concubines and wives, and the swathes [1048] of Omphale, and his base desertion of the Argonauts because he had lost his beautiful boy. [1049] To this mark of baseness add for his glorification likewise his attacks of madness, adore the arrows which slew his sons and wife. This was the man who, after deeming himself worthy of a funeral pile in the anguish of his remorse for his parricides, [1050] deserved rather to die the unhonoured death which awaited him, arrayed in the poisoned robe which his wife sent him on account of his lascivious attachment (to another). You, however, raised him from the pyre to the sky, with the same facility with which (you have distinguished in like manner) another hero [1051] also, who was destroyed by the violence of a fire from the gods. He having devised some few experiments, was said to have restored the dead to life by his cures. He was the son of Apollo, half human, although the grandson of Jupiter, and great-grandson of Saturn (or rather of spurious origin, because his parentage was uncertain, as Socrates of ἀργόν has related; he was exposed also, and found in a worse tutelage than even Jove's, suckled even at the dugs of a dog); nobody can deny that he deserved the end which befell him when he perished by a stroke of lightning. In this transaction, however, your most excellent Jupiter is once more found in the wrong--impious to his grandson, envious of his artistic skill. Pindar, indeed, has not concealed his true desert; according to him, he was punished for his avarice and love of gain, influenced by which he would bring the living to their death, rather than the dead to life, by the perverted use of his medical art which he put up for sale. [1052] It is said that his mother was killed by the same stroke, and it was only right that she, who had bestowed so dangerous a beast on the world, [1053] should escape to heaven by the same ladder.

And yet the Athenians will not be at a loss how to sacrifice to gods of such a fashion, for they pay divine honours to Æsculapius and his mother amongst their dead (worthies). As if, too, they had not ready to hand [1054] their own Theseus to worship, so highly deserving a god's distinction! Well, why not? Did he not on a foreign shore abandon the preserver of his life, [1055] with the same indifference, nay heartlessness, [1056] with which he became the cause of his father's death?

Chapter XV - The Constellations and the Genii Very Indifferent Gods. The Roman Monopoly of Gods Unsatisfactory. Other Nations Require Deities Quite as Much

It would be tedious to take a survey of all those, too, whom you have buried amongst the constellations, and audaciously minister to as gods. [1057] I suppose your Castors, and Perseus, and Erigona, [1058] have just the same claims for the honours of the sky as Jupiter's own big boy[1059] had. But why should we wonder? You have transferred to heaven even dogs, and scorpions, and crabs. I postpone all remarks [1060] concerning those whom you worship in your oracles. That this worship exists, is attested by him who pronounces the oracle. [1061] Why; you will have your gods to be spectators even of sadness,[1062] as is Viduus, who makes a widow of the soul, by parting it from the body, and whom you have condemned, by not permitting him to be enclosed within your city-walls; there is Cæculus also, to deprive the eyes of their perception; and Orbana, to bereave seed of its vital power; moreover, there is the goddess of death herself. To pass hastily by all others,[1063] you account as gods the sites of places or of the city; such are Father Janus (there being, moreover, the archer-goddess [1064] Jana [1065]), and Septimontius of the seven hills.

Men sacrifice [1066] to the same Genii, whilst they have altars or temples in the same places; but to others besides, when they dwell in a strange place, or live in rented houses. [1067] I say nothing about Ascensus, who gets his name for his climbing propensity, and Clivicola, from her sloping (haunts); I pass silently by the deities called Forculus from doors, and Cardea from hinges, and Limentinus the god of thresholds, and whatever others are worshipped by your neighbours as tutelar deities of their street doors. [1068] There is nothing strange in this, since men have their respective gods in their brothels, their kitchens, and even in their prison. Heaven, therefore, is crowded with innumerable gods of its own, both these and others belonging to the Romans, which have distributed amongst them the functions of one's whole life, in such a way that there is no want of the other [1069] gods. Although, it is true, [1070] the gods which we have enumerated are reckoned as Roman peculiarly, and as not easily recognised abroad; yet how do all those functions and circumstances, over which men have willed their gods to preside, come about, [1071] in every part of the human race, and in every nation, where their guarantees [1072] are not only without an official recognition, but even any recognition at all?

Chapter XVI - Inventors of Useful Arts Unworthy of Deification. They Would Be the First to Acknowledge a Creator. The Arts Changeable from Time to Time, and Some Become Obsolete

Well, but [1073] certain men have discovered fruits and sundry necessaries of life, (and hence are worthy of deification). [1074] Now let me ask, when you call these persons "discoverers," do you not confess that what they discovered was already in existence? Why then do you not prefer to honour the Author, from whom the gifts really come, instead of converting the Author into mere discoverers?

Previously he who made the discover, the inventor himself no doubt expressed his gratitude to the Author; no doubt, too, he felt that He was God, to whom really belonged the religious service, [1075] as the Creator (of the gift), by whom also both he who discovered and that which was discovered were alike created.

The green fig of Africa nobody at Rome had heard of when Cato introduced it to the Senate, in order that he might show how near was that province of the enemy [1076] whose subjugation he was constantly urging.

The cherry was first made common in Italy by Cn. Pompey, who imported it from Pontus. I might possibly have thought the earliest introducers of apples amongst the Romans deserving of the public honour [1077] of deification. This, however, would be as foolish a ground for making gods as even the invention of the useful arts. And yet if the skilful men [1078] of our own time be compared with these, how much more suitable would deification be to the later generation than to the former! For, tell me, have not all the extant inventions superseded antiquity, [1079] whilst daily experience goes on adding to the new stock? Those, therefore, whom you regard as divine because of their arts, you are really injuring by your very arts, and challenging (their divinity) by means of rival attainments, which cannot be surpassed. [1080]

Chapter XVII [1081] - Conclusion, the Romans Owe Not Their Imperial Power to Their Gods. The Great God Alone Dispenses Kingdoms, He is the God of the Christians

In conclusion, without denying all those whom antiquity willed and posterity has believed to be gods, to be the guardians of your religion, there yet remains for our consideration that very large assumption of the Roman superstitions which we have to meet in opposition to you, O heathen, viz. that the Romans have become the lords and masters of the whole world, because by their religious offices they have merited this dominion to such an extent that they are within a very little of excelling even their own gods in power. One cannot wonder that Sterculus, and Mutunus, and Larentina, have severally[1082] advanced this empire to its height! The Roman people has been by its gods alone ordained to such dominion. For I could not imagine that any foreign gods would have preferred doing more for a strange nation than for their own people, and so by such conduct become the deserters and neglecters, nay, the betrayers of the native land wherein they were born and bred, and ennobled and buried.

Thus not even Jupiter could suffer his own Crete to be subdued by the Roman fasces, forgetting that cave of Ida, and the brazen cymbals of the Corybantes, and the most pleasant odour of the goat which nursed him on that dear spot. Would he not have made that tomb of his superior to the whole Capitol, so that that land should most widely rule which covered the ashes of Jupiter?

Would Juno, too, be willing that the Punic city, for the love of which she even neglected Samos, should be destroyed, and that, too, by the fires of the sons of Æneas? Although I am well aware that

"Hic illius arma,
Hic currus fuit, hoc regnum des gentibus esse,
Si qua fata sinant, jam tunc tenditque fovetque." [1083]
"Here were her arms, her chariot here,
Here goddess-like, to fix one day
The seat of universal sway,
Might fate be wrung to yield assent,
E'έν then her schemes, her cares were bent." [1084]

Still the unhappy (queen of gods) had no power against the fates! And yet the Romans did not accord as much honour to the fates, although they gave them Carthage, as they did to Larentina. But surely those gods of yours have not the power of conferring empire. For when Jupiter reigned in Crete, and Saturn in Italy, and Isis in Egypt, it was even as men that they reigned, to whom also were assigned many to assist them. [1085] Thus he who serves also makes masters, and the bond-slave [1086] of Admetus [1087] aggrandizes with empire the citizens of Rome, although he destroyed his own liberal votary Croesus by deceiving him with ambiguous oracles. [1088] Being a god, why was he afraid boldly to foretell to him the truth that he must lose his kingdom. Surely those who were aggrandized with the power of wielding empire might always have been able to keep an eye, as it were, [1089] on their own cities. If they were strong enough to confer empire on the Romans, why did not Minerva defend Athens from Xerxes? Or why did not Apollo rescue Delphi out of the hand of Pyrrhus? They who lost their own cities preserve the city of Rome, since (forsooth) the religiousness [1090] of Rome has merited the protection! But is it not rather the fact that this excessive devotion [1091] has been devised since the empire has attained its glory by the increase of its power? No doubt sacred rites were introduced by Numa, but then your proceedings were not marred by a religion of idols and temples. Piety was simple, [1092] and worship humble; altars were artlessly reared, [1093] and the vessels (thereof) plain, and the incense from them scant, and the god himself nowhere. Men therefore were not religious before they achieved greatness, (nor great) because they were religious. But how can the Romans possibly seem to have acquired their empire by an excessive religiousness and very profound respect for the gods, when that empire was rather increased after the gods had been slighted? [1094] Now, if I am not mistaken, every kingdom or empire is acquired and enlarged by wars, whilst they and their gods also are injured by conquerors. For the same ruin affects both city-walls and temples; similar is the carnage both of civilians and of priests; identical the plunder of profane things and of sacred. To the Romans belong as many sacrileges as trophies; and then as many triumphs over gods as over nations. Still remaining are their captive idols amongst them; and certainly, if they can only see their conquerors, they do not give them their love. Since, however, they have no perception, they are injured with impunity; and since they are injured with impunity, they are worshipped to no purpose. The nation, therefore, which has grown to its powerful height by victory after victory, cannot seem to have developed owing to the merits of its religion--whether they have injured the religion by augmenting their power, or augmented their power by injuring the religion. All nations have possessed empire, each in its proper time, as the Assyrians, the Medes, the Persians, the Egyptians; empire is even now also in the possession of some, and yet they that have lost their power used not to behave[1095] without attention to religious services and the worship of the gods, even after these had become unpropitious to them, [1096] until at last almost universal dominion has accrued to the Romans. It is the fortune of the times that has thus constantly shaken kingdoms with revolution.[1097] Inquire who has ordained these changes in the times. It is the same (great Being) who dispenses kingdoms, [1098] and has now put the supremacy of them into the hands of the Romans, very much as if[1099] the tribute of many nations were after its exaction amassed in one (vast) coffer. What He has determined concerning it, they know who are the nearest to Him. [1100]

Appendix - A Fragment Concerning the Execrable Gods of the Heathen

So great blindness has fallen on the Roman race, that they call their enemy Lord, and preach the filcher of blessings as being their very giver, and to him they give thanks. They call those (deities), then, by human names, not by their own, for their own names they know not. That they are dæmons [1101] they understand: but they read histories of the old kings, and then, though they see that their character [1102] was mortal, they honour them with a deific name.

As for him whom they call Jupiter, and think to be the highest god, when he was born the years (that had elapsed) from the foundation of the world [1103] to him [1104] were some three thousand. He is born in Greece, from Saturnus and Ops; and, for fear he should be killed by his father (or else, if it is lawful to say so, should be begotten [1105] anew), is by the advice of his mother carried down into Crete, and reared in a cave of Ida; is concealed from his father's search by (the aid of) Cretans--born men! [1106] -- rattling their arms; sucks a she-goat's dugs; flays her; clothes himself in her hide; and (thus) uses his own nurse's hide, after killing her, to be sure, with his own hand! but he sewed thereon three golden tassels worth the price of an hundred oxen each, as their author Homer [1107] relates, if it is fair to believe it.

This Jupiter, in adult age, waged war several years with his father; overcame him; made a parricidal raid on his home; violated his virgin sisters; [1108] selected one of them in marriage; drave [1109] his father by dint of arms. The remaining scenes, moreover, of that act have been recorded. Of other folks' wives, or else of violated virgins, he begat him sons; defiled freeborn boys; oppressed peoples lawlessly with despotic and kingly sway. The father, whom they erringly suppose to have been the original god, was ignorant that this (son of his) was lying concealed in Crete; the son, again, whom they believe the mightier god, knows not that the father whom himself had banished is lurking in Italy. If he was in heaven, when would he not see what was doing in Italy? For the Italian land is "not in a corner."[1110] And yet, had he been a god, nothing ought to have escaped him. But that he whom the Italians call Saturnus did lurk there, is clearly evidenced on the face of it, from the fact that from his lurking [1111] the Hesperian [1112] tongue is to this day called Latin, [1113] as likewise their author Virgil relates. [1114] (Jupiter,) then, is said to have been born on earth, while (Saturnus his father) fears lest he be driven by him from his kingdom, and seeks to kill him as being his own rival, and knows not that he has been stealthily carried off, and is in hiding; and afterwards the son-god pursues his father, immortal seeks to slay immortal (is it credible? [1115]), and is disappointed by an interval of sea, and is ignorant of (his quarry's) flight; and while all this is going on between two gods on earth, heaven is deserted. No one dispensed the rains, no one thundered, no one governed all this mass of world. [1116] For they cannot even say that their action and wars took place in heaven; for all this was going on on Mount Olympus in

Greece. Well, but heaven is not called Olympus, for heaven is heaven.

These, then, are the actions of theirs, which we will treat of first--nativity, lurking, ignorance, parricide, adulteries, obscenities--things committed not by a god, but by most impure and truculent human beings; beings who, had they been living in these days, would have lain under the impeachment of all laws--laws which are far more just and strict than their actions. "He drave his father by dint of arms." The Falcidian and Sempronian law would bind the parricide in a sack with beasts. "He violated his sisters." The Papinian law would punish the outrage with all penalties, limb by limb. "He invaded others' wedlock." The Julian law would visit its adulterous violator capitally. "He defiled freeborn boys." The Cornelian law would condemn the crime of transgressing the sexual bond with novel severities, sacrilegiously guilty as it is of a novel union. [1117] This being is shown to have had no divinity either, for he was a human being; his father's flight escaped him. To this human being, of such a character, to so wicked a king, so obscene and so cruel, God's honour has been assigned by men. Now, to be sure, if on earth he were born and grew up through the advancing stages of life's periods, and in it committed all these evils, and yet is no more in it, what is thought [1118] (of him) but that he is dead? Or else does foolish error think wings were born him in his old age, whence to fly heavenward? Why, even this may possibly find credit among men bereft of sense, [1119] if indeed they believe, (as they do,) that he turned into a swan, to beget the Castors; [1120] an eagle, to contaminate Ganymede; a bull, to violate Europa; gold, to violate Danaë; a horse, to beget Pirithoüs; a goat, to beget Egyppa [1121] from a she-goat; a Satyr, to embrace Antiope. Beholding these adulteries, to which sinners are prone, they therefore easily believe that sanctions of misdeed and of every filthiness are borrowed from their feigned god. Do they perceive how void of amendment are the rest of his career's acts which can find credit, which are indeed true, and which, they say, he did without self transformation? Of Semele, he begets Liber; [1122] of Latona, Apollo and Diana; of Maia, Mercury; of Alcmena, Hercules. But the rest of his corruptions, which they themselves confess, I am unwilling to record, lest turpitude, once buried, be again called to men's ears. But of these few (offsprings of his) I have made mention; off-springs whom in their error they believe to be themselves, too, gods--born, to wit, of an incestuous father; adulterous births, supposititious births.

And the living, [1123] eternal God, of sempiternal divinity, prescient of futurity, immeasurable, [1124] they have dissipated (into nothing, by associating Him) with crimes so unspeakable.

Elucidation

This Fragment is noted as spurious, by Oehler who attributes it to somebody only moderately acquainted with Tertullian's style and teaching. [1125] I do not find it mentioned by Dupin, nor by Routh. This translation is by Thelwall.

Footnotes:

773. In this part of his work the author reviews the heathen mythology, and exposes the absurdity of the polytheistic worship in the various classes of the gods, according to the distribution of Varro.
774. Miserandæ.
775. Literally, "unwilling to know."
776. i.e., it does not know that it is error.
777. Nescit.
778. Agnoscit.
779. Liceret.
780. Discuti, or, in the logical sense, "be tested."
781. Nunciatio (legally, this is "an information lodged against a wrong.")
782. Excidere, "falls through."
783. Sed enim.
784. Quidni?
785. Receptorum.
786. Necessitatem, answering to the "leges dominantium."
787. Adulterinam.
788. St. Augustine, in his de Civit. Dei, makes similar use of Varro's work on the heathen gods, Liber Divinarum.
789. Scopum, perhaps "mark."
790. Insinuatores.
791. Volutetur.
792. Adoptionibus.
793. Adoptatio.
794. Passiva, "a jumble."
795. Argumentationibus.
796. Historia. This word seems to refer to the class of mythical divinity above mentioned. It therefore means "fable" or "absurd story" (see above).
797. Adoptivum.
798. Patrocinatur.
799. Mancipium.
800. Prov. ix. 10; Ps. cxi. 10.
801. Porro.
802. Deum omnium notititam et veritatem adsecutus, i.e., "following the God of all as knowledge and truth."
803. Nutat.
804. Passivæ fidei.
805. Solummodo.
806. Otiosum.

807. "A nobody."
808. Nisi ut sint expedire.
809. Aliquot commeatus.
810. Quasi certus.
811. Istos deos.
812. Non tenebat.
813. De mundo deo didicimus.
814. Istud.
815. Ad præsentem speciem, the physical class.
816. Or, classification.
817. Ut jam hinc præjudicatum sit.
818. Ad illam agnatorum speciem.
819. Scitum.
820. Non-deum.
821. "Quod," with a subj. mood.
822. Mundus iste.
823. Summaliter.
824. Humanitas.
825. Duritia.
826. Censetur.
827. i.e., "iste mundus."
828. Mundi, i.e., the universe; see above.
829. The best reading is "vobis credi;" this is one of Tertullian's "final infinitives."
830. Compare Augustine, de Civit. Dei, vii. 6, 23, 24, 28.
831. Formam.
832. Ratione.
833. Motatorem.
834. Alia sane vanitate.
835. This seems to mean: "because θέειν has also the sense of σείεσθαι (motion as well as progression)."
836. "Dominatione" is Oehler's reading, but he approves of "denominatione" (Rigault's reading); this would signify "designation of godhead."
837. Opinione.
838. Rescinditur.
839. Interpretatorium.
840. Reprehensum.
841. Docete.
842. Sine capite.
843. Scilicet.
844. Aciem.
845. Majorem orbem. Another reading has "majorem orbe," q.d. "as larger than the world."
846. Morositatis.
847. Cecidit turpiter.
848. Scilicet.
849. Habituros.
850. Humaniorem.
851. Conjectura.
852. Suffragio.
853. Sationem.
854. Temperamento.
855. Foederata.
856. Circulorum conditionibus.
857. Tanquam.
858. Jure.
859. Domina.
860. Scilicet.
861. Vi suavitatis.
862. Lanis.
863. Caput facti.
864. Invenitur.
865. Servitutis artem. "Artem" Oehler explains by "artificiose institutum."
866. We subjoin Oehler's text of this obscure sentence: "Non in ista investigatione alicujus artificis intus et domini servitudi artem ostendimus elementorum certis ex operis" (for "operibis," not unusual in Tertullian) "eorum quas facis potestatis?"
867. Aut.
868. De licentia passivitatis libertas approbetur.
869. Meminerunt.
870. Num non.
871. Universa negotiatio mundialis.
872. Felicitas.
873. These are the moon's monthly changes.
874. Tertullian refers to the Magian method of watching eclipses, the ἐνοπτρομαντεία.
875. Instead of "non valet," there is the reading "non volet," "God would not consent," etc.
876. Viderint igitur "Let them look to themselves," "never mind them."
877. Alias.
878. Ista.
879. Sedenim.
880. Mortalitas.
881. See above, c. i. [Note 19, p. 129.]
882. See The Apology, especially cc. xxii. and xxiii.
883. Pejerantes.
884. Lancinatis.
885. Repercutitus.
886. Vulgo.
887. Sapere. The infinitive of purpose is frequent in our author.
888. Distribuendis.
889. An allusion to Antinous, who is also referred to in The Apology, xiii. ["Court-page." See, p. 29, Supra.]
890. Inhoneste institutos.
891. By the "legibus" Tertullian refers to the divine honours ordered to be paid, by decrees of the Senate, to deceased emperors. Comp. Suetonius, Octav. 88; and Pliny, Paneg. 11 (Oehler).
892. Ultro siletur.
893. Ejusmodi.
894. Insuper.
895. Denique.
896. Ingenuitatis.
897. Initiatricem.
898. Sane.
899. Fides.

900. Polluuntur.
901. Relationibus.
902. Comp. The Apology, ix. [See, p. 25, Supra.]
903. Comp. Minucius Felix, Octav. xxi.; Arnobius, adv. Nat. v. 6, 7; Augustine, Civ. Dei, vi. 7.
904. This is the force of the subjunctive verb.
905. By divine scandals, he means such as exceed in their atrocity even human scandals.
906. See above, c. i. [p. 129.]
907. Municipes. "Their local worshippers or subjects."
908. Perceperint.
909. Literally, "Have men heard of any Nortia belonging to the Vulsinensians?"
910. Deos decuriones, in allusion to the small provincial senates which in the later times spread over the Roman colonies and municipia.
911. Privatas.
912. Compare Suidas, s. v. Σαράπις; Rufinus, Hist. Eccl. ii. 23. As Serapis was Joseph in disguise, so was Joseph a type of Christ, according to the ancient Christians, who were fond of subordinating heathen myths to Christian theology.
913. Tertullian is not the only writer who has made mistakes in citing from memory Scripture narratives. Comp. Arnobius.
914. Suggestu.
915. Modialis.
916. Super caput esse, i.e., was entrusted to him.
917. Canem dicaverunt.
918. Compressa.
919. Isis; comp. The Apology, xvi. [See p. 31, supra.]
920. Consecrasse.
921. Recontrans.
922. Vitii pueritatem.
923. Recipere (with a dative).
924. Ignotis Deis. Comp. Acts xvii. 23.
925. Ut bulbi. This is the passage which Augustine quotes (de Civit. Dei, vii. 1) as "too facetious."
926. Adventicii, "coming from abroad."
927. Touching these gods of the vanquished nations, compare The Apology, xxv.; below, c. xvii.; Minucius Felix, Octav. xxv.
928. Diligentem.
929. See Homer, Il. v. 300.
930. Invenitur.
931. Referred to also above, i. 18.
932. The obscure "formam et patrem" is by Oehler rendered "pulchritudinem et generis nobilitatem."
933. The word is "eorum" (possessive of "principum"), not "suæ."
934. Dejerant adversus.
935. What Tertullian himself thinks on this point, see his de Corona, xi.
936. Cleobis and Biton; see Herodotus i. 31.
937. See Valerius Maximus, v. 4, 1.
938. We need not stay to point out the unfairness of this statement, in contrast with the exploits of Æneas against Turnus, as detailed in the last books of the Æneid.
939. Usque in.
940. We have thus rendered "quiritatem est," to preserve as far as one could the pun on the deified hero of the Quirites.
941. We insert the Latin, to show the pun on Sterculus; see The Apology, c. xxv. [See p. 40, supra.]
942. Curaria quam consecrari.
943. Bona Dea, i.e., the daughter of Faunus just mentioned.
944. See Livy, viii. 20, xxxii. 1; Ovid, Fasti, vi. 213, etc. Compare also Augustine, de Civ. Dei, xviii. 19.
[Tom. vii. p. 576.]
945. Compare Augustine, de Civ. Dei, vi. 7. [Tom. vii. p. 184.]
946. Æditum ejus.
947. That is, when he mounted the pyre.
948. Herculi functam. "Fungi alicui" means to satisfy, or yield to.
949. The well-known Greek saying, Ἄλλος οὗτος Ἡρακλῆς.
950. Pluto; Proserpine, the daughter of Ceres, is meant. Oehler once preferred to read, "Hebe, quæ mortuo placuit," i.e., "than Hebe, who gratified Hercules after death."
951. Tertullian often refers indignantly to this atrocious case.
952. Subigitis.
953. Efflagitant coelo et sanciunt, (i.e., "they insist on deifying.")
954. Comp. Augustine, de Civ. Dei, vi. 9.
955. A name of Juno, in reference to her office to mothers, "quia eam sanguinis fluorem in conceptu retinere putabant." Comp. August. de Civ. Dei, iii. 2.
956. Comp. August. de Civ. Dei, vii. 2, 3.
957. Comp. August. de Civ. Dei, iv. 11.
958. Such as Lucina, Partula, Nona, Decima, Alemona.
959. Or, Prorsa.
960. "Quæ infantes in cunis (in their cradle) tuetur." Comp. August. de Civ. Dei, iv. 11.
961. Educatrix; Augustine says: "Ipse levet de terra et vocetur dea Levana" (de Civ. Dei, iv. 11).
962. From the old word ruma, a teat.
963. Comp. August. de Civ. Dei, iv. 9,

11, 36.

964. See also Tertullian's de Anima, xxxix.; and Augustine's de Civ. Dei, iv. 21, where the god has the masculine name of Statilinus.

965. See Augustine, de Civ. Dei, vi. 9 and vii. 3.

966. Ibid. iv. 21, vii. 3.

967. Ibid. iv. 21.

968. Ibid. iv. 11, vii. 22.

969. Ibid. iv. 11. [N.B.--Augustine's borrowing from our author.]

970. Arnobius, adv. Nationes, iv. 3.

971. Augustine, de Civ. Dei. [iv. 11 and 16] mentions Agenoria.

972. On Fortuna Barbata, see Augustine, de Civ. Dei, iv. 11, where he also names Consus and Juventa.

973. Tertullian, in Apol. xxv. sarcastically says, "Sterculus, and Mutunus, and Larentina, have raised the empire to its present height."

974. Arnobius, adv. Nationes, iv. 7, 11; August. de Civ. Dei, vi. 9.

975. For these three gods, see Augustine, de Civ. Dei, vi. 9; and Arnobius, adv. Nationes, iv. 7.

976. Agrees with The Apology, c. x.

977. Bona fide.

978. Censum.

979. There is here an omitted clause, supplied in The Apology, "but rather to recall it to your memory."

980. Ab ipsa ratione.

981. Signatur.

982. Undeunde.

983. Tantam proceritatem.

984. Insolescere, i.e., at the commencement of puberty.

985. Lapilliscere, i.e., to indicate maturity.

986. The nominative "coelum" is used.

987. It is not very clear what is the force of "sed et pepererit," as read by Oehler; we have given the clause an impersonal turn.

988. "Certe" is sometime "certo" in our author.

989. Distulit.

990. That is, to rain and cloud.

991. Abalienato.

992. The word is "coelum" here.

993. Eleganter.

994. i.e., as representing Time.

995. So Augustine, de Civ. Dei, iv. 10; Arnobius, adv. Nationes, iii. 29; Cicero, de Nat. Deor. ii. 25.

996. As if from "sero," satum.

997. Translatio.

998. Utrumque corporale.

999. Mentitis argumentationibus.

1000. Census.

1001. See his Histories, v. 2, 4.

1002. Antiquitatem canos, "hoary antiquity."

1003. Jano sive Jane.

1004. Depalaverat, "marked out with stakes."

1005. Coelitem.

1006. Magis proximis quoniam illius ætatis.

1007. Prosapia.

1008. Qualitas. [n.b. Our author's use of Præscriptio.]

1009. Comparantur.

1010. Monumenta liquent.

1011. Comp. The Apology, c. xi. [p. 27. Supra.]

1012. Allecti.

1013. This is not so terse as Tertullian's "nomen et numen."

1014. Præstare.

1015. Mancipem.

1016. In cunabulis temporalitatis.

1017. The ill-fame of the Cretans is noted by St. Paul, Tit. i. 12.

1018. Virgil, Georg. i. 125.

1019. Sewell.

1020. Ipsa.

1021. Jupiter's, of course.

1022. The law which prescribed the penalty of the paracide, that he be sewed up in a sack with an ape, a serpent, and a cock, and be thrown into the sea.

1023. In duos culleos dividi.

1024. De quo.

1025. De fugitivo.

1026. Abusui nundinare.

1027. The "operam ejus"=ingenia et artificia (Oehler).

1028. Percontationi alienæ.

1029. In the case of Europa.

1030. In the case of Danäe.

1031. Similitudines actuum ipsas.

1032. In the case of Ganymede.

1033. In the case of Leda.

1034. Quos.

1035. Plebs.

1036. Morata.

1037. Proseminatoribus.

1038. Alibi.

1039. Optimum.

1040. There would seem to be a jest here; "æquus" is not only just but equal, i.e., "on a par with" others--in evil, of course, as well as good.

1041. Inter nativos et factos. See above, c. ii., p. 131.

1042. Summa responsionis.

1043. Famulatoria mendicitas.

1044. Vaccula.

1045. Subegisse oculis, "reduced to his own eyesight."

1046. Byrsæ.

1047. Magis obtinendus divinitati

deputatur.

1048. Fascias.

1049. Hylas.

1050. Rather murders of children and other kindred.

1051. Æsculapius.

1052. Tertullian does not correctly quote Pindar (Pyth. iii. 54-59), who notices the skilful hero's love of reward, but certainly ascribes to him the merit of curing rather than killing:

Ἀλλὰ κέρδει καὶ σοφία δέδεται ἔτραπεν καὶ κἀκεῖνον ἀγάνορι μισθῷ χρυσὸς ἐν χερσὶν φανεὶς ἄνδρ ἐκ θανάτου κομίσαι ἤδη ἁλωκότα· χερσὶ δ᾽ ἄρα Κρονίων ῥίψαις δὶ ἀμφοῖν ἀμπνοὰν στέρνων καθέλεν ὠκέως, αἴθων δὲ κεραυνὸς ἐνέσκιμψεν μόρον--"Even wisdom has been bound by love of gain, and gold shining in the hand by a magnificent reward induced even him to restore from death a man already seized by it; and then the son of Saturn, hurling with his hands a bolt through both, speedily took away the breath of their breasts, and the flashing bolt inflicted death" (Dawson Turner).

1053. Tertullian does not follow the legend which is usually received.

He wishes to see no good in the object of his hatred, and so takes the worst view, and certainly improves upon it. The "bestia" is out of reason. [He doubtless followed some copy now lost.]

1054. Quasi non et ipsi.

1055. Ariadne.

1056. Amentia.

1057. Deis ministratis.

1058. The constellation Virgo.

1059. Jovis exoletus, Ganymede, or Aquarius.

1060. He makes a similar postponement above, in c. vii., to The Apology, cc. xxii. xxiii.

1061. Divini.

1062. Et tristitiæ arbitros.

1063. Transvolem.

1064. Diva arquis.

1065. Perhaps another form of Diana.

1066. Faciunt = ῥίζουσι.

1067. This seems to be the meaning of an almost unintelligible sentence, which we subjoin: "Geniis eisdem illi faciunt qui in isdem locis aras vel ædes habent; præterea aliis qui in alieno loco aut mercedibus habitant." Oehler, who makes this text, supposes that in each clause the name of some god has dropped out.

1068. Numinum janitorum.

1069. Ceteris.

1070. Immo cum.

1071. Proveniunt.

1072. Prædes.

1073. Sedenim.

1074. We insert this clause at Oehler's suggestion.

1075. Ministerium.

1076. The incident, which was closely connected with the third Punic war, is described pleasantly by Pliny, Hist. Nat. xv. 20.

1077. Præconium.

1078. Artifices.

1079. "Antiquitas" is here opposed to "novitas," and therefore means "the arts of old times."

1080. In æmulis. "In," in our author, often marks the instrument.

1081. Compare The Apology, xxv. xxvi., pp. 39, 40.

1082. The verb is in the singular number.

1083. Æneid, i. 16-20.

1084. Conington.

1085. Operati plerique.

1086. Dediticius.

1087. Apollo; comp. The Apology, c. xiv., p. 30.

1088. See Herodot. i. 50.

1089. Veluti tueri.

1090. Religiositas.

1091. Superstitio.

1092. Frugi.

1093. Temeraria.

1094. Læsis.

1095. Morabantur. We have taken this word as if from "mores" (character). Tertullian often uses the participle "moratus" in this sense.

1096. Et depropitiorum.

1097. Volutavit.

1098. Compare The Apology, c. xxvi.

1099. We have treated this "tanquam" and its clause as something more than a mere simile. It is, in fact, an integral element of the supremacy which the entire sentence describes as conferred on the Romans by the Almighty.

1100. That is, the Christians, who are well aware of God's purposes as declared in prophecy.

St. Paul tells the Thessalonians what the order of the great events subsequent to the Roman power was to be:

the destruction of that power was to be followed by the development and reign of Antichrist; and then the end of the world would come.

1101. Dæmons. Gr. δαίμων, which some hold to = δαήμων, "knowing," "skilful," in which case it would come to be used of any superhuman intelligence; others, again, derive from δαίω, "to divide, distribute," in which case it would mean a distributor of destinies; which latter derivation and meaning Liddell and Scott incline to.

1102. Actum: or "career."

1103. Mundi.

1104. i.e., till his time.

1105. Pareretur. As the word seems to be used here with reference to his father, this, although not by any means a usual meaning, would seem to be the sense. [As in the equivalent Greek.]

1106. A Cretibus, hominibus natis. The force seems to be in the absurdity of supposing that, 1st, there should be human beings (hominibus) born, (as Jupiter is said to have been "born,") already existing at the time of the "birth" of "the highest god;" 2ndly, that these should have had the power to do him so essential service as to conceal him from the search of his own father, likewise a mighty deity, by the simple expedient of rattling their arms.

1107. See Hom. Il. ii. 446-9; but Homer says there were 100 such tassels.

1108. Oehler's "virginis" must mean "virgines."

1109. So Scott: "He drave my cows last Fastern's night."--Lay of Last Minstrel.

1110. See Acts xxvi. 26.

1111. Latitatio.

1112. i.e., Western: here=Italian, as being west of Greece.

1113. Latina.

1114. See Virg. Æn. viii. 319-323: see also Ov. Fast. i. 234-238.

1115. Oehler does not mark this as a question. If we follow him, we may render, "this can find belief."

Above, it seemed necessary to introduce the parenthetical words to make some sense. The Latin is throughout very clumsy and incoherent.

1116. Orbis.

1117. Lex Cornelia transgressi foederis ammissum novis exemplis novi coitus sacrilegum damnaret. After consulting Dr. Holmes, I have rendered, but not without hesitation, as above. "Foedus" seems to have been technically used, especially in later Latin, of the marriage compact; but what "lex Cornelia" is meant I have sought vainly to discover, and whether "lex Cornelia transgressi foederis" ought not to go together I am not sure. For "ammissum" (=admissum) Migne's ed. reads "amissum," a very different word. For "sacrilegus" with a genitive, see de Res. Carn, c. xlii. med.

1118. Quid putatur (Oehler) putatus (Migne).

1119. Or, "feeling"--"sensu."

1120. The Dioscuri, Castor and Pollux.

1121. Perhaps Ægipana (marginal reading of the ms. as given in Oehler and Migne).

1122. i.e., Bacchus.

1123. Oehler reads "vide etem;" but Migne's "viventem" seems better: indeed, Oehler's is probably a misprint. The punctuation of this treatise in Oehler is very faulty throughout, and has been disregarded.

1124. "Immensum," rendered "incomprehensible" in the "Athanasian Creed.

1125. See page 14, supra.

VII – An Answer to the Jews [1126]
[Translated by the Rev. S. Thelwall.]

Chapter I - Occasion of Writing. Relative Position of Jews and Gentiles Illustrated

It happened very recently a dispute was held between a Christian and a Jewish proselyte. Alternately with contentious cable they each spun out the day until evening. By the opposing din, moreover, of some partisans of the individuals, truth began to be overcast by a sort of cloud. It was therefore our pleasure that that which, owing to the confused noise of disputation, could be less fully elucidated point by point, should be more carefully looked into, and that the pen should determine, for reading purposes, the questions handled.

For the occasion, indeed, of claiming Divine grace even for the Gentiles derived a pre-eminent fitness from this fact, that the man who set up to vindicate God's Law as his own was of the Gentiles, and not a Jew "of the stock of the Israelites." [1127] For this fact--that Gentiles are admissible to God's Law--is enough to prevent Israel from priding himself on the notion that "the Gentiles are accounted as a little drop of a bucket," or else as "dust out of a threshing-floor:" [1128] although we have God Himself as an adequate engager and faithful promiser, in that He promised to Abraham that "in his seed should be blest all nations of the earth;" [1129] and that [1130] out of the womb of Rebecca "two peoples and two nations were about to proceed," [1131] --of course those of the Jews, that is, of Israel; and of the Gentiles, that is ours. Each, then, was called a people and a nation; lest, from the nuncupative appellation, any should dare to claim for himself the privilege of grace.

For God ordained "two peoples and two nations" as about to proceed out of the womb of one woman: nor did grace [1132] make distinction in the nuncupative appellation, but in the order of birth; to the effect that, which ever was to be prior in proceeding from the womb, should be subjected to "the less," that is, the posterior. For thus unto Rebecca did God speak: "Two nations are in thy womb, and two peoples shall be divided from thy bowels; and people shall overcome people, and the greater shall serve the less." [1133] Accordingly, since the people or nation of the Jews is anterior in time, and "greater" through the grace of primary favour in the Law, whereas ours is understood to be "less" in the age of times, as having in the last Ἥρα of the world [1134] attained the knowledge of divine mercy:

beyond doubt, through the edict of the divine utterance, the prior and "greater" people--that is, the Jewish--must necessarily serve the "less;" and the "less" people--that is, the Christian--overcome the "greater." For, withal, according to the memorial records of the divine Scriptures, the people of the Jews--that is, the more ancient--quite forsook God, and did degrading service to idols, and, abandoning the Divinity, was surrendered to images; while "the people" said to Aaron, "Make us gods to go before us." [1135] And when the gold out of the necklaces of the women and the rings of the men had been wholly smelted by fire, and there had come forth a calf-like head, to this figment Israel with one consent (abandoning God) gave honour, saying, "These are the gods who brought us from the land of Egypt." [1136] For thus, in the later times in which kings were governing them, did they again, in conjunction with Jeroboam, worship golden kine, and groves, and enslave themselves to Baal. [1137] Whence is proved that they have ever been depicted, out of the volume of the divine Scriptures, as guilty of the crime of idolatry; whereas our "less"--that is, posterior--people, quitting the idols which formerly it used slavishly to serve, has been converted to the same God from whom Israel, as we have above related, had departed. [1138] For thus has the "less"--that is, posterior--people overcome the "greater people," while it attains the grace of divine favour, from which Israel has been divorced.

Chapter II - The Law Anterior to Moses

Stand we, therefore, foot to foot, and determine we the sum and substance of the actual question within definite lists.

For why should God, the founder of the universe, the Governor of the whole world, [1139] the Fashioner of humanity, the Sower [1140] of universal nations be believed to have given a law through Moses to one people, and not be said to have assigned it to all nations? For unless He had given it to all by no means would He have habitually permitted even proselytes out of the nations to have access to it. But--as is congruous with the goodness of God, and with His equity, as the Fashioner of mankind--He gave to all nations the selfsame law, which at definite and stated times He enjoined should be observed, when He willed, and through whom He willed, and as He willed. For in the beginning of the world He gave to Adam himself and Eve a law, that they were not to eat of the fruit of the tree planted in the midst of paradise; but that, if they did contrariwise, by death they were to die. [1141] Which law had continued enough for them, had it been kept. For in this law given to Adam we recognise in embryo [1142] all the precepts which afterwards sprouted forth when given through Moses; that is, Thou shalt love the Lord thy God from thy whole heart and out of thy whole soul; Thou shalt love thy neighbour as thyself;[1143] Thou shalt not kill; Thou shalt not commit adultery; Thou shalt not steal; False witness thou shalt not utter; Honour thy father and mother; and, That which is another's, shalt thou not covet.

For the primordial law was given to Adam and Eve in paradise, as the womb of all the precepts of God. In short, if they had loved the Lord their God, they would not have contravened His precept; if they had habitually loved their neighbour--that is, themselves [1144] --they would not have believed the persuasion of the serpent, and thus would not have committed murder upon themselves, [1145] by falling[1146] from immortality, by contravening God's precept; from theft also they would have abstained, if they had not stealthily tasted of the fruit of the tree, nor had been anxious to skulk beneath a tree to escape the view of the Lord their God; nor would they have been made partners with the falsehood-asseverating devil, by believing him that they would be "like God;" and thus they would not have offended God either, as their Father, who had fashioned them from clay of the earth, as out of the womb of a mother; if they had not coveted another's, they would not have tasted of the unlawful fruit.

Therefore, in this general and primordial law of God, the observance of which, in the case of the tree's fruit, He had sanctioned, we recognise enclosed all the precepts specially of the posterior Law, which germinated when disclosed at their proper times. For the subsequent superinduction of a law is the work of the same Being who had before premised a precept; since it is His province withal subsequently to train, who had before resolved to form, righteous creatures. For what wonder if He extends a discipline who institutes it? if He advances who begins? In short, before the Law of Moses,[1147] written in stone-tables, I contend that there was a law unwritten, which was habitually understood naturally, and by the fathers was habitually kept. For whence was Noah "found righteous," [1148] if in his case the righteousness of a natural law had not preceded? Whence was Abraham accounted "a friend of God," [1149] if not on the ground of equity and righteousness, (in the observance) of a natural law? Whence was Melchizedek named "priest of the most high God," [1150] if, before the priesthood of the Levitical law, there were not levites who were wont to offer sacrifices to God?

For thus, after the above-mentioned patriarchs, was the Law given to Moses, at that (well-known) time after their exode from Egypt, after the interval and spaces of four hundred years.

In fact, it was after Abraham's "four hundred and thirty years" [1151] that the Law was given. Whence we understand that God's law was anterior even to Moses, and was not first (given) in Horeb, nor in Sinai and in the desert, but was more ancient; (existing) first in paradise, subsequently reformed for the patriarchs, and so again for the Jews, at definite periods: so that we are not to give heed to Moses' Law as to the primitive law, but as to a subsequent, which at a definite period God has set forth to the Gentiles too and, after repeatedly promising so to do through the prophets, has reformed for the better; and has premonished that it should come to pass that, just as "the law was given through Moses" [1152] at a definite time, so it should be believed to have been temporarily observed and kept. And let us not annul this power which God has, which reforms the law's precepts answerably to the circumstances of the times, with a view to man's salvation. In fine, let him who contends that the Sabbath is still to be observed as a balm of salvation, and circumcision on the eighth day because of the threat of death, teach us that, for the time past, righteous men kept the Sabbath, or practised circumcision, and were thus rendered "friends of God." For if circumcision purges a man since God made Adam uncircumcised, why did He not circumcise him, even after his sinning, if circumcision purges? At all events, in settling him in paradise, He appointed one uncircumcised as colonist of paradise. Therefore, since God originated Adam uncircumcised, and inobservant of the Sabbath, consequently his offspring also, Abel, offering Him sacrifices, uncircumcised and inobservant of the Sabbath, was by Him commended; while He accepted [1153] what he was offering in simplicity of heart, and reprobated the sacrifice of his brother Cain, who was not rightly dividing what he was offering. [1154] Noah also, uncircumcised--yes, and inobservant of the Sabbath--God freed from the deluge. [1155] For Enoch, too, most righteous man, uncircumcised and inobservant of the Sabbath, He translated from this world; [1156] who did not first taste[1157] death, in order that, being a candidate for eternal life, [1158] he might by this time show us that we also may, without the burden of the law of Moses, please God. Melchizedek also, "the priest of the most high God," uncircumcised and inobservant of the Sabbath, was chosen to the priesthood of God. [1159] Lot, withal, the brother[1160] of Abraham, proves that it was for the merits of righteousness, without observance of the law, that he was freed from the conflagration of the Sodomites. [1161]

Chapter III - Of Circumcision and the Supercession of the Old Law

But Abraham, (you say,) was circumcised. Yes, but he pleased God before his circumcision;[1162] nor yet did he observe the Sabbath. For he had "accepted"[1163] circumcision; but such as was to be for "a sign" of that time, not for a prerogative title to salvation. In fact, subsequent patriarchs were uncircumcised, like Melchizedek, who, uncircumcised, offered to Abraham himself, already circumcised, on his return from battle, bread and wine.[1164] "But again," (you say) "the son of Moses would upon one occasion have been choked by an angel, if Zipporah,[1165] had not circumcised the foreskin of the infant with a pebble; whence, "there is the greatest peril if any fail to circumcise the foreskin of his flesh." Nay, but if circumcision altogether brought salvation, even Moses himself, in the case of his own son, would not have omitted to circumcise him on the eighth day; whereas it is agreed that Zipporah did it on the journey, at the compulsion of the angel. Consider we, accordingly, that one single infant's compulsory circumcision cannot have prescribed to every people, and founded, as it were, a law for keeping this precept. For God, foreseeing that He was about to give this circumcision to the people of Israel for "a sign," not for salvation, urges the circumcision of the son of Moses, their future leader, for this reason; that, since He had begun, through him, to give the People the precept of circumcision, the people should not despise it, from seeing this example (of neglect) already exhibited conspicuously in their leader's son. For circumcision had to be given; but as "a sign," whence Israel in the last time would have to be distinguished, when, in accordance with their deserts, they should be prohibited from entering the holy city, as we see through the words of the prophets, saying, "Your land is desert; your cities utterly burnt with fire; your country, in your sight, strangers shall eat up; and, deserted and subverted by strange peoples, the daughter of Zion shall be derelict, like a shed in a vineyard, and like a watchhouse in a cucumber-field, and as it were a city which is being stormed."[1166] Why so?

Because the subsequent discourse of the prophet reproaches them, saying, "Sons have I begotten and upraised, but they have reprobated me;"[1167] and again, "And if ye shall have outstretched hands, I will avert my face from you; and if ye shall have multiplied prayers, I will not hear you: for your hands are full of blood;"[1168] and again, "Woe! sinful nation; a people full of sins; wicked sons; ye have quite forsaken God, and have provoked unto indignation the Holy One of Israel."[1169] This, therefore, was God's foresight,--that of giving circumcision to Israel, for a sign whence they might be distinguished when the time should arrive wherein their above-mentioned deserts should prohibit their admission into Jerusalem:

which circumstance, because it was to be, used to be announced; and, because we see it accomplished, is recognised by us. For, as the carnal circumcision, which was temporary, was in wrought for "a sign" in a contumacious people, so the spiritual has been given for salvation to an obedient people; while the prophet Jeremiah says, "Make a renewal for you, and sow not in thorns; be circumcised to God, and circumcise the foreskin of your heart:"[1170] and in another place he says, "Behold, days shall come, saith the Lord, and I will draw up, for the house of Judah and for the house of Jacob,[1171] a new testament; not such as I once gave their fathers in the day wherein I led them out from the land of Egypt."[1172] Whence we understand that the coming cessation of the former circumcision then given, and the coming procession of a new law (not such as He had already given to the fathers), are announced: just as Isaiah foretold, saying that in the last days the mount of the Lord and the house of God were to be manifest above the tops of the mounts: "And it shall be exalted," he says, "above the hills; and there shall come over it all nations; and many shall walk, and say, Come, ascend we unto the mount of the Lord, and unto the house of the God of Jacob,"[1173] --not of Esau, the former son, but of Jacob, the second; that is, of our "people," whose "mount" is Christ, "præcised without concisors' hands,[1174] filling every land," shown in the book of Daniel.[1175] In short, the coming procession of a new law out of this "house of the God of Jacob" Isaiah in the ensuing words announces, saying, "For from Zion shall go out a law, and the word of the Lord out of Jerusalem, and shall judge among the nations,"--that is, among us, who have been called out of the nations,--"and they shall join to beat their glaives into ploughs, and their lances into sickles; and nations shall not take up glaive against nation, and they shall no more learn to fight."[1176] Who else, therefore, are understood but we, who, fully taught by the new law, observe these practices,--the old law being obliterated, the coming of whose abolition the action itself[1177] demonstrates? For the wont of the old law was to avenge itself by the vengeance of the glaive, and to pluck out "eye for eye," and to inflict retaliatory revenge for injury.[1178] But the new law's wont was to point to clemency, and to convert to tranquillity the pristine ferocity of "glaives" and "lances," and to remodel the pristine execution of "war" upon the rivals and foes of the law into the pacific actions of "ploughing" and "tilling" the land.[1179] Therefore as we have shown above that the coming cessation of the old law and of the carnal circumcision was declared, so, too, the observance of the new law and the spiritual circumcision has shone out into the voluntary obediences[1180] of peace. For "a people," he says, "whom I knew not hath served me; in obedience of the ear it hath obeyed me." [1181] Prophets made the announcement. But what is the "people" which was ignorant of God, but ours, who in days bygone knew not God? and who, in the hearing of the ear, gave heed to Him, but we, who, forsaking idols, have been converted to God? For Israel--who had been known to God, and who had by Him been "upraised" [1182] in Egypt, and was transported through the Red Sea, and who in the desert, fed forty years with manna, was wrought to the semblance of eternity, and not contaminated with human passions, [1183] or fed on this world's [1184] meats, but fed on "angel's loaves" [1185] --the manna--and sufficiently bound to God by His benefits--forgot his Lord and God, saying to Aaron: "Make us gods, to go before us: for that Moses, who ejected us from the land of Egypt, hath quite forsaken us; and what hath befallen him we know not." And accordingly we, who "were not the people of God" in days bygone, have been made His people, [1186] by accepting the new law above mentioned, and the new circumcision before foretold.

Chapter IV - Of the Observance of the Sabbath

It follows, accordingly, that, in so far as the abolition of carnal circumcision and of the old law is demonstrated as having been consummated at its specific times, so also the observance of the Sabbath is demonstrated to have been temporary.

For the Jews say, that from the beginning God sanctified the seventh day, by resting on it from all His works which He made; and that thence it was, likewise, that Moses said to the People: "Remember the day of the sabbaths, to sanctify it:

every servile work ye shall not do therein, except what pertaineth unto life." [1187] Whence we (Christians) understand that we still more ought to observe a sabbath from all "servile work"[1188] always, and not only every seventh day, but through all time. And through this arises the question for us, what sabbath God willed us to keep? For the Scriptures point to a sabbath eternal and a sabbath temporal. For Isaiah the prophet says, "Your sabbaths my soul hateth;" [1189] and in another place he says, "My sabbaths ye have profaned." [1190] Whence we discern that the temporal sabbath is human, and the eternal sabbath is accounted divine; concerning which He predicts through Isaiah: "And there shall be," He says, "month after month, and day after day, and sabbath after sabbath; and all flesh shall come to adore in Jerusalem, saith the Lord;" [1191] which we understand to have been fulfilled in the times of Christ, when "all flesh"--that is, every nation--"came to adore in Jerusalem" God the Father, through Jesus Christ His Son, as was predicted through the prophet: "Behold, proselytes through me shall go unto Thee." [1192] Thus, therefore, before this temporal sabbath, there was withal an eternal sabbath foreshown and foretold; just as before the carnal circumcision there was withal a spiritual circumcision foreshown. In short, let them teach us, as we have already premised, that Adam observed the sabbath; or that Abel, when offering to God a holy victim, pleased Him by a religious reverence for the sabbath; or that Enoch, when translated, had been a keeper of the sabbath; or that Noah the ark-builder observed, on account of the deluge, an immense sabbath; or that Abraham, in observance of the sabbath, offered Isaac his son; or that Melchizedek in his priesthood received the law of the sabbath.

But the Jews are sure to say, that ever since this precept was given through Moses, the observance has been binding. Manifest accordingly it is, that the precept was not eternal nor spiritual, but temporary, [1193] which would one day cease. In short, so true is it that it is not in the exemption from work of the sabbath--that is, of the seventh day--that the celebration of this solemnity is to consist, that Joshua the son of Nun, at the time that he was reducing the city Jericho by war, stated that he had received from God a precept to order the People that priests should carry the ark of the testament of God seven days, making the circuit of the city; and thus, when the seventh day's circuit had been performed, the walls of the city would spontaneously fall. [1194] Which was so done; and when the space of the seventh day was finished, just as was predicted, down fell the walls of the city. Whence it is manifestly shown, that in the number of the seven days there intervened a sabbath-day. For seven days, whencesoever they may have commenced, must necessarily include within them a sabbath-day; on which day not only must the priests have worked, but the city must have been made a prey by the edge of the sword by all the people of Israel. Nor is it doubtful that they "wrought servile work," when, in obedience to God's precept, they drave the preys of war. For in the times of the Maccabees, too, they did bravely in fighting on the sabbaths, and routed their foreign foes, and recalled the law of their fathers to the primitive style of life by fighting on the sabbaths. [1195] Nor should I think it was any other law which they thus vindicated, than the one in which they remembered the existence of the prescript touching "the day of the sabbaths." [1196]

Whence it is manifest that the force of such precepts was temporary, and respected the necessity of present circumstances; and that it was not with a view to its observance in perpetuity that God formerly gave them such a law.

Chapter V - Of Sacrifices

So, again, we show that sacrifices of earthly oblations and of spiritual sacrifices [1197] were predicted; and, moreover, that from the beginning the earthly were foreshown, in the person of Cain, to be those of the "elder son," that is, of Israel; and the opposite sacrifices demonstrated to be those of the "younger son," Abel, that is, of our people. For the elder, Cain, offered gifts to God from the fruit of the earth; but the younger son, Abel, from the fruit of his ewes. "God had respect unto Abel, and unto his gifts; but unto Cain and unto his gifts He had not respect. And God said unto Cain, Why is thy countenance fallen? hast thou not--if thou offerest indeed aright, but dost not divide aright--sinned? Hold thy peace. For unto thee shalt thy conversion be and he shall lord it over thee.

And then Cain said unto Abel his brother, Let us go into the field: and he went away with him thither, and he slew him. And then God said unto Cain, Where is Abel thy brother? And he said, I know not: am I my brother's keeper? To whom God said, The voice of the blood of thy brother crieth forth unto me from the earth. Wherefore cursed is the earth, which hath opened her mouth to receive the blood of thy brother. Groaning and trembling shalt thou be upon the earth, and every one who shall have found thee shall slay thee." [1198] From this proceeding we gather that the twofold sacrifices of "the peoples" were even from the very beginning foreshown. In short, when the sacerdotal law was being drawn up, through Moses, in Leviticus, we find it prescribed to the people of Israel that sacrifices should in no other place be offered to God than in the land of promise; which the Lord God was about to give to "the people" Israel and to their brethren, in order that, on Israel's introduction thither, there should there be celebrated sacrifices and holocausts, as well for sins as for souls; and nowhere else but in the holy land. [1199] Why, accordingly, does the Spirit afterwards predict, through the prophets, that it should come to pass that in every place and in every land there should be offered sacrifices to God? as He says through the angel Malachi, one of the twelve prophets:

"I will not receive sacrifice from your hands; for from the rising sun unto the setting my Name hath been made famous among all the nations, saith the Lord Almighty: and in every place they offer clean sacrifices to my Name." [1200] Again, in the Psalms, David says: "Bring to God, ye countries of the nations"--undoubtedly because "unto every land" the preaching of the apostles had to "go out" [1201] -- "bring to God fame and honour; bring to God the sacrifices of His name: take up [1202] victims and enter into His courts." [1203] For that it is not by earthly sacrifices, but by spiritual, that offering is to be made to God, we thus read, as it is written, An heart contribulate and humbled is a victim for God;" [1204] and elsewhere, "Sacrifice to God a sacrifice of praise, and render to the Highest thy vows." [1205] Thus, accordingly, the spiritual "sacrifices of praise" are pointed to, and "an heart contribulate" is demonstrated an acceptable sacrifice to God. And thus, as carnal sacrifices are understood to be reprobated--of which Isaiah withal speaks, saying, "To what end is the multitude of your sacrifices to me? saith the Lord" [1206] --so spiritual sacrifices are predicted [1207] as accepted, as the prophets announce.

For, "even if ye shall have brought me," He says, "the finest wheat flour, it is a vain supplicatory gift: a thing execrable to me;" and again He says, "Your holocausts and sacrifices, and the fat of goats, and blood of bulls, I will not, not even if ye come to be seen by me: for who hath required these things from your hands?" [1208] for "from the rising sun unto the setting, my Name hath been made famous among all the nations, saith the Lord." [1209] But of the spiritual sacrifices He adds, saying, "And in every place they offer clean sacrifices to my Name, saith the Lord."[1210]

Chapter VI - Of the Abolition and the Abolisher of the Old Law

Therefore, since it is manifest that a sabbath temporal was shown, and a sabbath eternal foretold; a circumcision carnal foretold, and a circumcision spiritual pre-indicated; a law temporal and a law eternal formally declared; sacrifices carnal and sacrifices spiritual foreshown; it follows that, after all these precepts had been given carnally, in time preceding, to the people Israel, there was to supervene a time whereat the precepts of the ancient Law and of the old ceremonies would cease, and the promise[1211] of the new law, and the recognition of spiritual sacrifices, and the promise of the New Testament, supervene; [1212] while the light from on high would beam upon us who were sitting in darkness, and were being detained in the shadow of death. [1213] And so there is incumbent on us a necessity [1214] binding us, since we have premised that a new law was predicted by the prophets, and that not such as had been already given to their fathers at the time when He led them forth from the land of Egypt, [1215] to show and prove, on the one hand, that that old Law has ceased, and on the other, that the promised new law is now in operation.

And, indeed, first we must inquire whether there be expected a giver of the new law, and an heir of the new testament, and a priest of the new sacrifices, and a purger of the new circumcision, and an observer of the eternal sabbath, to suppress the old law, and institute the new testament, and offer the new sacrifices, and repress the ancient ceremonies, and suppress [1216] the old circumcision together with its own sabbath, [1217] and announce the new kingdom which is not corruptible. Inquire, I say, we must, whether this giver of the new law, observer of the spiritual sabbath, priest of the eternal sacrifices, eternal ruler of the eternal kingdom, be come or no: that, if he is already come, service may have to be rendered him; if he is not yet come, he may have to be awaited, until by his advent it be manifest that the old Law's precepts are suppressed, and that the beginnings of the new law ought to arise.

And, primarily, we must lay it down that the ancient Law and the prophets could not have ceased, unless He were come who was constantly announced, through the same Law and through the same prophets, as to come.

Chapter VII - The Question Whether Christ Be Come Taken Up

Therefore upon this issue plant we foot to foot, whether the Christ who was constantly announced as to come be already come, or whether His coming be yet a subject of hope. For proof of which question itself, the times likewise must be examined by us when the prophets announced that the Christ would come; that, if we succeed in recognising that He has come within the limits of those times, we may without doubt believe Him to be the very one whose future coming was ever the theme of prophetic song, upon whom we--the nations, to wit--were ever announced as destined to believe; and that, when it shall have been agreed that He is come, we may undoubtedly likewise believe that the new law has by Him been given, and not disavow the new testament in Him and through Him drawn up for us. For that Christ was to come we know that even the Jews do not attempt to disprove, inasmuch as it is to His advent that they are directing their hope.

Nor need we inquire at more length concerning that matter, since in days bygone all the prophets have prophesied of it; as Isaiah: "Thus saith the Lord God to my Christ (the) Lord, [1218] whose right hand I have holden, that the nations may hear Him: the powers of kings will I burst asunder; I will open before Him the gates, and the cities shall not be closed to Him." Which very thing we see fulfilled. For whose right hand does God the Father hold but Christ's, His Son?--whom all nations have heard, that is, whom all nations have believed,--whose preachers, withal, the apostles, are pointed to in the Psalms of David: "Into the universal earth," says he, "is gone out their sound, and unto the ends of the earth their words." [1219] For upon whom else have the universal nations believed, but upon the Christ who is already come? For whom have the nations believed,--Parthians, Medes, Elamites, and they who inhabit Mesopotamia, Armenia, Phrygia, Cappadocia, and they who dwell in Pontus, and Asia, and Pamphylia, tarriers in Egypt, and inhabiters of the region of Africa which is beyond Cyrene, Romans and sojourners, yes, and in Jerusalem Jews,[1220] and all other nations; as, for instance, by this time, the varied races of the Gætulians, and manifold confines of the Moors, all the limits of the Spains, and the diverse nations of the Gauls, and the haunts of the Britons--inaccessible to the Romans, but subjugated to Christ, and of the Sarmatians, and Dacians, and Germans, and Scythians, and of many remote nations, and of provinces and islands many, to us unknown, and which we can scarce enumerate? In all which places the name of the Christ who is already come reigns, as of Him before whom the gates of all cities have been opened, and to whom none are closed, before whom iron bars have been crumbled, and brazen gates [1221] opened. Although there be withal a spiritual sense to be affixed to these expressions,--that the hearts of individuals, blockaded in various ways by the devil, are unbarred by the faith of Christ,--still they have been evidently fulfilled, inasmuch as in all these places dwells the "people" of the Name of Christ. For who could have reigned over all nations but Christ, God's Son, who was ever announced as destined to reign over all to eternity? For if Solomon "reigned," why, it was within the confines of Judea merely:

"from Beersheba unto Dan" the boundaries of his kingdom are marked. [1222] If, moreover, Darius "reigned" over the Babylonians and Parthians, he had not power over all nations; if Pharaoh, or whoever succeeded him in his hereditary kingdom, over the Egyptians, in that country merely did he possess his kingdom's dominion; if Nebuchadnezzar with his petty kings, "from India unto Ethiopia" he had his kingdom's boundaries; [1223] if Alexander the Macedonian he did not hold more than universal Asia, and other regions, after he had quite conquered them; if the Germans, to this day they are not suffered to cross their own limits; the Britons are shut within the circuit of their own ocean; the nations of the Moors, and the barbarism of the Gætulians, are blockaded by the Romans, lest they exceed the confines of their own regions. What shall I say of the Romans themselves, [1224] who fortify their own empire with garrisons of their own legions, nor can extend the might of their kingdom beyond these nations? But Christ's Name is extending everywhere, believed everywhere, worshipped by all the above-enumerated nations, reigning everywhere, adored everywhere, conferred equally everywhere upon all. No king, with Him, finds greater favour, no barbarian lesser joy; no dignities or pedigrees enjoy distinctions of merit; to all He is equal, to all King, to all Judge, to all "God and Lord." [1225] Nor would you hesitate to believe what we asseverate, since you see it taking place.

Chapter VIII - Of the Times of Christ's Birth and Passion, and of Jerusalem's Destruction

Accordingly the times must be inquired into of the predicted and future nativity of the Christ, and of His passion, and of the extermination of the city of Jerusalem, that is, its devastation. For Daniel says, that "both the holy city and the holy place are exterminated together with the coming Leader, and that the pinnacle is destroyed unto ruin." [1226] And so the times of the coming Christ, the Leader, [1227] must be inquired into, which we shall trace in Daniel; and, after computing them, shall prove Him to be come, even on the ground of the times prescribed, and of competent signs and operations of His.

Which matters we prove, again, on the ground of the consequences which were ever announced as to follow His advent; in order that we may believe all to have been as well fulfilled as foreseen.

In such wise, therefore, did Daniel predict concerning Him, as to show both when and in what time He was to set the nations free; and how, after the passion of the Christ, that city had to be exterminated. For he says thus: "In the first year under Darius, son of Ahasuerus, of the seed of the Medes, who reigned over the kingdom of the Chaldees, I Daniel understood in the books the number of the years....And while I was yet speaking in my prayer, behold, the man Gabriel, whom I saw in the vision in the beginning, flying; and he touched me, as it were, at the hour of the evening sacrifice, and made me understand, and spake with me, and said, Daniel I am now come out to imbue thee with understanding; in the beginning of thy supplication went out a word. And I am come to announce to thee, because thou art a man of desires; [1228] and ponder thou on the word, and understand in the vision. Seventy hebdomads have been abridged [1229] upon thy commonalty, and upon the holy city, until delinquency be made inveterate, and sins sealed, and righteousness obtained by entreaty, and righteousness eternal introduced; and in order that vision and prophet may be sealed, and an holy one of holy ones anointed.

And thou shalt know, and thoroughly see, and understand, from the going forth of a word for restoring and rebuilding Jerusalem unto the Christ, the Leader, hebdomads (seven and an half, and[1230]) lxii and an half: and it shall convert, and shall be built into height and entrenchment, and the times shall be renewed: and after these lxii hebdomads shall the anointing be exterminated, and shall not be; and the city and the holy place shall he exterminate together with the Leader, who is making His advent; and they shall be cut short as in a deluge, until (the) end of a war, which shall be cut short unto ruin. And he shall confirm a testament in many. In one hebdomad and the half of the hebdomad shall be taken away my sacrifice and libation, and in the holy place the execration of devastation, (and [1231]) until the end of (the) time consummation shall be given with regard to this devastation." [1232]

Observe we, therefore, the limit,--how, in truth, he predicts that there are to be lxx hebdomads, within which if they receive Him, "it shall be built into height and entrenchment, and the times shall be renewed." But God, foreseeing what was to be--that they will not merely not receive Him, but will both persecute and deliver Him to death--both recapitulated, and said, that in lx and ii and an half of an hebdomad He is born, and an holy one of holy ones is anointed; but that when vii hebdomads [1233] and an half were fulfilling, He had to suffer, and the holy city had to be exterminated after one and an half hebdomad--whereby namely, the seven and an half hebdomads have been completed. For he says thus: "And the city and the holy place to be exterminated together with the leader who is to come; and they shall be cut short as in a deluge; and he shall destroy the pinnacle unto ruin." [1234] Whence, therefore, do we show that the Christ came within the lxii and an half hebdomads?

We shall count, moreover, from the first year of Darius, as at this particular time is shown to Daniel this particular vision; for he says, "And understand and conjecture that at the completion of thy word [1235] I make thee these answers." Whence we are bound to compute from the first year of Darius, when Daniel saw this vision.

Let us see, therefore, how the years are filled up until the advent of the Christ:--

For Darius reigned...xviiii [1236] years (19).
Artaxerxes reigned...xl and i years (41).
Then King Ochus (who is also called Cyrus) reigned...xxiiii years (24).
Argus...one year.
Another Darius, who is also named Melas...xxi years (21).
Alexander the Macedonian...xii years (12).
Then, after Alexander, who had reigned over both Medes and Persians, whom he had reconquered, and had established his kingdom firmly in Alexandria, when withal he called that (city) by his own name; [1237] after him reigned, (there, in Alexandria,)

Soter...xxxv years (35).
To whom succeeds Philadelphus, reigning...xxx and viii years (38).

To him succeeds Euergetes...xxv years (25).
Then Philopator...xvii years (17).
After him Epiphanes...xxiiii years (24).
Then another Euergetes...xxviiii years (29).
Then another Soter,...xxxviii years (38).
Ptolemy...xxxvii years (37).
Cleopatra,...xx years v months (20 5-12).
Yet again Cleopatra reigned jointly with Augustus...xiii years (13).
After Cleopatra, Augustus reigned other...xliii years (43).
For all the years of the empire of Augustus were...lvi years (56).

Let us see, moreover, how in the forty-first year of the empire of Augustus, when he has been reigning for xx and viii years after the death of Cleopatra, the Christ is born.

(And the same Augustus survived, after Christ is born, xv years; and the remaining times of years to the day of the birth of Christ will bring us to the xl first year, which is the xx and viii^th of Augustus after the death of Cleopatra.) There are, (then,) made up cccxxx and vii years, v months: (whence are filled up lxii hebdomads and an half:

which make up ccccxxxvii years, vi months:) on the day of the birth of Christ. And (then) "righteousness eternal" was manifested, and "an Holy One of holy ones was anointed"--that is, Christ-- and "sealed was vision and prophet," and "sins" were remitted, which, through faith in the name of Christ, are washed away [1238] for all who believe on Him. But what does he mean by saying that "vision and prophecy are sealed?" That all prophets ever announced of Him that He was to come and had to suffer. Therefore, since the prophecy was fulfilled through His advent, for that reason he said that "vision and prophecy were sealed;" inasmuch as He is the signet of all prophets, fulfilling all things which in days bygone they had announced of Him. [1239] For after the advent of Christ and His passion there is no longer "vision or prophet" to announce Him as to come. In short, if this is not so, let the Jews exhibit, subsequently to Christ, any volumes of prophets, visible miracles wrought by any angels, (such as those) which in bygone days the patriarchs saw until the advent of Christ, who is now come; since which event "sealed is vision and prophecy," that is, confirmed.

And justly does the evangelist [1240] write, "The law and the prophets (were) until John" the Baptist. For, on Christ's being baptized, that is, on His sanctifying the waters in His own baptism,[1241] all the plenitude of bygone spiritual grace-gifts ceased in Christ, sealing as He did all vision and prophecies, which by His advent He fulfilled. Whence most firmly does he assert that His advent "seals visions and prophecy."

Accordingly, showing, (as we have done,) both the number of the years, and the time of the lx two and an half fulfilled hebdomads, on completion of which, (we have shown) that Christ is come, that is, has been born, let us see what (mean) other "vii and an half hebdomads," which have been subdivided in the abscision of [1242] the former hebdomads; (let us see, namely,) in what event they have been fulfilled:--

For, after Augustus who survived after the birth of Christ, are made up...xv years (15).
To whom succeeded Tiberius Cæsar, and held the empire...xx years, vii months, xxviii days (20 etc.).
(In the fiftieth year of his empire Christ suffered, being about xxx years of age when he suffered.)
Again Caius Cæsar, also called Caligula,...iii years, viii months, xiii days (3 etc.).
Nero Cæsar,...xi years, ix months, xiii days (11 etc.).
Galba...vii months, vi days. (7 etc.).
Otho...iii days.
Vitellius,...viii mos., xxvii days (8 mos.).
Vespasian, in the first year of his empire, subdues the Jews in war; and there are made lii years, vi months.

For he reigned xi years. And thus, in the day of their storming, the Jews fulfilled the lxx hebdomads predicted in Daniel.

Therefore, when these times also were completed, and the Jews subdued, there afterwards ceased in that place "libations and sacrifices," which thenceforward have not been able to be in that place celebrated; for "the unction," too, [1243] was "exterminated" in that place after the passion of Christ. For it had been predicted that the unction should be exterminated in that place; as in the Psalms it is prophesied, "They exterminated my hands and feet." [1244] And the suffering of this "extermination" was perfected within the times of the lxx hebdomads, under Tiberius Cæsar, in the consulate of Rubellius Geminus and Fufius Geminus, in the month of March, at the times of the passover, on the eighth day before the calends of April, [1245] on the first day of unleavened bread, on which they slew the lamb at even, just as had been enjoined by Moses. [1246] Accordingly, all the synagogue of Israel did slay Him, saying to Pilate, when he was desirous to dismiss Him, "His blood be upon us, and upon our children;"[1247] and, "If thou dismiss him, thou art not a friend of Cæsar;" [1248] in order that all things might be fulfilled which had been written of Him. [1249]

Chapter IX - Of the Prophecies of the Birth and Achievements of Christ

Begin we, therefore, to prove that the Birth of Christ was announced by prophets; as Isaiah (e.g.,) foretells, "Hear ye, house of David; no petty contest have ye with men, since God is proposing a struggle. Therefore God Himself will give you a sign; Behold, the virgin [1250] shall conceive, and bear a son, and ye shall call his name Emmanuel" [1251] (which is, interpreted, "God with us" [1252]): "butter and honey shall he eat;" [1253] : "since, ere the child learn to call father or mother, he shall receive the power of Damascus and the spoils of Samaria, in opposition to the king of the Assyrians." [1254]

Accordingly the Jews say: Let us challenge that prediction of Isaiah, and let us institute a comparison whether, in the case of the Christ who is already come, there be applicable to Him, firstly, the name which Isaiah foretold, and (secondly) the signs of it [1255] which he announced of Him.

Well, then, Isaiah foretells that it behoves Him to be called Emmanuel; and that subsequently He is to take the power of Damascus and the spoils of Samaria, in opposition to the king of the Assyrians. "Now," say they, "that (Christ) of yours, who is come, neither was called by that name, nor engaged in warfare." But we, on the contrary, have thought they ought to be admonished to recall to mind the context of this passage as well. For subjoined is withal the interpretation of Emmanuel--"God with us"[1256] --in order that you may regard not the sound only of the name, but the sense too. For the Hebrew sound, which is Emmanuel, has an interpretation, which is, God with us. Inquire, then, whether this speech, "God with us" (which is Emmanuel), be commonly applied to Christ ever since Christ's light has dawned, and I think you will not deny it. For they who out of Judaism believe in Christ, ever since their believing on Him, do, whenever they shall wish to say [1257] Emmanuel, signify that God is with us:

and thus it is agreed that He who was ever predicted as Emmanuel is already come, because that which Emmanuel signifies is come--that is, "God with us." Equally are they led by the sound of the name when they so understand "the power of Damascus," and "the spoils of Samaria," and "the kingdom of the Assyrians," as if they portended Christ as a warrior; not observing that Scripture premises, "since, ere the child learn to call father or mother, he shall receive the power of Damascus and the spoils of Samaria, in opposition to the king of the Assyrians." For the first step is to look at the demonstration of His age, to see whether the age there indicated can possibly exhibit the Christ as already a man, not to say a general. Forsooth, by His babyish cry the infant would summon men to arms, and would give the signal of war not with clarion, but with rattle, and point out the foe, not from His charger's back or from a rampart, but from the back or neck of His suckler and nurse, and thus subdue Damascus and Samaria in place of the breast. (It is another matter if, among you, infants rush out into battle,--oiled first, I suppose, to dry in the sun, and then armed with satchels and rationed on butter,--who are to know how to lance sooner than how to lacerate the bosom!) [1258] Certainly, if nature nowhere allows this,--(namely,) to serve as a soldier before developing into manhood, to take "the power of Damascus" before knowing your father,--it follows that the pronouncement is visibly figurative.

"But again," say they, "nature suffers not a virgin' to be a parent; and yet the prophet must be believed."

And deservedly so; for he bespoke credit for a thing incredible, by saying that it was to be a sign. "Therefore," he says, "shall a sign be given you. Behold, a virgin shall conceive in womb, and bear a son." But a sign from God, unless it had consisted in some portentous novelty, would not have appeared a sign. In a word, if, when you are anxious to cast any down from (a belief in) this divine prediction, or to convert whoever are simple, you have the audacity to lie, as if the Scripture contained (the announcement), that not "a virgin," but "a young female," was to conceive and bring forth; you are refuted even by this fact, that a daily occurrence--the pregnancy and parturition of a young female, namely--cannot possibly seem anything of a sign. And the setting before us, then, of a virgin-mother is deservedly believed to be a sign; but not equally so a warrior-infant. For there would not in this case again be involved the question of a sign; but, the sign of a novel birth having been awarded, the next step after the sign is, that there is enunciated a different ensuing ordering[1259] of the infant, who is to eat "honey and butter." Nor is this, of course, for a sign.

It is natural to infancy. But that he is to receive [1260] "the power of Damascus and the spoils of Samaria in opposition to the king of the Assyrians," this is a wondrous sign. Keep to the limit of (the infant's) age, and inquire into the sense of the prediction; nay, rather, repay to truth what you are unwilling to credit her with, and the prophecy becomes intelligible by the relation of its fulfilment. Let those Eastern magi be believed, dowering with gold and incense the infancy of Christ as a king; [1261] and the infant has received "the power of Damascus" without battle and arms. For, besides the fact that it is known to all that the "power"--for that is the "strength"--of the East is wont to abound in gold and odours, certain it is that the divine Scriptures regard "gold" as constituting the "power" also of all other nations; as it says [1262] through Zechariah: "And Judah keepeth guard at Jerusalem, and shall amass all the vigour of the surrounding peoples, gold and silver." [1263] For of this gift of "gold" David likewise says, "And to Him shall be given of the gold of Arabia;" [1264] and again, "The kings of the Arabs and Saba shall bring Him gifts." [1265] For the East, on the one hand, generally held the magi (to be) kings; and Damascus, on the other hand, used formerly to be reckoned to Arabia before it was transferred into Syrophoenicia on the division of the Syrias: the "power" whereof Christ then "received" in receiving its ensigns,--gold, to wit, and odours. "The spoils," moreover, "of Samaria" (He received in receiving) the magi themselves, who, on recognising Him, and honouring Him with gifts, and adoring Him on bended knee as Lord and King, on the evidence of the guiding and indicating star, became "the spoils of Samaria," that is, of idolatry--by believing, namely, on Christ.

For (Scripture) denoted idolatry by the name of "Samaria," Samaria being ignominious on the score of idolatry; for she had at that time revolted from God under King Jeroboam. For this, again, is no novelty to the Divine Scriptures, figuratively to use a transference of name grounded on parallelism of crimes. For it [1266] calls your rulers "rulers of Sodom," and your people the "people of Gomorrha," [1267] when those cities had already long been extinct. [1268] And elsewhere it says, through a prophet, to the people of Israel, "Thy father (was) an Amorite, and thy mother an Hittite;" [1269] of whose race they were not begotten, but (were called their sons) by reason of their consimilarity in impiety, whom of old (God) had called His own sons through Isaiah the prophet: "I have generated and exalted sons." [1270] So, too, Egypt is sometimes understood to mean the whole world [1271] in that prophet, on the count of superstition and malediction. [1272] So, again, Babylon, in our own John, is a figure of the city Rome, as being equally great and proud of her sway, and triumphant over the saints. [1273] On this wise, accordingly, (Scripture)[1274] entitled the magi also with the appellation of "Samaritans,"--"despoiled" (of that) which they had had in common with the Samaritans, as we have said--idolatry in opposition to the Lord.

(It [1275] adds), "in opposition," moreover, "to the king of the Assyrians,"--in opposition to the devil, who to this hour thinks himself to be reigning, if he detrudes the saints from the religion of God.

Moreover, this our interpretation will be supported while (we find that) elsewhere as well the Scriptures designate Christ a warrior, as we gather from the names of certain weapons, and words of that kind. But by a comparison of the remaining senses the Jews shall be convicted.

"Gird thee," says David, "the sword upon the thigh." [1276] But what do you read above concerning the Christ? "Blooming in beauty above the sons of men; grace is outpoured in thy lips."[1277] But very absurd it is if he was complimenting on the bloom of his beauty and the grace of his lips, one whom he was girding for war with a sword; of whom he proceeds subjunctively to say, "Outstretch and prosper, advance and reign!" And he has added, "because of thy lenity and justice." [1278] Who will ply the sword without practising the contraries to lenity and justice; that is, guile, and asperity, and injustice, proper (of course) to the business of battles?

See we, then, whether that which has another action be not another sword,--that is, the Divine word of God, doubly sharpened [1279] with the two Testaments of the ancient law and the new law; sharpened by the equity of its own wisdom; rendering to each one according to his own action.[1280] Lawful, then, it was for the Christ of God to be precinct, in the Psalms, without warlike achievements, with the figurative sword of the word of God; to which sword is congruous the predicated "bloom," together with the "grace of the lips;" with which sword He was then "girt upon the thigh," in the eye of David, when He was announced as about to come to earth in obedience to God the Father's decree. "The greatness of thy right hand," he says, "shall conduct thee" [1281] --the virtue to wit, of the spiritual grace from which the recognition of Christ is deduced. "Thine arrows," he says, "are sharp," [1282] --God's everywhere-flying precepts (arrows) threatening the exposure [1283] of every heart, and carrying compunction and transfixion to each conscience: "peoples shall fall beneath thee," [1284] --of course, in adoration. Thus mighty in war and weapon-bearing is Christ; thus will He "receive the spoils," not of "Samaria" alone, but of all nations as well.

Acknowledge that His "spoils" are figurative whose weapons you have learnt to be allegorical. And thus, so far, the Christ who is come was not a warrior, because He was not predicted as such by Isaiah.

"But if the Christ," say they, "who is believed to be coming is not called Jesus, why is he who is come called Jesus Christ?" Well, each name will meet in the Christ of God, in whom is found likewise the appellation [1285] Jesus. Learn the habitual character of your error. In the course of the appointing of a successor to Moses, Oshea [1286] the son of Nun [1287] is certainly transferred from his pristine name, and begins to be called Jesus. [1288] Certainly, you say. This we first assert to have been a figure of the future. For, because Jesus Christ was to introduce the second people (which is composed of us nations, lingering deserted in the world [1289] aforetime) into the land of promise, "flowing with milk and honey"[1290] (that is, into the possession of eternal life, than which nought is sweeter); and this had to come about, not through Moses (that is, not through the Law's discipline), but through Joshua (that is, through the new law's grace), after our circumcision with "a knife of rock" [1291] (that is, with Christ's precepts, for Christ is in many ways and figures predicted as a rock [1292]); therefore the man who was being prepared to act as images of this sacrament was inaugurated under the figure of the Lord's name, even so as to be named Jesus.[1293] For He who ever spake to Moses was the Son of God Himself; who, too, was always seen. [1294] For God the Father none ever saw, and lived. [1295] And accordingly it is agreed that the Son of God Himself spake to Moses, and said to the people, "Behold, I send mine angel before thy"--that is, the people's--"face, to guard thee on the march, and to introduce thee into the land which I have prepared thee: attend to him, and be not disobedient to him; for he hath not escaped[1296] thy notice, since my name is upon him." [1297] For Joshua was to introduce the people into the land of promise, not Moses. Now He called him an "angel," on account of the magnitude of the mighty deeds which he was to achieve (which mighty deeds Joshua the son of Nun did, and you yourselves read), and on account of his office of prophet announcing (to wit) the divine will; just as withal the Spirit, speaking in the person of the Father, calls the forerunner of Christ, John, a future "angel," through the prophet: "Behold, I send mine angel before Thy"--that is, Christ's--"face, who shall prepare Thy way before Thee." [1298] Nor is it a novel practice to the Holy Spirit to call those "angels" whom God has appointed as ministers of His power. For the same John is called not merely an "angel" of Christ, but withal a "lamp" shining before Christ: for David predicts, "I have prepared the lamp for my Christ;" [1299] and him Christ Himself, coming "to fulfil the prophets," [1300] called so to the Jews. "He was," He says, "the burning and shining lamp;" [1301] as being he who not merely "prepared His ways in the desert," [1302] but withal, by pointing out "the Lamb of God," [1303] illumined the minds of men by his heralding, so that they understood Him to be that Lamb whom Moses was wont to announce as destined to suffer.

Thus, too, (was the son of Nun called) Joshua, on account of the future mystery [1304] of his name: for that name (He who spake with Moses) confirmed as His own which Himself had conferred on him, because He had bidden him thenceforth be called, not "angel" nor "Oshea," but "Joshua." Thus, therefore, each name is appropriate to the Christ of God--that He should be called Jesus as well (as Christ).

And that the virgin of whom it behoved Christ to be born (as we have above mentioned) must derive her lineage of the seed of David, the prophet in subsequent passages evidently asserts. "And there shall be born," he says, "a rod from the root of Jesse"--which rod is Mary--"and a flower shall ascend from his root: and there shall rest upon him the Spirit of God, the spirit of wisdom and understanding, the spirit of discernment and piety, the spirit of counsel and truth; the spirit of God's fear shall fill Him."[1305] For to none of men was the universal aggregation of spiritual credentials appropriate, except to Christ; paralleled as He is to a "flower" by reason of glory, by reason of grace; but accounted "of the root of Jesse," whence His origin is to be deduced,--to wit, through Mary. [1306] For He was from the native soil of Bethlehem, and from the house of David; as, among the Romans, Mary is described in the census, of whom is born Christ. [1307]

I demand, again--granting that He who was ever predicted by prophets as destined to come out of Jesse's race, was withal to exhibit all humility, patience, and tranquillity--whether He be come? Equally so (in this case as in the former), the man who is shown to bear that character will be the very Christ who is come. For of Him the prophet says, "A man set in a plague, and knowing how to bear infirmity;" who "was led as a sheep for a victim; and, as a lamb before him who sheareth him, opened not His mouth." [1308] If He "neither did contend nor shout, nor was His voice heard abroad," who "crushed not the bruised reed"--Israel's faith, who "quenched not the burning flax" [1309] --that is, the momentary glow of the Gentiles--but made it shine more by the rising of His own light,--He can be none other than He who was predicted. The action, therefore, of the Christ who is come must be examined by being placed side by side with the rule of the Scriptures. For, if I mistake not, we find Him distinguished by a twofold operation,--that of preaching and that of power. Now, let each count be disposed of summarily. Accordingly, let us work out the order we have set down, teaching that Christ was announced as a preacher; as, through Isaiah: "Cry out," he says, "in vigour, and spare not; lift up, as with a trumpet, thy voice, and announce to my commonalty their crimes, and to the house of Jacob their sins.

Me from day to day they seek, and to learn my ways they covet, as a people which hath done righteousness, and hath not forsaken the judgment of God," and so forth: [1310] that, moreover, He was to do acts of power from the Father: "Behold, our God will deal retributive judgment; Himself will come and save us:

then shall the infirm be healed, and the eyes of the blind shall see, and the ears of the deaf shall hear, and the mutes' tongues shall be loosed, and the lame shall leap as an hart," [1311] and so on; which works not even you deny that Christ did, inasmuch as you were wont to say that, "on account of the works ye stoned Him not, but because He did them on the Sabbaths." [1312]

Chapter X - Concerning the Passion of Christ, and Its Old Testament Predictions and Adumbrations

Concerning the last step, plainly, of His passion you raise a doubt; affirming that the passion of the cross was not predicted with reference to Christ, and urging, besides, that it is not credible that God should have exposed His own Son to that kind of death; because Himself said, "Cursed is every one who shall have hung on a tree." [1313] But the reason of the case antecedently explains the sense of this malediction; for He says in Deuteronomy: "If, moreover, (a man) shall have been (involved) in some sin incurring the judgment of death, and shall die, and ye shall suspend him on a tree, his body shall not remain on the tree, but with burial ye shall bury him on the very day; because cursed by God is every one who shall have been suspended on a tree; and ye shall not defile the land which the Lord thy God shall give thee for (thy) lot." [1314] Therefore He did not maledictively adjudge Christ to this passion, but drew a distinction, that whoever, in any sin, had incurred the judgment of death, and died suspended on a tree, he should be "cursed by God," because his own sins were the cause of his suspension on the tree. On the other hand, Christ, who spoke not guile from His mouth, [1315] and who exhibited all righteousness and humility, not only (as we have above recorded it predicted of Him) was not exposed to that kind of death for his own deserts, but (was so exposed) in order that what was predicted by the prophets as destined to come upon Him through your means [1316] might be fulfilled; just as, in the Psalms, the Spirit Himself of Christ was already singing, saying, "They were repaying me evil for good;" [1317] and, "What I had not seized I was then paying in full;" [1318] "They exterminated my hands and feet;" [1319] and, "They put into my drink gall, and in my thirst they slaked me with vinegar;" [1320] "Upon my vesture they did cast (the) lot;" [1321] just as the other (outrages) which you were to commit on Him were foretold,--all which He, actually and thoroughly suffering, suffered not for any evil action of His own, but "that the Scriptures from the mouth of the prophets might be fulfilled."[1322]

And, of course, it had been meet that the mystery [1323] of the passion itself should be figuratively set forth in predictions; and the more incredible (that mystery), the more likely to be "a stumbling-stone," [1324] if it had been nakedly predicted; and the more magnificent, the more to be adumbrated, that the difficulty of its intelligence might seek (help from) the grace of God.

Accordingly, to begin with, Isaac, when led by his father as a victim, and himself bearing his own "wood," [1325] was even at that early period pointing to Christ's death; conceded, as He was, as a victim by the Father; carrying, as He did, the "wood" of His own passion. [1326]

Joseph, again, himself was made a figure of Christ [1327] in this point alone (to name no more, not to delay my own course), that he suffered persecution at the hands of his brethren, and was sold into Egypt, on account of the favour of God; [1328] just as Christ was sold by Israel--(and therefore,) "according to the flesh," by His "brethren" [1329] --when He is betrayed by Judas.[1330] For Joseph is withal blest by his father [1331] after this form: "His glory (is that) of a bull; his horns, the horns of an unicorn; on them shall he toss nations alike unto the very extremity of the earth."

Of course no one-horned rhinoceros was there pointed to, nor any two-horned minotaur. But Christ was therein signified: "bull," by reason of each of His two characters,--to some fierce, as Judge; to others gentle, as Saviour; whose "horns" were to be the extremities of the cross. For even in a ship's yard--which is part of a cross--this is the name by which the extremities are called; while the central pole of the mast is a "unicorn." By this power, in fact, of the cross, and in this manner horned, He does now, on the one hand, "toss" universal nations through faith, wafting them away from earth to heaven; and will one day, on the other, "toss" them through judgment, casting them down from heaven to earth.

He, again, will be the "bull" elsewhere too in the same scripture. [1332] When Jacob pronounced a blessing on Simeon and Levi, he prophesies of the scribes and Pharisees; for from them [1333] is derived their [1334] origin. For (his blessing) interprets spiritually thus: "Simeon and Levi perfected iniquity out of their sect," [1335] --whereby, to wit, they persecuted Christ: "into their counsel come not my soul! and upon their station rest not my heart! because in their indignation they slew men"--that is, prophets--"and in their concupiscence they hamstrung a bull!"[1336] --that is, Christ, whom--after the slaughter of prophets--they slew, and exhausted their savagery by transfixing His sinews with nails.

Else it is idle if, after the murder already committed by them, he upbraids others, and not them, with butchery. [1337]

But, to come now to Moses, why, I wonder, did he merely at the time when Joshua was battling against Amalek, pray sitting with hands expanded, when, in circumstances so critical, he ought rather, surely, to have commended his prayer by knees bended, and hands beating his breast, and a face prostrate on the ground; except it was that there, where the name of the Lord Jesus was the theme of speech--destined as He was to enter the lists one day singly against the devil--the figure of the cross was also necessary, (that figure) through which Jesus was to win the victory?[1338] Why, again, did the same Moses, after the prohibition of any "likeness of anything,"[1339] set forth a brazen serpent, placed on a "tree," in a hanging posture, for a spectacle of healing to Israel, at the time when, after their idolatry, [1340] they were suffering extermination by serpents, except that in this case he was exhibiting the Lord's cross on which the "serpent" the devil was "made a show of," [1341] and, for every one hurt by such snakes--that is, his angels[1342] --on turning intently from the peccancy of sins to the sacraments of Christ's cross, salvation was outwrought? For he who then gazed upon that (cross) was freed from the bite of the serpents. [1343]

Come, now, if you have read in the utterance of the prophet in the Psalms, "God hath reigned from the tree," [1344] I wait to hear what you understand thereby; for fear you may perhaps think some carpenter-king [1345] is signified, and not Christ, who has reigned from that time onward when he overcame the death which ensued from His passion of "the tree."

Similarly, again, Isaiah says: "For a child is born to us, and to us is given a son." [1346] What novelty is that, unless he is speaking of the "Son" of God?--and one is born to us the beginning of whose government has been made "on His shoulder." What king in the world wears the ensign of his power on his shoulder, and does not bear either diadem on his head, or else sceptre in his hand, or else some mark of distinctive vesture? But the novel "King of ages," Christ Jesus, alone reared "on His shoulder" His own novel glory, and power, and sublimity,--the cross, to wit; that, according to the former prophecy, the Lord thenceforth "might reign from the tree." For of this tree likewise it is that God hints, through Jeremiah, that you would say, "Come, let us put wood [1347] into his bread, and let us wear him away out of the land of the living; and his name shall no more be remembered." [1348] Of course on His body that "wood" was put; [1349] for so Christ has revealed, calling His body "bread," [1350] whose body the prophet in bygone days announced under the term "bread." If you shall still seek for predictions of the Lord's cross, the twenty-first Psalm will at length be able to satisfy you, containing as it does the whole passion of Christ; singing, as He does, even at so early a date, His own glory. [1351] "They dug," He says, "my hands and feet" [1352] --which is the peculiar atrocity of the cross; and again when He implores the aid of the Father, "Save me," He says, "out of the mouth of the lion"--of course, of death--"and from the horn of the unicorns my humility," [1353] --from the ends, to wit, of the cross, as we have above shown; which cross neither David himself suffered, nor any of the kings of the Jews: that you may not think the passion of some other particular man is here prophesied than His who alone was so signally crucified by the People.

Now, if the hardness of your heart shall persist in rejecting and deriding all these interpretations, we will prove that it may suffice that the death of the Christ had been prophesied, in order that, from the fact that the nature of the death had not been specified, it may be understood to have been affected by means of the cross [1354] and that the passion of the cross is not to be ascribed to any but Him whose death was constantly being predicted. For I desire to show, in one utterance of Isaiah, His death, and passion, and sepulture. "By the crimes," he says, "of my people was He led unto death; and I will give the evil for His sepulture, and the rich for His death, because he did not wickedness, nor was guile found in his mouth; and God willed to redeem His soul from death," [1355] and so forth. He says again, moreover: "His sepulture hath been taken away from the midst." [1356] For neither was He buried except He were dead, nor was His sepulture removed from the midst except through His resurrection. Finally, he subjoins: "Therefore He shall have many for an heritage, and of many shall He divide spoils:" [1357] who else (shall so do) but He who "was born," as we have above shown?--"in return for the fact that His soul was delivered unto death?" For, the cause of the favour accorded Him being shown,--in return, to wit, for the injury of a death which had to be recompensed,--it is likewise shown that He, destined to attain these rewards because of death, was to attain them after death--of course after resurrection. For that which happened at His passion, that mid-day grew dark, the prophet Amos announces, saying, "And it shall be," he says, "in that day, saith the Lord, the sun shall set at mid-day, and the day of light shall grow dark over the land:

and I will convert your festive days into grief, and all your canticles into lamentation; and I will lay upon your loins sackcloth, and upon every head baldness; and I will make the grief like that for a beloved (son), and them that are with him like a day of mourning." [1358] For that you would do thus at the beginning of the first month of your new (years) even Moses prophesied, when he was foretelling that all the community of the sons of Israel was [1359] to immolate at eventide a lamb, and were to eat [1360] this solemn sacrifice of this day (that is, of the passover of unleavened bread) with bitterness;" and added that "it was the passover of the Lord," [1361] that is, the passion of Christ. Which prediction was thus also fulfilled, that "on the first day of unleavened bread"[1362] you slew Christ; [1363] and (that the prophecies might be fulfilled) the day hasted to make an "eventide,"--that is, to cause darkness, which was made at mid-day; and thus "your festive days God converted into grief, and your canticles into lamentation." For after the passion of Christ there overtook you even captivity and dispersion, predicted before through the Holy Spirit.

Chapter XI - Further Proofs, from Ezekiel. Summary of the Prophetic Argument Thus Far

For, again, it is for these deserts of yours that Ezekiel announces your ruin as about to come: and not only in this age [1364] --a ruin which has already befallen--but in the "day of retribution,"[1365] which will be subsequent. From which ruin none will be freed but he who shall have been frontally sealed [1366] with the passion of the Christ whom you have rejected. For thus it is written: "And the Lord said unto me, Son of man, thou hast seen what the elders of Israel do, each one of them in darkness, each in a hidden bed-chamber: because they have said, The Lord seeth us not; the Lord hath derelinquished the earth. And He said unto me, Turn thee again, and thou shalt see greater enormities which these do. And He introduced me unto the thresholds of the gate of the house of the Lord which looketh unto the north; and, behold, there, women sitting and bewailing Thammuz.

And the Lord said unto me, Son of man, hast thou seen? Is the house of Judah moderate, to do the enormities which they have done? And yet thou art about to see greater affections of theirs. And He introduced me into the inner shrine of the house of the Lord; and, behold, on the thresholds of the house of the Lord, between the midst of the porch and between the midst of the altar, [1367] as it were twenty and five men have turned their backs unto the temple of the Lord, and their faces over against the east; these were adoring the sun. And He said unto me, Seest thou, son of man? Are such deeds trifles to the house of Judah, that they should do the enormities which these have done? because they have filled up (the measure of) their impieties, and, behold, are themselves, as it were, grimacing; I will deal with mine indignation, [1368] mine eye shall not spare, neither will I pity; they shall cry out unto mine ears with a loud voice, and I will not hear them, nay, I will not pity. And He cried into mine ears with a loud voice, saying, The vengeance of this city is at hand; and each one had vessels of extermination in his hand. And, behold, six men were coming toward the way of the high gate which was looking toward the north, and each one's double-axe of dispersion was in his hand: and one man in the midst of them, clothed with a garment reaching to the feet, [1369] and a girdle of sapphire about his loins:

and they entered, and took their stand close to the brazen altar. And the glory of the God of Israel, which was over the house, in the open court of it, [1370] ascended from the cherubim: and the Lord called the man who was clothed with the garment reaching to the feet, who had upon his loins the girdle; and said unto him, Pass through the midst of Jerusalem, and write the sign Tau[1371] on the foreheads of the men who groan and grieve over all the enormities which are done in their midst. And while these things were doing, He said unto an hearer, [1372] Go ye after him into the city, and cut short; and spare not with your eyes, and pity not elder or youth or virgin; and little ones and women slay ye all, that they may be thoroughly wiped away; but all upon whom is the sign Tau approach ye not; and begin with my saints."[1373] Now the mystery of this "sign" was in various ways predicted; (a "sign") in which the foundation of life was forelaid for mankind; (a "sign") in which the Jews were not to believe: just as Moses beforetime kept on announcing in Exodus, [1374] saying, "Ye shall be ejected from the land into which ye shall enter; and in those nations ye shall not be able to rest:

and there shall be instability of the print [1375] of thy foot: and God shall give thee a wearying heart, and a pining soul, and failing eyes, that they see not: and thy life shall hang on the tree [1376] before thine eyes; and thou shalt not trust thy life."

And so, since prophecy has been fulfilled through His advent--that is, through the nativity, which we have above commemorated, and the passion, which we have evidently explained--that is the reason withal why Daniel said, "Vision and prophet were sealed;" because Christ is the "signet" of all prophets, fulfilling all that had in days bygone been announced concerning Him: for, since His advent and personal passion, there is no longer "vision" or "prophet;" whence most emphatically he says that His advent "seals vision and prophecy." And thus, by showing "the number of the years, and the time of the lxii and an half fulfilled hebdomads," we have proved that at that specified time Christ came, that is, was born; and, (by showing the time) of the "seven and an half hebdomads," which are subdivided so as to be cut off from the former hebdomads, within which times we have shown Christ to have suffered, and by the consequent conclusion of the "lxx hebdomads," and the extermination of the city, (we have proved) that "sacrifice and unction" thenceforth cease.

Sufficient it is thus far, on these points, to have meantime traced the course of the ordained path of Christ, by which He is proved to be such as He used to be announced, even on the ground of that agreement of Scriptures, which has enabled us to speak out, in opposition to the Jews, on the ground [1377] of the prejudgment of the major part.

For let them not question or deny the writings we produce; that the fact also that things which were foretold as destined to happen after Christ are being recognised as fulfilled may make it impossible for them to deny (these writings) to be on a par with divine Scriptures. Else, unless He were come after whom the things which were wont to be announced had to be accomplished, would such as have been completed be proved? [1378]

Chapter XII - Further Proofs from the Calling of the Gentiles

Look at the universal nations thenceforth emerging from the vortex of human error to the Lord God the Creator and His Christ; and if you dare to deny that this was prophesied, forthwith occurs to you the promise of the Father in the Psalms, which says, "My Son art Thou; to-day have I begotten Thee.

Ask of Me, and I will give Thee Gentiles as Thine heritage, and as Thy possession the bounds of the earth." [1379] For you will not be able to affirm that "son" to be David rather than Christ; or the "bounds of the earth" to have been promised rather to David, who reigned within the single (country of) Judea, than to Christ, who has already taken captive the whole orb with the faith of His gospel; as He says through Isaiah:

"Behold, I have given Thee for a covenant [1380] of my family, for a light of Gentiles, that Thou mayst open the eyes of the blind"--of course, such as err--"to outloose from bonds the bound"--that is, to free them from sins--"and from the house of prison"--that is, of death--"such as sit in darkness" [1381] --of ignorance, to wit. And if these blessings accrue through Christ, they will not have been prophesied of another than Him through whom we consider them to have been accomplished. [1382]

Chapter XIII - Argument from the Destruction of Jerusalem and Desolation of Judea

Therefore, since the sons of Israel affirm that we err in receiving the Christ, who is already come, let us put in a demurrer against them out of the Scriptures themselves, to the effect that the Christ who was the theme of prediction is come; albeit by the times of Daniel's prediction we have proved that the Christ is come already who was the theme of announcement. Now it behoved Him to be born in Bethlehem of Judah. For thus it is written in the prophet: "And thou, Bethlehem, are not the least in the leaders of Judah: for out of thee shall issue a Leader who shall feed my People Israel." [1383] But if hitherto he has not been born, what "leader" was it who was thus announced as to proceed from the tribe of Judah, out of Bethlehem? For it behoves him to proceed from the tribe of Judah and from Bethlehem. But we perceive that now none of the race of Israel has remained in Bethlehem; and (so it has been) ever since the interdict was issued forbidding any one of the Jews to linger in the confines of the very district, in order that this prophetic utterance also should be perfectly fulfilled:

"Your land is desert, your cities burnt up by fire,"--that is, (he is foretelling) what will have happened to them in time of war "your region strangers shall eat up in your sight, and it shall be desert and subverted by alien peoples." [1384] And in another place it is thus said through the prophet: "The King with His glory ye shall see,"--that is, Christ, doing deeds of power in the glory of God the Father; [1385] "and your eyes shall see the land from afar," [1386] --which is what you do, being prohibited, in reward of your deserts, since the storming of Jerusalem, to enter into your land; it is permitted you merely to see it with your eyes from afar: "your soul," he says, "shall meditate terror," [1387] --namely, at the time when they suffered the ruin of themselves. [1388] How, therefore, will a "leader" be born from Judea, and how far will he "proceed from Bethlehem," as the divine volumes of the prophets do plainly announce; since none at all is left there to this day of (the house of) Israel, of whose stock Christ could be born?

Now, if (according to the Jews) He is hitherto not come, when He begins to come whence will He be anointed? [1389] For the Law enjoined that, in captivity, it was not lawful for the unction of the royal chrism to be compounded. [1390] But, if there is no longer "unction" there [1391] as Daniel prophesied (for he says, "Unction shall be exterminated"), it follows that they [1392] no longer have it, because neither have they a temple where was the "horn" [1393] from which kings were wont to be anointed.

If, then, there is no unction, whence shall be anointed the "leader" who shall be born in Bethlehem? or how shall he proceed "from Bethlehem," seeing that of the seed of Israel none at all exists in Bethlehem.

A second time, in fact, let us show that Christ is already come, (as foretold) through the prophets, and has suffered, and is already received back in the heavens, and thence is to come accordingly as the predictions prophesied. For, after His advent, we read, according to Daniel, that the city itself had to be exterminated; and we recognise that so it has befallen. For the Scripture says thus, that "the city and the holy place are simultaneously exterminated together with the leader," [1394] --undoubtedly (that Leader) who was to proceed "from Bethlehem," and from the tribe of "Judah." Whence, again, it is manifest that "the city must simultaneously be exterminated" at the time when its "Leader" had to suffer in it, (as foretold) through the Scriptures of the prophets, who say: "I have outstretched my hands the whole day unto a People contumacious and gainsaying Me, who walketh in a way not good, but after their own sins." [1395] And in the Psalms, David says: "They exterminated my hands and feet: they counted all my bones; they themselves, moreover, contemplated and saw me, and in my thirst slaked me with vinegar."[1396] These things David did not suffer, so as to seem justly to have spoken of himself; but the Christ who was crucified.

Moreover, the "hands and feet," are not "exterminated,"[1397] except His who is suspended on a "tree." Whence, again, David said that "the Lord would reign from the tree:"[1398] for elsewhere, too, the prophet predicts the fruit of this "tree," saying "The earth hath given her blessings,"[1399] --of course that virgin-earth, not yet irrigated with rains, nor fertilized by showers, out of which man was of yore first formed, out of which now Christ through the flesh has been born of a virgin; "and the tree,"[1400] he says, "hath brought his fruit,"[1401] --not that "tree" in paradise which yielded death to the protoplasts, but the "tree" of the passion of Christ, whence life, hanging, was by you not believed![1402] For this "tree" in a mystery,[1403] it was of yore wherewith Moses sweetened the bitter water; whence the People, which was perishing of thirst in the desert, drank and revived;[1404] just as we do, who, drawn out from the calamities of the heathendom[1405] in which we were tarrying perishing with thirst (that is, deprived of the divine word), drinking, "by the faith which is on Him,"[1406] the baptismal water of the "tree" of the passion of Christ, have revived,--a faith from which Israel has fallen away, (as foretold) through Jeremiah, who says, "Send, and ask exceedingly whether such things have been done, whether nations will change their gods (and these are not gods!). But My People hath changed their glory: whence no profit shall accrue to them: the heaven turned pale thereat" (and when did it turn pale? undoubtedly when Christ suffered), "and shuddered," he says, "most exceedingly;"[1407] and "the sun grew dark at mid-day:"[1408] (and when did it "shudder exceedingly" except at the passion of Christ, when the earth also trembled to her centre, and the veil of the temple was rent, and the tombs were burst asunder?[1409] "because these two evils hath My People done; Me," He says, "they have quite forsaken, the fount of water of life,[1410] and they have digged for themselves worn-out tanks, which will not be able to contain water." Undoubtedly, by not receiving Christ, the "fount of water of life," they have begun to have "worn-out tanks," that is, synagogues for the use of the "dispersions of the Gentiles,"[1411] in which the Holy Spirit no longer lingers, as for the time past He was wont to tarry in the temple before the advent of Christ, who is the true temple of God. For, that they should withal suffer this thirst of the Divine Spirit, the prophet Isaiah had said, saying: "Behold, they who serve Me shall eat, but ye shall be hungry; they who serve Me shall drink, but ye shall thirst, and from general tribulation of spirit shall howl: for ye shall transmit your name for a satiety to Mine elect, but you the Lord shall slay; but for them who serve Me shall be named a new name, which shall be blessed in the lands."[1412]

Again, the mystery of this "tree"[1413] we read as being celebrated even in the Books of the Reigns. For when the sons of the prophets were cutting "wood"[1414] with axes on the bank of the river Jordan, the iron flew off and sank in the stream; and so, on Elisha[1415] the prophet's coming up, the sons of the prophets beg of him to extract from the stream the iron which had sunk. And accordingly Elisha, having taken "wood," and cast it into that place where the iron had been submerged, forthwith it rose and swam on the surface,[1416] and the "wood" sank, which the sons of the prophets recovered.[1417] Whence they understood that Elijah's spirit was presently conferred upon him.[1418] What is more manifest than the mystery[1419] of this "wood,"--that the obduracy of this world[1420] had been sunk in the profundity of error, and is freed in baptism by the "wood" of Christ, that is, of His passion; in order that what had formerly perished through the "tree" in Adam, should be restored through the "tree" in Christ?[1421] while we, of course, who have succeeded to, and occupy, the room of the prophets, at the present day sustain in the world[1422] that treatment which the prophets always suffered on account of divine religion: for some they stoned, some they banished; more, however, they delivered to mortal slaughter,[1423] --a fact which they cannot deny.[1424]

This "wood," again, Isaac the son of Abraham personally carried for his own sacrifice, when God had enjoined that he should be made a victim to Himself. But, because these had been mysteries[1425] which were being kept for perfect fulfilment in the times of Christ, Isaac, on the one hand, with his "wood," was reserved, the ram being offered which was caught by the horns in the bramble;[1426] Christ, on the other hand, in His times, carried His "wood" on His own shoulders, adhering to the horns of the cross, with a thorny crown encircling His head. For Him it behoved to be made a sacrifice on behalf of all Gentiles, who "was led as a sheep for a victim, and, like a lamb voiceless before his shearer, so opened not His mouth" (for He, when Pilate interrogated Him, spake nothing[1427]); for "in humility His judgment was taken away:

His nativity, moreover, who shall declare?" Because no one at all of human beings was conscious of the nativity of Christ at His conception, when as the Virgin Mary was found pregnant by the word of God; and because "His life was to be taken from the land."[1428] Why, accordingly, after His resurrection from the dead, which was effected on the third day, did the heavens receive Him back? It was in accordance with a prophecy of Hosea, uttered on this wise:

"Before daybreak shall they arise unto Me, saying, Let us go and return unto the Lord our God, because Himself will draw us out and free us. After a space of two days, on the third day"[1429] --which is His glorious resurrection--He received back into the heavens (whence withal the Spirit Himself had come to the Virgin [1430]) Him whose nativity and passion alike the Jews have failed to acknowledge. Therefore, since the Jews still contend that the Christ is not yet come, whom we have in so many ways approved [1431] to be come, let the Jews recognise their own fate,--a fate which they were constantly foretold as destined to incur after the advent of the Christ, on account of the impiety with which they despised and slew Him. For first, from the day when, according to the saying of Isaiah, "a man cast forth his abominations of gold and silver, which they made to adore with vain and hurtful (rites)," [1432] -- that is, ever since we Gentiles, with our breast doubly enlightened through Christ's truth, cast forth (let the Jews see it) our idols,--what follows has likewise been fulfilled. For "the Lord of Sabaoth hath taken away, among the Jews from Jerusalem," among the other things named, "the wise architect" too, [1433] who builds the church, God's temple, and the holy city, and the house of the Lord. For thenceforth God's grace desisted (from working) among them. And "the clouds were commanded not to rain a shower upon the vineyard of Sorek," [1434] --the clouds being celestial benefits, which were commanded not to be forthcoming to the house of Israel; for it "had borne thorns"--whereof that house of Israel had wrought a crown for Christ--and not "righteousness, but a clamour,"--the clamour whereby it had extorted His surrender to the cross. [1435] And thus, the former gifts of grace being withdrawn, "the law and the prophets were until John," [1436] and the fishpool of Bethsaida [1437] until the advent of Christ: thereafter it ceased curatively to remove from Israel infirmities of health; since, as the result of their perseverance in their frenzy, the name of the Lord was through them blasphemed, as it is written: "On your account the name of God is blasphemed among the Gentiles:" [1438] for it is from them that the infamy (attached to that name) began, and (was propagated during) the interval from Tiberius to Vespasian. And because they had committed these crimes, and had failed to understand that Christ "was to be found" [1439] in "the time of their visitation," [1440] their land has been made "desert, and their cities utterly burnt with fire, while strangers devour their region in their sight: the daughter of Sion is derelict, as a watch-tower in a vineyard, or as a shed in a cucumber garden,"--ever since the time, to wit, when "Israel knew not" the Lord, and "the People understood Him not;" but rather "quite forsook, and provoked unto indignation, the Holy One of Israel." [1441] So, again, we find a conditional threat of the sword: "If ye shall have been unwilling, and shall not have been obedient, the glaive shall eat you up." [1442] Whence we prove that the sword was Christ, by not hearing whom they perished; who, again, in the Psalm, demands of the Father their dispersion, saying, "Disperse them in Thy power;" [1443] who, withal, again through Isaiah prays for their utter burning. "On My account," He says, "have these things happened to you; in anxiety shall ye sleep." [1444]

Since, therefore, the Jews were predicted as destined to suffer these calamities on Christ's account, and we find that they have suffered them, and see them sent into dispersion and abiding in it, manifest it is that it is on Christ's account that these things have befallen the Jews, the sense of the Scriptures harmonizing with the issue of events and of the order of the times. Or else, if Christ is not yet come, on whose account they were predicted as destined thus to suffer, when He shall have come it follows that they will thus suffer. And where will then be a daughter of Sion to be derelict, who now has no existence? where the cities to be exust, which are already exust and in heaps? where the dispersion of a race which is now in exile? Restore to Judea the condition which Christ is to find; and (then, if you will), contend that some other (Christ) is coming.

Chapter XIV - Conclusion. Clue to the Error of the Jews

Learn now (over and above the immediate question) the clue to your error.

We affirm, two characters of the Christ demonstrated by the prophets, and as many advents of His forenoted:

one, in humility (of course the first), when He has to be led "as a sheep for a victim; and, as a lamb voiceless before the shearer, so He opened not His mouth," not even in His aspect comely.

For "we have announced," says the prophet, "concerning Him, (He is) as a little child, as a root in a thirsty land; and there was not in Him attractiveness or glory. And we saw Him, and He had not attractiveness or grace; but His mien was unhonoured, deficient in comparison of the sons of men," [1445] "a man set in the plague, [1446] and knowing how to bear infirmity:" to wit as having been set by the Father "for a stone of offence," [1447] and "made a little lower" by Him "than angels." [1448] He pronounces Himself "a worm, and not a man, an ignominy of man, and the refuse of the People." [1449] Which evidences of ignobility suit the First Advent, just as those of sublimity do the Second; when He shall be made no longer "a stone of offence nor a rock of scandal," but "the highest corner-stone," [1450] after reprobation (on earth) taken up (into heaven) and raised sublime for the purpose of consummation, [1451] and that "rock"--so we must admit--which is read of in Daniel as forecut from a mount, which shall crush and crumble the image of secular kingdoms. [1452] Of which second advent of the same (Christ) Daniel has said: "And, behold, as it were a Son of man, coming with the clouds of the heaven, came unto the Ancient of days, and was present in His sight; and they who were standing by led (Him) unto Him. And there was given Him royal power; and all nations of the earth, according to their race, and all glory, shall serve Him: and His power is eternal, which shall not be taken away, and His kingdom one which shall not be corrupted." [1453] Then, assuredly, is He to have an honourable mien, and a grace not "deficient more than the sons of men;" for (He will then be) "blooming in beauty in comparison with the sons of men." [1454] "Grace," says the Psalmist, "hath been outpoured in Thy lips: wherefore God hath blessed Thee unto eternity. Gird Thee Thy sword around Thy thigh, most potent in Thy bloom and beauty!" [1455] while the Father withal afterwards, after making Him somewhat lower than angels, "crowned Him with glory and honour and subjected all things beneath His feet." [1456] And then shall they "learn to know Him whom they pierced, and shall beat their breasts tribe by tribe;" [1457] of course because in days bygone they did not know Him when conditioned in the humility of human estate. Jeremiah says: "He is a human being, and who will learn to know Him?" [1458] because, "His nativity," says Isaiah, "who shall declare?" So, too, in Zechariah, in His own person, nay, in the very mystery [1459] of His name withal, the most true Priest of the Father, His own [1460] Christ, is delineated in a twofold garb with reference to the two advents. [1461] First, He was clad in "sordid attire," that is, in the indignity of passible and mortal flesh, when the devil, withal, was opposing himself to Him--the instigator, to wit, of Judas the traitor [1462] --who even after His baptism had tempted Him.

In the next place, He was stripped of His former sordid raiment, and adorned with a garment down to the foot, and with a turban and a clean mitre, that is, (with the garb) of the second advent; since He is demonstrated as having attained "glory and honour." Nor will you be able to say that the man (there depicted) is "the son of Jozadak," [1463] who was never at all clad in a sordid garment, but was always adorned with the sacerdotal garment, nor ever deprived of the sacerdotal function. But the "Jesus" [1464] there alluded to is Christ, the Priest of God the most high Father; who at His first advent came in humility, in human form, and passible, even up to the period of His passion; being Himself likewise made, through all (stages of suffering) a victim for us all; who after His resurrection was "clad with a garment down to the foot," [1465] and named the Priest of God the Father unto eternity. [1466] So, again, I will make an interpretation of the two goats which were habitually offered on the fast-day. [1467] Do not they, too, point to each successive stage in the character of the Christ who is already come? A pair, on the one hand, and consimilar (they were), because of the identity of the Lord's general appearance, inasmuch as He is not to come in some other form, seeing that He has to be recognised by those by whom He was once hurt. But the one of them, begirt with scarlet, amid cursing and universal spitting, and tearing, and piercing, was cast away by the People outside the city into perdition, marked with manifest tokens of Christ's passion; who, after being begirt with scarlet garment, and subjected to universal spitting, and afflicted with all contumelies, was crucified outside the city. [1468] The other, however, offered for sins, and given as food to the priests merely of the temple, [1469] gave signal evidences of the second appearance; in so far as, after the expiation of all sins, the priests of the spiritual temple, that is, of the church, were to enjoy [1470] a spiritual public distribution (as it were) of the Lord's grace, while all others are fasting from salvation.

Therefore, since the vaticinations of the first advent obscured it with manifold figures, and debased it with every dishonour, while the second (was foretold as) manifest and wholly worthy of God, it has resulted therefrom, that, by fixing their gaze on that one alone which they could easily understand and believe (that is, the second, which is in honour and glory), they have been (not undeservedly) deceived as to the more obscure--at all events, the more unworthy--that is, the first. And thus to the present moment they affirm that their Christ is not come, because He is not come in majesty; while they are ignorant of [1471] the fact that He was first to come in humility.

Enough it is, meantime, to have thus far followed the stream downward of the order of Christ's course, whereby He is proved such as He was habitually announced: in order that, as a result of this harmony of the Divine Scriptures, we may understand; and that the events which used to be predicted as destined to take place after Christ may be believed to have been accomplished as the result of a divine arrangement. For unless He come after whom they had to be accomplished, by no means would the events, the future occurrence whereof was predictively assigned to His advent, have come to pass.

Therefore, if you see universal nations thenceforth emerging from the profundity of human error to God the Creator and His Christ (which you dare not assert to have not been prophesied, because, albeit you were so to assert, there would forthwith--as we have already premised [1472] --occur to you the promise of the Father saying, "My Son art Thou; I this day have begotten Thee; ask of Me, and I will give Thee Gentiles as Thine heritage, and as Thy possession the boundaries of the earth."

Nor will you be able to vindicate, as the subject of that prediction, rather the son of David, Solomon, than Christ, God's Son; nor "the boundaries of the earth," as promised rather to David's son, who reigned within the single land of Judea, than to Christ the Son of God, who has already illumined the whole world [1473] with the rays of His gospel. In short, again, a throne "unto the age" [1474] is more suitable to Christ, God's Son, than to Solomon,--a temporal king, to wit, who reigned over Israel alone. For at the present day nations are invoking Christ which used not to know Him; and peoples at the present day are fleeing in a body to the Christ of whom in days bygone they were ignorant [1475]), you cannot contend that is future which you see taking place. [1476] Either deny that these events were prophesied, while they are seen before your eyes; or else have been fulfilled, while you hear them read: or, on the other hand, if you fail to deny each position, they will have their fulfilment in Him with respect to whom they were prophesied.

Footnotes:

1126. [This treatise was written while our author was a Catholic. This seems to me the best supported of the theories concerning it. Let us accept Pamelius, for once and date it a.d. 198. Dr. Allix following Baronius, will have it as late as a.d. 208. Neander thinks the work, after the quotation from Isaiah in the beginning of chapter ninth, is not our author's, but was finished by another hand, clumsily annexing what is said on the same chapter of Isaiah in the Third Book against Marcion. It is only slightly varied. Bp. Kaye admits the very striking facts instanced by Neander, in support of this theory, but demolishes, with a word any argument drawn from thence that the genuine work was written after the author's lapse. This treatise is sufficiently annotated by Thelwall, and covers ground elsewhere gone over in this Series. My own notes are therefore very few.]

1127. Comp. Phil. iii. 5.

1128. See Isa. xl. 15: "dust of the balance," Eng. Ver.; ῥοπὴ ζυγοῦ LXX. For the expression "dust out of a threshing-floor," however, see Ps. i. 4, Dan. ii. 35.

1129. See Gen. xxii. 18; and comp. Gal. iii. 16, and the reference in both places.

1130. This promise may be said to have been given "to Abraham," because (of course) he was still living at the time; as we see by comparing Gen. xxi. 5 with xxv. 7 and 26. See, too, Heb. xi. 9.

1131. Or, "nor did He make, by grace, a distinction."

1132. Or, "nor did He make, by grace, a distinction."

1133. See Gen. xxv. 21-23, especially in the LXX.; and comp. Rom. ix. 10-13.

1134. Sæculi.

1135. Ex. xxxii. 1, 23; Acts vii. 39, 40.

1136. Ex. xxxii. 4: comp. Acts vii. 38-41; 1 Cor. x. 7; Ps. cvi. 19-22.

1137. Comp. 1 Kings xii. 25-33; 2 Kings xvii. 7-17 (in LXX. 3 and 4 Kings). The Eng. ver. speaks of "calves;" the LXX. call them "heifers."

1138. Comp. 1 Thess. i. 9, 10.

1139. Mundi.

1140. Comp. Jer. xxxi. 27 (in LXX. it is xxxviii. 27); Hos. ii. 23; Zech. x. 9; Matt. xiii. 31-43.

1141. See Gen. ii. 16, 17; iii. 2, 3.

1142. Condita.

1143. Deut. vi. 4, 5; Lev. xix. 18; comp. Matt. xxii. 34-40; Mark xii. 28-34; Luke x. 25-28; and for the rest, Ex. xx. 12-17; Deut. v. 16-21; Rom. xiii. 9.

1144. Semetipsos. ? Each other.

1145. Semetipsos. ? Each other.

1146. Excidendo; or, perhaps, "by self-excision," or "mutual excision."

1147. Or, "the Law written for Moses in stone-tables."

1148. Gen. vi. 9; vii. 1; comp. Heb. xi. 7.

1149. See Isa. xli. 8; Jas. ii. 23.

1150. Gen. xiv. 18, Ps. cx. (cix. in. LXX.) 4; Heb. v. 10, vii. 1-3, 10, 15, 17.

1151. Comp. Gen. xv. 13 with Ex. xii. 40-42 and Acts vii. 6.

1152. John i. 17.

1153. Or, "credited him with."

1154. Gen. iv. 1-7, especially in the LXX.; comp. Heb. xi. 4.

1155. Gen. vi. 18; vii. 23; 2 Pet. ii. 5.

1156. See Gen. v. 22, 24; Heb. xi. 5.

1157. Or, perhaps, "has not yet tasted."

1158. Æternitatis candidatus. Comp. ad Ux. l. i. c. vii., and note 3 there.

1159. See above.

1160. i.e., nephew. See Gen. xi. 31; xii. 5.

1161. See Gen. xix. 1-29; and comp. 2 Pet. ii. 6-9.

1162. See Gen. xii.-xv. compared with xvii. and Rom. iv.

1163. Acceperat. So Tertullian renders, as it appears to me, the ἔλαβε of St. Paul in Rom. iv. 11. q. v.

1164. There is, if the text be genuine, some confusion here. Melchizedek does not appear to have been, in any sense, "subsequent" to Abraham, for he probably was senior to him; and, moreover, Abraham does not appear to have been "already circumcised" carnally when Melchizedek met him. Comp. Gen. xiv. with Gen. xvii.

1165. Tertullian writes Seffora; the LXX. in loco, Σεπφώρα Ex. iv. 24-26, where the Eng. ver. says, "the Lord met him," etc.; the LXX ἄγγελος Κυρίου.

1166] Isa. i. 7, 8. See c. xiii. sub fin.

1167. Again an error; for these words precede the others. These are found in Isa. i. 2.

1168. Isa. i. 15.

1169. Isa. i. 4.

1170. Jer. iv. 3, 4. In Eng. ver., "break up your fallow ground;" but comp. de Pu. c. vi. ad init.

1171. So Tertullian. In Jer. ibid. "Israel

and...Judah."

1172. Jer. xxxi. 31, 32 (in LXX. ibid. xxxviii. 31, 32); comp. Heb. viii. 8-13.

1173. Isa. ii. 2, 3.

1174. Perhaps an allusion to Phil. iii. 1, 2.

1175. See Dan. ii. 34, 35, 44, 45. See c. xiv. below.

1176. Isa. ii. 3, 4.

1177. i.e., of beating swords into ploughs, etc.

1178. Comp. Ex. xxi. 24, 25; Lev. xxiv. 17-22; Deut. xix. 11-21; Matt. v. 38.

1179. Especially spiritually. Comp. 1 Cor. iii. 6-9; ix. 9, 10, and similar passages.

1180. Obsequia. See de Pa. c. iv. note 1.

1181. See Ps. xviii. 43, 44 (xvii. 44, 45 in LXX.), where the Eng. ver. has the future; the LXX., like Tertullian, the past. Comp. 2 Sam. (in LXX. 2 Kings) xxii. 44, 45, and Rom. x. 14-17.

1182. Comp. Isa. i. 2 as above, and Acts xiii. 17.

1183. Sæculi.

1184. Or, perhaps, "not affected, as a body, with human sufferings;" in allusion to such passages as Deut. viii. 4; xxix. 5; Neh. ix. 21.

1185. Ps. lxxviii. (lxxvii. in LXX.) 25; comp. John vi. 31, 32.

1186. See Hos. i. 10; 1 Pet. ii. 10.

1187. Comp. Gal. v. 1; iv. 8, 9.

1188. See Ex. xx. 8-11 and xii. 16 (especially in the LXX.).

1189. Isa. i. 13.

1190. This is not said by Isaiah; it is found in substance in Ezek. xxii. 8.

1191. Isa. lxvi. 23 in LXX.

1192. I am not acquainted with any such passage. Oehler refers to Isa. xlix. in his margin, but gives no verse, and omits to notice this passage of the present treatise in his index.

1193. Or, "temporal."

1194. Josh. vi. 1-20.

1195. See 1 Macc. ii. 41, etc.

1196. See Ex. xx. 8; Deut. v. 12, 15: in LXX.

1197. This tautology is due to the author, not to the translator: "sacrificia...spiritalium sacrificiorum."

1198. See Gen. iv. 2-14. But it is to be observed that the version given in our author differs widely in some particulars from the Heb. and the LXX.

1199. See Lev. xvii. 1-9; Deut. xii. 1-26.

1200. See Mal. i. 10, 11, in LXX.

1201. Comp. Matt. xxviii. 19, 20, Mark xvi. 15, 16, Luke xxiv. 45-48, with Ps. xix. 4 (xviii. 5 in LXX.), as explained in Rom. x. 18.

1202. Tollite = Gr. ἄρατε. Perhaps ="away with."

1203. See Ps. xcvi. (xcv. in LXX.) 7, 8; and comp. xxix. (xxviii. in LXX.) 1, 2.

1204. See Ps. li. 17 (in LXX. l. 19).

1205. Ps. l. (xlix. in LXX.) 14.

1206. Isa. i. 11.

1207. Or, "foretold."

1208. Comp. Isa. i. 11-14, especially in the LXX.

1209. See Mal. i. as above.

1210. See Mal. i. as above.

1211. Or, "sending forth"--promissio.

1212. The tautology is again due to the author.

1213. Comp. Luke i. 78, 79, Isa. ix. 1, 2, with Matt. iv. 12-16.

1214. Comp. 1 Cor. ix. 16.

1215. See ch. iii. above.

1216. Here again the repetition is the author's.

1217. Cum suo sibi sabbato. Unless the meaning be--which the context seems to forbid--"together with a sabbath of His own:" the Latinity is plainly incorrect.

1218. The reference is to Isa. xlv. 1. A glance at the LXX. will at once explain the difference between the reading of our author and the genuine reading. One letter--an "i"-- makes all the difference. For Κύρῳ has been read Κυρίῳ. In the Eng. ver. we read "His Anointed."

1219. Ps. xix. 4 (xviii. 5. in LXX.) and Rom. x. 18.

1220. See Acts ii. 9, 10; but comp. ver. 5.

1221. See Isa. xlv. 1, 2 (especially in Lowth's version and the LXX.).

1222. See 1 Kings iv. 25. (In the LXX. it is 3 Kings iv. 25; but the verse is omitted in Tischendorf's text, ed. Lips. 1860, though given in his footnotes there.) The statement in the text differs slightly from Oehler's reading; where I suspect there is a transposition of a syllable, and that for "in finibus Judæ tantum, a Bersabeæ," we ought to read "in finibus Judææ tantum, a Bersabe." See de Jej. c. ix.

1223. See Esth. i. 1; viii. 9.

1224. [Dr. Allix thinks these statements define the Empire after Severus, and hence accepts the date we have mentioned, for this treatise.]

1225. Comp. John xx. 28.

1226. See Dan. ix. 26 (especially in the LXX.).

1227. Comp. Isa. lv. 4.

1228. Vir desideriorum; Gr. ἀνὴρ ἐπιθυμιῶν; Eng. ver. "a man greatly beloved." Elsewhere Tertullian has another rendering-- "miserabilis." See de Jej. cc. vii, ix.

1229. Or, "abbreviated;" breviatæ sunt; Gr. συνετμήθησαν. For this rendering, and the interpretations which in ancient and modern days have been founded on it, see G. S.

Faber's Dissert. on the prophecy of the seventy weeks, pp. 5, 6, 109-112. (London, 1811.) The whole work will repay perusal.

1230. These words are given, by Oehler and Rig., on the authority of Pamelius. The mss. and early editions are without them.

1231. Also supplied by Pamelius.

1232. See Dan. ix . 24-27. It seemed best to render with the strictest literality, without regard to anything else; as an idea will thus then be given of the condition of the text, which, as it stands, differs widely, as will be seen, from the Hebrew and also from the LXX., as it stands in the ed. Tisch. Lips. 1860, to which I always adapt my references.

1233. Hebdomades is preferred to Oehler's -as, a reading which he follows apparently on slender authority.

1234. There is no trace of these last words in Tischendorf's LXX. here; and only in his footnotes is the "pinnacle" mentioned.

1235. Or, "speech." The reference seems to be to ver. 23, but there is no such statement in Daniel.

1236. So Oehler; and I print all these numbers uniformly--as in the former part of the present chapter--exactly in accordance with the Latin forms, for the sake of showing how easily, in such calculations, errors may creep in.

1237. Comp. Ps. xlix. 11 (in LXX. Ps. xlviii. 12).

1238. Diluuntur. So Oehler has amended for the reading of the mss. and edd., "tribuuntur."

1239. Comp. Pusey on Daniel, pp. 178, 179, notes 6, 7, 8, and the passages therein referred to. And for the whole question of the seventy weeks, and of the LXX. version of Daniel, comp. the same book, Lect. iv. and Note E (2d thousand, 1864). See also pp. 376-381 of the same book; and Faber (as above), pp. 293-297.

1240. Or rather, our Lord Himself. See Matt. xi. 13; Luke xvi. 16.

1241. Comp. the very obscure passage in de Pu. c. vi., towards the end, on which this expression appears to cast some light.

1242. Or, "in abscision from."

1243. And, without "unction"--i.e. without a priesthood, the head whereof, or high priest, was always anointed--no "sacrifices" were lawful.

1244. See Ps. xxii. 16 (xxi. 17 in LXX.)

1245. i.e., March 25.

1246. Comp. Ex. xii. 6 with Mark xiv. 12, Luke xxii. 7.

1247. See Matt. xxvii. 24, 25, with John xix. 12 and Acts iii. 13.

1248. John xix. 12.

1249. Comp. Luke xxiv. 44, etc.

1250. "A virgin," Eng. ver.; ἡ παρθένος, LXX.; "the virgin," Lowth.

1251. See Isa. vii. 13, 14.

1252. See Matt. i. 23.

1253. See Isa vii. 15.

1254. See Isa. viii. 4. (All these passages should be read in the LXX.)

1255. i.e., of the predicted name. [Here compare Against Marcion, Book III. (vol. vii. Edin. series) Cap. xii. p. 142. See my note (1) on Chapter First; and also Kaye, p. xix.]

1256. In Isa. viii. 8, 10, compared with vii. 14 in the Eng. ver. and the LXX., and also Lowth, introductory remarks on ch. viii.

1257. Or, "to call him."

1258. See adv. Marc. l. iii. c. xiii., which, with the preceding chapter, should be compared throughout with the chapter before us.

1259. Comp. Judg. xiii. 12; Eng. ver. "How shall we order the child?"

1260. Or, "accept."

1261. See Matt. ii. 1-12.

1262. Of course he ought to have said, "they say."

1263. Zech. xiv. 14, omitting the last clause.

1264. Ps. lxxii. 15 (lxxi. 15 in LXX.): "Sheba" in Eng. ver.; "Arabia" in the "Great Bible" of 1539; and so the LXX.

1265. Ps. lxxii. 10, in LXX, and "Great Bible;" "Sheba and Seba," Eng. ver.

1266. Strictly, Tertullian ought to have said "they call," having above said "Divine scriptures;" as above on the preceding page.

1267. Isa. i. 10.

1268. See Gen. xix. 23-29.

1269. Ezek. xvi. 3, 45.

1270. Isa. i. 2, as before.

1271. Orbis.

1272. Oehler refers to Isa. xix. 1. See, too, Isa. xxx. and xxxi.

1273. See Rev. xvii., etc.

1274. Or we may supply here ["Isaiah"].

1275. Or, "he."

1276. Ps. xlv. 3, clause 1 (in LXX. Ps. xliv. 4).

1277. See Ps. xlv. 2 (xliv. 3 in LXX.).

1278. Ps. xlv. 4 (xliv. 5 in LXX.).

1279. Comp. Heb. iv. 12; Rev. i. 16; ii. 12; xix. 15, 21; also Eph. vi. 17.

1280. Comp. Ps. lxii. 12 (lxi. 13 in LXX.); Rom. ii. 6.

1281. See Ps. xlv. 5 (xliv. in LXX.).

1282. Ps. xlv. 5 (xliv. 6 in LXX.).

1283. Traductionem (comp. Heb. iv. 13).

1284. Ps. xlv. 5.

1285. I can find no authority for "appellatus" as a substantive, but such forms are familiar with Tertullian. Or perhaps we may render: "in that He is found to have been likewise called Jesus."

1286. Auses; Αὐσή in LXX.

1287. Nave; Ναυή in LXX.

1288. Jehoshua, Joshua, Jeshua, Jesus, are all forms of the same name.

But the change from Oshea or Hoshea to Jehoshua appears to have been made when he was sent to spy the land.

See Num. xiii. 16 (17 in LXX., who call it a surnaming).

1289. If Oehler's "in sæculo desertæ" is to be retained, this appears to be the construction. But this passage, like others above noted, is but a reproduction of parts of the third book in answer to Marcion; and there the reading is "in sæculi desertis"="in the desert places of the world," or "of heathendom."

1290. See Ex. iii. 8, and the references there.

1291. See Josh. v. 2-9, especially in LXX. Comp. the margin in the Eng. ver. in ver. 2, "flint knives," and Wordsworth in loc., who refers to Ex. iv. 25, for which see ch. iii. above.

1292. See especially 1 Cor. x. 4.

1293. Or, "Joshua."

1294. Comp. Num. xii. 5-8.

1295. Comp. Ex. xxxiii. 20; John i. 18; xiv. 9; Col. i. 15; Heb. i. 3.

1296. Oehler and others read "celavit"; but the correction of Fr. Junius and Rig., "celabit," is certainly more agreeable to the LXX. and the Eng. ver.

1297. Ex. xxiii. 20, 21.

1298. Mal. iii. 1: comp. Matt. xi. 10; Mark i. 2; Luke vii. 27.

1299. See Ps. cxxxii. 17 (cxxi. 17 in LXX.).

1300. Matt. v. 17, briefly; a very favourite reference with Tertullian.

1301. John v. 35, ὁ λύχνος ὁ καιόμενος καὶ φαίνων.

1302. Comp. reference 8, p. 232; and Isa. xl. 3, John i. 23.

1303. See John i. 29, 36.

1304. Sacramentum.

1305. See Isa. xi. 1, 2, especially in LXX.

1306. See Luke i. 27.

1307. See Luke ii. 1-7.

1308. See Isa. liii. 3, 7, in LXX.; and comp. Ps. xxxviii. 17 (xxxvii. 18 in LXX.) in the "Great Bible" of 1539.

1309. See Isa. xlii. 2, 3, and Matt. xii. 19, 20.

1310. See Isa. lviii. 1, 2, especially in LXX.

1311. See Isa. xxxv. 4, 5, 6.

1312. See John v. 17, 18, compared with x. 31-33.

1313. Comp. Deut. xxi. 23 with Gal. iii. 13, with Prof. Lightfoot on the latter passage.

1314. Deut. xxi. 22, 23 (especially in the LXX.).

1315. See 1 Pet. ii. 22 with Isa. liii. 9.

1316. Oehler's pointing is disregarded.

1317. Ps. xxxv. (xxxiv. in LXX.) 12.

1318. Ps. lxix. 4 (lxviii. 5 in LXX.).

1319. Ps. xxii. 16 (xxi. 17 in LXX.).

1320. Ps. lxix. 21 (lxviii. 5 in LXX.).

1321. Ps. xxii. 18 (xxi. 19 in LXX.).

1322. See Matt. xxvi. 56; xxvii. 34, 35; John xix. 23, 24, 28, 32-37.

1323. Sacramentum.

1324. See Rom. ix. 32, 33, with Isa. xxviii. 16; 1 Cor. i. 23; Gal. v. 11.

1325. Lignum = ξύλον; constantly used for "tree."

1326. Comp. Gen. xxii. 1-10 with John xix. 17.

1327. "Christum figuratus" is Oehler's reading, after the two mss. and the Pamelian ed. of 1579; the rest read "figurans" or "figuravit."

1328. Manifested e.g., in his two dreams. See Gen. xxxvii.

1329. Comp. Rom. ix. 5.

1330. Or, "Judah."

1331. This is an error. It is not "his father," Jacob, but Moses, who thus blesses him. See Deut. xxxiii. 17. The same error occurs in adv. Marc. 1. iii. c. xxiii.

1332. Not strictly "the same;" for here the reference is to Gen. xlix. 5-7.

1333. i.e., Simeon and Levi.

1334. i.e., the scribes and Pharisees.

1335. Perfecerunt iniquitatem ex sua secta. There seems to be a play on the word "secta" in connection with the outrage committed by Simeon and Levi, as recorded in Gen. xxxiv. 25-31; and for συνετέλεσαν ἀδικίαν ἐξαιρέσεως αὐτῶν (which is the reading of the LXX., ed. Tisch. 3, Lips. 1860), Tertullian's Latin seems to have read, συνετέλεσαν ἀδικίαν ἐξ αἱρέσεως αὐτῶν.

1336. See Gen. xlix. 5-7 in LXX.; and comp. the margin of Eng. ver. on ver. 7, and Wordsworth in loc., who incorrectly renders ταῦρον an "ox" here.

1337. What the sense of this is it is not easy to see. It appears to have puzzled Pam. and Rig. so effectually that they both, conjecturally and without authority, adopted the reading found in adv. Marc. l. iii. c. xviii. (from which book, as usual, the present passage is borrowed), only altering illis to ipsis.

1338. See Ex. xvii. 8-16; and comp. Col. ii. 14, 15.

1339. Ex. xx. 4.

1340. Their sin was "speaking against God and against Moses" (Num. xxi. 4-9).

1341. Comp. Col. ii. 14, 15, as before; also Gen. iii. 1, etc.; 2 Cor. xi. 3; Rev. xii. 9.

1342. Comp. 2 Cor. xi. 14, 15; Matt.

xxv. 41; Rev. xii. 9.

1343. Comp. de Idol. c. v.; adv. Marc. l. iii. c. xviii.

1344. A ligno. Oehler refers us to Ps. xcvi. 10 (xcv. 10 in LXX.); but the special words "a ligno" are wanting there, though the text is often quoted by the Fathers.

1345. Lignarium aliquem regem. It is remarkable, in connection herewith, that our Lord is not only called by the Jews "the carpenter's son" (Matt. xiii. 55; Luke iv. 22), but "the carpenter" (Mark vi. 3).

1346. See Isa. ix. 6.

1347. Lignum.

1348. See Jer. xi. 19 (in LXX.).

1349. i.e., when they laid on Him the crossbeam to carry. See John xix. 17.

1350. See John vi. passim, and the various accounts of the institution of the Holy Supper.

1351. It is Ps. xxii. in our Bibles, xxi. in LXX.

1352. Ver. 16 (17 in LXX.).

1353. Ps. xxii. 21 (xxi. 22 in LXX., who render it as Tertullian does).

1354. i.e., perhaps, because of the extreme ignominy attaching to that death, which prevented its being expressly named.

1355. Isa. liii. 8, 9, 10, (in LXX.).

1356. Isa. lvii. 2 (in LXX.).

1357. Isa. liii. 12 (in LXX.). Comp., too, Bp. Lowth. Oehler's pointing again appears to be faulty.

1358. See Amos viii. 9, 10 (especially in the LXX.).

1359. Oehler's "esset" appears to be a mistake for "esse."

1360. The change from singular to plural is due to the Latin, not to the translator.

1361. See Ex. xii. 1-11.

1362. See Matt. xxvi. 17; Mark xiv. 12; Luke xxii. 7; John xviii. 28.

1363. Comp. 1 Cor. v. 7.

1364. Sæculo.

1365. Comp. Isa. lxi. 2.

1366. Or possibly, simply, "sealed"-- obsignatus.

1367. Inter mediam elam et inter medium altaris: i.e., probably ="between the porch and the altar," as the Eng. ver. has.

1368. So Oehler points, and Tischendorf in his edition of the LXX. points not very differently. I incline to read: "Because they have filled up the measure of their impieties, and, behold (are) themselves, as it were, grimacing, I will," etc.

1369. Comp. Rev. i. 13.

1370. "Quæ fuit super eam" (i.e. super domum) "in subdivali domûs" is Oehler's reading; but it differs from the LXX.

1371. The ms. which Oehler usually follows omits "Tau;" so do the LXX.

1372. Et in his dixit ad audientem. But the LXX. reading agrees almost verbatim with the Eng. ver.

1373. Ezek. viii. 12-ix. 6 (especially in the LXX.). Comp. adv. Marc. l. iii. c. xxii. But our author differs considerably even from the LXX.

1374. Or rather in Deuteronomy. See xxviii. 65 sqq.

1375. Or, "sole."

1376. In ligno. There are no such words in the LXX. If the words be retained, "thy life" will mean Christ, who is called "our Life" in Col. iii. 4. See also John i. 4; xiv. 6; xi. 25. And so, again, "Thou shalt not trust (or believe) thy life" would mean, "Thou shalt not believe Christ."

1377. Or, "in accordance with."

1378. i.e., Would they have happened? and, by happening, have been their own proof?

1379. Ps. ii. 7, 8.

1380. Dispositionem; Gr. διαθήκην.

1381. Isa. xlii. 6, 7, comp. lxi. 1; Luke iv. 14-18.

1382. Comp. Luke ii. 25-33.

1383. Mic. v. 2; Matt. ii. 3-6. Tertullian's Latin agrees rather with the Greek of St. Matthew than with the LXX.

1384. See Isa. i. 7.

1385. Comp. John v. 43; x. 37, 38.

1386. Isa. xxxiii. 17.

1387. Isa. xxxiii. 18.

1388. Comp. the "failing eyes" in the passage from Deuteronomy given in c. xi., if "eyes" is to be taken as the subject here. If not, we have another instance of the slipshod writing in which this treatise abounds.

1389. As His name "Christ" or "Messiah" implies.

1390. Comp. Ex. xxx. 22-33.

1391. i.e., in Jerusalem or Judea.

1392. The Jews.

1393. Comp. 1 Kings (3 Kings in LXX.) i. 39, where the Eng. ver. has "an horn;" the LXX. τὸ κέρας, "the horn;" which at that time, of course, was in David's tabernacle (2 Sam.-- 2 Kings in LXX.--vi. 17,) for "temple" there was yet none.

1394. Dan. ix. 26.

1395. See Isa. lxv. 2; Rom. x. 21.

1396. Ps. xxii. 16, 17 (xxi. 17, 18, in LXX.), and lxix. 21 (lxviii. 22 in LXX.).

1397. i.e., displaced, dislocated.

1398. See c. x. above.

1399. See Ps. lxvii. 6 (lxvi. 7 in LXX.), lxxxv. 12 (lxxxiv. 13 in LXX.).

1400. "Lignum," as before.

1401. See Joel ii. 22.

1402. See c. xi. above, and the note there.

1403. Sacramento.

1404. See Ex. xv. 22-26.
1405. Sæculi.
1406. See Acts xxvi. 18, ad fin.
1407. See Jer. ii. 10-12.
1408. See Amos viii. 9, as before, in c.x.
1409. See Matt. xxvii. 45, 50-52; Mark xv. 33, 37, 38, Luke xxiii. 44, 45.
1410. ὕδατος ζωῆς in the LXX. here (ed. Tischendorf, who quotes the Cod. Alex. as reading, however, ὕδατος ζῶντος). Comp. Rev. xxii. 1, 17, and xxi. 6; John vii. 37-39. (The reference, it will be seen, is still to Jer. ii. 10-13; but the writer has mixed up words of Amos therewith.)
1411. Comp. The τὴν διασπορὰν τῶν Ἑλλήνων of John vii. 35; and see 1 Pet. i. 1.
1412. See Isa. lxv. 13-16 in LXX.
1413. Hujus ligni sacramentum.
1414. Lignum.
1415. Helisæo. Comp. Luke iv. 27.
1416. The careless construction of leaving the nominative "Elisha" with no verb to follow it is due to the original, not to the translator.
1417. See 2 Kings vi. 1-7 (4 Kings vi. 1-7 in LXX). It is not said, however, that the wood sank.
1418. This conclusion they had drawn before, and are not said to have drawn, consequently, upon this occasion. See 2 Kings (4 Kings in LXX.) ii. 16.
1419. Sacramento.
1420. "Sæculi," or perhaps here "heathendom."
1421. For a similar argument, see Anselm's Cur Deus Homo? l. i. c. iii. sub fin.
1422. Sæculo.
1423. Mortis necem.
1424. Comp. Acts vii. 51, 52; Heb. xi. 32-38.
1425. Sacramenta.
1426. See Gen. xxii. 1-14.
1427. See Matt. xxvii. 11-14; Mark xv. 1-5; John xix. 8-12.
1428. See Isa. liii. 7, 8.
1429. Oehler refers to Hos. vi. 1; add 2 (ad init.).
1430. See Luke i. 35.
1431. For this sense of the word "approve," comp. Acts ii. 22, Greek and English, and Phil. i. 10, Greek and English.
1432. See Isa. ii. 20.
1433. See Isa. iii. 1, 3; and comp. 1 Cor. iii. 10; Eph. ii. 20, 21; 1 Pet. ii. 4-8, and many similar passages.
1434. Comp. Isa. v. 2 in LXX. and Lowth.
1435. Comp. Isa. v. 6, 7, with Matt. xxvii. 20-25, Mark xv. 8-15, Luke xxiii. 13-25, John xix. 12-16.
1436. Matt. xi. 13; Luke xvi. 16.
1437. See John v. 1-9; and comp. de Bapt. c. v., and the note there.
1438. See Isa. lii. 5; Ezek. xxxvi. 20, 23; Rom. ii. 24. (The passage in Isaiah in the LXX. agrees with Rom. ii. 24.)
1439. See Isa. lv. 6, 7.
1440. See Luke xix. 41-44.
1441. See Isa. i. 7, 8, 4.
1442. Isa. i. 20.
1443. See Ps. lix. 11 (lviii. 12 in LXX.)
1444. See Isa. l. 11 in LXX.
1445. See Isa. liii. 2 in LXX.
1446. See Ps. xxxviii. 17 in the "Great Bible" (xxxvii. 18 in LXX.). Also Isa. liii. 3 in LXX.
1447. See Isa. viii. 14 (where, however, the LXX. rendering is widely different) with Rom. ix. 32, 33; Ps. cxviii. 22 (cxvii. 22 in LXX.); 1 Pet. ii. 4.
1448. See Ps. viii. 5 (viii. 6 in LXX.) with Heb. ii. 5-9.
1449. See Ps. xxii. 6 (xxi. 7 in LXX., the Alex. ms. of which here agrees well with Tertullian).
1450. See reference 3 above, with Isa. xxviii. 16.
1451. Comp. Eph. i. 10.
1452. Or, "worldly kingdoms." See Dan. ii. 34, 35, 44, 45.
1453. See Dan. vii. 13, 14.
1454. See c. ix. med.
1455. See c. ix. med.
1456. See Ps. viii. 5, 6 (6, 7 in LXX.); Heb. ii. 6-9.
1457. See Zech. xii. 10, 12 (where the LXX., as we have it, differs widely from our Eng. ver. in ver. 10); Rev. i. 7.
1458. See Jer. xvii. 9 in LXX.
1459. Sacramento.
1460. The reading which Oehler follows, and which seems to have the best authority, is "verissimus sacerdos Patris, Christus Ipsius," as in the text.
But Rig., whose judgment is generally very sound, prefers, with some others, to read, "verus summus sacerdos Patris Christus Jesus;" which agrees better with the previous allusion to "the mystery of His name withal:" comp. c. ix. above, towards the end.
1461. See Zech. iii. "The mystery of His name" refers to the meaning of "Jeshua," for which see c. ix. above.
1462. Comp. John vi. 70 and xiii. 2 (especially in Greek, where the word διάβολος is used in each case).
1463. Or "Josedech," as Tertullian here writes, and as we find in Hag. i. 1, 12; ii. 2, 4; Zech. vi. 11, and in the LXX.
1464. Or, "Jeshua."
1465. See Rev. i. 13.
1466. See Ps. cx. (cix. in LXX.) 4; Heb. v. 5-10.
1467. See Lev. xvi.

1468. Comp. Heb. xiii. 10-13. It is to be noted, however, that all this spitting, etc., formed no part of the divinely ordained ceremony.

1469. This appears to be an error. See Lev. vi. 30.

1470. Unless Oehler's "fruerentur" is an error for "fruentur" ="will enjoy."

1471. Or, "ignore."

1472. See cc. xi. xii. above.

1473. Orbem.

1474. Or, "unto eternity." Comp. 2 Sam. (2 Kings in LXX.) vii. 13; 1 Chron. xvii. 12; Ps. lxxxix. 3, 4, 29, 35, 36, 37 (in LXX. Ps. lxxxviii. 4, 5, 30, 36, 37, 38).

1475. See Isa. lv. 5 (especially in the LXX).

1476. Oehler's pointing is discarded. The whole passage, from "which you dare not assert" down to "ignorant," appears to be parenthetical; and I have therefore marked it as such.

VIII - The Soul's Testimony [1477]
[Translated by the Rev. S. Thelwall.]

Chapter I

If, with the object of convicting the rivals and persecutors of Christian truth, from their own authorities, of the crime of at once being untrue to themselves and doing injustice to us, one is bent on gathering testimonies in its favour from the writings of the philosophers, or the poets, or other masters of this world's learning and wisdom, he has need of a most inquisitive spirit, and a still greater memory to carry out the research.

Indeed, some of our people, who still continued their inquisitive labours in ancient literature, and still occupied memory with it, have published works we have in our hands of this very sort; works in which they relate and attest the nature and origin of their traditions, and the grounds on which opinions rest, and from which it may be seen at once that we have embraced nothing new or monstrous--nothing for which we cannot claim the support of ordinary and well-known writings, whether in ejecting error from our creed, or admitting truth into it. But the unbelieving hardness of the human heart leads them to slight even their own teachers, otherwise approved and in high renown, whenever they touch upon arguments which are used in defence of Christianity. Then the poets are fools, when they describe the gods with human passions and stories; then the philosophers are without reason, when they knock at the gates of truth.

He will thus far be reckoned a wise and sagacious man who has gone the length of uttering sentiments that are almost Christian; while if, in a mere affectation of judgment and wisdom, he sets himself to reject their ceremonies, or to convicting the world of its sin, he is sure to be branded as a Christian. We will have nothing, then, to do with the literature and the teaching, perverted in its best results, which is believed in its errors rather than its truth. We shall lay no stress on it, if some of their authors have declared that there is one God, and one God only. Nay, let it be granted that there is nothing in heathen writers which a Christian approves, that it may be put out of his power to utter a single word of reproach.

For all are not familiar with their teachings; and those who are, have no assurance in regard to their truth.

Far less do men assent to our writings, to which no one comes for guidance unless he is already a Christian.

I call in a new testimony, yea, one which is better known than all literature, more discussed than all doctrine, more public than all publications, greater than the whole man--I mean all which is man's. Stand forth, O soul, whether thou art a divine and eternal substance, as most philosophers believe if it be so, thou wilt be the less likely to lie,--or whether thou art the very opposite of divine, because indeed a mortal thing, as Epicurus alone thinks--in that case there will be the less temptation for thee to speak falsely in this case: whether thou art received from heaven, or sprung from earth; whether thou art formed of numbers, or of atoms; whether thine existence begins with that of the body, or thou art put into it at a later stage; from whatever source, and in whatever way, thou makest man a rational being, in the highest degree capable of thought and knowledge,--stand forth and give thy witness. But I call thee not as when, fashioned in schools, trained in libraries, fed in Attic academies and porticoes, thou belchest wisdom.

I address thee simple, rude, uncultured and untaught, such as they have thee who have thee only; that very thing of the road, the street, the work-shop, wholly. I want thine inexperience, since in thy small experience no one feels any confidence. I demand of thee the things thou bringest with thee into man, which thou knowest either from thyself, or from thine author, whoever he may be. Thou art not, as I well know, Christian; for a man becomes a Christian, he is not born one. Yet Christians earnestly press thee for a testimony; they press thee, though an alien, to bear witness against thy friends, that they may be put to shame before thee, for hating and mocking us on account of things which convict thee as an accessory.

Chapter II

We give offence by proclaiming that there is one God, to whom the name of God alone belongs, from whom all things come, and who is Lord of the whole universe.[1478] Bear thy testimony, if thou knowest this to be the truth; for openly and with a perfect liberty, such as we do not possess, we hear thee both in private and in public exclaim, "Which may God grant," and, "If God so will." By expressions such as these thou declarest that there is one who is distinctively God, and thou confessest that all power belongs to him to whose will, as Sovereign, thou dost look. At the same time, too, thou deniest any others to be truly gods, in calling them by their own names of Saturn, Jupiter, Mars, Minerva; for thou affirmest Him to be God alone to whom thou givest no other name than God; and though thou sometimes callest these others gods, thou plainly usest the designation as one which does not really belong to them, but is, so to speak, a borrowed one. Nor is the nature of the God we declare unknown to thee: "God is good, God does good," thou art wont to say; plainly suggesting further, "But man is evil." In asserting an antithetic proposition, thou, in a sort of indirect and figurative way, reproachest man with his wickedness in departing from a God so good. So, again, as among us, as belonging to the God of benignity and goodness, "Blessing" is a most sacred act in our religion and our life, thou too sayest as readily as a Christian needs, "God bless thee;" and when thou turnest the blessing of God into a curse, in like manner thy very words confess with us that His power over us is absolute and entire. There are some who, though they do not deny the existence of God, hold withal that He is neither Searcher, nor Ruler, nor Judge; treating with especial disdain those of us who go over to Christ out of fear of a coming judgment, as they think, honouring God in freeing Him from the cares of keeping watch, and the trouble of taking note,--not even regarding Him as capable of anger. For if God, they say, gets angry, then He is susceptible of corruption and passion; but that of which passion and corruption can be affirmed may also perish, which God cannot do. But these very persons elsewhere, confessing that the soul is divine, and bestowed on us by God, stumble against a testimony of the soul itself, which affords an answer to these views. For if either divine or God-given, it doubtless knows its giver; and if it knows Him, it undoubtedly fears Him too, and especially as having been by Him endowed so amply. Has it no fear of Him whose favour it is so desirous to possess, and whose anger it is so anxious to avoid? Whence, then, the soul's natural fear of God, if God cannot be angry? How is there any dread of Him whom nothing offends? What is feared but anger? Whence comes anger, but from observing what is done? What leads to watchful oversight, but judgment in prospect? Whence is judgment, but from power? To whom does supreme authority and power belong, but to God alone? So thou art always ready, O soul, from thine own knowledge, nobody casting scorn upon thee, and no one preventing, to exclaim, "God sees all," and "I commend thee to God," and "May God repay," and "God shall judge between us." How happens this, since thou art not Christian? How is it that, even with the garland of Ceres on the brow, wrapped in the purple cloak of Saturn, wearing the white robe of the goddess Isis, thou invokest God as judge? Standing under the statue of Æsculapius, adorning the brazen image of Juno, arraying the helmet of Minerva with dusky figures, thou never thinkest of appealing to any of these deities. In thine own forum thou appealest to a God who is elsewhere; thou permittest honour to be rendered in thy temples to a foreign god. Oh, striking testimony to truth, which in the very midst of demons obtains a witness for us Christians!

Chapter III

But when we say that there are demons--as though, in the simple fact that we alone expel them from the men's bodies,[1479] we did not also prove their existence--some disciple of Chrysippus begins to curl the lip. Yet thy curses sufficiently attest that there are such beings, and that they are objects of thy strong dislike.[1480] As what comes to thee as a fit expression of thy strong hatred of him, thou callest the man a dæmon who annoys thee with his filthiness, or malice, or insolence, or any other vice which we ascribe to evil spirits. In expressing vexation, contempt, or abhorrence, thou hast Satan constantly upon thy lips;[1481] the very same we hold to be the angel of evil, the source of error, the corrupter of the whole world, by whom in the beginning man was entrapped into breaking the commandment of God. And (the man) being given over to death on account of his sin, the entire human race, tainted in their descent from him, were made a channel for transmitting his condemnation. Thou seest, then, thy destroyer; and though he is fully known only to Christians, or to whatever sect [1482] confesses the Lord, yet, even thou hast some acquaintance with him while yet thou abhorrest him!

Chapter IV

Even now, as the matter refers to thy opinion on a point the more closely belonging to thee, in so far as it bears on thy personal well-being, we maintain that after life has passed away thou still remainest in existence, and lookest forward to a day of judgment, and according to thy deserts art assigned to misery or bliss, in either way of it for ever; that, to be capable of this, thy former substance must needs return to thee, the matter and the memory of the very same human being: for neither good nor evil couldst thou feel if thou wert not endowed again with that sensitive bodily organization, and there would be no grounds for judgment without the presentation of the very person to whom the sufferings of judgment were due. That Christian view, though much nobler than the Pythagorean, as it does not transfer thee into beasts; though more complete than the Platonic, since it endows thee again with a body; though more worthy of honour than the Epicurean, as it preserves thee from annihilation,--yet, because of the name connected with it, it is held to be nothing but vanity and folly, and, as it is called, a mere presumption. But we are not ashamed of ourselves if our presumption is found to have thy support.

Well, in the first place, when thou speakest of one who is dead, thou sayest of him, "Poor man"--poor, surely, not because he has been taken from the good of life, but because he has been given over to punishment and condemnation. But at another time thou speakest of the dead as free from trouble; thou professest to think life a burden, and death a blessing. Thou art wont, too, to speak of the dead as in repose, [1483] when, returning to their graves beyond the city gates [1484] with food and dainties, thou art wont to present offerings to thyself rather than to them; or when, coming from the graves again, thou art staggering under the effects of wine. But I want thy sober opinion. Thou callest the dead poor when thou speakest thine own thoughts, when thou art at a distance from them. For at their feast, where in a sense they are present and recline along with thee, it would never do to cast reproach upon their lot. Thou canst not but adulate those for whose sake thou art feasting it so sumptuously. Dost thou then speak of him as poor who feels not? How happens it that thou cursest, as one capable of suffering from thy curse, the man whose memory comes back on thee with the sting in it of some old injury?

It is thine imprecation that "the earth may lie heavy on him," and that there may be trouble "to his ashes in the realm of the dead." In like manner, in thy kindly feeling to him to whom thou art indebted for favours, thou entreatest "repose to his bones and ashes," and thy desire is that among the dead he may "have pleasant rest." If thou hast no power of suffering after death, if no feeling remains,--if, in a word, severance from the body is the annihilation of thee, what makes thee lie against thyself, as if thou couldst suffer in another state? Nay, why dost thou fear death at all? There is nothing after death to be feared, if there is nothing to be felt. For though it may be said that death is dreadful not for anything it threatens afterwards, but because it deprives us of the good of life; yet, on the other hand, as it puts an end to life's discomforts, which are far more numerous, death's terrors are mitigated by a gain that more than outweighs the loss.

And there is no occasion to be troubled about a loss of good things, which is amply made up for by so great a blessing as relief from every trouble. There is nothing dreadful in that which delivers from all that is to be dreaded. If thou shrinkest from giving up life because thy experience of it has been sweet, at any rate there is no need to be in any alarm about death if thou hast no knowledge that it is evil. Thy dread of it is the proof that thou art aware of its evil. Thou wouldst never think it evil--thou wouldst have no fear of it at all--if thou wert not sure that after it there is something to make it evil, and so a thing of terror. [1485] Let us leave unnoted at this time that natural way of fearing death. It is a poor thing for any one to fear what is inevitable. I take up the other side, and argue on the ground of a joyful hope beyond our term of earthly life; for desire of posthumous fame is with almost every class an inborn thing. [1486] I have not time to speak of the Curtii, and the Reguli, or the brave men of Greece, who afford us innumerable cases of death despised for after renown. Who at this day is without the desire that he may be often remembered when he is dead? Who does not give all endeavour to preserve his name by works of literature, or by the simple glory of his virtues, or by the splendour even of his tomb?

How is it the nature of the soul to have these posthumous ambitions and with such amazing effort to prepare the things it can only use after decease? It would care nothing about the future, if the future were quite unknown to it.

But perhaps thou thinkest thyself surer, after thy exit from the body, of continuing still to feel, than of any future resurrection, which is a doctrine laid at our door as one of our presumptuous suppositions. But it is also the doctrine of the soul; for if any one inquires about a person lately dead as though he were alive, it occurs at once to say, "He has gone." He is expected to return, then.

Chapter V

These testimonies of the soul are simple as true, commonplace as simple, universal as commonplace, natural as universal, divine as natural.

I don't think they can appear frivolous or feeble to any one, if he reflect on the majesty of nature, from which the soul derives its authority. [1487] If you acknowledge the authority of the mistress, you will own it also in the disciple.

Well, nature is the mistress here, and her disciple is the soul. But everything the one has taught or the other learned, has come from God--the Teacher of the teacher. And what the soul may know from the teachings of its chief instructor, thou canst judge from that which is within thee. Think of that which enables thee to think; reflect on that which in forebodings is the prophet, the augur in omens, the foreseer of coming events. Is it a wonderful thing, if, being the gift of God to man, it knows how to divine? Is it anything very strange, if it knows the God by whom it was bestowed? Even fallen as it is, the victim of the great adversary's machinations, it does not forget its Creator, His goodness and law, and the final end both of itself and of its foe. Is it singular then, if, divine in its origin, its revelations agree with the knowledge God has given to His own people? But he who does not regard those outbursts of the soul as the teaching of a congenital nature and the secret deposit of an inborn knowledge, will say that the habit and, so to say, the vice of speaking in this way has been acquired and confirmed from the opinions of published books widely spread among men.

Unquestionably the soul existed before letters, and speech before books, and ideas before the writing of them, and man himself before the poet and philosopher. [1488] Is it then to be believed, that before literature and its publication no utterances of the sort we have pointed out came from the lips of men? Did nobody speak of God and His goodness, nobody of death, nobody of the dead? Speech went a-begging, I suppose; nay, (the subjects being still awanting, without which it cannot even exist at this day, when it is so much more copious, and rich, and wise), it could not exist at all if the things which are now so easily suggested, that cling to us so constantly, that are so very near to us, that are somehow born on our very lips, had no existence in ancient times, before letters had any existence in the world--before there was a Mercury, I think, at all. And whence was it, I pray, that letters themselves came to know, and to disseminate for the use of speech, what no mind had ever conceived, or tongue put forth, or ear taken in? But, clearly, since the Scriptures of God, whether belonging to Christians or to Jews, into whose olive tree we have been grafted--are much more ancient than any secular literature, (or, let us only say, are of a somewhat earlier date, as we have shown in its proper place when proving their trustworthiness); if the soul have taken these utterances from writings at all, we must believe it has taken them from ours, and not from yours, its instruction coming more naturally from the earlier than the later works. Which latter indeed waited for their own instruction from the former, and though we grant that light has come from you, still it has flowed from the first fountainhead originally; and we claim as entirely ours, all you may have taken from us and handed down. Since it is thus, it matters little whether the soul's knowledge was put into it by God or by His book. Why, then, O man, wilt thou maintain a view so groundless, as that those testimonies of the soul have gone forth from the mere human speculations of your literature, and got hardening of common use?

Chapter VI

Believe, then, your own books, and as to our Scriptures so much the more believe writings which are divine, but in the witness of the soul itself give like confidence to Nature. Choose the one of these you observe to be the most faithful friend of truth. If your own writings are distrusted, neither God nor Nature lie. And if you would have faith in God and Nature, have faith in the soul; thus you will believe yourself. Certainly you value the soul as giving you your true greatness,--that to which you belong; which is all things to you; without which you can neither live nor die; on whose account you even put God away from you. Since, then, you fear to become a Christian, call the soul before you, and put her to the question. Why does she worship another? why name the name of God? Why does she speak of demons, when she means to denote spirits to be held accursed? Why does she make her protestations towards the heavens, and pronounce her ordinary execrations earthwards? Why does she render service in one place, in another invoke the Avenger? Why does she pass judgments on the dead? What Christian phrases are those she has got, though Christians she neither desires to see nor hear? Why has she either bestowed them on us, or received them from us?

Why has she either taught us them, or learned them as our scholar? Regard with suspicion this accordance in words, while there is such difference in practice. It is utter folly--denying a universal nature--to ascribe this exclusively to our language and the Greek, which are regarded among us as so near akin. The soul is not a boon from heaven to Latins and Greeks alone. Man is the one name belonging to every nation upon earth: there is one soul and many tongues, one spirit and various sounds; every country has its own speech, but the subjects of speech are common to all.

God is everywhere, and the goodness of God is everywhere; demons are everywhere, and the cursing of them is everywhere; the invocation of divine judgment is everywhere, death is everywhere, and the sense of death is everywhere, and all the world over is found the witness of the soul. There is not a soul of man that does not, from the light that is in itself, proclaim the very things we are not permitted to speak above our breath. Most justly, then, every soul is a culprit as well as a witness: in the measure that it testifies for truth, the guilt of error lies on it; and on the day of judgment it will stand before the courts of God, without a word to say.

Thou proclaimedst God, O soul, but thou didst not seek to know Him: evil spirits were detested by thee, and yet they were the objects of thy adoration; the punishments of hell were foreseen by thee, but no care was taken to avoid them; thou hadst a savour of Christianity, and withal wert the persecutor of Christians.

Elucidations

I.
(Recognition of the Supreme God, cap. ii)

The passage referred to in the note, begins thus in Jowett's rendering:
"The Ruler of the Universe has ordered all things with a view to the preservation and perfection of the whole etc."

So, in the same book: "Surely God must not be supposed to have a nature which he himself hates." Again:

"Let us not, then, deem God inferior to human workmen, who in proportion to their skill finish and perfect their works...or that God, the wisest of beings, who is willing and able to extend his care to all things, etc." Now, it is a sublime plan which our author here takes up, (making only slight reference to the innumerable citations which were behind his apostrophe to the soul if any one should dispute it) to bid the soul stand forth and confess its consciousness of God.

II.
(Dæmons, cap. vi)

Those who would pursue the subject of Demonology, which Tertullian opens in this admirable treatise, should follow it up in a writer whom Tertullian greatly influenced, in many particulars, even when he presents a remarkable contrast. The Ninth Book of the City of God is devoted to inquiries which throw considerable light on some of the startling sayings of our author as to the heathen systems, and their testimony to the Soul's Consciousness of God and of the great enemy of God and the inferior spirit of Evil.

Footnotes:

1477. [The tract De Testimonio Animæ is cast into an apologetic form and very properly comes into place here.

It was written in Orthodoxy and forms a valuable preface to the De Anima, of which we cannot say that it is quite free from errors. As it refers to the Apology, we cannot place it before that work, and perhaps we shall not greatly err if we consider it a sequel to the Apology. If it proves to others the source of as much enjoyment as it affords to me, it will be treasured by them as one of the most precious testimonies to the Gospel, introducing Man to himself.]

1478. [The student of Plato will recall such evidence, readily. See The Laws, in Jowett's Translation, vol. iv. p. 416. Also Elucidation I.]

1479. [The existence of demoniacal possessions in heathen countries is said to be probable, even in our days. The Fathers unanimously assert the effectual exorcisms of their days.]

1480. [e.g. Horace, Epodes, Ode V.]

1481. [Satanan, in omni vexatione...pronuntias. Does he mean that they used this word? Rather, he means the demon is none other than Satan.]

1482. [I have been obliged, somewhat, to simplify the translation here.]

1483. [This whole passage is useful as a commentary on classic authors who use these poetical expressions. Coelo Musa beat (Hor. Ode viii. B. 4.) but the real feeling comes out in such expressions as one finds in Horace's odes to Sextius, (B. i. Ode 4.), or to Postumus, B. ii. Od. 14.]

1484. [The tombs, by the roadside, of which the traveller still sees specimens, used to be scenes of debauchery when the dead were honoured in this way. Now, the funeral honours (See De Corona, cap. iii.) which Christians substituted for these were Eucharistic alms and oblations: thanking God for their holy lives and perpetuating relations with them in the Communion of Saints.]

1485. [Butler, Analogy, Part I. chap. i.]

1486. [Horace, Book III. Ode 30.]

1487. [This appeal to the universal conscience and consciousness of mankind is unanswerable, and assures us that counter-theories will never prevail.

See Bossuet, De la Connoisance de Dieu et de Soi-même. OEuvres, Tom. V. pp. 86 et. seqq. Ed. Paris, 1846.]

1488.] [Compare the heathen ideas in Plato: e.g. the story Socrates tells in the Gorgias, (near the close) about death and Judgment.]

IX - A Treatise on the Soul [1489]
[Translated by Peter Holmes, D.D.]

Chapter I - It is Not to the Philosophers that We Resort for Information About the Soul But to God. [1490]

Having discussed with Hermogenes the single point of the origin of the soul, so far as his assumption led me, that the soul consisted rather in an adaptation [1491] of matter than of the inspiration [1492] of God, I now turn to the other questions incidental to the subject; and (in my treatment of these) I shall evidently have mostly to contend with the philosophers. In the very prison of Socrates they skirmished about the state of the soul. I have my doubts at once whether the time was an opportune one for their (great) master--(to say nothing of the place), although that perhaps does not much matter. For what could the soul of Socrates then contemplate with clearness and serenity? The sacred ship had returned (from Delos), the hemlock draft to which he had been condemned had been drunk, death was now present before him: (his mind) was, [1493] as one may suppose, [1494] naturally excited [1495] at every emotion; or if nature had lost her influence, it must have been deprived of all power of thought. [1496] Or let it have been as placid and tranquil so you please, inflexible, in spite of the claims of natural duty, [1497] at the tears of her who was so soon to be his widow, and at the sight of his thenceforward orphan children, yet his soul must have been moved even by its very efforts to suppress emotion; and his constancy itself must have been shaken, as he struggled against the disturbance of the excitement around him. Besides, what other thoughts could any man entertain who had been unjustly condemned to die, but such as should solace him for the injury done to him?

Especially would this be the case with that glorious creature, the philosopher, to whom injurious treatment would not suggest a craving for consolation, but rather the feeling of resentment and indignation. Accordingly, after his sentence, when his wife came to him with her effeminate cry, O Socrates, you are unjustly condemned! he seemed already to find joy in answering, Would you then wish me justly condemned? It is therefore not to be wondered at, if even in his prison, from a desire to break the foul hands of Anytus and Melitus, he, in the face of death itself, asserts the immortality of the soul by a strong assumption such as was wanted to frustrate the wrong (they had inflicted upon him). So that all the wisdom of Socrates, at that moment, proceeded from the affectation of an assumed composure, rather than the firm conviction of ascertained truth. For by whom has truth ever been discovered without God? By whom has God ever been found without Christ? By whom has Christ ever been explored without the Holy Spirit?

By whom has the Holy Spirit ever been attained without the mysterious gift of faith? [1498] Socrates, as none can doubt, was actuated by a different spirit. For they say that a demon clave to him from his boyhood--the very worst teacher certainly, notwithstanding the high place assigned to it by poets and philosophers--even next to, (nay, along with) the gods themselves. The teachings of the power of Christ had not yet been given--(that power) which alone can confute this most pernicious influence of evil that has nothing good in it, but is rather the author of all error, and the seducer from all truth. Now if Socrates was pronounced the wisest of men by the oracle of the Pythian demon, which, you may be sure, neatly managed the business for his friend, of how much greater dignity and constancy is the assertion of the Christian wisdom, before the very breath of which the whole host of demons is scattered!

This wisdom of the school of heaven frankly and without reserve denies the gods of this world, and shows no such inconsistency as to order a "cock to be sacrificed to Æsculapius:" [1499] no new gods and demons does it introduce, but expels the old ones; it corrupts not youth, but instructs them in all goodness and moderation; and so it bears the unjust condemnation not of one city only, but of all the world, in the cause of that truth which incurs indeed the greater hatred in proportion to its fulness:

so that it tastes death not out of a (poisoned) cup almost in the way of jollity; but it exhausts it in every kind of bitter cruelty, on gibbets and in holocausts. [1500] Meanwhile, in the still gloomier prison of the world amongst your Cebeses and Phædos, in every investigation concerning (man's) soul, it directs its inquiry according to the rules of God. At all events, you can show us no more powerful expounder of the soul than the Author thereof. From God you may learn about that which you hold of God; but from none else will you get this knowledge, if you get it not from God. For who is to reveal that which God has hidden? To that quarter must we resort in our inquiries whence we are most safe even in deriving our ignorance. For it is really better for us not to know a thing, because He has not revealed it to us, than to know it according to man's wisdom, because he has been bold enough to assume it.

Chapter II - The Christian Has Sure and Simple Knowledge Concerning the Subject Before Us

Of course we shall not deny that philosophers have sometimes thought the same things as ourselves. The testimony of truth is the issue thereof. It sometimes happens even in a storm, when the boundaries of sky and sea are lost in confusion, that some harbour is stumbled on (by the labouring ship) by some happy chance; and sometimes in the very shades of night, through blind luck alone, one finds access to a spot, or egress from it. In nature, however, most conclusions are suggested, as it were, by that common intelligence wherewith God has been pleased to endow the soul of man. This intelligence has been caught up by philosophy, and, with the view of glorifying her own art, has been inflated (it is not to be wondered at that I use this language) with straining after that facility of language which is practised in the building up and pulling down of everything, and which has greater aptitude for persuading men by speaking than by teaching. She assigns to things their forms and conditions; sometimes makes them common and public, sometimes appropriates them to private use; on certainties she capriciously stamps the character of uncertainty; she appeals to precedents, as if all things are capable of being compared together; she describes all things by rule and definition, allotting diverse properties even to similar objects; she attributes nothing to the divine permission, but assumes as her principles the laws of nature. I could bear with her pretensions, if only she were herself true to nature, and would prove to me that she had a mastery over nature as being associated with its creation. She thought, no doubt, that she was deriving her mysteries from sacred sources, as men deem them, because in ancient times most authors were supposed to be (I will not say godlike, but) actually gods: as, for instance, the Egyptian Mercury, [1501] to whom Plato paid very great deference; [1502] and the Phrygian Silenus, to whom Midas lent his long ears, when the shepherds brought him to him; and Hermotimus, to whom the good people of Clazomenæ built a temple after his death; and Orpheus; and Musæus; and Pherecydes, the master of Pythagoras. But why need we care, since these philosophers have also made their attacks upon those writings which are condemned by us under the title of apocryphal, [1503] certain as we are that nothing ought to be received which does not agree with the true system of prophecy, which has arisen in this present age; [1504] because we do not forget that there have been false prophets, and long previous to them fallen spirits, which have instructed the entire tone and aspect of the world with cunning knowledge of this (philosophic) cast? It is, indeed, not incredible that any man who is in quest of wisdom may have gone so far, as a matter of curiosity, as to consult the very prophets; (but be this as it may), if you take the philosophers, you would find in them more diversity than agreement, since even in their agreement their diversity is discoverable. Whatever things are true in their systems, and agreeable to prophetic wisdom, they either recommend as emanating from some other source, or else perversely apply[1505] in some other sense. This process is attended with very great detriment to the truth, when they pretend that it is either helped by falsehood, or else that falsehood derives support from it. The following circumstance must needs have set ourselves and the philosophers by the ears, especially in this present matter, that they sometimes clothe sentiments which are common to both sides, in arguments which are peculiar to themselves, but contrary in some points to our rule and standard of faith; and at other times defend opinions which are especially their own, with arguments which both sides acknowledge to be valid, and occasionally conformable to their system of belief. The truth has, at this rate, been well-nigh excluded by the philosophers, through the poisons with which they have infected it; and thus, if we regard both the modes of coalition which we have now mentioned, and which are equally hostile to the truth, we feel the urgent necessity of freeing, on the one hand, the sentiments held by us in common with them from the arguments of the philosophers, and of separating, on the other hand, the arguments which both parties employ from the opinions of the same philosophers. And this we may do by recalling all questions to God's inspired standard, with the obvious exception of such simple cases as being free from the entanglement of any preconceived conceits, one may fairly admit on mere human testimony; because plain evidence of this sort we must sometimes borrow from opponents, when our opponents have nothing to gain from it. Now I am not unaware what a vast mass of literature the philosophers have accumulated concerning the subject before us, in their own commentaries thereon--what various schools of principles there are, what conflicts of opinion, what prolific sources of questions, what perplexing methods of solution. Moreover, I have looked into Medical Science also, the sister (as they say) of Philosophy, which claims as her function to cure the body, and thereby to have a special acquaintance with the soul. From this circumstance she has great differences with her sister, pretending as the latter does to know more about the soul, through the more obvious treatment, as it were, of her in her domicile of the body. But never mind all this contention between them for pre-eminence!

For extending their several researches on the soul, Philosophy, on the one hand, has enjoyed the full scope of her genius; while Medicine, on the other hand, has possessed the stringent demands of her art and practice. Wide are men's inquiries into uncertainties; wider still are their disputes about conjectures. However great the difficulty of adducing proofs, the labour of producing conviction is not one whit less; so that the gloomy Heraclitus was quite right, when, observing the thick darkness which obscured the researches of the inquirers about the soul, and wearied with their interminable questions, he declared that he had certainly not explored the limits of the soul, although he had traversed every road in her domains. To the Christian, however, but few words are necessary for the clear understanding of the whole subject. But in the few words there always arises certainty to him; nor is he permitted to give his inquiries a wider range than is compatible with their solution; for "endless questions" the apostle forbids. [1506] It must, however, be added, that no solution may be found by any man, but such as is learned from God; and that which is learned of God is the sum and substance of the whole thing.

Chapter III - The Soul's Origin Defined Out of the Simple Words of Scripture

Would to God that no "heresies had been ever necessary, in order that they which are approved may be made manifest!" [1507] We should then be never required to try our strength in contests about the soul with philosophers, those patriarchs of heretics, as they may be fairly called.[1508] The apostle, so far back as his own time, foresaw, indeed, that philosophy would do violent injury to the truth. [1509] This admonition about false philosophy he was induced to offer after he had been at Athens, had become acquainted with that loquacious city, [1510] and had there had a taste of its huckstering wiseacres and talkers. In like manner is the treatment of the soul according to the sophistical doctrines of men which "mix their wine with water." [1511] Some of them deny the immortality of the soul; others affirm that it is immortal, and something more. Some raise disputes about its substance; others about its form; others, again, respecting each of its several faculties. One school of philosophers derives its state from various sources, while another ascribes its departure to different destinations. The various schools reflect the character of their masters, according as they have received their impressions from the dignity [1512] of Plato, or the vigour[1513] of Zeno, or the equanimity [1514] of Aristotle, or the stupidity [1515] of Epicurus, or the sadness [1516] of Heraclitus, or the madness [1517] of Empedocles. The fault, I suppose, of the divine doctrine lies in its springing from Judæa [1518] rather than from Greece. Christ made a mistake, too, in sending forth fishermen to preach, rather than the sophist. Whatever noxious vapours, accordingly, exhaled from philosophy, obscure the clear and wholesome atmosphere of truth, it will be for Christians to clear away, both by shattering to pieces the arguments which are drawn from the principles of things--I mean those of the philosophers--and by opposing to them the maxims of heavenly wisdom--that is, such as are revealed by the Lord; in order that both the pitfalls wherewith philosophy captivates the heathen may be removed, and the means employed by heresy to shake the faith of Christians may be repressed. We have already decided one point in our controversy with Hermogenes, as we said at the beginning of this treatise, when we claimed the soul to be formed by the breathing [1519] of God, and not out of matter. We relied even there on the clear direction of the inspired statement which informs us how that "the Lord God breathed on man's face the breath of life, so that man became a living soul" [1520] --by that inspiration of God, of course. On this point, therefore, nothing further need be investigated or advanced by us. It has its own treatise, [1521] and its own heretic. I shall regard it as my introduction to the other branches of the subject.

Chapter IV - In Opposition to Plato, the Soul Was Created and Originated at Birth. After settling the origin of the soul, its condition or state comes up next

For when we acknowledge that the soul originates in the breath of God, it follows that we attribute a beginning to it.

This Plato, indeed, refuses to assign to it, for he will have the soul to be unborn and unmade.[1522] We, however, from the very fact of its having had a beginning, as well as from the nature thereof, teach that it had both birth and creation. And when we ascribe both birth and creation to it, we have made no mistake: for being born, indeed, is one thing, and being made is another,--the former being the term which is best suited to living beings. When distinctions, however, have places and times of their own, they occasionally possess also reciprocity of application among themselves. Thus, the being made admits of being taken in the sense of being brought forth; [1523] inasmuch as everything which receives being or existence, in any way whatever, is in fact generated. For the maker may really be called the parent of the thing that is made: in this sense Plato also uses the phraseology. So far, therefore, as concerns our belief in the souls being made or born, the opinion of the philosopher is overthrown by the authority of prophecy [1524] even.

Chapter V - Probable View of the Stoics, that the Soul Has a Corporeal Nature

Suppose one summons a Eubulus to his assistance, and a Critolaus, and a Zenocrates, and on this occasion Plato's friend Aristotle. They may very possibly hold themselves ready for stripping the soul of its corporeity, unless they happen to see other philosophers opposed to them in their purpose--and this, too, in greater numbers--asserting for the soul a corporeal nature. Now I am not referring merely to those who mould the soul out of manifest bodily substances, as Hipparchus and Heraclitus (do) out of fire; as Hippon and Thales (do) out of water; as Empedocles and Critias (do) out of blood; as Epicurus (does) out of atoms, since even atoms by their coherence form corporeal masses; as Critolaus and his Peripatetics (do) out of a certain indescribable quintessence, [1525] if that may be called a body which rather includes and embraces bodily substances;--but I call on the Stoics also to help me, who, while declaring almost in our own terms that the soul is a spiritual essence (inasmuch as breath and spirit are in their nature very near akin to each other), will yet have no difficulty in persuading (us) that the soul is a corporeal substance. Indeed, Zeno, defining the soul to be a spirit generated with (the body), [1526]) constructs his argument in this way:

That substance which by its departure causes the living being to die is a corporeal one. Now it is by the departure of the spirit, which is generated with (the body,) that the living being dies; therefore the spirit which is generated with (the body) is a corporeal substance. But this spirit which is generated with (the body) is the soul:

it follows, then, that the soul is a corporeal substance. Cleanthes, too, will have it that family likeness passes from parents to their children not merely in bodily features, but in characteristics of the soul; as if it were out of a mirror of (a man's) manners, and faculties, and affections, that bodily likeness and unlikeness are caught and reflected by the soul also.

It is therefore as being corporeal that it is susceptible of likeness and unlikeness. Again, there is nothing in common between things corporeal and things incorporeal as to their susceptibility. But the soul certainly sympathizes with the body, and shares in its pain, whenever it is injured by bruises, and wounds, and sores: the body, too, suffers with the soul, and is united with it (whenever it is afflicted with anxiety, distress, or love) in the loss of vigour which its companion sustains, whose shame and fear it testifies by its own blushes and paleness. The soul, therefore, is (proved to be) corporeal from this inter-communion of susceptibility. Chrysippus also joins hands in fellowship with Cleanthes when he lays it down that it is not at all possible for things which are endued with body to be separated from things which have not body; because they have no such relation as mutual contact or coherence. Accordingly Lucretius says: [1527]

"Tangere enim et tangi nisi corpus nulla potest res."

"For nothing but body is capable of touching or of being touched."

(Such severance, however, is quite natural between the soul and the body); for when the body is deserted by the soul, it is overcome by death. The soul, therefore, is endued with a body; for if it were not corporeal, it could not desert the body.

Chapter VI - The Arguments of the Platonists for the Soul's Incorporeality, Opposed, Perhaps Frivolously

These conclusions the Platonists disturb more by subtilty than by truth. Every body, they say, has necessarily either an animate nature [1528] or an inanimate one. [1529] If it has the inanimate nature, it receives motion externally to itself; if the animate one, internally, Now the soul receives motion neither externally nor internally: not externally, since it has not the inanimate nature; nor internally, because it is itself rather the giver of motion to the body. It evidently, then, is not a bodily substance, inasmuch as it receives motion neither way, according to the nature and law of corporeal substances. Now, what first surprises us here, is the unsuitableness of a definition which appeals to objects which have no affinity with the soul. For it is impossible for the soul to be called either an animate body or an inanimate one, inasmuch as it is the soul itself which makes the body either animate, if it be present to it, or else inanimate, if it be absent from it.

That, therefore, which produces a result, cannot itself be the result, so as to be entitled to the designation of an animate thing or an inanimate one. The soul is so called in respect of its own substance. If, then, that which is the soul admits not of being called an animate body or an inanimate one, how can it challenge comparison with the nature and law of animate and inanimate bodies? Furthermore, since it is characteristic of a body to be moved externally by something else, and as we have already shown that the soul receives motion from some other thing when it is swayed (from the outside, of course, by something else) by prophetic influence or by madness, therefore I must be right in regarding that as bodily substance which, according to the examples we have quoted, is moved by some other object from without. Now, if to receive motion from some other thing is characteristic of a body, how much more is it so to impart motion to something else!

But the soul moves the body, all whose efforts are apparent externally, and from without. It is the soul which gives motion to the feet for walking, and to the hands for touching, and to the eyes for sight, and to the tongue for speech--a sort of internal image which moves and animates the surface. Whence could accrue such power to the soul, if it were incorporeal? How could an unsubstantial thing propel solid objects? But in what way do the senses in man seem to be divisible into the corporeal and the intellectual classes? They tell us that the qualities of things corporeal, such as earth and fire, are indicated by the bodily senses--of touch and sight; whilst (the qualities) of incorporeal things--for instance, benevolence and malignity--are discovered by the intellectual faculties. And from this (they deduce what is to them) the manifest conclusion, that the soul is incorporeal, its properties being comprehended by the perception not of bodily organs, but of intellectual faculties.

Well, (I shall be much surprised) if I do not at once cut away the very ground on which their argument stands.

For I show them how incorporeal things are commonly submitted to the bodily senses--sound, for instance, to the organ of hearing; colour, to the organ of sight; smell, to the olfactory organ.

And, just as in these instances, the soul likewise has its contact with [1530] the body; not to say that the incorporeal objects are reported to us through the bodily organs, for the express reason that they come into contact with the said organs. Inasmuch, then, as it is evident that even incorporeal objects are embraced and comprehended by corporeal ones, why should not the soul, which is corporeal, be equally comprehended and understood by incorporeal faculties? It is thus certain that their argument fails. Among their more conspicuous arguments will be found this, that in their judgment every bodily substance is nourished by bodily substances; whereas the soul, as being an incorporeal essence, is nourished by incorporeal aliments--for instance, by the studies of wisdom. But even this ground has no stability in it, since Soranus, who is a most accomplished authority in medical science, affords us as answer, when he asserts that the soul is even nourished by corporeal aliments; that in fact it is, when failing and weak, actually refreshed oftentimes by food. Indeed, when deprived of all food, does not the soul entirely remove from the body? Soranus, then, after discoursing about the soul in the amplest manner, filling four volumes with his dissertations, and after weighing well all the opinions of the philosophers, defends the corporeality of the soul, although in the process he has robbed it of its immortality. For to all men it is not given to believe the truth which Christians are privileged to hold. As, therefore, Soranus has shown us from facts that the soul is nourished by corporeal aliments, let the philosopher (adopt a similar mode of proof, and) show that it is sustained by an incorporeal food. But the fact is, that no one has even been able to quench this man's [1531] doubts and difficulties about the condition of the soul with the honey-water of Plato's subtle eloquence, nor to surfeit them with the crumbs from the minute nostrums of Aristotle. But what is to become of the souls of all those robust barbarians, which have had no nurture of philosopher's lore indeed, and yet are strong in untaught practical wisdom, and which although very starvelings in philosophy, without your Athenian academies and porches, and even the prison of Socrates, do yet contrive to live? For it is not the soul's actual substance which is benefited by the aliment of learned study, but only its conduct and discipline; such ailment contributing nothing to increase its bulk, but only to enhance its grace. It is, moreover, a happy circumstance that the Stoics affirm that even the arts have corporeality; since at the rate the soul too must be corporeal, since it is commonly supposed to be nourished by the arts.

Such, however, is the enormous preoccupation of the philosophic mind, that it is generally unable to see straight before it. Hence (the story of) Thales falling into the well. [1532] It very commonly, too, through not understanding even its own opinions, suspects a failure of its own health. Hence (the story of) Chrysippus and the hellebore. Some such hallucination, I take it, must have occurred to him, when he asserted that two bodies could not possibly be contained in one: he must have kept out of mind and sight the case of those pregnant women who, day after day, bear not one body, but even two and three at a time, within the embrace of a single womb. One finds likewise, in the records of the civil law, the instance of a certain Greek woman who gave birth to a quint [1533] of children, the mother of all these at one parturition, the manifold parent of a single brood, the prolific produce from a single womb, who, guarded by so many bodies--I had almost said, a people--was herself no less then the sixth person! The whole creation testifies how that those bodies which are naturally destined to issue from bodies, are already (included) in that from which they proceed. Now that which proceeds from some other thing must needs be second to it. Nothing, however, proceeds out of another thing except by the process of generation; but then they are two (things).

Chapter VII - The Soul's Corporeality Demonstrated Out of the Gospels

So far as the philosophers are concerned, we have said enough. As for our own teachers, indeed, our reference to them is ex abundanti--a surplusage of authority: in the Gospel itself they will be found to have the clearest evidence for the corporeal nature of the soul. In hell the soul of a certain man is in torment, punished in flames, suffering excruciating thirst, and imploring from the finger of a happier soul, for his tongue, the solace of a drop of water. [1534] Do you suppose that this end of the blessed poor man and the miserable rich man is only imaginary? Then why the name of Lazarus in this narrative, if the circumstance is not in (the category of) a real occurrence? But even if it is to be regarded as imaginary, it will still be a testimony to truth and reality. For unless the soul possessed corporeality, the image of a soul could not possibly contain a finger of a bodily substance; nor would the Scripture feign a statement about the limbs of a body, if these had no existence. But what is that which is removed to Hades [1535] after the separation of the body; which is there detained; which is reserved until the day of judgment; to which Christ also, on dying, descended? I imagine it is the souls of the patriarchs. But wherefore (all this), if the soul is nothing in its subterranean abode?

For nothing it certainly is, if it is not a bodily substance. For whatever is incorporeal is incapable of being kept and guarded in any way; it is also exempt from either punishment or refreshment. That must be a body, by which punishment and refreshment can be experienced. Of this I shall treat more fully in a more fitting place. Therefore, whatever amount of punishment or refreshment the soul tastes in Hades, in its prison or lodging, [1536] in the fire or in Abraham's bosom, it gives proof thereby of its own corporeality. For an incorporeal thing suffers nothing, not having that which makes it capable of suffering; else, if it has such capacity, it must be a bodily substance. For in as far as every corporeal thing is capable of suffering, in so far is that which is capable of suffering also corporeal. [1537]

Chapter VIII - Other Platonist Arguments Considered

Besides, it would be a harsh and absurd proceeding to exempt anything from the class of corporeal beings, on the ground that it is not exactly like the other constituents of that class. And where individual creatures possess various properties, does not this variety in works of the same class indicate the greatness of the Creator, in making them at the same time different and yet like, amicable yet rivals?

Indeed, the philosophers themselves agree in saying that the universe consists of harmonious oppositions, according to Empedocles' (theory of) friendship and enmity. Thus, then, although corporeal essences are opposed to incorporeal ones, they yet differ from each other in such sort as to amplify their species by their variety, without changing their genus, remaining all alike corporeal; contributing to God's glory in their manifold existence by reason of their variety; so various, by reason of their differences; so diverse, in that some of them possess one kind of perception, others another; some feeding on one kind of aliment, others on another; some, again, possessing visibility, while others are invisible; some being weighty, others light. They are in the habit of saying that the soul must be pronounced incorporeal on this account, because the bodies of the dead, after its departure from them, become heavier, whereas they ought to be lighter, being deprived of the weight of a body--since the soul is a bodily substance.

But what, says Soranus (in answer to this argument), if men should deny that the sea is a bodily substance, because a ship out of the water becomes a heavy and motionless mass? How much truer and stronger, then, is the soul's corporeal essence, which carries about the body, which eventually assumes so great a weight with the nimblest motion! Again, even if the soul is invisible, it is only in strict accordance with the condition of its own corporeality, and suitably to the property of its own essence, as well as to the nature of even those beings to which its destiny made it to be invisible. The eyes of the owl cannot endure the sun, whilst the eagle is so well able to face his glory, that the noble character of its young is determined by the unblinking strength of their gaze; while the eaglet, which turns away its eye from the sun's ray, is expelled from the nest as a degenerate creature! So true is it, therefore, than to one eye an object is invisible, which may be quite plainly seen by another,--without implying any incorporeality in that which is not endued with an equally strong power (of vision). The sun is indeed a bodily substance, because it is (composed of) fire; the object, however, which the eaglet at once admits the existence of, the owl denies, without any prejudice, nevertheless, to the testimony of the eagle. There is the selfsame difference in respect of the soul's corporeality, which is (perhaps) invisible to the flesh, but perfectly visible to the spirit. Thus John, being "in the Spirit" of God, [1538] beheld plainly the souls of the martyrs.[1539]

Chapter IX - Particulars of the Alleged Communication to a Montanist Sister

When we aver that the soul has a body of a quality and kind peculiar to itself, in this special condition of it we shall be already supplied with a decision respecting all the other accidents of its corporeity; how that they belong to it, because we have shown it to be a body, but that even they have a quality peculiar to themselves, proportioned to the special nature of the body (to which they belong); or else, if any accidents (of a body) are remarkable in this instance for their absence, then this, too, results from the peculiarity of the condition of the soul's corporeity, from which are absent sundry qualities which are present to all other corporeal beings. And yet, notwithstanding all this, we shall not be at all inconsistent if we declare that the more usual characteristics of a body, such as invariably accrue to the corporeal condition, belong also to the soul--such as form [1540] and limitation; and that triad of dimensions [1541] --I mean length, and breadth and height--by which philosophers gauge all bodies. What now remains but for us to give the soul a figure? [1542] Plato refuses to do this, as if it endangered the soul's immortality. [1543] For everything which has figure is, according to him, compound, and composed of parts; [1544] whereas the soul is immortal; and being immortal, it is therefore indissoluble; and being indissoluble, it is figureless:

for if, on the contrary, it had figure, it would be of a composite and structural formation. He, however, in some other manner frames for the soul an effigy of intellectual forms, beautiful for its just symmetry and tuitions of philosophy, but misshapen by some contrary qualities. As for ourselves, indeed, we inscribe on the soul the lineaments of corporeity, not simply from the assurance which reasoning has taught us of its corporeal nature, but also from the firm conviction which divine grace impresses on us by revelation. For, seeing that we acknowledge spiritual charismata, or gifts, we too have merited the attainment of the prophetic gift, although coming after John (the Baptist). We have now amongst us a sister whose lot it has been to be favoured with sundry gifts of revelation, which she experiences in the Spirit by ecstatic vision amidst the sacred rites of the Lord's day in the church: she converses with angels, and sometimes even with the Lord; she both sees and hears mysterious communications; [1545] some men's hearts she understands, and to them who are in need she distributes remedies. Whether it be in the reading of Scriptures, or in the chanting of psalms, or in the preaching of sermons, or in the offering up of prayers, in all these religious services matter and opportunity are afforded to her of seeing visions. It may possibly have happened to us, whilst this sister of ours was rapt in the Spirit, that we had discoursed in some ineffable way about the soul. After the people are dismissed at the conclusion of the sacred services, she is in the regular habit of reporting to us whatever things she may have seen in vision (for all her communications are examined with the most scrupulous care, in order that their truth may be probed).

"Amongst other things," says she, "there has been shown to me a soul in bodily shape, and a spirit has been in the habit of appearing to me; not, however, a void and empty illusion, but such as would offer itself to be even grasped by the hand, soft and transparent and of an etherial colour, and in form resembling that of a human being in every respect." This was her vision, and for her witness there was God; and the apostle most assuredly foretold that there were to be "spiritual gifts" in the church. [1546] Now, can you refuse to believe this, even if indubitable evidence on every point is forthcoming for your conviction? Since, then, the soul is a corporeal substance, no doubt it possesses qualities such as those which we have just mentioned, amongst them the property of colour, which is inherent in every bodily substance.

Now what colour would you attribute to the soul but an etherial transparent one? Not that its substance is actually the ether or air (although this was the opinion of Ænesidemus and Anaximenes, and I suppose of Heraclitus also, as some say of him), nor transparent light (although Heraclides of Pontus held it to be so). "Thunder-stones," [1547] indeed, are not of igneous substance, because they shine with ruddy redness; nor are beryls composed of aqueous matter, because they are of a pure wavy whiteness. How many things also besides these are there which their colour would associate in the same class, but which nature keeps widely apart! Since, however, everything which is very attenuated and transparent bears a strong resemblance to the air, such would be the case with the soul, since in its material nature [1548] it is wind and breath, (or spirit); whence it is that the belief of its corporeal quality is endangered, in consequence of the extreme tenuity and subtilty of its essence. Likewise, as regards the figure of the human soul from your own conception, you can well imagine that it is none other than the human form; indeed, none other than the shape of that body which each individual soul animates and moves about. This we may at once be induced to admit from contemplating man's original formation.

For only carefully consider, after God hath breathed upon the face of man the breath of life, and man had consequently become a living soul, surely that breath must have passed through the face at once into the interior structure, and have spread itself throughout all the spaces of the body; and as soon as by the divine inspiration it had become condensed, it must have impressed itself on each internal feature, which the condensation had filled in, and so have been, as it were, congealed in shape, (or stereotyped). Hence, by this densifying process, there arose a fixing of the soul's corporeity; and by the impression its figure was formed and moulded. This is the inner man, different from the outer, but yet one in the twofold condition. [1549] It, too, has eyes and ears of its own, by means of which Paul must have heard and seen the Lord; [1550] it has, moreover all the other members of the body by the help of which it effects all processes of thinking and all activity in dreams. Thus it happens that the rich man in hell has a tongue and poor (Lazarus) a finger and Abraham a bosom. [1551] By these features also the souls of the martyrs under the altar are distinguished and known. The soul indeed which in the beginning was associated with Adam's body, which grew with its growth and was moulded after its form proved to be the germ both of the entire substance (of the human soul) and of that (part of) creation.

Chapter X - The Simple Nature of the Soul is Asserted with Plato. The Identity of Spirit and Soul

It is essential to a firm faith to declare with Plato [1552] that the soul is simple; in other words uniform and uncompounded; simply that is to say in respect of its substance.

Never mind men's artificial views and theories, and away with the fabrications of heresy![1553] Some maintain that there is within the soul a natural substance--the spirit--which is different from it: [1554] as if to have life--the function of the soul--were one thing; and to emit breath--the alleged [1555] function of the spirit--were another thing.

Now it is not in all animals that these two functions are found; for there are many which only live but do not breathe in that they do not possess the organs of respiration--lungs and windpipes. [1556] But of what use is it, in an examination of the soul of man, to borrow proofs from a gnat or an ant, when the great Creator in His divine arrangements has allotted to every animal organs of vitality suited to its own disposition and nature, so that we ought not to catch at any conjectures from comparisons of this sort?

Man, indeed, although organically furnished with lungs and windpipes, will not on that account be proved to breathe by one process, and to live by another; [1557] nor can the ant, although defective in these organs, be on that account said to be without respiration, as if it lived and that was all. For by whom has so clear an insight into the works of God been really attained, as to entitle him to assume that these organic resources are wanting to any living thing? There is that Herophilus, the well-known surgeon, or (as I may almost call him) butcher, who cut up no end of persons, [1558] in order to investigate the secrets of nature, who ruthlessly handled [1559] human creatures to discover (their form and make): I have my doubts whether he succeeded in clearly exploring all the internal parts of their structure, since death itself changes and disturbs the natural functions of life, especially when the death is not a natural one, but such as must cause irregularity and error amidst the very processes of dissection.

Philosophers have affirmed it to be a certain fact, that gnats, and ants, and moths have no pulmonary or arterial organs. Well, then, tell me, you curious and elaborate investigator of these mysteries, have they eyes for seeing withal? But yet they proceed to whatever point they wish, and they both shun and aim at various objects by processes of sight: point out their eyes to me, show me their pupils. Moths also gnaw and eat: demonstrate to me their mandibles, reveal their jaw-teeth. Then, again, gnats hum and buzz, nor even in the dark are they unable to find their way to our ears:[1560] point out to me, then, not only the noisy tube, but the stinging lance of that mouth of theirs. Take any living thing whatever, be it the tiniest you can find, it must needs be fed and sustained by some food or other: show me, then, their organs for taking into their system, digesting, and ejecting food. What must we say, therefore? If it is by such instruments that life is maintained, these instrumental means must of course exist in all things which are to live, even though they are not apparent to the eye or to the apprehension by reason of their minuteness.

You can more readily believe this, if you remember that God manifests His creative greatness quite as much in small objects as in the very largest. If, however, you suppose that God's wisdom has no capacity for forming such infinitesimal corpuscles, you can still recognise His greatness, in that He has furnished even to the smallest animals the functions of life, although in the absence of the suitable organs,--securing to them the power of sight, even without eyes; of eating, even without teeth; and of digestion, even without stomachs. Some animals also have the ability to move forward without feet, as serpents, by a gliding motion; or as worms, by vertical efforts; or as snails and slugs, by their slimy crawl. Why should you not then believe that respiration likewise may be effected without the bellows of the lungs, and without arterial canals? You would thus supply yourself with a strong proof that the spirit or breath is an adjunct of the human soul, for the very reason that some creatures lack breath, and that they lack it because they are not furnished with organs of respiration. You think it possible for a thing to live without breath; then why not suppose that a thing might breathe without lungs? Pray, tell me, what is it to breathe? I suppose it means to emit breath from yourself. What is it not to live? I suppose it means not to emit breath from yourself. This is the answer which I should have to make, if "to breathe" is not the same thing as "to live." It must, however, be characteristic of a dead man not to respire:

to respire, therefore, is the characteristic of a living man. But to respire is likewise the characteristic of a breathing man: therefore also to breathe is the characteristic of a living man.

Now, if both one and the other could possibly have been accomplished without the soul, to breathe might not be a function of the soul, but merely to live. But indeed to live is to breathe, and to breathe is to live. Therefore this entire process, both of breathing and living, belongs to that to which living belongs--that is, to the soul.

Well, then, since you separate the spirit (or breath) and the soul, separate their operations also. Let both of them accomplish some act apart from one another--the soul apart, the spirit apart. Let the soul live without the spirit; let the spirit breathe without the soul. Let one of them quit men's bodies, let the other remain; let death and life meet and agree. If indeed the soul and the spirit are two, they may be divided; and thus, by the separation of the one which departs from the one which remains, there would accrue the union and meeting together of life and of death. But such a union never will accrue: therefore they are not two, and they cannot be divided; but divided they might have been, if they had been (two). Still two things may surely coalesce in growth. But the two in question never will coalesce, since to live is one thing, and to breathe is another. Substances are distinguished by their operations. How much firmer ground have you for believing that the soul and the spirit are but one, since you assign to them no difference; so that the soul is itself the spirit, respiration being the function of that of which life also is! But what if you insist on supposing that the day is one thing, and the light, which is incidental to the day, is another thing, whereas day is only the light itself?

There must, of course, be also different kinds of light, as (appears) from the ministry of fires. So likewise will there be different sorts of spirits, according as they emanate from God or from the devil. Whenever, indeed, the question is about soul and spirit, the soul will be (understood to be) itself the spirit, just as the day is the light itself. For a thing is itself identical with that by means of which itself exists.

Chapter XI - Spirit--A Term Expressive of an Operation of the Soul, Not of Its Nature

To Be Carefully Distinguished from the Spirit of God.

But the nature of my present inquiry obliges me to call the soul spirit or breath, because to breathe is ascribed to another substance. We, however, claim this (operation) for the soul, which we acknowledge to be an indivisible simple substance, and therefore we must call it spirit in a definitive sense--not because of its condition, but of its action; not in respect of its nature, but of its operation; because it respires, and not because it is spirit in any especial sense. [1561] For to blow or breathe is to respire. So that we are driven to describe, by (the term which indicates this respiration--that is to say) spirit--the soul which we hold to be, by the propriety of its action, breath. Moreover, we properly and especially insist on calling it breath (or spirit), in opposition to Hermogenes, who derives the soul from matter instead of from the afflatus or breath of God. He, to be sure, goes flatly against the testimony of

Scripture, and with this view converts breath into spirit, because he cannot believe that the (creature on which was breathed the) Spirit of God fell into sin, and then into condemnation; and therefore he would conclude that the soul came from matter rather than from the Spirit or breath of God. For this reason, we on our side even from that passage, maintain the soul to be breath and not the spirit, in the scriptural and distinctive sense of the spirit; and here it is with regret that we apply the term spirit at all in the lower sense, in consequence of the identical action of respiring and breathing.

In that passage, the only question is about the natural substance; to respire being an act of nature. I would not tarry a moment longer on this point, were it not for those heretics who introduce into the soul some spiritual germ which passes my comprehension: (they make it to have been) conferred upon the soul by the secret liberality of her mother Σοφία (Wisdom), without the knowledge of the Creator. [1562] But (Holy) Scripture, which has a better knowledge of the soul's Maker, or rather God, has told us nothing more than that God breathed on man's face the breath of life, and that man became a living soul, by means of which he was both to live and breathe; at the same time making a sufficiently clear distinction between the spirit and the soul, [1563] in such passages as the following, wherein God Himself declares: "My Spirit went forth from me, and I made the breath of each. And the breath of my Spirit became soul." [1564] And again:

"He giveth breath unto the people that are on the earth, and Spirit to them that walk thereon."[1565] First of all there comes the (natural) soul, that is to say, the breath, to the people that are on the earth,--in other words, to those who act carnally in the flesh; then afterwards comes the Spirit to those who walk thereon,--that is, who subdue the works of the flesh; because the apostle also says, that "that is not first which is spiritual, but that which is natural, (or in possession of the natural soul,) and afterward that which is spiritual." [1566] For, inasmuch as Adam straightway predicted that "great mystery of Christ and the church," [1567] when he said, "This now is bone of my bones, and flesh of my flesh; therefore shall a man leave his father and his mother, and shall cleave unto his wife, and they two shall become one flesh," [1568] he experienced the influence of the Spirit.

For there fell upon him that ecstasy, which is the Holy Ghost's operative virtue of prophecy. And even the evil spirit too is an influence which comes upon a man. Indeed, the Spirit of God not more really "turned Saul into another man," [1569] that is to say, into a prophet, when "people said one to another, What is this which is come to the son of Kish? Is Saul also among the prophets?"[1570] than did the evil spirit afterwards turn him into another man--in other words, into an apostate. Judas likewise was for a long time reckoned among the elect (apostles), and was even appointed to the office of their treasurer; he was not yet the traitor, although he was become fraudulent; but afterwards the devil entered into him. Consequently, as the spirit neither of God nor of the devil is naturally planted with a man's soul at his birth, this soul must evidently exist apart and alone, previous to the accession to it of either spirit: if thus apart and alone, it must also be simple and uncompounded as regards its substance; and therefore it cannot respire from any other cause than from the actual condition of its own substance.

Chapter XII - Difference Between the Mind and the Soul, and the Relation Between Them

In like manner the mind also, or animus, which the Greeks designate ΝΟΥΣ, is taken by us in no other sense than as indicating that faculty or apparatus [1571] which is inherent and implanted in the soul, and naturally proper to it, whereby it acts, whereby it acquires knowledge, and by the possession of which it is capable of a spontaneity of motion within itself, and of thus appearing to be impelled by the mind, as if it were another substance, as is maintained by those who determine the soul to be the moving principle of the universe [1572] --the god of Socrates, Valentinus' "only-begotten" of his father [1573] Bythus, and his mother Sige.

How confused is the opinion of Anaxagoras! For, having imagined the mind to be the initiating principle of all things, and suspending on its axis the balance of the universe; affirming, moreover, that the mind is a simple principle, unmixed, and incapable of admixture, he mainly on this very consideration separates it from all amalgamation with the soul; and yet in another passage he actually incorporates it with [1574] the soul. This (inconsistency) Aristotle has also observed: but whether he meant his criticism to be constructive, and to fill up a system of his own, rather than destructive of the principles of others, I am hardly able to decide. As for himself, indeed, although he postpones his definition of the mind, yet he begins by mentioning, as one of the two natural constituents of the mind,[1575] that divine principle which he conjectures to be impassible, or incapable of emotion, and thereby removes from all association with the soul. For whereas it is evident that the soul is susceptible of those emotions which it falls to it naturally to suffer, it must needs suffer either by the mind or with the mind. Now if the soul is by nature associated with the mind, it is impossible to draw the conclusion that the mind is impassible; or again, if the soul suffers not either by the mind or with the mind, it cannot possibly have a natural association with the mind, with which it suffers nothing, and which suffers nothing itself.

Moreover, if the soul suffers nothing by the mind and with the mind, it will experience no sensation, nor will it acquire any knowledge, nor will it undergo any emotion through the agency of the mind, as they maintain it will. For Aristotle makes even the senses passions, or states of emotion.

And rightly too. For to exercise the senses is to suffer emotion, because to suffer is to feel. In like manner, to acquire knowledge is to exercise the senses; and to undergo emotion is to exercise the senses; and the whole of this is a state of suffering.

But we see that the soul experiences nothing of these things, in such a manner as that the mind also is affected by the emotion, by which, indeed, and with which, all is effected. It follows, therefore, that the mind is capable of admixture, in opposition to Anaxagoras; and passible or susceptible of emotion, contrary to the opinion of Aristotle. Besides, if a separate condition between the soul and mind is to be admitted, so that they be two things in substance, then of one of them, emotion and sensation, and every sort of taste, and all action and motion, will be the characteristics; whilst of the other the natural condition will be calm, and repose, and stupor. There is therefore no alternative: either the mind must be useless and void, or the soul. But if these affections may certainly be all of them ascribed to both, then in that case the two will be one and the same, and Democritus will carry his point when he suppresses all distinction between the two. The question will arise how two can be one--whether by the confusion of two substances, or by the disposition of one?

We, however, affirm that the mind coalesces with [1576] the soul,--not indeed as being distinct from it in substance, but as being its natural function and agent. [1577]

Chapter XIII - The Soul's Supremacy

It next remains to examine where lies the supremacy; in other words, which of the two is superior to the other, so that with which the supremacy clearly lies shall be the essentially superior substance; [1578] whilst that over which this essentially superior substance shall have authority shall be considered as the natural functionary of the superior substance. Now who will hesitate to ascribe this entire authority to the soul, from the name of which the whole man has received his own designation in common phraseology?

How many souls, says the rich man, do I maintain? not how many minds. The pilot's desire, also, is to rescue so many souls from shipwreck, not so many minds; the labourer, too, in his work, and the soldier on the field of battle, affirms that he lays down his soul (or life), not his mind. Which of the two has its perils or its vows and wishes more frequently on men's lips--the mind or the soul? Which of the two are dying persons, said to have to do with the mind or the soul? In short, philosophers themselves, and medical men, even when it is their purpose to discourse about the mind, do in every instance inscribe on their title-page [1579] and table of contents, [1580] "De Anima" ("A treatise on the soul").

And that you may also have God's voucher on the subject, it is the soul which He addresses; it is the soul which He exhorts and counsels, to turn the mind and intellect to Him. It is the soul which Christ came to save; it is the soul which He threatens to destroy in hell; it is the soul (or life) which He forbids being made too much of; it is His soul, too (or life), which the good Shepherd Himself lays down for His sheep. It is to the soul, therefore, that you ascribe the supremacy; in it also you possess that union of substance, of which you perceive the mind to be the instrument, not the ruling power.

Chapter XIV - The Soul Variously Divided by the Philosophers; This Division is Not a Material Dissection

Being thus single, simple, and entire in itself, it is as incapable of being composed and put together from external constituents, as it is of being divided in and of itself, inasmuch as it is indissoluble. For if it had been possible to construct it and to destroy it, it would no longer be immortal. Since, however, it is not mortal, it is also incapable of dissolution and division. Now, to be divided means to be dissolved, and to be dissolved means to die. Yet (philosophers) have divided the soul into parts: Plato, for instance, into two; Zeno into three; Panætius, into five or six; Soranus, into seven; Chrysippus, into as many as eight; and Apollophanes, into as many as nine; whilst certain of the Stoics have found as many as twelve parts in the soul. Posidonius makes even two more than these: he starts with two leading faculties of the soul,--the directing faculty, which they designate ἡγεμονικόν; and the rational faculty, which they call λογικόν,--and ultimately subdivided these into seventeen [1581] parts. Thus variously is the soul dissected by the different schools. Such divisions, however, ought not to be regarded so much as parts of the soul, as powers, or faculties, or operations thereof, even as Aristotle himself has regarded some of them as being. For they are not portions or organic parts of the soul's substance, but functions of the soul--such as those of motion, of action, of thought, and whatsoever others they divide in this manner; such, likewise, as the five senses themselves, so well known to all-- seeing, hearing, tasting, touching, smelling. Now, although they have allotted to the whole of these respectively certain parts of the body as their special domiciles, it does not from that circumstance follow that a like distribution will be suitable to the sections of the soul; for even the body itself would not admit of such a partition as they would have the soul undergo. But of the whole number of the limbs one body is made up, so that the arrangement is rather a concretion than a division. Look at that very wonderful piece of organic mechanism by Archimedes,--I mean his hydraulic organ, with its many limbs, parts, bands, passages for the notes, outlets for their sounds, combinations for their harmony, and the array of its pipes; but yet the whole of these details constitute only one instrument. In like manner the wind, which breathes throughout this organ at the impulse of the hydraulic engine, is not divided into separate portions from the fact of its dispersion through the instrument to make it play: it is whole and entire in its substance, although divided in its operation. This example is not remote from (the illustration) of Strato, and Ænesidemus, and Heraclitus: for these philosophers maintain the unity of the soul, as diffused over the entire body, and yet in every part the same.[1582] Precisely like the wind blown in the pipes throughout the organ, the soul displays its energies in various ways by means of the senses, being not indeed divided, but rather distributed in natural order. Now, under what designations these energies are to be known, and by what divisions of themselves they are to be classified, and to what special offices and functions in the body they are to be severally confined, the physicians and the philosophers must consider and decide: for ourselves, a few remarks only will be proper.

Chapter XV - The Soul's Vitality and Intelligence. Its Character and Seat in Man

In the first place, (we must determine) whether there be in the soul some supreme principle of vitality and intelligence [1583] which they call "the ruling power of the soul"--τὸ ἡγεμονικόν for if this be not admitted, the whole condition of the soul is put in jeopardy. Indeed, those men who say that there is no such directing faculty, have begun by supposing that the soul itself is simply a nonentity. One Dicæarchus, a Messenian, and amongst the medical profession Andreas and Asclepiades, have thus destroyed the (soul's) directing power, by actually placing in the mind the senses, for which they claim the ruling faculty. Asclepiades rides rough-shod over us with even this argument, that very many animals, after losing those parts of their body in which the soul's principle of vitality and sensation is thought mainly to exist, still retain life in a considerable degree, as well as sensation: as in the case of flies, and wasps, and locusts, when you have cut off their heads; and of she-goats, and tortoises, and eels, when you have pulled out their hearts. (He concludes), therefore, that there is no especial principle or power of the soul; for if there were, the soul's vigour and strength could not continue when it was removed with its domiciles (or corporeal organs).

However, Dicæarchus has several authorities against him--and philosophers too--Plato, Strato, Epicurus, Democritus, Empedocles, Socrates, Aristotle; whilst in opposition to Andreas and Asclepiades (may be placed their brother) physicians Herophilus, Erasistratus, Diocles, Hippocrates, and Soranus himself; and better than all others, there are our Christian authorities. We are taught by God concerning both these questions--viz. that there is a ruling power in the soul, and that it is enshrined [1584] in one particular recess of the body.

For, when one reads of God as being "the searcher and witness of the heart;" [1585] when His prophet is reproved by His discovering to him the secrets of the heart; [1586] when God Himself anticipates in His people the thoughts of their heart, [1587] "Why think ye evil in your hearts?"[1588] when David prays "Create in me a clean heart, O God," [1589] and Paul declares, "With the heart man believeth unto righteousness,"[1590] and John says, "By his own heart is each man condemned;" [1591] when, lastly, "he who looketh on a woman so as to lust after her, hath already committed adultery with her in his heart," [1592] -- then both points are cleared fully up, that there is a directing faculty of the soul, with which the purpose of God may agree; in other words, a supreme principle of intelligence and vitality (for where there is intelligence, there must be vitality), and that it resides in that most precious part [1593] of our body to which God especially looks:

so that you must not suppose, with Heraclitus, that this sovereign faculty of which we are treating is moved by some external force; nor with Moschion, [1594] that it floats about through the whole body; nor with Plato, that it is enclosed in the head; nor with Zenophanes, that it culminates in the crown of the head; nor that it reposes in the brain, according to the opinion of Hippocrates; nor around the basis of the brain, as Herophilus thought; nor in the membranes thereof, as Strato and Erasistratus said; nor in the space between the eyebrows, as Strato the physician held; nor within the enclosure [1595] of the breast, according to Epicurus:

but rather, as the Egyptians have always taught, especially such of them as were accounted the expounders of sacred truths; [1596] in accordance, too, with that verse of Orpheus or Empedocles:

"Namque homini sanguis circumcordialis est sensus." [1597]

"Man has his (supreme) sensation in the blood around his heart."

Even Protagoras [1598] likewise, and Apollodorus, and Chrysippus, entertain this same view, so that (our friend) Asclepiades may go in quest of his goats bleating without a heart, and hunt his flies without their heads; and let all those (worthies), too, who have predetermined the character of the human soul from the condition of brute animals, be quite sure that it is themselves rather who are alive in a heartless and brainless state.

Chapter XVI - The Soul's Parts. Elements of the Rational Soul

That position of Plato's is also quite in keeping with the faith, in which he divides the soul into two parts--the rational and the irrational.

To this definition we take no exception, except that we would not ascribe this twofold distinction to the nature (of the soul). It is the rational element which we must believe to be its natural condition, impressed upon it from its very first creation by its Author, who is Himself essentially rational. For how should that be other than rational, which God produced on His own prompting; nay more, which He expressly sent forth by His own afflatus or breath? The irrational element, however, we must understand to have accrued later, as having proceeded from the instigation of the serpent--the very achievement of (the first) transgression--which thenceforward became inherent in the soul, and grew with its growth, assuming the manner by this time of a natural development, happening as it did immediately at the beginning of nature.

But, inasmuch as the same Plato speaks of the rational element only as existing in the soul of God Himself, if we were to ascribe the irrational element likewise to the nature which our soul has received from God, then the irrational element will be equally derived from God, as being a natural production, because God is the author of nature. Now from the devil proceeds the incentive to sin. All sin, however, is irrational: therefore the irrational proceeds from the devil, from whom sin proceeds; and it is extraneous to God, to whom also the irrational is an alien principle.

The diversity, then, between these two elements arises from the difference of their authors. When, therefore, Plato reserves the rational element (of the soul) to God alone, and subdivides it into two departments: the irascible, which they call θυμικόν, and the concupiscible, which they designate by the term ἐπιθυμητικόν (in such a way as to make the first common to us and lions, and the second shared between ourselves and flies, whilst the rational element is confined to us and God)--I see that this point will have to be treated by us, owing to the facts which we find operating also in Christ. For you may behold this triad of qualities in the Lord. There was the rational element, by which He taught, by which He discoursed, by which He prepared the way of salvation; there was moreover indignation in Him, by which He inveighed against the scribes and the Pharisees; and there was the principle of desire, by which He so earnestly desired to eat the passover with His disciples. [1599] In our own cases, accordingly, the irascible and the concupiscible elements of our soul must not invariably be put to the account of the irrational (nature), since we are sure that in our Lord these elements operated in entire accordance with reason. God will be angry, with perfect reason, with all who deserve His wrath; and with reason, too, will God desire whatever objects and claims are worthy of Himself.

For He will show indignation against the evil man, and for the good man will He desire salvation. To ourselves even does the apostle allow the concupiscible quality. "If any man," says he, "desireth the office of a bishop, he desireth a good work." [1600] Now, by saying "a good work," he shows us that the desire is a reasonable one. He permits us likewise to feel indignation.

How should he not, when he himself experiences the same? "I would," says he, "that they were even cut off which trouble you." [1601] In perfect agreement with reason was that indignation which resulted from his desire to maintain discipline and order. When, however, he says, "We were formerly the children of wrath," [1602] he censures an irrational irascibility, such as proceeds not from that nature which is the production of God, but from that which the devil brought in, who is himself styled the lord or "master" of his own class, "Ye cannot serve two masters," [1603] and has the actual designation of "father:"

"Ye are of your father the devil." [1604] So that you need not be afraid to ascribe to him the mastery and dominion over that second, later, and deteriorated nature (of which we have been speaking), when you read of him as "the sewer of tares," and the nocturnal spoiler of the crop of corn. [1605]

Chapter XVII - The Fidelity of the Senses, Impugned by Plato, Vindicated by Christ Himself

Then, again, when we encounter the question (as to the veracity of those five senses which we learn with our alphabet; since from this source even there arises some support for our heretics. They are the faculties of seeing, and hearing, and smelling, and tasting, and touching. The fidelity of these senses is impugned with too much severity by the Platonists, [1606] and according to some by Heraclitus also, and Diocles, and Empedocles; at any rate, Plato, in the Timæus, declares the operations of the senses to be irrational, and vitiated [1607] by our opinions or beliefs. Deception is imputed to the sight, because it asserts that oars, when immersed in the water, are inclined or bent, notwithstanding the certainty that they are straight; because, again, it is quite sure that that distant tower with its really quadrangular contour is round; because also it will discredit the fact of the truly parallel fabric of yonder porch or arcade, by supposing it to be narrower and narrower towards its end; and because it will join with the sea the sky which hangs at so great a height above it.

In the same way, our hearing is charged with fallacy: we think, for instance, that that is a noise in the sky which is nothing else than the rumbling of a carriage; or, if you prefer it [1608] the other way, when the thunder rolled at a distance, we were quite sure that it was a carriage which made the noise.

Thus, too, are our faculties of smell and taste at fault, because the selfsame perfumes and wines lose their value after we have used them awhile. On the same principle our touch is censured, when the identical pavement which seemed rough to the hands is felt by the feet to be smooth enough; and in the baths a stream of warm water is pronounced to be quite hot at first, and beautifully temperate afterwards. Thus, according to them, our senses deceive us, when all the while we are (the cause of the discrepancies, by) changing our opinions. The Stoics are more moderate in their views; for they do not load with the obloquy of deception every one of the senses, and at all times. The Epicureans, again, show still greater consistency, in maintaining that all the senses are equally true in their testimony, and always so--only in a different way. It is not our organs of sensation that are at fault, but our opinion. The senses only experience sensation, they do not exercise opinion; it is the soul that opines. They separated opinion from the senses, and sensation from the soul. Well, but whence comes opinion, if not from the senses? Indeed, unless the eye had descried a round shape in that tower, it could have had no idea that it possessed roundness. Again, whence arises sensation if not from the soul? For if the soul had no body, it would have no sensation. Accordingly, sensation comes from the soul, and opinion from sensation; and the whole (process) is the soul. But further, it may well be insisted on that there is a something which causes the discrepancy between the report of the senses and the reality of the facts.

Now, since it is possible, (as we have seen), for phenomena to be reported which exist not in the objects, why should it not be equally possible for phenomena to be reported which are caused not by the senses, but by reasons and conditions which intervene, in the very nature of the case? If so, it will be only right that they should be duly recognised. The truth is, that it was the water which was the cause of the oar seeming to be inclined or bent: out of the water, it was perfectly straight in appearance (as well as in fact).

The delicacy of the substance or medium which forms a mirror by means of its luminosity, according as it is struck or shaken, by the vibration actually destroys the appearance of the straightness of a right line. In like manner, the condition of the open space which fills up the interval between it and us, necessarily causes the true shape of the tower to escape our notice; for the uniform density of the surrounding air covering its angles with a similar light obliterates their outlines. So, again, the equal breadth of the arcade is sharpened or narrowed off towards its termination, until its aspect, becoming more and more contracted under its prolonged roof, comes to a vanishing point in the direction of its farthest distance. So the sky blends itself with the sea, the vision becoming spent at last, which had maintained duly the boundaries of the two elements, so long as its vigorous glance lasted. As for the (alleged cases of deceptive) hearing, what else could produce the illusion but the similarity of the sounds? And if the perfume afterwards was less strong to the smell, and the wine more flat to the taste, and the water not so hot to the touch, their original strength was after all found in the whole of them pretty well unimpaired. In the matter, however, of the roughness and smoothness of the pavement, it was only natural and right that limbs like the hands and the feet, so different in tenderness and callousness, should have different impressions. In this way, then, there cannot occur an illusion in our senses without an adequate cause. Now if special causes, (such as we have indicated,) mislead our senses and (through our senses) our opinions also, then we must no longer ascribe the deception to the senses, which follow the specific causes of the illusion, nor to the opinions we form; for these are occasioned and controlled by our senses, which only follow the causes. Persons who are afflicted with madness or insanity, mistake one object for another.

Orestes in his sister sees his mother; Ajax sees Ulysses in the slaughtered herd; Athamas and Agave descry wild beasts in their children. Now is it their eyes or their phrenzy which you must blame for so vast a fallacy?

All things taste bitter, in the redundancy of their bile, to those who have the jaundice. Is it their taste which you will charge with the physical prevarication, or their ill state of health? All the senses, therefore, are disordered occasionally, or imposed upon, but only in such a way as to be quite free of any fault in their own natural functions. But further still, not even against the specific causes and conditions themselves must we lay an indictment of deception. For, since these physical aberrations happen for stated reasons, the reasons do not deserve to be regarded as deceptions. Whatever ought to occur in a certain manner is not a deception. If, then, even these circumstantial causes must be acquitted of all censure and blame, how much more should we free from reproach the senses, over which the said causes exercise a liberal sway! Hence we are bound most certainly to claim for the senses truth, and fidelity, and integrity, seeing that they never render any other account of their impressions than is enjoined on them by the specific causes or conditions which in all cases produce that discrepancy which appears between the report of the senses and the reality of the objects. What mean you, then, O most insolent Academy? You overthrow the entire condition of human life; you disturb the whole order of nature; you obscure the good providence of God Himself: for the senses of man which God has appointed over all His works, that we might understand, inhabit, dispense, and enjoy them, (you reproach) as fallacious and treacherous tyrants! But is it not from these that all creation receives our services?

Is it not by their means that a second form is impressed even upon the world?--so many arts, so many industrious resources, so many pursuits, such business, such offices, such commerce, such remedies, counsels, consolations, modes, civilizations, and accomplishments of life! All these things have produced the very relish and savour of human existence; whilst by these senses of man, he alone of all animated nature has the distinction of being a rational animal, with a capacity for intelligence and knowledge--nay, an ability to form the Academy itself! But Plato, in order to disparage the testimony of the senses, in the Phædrus denies (in the person of Socrates) his own ability to know even himself, according to the injunction of the Delphic oracle; and in the Theætetus he deprives himself of the faculties of knowledge and sensation; and again, in the Phædrus he postpones till after death the posthumous knowledge, as he calls it, of the truth; and yet for all he went on playing the philosopher even before he died. We may not, I say, we may not call into question the truth of the (poor vilified) senses, [1609] lest we should even in Christ Himself, bring doubt upon [1610] the truth of their sensation; lest perchance it should be said that He did not really "behold Satan as lightning fall from heaven;" [1611] that He did not really hear the Father's voice testifying of Himself; [1612] or that He was deceived in touching Peter's wife's mother; [1613] or that the fragrance of the ointment which He afterwards smelled was different from that which He accepted for His burial; [1614] and that the taste of the wine was different from that which He consecrated in memory of His blood. [1615] On this false principle it was that Marcion actually chose to believe that He was a phantom, denying to Him the reality of a perfect body. Now, not even to His apostles was His nature ever a matter of deception. He was truly both seen and heard upon the mount; [1616] true and real was the draught of that wine at the marriage of (Cana in) Galilee; [1617] true and real also was the touch of the then believing Thomas. [1618] Read the testimony of John: "That which we have seen, which we have heard, which we have looked upon with our eyes, and our hands have handled, of the Word of life." [1619] False, of course, and deceptive must have been that testimony, if the witness of our eyes, and ears, and hands be by nature a lie.

Chapter XVIII - Plato Suggested Certain Errors to the Gnostics. Functions of the Soul

I turn now to the department of our intellectual faculties, such as Plato has handed it over to the heretics, distinct from our bodily functions, having obtained the knowledge of them before death. [1620] He asks in the Phædo, What, then, (do you think) concerning the actual possession of knowledge? Will the body be a hindrance to it or not, if one shall admit it as an associate in the search after knowledge? I have a similar question to ask: Have the faculties of their sight and hearing any truth and reality for human beings or not?

Is it not the case, that even the poets are always muttering against us, that we can never hear or see anything for certain? He remembered, no doubt, what Epicharmus the comic poet had said: "It is the mind which sees, the mind that hears--all else is blind and deaf." To the same purport he says again, that man is the wisest whose mental power is the clearest; who never applies the sense of sight, nor adds to his mind the help of any such faculty, but employs the intellect itself in unmixed serenity when he indulges in contemplation for the purpose of acquiring an unalloyed insight into the nature of things; divorcing himself with all his might from his eyes and ears and (as one must express himself) from the whole of his body, on the ground of its disturbing the soul, and not allowing it to possess either truth or wisdom, whenever it is brought into communication with it. We see, then, that in opposition to the bodily senses another faculty is provided of a much more serviceable character, even the powers of the soul, which produce an understanding of that truth whose realities are not palpable nor open to the bodily senses, but are very remote from men's everyday knowledge, lying in secret--in the heights above, and in the presence of God Himself. For Plato maintains that there are certain invisible substances, incorporeal, celestial, [1621] divine, and eternal, which they call ideas, that is to say, (archetypal) forms, which are the patterns and causes of those objects of nature which are manifest to us, and lie under our corporeal senses: the former, (according to Plato,) are the actual verities, and the latter the images and likenesses of them. Well, now, are there not here gleams of the heretical principles of the Gnostics and the Valentinians? It is from this philosophy that they eagerly adopt the difference between the bodily senses and the intellectual faculties,--a distinction which they actually apply to the parable of the ten virgins: making the five foolish virgins to symbolize the five bodily senses, seeing that these are so silly and so easy to be deceived; and the wise virgin to express the meaning of the intellectual faculties, which are so wise as to attain to that mysterious and supernal truth, which is placed in the pleroma. (Here, then, we have) the mystic original of the ideas of these heretics. For in this philosophy lie both their Æons and their genealogies. Thus, too, do they divide sensation, both into the intellectual powers from their spiritual seed, and the sensuous faculties from the animal, which cannot by any means comprehend spiritual things. From the former germ spring invisible things; from the latter, visible things which are grovelling and temporary, and which are obvious to the senses, placed as they are in palpable forms. [1622] It is because of these views that we have in a former passage stated as a preliminary fact, that the mind is nothing else than an apparatus or instrument of the soul, [1623] and that the spirit is no other faculty, separate from the soul, but is the soul itself exercised in respiration; although that influence which either God on the one hand, or the devil on the other, has breathed upon it, must be regarded in the light of an additional element. [1624] And now, with respect to the difference between the intellectual powers and the sensuous faculties, we only admit it so far as the natural diversity between them requires of us. (There is, of course, a difference) between things corporeal and things spiritual, between visible and invisible beings, between objects which are manifest to the view and those which are hidden from it; because the one class are attributed to sensation, and the other to the intellect. But yet both the one and the other must be regarded as inherent in the soul, and as obedient to it, seeing that it embraces bodily objects by means of the body, in exactly the same way that it conceives incorporeal objects by help of the mind, except that it is even exercising sensation when it is employing the intellect. For is it not true, that to employ the senses is to use the intellect? And to employ the intellect amounts to a use of the senses? [1625] What indeed can sensation be, but the understanding of that which is the object of the sensation? And what can the intellect or understanding be, but the seeing of that which is the object understood? Why adopt such excruciating means of torturing simple knowledge and crucifying the truth? Who can show me the sense which does not understand the object of its sensation, or the intellect which perceives not the object which it understands, in so clear a way as to prove to me that the one can do without the other? If corporeal things are the objects of sense, and incorporeal ones objects of the intellect, it is the classes of the objects which are different, not the domicile or abode of sense and intellect; in other words, not the soul (anima) and the mind (animus). By what, in short, are corporeal things perceived?

If it is by the soul, [1626] then the mind is a sensuous faculty, and not merely an intellectual power; for whilst it understands, it also perceives, because without the perception there is no understanding. If, however, corporeal things are perceived by the soul, then it follows that the soul's power is an intellectual one, and not merely a sensuous faculty; for while it perceives it also understands, because without understanding there is no perceiving. And then, again, by what are incorporeal things understood? If it is by the mind, [1627] where will be the soul? If it is by the soul, where will be the mind? For things which differ ought to be mutually absent from each other, when they are occupied in their respective functions and duties. It must be your opinion, indeed, that the mind is absent from the soul on certain occasions; for (you suppose) that we are so made and constituted as not to know that we have seen or heard something, on the hypothesis [1628] that the mind was absent at the time. I must therefore maintain that the very soul itself neither saw nor heard, since it was at the given moment absent with its active power--that is to say, the mind. The truth is, that whenever a man is out of his mind, [1629] it is his soul that is demented--not because the mind is absent, but because it is a fellow-sufferer (with the soul) at the time. [1630] Indeed, it is the soul which is principally affected by casualties of such a kind. Whence is this fact confirmed? It is confirmed from the following consideration: that after the soul's departure, the mind is no longer found in a man: it always follows the soul; nor does it at last remain behind it alone, after death. Now, since it follows the soul, it is also indissolubly attached to it; just as the understanding is attached to the soul, which is followed by the mind, with which the understanding is indissolubly connected. Granted now that the understanding is superior to the senses, and a better discoverer of mysteries, what matters it, so long as it is only a peculiar faculty of the soul, just as the senses themselves are? It does not at all affect my argument, unless the understanding were held to be superior to the senses, for the purpose of deducing from the allegation of such superiority its separate condition likewise. After thus combating their alleged difference, I have also to refute this question of superiority, previous to my approaching the belief (which heresy propounds) in a superior god. On this point, however, of a (superior) god, we shall have to measure swords with the heretics on their own ground. [1631] Our present subject concerns the soul, and the point is to prevent the insidious ascription of a superiority to the intellect or understanding. Now, although the objects which are touched by the intellect are of a higher nature, since they are spiritual, than those which are embraced by the senses, since these are corporeal, it will still be only a superiority in the objects--as of lofty ones contrasted with humble--not in the faculties of the intellect against the senses. For how can the intellect be superior to the senses, when it is these which educate it for the discovery of various truths? It is a fact, that these truths are learned by means of palpable forms; in other words, invisible things are discovered by the help of visible ones, even as the apostle tells us in his epistle: "For the invisible things of Him are clearly seen from the creation of the world, being understood by the things that are made;" [1632] and as Plato too might inform our heretics:

"The things which appear are the image [1633] of the things which are concealed from view,"[1634] whence it must needs follow that this world is by all means an image of some other: so that the intellect evidently uses the senses for its own guidance, and authority, and mainstay; and without the senses truth could not be attained.

How, then, can a thing be superior to that which is instrumental to its existence, which is also indispensable to it, and to whose help it owes everything which it acquires? Two conclusions therefore follow from what we have said: (1) That the intellect is not to be preferred above the senses, on the (supposed) ground that the agent through which a thing exists is inferior to the thing itself; and (2) that the intellect must not be separated from the senses, since the instrument by which a thing's existence is sustained is associated with the thing itself.

Chapter XIX - The Intellect Coeval with the Soul in the Human Being. An Example from Aristotle. Converted into Evidence Favourable to These Views

Nor must we fail to notice those writers who deprive the soul of the intellect even for a short period of time. They do this in order to prepare the way of introducing the intellect--and the mind also--at a subsequent time of life, even at the time when intelligence appears in a man. They maintain that the stage of infancy is supported by the soul alone, simply to promote vitality, without any intention of acquiring knowledge also, because not all things have knowledge which possess life. Trees, for instance, to quote Aristotle's example, [1635] have vitality, but have not knowledge; and with him agrees every one who gives a share to all animated beings of the animal substance, which, according to our view, exists in man alone as his special property,--not because it is the work of God, which all other creatures are likewise, but because it is the breath of God, which this (human soul) alone is, which we say is born with the full equipment of its proper faculties. Well, let them meet us with the example of the trees: we will accept their challenge, (nor shall we find in it any detriment to our own argument;) for it is an undoubted fact, that whilst trees are yet but twigs and sprouts, and before they even reach the sapling stage, there is in them their own proper faculty of life, as soon as they spring out of their native beds. But then, as time goes on, the vigour of the tree slowly advances, as it grows and hardens into its woody trunk, until its mature age completes the condition which nature destines for it. Else what resources would trees possess in due course for the inoculation of grafts, and the formation of leaves, and the swelling of their buds, and the graceful shedding of their blossom, and the softening of their sap, were there not in them the quiet growth of the full provision of their nature, and the distribution of this life over all their branches for the accomplishment of their maturity? Trees, therefore, have ability or knowledge; and they derive it from whence they also derive vitality--that is, from the one source of vitality and knowledge which is peculiar to their nature, and that from the infancy which they, too, begin with.

For I observe that even the vine, although yet tender and immature, still understands its own natural business, and strives to cling to some support, that, leaning on it, and lacing through it,[1636] it may so attain its growth. Indeed, without waiting for the husbandman's training, without an espalier, without a prop, whatever its tendrils catch, it will fondly cling to, [1637] and embrace with really greater tenacity and force by its own inclination than by your volition. It longs and hastens to be secure. Take also ivy-plants, never mind how young: I observe their attempts from the very first to grasp objects above them, and outrunning everything else, to hang on to the highest thing, preferring as they do to spread over walls with their leafy web and woof rather than creep on the ground and be trodden under by every foot that likes to crush them. On the other hand, in the case of such trees as receive injury from contact with a building, how do they hang off as they grow and avoid what injures them! You can see that their branches were naturally meant to take the opposite direction, and can very well understand the vital instincts [1638] of such a tree from its avoidance of the wall.

It is contented (if it be only a little shrub) with its own insignificant destiny, which it has in its foreseeing instinct thoroughly been aware of from its infancy, only it still fears even a ruined building. On my side, then, why should I not contend for these wise and sagacious natures of trees?

Let them have vitality, as the philosophers permit it; but let them have knowledge too, although the philosophers disavow it. Even the infancy of a log, then, may have an intellect (suitable to it): how much more may that of a human being, whose soul (which may be compared with the nascent sprout of a tree) has been derived from Adam as its root, and has been propagated amongst his posterity by means of woman, to whom it has been entrusted for transmission, and thus has sprouted into life with all its natural apparatus, both of intellect and of sense! I am much mistaken if the human person, even from his infancy, when he saluted life with his infant cries, does not testify to his actual possession of the faculties of sensation and intellect by the fact of his birth, vindicating at one and the same time the use of all his senses--that of seeing by the light, that of hearing by sounds, that of taste by liquids, that of smell by the air, that of touch by the ground. This earliest voice of infancy, then, is the first effort of the senses, and the initial impulse of mental perceptions. [1639] There is also the further fact, that some persons understand this plaintive cry of the infant to be an augury of affliction in the prospect of our tearful life, whereby from the very moment of birth (the soul) has to be regarded as endued with prescience, much more with intelligence. Accordingly by this intuition [1640] the babe knows his mother, discerns the nurse, and even recognises the waiting-maid; refusing the breast of another woman, and the cradle that is not his own, and longing only for the arms to which he is accustomed. Now from what source does he acquire this discernment of novelty and custom, if not from instinctive knowledge? How does it happen that he is irritated and quieted, if not by help of his initial intellect? It would be very strange indeed that infancy were naturally so lively, if it had not mental power; and naturally so capable of impression and affection, if it had no intellect. But (we hold the contrary): for Christ, by "accepting praise out of the mouth of babes and sucklings," [1641] has declared that neither childhood nor infancy is without sensibility, [1642] --the former of which states, when meeting Him with approving shouts, proved its ability to offer Him testimony; [1643] while the other, by being slaughtered, for His sake of course, knew what violence meant. [1644]

Chapter XX - The Soul, as to Its Nature Uniform, But Its Faculties Variously Developed. Varieties Only Accidental

And here, therefore, we draw our conclusion, that all the natural properties of the soul are inherent in it as parts of its substance; and that they grow and develope along with it, from the very moment of its own origin at birth.

Just as Seneca says, whom we so often find on our side: [1645] "There are implanted within us the seeds of all the arts and periods of life. And God, our Master, secretly produces our mental dispositions;" that is, from the germs which are implanted and hidden in us by means of infancy, and these are the intellect: for from these our natural dispositions are evolved.

Now, even the seeds of plants have, one form in each kind, but their development varies: some open and expand in a healthy and perfect state, while others either improve or degenerate, owing to the conditions of weather and soil, and from the appliance of labour and care; also from the course of the seasons, and from the occurrence of casual circumstances. In like manner, the soul may well be [1646] uniform in its seminal origin, although multiform by the process of nativity.[1647] And here local influences, too, must be taken into account. It has been said that dull and brutish persons are born at Thebes; and the most accomplished in wisdom and speech at Athens, where in the district of Colythus [1648] children speak--such is the precocity of their tongue--before they are a month old. Indeed, Plato himself tells us, in the Timæus, that Minerva, when preparing to found her great city, only regarded the nature of the country which gave promise of mental dispositions of this kind; whence he himself in The Laws instructs Megillus and Clinias to be careful in their selection of a site for building a city. Empedocles, however, places the cause of a subtle or an obtuse intellect in the quality of the blood, from which he derives progress and perfection in learning and science. The subject of national peculiarities has grown by this time into proverbial notoriety.

Comic poets deride the Phrygians for their cowardice; Sallust reproaches the Moors for their levity, and the Dalmatians for their cruelty; even the apostle brands the Cretans as "liars." [1649] Very likely, too, something must be set down to the score of bodily condition and the state of the health.

The Writings of Tertullian - Volume I

Stoutness hinders knowledge, but a spare form stimulates it; paralysis prostrates the mind, a decline preserves it. How much more will those accidental circumstances have to be noticed, which, in addition to the state of one's body or one's health, tend to sharpen or to dull the intellect! It is sharpened by learned pursuits, by the sciences, the arts, by experimental knowledge, business habits, and studies; it is blunted by ignorance, idle habits, inactivity, lust, inexperience, listlessness, and vicious pursuits.

Then, besides these influences, there must perhaps [1650] be added the supreme powers. Now these are the supreme powers: according to our (Christian) notions, they are the Lord God and His adversary the devil; but according to men's general opinion about providence, they are fate and necessity; and about fortune, it is man's freedom of will.

Even the philosophers allow these distinctions; whilst on our part we have already undertaken to treat of them, on the principles of the (Christian) faith, in a separate work. [1651] It is evident how great must be the influences which so variously affect the one nature of the soul, since they are commonly regarded as separate "natures." Still they are not different species, but casual incidents of one nature and substance--even of that which God conferred on Adam, and made the mould of all (subsequent ones). Casual incidents will they always remain, but never will they become specific differences.

However great, too, at present is the variety of men's maunders, it was not so in Adam, the founder of their race.

But all these discordances ought to have existed in him as the fountainhead, and thence to have descended to us in an unimpaired variety, if the variety had been due to nature.

Chapter XXI - As Free-Will Actuates an Individual So May His Character Change

Now, if the soul possessed this uniform and simple nature from the beginning in Adam, previous to so many mental dispositions (being developed out of it), it is not rendered multiform by such various development, nor by the triple [1652] form predicated of it in "the Valentinian trinity" (that we may still keep the condemnation of that heresy in view), for not even this nature is discoverable in Adam. What had he that was spiritual? Is it because he prophetically declared "the great mystery of Christ and the church?" [1653] "This is bone of my bone, and flesh of my flesh: she shall be called Woman. Therefore shall a man leave his father and mother, and he shall cleave unto his wife; and they two shall be one flesh." [1654] But this (gift of prophecy) only came on him afterwards, when God infused into him the ecstasy, or spiritual quality, in which prophecy consists. If, again, the evil of sin was developed in him, this must not be accounted as a natural disposition: it was rather produced by the instigation of the (old) serpent as far from being incidental to his nature as it was from being material in him, for we have already excluded belief in "Matter." [1655] Now, if neither the spiritual element, nor what the heretics call the material element, was properly inherent in him (since, if he had been created out of matter, the germ of evil must have been an integral part of his constitution), it remains that the one only original element of his nature was what is called the animal (the principle of vitality, the soul), which we maintain to be simple and uniform in its condition. Concerning this, it remains for us to inquire whether, as being called natural, it ought to be deemed subject to change. (The heretics whom we have referred to) deny that nature is susceptible of any change, [1656] in order that they may be able to establish and settle their threefold theory, or "trinity," in all its characteristics as to the several natures, because "a good tree cannot produce evil fruit, nor a corrupt tree good fruit; and nobody gathers figs of thorns, nor grapes of brambles." [1657] If so, then "God will not be able any longer to raise up from the stones children unto Abraham; nor to make a generation of vipers bring forth fruits of repentance." [1658] And if so, the apostle too was in error when he said in his epistle, "Ye were at one time darkness, (but now are ye light in the Lord:)" [1659] and, "We also were by nature children of wrath;" [1660] and, "Such were some of you, but ye are washed." [1661] The statements, however, of holy Scripture will never be discordant with truth. A corrupt tree will never yield good fruit, unless the better nature be grafted into it; nor will a good tree produce evil fruit, except by the same process of cultivation. Stones also will become children of Abraham, if educated in Abraham's faith; and a generation of vipers will bring forth the fruits of penitence, if they reject the poison of their malignant nature. This will be the power of the grace of God, more potent indeed than nature, exercising its sway over the faculty that underlies itself within us--even the freedom of our will, which is described as αὐτεξούσιος (of independent authority); and inasmuch as this faculty is itself also natural and mutable, in whatsoever direction it turns, it inclines of its own nature. Now, that there does exist within us naturally this independent authority (τὸ αὐτεξούσιον), we have already shown in opposition both to Marcion [1662] and to Hermogenes. [1663] If, then, the natural condition has to be submitted to a definition, it must be determined to be twofold--there being the category of the born and the unborn, the made and not-made. Now that which has received its constitution by being made or by being born, is by nature capable of being changed, for it can be both born again and re-made; whereas that which is not-made and unborn will remain for ever immoveable.

Since, however, this state is suited to God alone, as the only Being who is unborn and not-made (and therefore immortal and unchangeable), it is absolutely certain that the nature of all other existences which are born and created is subject to modification and change; so that if the threefold state is to be ascribed to the soul, it must be supposed to arise from the mutability of its accidental circumstances, and not from the appointment of nature.

Chapter XXII - Recapitulation. Definition of the Soul

Hermogenes has already heard from us what are the other natural faculties of the soul, as well as their vindication and proof; whence it may be seen that the soul is rather the offspring of God than of matter. The names of these faculties shall here be simply repeated, that they may not seem to be forgotten and passed out of sight.

We have assigned, then, to the soul both that freedom of the will which we just now mentioned, and its dominion over the works of nature, and its occasional gift of divination, independently of that endowment of prophecy which accrues to it expressly from the grace of God. We shall therefore now quit this subject of the soul's disposition, in order to set out fully in order its various qualities. [1664] The soul, then, we define to be sprung from the breath of God, immortal, possessing body, having form, simple in its substance, intelligent in its own nature, developing its power in various ways, free in its determinations, subject to be changes of accident, in its faculties mutable, rational, supreme, endued with an instinct of presentiment, evolved out of one (archetypal soul). It remains for us now to consider how it is developed out of this one original source; in other words, whence, and when, and how it is produced.

Chapter XXIII - The Opinions of Sundry Heretics Which Originate Ultimately with Plato

Some suppose that they came down from heaven, with as firm a belief as they are apt to entertain, when they indulge in the prospect of an undoubted return thither. Saturninus, the disciple of Menander, who belonged to Simon's sect, introduced this opinion: he affirmed that man was made by angels. A futile, imperfect creation at first, weak and unable to stand, he crawled upon the ground like a worm, because he wanted the strength to maintain an erect posture; but afterwards having, by the compassion of the Supreme Power (in whose image, which had not been fully understood, he was clumsily formed), obtained a slender spark of life, this roused and righted his imperfect form, and animated it with a higher vitality, and provided for its return, on its relinquishment of life, to its original principle. Carpocrates, indeed, claims for himself so extreme an amount of the supernal qualities, that his disciples set their own souls at once on an equality with Christ (not to mention the apostles); and sometimes, when it suits their fancy, even give them the superiority--deeming them, forsooth, to have partaken of that sublime virtue which looks down upon the principalities that govern this world. Apelles tells us that our souls were enticed by earthly baits down from their super-celestial abodes by a fiery angel, Israel's God and ours, who then enclosed them firmly within our sinful flesh. The hive of Valentinus fortifies the soul with the germ of Σοφία, or Wisdom; by means of which germ they recognise, in the images of visible objects, the stories and Milesian fables of their own Æons. I am sorry from my heart that Plato has been the caterer to all these heretics. For in the Phædo he imagines that souls wander from this world to that, and thence back again hither; whilst in the Timæus he supposes that the children of God, to whom had been assigned the production of mortal creatures, having taken for the soul the germ of immortality, congealed around it a mortal body,--thereby indicating that this world is the figure of some other. Now, to procure belief in all this--that the soul had formerly lived with God in the heavens above, sharing His ideas with Him, and afterwards came down to live with us on earth, and whilst here recollects the eternal patterns of things which it had learnt before--he elaborated his new formula, μαθήσεις ἀναμνήσεις, which means that "learning is reminiscence;" implying that the souls which come to us from thence forget the things amongst which they formerly lived, but that they afterwards recall them, instructed by the objects they see around them. Forasmuch, therefore, as the doctrines which the heretics borrow from Plato are cunningly defended by this kind of argument, I shall sufficiently refute the heretics if I overthrow the argument of Plato.

Chapter XXIV - Plato's Inconsistency. He Supposes the Soul Self-Existent, Yet Capable of Forgetting What Passed in a Previous State

In the first place, I cannot allow that the soul is capable of a failure of memory; because he has conceded to it so large an amount of divine quality as to put it on a par with God. He makes it unborn, which single attribute I might apply as a sufficient attestation of its perfect divinity; he then adds that the soul is immortal, incorruptible, incorporeal--since he believed God to be the same--invisible, incapable of delineation, uniform, supreme, rational, and intellectual. What more could he attribute to the soul, if he wanted to call it God? We, however, who allow no appendage to God [1665] (in the sense of equality), by this very fact reckon the soul as very far below God: for we suppose it to be born, and hereby to possess something of a diluted divinity and an attenuated felicity, as the breath (of God), though not His spirit; and although immortal, as this is an attribute of divinity, yet for all that passible, since this is an incident of a born condition, and consequently from the first capable of deviation from perfection and right, [1666] and by consequence susceptible of a failure in memory. This point I have discussed sufficiently with Hermogenes. [1667] But it may be further observed, that if the soul is to merit being accounted a god, by reason of all its qualities being equal to the attributes of God, it must then be subject to no passion, and therefore to no loss of memory; for this defect of oblivion is as great an injury to that of which you predicate it, as memory is the glory thereof, which Plato himself deems the very safeguard of the senses and intellectual faculties, and which Cicero has designated the treasury of all the sciences. Now we need not raise the doubt whether so divine a faculty as the soul was capable of losing memory: the question rather is, whether it is able to recover afresh that which it has lost. I could not decide whether that, which ought to have lost memory, if it once incurred the loss, would be powerful enough to recollect itself. Both alternatives, indeed, will agree very well with my soul, but not with Plato's. In the second place, my objection to him will stand thus: (Plato,) do you endow the soul with a natural competency for understanding those well-known ideas of yours? Certainly I do, will be your answer. Well, now, no one will concede to you that the knowledge, (which you say is) the gift of nature, of the natural sciences can fail.

But the knowledge of the sciences fails; the knowledge of the various fields of learning and of the arts of life fails; and so perhaps the knowledge of the faculties and affections of our minds fails, although they seem to be inherent in our nature, but really are not so:

because, as we have already said, [1668] they are affected by accidents of place, of manners and customs, of bodily condition, of the state of man's health--by the influences of the Supreme Powers, and the changes of man's free-will.

Now the instinctive knowledge of natural objects never fails, not even in the brute creation. The lion, no doubt, will forget his ferocity, if surrounded by the softening influence of training; he may become, with his beautiful mane, the plaything of some Queen Berenice, and lick her cheeks with his tongue.

A wild beast may lay aside his habits, but his natural instincts will not be forgotten. He will not forget his proper food, nor his natural resources, nor his natural alarms; and should the queen offer him fishes or cakes, he will wish for flesh; and if, when he is ill, any antidote be prepared for him, he will still require the ape; and should no hunting-spear be presented against him, he will yet dread the crow of the cock. In like manner with man, who is perhaps the most forgetful of all creatures, the knowledge of everything natural to him will remain ineradicably fixed in him,--but this alone, as being alone a natural instinct. He will never forget to eat when he is hungry; or to drink when he is thirsty; or to use his eyes when he wants to see; or his ears, to hear; or his nose, to smell; or his mouth, to taste; or his hand, to touch.

These are, to be sure, the senses, which philosophy depreciates by her preference for the intellectual faculties.

But if the natural knowledge of the sensuous faculties is permanent, how happens it that the knowledge of the intellectual faculties fails, to which the superiority is ascribed? Whence, now, arises that power of forgetfulness itself which precedes recollection? From long lapse of time, he says. But this is a shortsighted answer. Length of time cannot be incidental to that which, according to him, is unborn, and which therefore must be deemed most certainly eternal. For that which is eternal, on the ground of its being unborn, since it admits neither of beginning nor end of time, is subject to no temporal criterion. And that which time does not measure, undergoes no change in consequence of time; nor is long lapse of time at all influential over it. If time is a cause of oblivion, why, from the time of the soul's entrance into the body, does memory fail, as if thenceforth the soul were to be affected by time? for the soul, being undoubtedly prior to the body, was of course not irrespective of time. Is it, indeed, immediately on the soul's entrance into the body that oblivion takes place, or some time afterwards? If immediately, where will be the long lapse of the time which is as yet inadmissible in the hypothesis? [1669] Take, for instance, the case of the infant. If some time afterwards, will not the soul, during the interval previous to the moment of oblivion, still exercise its powers of memory? And how comes it to pass that the soul subsequently forgets, and then afterwards again remembers? How long, too, must the lapse of the time be regarded as having been, during which the oblivion oppressed the soul? The whole course of one's life, I apprehend, will be insufficient to efface the memory of an age which endured so long before the soul's assumption of the body.

But then, again, Plato throws the blame upon the body, as if it were at all credible that a born substance could extinguish the power of one that is unborn. There exist, however, among bodies a great many differences, by reason of their rationality, their bulk, their condition, their age, and their health. Will there then be supposed to exist similar differences in obliviousness? Oblivion, however, is uniform and identical. Therefore bodily peculiarity, with its manifold varieties, will not become the cause of an effect which is an invariable one. There are likewise, according to Plato's own testimony, many proofs to show that the soul has a divining faculty, as we have already advanced against Hermogenes. But there is not a man living, who does not himself feel his soul possessed with a presage and augury of some omen, danger, or joy. Now, if the body is not prejudicial to divination, it will not, I suppose, be injurious to memory. One thing is certain, that souls in the same body both forget and remember. If any corporeal condition engenders forgetfulness, how will it admit the opposite state of recollection? Because recollection, after forgetfulness, is actually the resurrection of the memory. Now, how should not that which is hostile to the memory at first, be also prejudicial to it in the second instance? Lastly, who have better memories than little children, with their fresh, unworn souls, not yet immersed in domestic and public cares, but devoted only to those studies the acquirement of which is itself a reminiscence? Why, indeed, do we not all of us recollect in an equal degree, since we are equal in our forgetfulness? But this is true only of philosophers! But not even of the whole of them. Amongst so many nations, in so great a crowd of sages, Plato, to be sure, is the only man who has combined the oblivion and the recollection of ideas. Now, since this main argument of his by no means keeps its ground, it follows that its entire superstructure must fall with it, namely, that souls are supposed to be unborn, and to live in the heavenly regions, and to be instructed in the divine mysteries thereof; moreover, that they descend to this earth, and here recall to memory their previous existence, for the purpose, of course, of supplying to our heretics the fitting materials for their systems.

Chapter XXV - Tertullian Refutes, Physiologically, the Notion that the Soul is Introduced After Birth

I shall now return to the cause of this digression, in order that I may explain how all souls are derived from one, when and where and in what manner they are produced. Now, touching this subject, it matters not whether the question be started by the philosopher, by the heretic, or by the crowd. Those who profess the truth care nothing about their opponents, especially such of them as begin by maintaining that the soul is not conceived in the womb, nor is formed and produced at the time that the flesh is moulded, but is impressed from without upon the infant before his complete vitality, but after the process of parturition. They say, moreover, that the human seed having been duly deposited ex concubiterin the womb, and having been by natural impulse quickened, it becomes condensed into the mere substance of the flesh, which is in due time born, warm from the furnace of the womb, and then released from its heat. (This flesh) resembles the case of hot iron, which is in that state plunged into cold water; for, being smitten by the cold air (into which it is born), it at once receives the power of animation, and utters vocal sound. This view is entertained by the Stoics, along with Ænesidemus, and occasionally by Plato himself, when he tells us that the soul, being quite a separate formation, originating elsewhere and externally to the womb, is inhaled[1670] when the new-born infant first draws breath, and by and by exhaled [1671] with the man's latest breath. We shall see whether this view of his is merely fictitious. Even the medical profession has not lacked its Hicesius, to prove a traitor both to nature and his own calling. These gentlemen, I suppose, were too modest to come to terms with women on the mysteries of childbirth, so well known to the latter. But how much more is there for them to blush at, when in the end they have the women to refute them, instead of commending them. Now, in such a question as this, no one can be so useful a teacher, judge, or witness, as the sex itself which is so intimately concerned. Give us your testimony, then, ye mothers, whether yet pregnant, or after delivery (let barren women and men keep silence),--the truth of your own nature is in question, the reality of your own suffering is the point to be decided.

(Tell us, then,) whether you feel in the embryo within you any vital force [1672] other than your own, with which your bowels tremble, your sides shake, your entire womb throbs, and the burden which oppresses you constantly changes its position? Are these movements a joy to you, and a positive removal of anxiety, as making you confident that your infant both possesses vitality and enjoys it? Or, should his restlessness cease, your first fear would be for him; and he would be aware of it within you, since he is disturbed at the novel sound; and you would crave for injurious diet, [1673] or would even loathe your food--all on his account; and then you and he, (in the closeness of your sympathy,) would share together your common ailments--so far that with your contusions and bruises would he actually become marked,--whilst within you, and even on the selfsame parts of the body, taking to himself thus peremptorily [1674] the injuries of his mother! Now, whenever a livid hue and redness are incidents of the blood, the blood will not be without the vital principle, [1675] or soul; or when disease attacks the soul or vitality, (it becomes a proof of its real existence, since) there is no disease where there is no soul or principle of life. Again, inasmuch as sustenance by food, and the want thereof, growth and decay, fear and motion, are conditions of the soul or life, he who experiences them must be alive. And, so, he at last ceases to live, who ceases to experience them.

And thus by and by infants are still-born; but how so, unless they had life? For how could any die, who had not previously lived? But sometimes by a cruel necessity, whilst yet in the womb, an infant is put to death, when lying awry in the orifice of the womb he impedes parturition, and kills his mother, if he is not to die himself.

Accordingly, among surgeons' tools there is a certain instrument, which is formed with a nicely-adjusted flexible frame for opening the uterus first of all, and keeping it open; it is further furnished with an annular blade, [1676] by means of which the limbs within the womb are dissected with anxious but unfaltering care; its last appendage being a blunted or covered hook, wherewith the entire foetus is extracted [1677] by a violent delivery. There is also (another instrument in the shape of) a copper needle or spike, by which the actual death is managed in this furtive robbery of life: they give it, from its infanticide function, the name of ἐμβρυοσφάκτης , the slayer of the infant, which was of course alive. Such apparatus was possessed both by Hippocrates, and Asclepiades, and Erasistratus, and Herophilus, that dissector of even adults, and the milder Soranus himself, who all knew well enough that a living being had been conceived, and pitied this most luckless infant state, which had first to be put to death, to escape being tortured alive. Of the necessity of such harsh treatment I have no doubt even Hicesius was convinced, although he imported their soul into infants after birth from the stroke of the frigid air, because the very term for soul, forsooth, in Greek answered to such a refrigeration! [1678] Well, then, have the barbarian and Roman nations received souls by some other process, (I wonder;) for they have called the soul by another name than ψυχή? How many nations are there who commence life [1679] under the broiling sun of the torrid zone, scorching their skin into its swarthy hue? Whence do they get their souls, with no frosty air to help them?

I say not a word of those well-warmed bed-rooms, and all that apparatus of heat which ladies in childbirth so greatly need, when a breath of cold air might endanger their life. But in the very bath almost a babe will slip into life, and at once his cry is heard! If, however, a good frosty air is to the soul so indispensable a treasure, then beyond the German and the Scythian tribes, and the Alpine and the Argæan heights, nobody ought ever to be born! But the fact really is, that population is greater within the temperate regions of the East and the West, and men's minds are sharper; whilst there is not a Sarmatian whose wits are not dull and humdrum. The minds of men, too, would grow keener by reason of the cold, if their souls came into being amidst nipping frosts; for as the substance is, so must be its active power. Now, after these preliminary statements, we may also refer to the case of those who, having been cut out of their mother's womb, have breathed and retained life--your Bacchuses [1680] and Scipios. [1681] If, however, there be any one who, like Plato, [1682] supposes that two souls cannot, more than two bodies could, co-exist in the same individual, I, on the contrary, could show him not merely the co-existence of two souls in one person, as also of two bodies in the same womb, but likewise the combination of many other things in natural connection with the soul--for instance, of demoniacal possession; and that not of one only, as in the case of Socrates' own demon; but of seven spirits as in the case of the Magdalene;[1683] and of a legion in number, as in the Gadarene. [1684] Now one soul is naturally more susceptible of conjunction with another soul, by reason of the identity of their substance, than an evil spirit is, owing to their diverse natures. But when the same philosopher, in the sixth book of The Laws, warns us to beware lest a vitiation of seed should infuse a soil into both body and soul from an illicit or debased concubinage, I hardly know whether he is more inconsistent with himself in respect of one of his previous statements, or of that which he had just made. For he here shows us that the soul proceeds from human seed (and warns us to be on our guard about it), not, (as he had said before,) from the first breath of the new-born child. Pray, whence comes it that from similarity of soul we resemble our parents in disposition, according to the testimony of Cleanthes,[1685] if we are not produced from this seed of the soul? Why, too, used the old astrologers to cast a man's nativity from his first conception, if his soul also draws not its origin from that moment? To this (nativity) likewise belongs the inbreathing of the soul, whatever that is.

Chapter XXVI - Scripture Alone Offers Clear Knowledge on the Questions We Have Been Controverting

Now there is no end to the uncertainty and irregularity of human opinion, until we come to the limits which God has prescribed. I shall at last retire within our own lines and firmly hold my ground there, for the purpose of proving to the Christian (the soundness of) my answers to the Philosophers and the Physicians. Brother (in Christ), on your own foundation [1686] build up your faith. Consider the wombs of the most sainted women instinct with the life within them, and their babes which not only breathed therein, but were even endowed with prophetic intuition. See how the bowels of Rebecca are disquieted,[1687] though her child-bearing is as yet remote, and there is no impulse of (vital) air. Behold, a twin offspring chafes within the mother's womb, although she has no sign as yet of the twofold nation. Possibly we might have regarded as a prodigy the contention of this infant progeny, which struggled before it lived, which had animosity previous to animation, if it had simply disturbed the mother by its restlessness within her.

But when her womb opens, and the number of her offspring is seen, and their presaged condition known, we have presented to us a proof not merely of the (separate) souls of the infants, but of their hostile struggles too. He who was the first to be born was threatened with detention by him who was anticipated in birth, who was not yet fully brought forth, but whose hand only had been born. Now if he actually imbibed life, and received his soul, in Platonic style, at his first breath; or else, after the Stoic rule, had the earliest taste of animation on touching the frosty air; what was the other about, who was so eagerly looked for, who was still detained within the womb, and was trying to detain (the other) outside? I suppose he had not yet breathed when he seized his brother's heel; [1688] and was still warm with his mother's warmth, when he so strongly wished to be the first to quit the womb. What an infant! so emulous, so strong, and already so contentious; and all this, I suppose, because even now full of life!

Consider, again, those extraordinary conceptions, which were more wonderful still, of the barren woman and the virgin: these women would only be able to produce imperfect offspring against the course of nature, from the very fact that one of them was too old to bear seed, and the other was pure from the contact of man. If there was to be bearing at all in the case, it was only fitting that they should be born without a soul, (as the philosopher would say,) who had been irregularly conceived. However, even these have life, each of them in his mother's womb. Elizabeth exults with joy, (for) John had leaped in her womb; [1689] Mary magnifies the Lord, (for) Christ had instigated her within. [1690] The mothers recognise each their own offspring, being moreover each recognised by their infants, which were therefore of course alive, and were not souls merely, but spirits also. Accordingly you read the word of God which was spoken to Jeremiah, "Before I formed thee in the belly, I knew thee." [1691] Since God forms us in the womb, He also breathes upon us, as He also did at the first creation, when "the Lord God formed man, and breathed into him the breath of life." [1692] Nor could God have known man in the womb, except in his entire nature: "And before thou camest forth out of the womb, I sanctified thee."[1693] Well, was it then a dead body at that early stage? Certainly not. For "God is not the God of the dead, but of the living."

Chapter XXVII - Soul and Body Conceived, Formed and Perfected in Element Simultaneously

How, then, is a living being conceived? Is the substance of both body and soul formed together at one and the same time? Or does one of them precede the other in natural formation? We indeed maintain that both are conceived, and formed, and perfectly simultaneously, as well as born together; and that not a moment's interval occurs in their conception, so that, a prior place can be assigned to either. [1694] Judge, in fact, of the incidents of man's earliest existence by those which occur to him at the very last. As death is defined to be nothing else than the separation of body and soul, [1695] life, which is the opposite of death, is susceptible of no other definition than the conjunction of body and soul.

If the severance happens at one and the same time to both substances by means of death, so the law of their combination ought to assure us that it occurs simultaneously to the two substances by means of life. Now we allow that life begins with conception, because we contend that the soul also begins from conception; life taking its commencement at the same moment and place that the soul does. Thus, then, the processes which act together to produce separation by death, also combine in a simultaneous action to produce life. If we assign priority to (the formation of) one of the natures, and a subsequent time to the other, we shall have further to determine the precise times of the semination, according to the condition and rank of each. And that being so, what time shall we give to the seed of the body, and what to the seed of the soul? Besides, if different periods are to be assigned to the seminations then arising out of this difference in time, we shall also have different substances. [1696] For although we shall allow that there are two kinds of seed--that of the body and that of the soul--we still declare that they are inseparable, and therefore contemporaneous and simultaneous in origin. Now let no one take offence or feel ashamed at an interpretation of the processes of nature which is rendered necessary (by the defence of the truth). Nature should be to us an object of reverence, not of blushes. It is lust, not natural usage, which has brought shame on the intercourse of the sexes.

It is the excess, not the normal state, which is immodest and unchaste: the normal condition has received a blessing from God, and is blest by Him: "Be fruitful, and multiply, (and replenish the earth.)" [1697] Excess, however, has He cursed, in adulteries, and wantonness, and chambering.[1698] Well, now, in this usual function of the sexes which brings together the male and the female in their common intercourse, we know that both the soul and the flesh discharge a duty together: the soul supplies desire, the flesh contributes the gratification of it; the soul furnishes the instigation, the flesh affords the realization. The entire man being excited by the one effort of both natures, his seminal substance is discharged, deriving its fluidity from the body, and its warmth from the soul. Now if the soul in Greek is a word which is synonymous with cold, [1699] how does it come to pass that the body grows cold after the soul has quitted it? Indeed (if I run the risk of offending modesty even, in my desire to prove the truth), I cannot help asking, whether we do not, in that very heat of extreme gratification when the generative fluid is ejected, feel that somewhat of our soul has gone from us? And do we not experience a faintness and prostration along with a dimness of sight?

This, then, must be the soul-producing seed, which arises at once from the out-drip of the soul, just as that fluid is the body-producing seed which proceeds from the drainage of the flesh.

Most true are the examples of the first creation. Adam's flesh was formed of clay. Now what is clay but an excellent moisture, whence should spring the generating fluid?

From the breath of God first came the soul. But what else is the breath of God than the vapour of the spirit, whence should spring that which we breathe out through the generative fluid? Forasmuch, therefore, as these two different and separate substances, the clay and the breath, combined at the first creation in forming the individual man, they then both amalgamated and mixed their proper seminal rudiments in one, and ever afterwards communicated to the human race the normal mode of its propagation, so that even now the two substances, although diverse from each other, flow forth simultaneously in a united channel; and finding their way together into their appointed seed-plot, they fertilize with their combined vigour the human fruit out of their respective natures.

And inherent in this human product is his own seed, according to the process which has been ordained for every creature endowed with the functions of generation. Accordingly from the one (primeval) man comes the entire outflow and redundance of men's souls--nature proving herself true to the commandment of God, "Be fruitful, and multiply." [1700] For in the very preamble of this one production, "Let us make man," [1701] man's whole posterity was declared and described in a plural phrase, "Let them have dominion over the fish of the sea," etc. [1702] And no wonder: in the seed lies the promise and earnest of the crop.

Chapter XXVIII - The Pythagorean Doctrine of Transmigration Sketched and Censured

What, then, by this time means that ancient saying, mentioned by Plato, [1703] concerning the reciprocal migration of souls; how they remove hence and go thither, and then return hither and pass through life, and then again depart from this life, and afterwards become alive from the dead? Some will have it that this is a saying of Pythagoras; Albinus supposes it to be a divine announcement, perhaps of the Egyptian Mercury. [1704] But there is no divine saying, except of the one true God, by whom the prophets, and the apostles, and Christ Himself declared their grand message. More ancient than Saturn a good deal (by some nine hundred years or so), and even than his grandchildren, is Moses; and he is certainly much more divine, recounting and tracing out, as he does, the course of the human race from the very beginning of the world, indicating the several births (of the fathers of mankind) according to their names and their epochs; giving thus plain proof of the divine character of his work, from its divine authority and word. If, indeed, the sophist of Samos is Plato's authority for the eternally revolving migration of souls out of a constant alternation of the dead and the living states, then no doubt did the famous Pythagoras, however excellent in other respects, for the purpose of fabricating such an opinion as this, rely on a falsehood, which was not only shameful, but also hazardous. Consider it, you that are ignorant of it, and believe with us.

He feigns death, he conceals himself underground, he condemns himself to that endurance for some seven years, during which he learns from his mother, who was his sole accomplice and attendant, what he was to relate for the belief of the world concerning those who had died since his seclusion; [1705]

and when he thought that he had succeeded in reducing the frame of his body to the horrid appearance of a dead old man, he comes forth from the place of his concealment and deceit, and pretends to have returned from the dead. Who would hesitate about believing that the man, whom he had supposed to have died, was come back again to life? especially after hearing from him facts about the recently dead,[1706] which he evidently could only have discovered in Hades itself! Thus, that men are made alive after death, is rather an old statement. But what if it be rather a recent one also? The truth does not desire antiquity, nor does falsehood shun novelty. This notable saying I hold to be plainly false, though ennobled by antiquity. How should that not be false, which depends for its evidence on a falsehood?-- How can I help believing Pythagoras to be a deceiver, who practises deceit to win my belief? How will he convince me that, before he was Pythagoras, he had been Æthalides, and Euphorbus, and the fisherman Pyrrhus, and Hermotimus, to make us believe that men live again after they have died, when he actually perjured himself afterwards as Pythagoras. In proportion as it would be easier for me to believe that he had returned once to life in his own person, than so often in the person of this man and that, in the same degree has he deceived me in things which are too hard to be credited, because he has played the impostor in matters which might be readily believed. Well, but he recognised the shield of Euphorbus, which had been formerly consecrated at Delphi, and claimed it as his own, and proved his claim by signs which were generally unknown. Now, look again at his subterranean lurking-place, and believe his story, if you can. For, as to the man who devised such a tricksty scheme, to the injury of his health, fraudulently wasting his life, and torturing it for seven years underground, amidst hunger, idleness, and darkness--with a profound disgust for the mighty sky--what reckless effort would he not make, what curious contrivance would he not attempt, to arrive at the discovery of this famous shield? Suppose now, that he found it in some of those hidden researches; suppose that he recovered some slight breath of report which survived the now obsolete tradition; suppose him to have come to the knowledge of it by an inspection which he had bribed the beadle to let him have,--we know very well what are the resources of magic skill for exploring hidden secrets: there are the catabolic spirits, which floor their victims; [1707] and the paredral spirits, which are ever at their side [1708] to haunt them; and the pythonic spirits, which entrance them by their divination and ventriloquistic[1709] arts. For was it not likely that Pherecydes also, the master of our Pythagoras, used to divine, or I would rather say rave and dream, by such arts and contrivances as these? Might not the self-same demon have been in him, who, whilst in Euphorbus, transacted deeds of blood? But lastly, why is it that the man, who proved himself to have been Euphorbus by the evidence of the shield, did not also recognise any of his former Trojan comrades? For they, too, must by this time have recovered life, since men were rising again from the dead.

Chapter XXIX - The Pythagorean Doctrine Refuted by Its Own First Principle, that Living Men are Formed from the Dead

It is indeed, manifest that dead men are formed from living ones; but it does not follow from that, that living men are formed from dead ones. For from the beginning the living came first in the order of things, and therefore also from the beginning the dead came afterwards in order. But these proceeded from no other source except from the living. The living had their origin in any other source (you please) than in the dead; whilst the dead had no source whence to derive their beginning, except from the living. If, then, from the very first the living came not from the dead, why should they afterwards (be said to) come from the dead? Had that original source, whatever it was, come to an end? Was the form or law thereof a matter for regret? Then why was it preserved in the case of the dead? Does it not follow that, because the dead came from the living at the first, therefore they always came from the living? For either the law which obtained at the beginning must have continued in both of its relations, or else it must have changed in both; so that, if it had become necessary for the living afterwards to proceed from the dead, it would be necessary, in like manner, for the dead also not to proceed from the living. For if a faithful adherence to the institution was not meant to be perpetuated in each respect, then contraries cannot in due alternation continue to be re-formed from contraries. We, too, will on our side adduce against you certain contraries, of the born and the unborn, of vision [1710] and blindness, of youth and old age, of wisdom and folly. Now it does not follow that the unborn proceeds from the born, on the ground that a contrary issues from a contrary; nor, again, that vision proceeds from blindness, because blindness happens to vision; nor, again, that youth revives from old age, because after youth comes the decrepitude of senility; nor that folly [1711] is born with its obtuseness from wisdom, because wisdom may possibly be sometimes sharpened out of folly.

Albinus has some fears for his (master and friend) Plato in these points, and labours with much ingenuity to distinguish different kinds of contraries; as if these instances did not as absolutely partake of the nature of contrariety as those which are expounded by him to illustrate his great master's principle--I mean, life and death.

Nor is it, for the matter of that, true that life is restored out of death, because it happens that death succeeds [1712] life.

Chapter XXX - Further Refutation of the Pythagorean Theory

The State of Contemporary Civilisation.

But what must we say in reply to what follows? For, in the first place, if the living come from the dead, just as the dead proceed from the living, then there must always remain unchanged one and the selfsame number of mankind, even the number which originally introduced (human) life. The living preceded the dead, afterwards the dead issued from the living, and then again the living from the dead. Now, since this process was evermore going on with the same persons, therefore they, issuing from the same, must always have remained in number the same. For they who emerged (into life) could never have become more nor fewer than they who disappeared (in death). We find, however, in the records of the Antiquities of Man, [1713] that the human race has progressed with a gradual growth of population, either occupying different portions of the earth as aborigines, or as nomad tribes, or as exiles, or as conquerors--as the Scythians in Parthia, the Temenidæ in Peloponnesus, the Athenians in Asia, the Phrygians in Italy, and the Phoenicians in Africa; or by the more ordinary methods of migration, which they call ἀποικίαι or colonies, for the purpose of throwing off redundant population, disgorging into other abodes their overcrowded masses. The aborigines remain still in their old settlements, and have also enriched other districts with loans of even larger populations. Surely it is obvious enough, if one looks at the whole world, that it is becoming daily better cultivated and more fully peopled than anciently. All places are now accessible, all are well known, all open to commerce; most pleasant farms have obliterated all traces of what were once dreary and dangerous wastes; cultivated fields have subdued forests; flocks and herds have expelled wild beasts; sandy deserts are sown; rocks are planted; marshes are drained; and where once were hardly solitary cottages, there are now large cities. No longer are (savage) islands dreaded, nor their rocky shores feared; everywhere are houses, and inhabitants, and settled government, and civilized life. What most frequently meets our view (and occasions complaint), is our teeming population: our numbers are burdensome to the world, which can hardly supply us from its natural elements; our wants grow more and more keen, and our complaints more bitter in all mouths, whilst Nature fails in affording us her usual sustenance. In very deed, pestilence, and famine, and wars, and earthquakes have to be regarded as a remedy for nations, as the means of pruning the luxuriance of the human race; and yet, when the hatchet has once felled large masses of men, the world has hitherto never once been alarmed at the sight of a restitution of its dead coming back to life after their millennial exile. [1714] But such a spectacle would have become quite obvious by the balance of mortal loss and vital recovery, if it were true that the dead came back again to life. Why, however, is it after a thousand years, and not at the moment, that this return from death is to take place, when, supposing that the loss is not at once supplied, there must be a risk of an utter extinction, as the failure precedes the compensation? Indeed, this furlough of our present life would be quite disproportioned to the period of a thousand years; so much briefer is it, and on that account so much more easily is its torch extinguished than rekindled.

Inasmuch, then, as the period which, on the hypothesis we have discussed, ought to intervene, if the living are to be formed from the dead, has not actually occurred, it will follow that we must not believe that men come back to life from the dead (in the way surmised in this philosophy).

Chapter XXXI - Further Exposure of Transmigration, Its Inextricable Embarrassment

Again, if this recovery of life from the dead take place at all, individuals must of course resume their own individuality. Therefore the souls which animated each several body must needs have returned separately to their several bodies. Now, whenever two, or three, or five souls are re-enclosed (as they constantly are) in one womb, it will not amount in such cases to life from the dead, because there is not the separate restitution which individuals ought to have; although at this rate, (no doubt,) the law of the primeval creation is signally kept, [1715] by the production still of several souls out of only one! Then, again, if souls depart at different ages of human life, how is it that they come back again at one uniform age? For all men are imbued with an infant soul at their birth. But how happens it that a man who dies in old age returns to life as an infant? If the soul, whilst disembodied, decreases thus by retrogression of its age, how much more reasonable would it be, that it should resume its life with a richer progress in all attainments of life after the lapse of a thousand years! At all events, it should return with the age it had attained at its death, that it might resume the precise life which it had relinquished. But even if, at this rate, they should reappear the same evermore in their revolving cycles, it would be proper for them to bring back with them, if not the selfsame forms of body, at least their original peculiarities of character, taste, and disposition, because it would be hardly possible [1716] for them to be regarded as the same, if they were deficient in those characteristics by means of which their identity should be proved. (You, however, meet me with this question): How can you possibly know, you ask, whether all is not a secret process? may not the work of a thousand years take from you the power of recognition, since they return unknown to you? But I am quite certain that such is not the case, for you yourself present Pythagoras to me as (the restored) Euphorbus. Now look at Euphorbus: he was evidently possessed of a military and warlike soul, as is proved by the very renown of the sacred shields. As for Pythagoras, however, he was such a recluse, and so unwarlike, that he shrank from the military exploits of which Greece was then so full, and preferred to devote himself, in the quiet retreat of Italy, to the study of geometry, and astrology, and music--the very opposite to Euphorbus in taste and disposition.

Then, again, the Pyrrhus (whom he represented) spent his time in catching fish; but Pythagoras, on the contrary, would never touch fish, abstaining from even the taste of them as from animal food. Moreover, Æthalides and Hermotimus had included the bean amongst the common esculents at meals, while Pythagoras taught his disciples not even to pass through a plot which was cultivated with beans. I ask, then, how the same souls are resumed, which can offer no proof of their identity, either by their disposition, or habits, or living? And now, after all, (we find that) only four souls are mentioned as recovering life [1717] out of all the multitudes of Greece. But limiting ourselves merely to Greece, as if no transmigrations of souls and resumptions of bodies occurred, and that every day, in every nation, and amongst all ages, ranks, and sexes, how is it that Pythagoras alone experiences these changes into one personality and another? Why should not I too undergo them? Or if it be a privilege monopolized by philosophers--and Greek philosophers only, as if Scythians and Indians had no philosophers--how is it that Epicurus had no recollection that he had been once another man, nor Chrysippus, nor Zeno, nor indeed Plato himself, whom we might perhaps have supposed to have been Nestor, from his honeyed eloquence?

Chapter XXXII - Empedocles Increased the Absurdity of Pythagoras by Developing the Posthumous Change of Men into Various Animals

But the fact is, Empedocles, who used to dream that he was a god, and on that account, I suppose, disdained to have it thought that he had ever before been merely some hero, declares in so many words: "I once was Thamnus, and a fish." Why not rather a melon, seeing that he was such a fool; or a cameleon, for his inflated brag? It was, no doubt, as a fish (and a queer one too!) that he escaped the corruption of some obscure grave, when he preferred being roasted by a plunge into Ætna; after which accomplishment there was an end for ever to his μετενσωμάτωσις or putting himself into another body-- (fit only now for) a light dish after the roast-meat. At this point, therefore, we must likewise contend against that still more monstrous presumption, that in the course of the transmigration beasts pass from human beings, and human beings from beasts. Let (Empedocles') Thamnuses alone. Our slight notice of them in passing will be quite enough: (to dwell on them longer will inconvenience us,) lest we should be obliged to have recourse to raillery and laughter instead of serious instruction. Now our position is this: that the human soul cannot by any means at all be transferred to beasts, even when they are supposed to originate, according to the philosophers, out of the substances of the elements. Now let us suppose that the soul is either fire, or water, or blood, or spirit, or air, or light; we must not forget that all the animals in their several kinds have properties which are opposed to the respective elements. There are the cold animals which are opposed to fire--water-snakes, lizards, salamanders, and what things soever are produced out of the rival element of water. In like manner, those creatures are opposite to water which are in their nature dry and sapless; indeed, locusts, butterflies, and chameleons rejoice in droughts. So, again, such creatures are opposed to blood which have none of its purple hue, such as snails, worms, and most of the fishy tribes. Then opposed to spirit are those creatures which seem to have no respiration, being unfurnished with lungs and windpipes, such as gnats, ants, moths, and minute things of this sort. Opposed, moreover, to air are those creatures which always live under ground and under water, and never imbibe air--things of which you are more acquainted with the existence than with the names. Then opposed to light are those things which are either wholly blind, or possess eyes for the darkness only, such as moles, bats, and owls. These examples (have I adduced), that I might illustrate my subject from clear and palpable natures. But even if I could take in my hand the "atoms" of Epicurus, or if my eye could see the "numbers" of Pythagoras, or if my foot could stumble against the "ideas" of Plato, or if I could lay hold of the "entelechies" of Aristotle, the chances would be, that even in these (impalpable) classes I should find such animals as I must oppose to one another on the ground of their contrariety. For I maintain that, of whichsoever of the before-mentioned natures the human soul is composed, it would not have been possible for it to pass for new forms into animals so contrary to each of the separate natures, and to bestow an origin by its passage on those beings, from which it would have to be excluded and rejected rather than to be admitted and received, by reason of that original contrariety which we have supposed it to possess, [1718] and which commits the bodily substance receiving it to an interminable strife; and then again by reason of the subsequent contrariety, which results from the development inseparable from each several nature. Now it is on quite different conditions [1719] that the soul of man has had assigned to it (in individual bodies [1720]) its abode, and aliment, and order, and sensation, and affection, and sexual intercourse, and procreation of children; also (on different conditions has it, in individual bodies, received especial) dispositions, as well as duties to fulfil, likings, dislikes, vices, desires, pleasures, maladies, remedies--in short, its own modes of living, its own outlets of death. How, then, shall that (human) soul which cleaves to the earth, and is unable without alarm to survey any great height, or any considerable depth, and which is also fatigued if it mounts many steps, and is suffocated if it is submerged in a fish-pond,--(how, I say, shall a soul which is beset with such weaknesses) mount up at some future stage into the air in an eagle, or plunge into the sea in an eel?

How, again, shall it, after being nourished with generous and delicate as well as exquisite viands, feed deliberately on, I will not say husks, but even on thorns, and the wild fare of bitter leaves, and beasts of the dung-hill, and poisonous worms, if it has to migrate into a goat or into a quail?--nay, it may be, feed on carrion, even on human corpses in some bear or lion? But how indeed (shall it stoop to this), when it remembers its own (nature and dignity)? In the same way, you may submit all other instances to this criterion of incongruity, and so save us from lingering over the distinct consideration of each of them in turn. Now, whatever may be the measure and whatever the mode of the human soul, (the question is forced upon us,) what it will do in far larger animals, or in very diminutive ones? It must needs be, that every individual body of whatever size is filled up by the soul, and that the soul is entirely covered by the body. How, therefore, shall a man's soul fill an elephant?

How, likewise, shall it be contracted within a gnat? If it be so enormously extended or contracted, it will no doubt be exposed to peril. And this induces me to ask another question: If the soul is by no means capable of this kind of migration into animals, which are not fitted for its reception, either by the habits of their bodies or the other laws of their being, will it then undergo a change according to the properties of various animals, and be adapted to their life, notwithstanding its contrariety to human life-- having, in fact, become contrary to its human self by reason of its utter change? Now the truth is, if it undergoes such a transformation, and loses what it once was, the human soul will not be what it was; and if it ceases to be its former self, the μετενσωμάτωσις, or adaptation of some other body, comes to nought, and is not of course to be ascribed to the soul which will cease to exist, on the supposition of its complete change. For only then can a soul be said to experience this process of the μετενσωμάτωσις, when it undergoes it by remaining unchanged in its own (primitive) condition. Since, therefore, the soul does not admit of change, lest it should cease to retain its identity; and yet is unable to remain unchanged in its original state, because it fails then to receive contrary (bodies),--I still want to know some credible reason to justify such a transformation as we are discussing. For although some men are compared to the beasts because of their character, disposition, and pursuits (since even God says, "Man is like the beasts that perish" [1721]), it does not on this account follow that rapacious persons become kites, lewd persons dogs, ill-tempered ones panthers, good men sheep, talkative ones swallows, and chaste men doves, as if the selfsame substance of the soul everywhere repeated its own nature in the properties of the animals (into which it passed). Besides, a substance is one thing, and the nature of that substance is another thing; inasmuch as the substance is the special property of one given thing, whereas the nature thereof may possibly belong to many things.

Take an example or two. A stone or a piece of iron is the substance: the hardness of the stone and the iron is the nature of the substance. Their hardness combines objects by a common quality; their substances keep them separate.

Then, again, there is softness in wool, and softness in a feather: their natural qualities are alike, (and put them on a par;) their substantial qualities are not alike, (and keep them distinct.) Thus, if a man likewise be designated a wild beast or a harmless one, there is not for all that an identity of soul. Now the similarity of nature is even then observed, when dissimilarity of substance is most conspicuous: for, by the very fact of your judging that a man resembles a beast, you confess that their soul is not identical; for you say that they resemble each other, not that they are the same. This is also the meaning of the word of God (which we have just quoted): it likens man to the beasts in nature, but not in substance. Besides, God would not have actually made such a comment as this concerning man, if He had known him to be in substance only bestial.

Tertullian

Chapter XXXIII - The Judicial Retribution of These Migrations Refuted with Raillery

Forasmuch as this doctrine is vindicated even on the principle of judicial retribution, on the pretence that the souls of men obtain as their partners the kind of animals which are suited to their life and deserts,--as if they ought to be, according to their several characters, either slain in criminals destined to execution, or reduced to hard work in menials, or fatigued and wearied in labourers, or foully disgraced in the unclean; or, again, on the same principle, reserved for honour, and love, and care, and attentive regard in characters most eminent in rank and virtue, usefulness, and tender sensibility,--I must here also remark, that if souls undergo a transformation, they will actually not be able to accomplish and experience the destinies which they shall deserve; and the aim and purpose of judicial recompense will be brought to nought, as there will be wanting the sense and consciousness of merit and retribution. And there must be this want of consciousness, if souls lose their condition; and there must ensue this loss, if they do not continue in one stay. But even if they should have permanency enough to remain unchanged until the judgment,--a point which Mercurius Ægyptius recognised, when he said that the soul, after its separation from the body, was not dissipated back into the soul of the universe, but retained permanently its distinct individuality, "in order that it might render," to use his own words, "an account to the Father of those things which it has done in the body;" --(even supposing all this, I say,) I still want to examine the justice, the solemnity, the majesty, and the dignity of this reputed judgment of God, and see whether human judgment has not too elevated a throne in it--exaggerated in both directions, in its office both of punishments and rewards, too severe in dealing out its vengeance, and too lavish in bestowing its favour. What do you suppose will become of the soul of the murderer? (It will animate), I suppose, some cattle destined for the slaughter-house and the shambles, that it may itself be killed, even as it has killed; and be itself flayed, since it has fleeced others; and be itself used for food, since it has cast to the wild beasts the ill-fated victims whom it once slew in woods and lonely roads. Now, if such be the judicial retribution which it is to receive, is not such a soul likely to find more of consolation than of punishment, in the fact that it receives its coup de grâce from the hands of most expert practitioners--is buried with condiments served in the most piquant styles of an Apicius or a Lurco, is introduced to the tables of your exquisite Ciceros, is brought up on the most splendid dishes of a Sylla, finds its obsequies in a banquet, is devoured by respectable (mouths) on a par with itself, rather than by kites and wolves, so that all may see how it has got a man's body for its tomb, and has risen again after returning to its own kindred race--exulting in the face of human judgments, if it has experienced them? For these barbarous sentences of death consign to various wild beasts, which are selected and trained even against their nature for their horrible office the criminal who has committed murder, even while yet alive; nay, hindered from too easily dying, by a contrivance which retards his last moment in order to aggravate his punishment. But even if his soul should have anticipated by its departure the sword's last stroke, his body at all events must not escape the weapon: retribution for his own crime is yet exacted by stabbing his throat and stomach, and piercing his side. After that he is flung into the fire, that his very grave may be cheated. [1722] In no other way, indeed, is a sepulture allowed him. Not that any great care, after all, is bestowed on his pyre, so that other animals light upon his remains. At any rate, no mercy is shown to his bones, no indulgence to his ashes, which must be punished with exposure and nakedness. The vengeance which is inflicted among men upon the homicide is really as great as that which is imposed by nature. Who would not prefer the justice of the world, which, as the apostle himself testifies, "beareth not the sword in vain," [1723] and which is an institute of religion when it severely avenges in defence of human life? When we contemplate, too, the penalties awarded to other crimes--gibbets, and holocausts, and sacks, and harpoons, and precipices--who would not think it better to receive his sentence in the courts of Pythagoras and Empedocles?

For even the wretches whom they will send into the bodies of asses and mules to be punished by drudgery and slavery, how will they congratulate themselves on the mild labour of the mill and the water-wheel, when they recollect the mines, and the convict-gangs, and the public works, and even the prisons and black-holes, terrible in their idle, do-nothing routine? Then, again, in the case of those who, after a course of integrity, have surrendered their life to the Judge, I likewise look for rewards, but I rather discover punishments. To be sure, it must be a handsome gain for good men to be restored to life in any animals whatsoever! Homer, so dreamt Ennius, remembered that he was once a peacock; however, I cannot for my part believe poets, even when wide awake. A peacock, no doubt, is a very pretty bird, pluming itself, at will, on its splendid feathers; but then its wings do not make amends for its voice, which is harsh and unpleasant; and there is nothing that poets like better than a good song. His transformation, therefore, into a peacock was to Homer a penalty, not an honour.

The world's remuneration will bring him a much greater joy, when it lauds him as the father of the liberal sciences; and he will prefer the ornaments of his fame to the graces of his tail! But never mind! let poets migrate into peacocks, or into swans, if you like, especially as swans have a respectable voice:

in what animal will you invest that righteous hero Æacus? In what beast will you clothe the chaste and excellent Dido?

What bird shall fall to the lot of Patience? what animal to the lot of Holiness? what fish to that of Innocence?

Now all creatures are the servants of man; all are his subjects, all his dependants. If by and by he is to become one of these creatures, he is by such a change debased and degraded, he to whom, for his virtues, images, statues, and titles are freely awarded as public honours and distinguished privileges, he to whom the senate and the people vote even sacrifices! Oh, what judicial sentences for gods to pronounce, as men's recompense after death! They are more mendacious than any human judgments; they are contemptible as punishments, disgusting as rewards; such as the worst of men could never fear, nor the best desire; such indeed, as criminals will aspire to, rather than saints,--the former, that they may escape more speedily the world's stern sentence,--the latter that they may more tardily incur it. How well, (forsooth), O ye philosophers do you teach us, and how usefully do you advise us, that after death rewards and punishments fall with lighter weight! whereas, if any judgment awaits souls at all, it ought rather to be supposed that it will be heavier at the conclusion of life than in the conduct [1724] thereof, since nothing is more complete than that which comes at the very last--nothing, moreover, is more complete than that which is especially divine. Accordingly, God's judgment will be more full and complete, because it will be pronounced at the very last, in an eternal irrevocable sentence, both of punishment and of consolation, (on men whose) souls are not to transmigrate into beasts, but are to return into their own proper bodies. And all this once for all, and on "that day, too, of which the Father only knoweth;" [1725] (only knoweth,) in order that by her trembling expectation faith may make full trial of her anxious sincerity, keeping her gaze ever fixed on that day, in her perpetual ignorance of it, daily fearing that for which she yet daily hopes.

Chapter XXXIV - These Vagaries Stimulated Some Profane Corruptions of Christianity. The Profanity of Simon Magus Condemned

No tenet, indeed, under cover of any heresy has as yet burst upon us, embodying any such extravagant fiction as that the souls of human beings pass into the bodies of wild beasts; but yet we have deemed it necessary to attack and refute this conceit, as a consistent sequel to the preceding opinions, in order that Homer in the peacock might be got rid of as effectually as Pythagoras in Euphorbus; and in order that, by the demolition of the metempsychosis and μετενσωμάτωσις by the same blow, the ground might be cut away which has furnished no inconsiderable support to our heretics. There is the (infamous) Simon of Samaria in the Acts of the Apostles, who chaffered for the Holy Ghost: after his condemnation by Him, and a vain remorse that he and his money must perish together, [1726] he applied his energies to the destruction of the truth, as if to console himself with revenge. Besides the support with which his own magic arts furnished him, he had recourse to imposture, and purchased a Tyrian woman of the name of Helen out of a brothel, with the same money which he had offered for the Holy Spirit,--a traffic worthy of the wretched man. He actually feigned himself to be the Supreme Father, and further pretended that the woman was his own primary conception, wherewith he had purposed the creation of the angels and the archangels; that after she was possessed of this purpose she sprang forth from the Father and descended to the lower spaces, and there anticipating the Father's design had produced the angelic powers, which knew nothing of the Father, the Creator of this world; that she was detained a prisoner by these from a (rebellious) motive very like her own, lest after her departure from them they should appear to be the offspring of another being; and that, after being on this account exposed to every insult, to prevent her leaving them anywhere after her dishonour, she was degraded even to the form of man, to be confined, as it were, in the bonds of the flesh. Having during many ages wallowed about in one female shape and another, she became the notorious Helen who was so ruinous to Priam, and afterwards to the eyes of Stesichorus, whom, she blinded in revenge for his lampoons, and then restored to sight to reward him for his eulogies. After wandering about in this way from body to body, she, in her final disgrace, turned out a viler Helen still as a professional prostitute. This wench, therefore, was the lost sheep, upon whom the Supreme Father, even Simon, descended, who, after he had recovered her and brought her back--whether on his shoulders or loins I cannot tell--cast an eye on the salvation of man, in order to gratify his spleen by liberating them from the angelic powers. Moreover, to deceive these he also himself assumed a visible shape; and feigning the appearance of a man amongst men, he acted the part of the Son in Judea, and of the Father in Samaria. O hapless Helen, what a hard fate is yours between the poets and the heretics, who have blackened your fame sometimes with adultery, sometimes with prostitution!

Only her rescue from Troy is a more glorious affair than her extrication from the brothel. There were a thousand ships to remove her from Troy; a thousand pence were probably more than enough to withdraw her from the stews. Fie on you, Simon, to be so tardy in seeking her out, and so inconstant in ransoming her! How different from Menelaus! As soon as he has lost her, he goes in pursuit of her; she is no sooner ravished than he begins his search; after a ten years' conflict he boldly rescues her:

there is no lurking, no deceiving, no cavilling. I am really afraid that he was a much better "Father," who laboured so much more vigilantly, bravely, and perseveringly, about the recovery of his Helen.

Chapter XXXV - The Opinions of Carpocrates, Another Offset from the Pythagorean Dogmas, Stated and Confuted

However, it is not for you alone, (Simon), that the transmigration philosophy has fabricated this story. Carpocrates also makes equally good use of it, who was a magician and a fornicator like yourself, only he had not a Helen. [1727] And why should he not? since he asserted that souls are reinvested with bodies, in order to ensure the overthrow by all means of divine and human truth. For, (according to his miserable doctrine,) this life became consummated to no man until all those blemishes which are held to disfigure it have been fully displayed in its conduct; because there is nothing which is accounted evil by nature, but simply as men think of it.

The transmigration of human souls, therefore, into any kind of heterogeneous bodies, he thought by all means indispensable, whenever any depravity whatever had not been fully perpetrated in the early stage of life's passage. Evil deeds (one may be sure) appertain to life. Moreover, as often as the soul has fallen short as a defaulter in sin, it has to be recalled to existence, until it "pays the utmost farthing," [1728] thrust out from time to time into the prison of the body. To this effect does he tamper with the whole of that allegory of the Lord which is extremely clear and simple in its meaning, and ought to be from the first understood in its plain and natural sense. Thus our "adversary" (therein mentioned [1729]) is the heathen man, who is walking with us along the same road of life which is common to him and ourselves. Now "we must needs go out of the world," [1730] if it be not allowed us to have conversation with them. He bids us, therefore, show a kindly disposition to such a man. "Love your enemies," says He, "pray for them that curse you,"[1731] lest such a man in any transaction of business be irritated by any unjust conduct of yours, and "deliver thee to the judge" of his own (nation [1732]), and you be thrown into prison, and be detained in its close and narrow cell until you have liquidated all your debt against him.[1733] Then, again, should you be disposed to apply the term "adversary" to the devil, you are advised by the (Lord's) injunction, "while you are in the way with him," to make even with him such a compact as may be deemed compatible with the requirements of your true faith. Now the compact you have made respecting him is to renounce him, and his pomp, and his angels. Such is your agreement in this matter. Now the friendly understanding you will have to carry out must arise from your observance of the compact: you must never think of getting back any of the things which you have abjured, and have restored to him, lest he should summon you as a fraudulent man, and a transgressor of your agreement, before God the Judge (for in this light do we read of him, in another passage, as "the accuser of the brethren," [1734] or saints, where reference is made to the actual practice of legal prosecution); and lest this Judge deliver you over to the angel who is to execute the sentence, and he commit you to the prison of hell, out of which there will be no dismissal until the smallest even of your delinquencies be paid off in the period before the resurrection. [1735] What can be a more fitting sense than this? What a truer interpretation? If, however, according to Carpocrates, the soul is bound to the commission of all sorts of crime and evil conduct, what must we from his system understand to be its "adversary" and foe? I suppose it must be that better mind which shall compel it by force to the performance of some act of virtue, that it may be driven from body to body, until it be found in none a debtor to the claims of a virtuous life. This means, that a good tree is known by its bad fruit--in other words, that the doctrine of truth is understood from the worst possible precepts.

I apprehend [1736] that heretics of this school seize with especial avidity the example of Elias, whom they assume to have been so reproduced in John (the Baptist) as to make our Lord's statement sponsor for their theory of transmigration, when He said, "Elias is come already, and they knew him not;" [1737] and again, in another passage, "And if ye will receive it, this is Elias, which was for to come." [1738] Well, then, was it really in a Pythagorean sense that the Jews approached John with the inquiry, "Art thou Elias?" [1739] and not rather in the sense of the divine prediction, "Behold, I will send you Elijah" the Tisbite? [1740] The fact, however, is, that their metempsychosis, or transmigration theory, signifies the recall of the soul which had died long before, and its return to some other body. But Elias is to come again, not after quitting life (in the way of dying), but after his translation (or removal without dying); not for the purpose of being restored to the body, from which he had not departed, but for the purpose of

215

revisiting the world from which he was translated; not by way of resuming a life which he had laid aside, but of fulfilling prophecy,--really and truly the same man, both in respect of his name and designation, as well as of his unchanged humanity. How, therefore could John be Elias? You have your answer in the angel's announcement: "And he shall go before the people," says he, "in the spirit and power of Elias"--not (observe) in his soul and his body. These substances are, in fact, the natural property of each individual; whilst "the spirit and power" are bestowed as external gifts by the grace of God and so may be transferred to another person according to the purpose and will of the Almighty, as was anciently the case with respect to the spirit of Moses. [1741]

Chapter XXXVI - The Main Points of Our Author's Subject. On the Sexes of the Human Race

For the discussion of these questions we abandoned, if I remember rightly, ground to which we must now return. We had established the position that the soul is seminally placed in man, and by human agency, and that its seed from the very beginning is uniform, as is that of the soul also, to the race of man; (and this we settled) owing to the rival opinions of the philosophers and the heretics, and that ancient saying mentioned by Plato (to which we referred above). [1742] We now pursue in their order the points which follow from them. The soul, being sown in the womb at the same time as the body, receives likewise along with it its sex; and this indeed so simultaneously, that neither of the two substances can be alone regarded as the cause of the sex.

Now, if in the semination of these substances any interval were admissible in their conception, in such wise that either the flesh or the soul should be the first to be conceived, one might then ascribe an especial sex to one of the substances, owing to the difference in the time of the impregnations, so that either the flesh would impress its sex upon the soul, or the soul upon the sex; even as Apelles (the heretic, not the painter [1743]) gives the priority over their bodies to the souls of men and women, as he had been taught by Philumena, and in consequence makes the flesh, as the later, receive its sex from the soul. They also who make the soul supervene after birth on the flesh predetermine, of course, the sex of the previously formed soul to be male or female, according to (the sex of) the flesh. But the truth is, the seminations of the two substances are inseparable in point of time, and their effusion is also one and the same, in consequence of which a community of gender is secured to them; so that the course of nature, whatever that be, shall draw the line (for the distinct sexes).

Certainly in this view we have an attestation of the method of the first two formations, when the male was moulded and tempered in a completer way, for Adam was first formed; and the woman came far behind him, for Eve was the later formed. So that her flesh was for a long time without specific form (such as she afterwards assumed when taken out of Adam's side); but she was even then herself a living being, because I should regard her at that time in soul as even a portion of Adam. Besides, God's afflatus would have animated her too, if there had not been in the woman a transmission from Adam of his soul also as well as of his flesh.

Chapter XXXVII - On the Formation and State of the Embryo. Its Relation with the Subject of This Treatise

Now the entire process of sowing, forming, and completing the human embryo in the womb is no doubt regulated by some power, which ministers herein to the will of God, whatever may be the method which it is appointed to employ. Even the superstition of Rome, by carefully attending to these points, imagined the goddess Alemona to nourish the foetus in the womb; as well as (the goddesses) Nona and Decima, called after the most critical months of gestation; and Partula, to manage and direct parturition; and Lucina, to bring the child to the birth and light of day. We, on our part, believe the angels to officiate herein for God. The embryo therefore becomes a human being in the womb from the moment that its form is completed. The law of Moses, indeed, punishes with due penalties the man who shall cause abortion, inasmuch as there exists already the rudiment of a human being, [1744] which has imputed to it even now the condition of life and death, since it is already liable to the issues of both, although, by living still in the mother, it for the most part shares its own state with the mother. I must also say something about the period of the soul's birth, that I may omit nothing incidental in the whole process. A mature and regular birth takes place, as a general rule, at the commencement of the tenth month. They who theorize respecting numbers, honour the number ten as the parent of all the others, and as imparting perfection to the human nativity. For my own part, I prefer viewing this measure of time in reference to God, as if implying that the ten months rather initiated man into the ten commandments; so that the numerical estimate of the time needed to consummate our natural birth should correspond to the numerical classification of the rules of our regenerate life. But inasmuch as birth is also completed with the seventh month, I more readily recognize in this number than in the eighth the honour of a numerical agreement with the sabbatical period; so that the month in which God's image is sometimes produced in a human birth, shall in its number tally with the day on which God's creation was completed and hallowed. Human nativity has sometimes been allowed to be premature, and yet to occur in fit and perfect accordance with an hebdomad or sevenfold number, as an auspice of our resurrection, and rest, and kingdom. The ogdoad, or eightfold number, therefore, is not concerned in our formation; [1745] for in the time it represents there will be no more marriage. [1746] We have already demonstrated the conjunction of the body and the soul, from the concretion of their very seminations to the complete formation of the foetus. We now maintain their conjunction likewise from the birth onwards; in the first place, because they both grow together, only each in a different manner suited to the diversity of their nature--the flesh in magnitude, the soul in intelligence--the flesh in material condition, the soul in sensibility. We are, however, forbidden to suppose that the soul increases in substance, lest it should be said also to be capable of diminution in substance, and so its extinction even should be believed to be possible; but its inherent power, in which are contained all its natural peculiarities, as originally implanted in its being, is gradually developed along with the flesh, without impairing the germinal basis of the substance, which it received when breathed at first into man. Take a certain quantity of gold or of silver--a rough mass as yet: it has indeed a compact condition, and one that is more compressed at the moment than it will be; yet it contains within its contour what is throughout a mass of gold or of silver. When this mass is afterwards extended by beating it into leaf, it becomes larger than it was before by the elongation of the original mass, but not by any addition thereto, because it is extended in space, not increased in bulk; although in a way it is even increased when it is extended: for it may be increased in form, but not in state.

Then, again, the sheen of the gold or the silver, which when the metal was any in block was inherent in it no doubt really, but yet only obscurely, shines out in developed lustre.

Afterwards various modifications of shape accrue, according to the feasibility in the material which makes it yield to the manipulation of the artisan, who yet adds nothing to the condition of the mass but its configuration. In like manner, the growth and developments of the soul are to be estimated, not as enlarging its substance, but as calling forth its powers.

Chapter XXXVIII - On the Growth of the Soul. Its Maturity Coincident with the Maturity of the Flesh in Man

Now we have already [1747] laid down the principle, that all the natural properties of the soul which relate to sense and intelligence are inherent in its very substance, and spring from its native constitution, but that they advance by a gradual growth through the stages of life and develope themselves in different ways by accidental circumstances, according to men's means and arts, their manners and customs their local situations, and the influences of the Supreme Powers; [1748] but in pursuance of that aspect of the association of body and soul which we have now to consider, we maintain that the puberty of the soul coincides with that of the body, and that they attain both together to this full growth at about the fourteenth year of life, speaking generally,--the former by the suggestion of the senses, and the latter by the growth of the bodily members; and (we fix on this age) not because, as Asclepiades supposes, reflection then begins, nor because the civil laws date the commencement of the real business of life from this period, but because this was the appointed order from the very first. For as Adam and Eve felt that they must cover their nakedness after their knowledge of good and evil so we profess to have the same discernment of good and evil from the time that we experience the same sensation of shame. Now from the before-mentioned age (of fourteen years) sex is suffused and clothed with an especial sensibility, and concupiscence employs the ministry of the eye, and communicates its pleasure to another, and understands the natural relations between male and female, and wears the fig-tree apron to cover the shame which it still excites, and drives man out of the paradise of innocence and chastity, and in its wild pruriency falls upon sins and unnatural incentives to delinquency; for its impulse has by this time surpassed the appointment of nature, and springs from its vicious abuse.

But the strictly natural concupiscence is simply confined to the desire of those aliments which God at the beginning conferred upon man. "Of every tree of the garden" He says, "ye shall freely eat;" [1749] and then again to the generation which followed next after the flood He enlarged the grant: "Every moving thing that liveth shall be meat for you; behold, as the green herb have I given you all these things," [1750] --where He has regard rather to the body than to the soul, although it be in the interest of the soul also. For we must remove all occasion from the caviller, who, because the soul apparently wants ailments, would insist on the soul's being from this circumstance deemed mortal, since it is sustained by meat and drink and after a time loses its rigour when they are withheld, and on their complete removal ultimately droops and dies. Now the point we must keep in view is not merely which particular faculty it is which desires these (aliments), but also for what end; and even if it be for its own sake, still the question remains, Why this desire, and when felt, and how long? Then again there is the consideration, that it is one thing to desire by natural instinct, and another thing to desire through necessity; one thing to desire as a property of being, another thing to desire for a special object. The soul, therefore, will desire meat and drink--for itself indeed, because of a special necessity; for the flesh, however, from the nature of its properties. For the flesh is no doubt the house of the soul, and the soul is the temporary inhabitant of the flesh. The desire, then, of the lodger will arise from the temporary cause and the special necessity which his very designation suggests,--with a view to benefit and improve the place of his temporary abode, while sojourning in it; not with the view, certainly, of being himself the foundation of the house, or himself its walls, or himself its support and roof, but simply and solely with the view of being accommodated and housed, since he could not receive such accommodation except in a sound and well-built house. (Now, applying this imagery to the soul,) if it be not provided with this accommodation, it will not be in its power to quit its dwelling-place, and for want of fit and proper resources, to depart safe and sound, in possession, too, of its own supports, and the aliments which belong to its own proper condition,--namely immortality, rationality, sensibility, intelligence, and freedom of the will.

Chapter XXXIX - The Evil Spirit Has Marred the Purity of the Soul from the Very Birth

All these endowments of the soul which are bestowed on it at birth are still obscured and depraved by the malignant being who, in the beginning, regarded them with envious eye, so that they are never seen in their spontaneous action, nor are they administered as they ought to be. For to what individual of the human race will not the evil spirit cleave, ready to entrap their souls from the very portal of their birth, at which he is invited to be present in all those superstitious processes which accompany childbearing? Thus it comes to pass that all men are brought to the birth with idolatry for the midwife, whilst the very wombs that bear them, still bound with the fillets that have been wreathed before the idols, declare their offspring to be consecrated to demons: for in parturition they invoke the aid of Lucina and Diana; for a whole week a table is spread in honour of Juno; on the last day the fates of the horoscope [1751] are invoked; and then the infant's first step on the ground is sacred to the goddess Statina. After this does any one fail to devote to idolatrous service the entire head of his son, or to take out a hair, or to shave off the whole with a razor, or to bind it up for an offering, or seal it for sacred use--in behalf of the clan, of the ancestry, or for public devotion? On this principle of early possession it was that Socrates, while yet a boy, was found by the spirit of the demon. Thus, too, is it that to all persons their genii are assigned, which is only another name for demons. Hence in no case (I mean of the heathen, of course) is there any nativity which is pure of idolatrous superstition. It was from this circumstance that the apostle said, that when either of the parents was sanctified, the children were holy; [1752] and this as much by the prerogative of the (Christian) seed as by the discipline of the institution (by baptism, and Christian education). "Else," says he, "were the children unclean" by birth: [1753] as if he meant us to understand that the children of believers were designed for holiness, and thereby for salvation; in order that he might by the pledge of such a hope give his support to matrimony, which he had determined to maintain in its integrity. Besides, he had certainly not forgotten what the Lord had so definitively stated:

"Except a man be born of water and of the Spirit, he cannot enter into the kingdom of God;"[1754] in other words, he cannot be holy.

Chapter XL - The Body of Man Only Ancillary to the Soul in the Commission of Evil

Every soul, then, by reason of its birth, has its nature in Adam until it is born again in Christ; moreover, it is unclean all the while that it remains without this regeneration; [1755] and because unclean, it is actively sinful, and suffuses even the flesh (by reason of their conjunction) with its own shame. Now although the flesh is sinful, and we are forbidden to walk in accordance with it,[1756] and its works are condemned as lusting against the spirit, [1757] and men on its account are censured as carnal, [1758] yet the flesh has not such ignominy on its own account. For it is not of itself that it thinks anything or feels anything for the purpose of advising or commanding sin. How should it, indeed? It is only a ministering thing, and its ministration is not like that of a servant or familiar friend--animated and human beings;

but rather that of a vessel, or something of that kind: it is body, not soul. Now a cup may minister to a thirsty man; and yet, if the thirsty man will not apply the cup to his mouth, the cup will yield no ministering service. Therefore the differentia, or distinguishing property, of man by no means lies in his earthy element; nor is the flesh the human person, as being some faculty of his soul, and a personal quality; but it is a thing of quite a different substance and different condition, although annexed to the soul as a chattel or as an instrument for the offices of life. Accordingly the flesh is blamed in the Scriptures, because nothing is done by the soul without the flesh in operations of concupiscence, appetite, drunkenness, cruelty, idolatry, and other works of the flesh,--operations, I mean, which are not confined to sensations, but result in effects. The emotions of sin, indeed, when not resulting in effects, are usually imputed to the soul: "Whosoever looketh on a woman to lust after, hath already in his heart committed adultery with her." [1759] But what has the flesh alone, without the soul, ever done in operations of virtue, righteousness, endurance, or chastity? What absurdity, however, it is to attribute sin and crime to that substance to which you do not assign any good actions or character of its own! Now the party which aids in the commission of a crime is brought to trial, only in such a way that the principal offender who actually committed the crime may bear the weight of the penalty, although the abettor too does not escape indictment. Greater is the odium which falls on the principal, when his officials are punished through his fault. He is beaten with more stripes who instigates and orders the crime, whilst at the same time he who obeys such an evil command is not acquitted.

Chapter XLI - Notwithstanding the Depravity of Man's Soul by Original Sin, There is Yet Left a Basis Whereon Divine Grace Can Work for Its Recovery by Spiritual Regeneration

There is, then, besides the evil which supervenes on the soul from the intervention of the evil spirit, an antecedent, and in a certain sense natural, evil which arises from its corrupt origin. For, as we have said before, the corruption of our nature is another nature having a god and father of its own, namely the author of (that) corruption. Still there is a portion of good in the soul, of that original, divine, and genuine good, which is its proper nature.

For that which is derived from God is rather obscured than extinguished. It can be obscured, indeed, because it is not God; extinguished, however, it cannot be, because it comes from God. As therefore light, when intercepted by an opaque body, still remains, although it is not apparent, by reason of the interposition of so dense a body; so likewise the good in the soul, being weighed down by the evil, is, owing to the obscuring character thereof, either not seen at all, its light being wholly hidden, or else only a stray beam is there visible where it struggles through by an accidental outlet. Thus some men are very bad, and some very good; but yet the souls of all form but one genus: even in the worst there is something good, and in the best there is something bad. For God alone is without sin; and the only man without sin is Christ, since Christ is also God. Thus the divinity of the soul bursts forth in prophetic forecasts in consequence of its primeval good; and being conscious of its origin, it bears testimony to God (its author) in exclamations such as: Good God! God knows! and Good-bye! [1760] Just as no soul is without sin, so neither is any soul without seeds of good.

Therefore, when the soul embraces the faith, being renewed in its second birth by water and the power from above, then the veil of its former corruption being taken away, it beholds the light in all its brightness. It is also taken up (in its second birth) by the Holy Spirit, just as in its first birth it is embraced by the unholy spirit. The flesh follows the soul now wedded to the Spirit, as a part of the bridal portion--no longer the servant of the soul, but of the Spirit. O happy marriage, if in it there is committed no violation of the nuptial vow!

Chapter XLII - Sleep, the Mirror of Death, as Introductory to the Consideration of Death

It now remains (that we discuss the subject) of death, in order that our subject-matter may terminate where the soul itself completes it; although Epicurus, indeed, in his pretty widely known doctrine, has asserted that death does not appertain to us. That, says he, which is dissolved lacks sensation; and that which is without sensation is nothing to us. Well, but it is not actually death which suffers dissolution and lacks sensation, but the human person who experiences death. Yet even he has admitted suffering to be incidental to the being to whom action belongs. Now, if it is in man to suffer death, which dissolves the body and destroys the senses, how absurd to say that so great a susceptibility belongs not to man! With much greater precision does Seneca say: "After death all comes to an end, even (death) itself." From which position of his it must needs follow that death will appertain to its own self, since itself comes to an end; and much more to man, in the ending of whom amongst the "all," itself also ends. Death, (says Epicurus) belongs not to us; then at that rate, life belongs not to us.

For certainly, if that which causes our dissolution have no relation to us, that also which compacts and composes us must be unconnected with us. If the deprivation of our sensation be nothing to us, neither can the acquisition of sensation have anything to do with us. The fact, however, is, he who destroys the very soul, (as Epicurus does), cannot help destroying death also. As for ourselves, indeed, (Christians as we are), we must treat of death just as we should of the posthumous life and of some other province of the soul, (assuming) that we at all events belong to death, if it does not pertain to us. And on the same principle, even sleep, which is the very mirror of death, is not alien from our subject-matter.

Chapter XLIII - Sleep a Natural Function as Shown by Other Considerations, and by the Testimony of Scripture

Let us therefore first discuss the question of sleep, and afterwards in what way the soul encounters [1761] death. Now sleep is certainly not a supernatural thing, as some philosophers will have it be, when they suppose it to be the result of causes which appear to be above nature. The Stoics affirm sleep to be "a temporary suspension of the activity of the senses;" [1762] the Epicureans define it as an intermission of the animal spirit; Anaxagoras and Xenophanes as a weariness of the same; Empedocles and Parmenides as a cooling down thereof; Strato as a separation of the (soul's) connatural spirit; Democritus as the soul's indigence; Aristotle as the interruption [1763] of the heat around the heart. As for myself, I can safely say that I have never slept in such a way as to discover even a single one of these conditions.

Indeed, we cannot possibly believe that sleep is a weariness; it is rather the opposite, for it undoubtedly removes weariness, and a person is refreshed by sleep instead of being fatigued.

Besides, sleep is not always the result of fatigue; and even when it is, the fatigue continues no longer. Nor can I allow that sleep is a cooling or decaying of the animal heat, for our bodies derive warmth from sleep in such a way that the regular dispersion of the food by means of sleep could not so easily go on if there were too much heat to accelerate it unduly, or cold to retard it, if sleep had the alleged refrigerating influence. There is also the further fact that perspiration indicates an over-heated digestion; and digestion is predicated of us as a process of concoction, which is an operation concerned with heat and not with cold.

In like manner, the immortality of the soul precludes belief in the theory that sleep is an intermission of the animal spirit, or an indigence of the spirit, or a separation of the (soul's) connatural spirit. The soul perishes if it undergoes diminution or intermission. Our only resource, indeed, is to agree with the Stoics, by determining the soul to be a temporary suspension of the activity of the senses, procuring rest for the body only, not for the soul also. For the soul, as being always in motion, and always active, never succumbs to rest,--a condition which is alien to immortality: for nothing immortal admits any end to its operation; but sleep is an end of operation. It is indeed on the body, which is subject to mortality, and on the body alone, that sleep graciously bestows [1764] a cessation from work. He, therefore, who shall doubt whether sleep is a natural function, has the dialectical experts calling in question the whole difference between things natural and supernatural--so that what things he supposed to be beyond nature he may, (if he likes,) be safe in assigning to nature, which indeed has made such a disposition of things, that they may seemingly be accounted as beyond it; and so, of course, all things are natural or none are natural, (as occasion requires.) With us (Christians), however, only that can receive a hearing which is suggested by contemplating God, the Author of all the things which we are now discussing. For we believe that nature, if it is anything, is a reasonable work of God.

Now reason presides over sleep; for sleep is so fit for man, so useful, so necessary, that were it not for it, not a soul could provide agency for recruiting the body, for restoring its energies, for ensuring its health, for supplying suspension from work and remedy against labour, and for the legitimate enjoyment of which day departs, and night provides an ordinance by taking from all objects their very colour.

Since, then, sleep is indispensable to our life, and health, and succour, there can be nothing pertaining to it which is not reasonable, and which is not natural. Hence it is that physicians banish beyond the gateway of nature everything which is contrary to what is vital, healthful, and helpful to nature; for those maladies which are inimical to sleep--maladies of the mind and of the stomach--they have decided to be contrariant to nature, and by such decision have determined as its corollary that sleep is perfectly natural.

Moreover, when they declare that sleep is not natural in the lethargic state, they derive their conclusion from the fact that it is natural when it is in its due and regular exercise. For every natural state is impaired either by defect or by excess, whilst it is maintained by its proper measure and amount.

That, therefore, will be natural in its condition which may be rendered non-natural by defect or by excess.

Well, now, what if you were to remove eating and drinking from the conditions of nature? if in them lies the chief incentive to sleep. It is certain that, from the very beginning of his nature, man was impressed with these instincts (of sleep). [1765] If you receive your instruction from God, (you will find) that the fountain of the human race, Adam, had a taste of drowsiness before having a draught of repose; slept before he laboured, or even before he ate, nay, even before he spoke; in order that men may see that sleep is a natural feature and function, and one which has actually precedence over all the natural faculties. From this primary instance also we are led to trace even then the image of death in sleep. For as Adam was a figure of Christ, Adam's sleep shadowed out the death of Christ, who was to sleep a mortal slumber, that from the wound inflicted on His side might, in like manner (as Eve was formed), be typified the church, the true mother of the living. This is why sleep is so salutary, so rational, and is actually formed into the model of that death which is general and common to the race of man. God, indeed, has willed (and it may be said in passing that He has, generally, in His dispensations brought nothing to pass without such types and shadows) to set before us, in a manner more fully and completely than Plato's example, by daily recurrence the outlines of man's state, especially concerning the beginning and the termination thereof; thus stretching out the hand to help our faith more readily by types and parables, not in words only, but also in things. He accordingly sets before your view the human body stricken by the friendly power of slumber, prostrated by the kindly necessity of repose immoveable in position, just as it lay previous to life, and just as it will lie after life is past: there it lies as an attestation of its form when first moulded, and of its condition when at last buried--awaiting the soul in both stages, in the former previous to its bestowal, in the latter after its recent withdrawal. Meanwhile the soul is circumstanced in such a manner as to seem to be elsewhere active, learning to bear future absence by a dissembling of its presence for the moment. We shall soon know the case of Hermotimus. But yet it dreams in the interval. Whence then its dreams? The fact is, it cannot rest or be idle altogether, nor does it confine to the still hours of sleep the nature of its immortality. It proves itself to possess a constant motion; it travels over land and sea, it trades, it is excited, it labours, it plays, it grieves, it rejoices, it follows pursuits lawful and unlawful; it shows what very great power it has even without the body, how well equipped it is with members of its own, although betraying at the same time the need it has of impressing on some body its activity again. Accordingly, when the body shakes off its slumber, it asserts before your eye the resurrection of the dead by its own resumption of its natural functions.

Such, therefore, must be both the natural reason and the reasonable nature of sleep. If you only regard it as the image of death, you initiate faith, you nourish hope, you learn both how to die and how to live, you learn watchfulness, even while you sleep.

Chapter XLIV - The Story of Hermotimus, and the Sleeplessness of the Emperor Nero. No Separation of the Soul from the Body Until Death

With regard to the case of Hermotimus, they say that he used to be deprived of his soul in his sleep, as if it wandered away from his body like a person on a holiday trip. His wife betrayed the strange peculiarity. His enemies, finding him asleep, burnt his body, as if it were a corpse: when his soul returned too late, it appropriated (I suppose) to itself the guilt of the murder. However the good citizens of Clazomenæ consoled poor Hermotimus with a temple, into which no woman ever enters, because of the infamy of this wife.

Now why this story? In order that, since the vulgar belief so readily holds sleep to be the separation of the soul from the body, credulity should not be encouraged by this case of Hermotimus. It must certainly have been a much heavier sort of slumber: one would presume it was the nightmare, or perhaps that diseased languor which Soranus suggests in opposition to the nightmare, or else some such malady as that which the fable has fastened upon Epimenides, who slept on some fifty years or so. Suetonius, however, informs us that Nero never dreamt, and Theopompus says the same thing about Thrasymedes; but Nero at the close of his life did with some difficulty dream after some excessive alarm. What indeed would be said, if the case of Hermotimus were believed to be such that the repose of his soul was a state of actual idleness during sleep, and a positive separation from his body? You may conjecture it to be anything but such a licence of the soul as admits of flights away from the body without death, and that by continual recurrence, as if habitual to its state and constitution.

If indeed such a thing were told me to have happened at any time to the soul--resembling a total eclipse of the sun or the moon--I should verily suppose that the occurrence had been caused by God's own interposition, for it would not be unreasonable for a man to receive admonition from the Divine Being either in the way of warning or of alarm, as by a flash of lightning, or by a sudden stroke of death; only it would be much the more natural conclusion to believe that this process should be by a dream, because if it must be supposed to be, (as the hypothesis we are resisting assumes it to be,) not a dream, the occurrence ought rather to happen to a man whilst he is wide awake.

Chapter XLV - Dreams, an Incidental Effect of the Soul's Activity. Ecstasy

We are bound to expound at this point what is the opinion of Christians respecting dreams, as incidents of sleep, and as no slight or trifling excitements of the soul, which we have declared to be always occupied and active owing to its perpetual movement, which again is a proof and evidence of its divine quality and immortality. When, therefore, rest accrues to human bodies, it being their own especial comfort, the soul, disdaining a repose which is not natural to it, never rests; and since it receives no help from the limbs of the body, it uses its own. Imagine a gladiator without his instruments or arms, and a charioteer without his team, but still gesticulating the entire course and exertion of their respective employments: there is the fight, there is the struggle; but the effort is a vain one. Nevertheless the whole procedure seems to be gone through, although it evidently has not been really effected. There is the act, but not the effect. This power we call ecstasy, in which the sensuous soul stands out of itself, in a way which even resembles madness. [1766] Thus in the very beginning sleep was inaugurated by ecstasy: "And God sent an ecstasy upon Adam, and he slept."[1767] The sleep came on his body to cause it to rest, but the ecstasy fell on his soul to remove rest: from that very circumstance it still happens ordinarily (and from the order results the nature of the case) that sleep is combined with ecstasy. In fact, with what real feeling, and anxiety, and suffering do we experience joy, and sorrow, and alarm in our dreams! Whereas we should not be moved by any such emotions, by what would be the merest fantasies of course, if when we dream we were masters of ourselves, (unaffected by ecstasy.) In these dreams, indeed, good actions are useless, and crimes harmless; for we shall no more be condemned for visionary acts of sin, than we shall be crowned for imaginary martyrdom. But how, you will ask, can the soul remember its dreams, when it is said to be without any mastery over its own operations? This memory must be an especial gift of the ecstatic condition of which we are treating, since it arises not from any failure of healthy action, but entirely from natural process; nor does it expel mental function--it withdraws it for a time. It is one thing to shake, it is another thing to move; one thing to destroy, another thing to agitate. That, therefore, which memory supplies betokens soundness of mind; and that which a sound mind ecstatically experiences whilst the memory remains unchecked, is a kind of madness. We are accordingly not said to be mad, but to dream, in that state; to be in the full possession also of our mental faculties, [1768] if we are at any time. For although the power to exercise these faculties [1769] may be dimmed in us, it is still not extinguished; except that it may seem to be itself absent at the very time that the ecstasy is energizing in us in its special manner, in such wise as to bring before us images of a sound mind and of wisdom, even as it does those of aberration.

Chapter XLVI - Diversity of Dreams and Visions. Epicurus Thought Lightly of Them, Though Generally Most Highly Valued. Instances of Dreams

We now find ourselves constrained to express an opinion about the character of the dreams by which the soul is excited. And when shall we arrive at the subject of death? And on such a question I would say, When God shall permit: that admits of no long delay which must needs happen at all events. Epicurus has given it as his opinion that dreams are altogether vain things; (but he says this) when liberating the Deity from all sort of care, and dissolving the entire order of the world, and giving to all things the aspect of merest chance, casual in their issues, fortuitous in their nature. Well, now, if such be the nature of things, there must be some chance even for truth, because it is impossible for it to be the only thing to be exempted from the fortune which is due to all things. Homer has assigned two gates to dreams, [1770] --the horny one of truth, the ivory one of error and delusion. For, they say, it is possible to see through horn, whereas ivory is untransparent.

Aristotle, while expressing his opinion that dreams are in most cases untrue, yet acknowledges that there is some truth in them. The people of Telmessus will not admit that dreams are in any case unmeaning, but they blame their own weakness when unable to conjecture their signification. Now, who is such a stranger to human experience as not sometimes to have perceived some truth in dreams? I shall force a blush from Epicurus, if I only glance at some few of the more remarkable instances. Herodotus[1771] relates how that Astyages, king of the Medes, saw in a dream issuing from the womb of his virgin daughter a flood which inundated Asia; and again, in the year which followed her marriage, he saw a vine growing out from the same part of her person, which overspread the whole of Asia. The same story is told prior to Herodotus by Charon of Lampsacus. Now they who interpreted these visions did not deceive the mother when they destined her son for so great an enterprise, for Cyrus both inundated and overspread Asia. Philip of Macedon, before he became a father, had seen imprinted on the pudenda of his consort Olympias the form of a small ring, with a lion as a seal. He had concluded that an offspring from her was out of the question (I suppose because the lion only becomes once a father), when Aristodemus or Aristophon happened to conjecture that nothing of an unmeaning or empty import lay under that seal, but that a son of very illustrious character was portended. They who know anything of Alexander recognise in him the lion of that small ring.

Ephorus writes to this effect.

Again, Heraclides has told us, that a certain woman of Himera beheld in a dream Dionysius' tyranny over Sicily.

Euphorion has publicly recorded as a fact, that, previous to giving birth to Seleucus, his mother Laodice foresaw that he was destined for the empire of Asia. I find again from Strabo, that it was owing to a dream that even Mithridates took possession of Pontus; and I further learn from Callisthenes that it was from the indication of a dream that Baraliris the Illyrian stretched his dominion from the Molossi to the frontiers of Macedon. The Romans, too, were acquainted with dreams of this kind.

From a dream Marcus Tullius (Cicero) had learnt how that one, who was yet only a little boy, and in a private station, who was also plain Julius Octavius, and personally unknown to (Cicero) himself, was the destined Augustus, and the suppressor and destroyer of (Rome's) civil discords. This is recorded in the Commentaries of Vitellius. But visions of this prophetic kind were not confined to predictions of supreme power; for they indicated perils also, and catastrophes: as, for instance, when Cæsar was absent from the battle of Philippi through illness, and thereby escaped the sword of Brutus and Cassius, and then although he expected to encounter greater danger still from the enemy in the field, he quitted his tent for it, in obedience to a vision of Artorius, and so escaped (the capture by the enemy, who shortly after took possession of the tent); as, again, when the daughter of Polycrates of Samos foresaw the crucifixion which awaited him from the anointing of the sun and the bath of Jupiter. [1772] So likewise in sleep revelations are made of high honours and eminent talents; remedies are also discovered, thefts brought to light, and treasures indicated. Thus Cicero's eminence, whilst he was still a little boy, was foreseen by his nurse. The swan from the breast of Socrates soothing men, is his disciple Plato.

The boxer Leonymus is cured by Achilles in his dreams. Sophocles the tragic poet discovers, as he was dreaming, the golden crown, which had been lost from the citadel of Athens. Neoptolemus the tragic actor, through intimations in his sleep from Ajax himself, saves from destruction the hero's tomb on the Rhoetean shore before Troy; and as he removes the decayed stones, he returns enriched with gold.

How many commentators and chroniclers vouch for this phenomenon? There are Artemon, Antiphon, Strato, Philochorus, Epicharmus, Serapion, Cratippus, and Dionysius of Rhodes, and Hermippus--the entire literature of the age.

I shall only laugh at all, if indeed I ought to laugh at the man who fancied that he was going to persuade us that Saturn dreamt before anybody else; which we can only believe if Aristotle, (who would fain help us to such an opinion,) lived prior to any other person.

Pray forgive me for laughing.

Epicharmus, indeed, as well as Philochorus the Athenian, assigned the very highest place among divinations to dreams.

The whole world is full of oracles of this description: there are the oracles of Amphiaraus at Oropus, of Amphilochus at Mallus, of Sarpedon in the Troad, of Trophonius in Boeotia, of Mopsus in Cilicia, of Hermione in Macedon, of Pasiphäe in Laconia. Then, again, there are others, which with their original foundations, rites, and historians, together with the entire literature of dreams, Hermippus of Berytus in five portly volumes will give you all the account of, even to satiety.

But the Stoics are very fond of saying that God, in His most watchful providence over every institution, gave us dreams amongst other preservatives of the arts and sciences of divination, as the especial support of the natural oracle. So much for the dreams to which credit has to be ascribed even by ourselves, although we must interpret them in another sense. As for all other oracles, at which no one ever dreams, what else must we declare concerning them, than that they are the diabolical contrivance of those spirits who even at that time dwelt in the eminent persons themselves, or aimed at reviving the memory of them as the mere stage of their evil purposes, going so far as to counterfeit a divine power under their shape and form, and, with equal persistence in evil, deceiving men by their very boons of remedies, warnings, and forecasts,--the only effect of which was to injure their victims the more they helped them; while the means whereby they rendered the help withdrew them from all search after the true God, by insinuating into their minds ideas of the false one? And of course so pernicious an influence as this is not shut up nor limited within the boundaries of shrines and temples: it roams abroad, it flies through the air, and all the while is free and unchecked. So that nobody can doubt that our very homes lie open to these diabolical spirits, who beset their human prey with their fantasies not only in their chapels but also in their chambers.

Chapter XLVII - Dreams Variously Classified. Some are God-Sent, as the Dreams of Nebuchadnezzar; Others Simply Products of Nature

We declare, then, that dreams are inflicted on us mainly by demons, although they sometimes turn out true and favourable to us. When, however, with the deliberate aim after evil, of which we have just spoken, they assume a flattering and captivating style, they show themselves proportionately vain, and deceitful, and obscure, and wanton, and impure. And no wonder that the images partake of the character of the realities. But from God--who has promised, indeed, "to pour out the grace of the Holy Spirit upon all flesh, and has ordained that His servants and His handmaids should see visions as well as utter prophecies" [1773] --must all those visions be regarded as emanating, which may be compared to the actual grace of God, as being honest, holy, prophetic, inspired, instructive, inviting to virtue, the bountiful nature of which causes them to overflow even to the profane, since God, with grand impartiality, "sends His showers and sunshine on the just and on the unjust." [1774] It was, indeed by an inspiration from God that Nebuchadnezzar dreamt his dreams; [1775] and almost the greater part of mankind get their knowledge of God from dreams. Thus it is that, as the mercy of God super-abounds to the heathen, so the temptation of the evil one encounters the saints, from whom he never withdraws his malignant efforts to steal over them as best he may in their very sleep, if unable to assault them when they are awake. The third class of dreams will consist of those which the soul itself apparently creates for itself from an intense application to special circumstances. Now, inasmuch as the soul cannot dream of its own accord (for even Epicharmus is of this opinion), how can it become to itself the cause of any vision? Then must this class of dreams be abandoned to the action of nature, reserving for the soul, even when in the ecstatic condition, the power of enduring whatever incidents befall it? Those, moreover, which evidently proceed neither from God, nor from diabolical inspiration, nor from the soul, being beyond the reach as well of ordinary expectation, usual interpretation, or the possibility of being intelligibly related, will have to be ascribed in a separate category to what is purely and simply the ecstatic state and its peculiar conditions.

Chapter XLVIII - Causes and Circumstances of Dreams. What Best Contributes to Efficient Dreaming

They say that dreams are more sure and clear when they happen towards the end of the night, because then the vigour of the soul emerges, and heavy sleep departs. As to the seasons of the year, dreams are calmer in spring, since summer relaxes, and winter somehow hardens, the soul; while autumn, which in other respects is trying to health, is apt to enervate the soul by the lusciousness of its fruits.

Then, again, as regards the position of one's body during sleep, one ought not to lie on his back, nor on his right side, nor so as to wrench [1776] his intestines, as if their cavity were reversely stretched: a palpitation of the heart would ensue, or else a pressure on the liver would produce a painful disturbance of the mind. But however this be, I take it that it all amounts to ingenious conjecture rather than certain proof (although the author of the conjecture be no less a man than Plato); [1777] and possibly all may be no other than the result of chance. But, generally speaking, dreams will be under control of a man's will, if they be capable of direction at all; for we must not examine what opinion on the one hand, and superstition on the other, have to prescribe for the treatment of dreams, in the matter of distinguishing and modifying different sorts of food.

As for the superstition, we have an instance when fasting is prescribed for such persons as mean to submit to the sleep which is necessary for receiving the oracle, in order that such abstinence may produce the required purity; while we find an instance of the opinion when the disciples of Pythagoras, in order to attain the same end, reject the bean as an aliment which would load the stomach, and produce indigestion. But the three brethren, who were the companions of Daniel, being content with pulse alone, to escape the contamination of the royal dishes, [1778] received from God, besides other wisdom, the gift especially of penetrating and explaining the sense of dreams. For my own part, I hardly know whether fasting would not simply make me dream so profoundly, that I should not be aware whether I had in fact dreamt at all. Well, then, you ask, has not sobriety something to do in this matter?

Certainly it is as much concerned in this as it is in the entire subject: if it contributes some good service to superstition, much more does it to religion. For even demons require such discipline from their dreamers as a gratification to their divinity, because they know that it is acceptable to God, since Daniel (to quote him again) "ate no pleasant bread" for the space of three weeks. [1779] This abstinence, however, he used in order to please God by humiliation, and not for the purpose of producing a sensibility and wisdom for his soul previous to receiving communication by dreams and visions, as if it were not rather to effect such action in an ecstatic state. This sobriety, then, (in which our question arises,) will have nothing to do with exciting ecstasy, but will rather serve to recommend its being wrought by God.

Chapter XLIX - No Soul Naturally Exempt from Dreams

As for those persons who suppose that infants do not dream, on the ground that all the functions of the soul throughout life are accomplished according to the capacity of age, they ought to observe attentively their tremors, and nods, and bright smiles as they sleep, and from such facts understand that they are the emotions of their soul as it dreams, which so readily escape to the surface through the delicate tenderness of their infantine body. The fact, however, that the African nation of the Atlantes are said to pass through the night in a deep lethargic sleep, brings down on them the censure that something is wrong in the constitution of their soul. Now either report, which is occasionally calumnious against barbarians, deceived Herodotus, [1780] or else a large force of demons of this sort domineers in those barbarous regions. Since, indeed, Aristotle remarks of a certain hero of Sardinia that he used to withhold the power of visions and dreams from such as resorted to his shrine for inspiration, it must lie at the will and caprice of the demons to take away as well as to confer the faculty of dreams; and from this circumstance may have arisen the remarkable fact (which we have mentioned [1781]) of Nero and Thrasymedes only dreaming so late in life. We, however, derive dreams from God. Why, then, did not the Atlantes receive the dreaming faculty from God, because there is really no nation which is now a stranger to God, since the gospel flashes its glorious light through the world to the ends of the earth? Could it then be that rumour deceived Aristotle, or is this caprice still the way of demons? (Let us take any view of the case), only do not let it be imagined that any soul is by its natural constitution exempt from dreams.

Chapter L - The Absurd Opinion of Epicurus and the Profane Conceits of the Heretic Menander on Death, Even Enoch and Elijah Reserved for Death

We have by this time said enough about sleep, the mirror and image of death; and likewise about the occupations of sleep, even dreams. Let us now go on to consider the cause of our departure hence--that is, the appointment and course of death--because we must not leave even it unquestioned and unexamined, although it is itself the very end of all questions and investigations. According to the general sentiment of the human race, we declare death to be "the debt of nature." So much has been settled by the voice of God; [1782] such is the contract with everything which is born: so that even from this the frigid conceit of Epicurus is refuted, who says that no such debt is due from us; and not only so, but the insane opinion of the Samaritan heretic Menander is also rejected, who will have it that death has not only nothing to do with his disciples, but in fact never reaches them. He pretends to have received such a commission from the secret power of One above, that all who partake of his baptism become immortal, incorruptible and instantaneously invested with resurrection-life. We read, no doubt, of very many wonderful kinds of waters: how, for instance, the vinous quality of the stream intoxicates people who drink of the Lyncestis; how at Colophon the waters of an oracle-inspiring fountain [1783] affect men with madness; how Alexander was killed by the poisonous water from Mount Nonacris in Arcadia. Then, again, there was in Judea before the time of Christ a pool of medicinal virtue. It is well known how the poet has commemorated the marshy Styx as preserving men from death; although Thetis had, in spite of the preservative, to lament her son. And for the matter of that, were Menander himself to take a plunge into this famous Styx, he would certainly have to die after all; for you must come to the Styx, placed as it is by all accounts in the regions of the dead. Well, but what and where are those blessed and charming waters which not even John Baptist ever used in his preministrations, nor Christ after him ever revealed to His disciples? What was this wondrous bath of Menander? He is a comical fellow, I ween. [1784] But why (was such a font) so seldom in request, so obscure, one to which so very few ever resorted for their cleansing? I really see something to suspect in so rare an occurrence of a sacrament to which is attached so very much security and safety, and which dispenses with the ordinary law of dying even in the service of God Himself, when, on the contrary, all nations have "to ascend to the mount of the Lord and to the house of the God of Jacob," who demands of His saints in martyrdom that death which He exacted even of His Christ. No one will ascribe to magic such influence as shall exempt from death, or which shall refresh and vivify life, like the vine by the renewal of its condition. Such power was not accorded to the great Medea herself--over a human being at any rate, if allowed her over a silly sheep. Enoch no doubt was translated, [1785] and so was Elijah; [1786] nor did they experience death: it was postponed, (and only postponed,) most certainly: they are reserved for the suffering of death, that by their blood they may extinguish Antichrist. [1787] Even John underwent death, although concerning him there had prevailed an ungrounded expectation that he would remain alive until the coming of the Lord. [1788] Heresies, indeed, for the most part spring hurriedly into existence, from examples furnished by ourselves: they procure their defensive armour from the very place which they attack. The whole question resolves itself, in short, into this challenge: Where are to be found the men whom Menander himself has baptized? whom he has plunged into his Styx? Let them come forth and stand before us--those apostles of his whom he has made immortal?

Let my (doubting) Thomas see them, let him hear them, let him handle them--and he is convinced.

Chapter LI - Death Entirely Separates the Soul from the Body

But the operation of death is plain and obvious: it is the separation of body and soul. Some, however, in reference to the soul's immortality, on which they have so feeble a hold through not being taught of God, maintain it with such beggarly arguments, that they would fain have it supposed that certain souls cleave to the body even after death. It is indeed in this sense that Plato, although he despatches at once to heaven such souls as he pleases, [1789] yet in his Republic[1790] exhibits to us the corpse of an unburied person, which was preserved a long time without corruption, by reason of the soul remaining, as he says, unseparated from the body. To the same purport also Democritus remarks on the growth for a considerable while of the human nails and hair in the grave. Now, it is quite possible that the nature of the atmosphere tended to the preservation of the above-mentioned corpse.

What if the air were particularly dry, and the ground of a saline nature? What, too, if the substance of the body itself were unusually dry and arid?

What, moreover, if the mode of the death had already eliminated from the corpse all corrupting matter? As for the nails, since they are the commencement of the nerves, they may well seem to be prolonged, owing to the nerves themselves being relaxed and extended, and to be protruded more and more as the flesh fails. The hair, again, is nourished from the brain, which would cause it endure for a long time as its secret aliment and defence. Indeed, in the case of living persons themselves, the whole head of hair is copious or scanty in proportion to the exuberance of the brain. You have medical men (to attest the fact). But not a particle of the soul can possibly remain in the body, which is itself destined to disappear when time shall have abolished the entire scene on which the body has played its part. And yet even this partial survival of the soul finds a place in the opinions of some men; and on this account they will not have the body consumed at its funeral by fire, because they would spare the small residue of the soul. There is, however, another way of accounting for this pious treatment, not as if it meant to favour the relics of the soul, but as if it would avert a cruel custom in the interest even of the body; since, being human, it is itself undeserving of an end which is also inflicted upon murderers. The truth is, the soul is indivisible, because it is immortal; (and this fact) compels us to believe that death itself is an indivisible process, accruing indivisibly to the soul, not indeed because it is immortal, but because it is indivisible. Death, however, would have to be divided in its operation, if the soul were divisible into particles, any one of which has to be reserved for a later stage of death.

At this rate, a part of death will have to stay behind for a portion of the soul. I am not ignorant that some vestige of this opinion still exists. I have found it out from one of my own people.

I am acquainted with the case of a woman, the daughter of Christian parents, [1791] who in the very flower of her age and beauty slept peacefully (in Jesus), after a singularly happy though brief married life.

Before they laid her in her grave, and when the priest began the appointed office, at the very first breath of his prayer she withdrew her hands from her side, placed them in an attitude of devotion, and after the holy service was concluded restored them to their lateral position. Then, again, there is that well-known story among our own people, that a body voluntarily made way in a certain cemetery, to afford room for another body to be placed near to it. If, as is the case, similar stories are told amongst the heathen, (we can only conclude that) God everywhere manifests signs of His own power--to His own people for their comfort, to strangers for a testimony unto them. I would indeed much rather suppose that a portent of this kind happened from the direct agency of God than from any relics of the soul:

for if there were a residue of these, they would be certain to move the other limbs; and even if they moved the hands, this still would not have been for the purpose of a prayer. Nor would the corpse have been simply content to have made way for its neighbour: it would, besides, have benefited its own self also by the change of its position.

But from whatever cause proceeded these phenomena, which you must put down amongst signs and portents, it is impossible that they should regulate nature. Death, if it once falls short of totality in operation, is not death. If any fraction of the soul remain, it makes a living state. Death will no more mix with life, than will night with day.

Chapter LII - All Kinds of Death a Violence to Nature, Arising from Sin.--Sin an Intrusion Upon Nature as God Created It

Such, then, is the work of death--the separation of the soul from the body.

Putting out of the question fates and fortuitous circumstances, it has been, according to men's views, distinguished in a twofold form--the ordinary and the extraordinary. The ordinary they ascribe to nature, exercising its quiet influence in the case of each individual decease; the extraordinary is said to be contrary to nature, happening in every violent death. As for our own views, indeed, we know what was man's origin, and we boldly assert and persistently maintain that death happens not by way of natural consequence to man, but owing to a fault and defect which is not itself natural; although it is easy enough, no doubt, to apply the term natural to faults and circumstances which seem to have been (though from the emergence of an external cause [1792]) inseparable to us from our very birth.

If man had been directly appointed to die as the condition of his creation, [1793] then of course death must be imputed to nature.

Now, that he was not thus appointed to die, is proved by the very law which made his condition depend on a warning, and death result from man's arbitrary choice. Indeed, if he had not sinned, he certainly would not have died.

That cannot be nature which happens by the exercise of volition after an alternative has been proposed to it, and not by necessity--the result of an inflexible and unalterable condition.

Consequently, although death has various issues, inasmuch as its causes are manifold, we cannot say that the easiest death is so gentle as not to happen by violence (to our nature). The very law which produces death, simple though it be, is yet violence. How can it be otherwise, when so close a companionship of soul and body, so inseparable a growth together from their very conception of two sister substances, is sundered and divided? For although a man may breathe his last for joy, like the Spartan Chilon, while embracing his son who had just conquered in the Olympic games; or for glory, like the Athenian Clidemus, while receiving a crown of gold for the excellence of his historical writings; or in a dream, like Plato; or in a fit of laughter, like Publius Crassus,--yet death is much too violent, coming as it does upon us by strange and alien means, expelling the soul by a method all its own, calling on us to die at a moment when one might live a jocund life in joy and honour, in peace and pleasure. That is still a violence to ships: although far away from the Capharean rocks, assailed by no storms, without a billow to shatter them, with favouring gale, in gliding course, with merry crews, they founder amidst entire security, suddenly, owing to some internal shock.

Not dissimilar are the shipwrecks of life,--the issues of even a tranquil death. It matters not whether the vessel of the human body goes with unbroken timbers or shattered with storms, if the navigation of the soul be overthrown.

Chapter LIII - The Entire Soul Being Indivisible Remains to the Last Act of Vitality; Never Partially or Fractionally Withdrawn from the Body

But where at last will the soul have to lodge, when it is bare and divested of the body? We must certainly not hesitate to follow it thither, in the order of our inquiry. We must, however, first of all fully state what belongs to the topic before us, in order that no one, because we have mentioned the various issues of death, may expect from us a special description of these, which ought rather to be left to medical men, who are the proper judges of the incidents which appertain to death, or its causes, and the actual conditions of the human body. Of course, with the view of preserving the truth of the soul's immortality, whilst treating this topic, I shall have, on mentioning death, to introduce phrases about dissolution of such a purport as seems to intimate that the soul escapes by degrees, and piece by piece; for it withdraws (from the body) with all the circumstances of a decline, seeming to suffer consumption, and suggests to us the idea of being annihilated by the slow process of its departure. But the entire reason of this phenomenon is in the body, and arises from the body. For whatever be the kind of death (which operates on man), it undoubtedly produces the destruction either of the matter, or of the region, or of the passages of vitality: of the matter, such as the gall and the blood; of the region, such as the heart and the liver; of the passages, such as the veins and the arteries.

Inasmuch, then, as these parts of the body are severally devastated by an injury proper to each of them, even to the very last ruin and annulling of the vital powers--in other words, of the ends, the sites, and the functions of nature--it must needs come to pass, amidst the gradual decay of its instruments, domiciles, and spaces, that the soul also itself, being driven to abandon each successive part, assumes the appearance of being lessened to nothing; in some such manner as a charioteer is assumed to have himself failed, when his horses, through fatigue, withdraw from him their energies. But this assumption applies only to the circumstances of the despoiled person, not to any real condition of suffering. Likewise the body's charioteer, the animal spirit, fails on account of the failure of its vehicle, not of itself--abandoning its work, but not its vigour--languishing in operation, but not in essential condition-- bankrupt in solvency, not in substance--because ceasing to put in an appearance, but not ceasing to exist. Thus every rapid death--such as a decapitation, or a breaking of the neck, [1794] which opens at once a vast outlet for the soul; or a sudden ruin, which at a stroke crushes every vital action, like that inner ruin apoplexy--retards not the soul's escape, nor painfully separates its departure into successive moments. Where, however, the death is a lingering one, the soul abandons its position in the way in which it is itself abandoned. And yet it is not by this process severed in fractions: it is slowly drawn out; and whilst thus extracted, it causes the last remnant to seem to be but a part of itself. No portion, however, must be deemed separable, because it is the last; nor, because it is a small one, must it be regarded as susceptible of dissolution. Accordant with a series is its end, and the middle is prolonged to the extremes; and the remnants cohere to the mass, and are waited for, but never abandoned by it.

And I will even venture to say, that the last of a whole is the whole; because while it is less, and the latest, it yet belongs to the whole, and completes it. Hence, indeed, many times it happens that the soul in its actual separation is more powerfully agitated with a more anxious gaze, and a quickened loquacity; whilst from the loftier and freer position in which it is now placed, it enunciates, by means of its last remnant still lingering in the flesh, what it sees, what it hears, and what it is beginning to know. In Platonic phrase, indeed, the body is a prison, [1795] but in the apostle's it is "the temple of God," [1796] because it is in Christ. Still, (as must be admitted,) by reason of its enclosure it obstructs and obscures the soul, and sullies it by the concretion of the flesh; whence it happens that the light which illumines objects comes in upon the soul in a more confused manner, as if through a window of horn. Undoubtedly, when the soul, by the power of death, is released from its concretion with the flesh, it is by the very release cleansed and purified: it is, moreover, certain that it escapes from the veil of the flesh into open space, to its clear, and pure, and intrinsic light; and then finds itself enjoying its enfranchisement from matter, and by virtue of its liberty it recovers its divinity, as one who awakes out of sleep passes from images to verities. Then it tells out what it sees; then it exults or it fears, according as it finds what lodging is prepared for it, as soon as it sees the very angel's face, that arraigner of souls, the Mercury of the poets.

Chapter LIV - Whither Does the Soul Retire When It Quits the Body? Opinions of Philosophers All More or Less Absurd. The Hades of Plato

To the question, therefore, whither the soul is withdrawn, we now give an answer. Almost all the philosophers, who hold the soul's immortality, notwithstanding their special views on the subject, still claim for it this (eternal condition), as Pythagoras, and Empedocles, and Plato, and as they who indulge it with some delay from the time of its quitting the flesh to the conflagration of all things, and as the Stoics, who place only their own souls, that is, the souls of the wise, in the mansions above. Plato, it is true, does not allow this destination to all the souls, indiscriminately, of even all the philosophers, but only of those who have cultivated their philosophy out of love to boys. So great is the privilege which impurity obtains at the hands of philosophers!

In his system, then, the souls of the wise are carried up on high into the ether: according to Arius,[1797] into the air; according to the Stoics, into the moon. I wonder, indeed, that they abandon to the earth the souls of the unwise, when they affirm that even these are instructed by the wise, so much their superiors.

For where is the school where they can have been instructed in the vast space which divides them? By what means can the pupil-souls have resorted to their teachers, when they are parted from each other by so distant an interval?

What profit, too, can any instruction afford them at all in their posthumous state, when they are on the brink of perdition by the universal fire? All other souls they thrust down to Hades, which Plato, in his Phædo, [1798] describes as the bosom of the earth, where all the filth of the world accumulates, settles, and exhales, and where every separate draught of air only renders denser still the impurities of the seething mass.

Chapter LV - The Christian Idea of the Position of Hades; The Blessedness of Paradise Immediately After Death. The Privilege of the Martyrs

By ourselves the lower regions (of Hades) are not supposed to be a bare cavity, nor some subterranean sewer of the world, but a vast deep space in the interior of the earth, and a concealed recess in its very bowels; inasmuch as we read that Christ in His death spent three days in the heart of the earth, [1799] that is, in the secret inner recess which is hidden in the earth, and enclosed by the earth, and superimposed on the abysmal depths which lie still lower down. Now although Christ is God, yet, being also man, "He died according to the Scriptures," [1800] and "according to the same Scriptures was buried."[1801] With the same law of His being He fully complied, by remaining in Hades in the form and condition of a dead man; nor did He ascend into the heights of heaven before descending into the lower parts of the earth, that He might there make the patriarchs and prophets partakers of Himself. [1802] (This being the case), you must suppose Hades to be a subterranean region, and keep at arm's length those who are too proud to believe that the souls of the faithful deserve a place in the lower regions. [1803] These persons, who are "servants above their Lord, and disciples above their Master," [1804] would no doubt spurn to receive the comfort of the resurrection, if they must expect it in Abraham's bosom. But it was for this purpose, say they, that Christ descended into hell, that we might not ourselves have to descend thither. Well, then, what difference is there between heathens and Christians, if the same prison awaits them all when dead? How, indeed, shall the soul mount up to heaven, where Christ is already sitting at the Father's right hand, when as yet the archangel's trumpet has not been heard by the command of God,[1805] --when as yet those whom the coming of the Lord is to find on the earth, have not been caught up into the air to meet Him at His coming, [1806] in company with the dead in Christ, who shall be the first to arise? [1807] To no one is heaven opened; the earth is still safe for him, I would not say it is shut against him. When the world, indeed, shall pass away, then the kingdom of heaven shall be opened.

Shall we then have to sleep high up in ether, with the boy-loving worthies of Plato; or in the air with Arius; or around the moon with the Endymions of the Stoics? No, but in Paradise, you tell me, whither already the patriarchs and prophets have removed from Hades in the retinue of the Lord's resurrection. How is it, then, that the region of Paradise, which as revealed to John in the Spirit lay under the altar, [1808] displays no other souls as in it besides the souls of the martyrs? How is it that the most heroic martyr Perpetua on the day of her passion saw only her fellow-martyrs there, in the revelation which she received of Paradise, if it were not that the sword which guarded the entrance permitted none to go in thereat, except those who had died in Christ and not in Adam? A new death for God, even the extraordinary one for Christ, is admitted into the reception-room of mortality, specially altered and adapted to receive the new-comer. Observe, then, the difference between a heathen and a Christian in their death: if you have to lay down your life for God, as the Comforter [1809] counsels, it is not in gentle fevers and on soft beds, but in the sharp pains of martyrdom: you must take up the cross and bear it after your Master, as He has Himself instructed you. [1810] The sole key to unlock Paradise is your own life's blood. [1811] You have a treatise by us, [1812] (on Paradise), in which we have established the position that every soul is detained in safe keeping in Hades until the day of the Lord.

Chapter LVI - Refutation of the Homeric View of the Soul's Detention from Hades Owing to the Body's Being Unburied. That Souls Prematurely Separated from the Body Had to Wait for Admission into Hades Also Refuted

There arises the question, whether this takes place immediately after the soul's departure from the body; whether some souls are detained for special reasons in the meantime here on earth; and whether it is permitted them of their own accord, or by the intervention of authority, to be removed from Hades [1813] at some subsequent time? Even such opinions as these are not by any means lacking persons to advance them with confidence. It was believed that the unburied dead were not admitted into the infernal regions before they had received a proper sepulture; as in the case of Homer's Patroclus, who earnestly asks for a burial of Achilles in a dream, on the ground that he could not enter Hades through any other portal, since the souls of the sepulchred dead kept thrusting him away. [1814] We know that Homer exhibited more than a poetic licence here; he had in view the rights of the dead. Proportioned, indeed, to his care for the just honours of the tomb, was his censure of that delay of burial which was injurious to souls. (It was also his purpose to add a warning), that no man should, by detaining in his house the corpse of a friend, only expose himself, along with the deceased, to increased injury and trouble, by the irregularity[1815] of the consolation which he nourishes with pain and grief. He has accordingly kept a twofold object in view in picturing the complaints of an unburied soul: he wished to maintain honour to the dead by promptly attending to their funeral, as well as to moderate the feelings of grief which their memory excited. But, after all, how vain is it to suppose that the soul could bear the rites and requirements of the body, or carry any of them away to the infernal regions! And how much vainer still is it, if injury be supposed to accrue to the soul from that neglect of burial which it ought to receive rather as a favour!

For surely the soul which had no willingness to die might well prefer as tardy a removal to Hades as possible. It will love the undutiful heir, by whose means it still enjoys the light. If, however, it is certain that injury accrues to the soul from a tardy interment of the body--and the gist of the injury lies in the neglect of the burial--it is yet in the highest degree unfair, that that should receive all the injury to which the faulty delay could not possibly be imputed, for of course all the fault rests on the nearest relations of the dead. They also say that those souls which are taken away by a premature death wander about hither and thither until they have completed the residue of the years which they would have lived through, had it not been for their untimely fate. Now either their days are appointed to all men severally, and if so appointed, I cannot suppose them capable of being shortened; or if, notwithstanding such appointment, they may be shortened by the will of God, or some other powerful influence, then (I say) such shortening is of no validity, if they still may be accomplished in some other way. If, on the other hand, they are not appointed, there cannot be any residue to be fulfilled for unappointed periods. I have another remark to make. Suppose it be an infant that dies yet hanging on the breast; or it may be an immature boy; or it may be, once more, a youth arrived at puberty:

suppose, moreover, that the life in each case ought to have reached full eighty years, how is it possible that the soul of either could spend the whole of the shortened years here on earth after losing the body by death? One's age cannot be passed without one's body, it being by help of the body that the period of life has its duties and labours transacted. Let our own people, moreover, bear this in mind, that souls are to receive back at the resurrection the self-same bodies in which they died.

Therefore our bodies must be expected to resume the same conditions and the same ages, for it is these particulars which impart to bodies their especial modes. By what means, then, can the soul of an infant so spend on earth its residue of years, that it should be able at the resurrection to assume the state of an octogenarian, although it had barely lived a month? Or if it shall be necessary that the appointed days of life be fulfilled here on earth, must the same course of life in all its vicissitudes, which has been itself ordained to accompany the appointed days, be also passed through by the soul along with the days? Must it employ itself in school studies in its passage from infancy to boyhood; play the soldier in the excitement and vigour of youth and earlier manhood; and encounter serious and judicial responsibilities in the graver years between ripe manhood and old age? Must it ply trade for profit, turn up the soil with hoe and plough, go to sea, bring actions at law, get married, toil and labour, undergo illnesses, and whatever casualties of weal and woe await it in the lapse of years? Well, but how are all these transactions to be managed without one's body? Life (spent) without life? But (you will tell me) the destined period in question is to be bare of all incident whatever, only to be accomplished by merely elapsing. What, then, is to prevent its being fulfilled in Hades, where there is absolutely no use to which you can apply it? We therefore maintain that every soul, whatever be its age on quitting the body, remains unchanged in the same, until the time shall come when the promised perfection shall be realized in a state duly tempered to the measure of the peerless angels. Hence those souls must be accounted as passing an exile in Hades, which people are apt to regard as carried off by violence, especially by cruel tortures, such as those of the cross, and the axe, and the sword, and the lion; but we do not account those to be violent deaths which justice awards, that avenger of violence.

So then, you will say, it is all the wicked souls that are banished in Hades. (Not quite so fast, is my answer.) I must compel you to determine (what you mean by Hades), which of its two regions, the region of the good or of the bad. If you mean the bad, (all I can say is, that) even now the souls of the wicked deserve to be consigned to those abodes; if you mean the good why should you judge to be unworthy of such a resting-place the souls of infants and of virgins, and [1816] those which, by reason of their condition in life were pure and innocent?

Chapter LVII - Magic and Sorcery Only Apparent in Their Effects. God Alone Can Raise the Dead

It is either a very fine thing to be detained in these infernal regions with the Aori, or souls which were prematurely hurried away; or else a very bad thing indeed to be there associated with the Biaeothanati, who suffered violent deaths. I may be permitted to use the actual words and terms with which magic rings again, that inventor of all these odd opinions--with its Ostanes, and Typhon, and Dardanus, and Damigeron, and Nectabis, and Berenice. There is a well-known popular bit of writing, [1817] which undertakes to summon up from the abode of Hades the souls which have actually slept out their full age, and had passed away by an honourable death, and had even been buried with full rites and proper ceremony. What after this shall we say about magic? Say, to be sure, what almost everybody says of it--that it is an imposture. But it is not we Christians only whose notice this system of imposture does not escape. We, it is true, have discovered these spirits of evil, not, to be sure, by a complicity with them, but by a certain knowledge which is hostile to them; nor is it by any procedure which is attractive to them, but by a power which subjugates them that we handle (their wretched system)--that manifold pest of the mind of man, that artificer of all error, that destroyer of our salvation and our soul at one swoop. [1818] In this way, even by magic, which is indeed only a second idolatry, wherein they pretend that after death they become demons, just as they were supposed in the first and literal idolatry to become gods (and why not? since the gods are but dead things), the before-mentioned Aori Biaeothanati are actually invoked,--and not unfairly, [1819] if one grounds his faith on this principle, that it is clearly credible for those souls to be beyond all others addicted to violence and wrong, which with violence and wrong have been hurried away by a cruel and premature death and which would have a keen appetite for reprisals.

Under cover, however, of these souls, demons operate, especially such as used to dwell in them when they were in life, and who had driven them, in fact, to the fate which had at last carried them off.

For, as we have already suggested, [1820] there is hardly a human being who is unattended by a demon; and it is well known to many, that premature and violent deaths, which men ascribe to accidents, are in fact brought about by demons.

This imposture of the evil spirit lying concealed in the persons of the dead, we are able, if I mistake not, to prove by actual facts, when in cases of exorcism (the evil spirit) affirms himself sometimes to be one of the relatives [1821] of the person possessed by him, sometimes a gladiator or a bestiarius, [1822] and sometimes even a god; always making it one of his chief cares to extinguish the very truth which we are proclaiming, that men may not readily believe that all souls remove to Hades, and that they may overthrow faith in the resurrection and the judgment. And yet for all that, the demon, after trying to circumvent the bystanders, is vanquished by the pressure of divine grace, and sorely against his will confesses all the truth. So also in that other kind of magic, which is supposed to bring up from Hades the souls now resting there, and to exhibit them to public view, there is no other expedient of imposture ever resorted to which operates more powerfully. Of course, why a phantom becomes visible, is because a body is also attached to it; and it is no difficult matter to delude the external vision of a man whose mental eye it is so easy to blind. The serpents which emerged from the magicians' rods, certainly appeared to Pharaoh and to the Egyptians as bodily substances. It is true that the verity of Moses swallowed up their lying deceit.[1823] Many attempts were also wrought against the apostles by the sorcerers Simon and Elymas, [1824] but the blindness which struck (them) was no enchanter's trick. What novelty is there in the effort of an unclean spirit to counterfeit the truth?

At this very time, even, the heretical dupes of this same Simon (Magus) are so much elated by the extravagant pretensions of their art, that they undertake to bring up from Hades the souls of the prophets themselves. And I suppose that they can do so under cover of a lying wonder. For, indeed, it was no less than this that was anciently permitted to the Pythonic (or ventriloquistic) spirit [1825] --even to represent the soul of Samuel, when Saul consulted the dead, after (losing the living) God.[1826] God forbid, however, that we should suppose that the soul of any saint, much less of a prophet, can be dragged out of (its resting-place in Hades) by a demon. We know that "Satan himself is transformed into an angel of light" [1827] --much more into a man of light--and that at last he will "show himself to be even God," [1828] and will exhibit "great signs and wonders, insomuch that, if it were possible, he shall deceive the very elect." [1829] He hardly [1830] hesitated on the before-mentioned occasion to affirm himself to be a prophet of God, and especially to Saul, in whom he was then actually dwelling. You must not imagine that he who produced the phantom was one, and he who consulted it was another; but that it was one and the same spirit, both in the sorceress and in the apostate (king), which easily pretended an apparition of that which it had already prepared them to believe as real--(even the spirit) through whose evil influence Saul's heart was fixed where his treasure was, and where certainly God was not. Therefore it came about, that he saw him through whose aid he believed that he was going to see, because he believed him through whose help he saw. But we are met with the objection, that in visions of the night dead persons are not unfrequently seen, and that for a set purpose. [1831] For instance, the Nasamones consult private oracles by frequent and lengthened visits to the sepulchres of their relatives, as one may find in Heraclides, or Nymphodorus, or Herodotus; [1832] and the Celts, for the same purpose, stay away all night at the tombs of their brave chieftains, as Nicander affirms.

Well, we admit apparitions of dead persons in dreams to be not more really true than those of living persons; but we apply the same estimate to all alike--to the dead and to the living, and indeed to all the phenomena which are seen. Now things are not true because they appear to be so, but because they are fully proved to be so. The truth of dreams is declared from the realization, not the aspect. Moreover, the fact that Hades is not in any case opened for (the escape of) any soul, has been firmly established by the Lord in the person of Abraham, in His representation of the poor man at rest and the rich man in torment. [1833] No one, (he said,) could possibly be despatched from those abodes to report to us how matters went in the nether regions,--a purpose which, (if any could be,) might have been allowable on such an occasion, to persuade a belief in Moses and the prophets. The power of God has, no doubt, sometimes recalled men's souls to their bodies, as a proof of His own transcendent rights; but there must never be, because of this fact, any agreement supposed to be possible between the divine faith and the arrogant pretensions of sorcerers, and the imposture of dreams, and the licence of poets. But yet in all cases of a true resurrection, when the power of God recalls souls to their bodies, either by the agency of prophets, or of Christ, or of apostles, a complete presumption is afforded us, by the solid, palpable, and ascertained reality (of the revived body), that its true form must be such as to compel one's belief of the fraudulence of every incorporeal apparition of dead persons.

Chapter LVIII - Conclusion. Points Postponed. All Souls are Kept in Hades Until the Resurrection, Anticipating Their Ultimate Misery or Bliss

All souls, therefore, are shut up within Hades: do you admit this? (It is true, whether) you say yes or no: moreover, there are already experienced there punishments and consolations; and there you have a poor man and a rich. And now, having postponed some stray questions [1834] for this part of my work, I will notice them in this suitable place, and then come to a close. Why, then, cannot you suppose that the soul undergoes punishment and consolation in Hades in the interval, while it awaits its alternative of judgment, in a certain anticipation either of gloom or of glory?

You reply: Because in the judgment of God its matter ought to be sure and safe, nor should there be any inkling beforehand of the award of His sentence; and also because (the soul) ought to be covered first by its vestment [1835] of the restored flesh, which, as the partner of its actions, should be also a sharer in its recompense. What, then, is to take place in that interval? Shall we sleep? But souls do not sleep even when men are alive: it is indeed the business of bodies to sleep, to which also belongs death itself, no less than its mirror and counterfeit sleep. Or will you have it, that nothing is there done whither the whole human race is attracted, and whither all man's expectation is postponed for safe keeping? Do you think this state is a foretaste of judgment, or its actual commencement? a premature encroachment on it, or the first course in its full ministration? Now really, would it not be the highest possible injustice, even[1836] in Hades, if all were to be still well with the guilty even there, and not well with the righteous even yet? What, would you have hope be still more confused after death? would you have it mock us still more with uncertain expectation? or shall it now become a review of past life, and an arranging of judgment, with the inevitable feeling of a trembling fear? But, again, must the soul always tarry for the body, in order to experience sorrow or joy? Is it not sufficient, even of itself, to suffer both one and the other of these sensations? How often, without any pain to the body, is the soul alone tortured by ill-temper, and anger, and fatigue, and very often unconsciously, even to itself? How often, too, on the other hand, amidst bodily suffering, does the soul seek out for itself some furtive joy, and withdraw for the moment from the body's importunate society? I am mistaken if the soul is not in the habit, indeed, solitary and alone, of rejoicing and glorifying over the very tortures of the body. Look for instance, at the soul of Mutius Scævola as he melts his right hand over the fire; look also at Zeno's, as the torments of Dionysius pass over it. [1837] The bites of wild beasts are a glory to young heroes, as on Cyrus were the scars of the bear. [1838] Full well, then, does the soul even in Hades know how to joy and to sorrow even without the body; since when in the flesh it feels pain when it likes, though the body is unhurt; and when it likes it feels joy though the body is in pain. Now if such sensations occur at its will during life, how much rather may they not happen after death by the judicial appointment of God! Moreover, the soul executes not all its operations with the ministration of the flesh; for the judgment of God pursues even simple cogitations and the merest volitions. "Whosoever looketh on a woman to lust after her, hath committed adultery with her already in his heart." [1839] Therefore, even for this cause it is most fitting that the soul, without at all waiting for the flesh, should be punished for what it has done without the partnership of the flesh. So, on the same principle, in return for the pious and kindly thoughts in which it shared not the help of the flesh, shall it without the flesh receive its consolation.

Nay more, [1840] even in matters done through the flesh the soul is the first to conceive them, the first to arrange them, the first to authorize them, the first to precipitate them into acts. And even if it is sometimes unwilling to act, it is still the first to treat the object which it means to effect by help of the body.

In no case, indeed, can an accomplished fact be prior to the mental conception [1841] thereof. It is therefore quite in keeping with this order of things, that that part of our nature should be the first to have the recompense and reward to which they are due on account of its priority. In short, inasmuch as we understand "the prison" pointed out in the Gospel to be Hades, [1842] and as we also interpret "the uttermost farthing" [1843] to mean the very smallest offence which has to be recompensed there before the resurrection, [1844] no one will hesitate to believe that the soul undergoes in Hades some compensatory discipline, without prejudice to the full process of the resurrection, when the recompense will be administered through the flesh besides. This point the Paraclete has also pressed home on our attention in most frequent admonitions, whenever any of us has admitted the force of His words from a knowledge of His promised spiritual disclosures. [1845] And now at last having, as I believe, encountered every human opinion concerning the soul, and tried its character by the teaching of (our holy faith,) we have satisfied the curiosity which is simply a reasonable and necessary one.

As for that which is extravagant and idle, there will evermore be as great a defect in its information, as there has been exaggeration and self-will in its researches.

Footnotes:

1489. [It is not safe to date this treatise before a.d. 203, and perhaps it would be unsafe to assign a later date. The note of the translator, which follows, relieves me from any necessity to add more, just here.]

1490. In this treatise we have Tertullian's speculations on the origin, the nature, and the destiny of the human soul. There are, no doubt, paradoxes startling to a modern reader to be found in it, such as that of the soul's corporeity; and there are weak and inconclusive arguments. But after all such drawbacks (and they are not more than what constantly occur in the most renowned speculative writers of antiquity), the reader will discover many interesting proofs of our author's character for originality of thought, width of information, firm grasp of his subject, and vivacious treatment of it, such as we have discovered in other parts of his writings. If his subject permits Tertullian less than usual of an appeal to his favourite Holy Scripture, he still makes room for occasional illustration from it, and with his characteristic ability; if, however, there is less of his sacred learning in it, the treatise teems with curious information drawn from the secular literature of that early age. Our author often measures swords with Plato in his discussions on the soul, and it is not too much to say that he shows himself a formidable opponent to the great philosopher. See Bp. Kaye, On Tertullian, pp. 199, 200.

1491. Suggestu. [Kaye, pp. 60 and 541.]

1492. Flatu "the breath."

1493. Utique.

1494. Consternata.

1495. Consternata.

1496. Externata. "Externatus = ἐκτὸς φρενῶν. Gloss. Philox.

1497. Pietatis.

1498. Fidei sacramento.

1499. The allusion is to the inconsistency of the philosopher, who condemned the gods of the vulgar, and died offering a gift to one of them.

1500. Vivicomburio.

1501. Mentioned below, c. xxxiii.; also Adv. Valent. c. xv.

1502. See his Phædrus, c. lix. (p. 274); also Augustin, De. Civ. Dei, viii. 11; Euseb. Præp. Evang. ix. 3.

1503. Or spurious; not to be confounded with our so-called Apocrypha, which were in

Tertullian's days called Libri Ecclesiastici.
1504. Here is a touch of Tertullian's Montanism.
1505. Subornant.
1506. 1 Tim. i. 4.
1507. 1 Cor. x. 19.
1508. Compare Tertullian's Adv. Hermog. c. viii.
1509. Col. ii. 8.
1510. Linguatam civitatem. Comp. Acts xvii. 21.
1511. Isa. i. 22.
1512. Honor.
1513. Vigor. Another reading has "rigor" (ακληρότης), harshness.
1514. Tenor.
1515. Stupor.
1516. Moeror.
1517. Furor.
1518. Isa. ii. 3.
1519. Flatu.
1520. Gen. ii. 7.
1521. Titulus.
1522. See his Phædrus, c. xxiv.
1523. Capit itaque et facturam provenisse poni.
1524. Or, "inspiration."
1525. Ex quinta nescio qua substantia. Comp. Cicero's Tuscul. i. 10.
1526. Consitum.
1527. De Nat. Rer. i. 305.
1528. Animale, "having the nature of soul."
1529. Inanimale.
1530. Accedit.
1531. We follow Oehler's view of this obscure passage, in preference to Rigaltius'.
1532. See Tertullian's Ad Nationes (our translation), p. 33, Supra..
1533. Quinionem.
1534. Luke xvi. 23, 24.
1535. Ad inferna. [See p. 59, supra.]
1536. Diversorio.
1537. Compare De Resur. Carnis, xvii. There is, however, some variation in Tertullian's language on this subject. In his Apol. xlviii. he speaks as if the soul could not suffer when separated from the body. See also his De Testimonio Animæ, ch. iv., p. 177, supra; and see Bp. Kaye, p. 183.
1538. Rev. i. 10.
1539. Rev. vi. 9.
1540. Habitum.
1541. Illud trifariam distantivum (Τριχῶς διαστηματικόν) Fr. Junius.
1542. Effigiem.
1543. See his Phædo, pp. 105, 106.
1544. Structile.
1545. Sacramenta.
1546. 1 Cor. xii. 1-11. [A key to our author's
1547. Cerauniis gemmis.

1548. Tradux.
1549. Dupliciter unus.
1550. 2 Cor. xii. 2-4.
1551. Luke xvi. 23, 24.
1552. See his Phædo, p. 80; Timæus, § 12, p. 35 (Bekker, pp. 264, 265).
1553. We have here combined two readings, effigies (Oehler's) and hæreses (the usual one).
1554. Aliam.
1555. This is the force of the subjunctive fiat.
1556. Arterias.
1557. Aliunde spirabit, aliunde vivet. "In the nature of man, life and breath are inseparable," Bp. Kaye, p. 184.
1558. Sexcentos.
1559. Odit.
1560. Aurium cæci.
1561. Proprie "by reason of its nature."
1562. See the tract Adv. Valentin., c. xxv. infra.
1563. Compare Adv. Hermog. xxxii. xxxiii.; also Irenæus, v. 12, 17. [See Vol. I. p. 527, this Series.]
1564. Tertullian's reading of Isa. lvii. 16.
1565. Isa. xlii. 5.
1566. 1 Cor. xv. 46.
1567. Eph. v. 31, 32.
1568. Gen. ii. 24, 25.
1569. 1 Sam. x. 6.
1570. 1 Sam. x. 11.
1571. Suggestum.
1572. Comp. The Apology, c. xlviii.; August. De Civ. Dei, xiii. 17.
1573. Comp. Adv. Valentin. vii. infra.
1574. Addicit.
1575. Alterum animi genus.
1576. Concretum.
1577. Substantiæ officium.
1578. Substantiæ massa.
1579. Faciem operis.
1580. Fontem materiæ.
1581. This is Oehler's text; another reading has twelve, which one would suppose to be the right one.
1582. Ubique ipsa.
1583. Sapientialis.
1584. Consecratum.
1585. Wisd. i. 6.
1586. Prov. xxiv. 12.
1587. Ps. cxxxix. 23.
1588. Matt. ix. 4.
1589. Ps. li. 12.
1590. Rom. x. 10.
1591. 1 John iii. 20.
1592. Matt. v. 28.
1593. In eo thesauro.
1594. Not Suidas' philosopher of that name, but a renowned physician mentioned by Galen and Pliny (Oehler).
1595. Lorica.

1596. The Egyptian hierophants.
1597. The original, as given in Stobæus, Eclog. i. p. 1026, is this hexameter: Αἷμα γὰρ ἀνθρώποις περικάρδιόν ἐστι νόημα.
1598. Or probably that Praxagoras the physician who is often mentioned by Athenæus and by Pliny (Pamel.).
1599. Luke xxii. 15.
1600. 1 Tim. iii. 1.
1601. Gal. v. 12.
1602. Eph. ii. 3.
1603. Matt. vi. 24.
1604. John vi. 44.
1605. Matt. xiii. 25.
1606. Academici.
1607. Coimplicitam "entangled" or "embarrassed." See the Timæus pp. 27, 28.
1608. Vel.
1609. Sensus istos.
1610. Deliberetur.
1611. Luke x. 18.
1612. Matt. iii. 17.
1613. Matt. viii. 15.
1614. Matt. xxvi. 7-12.
1615. Matt. xxvi. 27, 28; Luke xxii. 19, 20; 1 Cor. xi. 25.
1616. Matt. xvii. 3-8.
1617. John ii. 1-10.
1618. John xx. 27.
1619. 1 John i. 1.
1620. Said ironically, as if rallying Plato for inconsistency between his theory here and the fact.
1621. Supermundiales "placed above this world."
1622. Imaginibus.
1623. See above, c. xii. p. 192.
1624. Above, c. xi. p. 191.
1625. Intelligere sentire est.
1626. Oehler has "anima;" we should rather have expected "animo," which is another reading.
1627. "Animo" this time.
1628. Subjunctive verb, "fuerit."
1629. Dementit.
1630. The opposite opinion was held by Tertullian's opponents, who distinguished between the mind and the soul. They said, that when a man was out of his mind, his mind left him, but that his soul remained. (Lactantius, De Opif. xviii.; Instit. Div. vii. 12; La Cerda).
1631. See his treatise, Against Marcion.
1632. Rom. i. 20.
1633. Facies.
1634. Timæus, pp. 29, 30, 37, 38.
1635. His De Anima, ii. 2, 3.
1636. Innixa et innexa.
1637. Amabit.
1638. Animationem. The possession and use of an "anima."
1639. Intellectuam.
1640. Spiritu. The mental instinct, just mentioned.
1641. Ps. viii. 2; Matt. xxi. 16.
1642. Hebetes.
1643. Matt. xxi. 15.
1644. Matt. ii. 16-18.
1645. Sæpe noster.
1646. Licebit.
1647. Fetu.
1648. Tertullian perhaps mentions this "demus" of Athens as the birthplace of Plato (Oehler).
1649. Tit. i. 12.
1650. Si et alia.
1651. Tertullian wrote a work De Fato, which is lost. Fulgentius, p. 561, gives a quotation from it.
1652. i.e., the carnal, the animal, and the spiritual. Comp. Adv. Valentin. xxv., and De Resur. Carnis, lv.
1653. Eph. v. 32.
1654. Gen. ii. 23, 24.
1655. See Adv. Hermog. xiii.
1656. See Adv. Valentin. xxix.
1657. Luke vi. 43, 44.
1658. Matt. iii. 7-9.
1659. Eph. v. 8.
1660. Eph. ii. 3.
1661. 1 Cor. vi. 11.
1662. See our Anti-Marcion, ii. 5-7.
1663. In his work against this man, entitled De Censu Animæ, not now extant.
1664. Tertullian had shown that "the soul is the breath or afflatus of God," in ch. iv. and xi. above. He demonstrated its "immortality" in ch. ii.-iv., vi., ix., xiv.; and he will repeat his proof hereafter, in ch. xxiv., xxxviii., xlv., li., liii., liv. Moreover, he illustrates the soul's "corporeity" in ch. v.-viii.; its "endowment with form or figure," in ch. ix.; its "simplicity in substance" in ch. x. and xi.; its "inherent intelligence," in ch. xii.; its varied development, in ch. xiii.-xv. The soul's "rationality," "supremacy," and "instinctive divination," Tertullian treated of in his treatise De Censu Animæ against Hermogenes (as he has said in the text); but he has treated somewhat of the soul's "rational nature" in the sixteenth chapter above; in the fourteenth and fifteenth chapters he referred to the soul's "supremacy or hegemony;" whilst we have had a hint about its "divining faculty," even in infants, in ch. xix. The propagation of souls from the one archetypal soul is the subject of the chapter before us, as well as of the five succeeding ones (La Cerda).
1665. Nihil Deo appendimus.
1666. Exorbitationis.
1667. In his, now lost, treatise, De Censu Animæ.
1668. Above, in ch. xix. xx. pp. 200, 201.
1669. Or, "which has been too short for

calculation."

1670. "Inhaled" is Bp. Kaye's word for adduci, "taken up."

1671. Educi.

1672. Vivacitas.

1673. Ciborum vanitates.

1674. Rapiens.

1675. Anima.

1676. Anulocultro. [To be seen in the Museum at Naples.]

1677. Or, "the whole business (totem facinus) is despatched."

1678. So Plato, Cratylus, p. 399, c. 17.

1679. Censentur.

1680. Liberi aliqui.

1681. See Pliny, Natural History, vii. 9.

1682. See above, ch. x.

1683. Mark xvi. 9.

1684. Mark vi. 1-9.

1685. See above, ch. v.

1686. Of the Scriptures.

1687. Gen. xxv. 22, 23.

1688. Gen. xxv. 26.

1689. Luke i. 41-45.

1690. Luke i. 46.

1691. Jer. i. 5.

1692. Gen. ii. 7.

1693. Jer. i. 5.

1694. Comp. De Resurr. Carnis, xlv.

1695. So Plato, Phædo, p. 64.

1696. Materiæ.

1697. Gen. i. 28.

1698. Lupanaria.

1699. See above, c. xxv. p. 206.

1700. Gen. i. 28.

1701. Ver. 26.

1702. Ver. 26.

1703. Phædo, p. 70.

1704. [Hermes. See Bacon, De Aug. i. p. 99.]

1705. De posteris defunctis.

1706. De posteris defunctis.

1707. From καταβάλλειν, to knock down.

1708. From πάρεδος, sitting by one.

1709. From πυθωνικός, an attribute of Pythius Apollo; this class were sometimes called ἐγγαστρίμυθοι, ventriloquists.

1710. Visualitatis.

1711. Insipientiam. "Imbecility" is the meaning here, though the word takes the more general sense in the next clause.

1712. Deferatur.

1713. A probable allusion to Varro's work, De Antiqq. Rerum Humanarum.

1714. An allusion to Plato's notion that, at the end of a thousand years, such a restoration of the dead, took place. See his Phædrus, p. 248, and De Republ. x. p. 614.

1715. Signatur. Rigaltius reads "singulatur," after the Codex Agobard., as meaning, "The single origin of the human race is in principle maintained," etc.

1716. Temere.

1717. Recensentur.

1718. Hujus.

1719. Alias.

1720. This is the force of the objective nouns, which are all put in the plural form.

1721. Ps. xlix. 20.

1722. Or, "that he may be punished even in his sepulture."

1723. Rom. xiii. 4.

1724. In administratione.

1725. Mark xiii. 32.

1726. Acts viii. 18-21. [Vol. I. pp. 171, 182, 193, 347.]

1727. For Carpocrates, see Irenæus, i. 24; Eusebius, H. E. iv. 7; Epiphan. Hær. 27.

1728. Matt. v. 26.

1729. Ver. 25.

1730. 1 Cor. v. 10.

1731. Luke vi. 27.

1732. Matt. v. 25.

1733. Ver. 26.

1734. Rev. xii. 10.

1735. Morâ resurrectionis. For the force of this phrase, as apparently implying a doctrine of purgatory, and an explanation of Tertullian's teaching on this point, see Bp. Kaye on Tertullian, pp. 328, 329. [See p. 59, supra.]

1736. Spero.

1737. Matt. xvii. 12.

1738. Matt. xi. 14.

1739. John i. 21.

1740. Mal. iv. 5.

1741. Num. xii. 2.

1742. In ch. xxviii. at the beginning.

1743. See above, ch. xxiii. [Also p. 246, infra.]

1744. Causa hominis.

1745. The ogdoad, or number eight, mystically representing "heaven," where they do not marry.

1746. Beyond the hebdomad comes the resurrection, on which see Matt. xxii. 30.

1747. See above, in ch. xx.

1748. See above, in ch. xxiv.

1749. Gen. ii. 16.

1750. Gen. ix. 3.

1751. Fata Scribunda.

1752. 1 Cor. vii. 14.

1753. 1 Cor. vii. 14.

1754. John iii. 5.

1755. Rom. vi. 4.

1756. Gal. v. 16.

1757. Ver. 17.

1758. Rom. viii. 5.

1759. Matt. v. 28.

1760. Deo commendo = God be wi' ye. De Test. c. ii. p. 176, supra.

1761. Decurrat.

1762. So Bp. Kaye, p. 195.

1763. Marcorem, "the decay."
1764. Adulatur.
1765. Gen. ii. 21.
1766. We had better give Tertullian's own succinct definition: "Excessus sensûs et amentiæ instar."
1767. Gen. ii. 21.
1768. Prudentes.
1769. Sapere.
1770. See the Odyssey, xix. 562, etc. [Also, Æneid, vi. 894.]
1771. See i. 107, etc.
1772. See an account of her vision and its interpretation in Herodot. iv. 124.
1773. Joel iii. 1.
1774. Matt. v. 45.
1775. Dan. ii. 1, etc.
1776. Conresupinatis.
1777. See his Timæus, c. xxxii. p. 71.
1778. Dan. i. 8-14
1779. Dan. x. 2.
1780. Who mentions this story of the Atlantes in iv. 184.
1781. In ch. xliv. p. 223.
1782. Gen. ii. 17. [Not ex natura, but as penalty.]
1783. Scaturigo dæmonica.
1784. It is difficult to say what Tertullian means by his "comicum credo." Is it a playful parody on the heretic's name, the same as the comic poet's (Menander)?
1785. Gen. v. 24; Heb. xi. 5.
1786. 2 Kings ii. 11.
1787. Rev. xi. 3.
1788. John xxi. 23.
1789. See below, ch. liv.
1790. Ch. x. p. 614.
1791. Vernaculam ecclesiæ.
1792. Ex accidentia.
1793. In mortem directo institutus est. [See p. 227, supra.]
1794. We have made Tertullian's "cervicum messis" include both these modes of instantaneous death.
1795. Phædo, p. 62, c. 6.
1796. 1 Cor. iii. 16; vi. 19; 2 Cor. vi. 16.
1797. An Alexandrian philosopher in great repute with the Emperor Augustus.
1798. Phædo, pp. 112-114.
1799. Matt. xii. 40.
1800. 1 Cor. xv. 3.
1801. Ver. 4.
1802. 1 Pet. iii. 19.
1803. See Irenæus, adv. Hæres. v. [Vol. I. p. 566, this Series.]
1804. Matt. x. 24.
1805. 1 Cor. xv. 52 and 1 Thess. iv. 16.
1806. 1 Thess. iv. 17.
1807. Ver. 16.
1808. Rev. vi. 9.
1809. Paracletus.
1810. Matt. xvi. 24.
1811. The souls of the martyrs were, according to Tertullian, at once removed to Paradise (Bp. Kaye, p. 249).
1812. De Paradiso. [Compare, p. 216, note 9, supra.]
1813. Ab inferis.
1814. Iliad, xxiii. 72, etc.
1815. Enormitate.
1816. We have treated this particle as a conjunction but it may only be an intensive particle introducing an explanatory clause: "even those which were pure," etc. [a better rendering.]
1817. Litteratura.
1818. Oehler takes these descriptive clauses as meant of Satan, instead of being synonymes of magic, as the context seems to require.
1819. Æque.
1820. Above, in ch. xxxix. p. 219.
1821. Aliquem ex parentibus.
1822. One who fought with wild beasts in the public games, only without the weapons allowed to the gladiator.
1823. Ex. vii. 12.
1824. Acts viii. 9; xiii. 8.
1825. See above in ch. xxviii. p. 209, supra.
1826. 1 Sam. xxviii. 6-16.
1827. 2 Cor. xi. 14.
1828. 2 Thess. ii. 4.
1829. Matt. xxiv. 24.
1830. Si forte.
1831. Non frustra.
1832. In iv. 172.
1833. Luke xvi. 26. [Compare note 15, p. 231. supra.]
1834. Nescio quid.
1835. "Operienda" is Oehler's text; another reading gives "opperienda," q.d., "the soul must wait for the restored body."
1836. This "etiam" is "otium" in the Agobardine ms., a good reading; q.d. "a most iniquitous indifference to justice," etc.
1837. Comp. The Apology, last chapter.
1838. Xen. Cyropæd. p. 6.
1839. Matt. v. 28.
1840. Quid nunc si.
1841. Conscientia.
1842. Matt. v. 25.
1843. Ver. 26.
1844. Morâ resurrectionis. See above, on this opinion of Tertullian, in ch. xxxv.
1845. [A symptom of Montanism.]

www.ingramcontent.com/pod-product-compliance
Lightning Source LLC
Chambersburg PA
CBHW031140160426
43193CB00008B/206